THE NEW ANTHOLOGY OF AMERICAN POETRY

The New Anthology
of American Poetry

VOLUME TWO
Modernisms
1900–1950

✦   ✦   ✦   ✦   ✦   ✦   ✦   ✦   ✦   ✦   ✦   ✦   ✦

EDITED BY

Steven Gould Axelrod

Camille Roman

Thomas Travisano

RUTGERS UNIVERSITY PRESS
NEW BRUNSWICK, NEW JERSEY, AND LONDON

Fifth paperback printing, 2011

Produced by Wilsted & Taylor Publishing Services
    Copyediting: Melody Lacina
    Design and composition: Melissa Ehn

Manufactured in the United States of America

Library of Congress Cataloging-in-Publication Data

The new anthology of American poetry / edited by Steven Gould Axelrod,
    Camille Roman, and Thomas Travisano.
        p. cm.
    Vol. 2.
    Includes bibliographical references and index.
    Contents: v. 2. Modernisms, 1900–1950.
    ISBN 0-8135-3163-2 (cloth : alk. paper) — ISBN 0-8135-3164-0 (pbk. : alk. paper)
    1. American poetry.   I. Axelrod, Steven Gould, 1944–   II. Roman, Camille,
    1948–   III. Travisano, Thomas J., 1951–

PS586.N492003
811.008—dc21   2002070502

A British Cataloging-in-Publication record for this book is available from the
British Library.

To Our Families and Students

CONTENTS

PART TWO: SECOND-GENERATION MODERNISMS

PREFACE

WELCOME TO AN EXCITING PERIOD of American poetry and culture—the rise of modernisms. Modernisms are a variety of movements and ideas grouped under a single, now generally pluralized name. One of the hallmarks of modernist poems is change. The poets were often proud of breaking with the past in form or theme, even as they were conscious of the relations between their poems and those written in earlier times and other places. Another hallmark of these poems is diversity. Different poets and groups had alternative methods and aims, and their audiences varied. Some modernists emphasized formal issues—art for art's sake. Some emphasized epistemological or linguistic issues—the relations or lack of relations between word and world. And some emphasized social issues—the dilemmas of race, gender, ethnicity, sexuality, nationality, social standing, and economic disparity that have divided and burdened the country and the world. In the period approximately from 1900 to 1950, modernity was rich, confusing, and disturbing, and change was rapid and unpredictable. American poetic modernisms both reflected and helped create the sense of that time. They still provide an entry into that era for us today.

Many of the poems included in this volume are as inviting as the table laden with melon, grapes, and peaches depicted in Pierre Daura's modernist painting on this book's cover. The poems themselves often depict pleasant meals or happy parties. They offer what Gertrude Stein calls, in "Susie Asado," a "told tray sure." Stein's phrase may allude to a dependable tea tray filled with tempting things to eat and drink, an object so welcome that it is "told" about. Or, in Stein's trademark play of words, the phrase may suggest a "gold treasure"—a source of aesthetic and intellectual richness, bounty, and beauty. Whatever the range of meanings, the tea party or dance party that Stein's poem so giddily describes parallels the sustaining and joy-giving experience of reading many of these poems. Modernist poems give pleasure the way plums do in William Carlos Williams's "This Is Just to Say" and "To a Poor Old Woman." They "taste good" to us. The experimental poems exhibit the panache of forms and words used as never before. The more traditional poems exhibit the quiet glow of forms and words employed skillfully, with subtle changes rung on age-old usages.

Many of the texts, on the other hand, take us to dark places in social history and the human soul. These poems depict lonely disintegrations or communal sufferings. They offer what Langston Hughes calls "The Weary Blues":

> I got the Weary Blues
> And I can't be satisfied.
> Got the Weary Blues
> And can't be satisfied—
> I ain't happy no mo'
> And I wish that I had died.

The "weary blues" arrive for a variety of reasons to every imaginable individual and social group. They may take the form of Eliot's "I can connect nothing with nothing" in *The Waste Land*, a poem that for some readers has defined the age. Feelings of dejection may be expressed by Asian, Native American, or Latino individuals suffering the burdens of displacement and oppression, as in the line by a Chinese immigrant detained at Angel Island, "Sadness kills the person in the wooden building." Poets may meditate, with Robert Frost, their (and our) interior "desert places." Or they may capture the essence of fear, loneliness, and awe through apparently simple observation, as in Adelaide Crapsey's "November Night":

> Listen. .
> With faint dry sound,
> Like steps of passing ghosts,
> The leaves, frost-crisp'd, break from the trees
> And fall.

Some modernist poems offer a feast of delights, like the delicious-looking fruit in Daura's painting. Others address dilemmas and pathologies, cutting into them like the sharp knife Daura also depicted. Some poems are inscribed on what H. D. calls "the blank page of the new," while others meditate, with Wallace Stevens, "old" catastrophes. Pound focuses on silent "faces in the crowd," while W. C. Handy wonders what it would sound like "if Beale Street could talk." Poem topics range from Lorine Niedecker's "friend sun" and Amy Lowell's "beloved" to Robinson Jeffers's "hurt hawks" and Angelina Weld Grimké's evanescent "grey dreams." Each of the poems, in its own way, seeks to discover Hart Crane's perfectly imaged "Word," which holds "hushed willows anchored in its glow." As editors of this anthology, we are delighted to invite you inside to see for yourself the imaged words, the inventive forms, and the competing social discourses and perspectives that compose poetic modernisms. In the words of Robert Frost, "You come too."

ACKNOWLEDGMENTS

WE ARE DEEPLY INDEBTED to the numerous pathbreaking literary critics, historians, editors, and anthologists mentioned in our headnotes and the "Further Reading" sections of this anthology. We also thank our students at the University of California, Riverside, Washington State University, and Hartwick College for their lively sense of inquiry and their readiness to explore the unexpected.

Our special thanks go to Leslie Mitchner, our editor at Rutgers, for her enthusiasm, professionalism, imagination, and wise counsel. We are grateful as well to the rest of the staff at the press, particularly Molly Baab, Arlene Bacher, Penny Borden, Gary Fitzgerald, Alison Hack, Adi Hovav, Donna Liese, Jessica Pellien, and Jonathan Reilly. We also thank the people at Wilsted & Taylor Publishing Services, especially Christine Taylor, Melody Lacina, and Melissa Ehn for their skill in editing and designing this book. Melody, a poet herself, has helped make our prose sparkle.

For his invaluable professional assistance with Pierre Daura's painting *Melon and Chocolate Pot* (1928), which adorns the cover, we thank David Kencik, Collections Assistant for Data Management, San Diego Museum of Art. Daura (1896–1976) was born on the Spanish island of Minorca, grew up in Barcelona, Catalonia (a region of Spain), studied art with Picasso's father, and lived for many years in Paris. His Spanish citizenship was revoked after he fought with the anti-fascist forces in the Spanish Civil War. While he and his family were visiting Virginia, World War II broke out, preventing their return to France. Daura lived the rest of his life in the United States, becoming an American citizen. We hope that his inviting painting suggests the beauty, the innovative qualities, and the international influences that marked the arts in the modernist era.

Steven Gould Axelrod thanks Megan Fowler, Courtney Scarborough, and Sayaka Yamazaki for their expert research assistance. He also thanks the following scholars and lovers of the arts for their invaluable advice and help: Jeremiah B. C. Axelrod, Rise B. Axelrod, Elizabeth Barnett (of the Edna St. Vincent Millay Society), Lee A. Daniels (of the National Urban League), Bea Ganim, John Ganim, Gudrun Grabher, Jeffrey Gray, Burton Hatlen, Richard Hishmeh, Cynthia Hogue, Andrew Howe, Suzanne Juhasz, Marilyn Kane, Stephanie Kay, Kathryn

O'Rourke, Amy Robbins, Gail Sapiel, Miriam Shain, Christine Smedley, and Edith Vasquez. He is grateful to all the participants in a Ford Foundation conference at the Center for Ideas and Society at the University of California, Riverside, and particularly to Emory Elliott and Lisa Lowe, for their thoughtful response to his work on post-immigration poetry. He is also grateful to the students in his graduate seminar in literary modernisms for their stimulating ideas about modernist poems: Tucker Amidon, Hugh Bonar, Tammy Di Benedetto, Angelica Duran, Rachel Gardner, Matthew Heard, Jeremy Kaye, Ann Modzelewski, Michael Moreno, Zina Rodriguez, Hank Scotch, Mary Song, Lisa Sperber, Paul Tayyar, and Nick Valdez. Finally, he gratefully acknowledges the help of the librarians at the Tomás Rivera Library at the University of California, Riverside, and the financial support of the university's Research Committee.

Camille Roman especially wishes to thank Brian Hayakawa and Walter Lew for their discussions of Asian-American culture, history, and poetry; Ernie Harburg, of the E. Y. "Yip" Harburg Foundation, for his kind and generous permissions support and for his scholarship on musical theater song; and Melissa Bradshaw and Adrienne Munich, editors of *Amy Lowell, American Modern*, for sharing their collection of essays with us in advance of publication. She also expresses her appreciation for the kind permissions support of Franklin Odo, Director, Smithsonian Asian Pacific American Program and Curator, National Museum of American History; Karleen Chinen, editor, *The Hawaii Herald*; Lee A. Daniels, Vice President, Publications, and Editor, *Opportunity*, the National Urban League; Kay Nakano Yokoyama, translator in the "Poets Behind Barbed Wire" project; Machiko Wada, coordinator of the Japanese Community Service, Seattle, Washington; Jennifer Chartier, Business Administrator, Hal Leonard Corporation; Hope Chirino, Business Affairs official, Warner Brothers Music; Margaret Forster, Publications Fellow, *MANA: A South Pacific Journal of Art, Culture, Language, and Literature*, Institute of Pacific Studies, University of the South Pacific, Fiji; Diane Meuser, permissions editor, The New York Times Agency; and Kristen Hagenbuckle, Assistant to the Director, University of Arizona Press. She is grateful to Washington State University for an American Cultural Diversity Grant in 2001 and to the Department of English for its financial assistance.

Camille Roman would also like to thank her colleagues at Washington State University, and especially George Kennedy, Barbara Sitko, Jerrie Sinclair, Elizabeth Siler, Lynn Gordon, Amanda Espinosa-Aguilar, Nelly Zamora, Stan Linden, Nick Kiessling, Carol Siegel, Jijo Magee, Ann Berry, Victor Villanueva, Jana Argersinger, Alex Hammond, Debbie Lee, Elwood Hartman, Mary Anderson, Jingyu Wang, Jason Miller, and Paula Coomer, for their generous support during a family emergency. She thanks Jennifer Stevens and Paula Elliott of the Washington State University Libraries for their work in compiling reference sources for poetry after 1900 and for building up their holdings in this area. She is grateful to her editorial assistants, Jason Miller and Drew Piper, for their enthusiastic and dedicated work on this volume. She also acknowledges her energizing research assistants Christy Kord, Jingyu Wang, Rajaa al Khalili, and Keely Kuhlman. She expresses her appreciation to her undergraduate and graduate students from 2001 to 2003 in Modern American Literature, Modern American Poetry, and World War II Poetry. She wishes to thank Douglas Hancock, Dave Stover, and Francine and Jeff Reingold for their goodwill during emergencies and, especially, Jane Betts-Stover, for her unflagging support. Finally, she thanks Chris D. Frigon, her husband and coeditor of Twayne's Music Book Series, for his deep commitment to seeing this project into print.

Thomas Travisano would like to thank research assistants Ashley Beadore, Amy Norkus, and Zach Sanzone for their dedicated and enthusiastic work in support of this project. He thanks the reference department of the Hartwick College Library, especially Sue Stevens, for their energy and persistence in searching for rare and elusive out-of-print books. He also is grateful to the Board of Trustees of Hartwick College and the Office of Academic Affairs for their generous and ongoing support. He thanks his Hartwick classes, especially in the courses Reading American Poetry and Four Modern American Poets, for their excellent questions and inquiring attitude. He also wishes to thank Michael Webster for his alert suggestions regarding E. E. Cummings. Most of all, he thanks his wife, Elsa Travisano, for her computer expertise and literary judgment as well as her resilience, patience, good humor, and good counsel.

Each of the editors wishes to acknowledge the generous support and insight of the others in what has been, from the beginning of Volume One to the end of Volume Two, an extremely gratifying and enlightening collaboration. And thanks, too, to you, our readers.

PART ONE

◆

First-Generation Modernisms

INTRODUCTION

THE INITIAL STAGE of the modernist enterprise, which we are calling "first-generation modernisms," peaked between about 1910 and 1930. This stage emphasized poetic innovations of various kinds, and internationalist connections went to its heart. The spirit of change was in the air. Poets explored new methods of assembling poetic language and portraying self, community, and world—or they contested these new methods. Poems came from multiple sources—cultivated and popular—and they absorbed many global influences.

Material conditions and social arrangements were rapidly altering in the first decades of the twentieth century. The period included such phenomena as large-scale immigration and within-border migrations, urbanization, industrialization, prohibition, accelerating speed and mobility, technological breakthroughs, advances in the arts and sciences, widening gaps between rich and poor, conflict between social groups arranged in hierarchal systems, women's struggles for suffrage and other rights, the expatriation of artists, and, alongside it all, the incredible, traumatic carnage of World War I, the first fully mechanized war. Many sensed that the United States epitomized modernity and that modernity itself was a surprising and confusing thing. Modernity generated hope, anticipation, and excitement, but its boisterous changes also provoked feelings of loss and disorientation. Many in the working classes felt that their social space was endangered, whereas many in more apparently comfortable situations worried about what the future held, and they looked back with longing toward a more settled past.

This confused sense of hope and dread was both a cause and a product of revolutionary advances in the arts. American poetry witnessed the arrival of many new movements, including the visual poetry of imagism and the more auditory poetry of the Harlem Renaissance. Forms, language, and social attitudes changed dramatically in the work of many modernist poets. Such changes were contested in the work of others. Little consensus existed at the time about who the "central" figures were—and even less agreement is evident today. For the purposes of charting this poetic landscape, providing the roughest of rough guides to the terrain, we posit that first-generation modernisms were invented and performed by poets born between 1873 and 1894. Within this generation, we describe four often intertwined groups of poets: the experimental modernists, the Harlem Renaissance poets, the traditionalist modernists, and the popular culture modernists.

3

The experimental modernists produced a poetry based on formal innovation. This pioneering group may be further subdivided, as critic Peter Nicholls has suggested, into a pair of "high" modernists, who made the biggest initial splash, and a larger set of "other" modernists, who now match the initial pair in prominence. The "high" modernists, sometimes also called the "men of 1914," were Ezra Pound and T. S. Eliot. This pair mutually established the idea of a poetic project, and they produced its first recognized masterpiece in Eliot's *The Waste Land*. Pound and Eliot consciously broke away from nineteenth-century norms. They sought to elucidate through juxtaposition, irony, and mythic correspondences rather than through direct statement. They prized imagery over explanation, fragmentation over cohesion, allusiveness over monologue, and impersonality over sentiment. Stylists rather than rhetoricians, they took the risk of obscurity, believing that readers must make the effort to come to them. Devoted to the idea of elite cultural and aesthetic productions, they often combined an invigorating cosmopolitanism and historicism with a countervailing sense of isolation, vulnerability, and loss. Pound's oft-repeated slogan was "make it new." Both poets believed that poetry must treat the modern world in innovative ways, but at the same time they often lamented the very changes their work evoked and exemplified.

Although Pound and Eliot initially succeeded in defining experimental modernism in their own image, attention has increasingly drifted to a second, much larger set of experimentalists. Some of these poets were closely aligned with Eliot and Pound, at least for a time, but they eventually went their own ways. Poets as diverse as H.D., Gertrude Stein, William Carlos Williams, Wallace Stevens, Marianne Moore, Amy Lowell, Adelaide Crapsey, Mina Loy, E. E. Cummings, Charles Reznikoff, and the New York Dadaists may all be placed in this category. H.D. actually invented and practiced imagism before Pound named it as such. But H.D. ultimately moved from her resonant evocations of hard-edged natural objects, contained within carefully honed free verse, to an expansive, woman-centered mythic discourse that sought to redefine and transform the world. Stein, whom Pound called "old tub of guts" and Eliot thought a "barbarian," experimented with language in ways that were radically productive but increasingly at odds with the innovations of the "men of 1914." Instead of valuing verbal economy and "direct treatment of the thing," as Pound advocated, she explored the resources of repetition, abstraction, and verbal play. Whereas Pound's "direct treatment" and Eliot's "objective correlative" sought to diminish the gap between word and thing, Stein's lively words emphasized the gap, highlighting the materiality of language. In addition, both H.D. and Stein—along with such other modernists as Moore, Lowell, Crapsey, and Loy—produced what critics Margaret Dickey and Thomas Travisano have called "gendered modernisms," in contrast to the more traditional, male-centered gender depictions of Pound and Eliot.

William Carlos Williams admired both Pound *and* Stein, though he deemed

Eliot's *The Waste Land* a "great disaster" because of its learned quality, which he thought "returned poetry to the classroom." But Williams also disapproved of the whole expatriate motive underlying Eliot's work—and that of Pound, H.D., and Stein as well. The expatriates had made a permanent home in Europe, returning to the United States infrequently and, in Pound's case, involuntarily. Williams, in contrast, wished to explore the resources of his own native land, its languages and peoples. Using imagistic techniques indebted to H.D. and Pound, his poems often circle around everyday occurrences such as a drive in the car or a note taped to an icebox—humdrum events and objects that, on inspection, aren't humdrum at all. Williams wrote about the lives of working-class people in language, he was later to say, that came "from the mouths of Polish mothers"—that is, from the immigrants and laborers he encountered on the street. He named his epic poem not for Dante (as Pound did his *Cantos*) but for an "anywhere" that was "everywhere": the aging industrial city of Paterson, New Jersey.

Wallace Stevens and Marianne Moore stayed in the United States, too, but neither of them had the gregarious impulses that underlay Williams's work. Stevens produced a meditational poetry, one that prized the beauty of the physical world, just as Williams's did, but one that was firmly rooted in the abstractions of mind and language. Stevens believed that "it's a world of words to the end of it"—that words mediate everything, even the perception of nature. He also posited that "God and the imagination are one," implying that the aesthetic operations of the meditative mind are the best antidote for the pain and loss of human experience. Marianne Moore, in contrast, produced collage-like effects by stringing together allusions and quotations within a discourse of precisely observed and morally resonant detail. Her poems explore the natural world as it is contained in zoos or conveyed by books—and they tease out the emotional and ethical dimensions of what is seen. Her poems, which embed the most serious ideas in the most delightful description, have a clarity lacking in the work of some other experimental modernists. They also suggest a gendered and feminist awareness, an aversion to egotism and bravado, that puts them into conversation with the poetry of other women poets of the period.

Amy Lowell, who fought Pound for leadership of the imagist movement, imbued her poetic practice with an erotic and emotional fervor, a sense of female values, and a rich and cultivated awareness of foreign cultures, particularly those of East Asia. Adelaide Crapsey, writing by herself and in failing health, did as much with a simple visual or auditory image as anyone has ever done. Mina Loy employed a style of obscurity, fragmentation, and cosmopolitanism that may recall that of Pound and Eliot, but she merged that style with a feminist perspective that had nothing to do with their worldview. E. E. Cummings lent to his verbal improvisations a witty exuberance that few other experimental modernists matched. Finally, Charles Reznikoff, a child of immigrant culture, used imagistic techniques to tell the stories of the urban poor. His poetry has links to both the concision of H.D. and the urban vitality of the Harlem Renaissance. Like Williams but even more so, he brought experimental modernism into close contact with working-class life.

The Harlem Renaissance of 1922–30 opposes, informs, and complements experimental modernism. Whereas experimental modernism grew from cultures both elite (Pound, Eliot, Moore, Lowell) and immigrant (Stein, Williams, Loy, Reznikoff), the Harlem Renaissance represented a great flowering of African-American culture. It arrived about a decade after the onset of experimental modernism, though some of its pioneering representatives—such as Claude McKay, Alice Dunbar-Nelson, Jessie Fauset, Georgia Douglas Johnson, Angelina Weld Grimké, and Jean Toomer—were of the same generation as the experimentalists. Some, like Toomer, were influenced by modernist experiments, whereas others, like McKay and Grimké, resisted such innovations. Michael North has pointed out that Pound and Eliot occasionally used a distorted and patronizing version of black dialect. In contrast, many poets of the Harlem Renaissance (for example, McKay, Johnson, and Grimké) avoided dialect in their mature work, believing it hopelessly contaminated by the traditions of white minstrelsy and the entertainment demands of the white audience. Other Harlem Renaissance poets (especially those of the second generation, to be discussed in the Introduction to Part Two) used street vernacular and the rhythms of jazz and the blues, thereby producing a new language for American poetry.

Whether the Harlem Renaissance poets employed traditional English-language forms and vocabularies, or whether they made use of the sounds and rhythms they heard around them in the African-American community, their writing was both a challenge to white systems of exclusion and a celebration of black culture. The critic Houston Baker terms the Renaissance poets' adherence to tradition a "mastery of form" and their use of the vernacular a "deformation of mastery." Both styles emphasize the "sounding" voice, in contrast to the intense visuality of most poems influenced by imagism. Whereas the elite brands of experimental modernism depict a normatively white world in which people of color are subordinated, Harlem Renaissance poetry depicts the richness of African, African-American, and urban polyglot cultures. It suggests a world in which race is central to social understanding and opportunity. It presents black characters who try to survive and alter iniquitous systems while maintaining their own vibrant cultural reality.

A third, disparate group might be assembled of poets who in some way resisted the challenges of formal innovation. These traditionalists, or anti-modernist modernists, include Robert Frost and Robinson Jeffers. Both of these poets rejected what Jeffers termed modernist "trickiness," by which he must have meant the opacity and fragmentation of the text. Frost, writing from rural New England, captured the cosmic pessimism so common in modernity, but he did so in a dazzling array of time-honored rhythms and forms. Like Stevens, he provided an image of the mind in motion, but unlike many other great writers of his time, he never stopped wanting to represent the natural and human world in a recognizable way. Jeffers, writing from the central California coast, also explored the natural and human world. His moods, however, were often more dramatic and extreme than those of Frost, and he had no talent for Frost's gentle humor. Both Frost and Jeffers carry traditional lyric forms to new places, while evoking an ecological awareness that is as powerful today as when the poems were written. In their environmentalism, these poets connect back in unexpected ways to such experimental modernists as H.D., Williams, Stevens, Moore, and Reznikoff.

Sara Teasdale, Elinor Wylie, and Edna St. Vincent Millay may also be placed among the traditionalist modernists, at least in a stylistic sense. Like Frost and Jeffers, these women writers resisted the extremes of formal innovation, exploring instead the euphonious and semantic potential of inherited forms, rhythms, and vocabularies. But these poets explored women's perspectives in ways that have little to do with Frost or Jeffers. As women writers, they have a great deal in common with such experimentalists as H.D., Moore, Lowell, Crapsey, and Loy as well as with such Harlem Renaissance poets as Dunbar-Nelson, Johnson, and Grimké. Teasdale's and Wylie's lyrics tend to be elegant, graceful, stringent, and austere, as critic Cheryl Walker has observed. Millay's, in contrast, are outrageous and assertive. Teasdale and Wylie explored the slow psychological effects of loss, loneliness, and sadness. Millay dramatized a woman's emotional highs and lows, while making clear her feminist and progressive political views. She sometimes made a spectacle of her body, which may be interpreted as either an act of self-commodification or a subversive theatricalization of gender asymmetries. Writing in time-honored forms, Teasdale, Wylie, and Millay explored women's perspectives in ways that are often excitingly new.

Finally, the period is enhanced by a wide variety of popular poems and songs that helped create and interpret the very notion of modernity. Native Americans produced powerful poems of social observation and protest as well as ghost dance lyrics reflecting the sadness and anger of loss. Immigrant groups from East Asia, South Asia, the Middle East, and Europe provided poems that have stunning social or spiritual meanings. Poets and songwriters from Mexico, Puerto Rico, and Central and South America spoke memorably of imperialism, the struggle for survival, and love of the land. White and immigrant writers composed parlor songs that shaped the awareness of the nation. And African-American lyricists and musicians produced two new cultural forms that transformed the nation: the blues and jazz. The reciprocal relations between popular and elite forms—a dichotomy sometimes termed "high" and "low"—invigorated both kinds of poetry. This mutual influence is a relatively untold story of American poetry, and we hope that this anthology will bring it to the fore.

As we have suggested, modernist poetry is a low-consensus field. Different readers respond strongly to different groups and movements, different poets and poems. Back in 1950, F. O. Matthiessen suggested that the two top modernist poets were Frost and Eliot. Contemporary critics such as Houston Baker, Michael Cooke, Maureen Honey, and Venetria Patton have made convincing cases for the centrality of Harlem Renaissance poets such as McKay, Grimké, and Toomer. Marjorie Perloff, privileging the formal experiments of the avant-garde, concentrates her attention on Pound, Stein, Eliot, and Williams. Harold Bloom, valorizing the romantic traditions of poetry, locates a central quartet in Stevens, Crane (a second-generation poet), Frost, and Eliot, surrounding them with such lesser but still fascinating figures as Williams, Moore, Pound, H.D., John Crowe Ransom, and Conrad Aiken. Readers who focus on social issues often consider Williams, McKay, Grimké, Reznikoff, Lola Ridge, and Genevieve Taggard to be particularly valuable, along with the popular forms of immigrant poetry, corridos, parlor songs, blues, and jazz. Other readers, looking through the lens of gender and sexuality, find great power in the work of H.D., Stein, Moore, Lowell, Crapsey, Loy, Johnson, and Grimké. Yet other readers admire such independent spirits and stylistic masters as Cummings, Jeffers, and Ransom.

There exist as many modernisms as there are informed readers. The era's various poems and movements were often generated by a desire for aesthetic or cultural change—or by a principled resistance to such changes. In 1926, Gertrude Stein called modernist poems "wonderfully beautiful" and also "irritating annoying stimulating." So they were then, and so they still are today.

NATIVE-AMERICAN
SONGS AND POETRY

ALTHOUGH THE LAST DECADES of the nineteenth century saw the publication of numerous volumes of Native-American songs, ways, and poems, many important texts were yet to be collected and published. Ethnomusicologist Frances Densmore did much to fill in the gaps in the early part of the twentieth century. Born in Red Wing, Minnesota, Densmore devoted much of her time to the study of Chippewa music and published a book on that topic in 1910. A leader in the collection of Native-American music, she typically visited the federal reservations, transcribed and recorded the songs she heard, and interviewed the tribal members. The texts of several of her transcribed songs in English are anthologized here, along with songs and poems from other tribes that she and others studied.

Although the Native Americans were often restricted to reservations, they continued their cultural and ceremonial lives under this subjugation and retained their tribal identities in the face of federal pressures. These songs and poems are part of ever-evolving cultural traditions and should be approached in this way rather than simply as historical or anthropological texts. The written transcriptions included here are, at best, approximations of the songs and poems as actually performed because the performances vary from singer to singer, who improvises as he or she wishes. Moreover, the transcriber inevitably mediated the inscribed words.

FURTHER READING

John Bierhorst, ed. *The Sacred Path: Spells, Prayers and Power Songs of the American Indians*. New York: William Morrow, 1983.

William Brandon, ed. *The Magic World: American Indian Songs and Poems*. New York: William Morrow, 1971.

Frances Densmore. *Chippewa Music*. 1910; reprint, New York: Da Capo Press, 1972.

Brian Swann. *Native American Songs: An Anthology*. Mineola, N.Y.: Dover, 1996.

Paul Zolbrod. *Reading the Voice: Native American Oral Poetry on the Written Page*. Salt Lake City: University of Utah Press, 1995.

[CHIPPEWA]   *Song of the Crows*

> The first to come
> I am called
> Among the birds

> I bring the rain
> Crow is my name.
>
> *n.d.*

Densmore explains that the crows are believed to have given this song to a young man who was fasting. They then became his spirit power. The crows are the first birds to return to Chippewa lands in the spring, and they are said to bring the spring rain.

[CHIPPEWA]

Love-Charm Song

> What are you saying to me?
> I am arrayed like the roses
> And beautiful as they.
>
> *n.d.*

Love-charm songs are considered very powerful. Generally the person visualizes the desired result or goal while singing it, thereby gaining access to spiritual power as well.

[CHIPPEWA]

The Approach of the Storm

> From the half of the sky
> That which lives there
> Is coming, and makes a noise.
>
> *n.d.*

The Chippewa believe that thunder is a spirit of an incoming storm and is sent to warn the world of severe weather.

Song of the Captive Sioux Woman

> Any Chippewa
> Whenever I see
> I will greet him with a kiss
> Truly
> He pities me
>
> *n.d.*

According to Densmore, this song recalls an actual event during war. A Sioux woman who was defending her children was captured by the Chippewa. Before she was to be shot, she was given the chance to sing. Although her song is not known, it moved the elder brother of a chief so much that he rescued her. She later thanked the warriors for sparing her life and sang this song for them.

[CHIPPEWA]

As my eyes search the prairie

As my eyes search the prairie
I feel the summer in the spring
n.d.

This two-line song relies on rhyming thoughts rather than rhyming words for its organization.

[TETON SIOUX]

You Have No Horses

Well, when I was courting
"Horses you have none,"
To me was said.

Therefore, over the land
I roam.
n.d.

Horses were highly regarded property for a courting male.

[CHIPPEWA]

Arrow Song

Scarlet
Is its head.
n.d.

This brief poem reminds one of Japanese haiku, a favorite way of transcribing Native-American songs and poetry. While such songs are meant to be read as poems, it is important to remember that the songs are also sung and that words may be repeated many times as the singer improvises.

[OSAGE]

The Rising of the Buffalo Men

I rise, I rise,
I, whose tread make the earth to rumble.

❋   ❋   ❋

I rise, I rise,
I, in whose thighs there is strength.

I rise, I rise,
I, who whips his back with his tail in rage.

I rise, I rise,
I, in whose humped shoulders there is power.

I rise, I rise,
I, who shake his mane when angered.

I rise, I rise,
I, whose horns are sharp and curved.

n.d.

"The Rising of the Buffalo Men" is from the Osage rite of vigil. Such ritual songs helped the men prepare mentally and physically for the arduous experience of buffalo hunting, a major event in the life of Plains Indians.

[PAWNEE]   ## Song to the Pleiades

Look as they rise, rise
Over the line where sky meets the earth;
Pleiades![1]
Lo! They are ascending, come to guide us,
Leading us safely, keeping us one,
Pleiades,
Teach us to be, like you, united.

n.d.

"Song to the Pleiades," from the Hako ceremony performed whenever these stars are visible, is a plea for unity to the spirits, whom the Pawnee wish to emulate.

---

1. A readily visible cluster of stars in the constellation Taurus that contains six stars forming a tiny dipper.

THE GHOST DANCE RITUAL of the Upper Plains, with its songs that James Mooney of the Bureau of American Ethnology studied sympathetically at the end of the nineteenth century, continued to reach interested English-speaking readers into the twentieth century and to influence mainstream cultural perceptions of the Native-American plight. Mooney published his first translations of the songs in 1896 in collaboration with tribal leaders. The ghost dance religion, which combined Comanche, Arapaho, and Sioux spiritual beliefs with Christian motifs, is thought to be a response to battleground defeat, poverty, the remorseless seizure of land, and internment on reservations. Like earlier round dances, the ghost dances took place with dancers joined together in a loose circle. The songs continually varied and changed, depending on the wishes and feelings of the individual dancers, who would fall into trances and then sing about what they had met in the spirit world. The songs referred not only to spiritual beliefs but also to the daily lives and losses of the tribal members.

FURTHER READING

John Bierhorst, ed. *The Sacred Path: Spells, Prayers and Power Songs of the American Indians.* New York: William Morrow, 1983.

William Brandon, ed. *The Magic World: American Indian Songs and Poems.* New York: William Morrow, 1971.

A. LaVonne Brown Ruoff. *American Indian Literatures.* New York: Modern Language Association, 1990.

Brian Swann, ed. *Native American Songs and Poems: An Anthology.* Mineola, N.Y.: Dover, 1996.

Father, Have Pity on Me

Father, have pity on me,
Father, have pity on me;
I am crying for thirst,
I am crying for thirst;
All is gone — I have nothing to eat,
All is gone — I have nothing to eat.

1880s–1890s

While this song contains a recognizable Christian allusion to Jesus Christ on the Cross crying out, it also reflects on the pain and suffering of the tribes.

My Children, When at First I Liked the Whites

My children, when at first I liked the whites,
My children, when at first I liked the whites,
I gave them fruits,
I gave them fruits.

1880s–1890s

This song recalls a more promising time in the relationship between European settlers and
Native Americans, relating the Native American's generosity toward the newcomers.

When I Met Him Approaching

He! When I met him approaching —
He! When I met him approaching —
My children, my children —
I then saw the multitude plainly,
I then saw the multitude plainly.

1880s–1890s

This song originated with Sitting Bull. A dancer saw the messiah at the end of a spirit army
and sang about his vision.

My Son, Let Me Grasp Your Hand

My son, let me grasp your hand,
My son, let me grasp your hand,
Says the father,
Says the father.
You shall live,
You shall live,
Says the father,
Says the father.
I bring you a pipe,
I bring you a pipe,
Says the father,
Says the father.
By means of it you shall live,

By means of it you shall live,
Says the father,
Says the father.

1880s–1890s

"My Son, Let Me Grasp Your Hand" emphasizes the bond between father and son and the role of the pipe.

The Spirit Host Is Advancing, They Say

The spirit host is advancing, they say,
The spirit host is advancing, they say,
They are coming with the buffalo, they say,
They are coming with the buffalo, they say.
They are coming with the new earth, they say,
They are coming with the new earth, they say.

1880s–1890s

"The Spirit Host Is Advancing, They Say" expresses a vision of Native Americans' renewed strength with the return of the buffalo and the new earth.

He'Yoho'Ho! He'Yoho'Ho!

He'yoho'ho! He'yoho'ho!
The yellow-hide, the white skin
I have now put him aside —
I have now put him aside —
I have no more sympathy with him,
I have no more sympathy with him.
He'yoho'ho! He'yoho'ho!

1880s–1890s

This song expresses anger and disdain for the European Americans.

I'Yehe! My Children — Uhi'Yeye'heye!

I'yehe! my children — Uhi'yeye'heye!
I'yehe! my children — Uhi'yeye'heye!

I'yehe! we have rendered them desolate—Eye 'ae 'yuhe' yu!
I'yehe! we have rendered them desolate—Eye 'ae 'yuhe' yu!
The whites are crazy—Ahe 'yuhe' yu!

1880s–1890s

The speaker in this song imagines rendering the European Americans desolate and crazy.

SONGS OF DISPLACEMENT, MIGRATION, AND WORK I

Many oral and written traditions about displacement, migration, and work infused new voices, images, and poetic forms into American poetry from its cultural borders. Such communities as Chinese and Japanese mainland laborers, ethnically diverse Hawaiian plantation workers, and Russian and eastern European Jewish immigrant "sweatshop" employees relied on poetry to preserve their specific communal memory and culture and to tell stories about life in their new homes. Heterogeneous voices created lyrics about various subjects such as captivity, labor exploitation, loss, brutality, nostalgia, love, social activism, daily life and pleasures, freedom, self-empowerment, and ghettos. The poetry in this first grouping not only represents the lives and dreams of the communities included here but also draws attention to the poetic traditions of others in similar conditions at this time in the United States. At the end of this section of first-generation modernisms, a second grouping of poems addresses the cultures and lives of Chicanos, the ethnically diverse detainees at Angel Island, Asian Indians, Koreans, and Filipinos.

JINSHAN GE/SONGS OF GOLD MOUNTAIN

As soon as Cantonese men, who left China to escape severe economic depression, arrived on the West Coast of the United States during the 1830s, they began developing new folk songs and rhymed narratives to relate their experiences. (The earliest known poem is included in the first volume of this anthology.) Originally the men worked in mining, railroad construction, and farming, hoping to earn enough money to return to Canton. According to U.S. laws, initially they were not allowed to bring their wives or families. Because many men could not afford passage home or chose not to return, they began to settle into primarily male communities that formed the first Chinatowns in such cities as San Francisco. With the passage of the Chinese Exclusion Act of 1882, the first federal act to discriminate among immigrants on the basis of race and national identity, Chinese immigration came to a near halt. Nevertheless, the Chinese enclaves, composed of Cantonese settlers and the families of wealthy middle-class Chinese immigrant merchants, prospered.

Literary life in the Chinatowns was highly valued. Children learned from traditional Chinese texts that included classics, poetry, fiction, drama, and historical writings. Community Chinese-language newspapers published daily supplements of many genres, including poetry and the popular Cantonese vernacular rhymes and satires. Adult literary societies flourished, sponsoring poetry contests that drew submissions from Chinese poets in Peru, Mexico, Canada, and Cuba as well as throughout the United States. Marlon Hom reports that in July 1915 the topic for one such competition was "Hardships of the Chinese Overseas." The selections included here offer a range of attitude toward those hardships.

FURTHER READING

Iris Chang. *The Chinese in America*. New York: Viking, 2003.
Marlon K. Hom. *Songs of Gold Mountain: Cantonese Rhymes from San Francisco Chinatown*. Berkeley: University of California Press, 1992.

走盡天涯路。風塵跋涉多。

勞勞碌碌爲窮途。景遇未逢眞不妥。

朝夕思。憑誰救涸鮒。

遠念高堂妻共子。柴米油鹽尚有無。

[TRANS.] I have walked to
the very ends of the earth

I have walked to the very ends of the earth,
A dusty, windy journey.
I've toiled and I'm worn out, all for a miserable lot.
Nothing is ideal when I am down and out.
I think about it day and night—
Who can save a fish out of water?
From far away, I worry for my parents, my wife, my boy:
Do they still have enough firewood, rice, salt, and
    cooking oil?

n.d.

離愁觸起情何已。回憶長亭折柳枝。

陌頭飛絮入羅幃。惱煞鶯啼驚妾耳。

心癡癡。孤枕難成寐。

夫婿棲何地。臨粧懶畫眉。

[TRANS.] Where is my husband now?

Where is my husband now?
Before the vanity,[1] I no longer care to paint my brows.
Spring catkins from the fields fly in through the curtains;
Orioles' cries startle and frustrate me.
O, silly me—
I cannot sleep with only a pillow.
Aroused by the sorrow of parting, a sorrow without an end,
I longingly recall plucking willow branches at the
      Farewell Pavilion.[2]

n.d.

One of the wives of the "Gold Mountain men" (the term for the Cantonese men who left for the United States) wrote this poem of agonizing longing. Although such women led comfortable lives and were the envy of those who did not have connections in the United States, they suffered emotionally during separation from their husbands. Chinese women normally went to great effort to paint their eyebrows, and painting them in the shape of willows was popular. In line two, the speaker indicates her loss of interest in painting her brows, perhaps because she is depressed or because her husband is no longer there to admire them.

怎得重逢同作伴。免吾寮宿枕衾寒。

掛胆肝。癡情難割斷。

幾回惱煞月團圓。令我腸回更九轉。

意中人隔遠。獨自倚欄看。

[TRANS.] My loved one is far away

My loved one is far away.
Alone, by the railing, I look around aimlessly
Many times, depressed by a bright, full moon,[1]
My body aches and twists with ninefold grief and pain.
A heart left hanging.
A deep love that cannot be severed.
Just how can we be reunited and share companionship
      again?
Spare me from sleeping with only a cold quilt and pillow.

n.d.

In this poem, a sojourner to the United States expresses his feelings of loneliness and longing. Such expression by a man is unusual in Chinese literature. More often, male poets adopt female personae to express emotion.

---

1. Vanity table with mirror.
2. Plucking willow branches at the Farewell Pavilion refers to a lovers' parting. The reference was popularized by a Chinese Yuan dynasty drama

based on a T'ang dynasty story of premarital romance
1. The full moon implies the reunion of lovers, families, and friends.

子孫心肝蒂。財為養命基。

要纏十萬相扶持。烏鳥私情難比擬。

要緊記。利權歸自己。

縱使鳳毛稱濟美。孔方弗可須臾離。

[TRANS.] Sons and grandsons are dearest to one's heart

Sons and grandsons are dearest to one's heart.
Yet money is a foundation of life.
A hundred thousand dollars in a money belt will enable
    you to survive;
Even the filiality of a crow is no comparison.
Remember, by all means:
Profits and privileges are all in your possession.
A son may be illustrious and outstanding,
But you and your money should never have a separation!

          n.d.

Since so many Chinese men who came to the United States had no sons here, bachelor poets often consoled themselves with the thought that money can help out in life when one has no family.

由美返香港。腰纏十萬方。

髮長面垢似花郎。穿件驟布如爛網。

上瓊芳。公廳問唔講。

長衫客來着眼望。茶煙奉罷又檳榔。

[TRANS.] I've returned to Hong Kong from America

I've returned to Hong Kong from America,
With one hundred thousand dollars securely wrapped
    around my waist.
My hair is long, my face dirty, like a beggar;
My denim mule clothes are like a net, all torn and
    tattered.
I went up to King Fong Restaurant.
The maître d'hôtel[1] ignored me.
Then a gentleman in a long gown came over and
    sized me up;
After tea and tobacco, they even offered me betel nuts.

          n.d.

I've returned to Hong Kong from America tells of a Cantonese man's experience upon returning to Hong Kong, where he is not treated well by the maître d'hôtel. But apparently the hotel manager or owner, dressed in a traditional long gown, realizes that the poet is a sojourner from the United States and has money in spite of his appearance. The offer of betel nuts signals the attempt to court his favor after the initial social blunder.

1. Restaurant host.

寧可抵窮無米煮。要冲幾件光棍皮。

有誰知。藍褸看唔起。

不分庸與濁清奇。縱使談書和識理。

睇下副皮鼠。接待禮頻施。

[TRANS.] With a mere glance at the fur coat

With a mere glance at the fur coat,
Courtesy and hospitality are accorded in earnest,
Regardless of one's vulgarity or sophistication;
So what if you are learned and civil?
Who is to know?
A blue garb is simply despicable.
So, even if you face poverty and an empty rice bowl,
You must by all means put up a front with a few
      items of smart apparel.

n.d.

The Chinese-American immigrant who wrote *With a mere glance at the fur coat* realizes that in the United States one must dress well according to American standards in order to be accepted and to be judged as learned and sophisticated. The traditional Chinese blue clothing brings only discrimination and mistreatment. The poet suggests that it is better to go hungry than to dress as a traditional Chinese man.

淑性陶情眞消灑。同人漫笑我爲沙。

即管駕。動機隨街下。

公園物院幾繁華。快倩自由車一架。

學堂放暑假。未可遽回家。

[TRANS.] School lets out for the summer

School lets out for the summer.
No need to go home right away.
Bustling are the parks and museums;
So, hurry and rent a bicycle
Just to ride around.
Start pedaling, roll down the streets!
It's soothing and pleasing to the soul,
      a truly dashing experience.
But my companions tease me about
      what a big show-off I am.

n.d.

A Chinese schoolchild wrote this poem about anticipating summer without school and the luxury of riding a bicycle. Apparently a bicycle is highly coveted.

獅吼河東再復遇。○季常那有樂歡娛。○

當作吹。○還重口嘴嘴。○

蘭房不睦若何如。○角枕教訓毫不懼。○

娶着自由女。拓張脂虎威。○

[TRANS.] I married an emancipated woman

I married an emancipated woman,
Who flexes her tigress might.
What can I do about harmony in the bedroom?
She has no fear of lectures from the pillow side.
For her, they are so much wind.
She talks back all the more.
It's a repeat of the lioness roaring at the eastern riverbank.[1]
O, how did that Gwaiseung[2] ever have any fun?

n.d.

Many Chinese-American male immigrants disliked the way that female immigrants adopted Western standards of emancipation because it interfered with traditional marital roles. This poet bemoans his marriage to such a "tigress."

夫婿智愚隨我採。○縱然爹媽阻唔來。○

得意哉。○身處專制外。○

從今巾幗起高才。○男婦平權無更改。○

敬告眾姊妹。○何必心先灰。○

[TRANS.] In all earnestness, I speak to all my sisters

In all earnestness, I speak to all my sisters:
Why be so easily discouraged?
From now on, superior talents will arise among us
    women;
Men and women will have equal rights, and that will not
    change!
Won't that be wonderful?
A life without oppression!
We can choose our own mate, be he a wise man or a fool.
Even our parents can't interfere with us anymore!

n.d.

The female poet, an emancipated Chinese-American immigrant, urges other women to rejoice in emancipation. She directly addresses the traditional practice of arranged marriages that can be discarded in this new life in favor of selecting one's own husband.

1. Refers to a woman's outrage at her husband as well as her domination of him.

2. A henpecked husband, according to Chinese legends.

丈夫氣蓋世。紅粉豈能迷。

無奈人情慕少艾。軟索緊纏終莫擺。

困色界。溫柔鄉久滯。

任爾拔山霸力大。香幃攔住也頭低。

[TRANS.] A man's ambition is
to conquer the world

A man's ambition is to conquer the world.
He cannot let rouge and women bewitch him.
Admiration for the young and beautiful is natural;
　　so what can he do?
Escape from their tender demands and intimate
　　bonds is just impossible.
Stranded in the realm of lust,
You've stayed in the paradise of comfort far too long;
You may have the might to move mountains,
But you must bow to the fragrant curtain that blocks
　　your way.

n.d.

重逢甲子秋。鬢白不知憂。

穿紅着綠又穿綢。舉步身搖如擺柳。

性嗜酒。臨邛尋愛友。

醉向嫦娥細研究。巫山雲雨樂優游。

[TRANS.] I'm sixty, this autumn

I'm sixty, this autumn.
White hair on my temples, but I am not worried.
I dress in red and green, all fine silk;
When I walk, my body moves like a bending willow.
I indulge in wine,
And seek out a playmate in Laamkung.[1]
Tipsy, I turn to Seung Ngo[2] and examine her fine details.
The clouds and rain atop Wu Mountain[3] are the
　　wonders of making love.

n.d.

In *I'm sixty, this autumn*, the poet brags about his sexual
prowess. Like many of the Cantonese immigrants to the
United States, he is an elderly bachelor with no family here
but with wealth to spend on a life of pleasure.

---

1. A house of prostitution.　　　　　　　3. Wu Mountain is a symbol for sexual intimacy.
2. A woman with goddess-like beauty.

[TRANS.] Face haggard, turning yellow and puffy

Face haggard, turning yellow and puffy,
Waist, bent like a drawn bow.
Lying on his side next to a small lit lamp,
He holds the pipe as his family fortune goes down its hole.
Look at him:
Soon he will be six feet underground.
Lazy, remiss, he won't move even if you drag him.
He's about to meet King Yimlo at Hell's tenth palace.[1]

n.d.

This poem suggests the fate of an opium addict. Opium dens prospered in the early Chinatowns, and many men lost everything to this addiction.

面已變黃腫。腰似一枝弓。

側身點着小燈籠。扛起家財過斗孔。

看形容。就入埋人塚。

懶性懶情拖不動。將會閻王十殿宮。

[TRANS.] A green mansion is a place of filth and shame

A green mansion is a place of filth and shame,
Of lost chastity and lost virtue.
Most repulsive is it to kiss the customers on the lips
And let them fondle every part of my body.
I hesitate, I resist;
All the more ashamed, beyond words.
I must by all means leave this troupe of flowers and rouge;
Find a nice man and follow him as his woman.

n.d.

In *A green mansion*, a prostitute relates the sordidness of her life, along with her hope of finding a nice man to rescue her from it. Many young Chinese-American women found prostitution very lucrative in the early Chinatowns because so many elderly wealthy bachelors lived there.

蒙污青樓處。節烈盡喪除。

最恥同人來接嘴。任教旅客舞全軀。

妾豫推。益覺羞難語。

拚命要難花粉隊。跟個好老樂唱隨。

---

1. According to popular Chinese legend, hell has eighteen palaces. The eighteenth palace contains the most severe punishments, so the opium addict faces an unpleasant end.

HAWAIIAN PLANTATION WORK SONGS

When Hawai'i became a U.S. territory in 1900, a large-scale migration of Chinese, Japanese, Filipino, Puerto Rican, and Korean laborers to work in the sugarcane plantations had been under way for several decades. By 1920, more than three hundred thousand Asians had arrived to work in squalid conditions. The work of cutting and transporting sugarcane was dangerous and inhumane. Wages were poor. As a result, workers began to strike to improve conditions and wages. Much violence resulted, but eventually concessions from plantation owners were won. The work songs record the plight of the plantation laborers—men, women, and sometimes children—as they tried to make new lives for themselves in a new land.

Many of these songs were called *hole hole bushi*, a kind of Japanese blues. "Hole hole" refers to the work of stripping sugarcane off the stalk. "Bushi" refers to the tune, often taken from a Japanese folk song, to which the workers would spontaneously put their words and feelings as they worked and went about their daily lives. The songs tell of injustice but also of loneliness, love, and other emotions. As workers' contracts expired, many workers chose to move to the mainland or to go elsewhere, leaving the plantations to struggle to attract and retain laborers—as implied in *The laborers keep on coming*. These work songs look back to earlier plantation songs (included in the first volume of this anthology), and they have inspired such contemporary poets as Cathy Song and Garrett Hongo. They have been written down in English, in pidgin English (a mixture of languages), and sometimes in both Japanese and English. Our selections begin with bilingual versions and conclude with English-only versions.

FURTHER READING

Juliana Chang, ed. *Quiet Fire: A Historical Anthology of Asian American Poetry, 1892–1970.* New Brunswick, N.J.: Rutgers University Press, 1996.

Gail Miyasaki. "Hole Hole Bushi: The Only Song of the Japanese in Hawai'i." *Hawai'i Herald* (Honolulu). February 2, 1973, 4–5.

Franklin S. Odo. "Hole Hole Bushi: Songs of Hawai'i's Japanese Immigrants." *Mana: A South Pacific Journal of Art, Culture, Language, and Literature* (Suva, Fiji: Institute of Pacific Studies) 6, no. 1 (1981). With Harry Urata.

Ronald Takaki. *Strangers from a Different Shore: A History of Asian Americans.* Boston: Back Bay Books, 1998.

Yukuo Uyehara. "'The Hore-Hore-Bushi': A Type of Japanese Folksong Developed and Sung Among Early Immigrants in Hawaii." *Social Process in Hawaii* 28 (1980–81): 110–20.

Dekasegi wa kuru kuru

Dekasegi wa kuru kuru
Hawai'i wa tsumaru
Ai no Nakayama
Kane ga furo

[TRANS.] The laborers keep on coming

The laborers keep on coming
Overflowing these Islands
But it's only Inspector
Nakayama
Who rakes in the profits.

n.d.

Joyaku wa kirerushi

Joyaku wa kirerushi
Miren wa nokoru
Danburo no wahine nya
Ki ga nokoru

[TRANS.] The contract is over and yet

The contract is over and yet
I hate to give up my work
If I do, I'll miss the
Woman who lives
Outside the camp.

n.d.

Sodo okoshite

Sodo okoshite
Sowareru mi narya
Hayaku sodo ga
Okosohitai

[TRANS.] If we can get married

If we can get married
By stirring up troubles,
I'd like to start the troubles
Very soon.

n.d.

In the rush at pau hana

In the rush at pau hana
I get caught in cane leaves,
When I stumble and fall,
They prickle, they jab.

n.d.

I hate hole hole work

I hate hole hole[1] work
Let's finish cutting cane
And go to Honolulu.

n.d.

---

1. Stripping sugarcane (Japanese).

With one woven basket

With one woven basket
Alone I came
Now I have children
And even grandchildren too.

n.d.

Should I return to Japan?

Should I return to Japan?
I'm lost in thoughts
Here in Hawai'i.

n.d.

JAPANESE IMMIGRANT POETRY

First-generation Japanese immigrants, or the Issei, began traveling to Hawaii during the 1880s and then to the U.S. mainland in the 1890s. The Japanese government, under the Meiji dynasty, financed the industrialization and militarization of a modern and more Western Japanese nation by taxing farmland and depressing the price of rice. As a result, many Japanese farmers lost their land and sought work in the United States. Because of the Chinese immigration experience, which resulted in a large initial generation of bachelors in Chinatowns, the Japanese government encouraged women and entire families to resettle with the men. Spirits were at first high. But the Japanese immigrants soon found that they faced discrimination as well. Their poetry, written primarily in haiku, reflects both their hopes and their shattered dreams. It has inspired later generations of Japanese-American poets.

FURTHER READING

Ronald Takaki. *Strangers from a Different Shore: A History of Asian Americans*. Boston: Back Bay Books, 1998.

Day of vast dreaming

Day of vast dreaming!
I sailed for America
Billowing with hope.

n.d.

Family treasures

Family treasures
Tarnish in the wicker trunk
I carry on board.

n.d.

With eyes filled with tears

With eyes filled with tears
I look back to my homeland,
Glimpsing one last time.

n.d.

Once a Meiji voice

Once a Meiji voice,
Traveling the Pacific,
It has grown rougher.

n.d.

Following U.S. Commodore Matthew Perry's forced opening of Japan for trade in 1853, the Meiji dynasty pursued a program of modernization and westernization.

Streamers of farewell

Streamers of farewell
I press between my fingers
Until blood flows through.

n.d.

My island spirit

My island spirit
Cast behind to cross the sea.
Ah, the spacious world!

n.d.

Loud waves up and down

Loud waves up and down
Over the North Pacific
Crossing the wide sea
I stand on white-washed decks
And am wet with salty spray.

n.d.

Just for a while

Just for a while
Meeting up with a person
Who was anti-Japanese,
I scraped against a spirit
Dissonant with mine.

n.d.

Eager to become

Eager to become
One with the alien land,
I make a home.

n.d.

A barren grassland

A barren grassland
Turned to fruitful fields by sweat
Of my husbandry:
But I, made dry and yellow
By permitting others' insults.

n.d.

America . . . then

America . . . then
An image of hope and desire,
Now a time of tears.

n.d.

Issei's history—

Issei's history—
Gritting of one's will
Against exclusion.

n.d.

JEWISH LABOR POETRY

Between the 1880s and World War I, nearly one-third of all Jews in Russia and east-
ern Europe immigrated, mostly to the United States, as they faced pogrom after
pogrom aimed at their annihilation in their homelands. By 1905 about a half-
million Jews had settled in the Lower East Side of New York City, bringing with
them their communal and religious customs, a lively intellectual and cultural life
(epitomized by such institutions as the Yiddish Theater), and a strong determina-
tion to become permanent citizens. Men, women, and children survived by work-
ing in the garment industry and in other menial jobs. Many found themselves
in life-threatening conditions in sweatshops, which they memorialized in both
poetry and song. Whereas Charles Reznikoff (included in this anthology) wrote
about such lives in English, many other poets, like Morris Rosenfeld represented
in this entry, wrote in their native language, which in most cases was Yiddish—a
hybridized language derived from Hebrew, German, and other European lan-
guages. Labor union efforts gradually transformed working conditions for the bet-
ter, and access to education eventually allowed children or grandchildren to find
less punishing work. One such child, whose family worked in the sweatshops and
who began working in the garment trade himself, was Yip Harburg (included in
the Jazz and Musical Theater Lyrics entry of this anthology). He wrote the lyrics
to the American classic "Over the Rainbow" and enjoyed an outstanding career as
a lyricist in theater and film.

FURTHER READING

Jules Chametzky, John Felstiner, Hilene Flanzbaum, and Kathryn Hellerstein, eds. *Jewish Amer-
ican Literature: A Norton Anthology*. New York: Norton, 2001.
Irving Howe and Kenneth Libo, eds. *How We Lived: A Documentary History of Immigrant Jews
in America, 1880–1930*. New York: Richard Mark Publishers, 1979.
Leon Stein. *The Triangle Fire*. Ithaca, N.Y.: Cornell University Press, 2001.
Barbara Wertheimer. *We Were There*. New York: Pantheon Books, 1977.

Memorial to Triangle Fire Victims

Morris Rosenfeld

Neither battle nor fiendish pogrom
Fills this great city with sorrow;
Nor does the earth shudder or lightning rend the heavens,
No clouds darken, no cannon's roar shatters the air.
Only hell's fire engulfs these slave stalls
And Mammon devours our sons and daughters.
Wrapt in scarlet flames, they drop to death from his maw
And death receives them all.
Hear my sorrow:
See where the dead are hidden in dark corners,
Where life is choked from those who labor.
Oh, woe is me, and woe is to the world
On this Sabbath
When an avalanche of red blood and fire
Pours forth from the god of gold on high
As now my tears stream forth unceasingly.
Damned be the rich!
Damned be the system!
Damned be the world!
Over whom shall we weep first?
Over the burned ones?
Over those beyond recognition?
Over those who have been crippled?
Or driven senseless?
Or smashed?
I weep for them all.
Now let us light the holy candles
And mark the sorrow
Of Jewish masses in darkness and poverty.
This is our funeral,
These our graves,
Our children,
The beautiful, beautiful flowers destroyed,
Our lovely ones burned,
Their ashes buried under a mountain of caskets.
There will come a time
When your time will end, you golden princes. Meanwhile,
Let this haunt your consciences:
Let the burning building, our daughters in flame

Be the nightmare that destroys your sleep,
The poison that embitters your lives,
The horror that kills your joy.
And in the midst of celebrations for your children,
May you be struck blind with fear over the
Memory of this red avalanche
Until time erases you.

1911

This poem commemorates the 1911 Triangle Shirtwaist Company fire in New York City, in which 146 young Jewish and Italian female workers died. Eight hundred were trapped in the building in one of the worst industrial fires in U.S. history, and many fell to their deaths as the flames engulfed the structure. More than fifty thousand mourners marched in a memorial parade to bury the workers together in the Workmen's Circle Cemetery. In 1909–10, the shirtwaist workers at this factory had struck, unsuccessfully, to demand safer working conditions and a more sanitary environment. Rosenfeld, who was known as the "poet laureate of the slum and sweatshops," wrote the poem several days after the fire and presented it at the memorial held at the Metropolitan Opera House. *The Jewish Daily Forward* printed the poem alone on its front page as a tribute to the victims and their families. Rosenfeld labored in the sweatshops until working conditions left him too disabled to work there. In spite of his hardships, he wrote frequently for the Jewish press and Yiddish Theater and published several volumes of poetry. This poem was translated by Leon Stein.

The Uprising of the 20,000

In the black winter of 1909
When we froze and bled on the picket line
We showed the world that women could fight
And we rose and we won with women's might.

Hail the waist makers of 1909
Making their stand on the picket line
Breaking the power of those who reign
Pointing the way and smashing the chain.

And we gave new courage to the men
Who carried on in 1910
And shoulder to shoulder we'll win through
Led by the ILGWU.

n.d.

The International Ladies' Garment Workers' Union (ILGWU) strike described in this lyric initiated a wave of labor union organization that changed working conditions between 1909 and 1920. As a result of this strike, more than 300 of the 450 garment firms in New York were forced to agree to a fifty-two-hour workweek and overtime pay, and to recognize the legitimacy of organized labor unions. The strike began when nineteen-year-old Clara Lemlich spoke out in Yiddish to the workers, urging her mainly Jewish audience to walk out of their meeting. Italian and Irish workers joined the strike.

WILLA CATHER
1873–1947

WILLA CATHER, one of the outstanding American fiction writers of the early twentieth century, is best known for her novels of pioneer life on the Nebraska prairie and elsewhere, including *O Pioneers!* (1913), *My Ántonia* (1918), and *Death Comes for the Archbishop* (1927). Cather was prolific throughout a long and versatile writing career as a fiction writer, journalist, editor, critic, and poet. Her poems, written early in her career, explore the passionate nature of women and men living on the rolling prairies of the Midwest.

Born in rural Virginia in 1873, Cather moved with her family to Nebraska when she was eight, living first on a farm with her grandparents, then in the town of Red Cloud, where her father opened an insurance office. Upon her graduation from the University of Nebraska in 1895, Cather moved to Pittsburgh, where she worked as a journalist and editor and published her first book of poems, *April Twilights*, in 1903. In 1906, she moved to New York City to begin a successful career as a magazine editor with *McClure's* magazine. Under the influence of fiction writer Sarah Orne Jewett, who wrote brilliantly about her native Maine, Cather focused her own fiction on her native soil, the Nebraska prairie of her childhood. In 1912 Cather left her editorial post at *McClure's* to devote herself to writing fiction, and a year later she published her first masterpiece, *O Pioneers!* (which was dedicated to Jewett's memory).

Cather was less prolific in poetry than in fiction, telling a critic in 1925 that "I do not take myself seriously as a poet." Nevertheless, her poems, mostly written before 1904, show the same immersion in the prairie rhythms of Nebraska and the same empathic attention to interior states of mind and feeling.

FURTHER READING

Willa Cather. *Stories, Poems, and Other Writings*. Ed. Sharon O'Brien. New York: Library of America, 1992.

Prairie Spring

Evening and the flat land,
Rich and sombre and always silent;
The miles of fresh-plowed soil,
Heavy and black, full of strength and harshness;
The growing wheat, the growing weeds,
The toiling horses, the tired men;
The long empty roads,
Sullen fires of sunset, fading,
The eternal, unresponsive sky.
Against all this, Youth,
Flaming like the wild roses,
Singing like the larks over the plowed fields,
Flashing like a star out of the twilight;
Youth with its insupportable sweetness,
Its fierce necessity,
Its sharp desire,
Singing and singing,
Out of the lips of silence,
Out of the earthy dusk.

1903

"Prairie Spring," written in free verse, served later as the lyric prologue to Cather's novel
O Pioneers!

Macon Prairie

(NEBRASKA)

She held me for a night against her bosom,
The aunt who died when I was yet a baby,
The girl who scarcely lived to be a woman.
Stricken, she left familiar earth behind her,
Mortally ill, she braved the boisterous ocean,
Dying, she crossed irrevocable rivers,
Hailed the blue Lakes, and saw them fade forever,
Hungry for distances;—her heart exulting
That God had made so many seas and countries
To break upon the eye and sweep behind her.
From one whose love was tempered by discretion,
From all the net of caution and convenience

She snatched her high heart for the great adventure,
Broke her bright bubble under far horizons, —
Among the skirmishers that teased the future,
Precursors of the grave slow-moving millions
Already destined to the Westward-faring.

They came, at last, to where the railway ended,
The strange troop captained by a dying woman;
The father, the old man of perfect silence,
The mother, unresisting, broken-hearted,
The gentle brother and his wife, both timid,
Not knowing why they left their native hamlet;
Going as in a dream, but ever going.

In all the glory of an Indian summer,
The lambent transmutations of October,
They started with the great ox-teams from Hastings
And trekked in a southwesterly direction,
Boring directly toward the fiery sunset.
Over the red grass prairies, shaggy-coated,
Without a goal the caravan proceeded;
Across the tablelands and rugged ridges,
Through the coarse grasses which the oxen breasted,
Blue-stem and bunch-grass, red as sea-marsh samphire.[1]
Always the similar, soft undulations
Of the free-breathing earth in golden sunshine,
The hardy wind, and dun hawks flying over
Against the unstained firmament of heaven.

In the front wagon, under the white cover,
Stretched on her feather-bed and propped with pillows,
Never dismayed by the rude oxen's scrambling,
The jolt of the tied wheel or brake or hold-back,
She lay, the leader of the expedition;
And with her burning eyes she took possession
Of the red waste, — for hers, and theirs, forever.

A wagon-top, rocking in seas of grasses,
A camp-fire on a prairie chartless, trackless,
A red spark under the dark tent of heaven.

---

1. A common coastal plant.

Surely, they said, by day she saw a vision,
Though her exhausted strength could not impart it, —
Her breathing hoarser than the tired cattle.

When cold, bright stars the sunburnt days succeeded,
She took me in her bed to sleep beside her, —
A sturdy bunch of life, born on the ocean.
Always she had the wagon cover lifted
Before her face. The sleepless hours till daybreak
She read the stars.

"Plenty of time for sleep," she said, "hereafter."

She pointed out the spot on Macon Prairie,
Telling my father that she wished to lie there.
"And plant, one day, an apple orchard round me,
In memory of woman's first temptation,
And man's first cowardice."
That night, within her bosom,
I slept.
             Before the morning
I cried because the breast was cold to me.
Now, when the sky blazes like blue enamel,
Brilliant and hard over the blond cornfields,
And through the autumn days our wind is blowing
Like the creative breath of God Almighty —
Then I rejoice that offended love demanded
Such wide retreat, and such self-restitution;
Forged an explorer's will in a frail woman,
Asked of her perfect faith and renunciation,
Hardships and perils, prophecy and vision,
The leadership of kin, and happy ending
On the red rolling land of Macon Prairie.

1903

Macon Prairie is in south-central Nebraska.

ALEXANDER POSEY
1873–1908

ALEXANDER POSEY is best known for his involvement in Native-American territorial politics, his editorship of the *Eufala Indian Journal* in Oklahoma, the first Native American–published daily newspaper in the nation, and the comic letters written by his fictional persona, *Fus Fixico* (Heartless Bird). But Posey also wrote poetry that appeared in publications in Native-American territories as well as the Eastern and Midwestern United States. His poetry reflects his reading as a student at Bacone Indian University in Muskogee (in what is now Oklahoma), where he was introduced to the work of John Greenleaf Whittier, Henry Wadsworth Longfellow, Alfred Tennyson, Henry David Thoreau, John Burroughs, and other nineteenth-century writers. Posey was also influenced by the popular dialect literature of the time, which hearkened back to the poetry of the Scottish bard Robert Burns and included as its apex the work of the African-American poet Paul Laurence Dunbar (included in the first volume of this anthology). Dissatisfied with the way Creek cultural experience was usually translated into English, Posey tried to imitate the rhythms and cadences of the musical Creek language in his poetry.

Born and raised in the Native-American territories of what is now Oklahoma, Posey belonged to the Wind clan of the Tuskegee Creek nation. His mother was half Creek and half Chickasaw, but because Creek membership followed matrilineal lines, he was deemed Creek. Although his father was born to white (Scotch-Irish) parents, he too called himself Creek. Posey originally spoke only Creek, learning native traditions and history from his mother. Later, his father forced him to speak only English in order to gain a formal education. Perhaps as a result of his estrangement from the Creek language, his mixed-blood status, and his education, Posey questioned Creek culture and politics with a satirical voice. Believing that Native Americans should assimilate to European-American customs in the interests of survival, yet reverent toward the landscape of his youth, Posey wrote a critical and humorous discourse from a position within the Creek nation.

FURTHER READING

Daniel F. Littlefield. *Alex Posey: Creek Poet, Journalist, and Humorist*. Lincoln: University of Nebraska Press, 1997.

Alexander Posey. *The Poems of Alexander Posey*. Ed. Minnie Posey. New York: Houghton Mifflin, 1910.

Ode to Sequoyah

The names of Waitie[1] and Boudinot—
    The valiant warrior and gifted sage—
And other Cherokees, may be forgot,
    But thy name shall descend to every age;
The mysteries enshrouding Cadmus'[2] name
Cannot obscure thy claim to fame.

The people's language cannot perish, — nay,
    When from the face of this great continent
    Inevitable doom hath swept away
The last memorial—the last fragment
    Of tribes, — some scholar learned shall pore
Upon thy letters, seeking ancient lore.

Some bard shall lift a voice in praise of thee,
    In moving numbers tell the world how men
Scoffed thee, hissed thee, charged with lunacy![3]
    And who could not give 'nough honor when
At length, in spite of jeers, of want and need,
Thy genius shaped a dream into a deed.

By cloud-capped summits in the boundless west
    Or mighty river rolling to the sea,
Where'er thy footsteps led thee on that quest,
    Unknown, rest thee, illustrious Cherokee![4]

1899

This ode is to the well-known inventor of the Cherokee syllabary (listing of syllables), Sequoyah, or George Guess (1770–1843). Sequoyah was also the name of the proposed but never fulfilled Native-American state to be carved out of Oklahoma Territory at the same time that a state for whites was formed.

1. A leader of the Cherokee Treaty Party, Stand Watie advocated the removal of the tribe from the Southeast to Oklahoma. His brother Elias Boudinot, also a leader of this party, edited the *Cherokee Phoenix*, the Cherokee national newspaper. Watie was assassinated for his pro-removal views in 1839, the year of the enforced death march known as the "Trail of Tears," which resulted in the death of as many as four thousand Cherokees.

2. Cadmus introduced the alphabet to Greece in Greek myth.
3. Sequoyah was accused of lunacy while attempting to compile a list of Cherokee syllables because of the characters he wrote down.
4. Sequoyah's burial site is unknown. He disappeared during his search for tribesmen who had decided to go to Mexico rather than move to the Oklahoma Indian Territory.

Hotgun on the Death of Yadeka Harjo

"Well so," Hotgun say,
    "My ol'-time frien', Yadeka Harjo,[1] he
Was died the other day,
    An' they was no ol'-timer left but me.

"Hotulk Emathla he
    Was go to be good Injin long time 'go,
An' Woxie Harjoche
    Been dead ten years, or twenty, maybe so.

"All had to die at las';
    I live long time, but now my days was few;
'Fore long poke-weeds an' grass
    Be growin' all aroun' my grave-house[2] too."

Wolf Warrior he listen close,
    An' Kono Harjo pay close 'tention, too;
Tookpafka Micco he almos'
    Let his pipe go out a time or two.

                                        1908

This dialect poem includes many of the characters that appear in Posey's famous *Fus Fixico* letters. The letters' central figure, Hotgun (Mitchka Hiyah), was, according to Posey, "a philosopher, carpenter, blacksmith, fiddler, clockmaker, worker in metals, and a maker of medicines." Wolf Warrior, Kono Harjo, and Tookpafka Micco also appear in the letters. The other characters in the poem are either real persons or based on real persons. Hotulk Emathla (Edward Bullet) was principal chief of the Creeks in 1895.

LOLA RIDGE
1873–1941

ALTHOUGH LITTLE KNOWN today, Lola Ridge was a notable poet in her own time. When she died, William Rose Benét called her "a rebel . . . in the lineage of Spartacus," a poet who espoused "the cause of the downtrodden everywhere." Some of her poems, such as "The Fifth-Floor Window" and "Phyllis," evoke mo-

---

1. Yadeka Harjo was a well-known figure in the Creek nation who lived more than ninety years.

2. Traditional Creeks build roofed houses over graves.

ments in the lives of the kinds of people that respectable society chooses not to see. These sharply observed poems brim with the textures and hurts of everyday life among the urban poor. Other poems, such as "Morning Ride" and "Stone Face," protest gross miscarriages of justice. Ridge inserted an almost reportorial narrative style, a sensitivity to the modern ambience, an eye for telling images, and a powerful social conscience into the poetry of her time.

Of Irish origin, Ridge spent her formative years in New Zealand and Australia, living in poverty with her mother. After a failed marriage and a period of art study in Sydney, she immigrated to the United States at the age of thirty-four. Residing in New York, she supported herself by means of factory work, modeling, and other jobs. She also changed her first name from Rose Emily to Lola, becoming active in the worlds of radical politics and avant-garde poetry. Involved in Emma Goldman's anarchist movement, she advocated the causes of women, working people, and immigrants, and she attacked injustice. She published five volumes of poetry as well as individual poems in such important journals as *Mother Earth*, the *New Republic*, the *Nation*, the *Dial*, the *New Masses*, and *Poetry*. She served as editor of the literary magazines *Others* and *Broom*. "Harassed by bodily infirmity," in her friend Benét's words, she died at home in Brooklyn at the age of sixty-seven, "valiant to the end."

FURTHER READING

William Rose Benét. "Lola Ridge: 1873–1941." *The Saturday Review of Literature*, May 31, 1941: 8.

Nancy Berke. *Women Poets on the Left: Lola Ridge, Genevieve Taggard, Margaret Walker.* Gainesville: University of Florida Press, 2001.

Lola Ridge. *Dance of Fire*. New York: Harrison Smith and Robert Haas, 1935.

——. *Red Flag*. New York: Viking Press, 1927.

The Fifth-Floor Window

Walls . . . iridescent with eyes
that stare into the courtyard
at the still thing lying
in the turned-back snow
stark precipice of walls
with a foam of white faces
lathering their stone lips . . .
faces of the shawled women
the walls pour forth without aim
under the vast pallor of the sky.

They point at the fifth-floor window
and whisper one to the other:

"It's hard on a man out of work
an' the mother gone out of his door
with a younger lover . . ."

The blanched morning stares
in like a face flattened against the pane
where the little girl used to cry all day
with a feeble and goading cry.
Her father, with his eyes at bay
before the vague question of the light,
says that she fell . . .
Between his twitching lips
a stump of cigarette
smoulders, like a burning root.

Only the wind was abroad
in high cold hours
of the icy and sightless night
with back to the stars—
night growing white and still as a pillar of salt
and the snow mushing without sound—
when something hurtled through the night
and drifted like a larger snow-flake
in the trek of the blind snow
that stumbled over it in heaps—
only white-furred wind
pawed at the fifth-floor window
and nosed cigarette-butts on the sill . . .
till the window closed down softly
on the silvery fleece of wind
that tore and left behind its flying fringes.

Now the wind
down the valley of the tenements
sweeps in weakened rushes
and meddles with the clothes-lines
where little white pinafores sway stiffly
like dead geese.
Over the back-yards
that are laid out smooth and handsome as a corpse
under the seamless snow,

the sky is a vast ash-pit
where the buried sun
rankles in a livid[1] spot.

1926

Phyllis

Phyllis' face is a weathered sign
to the palace of gliding cars
over the line where the trolley dips:
a dime for a wired rose —
nickel a ride to the zigzag stars —
and the men in elegant clothes
who feed you on cardboard ships . . .
and the sea floats so fine!
like a green and gorgeous bubble
God blew out of his lips. . . .

When Phyllis carries down the stair
the ritual of her face,
your greeting takes her unaware
and her glance is timid-bold
as a dog's . . . unsure of its place.
With that hair of the rubbed-off gold
of a wedding-ring worn to a thread,
and those luminous eyes in their rims of paint,
she looks a bedizened saint.

But when the worn moon
like a face
still beautiful . . .
wavers above the Battery[1]
and light comes in, mauve-grey,
squeezing through shutters of furnished rooms,
till only corners hold spots of darkness
as a table-cloth its purple stains
when a festival is ended . . .
then Phyllis creeps into the house.

---

1. Grayish or bluish, like a bruise.
1. An area along the docks in Lower Manhattan. In the 1920s it was a slum populated by impoverished immigrants.

* * *

The paint is lonesome on her cheek . . .
the paint is gone from off her mouth
that curls back loosely from her teeth.
She pushes slackly at the dawn
that crawls upon the yellow blind,
and enters like an aimless moth
whose dim wings hover and alight
upon the blurred face of the clock
or on the pallor of her feet
or anything that's white . . .
until dispersed upon the sheet,
all limp . . . her waxen body lies
in its delinquent grace
like a warm bent candle
that flears[2] about its place.

1926

Morning Ride

Headlines chanting—
youth
lynched ten years ago cleared—
Skyscrapers
seeming still
whirling on their concrete
bases,
windows fanged—
leo frank
lynched ten
            say it with flowers
wrigley's spearmint gum
            carter's little liver[1]—
lean
to the soft blarney of the wind
fooling with your hair,
look

2. Perhaps flares; perhaps floors (grins mockingly).
1. News of Frank's subsequent exoneration alternates with advertisements for flowers, gum, and Carter's Little Liver Pills.

milk-clouds oozing over the blue
Step lively Please
Let 'Em Out First Let 'Em Out
did he too feel it on his forehead,
the gentle raillery of the wind,
as the rope pulled taut over the tree
in the cool dawn?

1926

"Morning Ride," set in busy midtown Manhattan in the mid-1920s, recalls the notorious lynching of Leo Frank (1884–1915) in Georgia ten years before. Frank, a Jew living in Atlanta, was falsely accused of murdering a twelve-year-old white Protestant girl named Mary Phagan. (The real murderer was another white Protestant named Jim Conley.) Convicted as a result of religious prejudice, Frank was sentenced to death but had his sentence commuted to life imprisonment. Two months later twenty-five armed members of the Ku Klux Klan broke into Georgia State Prison, abducted Frank, and hanged him in a grove outside of Marietta, Georgia. Crowds gathered to see Frank's body, and photographs were taken, one of which became a souvenir postcard. No one was ever prosecuted for Frank's murder.

Stone Face

They have carved you into a stone face, Tom Mooney,
You, there lifted high in California
Over the salt wash of the Pacific,
With your eyes . . . crying in many tongues,
Goading, innumerable eyes of the multitudes,
Holding in them all hopes, fears, persecutions,
Forever straining one way.

Even in the Sunday papers, and your face tight-bitten like a pierced fist,
The eyes have a transfixed gleam as they had glimpsed some vision and there hung
Impaled as on a bright lance.

Too much lip-foam has dripped on you, too many
And disparate signatures are scrawled on your stone face that all
Have set some finger on, to say who made you for the years
To mouth as waves mouth rock . . . you, a rough man,
Rude-nurtured, casually shouldering
Through a May-day crowd in San Francisco,
To be cast up out of the dark mass—terribly gestating, swarming without feature,
And raised with torsion to identity.

* * *

Now they—who wrote you plain, with Sacco and the fish-monger,[1]
High on the scroll of the Republic—
Look up with a muddled irritation at your clenched face,
It is set up in full sight under the long
Gaze of the generations—to be there
Haggard in the sunrise, when San Quentin
Prison shall be caved in and its steel ribs
Food for the ant-rust . . . and Governor Rolph[2]
A fleck of dust among the archives.

1935

Tom Mooney (1892–1942) was a labor leader falsely convicted of murder after a bomb exploded at a San Francisco labor demonstration in 1916. Mooney had been nowhere near the scene, and the testimony against him was perjured. He eventually received a pardon in 1939, after spending twenty-three years in jail.

ROBERT FROST
1874–1963

ROBERT FROST holds a position in American poetry similar to that of Emily Dickinson, his favorite poet. He is one of the international stars. Two mythic images of Frost dominate in the public's mind. He is viewed first and foremost as a nature poet. Many link him to the American Transcendentalists, including Ralph Waldo Emerson and Henry David Thoreau. Yet this perspective is incomplete. He revered Dickinson above Emerson and Thoreau, embracing her ability to use nature as a way of contemplating human character and feelings. Frost himself stated that his nature poetry really addressed "outer and inner weather." Equally important, Frost is seen as a poet in the tradition of poet-sages and statesmen like the Roman Horace. This mythic image also is only a partial view as well, even though the most popular photos show him near the end of his life at the inaugural of President

1. Nicola Sacco, a shoemaker, and Bartolomeo Vanzetti, a fish peddler, were wrongly convicted of murder in Massachusetts in 1921, probably because of their anarchist beliefs and immigrant backgrounds. They were executed in 1927.
2. James Rolph (1869–1934) was the Republican governor of California in 1931–34. An alcoholic and supporter of lynch mobs, he refused to pardon Mooney, reputedly following the orders of Herbert Fleishacker, president of the Anglo-California National Bank.

John F. Kennedy in 1961, bravely reciting his poetry in spite of frigid winds that swept away his manuscript. He fully entered the public life of the nation little more than a decade before his death. The most comprehensive appraisals of his poetry acknowledge these two outstanding contributions — but they also ascribe to him a near-existential, stoic vision of terror and fortitude. He found such qualities in the New England Appalachian culture and dialect that dominate not only his nature lyrics but also his psychological portraits and his philosophical and reflective poems.

Because Frost was an upwardly mobile, European-American, educated male who was eventually successful enough as a poet to support himself through his published poetry, public readings, and teaching, many assume that his life was dominated by a pattern of prosperity, success, and happiness. But this was not the case. His legendary stoicism is grounded in his own life. He was born in California, not (as many think) in New England. His move to Lawrence, Massachusetts, at age eleven occurred when his father committed suicide after losing a political election. This experience, he said, made him wary of politics. After the death, his mother uprooted the family to give them a fresh start in Massachusetts, supporting them by teaching. After Frost graduated from high school in 1891, he married and began a family. For the next twenty years, until 1912, he struggled with poverty, taking jobs as a mill worker, dairy farmer, schoolteacher, and college instructor. He attended classes at both Dartmouth and Harvard during this time and worked on his poetry. An infant daughter and three-year-old son died during this period, but four children survived into adulthood.

In 1912, Frost decided to move his family to England to jump-start his career as a poet. This change proved to be a turning point. He met the English Georgian poets and wrote full-time, becoming especially close to Edward Thomas. He also met Ezra Pound and other poets such as William Butler Yeats. His association with Pound proved to be the key that he was hoping for. Pound embraced Frost's work, fostering the publication of his first collection, *A Boy's Will*, in London. Pound's sponsorship also resulted in the publication of Frost's second book, *North of Boston*, in London. This collection was then published in the United States; and Frost's career trajectory changed from that of a struggling unknown poet to that of a rising star.

Frost returned to the United States because of his success in locating a U.S. publisher and because World War I was beginning. This move back proved fortuitous. Amy Lowell, Pound's rival, also decided to mentor Frost, featuring him in her edited *Tendencies in Modern American Poetry* and writing a legendary review of *North of Boston*. Although Frost privately chafed at her sponsorship, without her he could not have made the quick transition to being a successful poet on the teaching, lecture, and public reading circuit. Lowell, who was not easily impressed by any poet, took to Frost from her first reading of him. She found *North of Boston* at the Poetry Bookshop in London and said, "I immediately took off my hat to the unknown poet, and I have been taking it off ever since in a positively wearying repetition."

Frost enjoyed a career path of success from this point forward, winning Pulitzer Prizes in 1924, 1931, 1937, and 1943 and serving as the nation's poet laureate in 1958–59. But his personal life was tragic. One of his daughters died of a prolonged illness in 1934. His wife died in 1938. His son committed suicide in 1940. Finally, another daughter was hospitalized for mental illness following a collapse in 1947. Although Frost's sister also suffered from mental illness and he himself admitted to contemplating suicide, especially during his twenty years of career struggle, the suicide and mental breakdown of his children bore down on him heavily.

Frost entered the nation's public life during the 1950s, largely at the encouragement of his daughter Lesley as well as his friend Sherman Adams, who was chief of staff to President Dwight D. Eisenhower. In 1954 and 1957 Frost undertook visits to South America and England, sponsored by the State Department led by John Foster Dulles. Frost successfully lobbied for the release of Pound from internment at St. Elizabeths Hospital, where he had been living since actively supporting the Axis in World War II. In 1961, Frost memorably participated in President Kennedy's inauguration, fulfilling a lifelong dream to bring poetry into the national life. In 1962, he visited the Soviet Union at Kennedy's request. But he was skeptical about the nation's Cold War foreign policy, a skepticism that undoubtedly grew after he gave a public reading in Rio de Janeiro, Brazil, where the U.S. ambassador, an insurance executive from the Midwest, insulted everyone by sitting with an unlit cigar in his mouth between Frost and his daughter. Frost ended his life as a beloved public figure, and he lives on through his role as an observant, eloquent, funny, thoughtful, highly skilled, and very private master of poetic language.

FURTHER READING

Robert Faggen, ed. *The Cambridge Companion to Robert Frost*. Cambridge: Cambridge University Press, 2001.

Robert Frost. *Poetry*. Ed. Edward Connery Lathem. New York: Holt, 1969.

Tyler Hoffman. *Robert Frost and the Politics of Poetry*. Hanover, N.H.: University Press of New England, 2001.

Karen Kilcup. *Robert Frost and Feminine Literary Tradition*. Ann Arbor: University of Michigan Press, 1998.

Jay Parini. *Robert Frost: A Life*. New York: Owl Books, 2000.

Mark Richardson. *The Ordeal of Robert Frost: The Poet and His Poetics*. Urbana: University of Illinois Press, 1997.

Camille Roman. "Robert Frost and Three Female Modern Poets: Amy Lowell, Louise Bogan, and Edna Millay." *The Robert Frost Review* (1995): 62–69.

Nancy Lewis Tuten and John Zubizarreta, eds. *The Robert Frost Encyclopedia*. Westport, Conn.: Greenwood, 2000.

Earl Wilcox and Jonathan Barron, eds. *Roads Not Taken: Rereading Robert Frost*. Columbia: University of Missouri Press, 2000.

The Tuft of Flowers

I went to turn the grass once after one
Who mowed it in the dew before the sun.

The dew was gone that made his blade so keen
Before I came to view the leveled scene.

I looked for him behind an isle of trees;
I listened for his whetstone on the breeze.

But he had gone his way, the grass all mown,
And I must be, as he had been—alone,

"As all must be," I said within my heart,
"Whether they work together or apart."

But as I said it, swift there passed me by
On noiseless wing a bewildered butterfly,

Seeking with memories grown dim o'er night
Some resting flower of yesterday's delight.

And once I marked his flight go round and round,
As where some flower lay withering on the ground.

And then he flew as far as eye could see,
And then on tremulous wing came back to me.

I thought of questions that have no reply,
And would have turned to toss the grass to dry;

But he turned first, and led my eye to look
At a tall tuft of flowers beside a brook,

A leaping tongue of bloom the scythe had spared
Beside a reedy brook the scythe had bared.

The mower in the dew had loved them thus,
By leaving them to flourish, not for us,

Nor yet to draw one thought of ours to him,
But from sheer morning gladness at the brim.

The butterfly and I had lit upon,
Nevertheless, a message from the dawn,

     *   *   *

That made me hear the wakening birds around,
And hear his long scythe whispering to the ground,

And feel a spirit kindred to my own;
So that henceforth I worked no more alone;

But glad with him, I worked as with his aid,
And weary, sought at noon with him the shade;

And dreaming, as it were, held brotherly speech
With one whose thought I had not hoped to reach.

"Men work together," I told him from the heart,
"Whether they work together or apart."

1906

The Pasture

I'm going out to clean the pasture spring;
I'll only stop to rake the leaves away
(And wait to watch the water clear, I may):
I shan't be gone long. —You come too.

I'm going out to fetch the little calf
That's standing by the mother. It's so young
It totters when she licks it with her tongue.
I shan't be gone long. —You come too.

1914

Mending Wall

Something there is that doesn't love a wall,
That sends the frozen-ground-swell under it,
And spills the upper boulders in the sun;
And makes gaps even two can pass abreast.
The work of hunters is another thing:
I have come after them and made repair
Where they have left not one stone on a stone,
But they would have the rabbit out of hiding,
To please the yelping dogs. The gaps I mean,
No one has seen them made or heard them made,
But at spring mending-time we find them there.
I let my neighbor know beyond the hill;

And on a day we meet to walk the line
And set the wall between us once again.
We keep the wall between us as we go.
To each the boulders that have fallen to each.
And some are loaves and some so nearly balls
We have to use a spell to make them balance:
"Stay where you are until our backs are turned!"
We wear our fingers rough with handling them.
Oh, just another kind of outdoor game,
One on a side. It comes to little more:
There where it is we do not need the wall:
He is all pine and I am apple orchard.
My apple trees will never get across
And eat the cones under his pines, I tell him.
He only says, "Good fences make good neighbors."
Spring is the mischief in me, and I wonder
If I could put a notion in his head:
"*Why* do they make good neighbors? Isn't it
Where there are cows? But here there are no cows.
Before I built a wall I'd ask to know
What I was walling in or walling out,
And to whom I was like to give offense.
Something there is that doesn't love a wall,
That wants it down." I could say "Elves" to him,
But it's not elves exactly, and I'd rather
He said it for himself. I see him there,
Bringing a stone grasped firmly by the top
In each hand, like an old-stone savage armed.
He moves in darkness as it seems to me,
Not of woods only and the shade of trees.
He will not go behind his father's saying,
And he likes having thought of it so well
He says again, "Good fences make good neighbors."

1914

The Death of the Hired Man

Mary sat musing on the lamp-flame at the table,
Waiting for Warren. When she heard his step,
She ran on tiptoe down the darkened passage
To meet him in the doorway with the news

And put him on his guard. "Silas is back."
She pushed him outward with her through the door
And shut it after her. "Be kind," she said.
She took the market things from Warren's arms
And set them on the porch, then drew him down
To sit beside her on the wooden steps.

"When was I ever anything but kind to him?
But I'll not have the fellow back," he said.
"I told him so last haying, didn't I?
If he left then, I said, that ended it.
What good is he? Who else will harbor him
At his age for the little he can do?
What help he is there's no depending on.
Off he goes always when I need him most.
He thinks he ought to earn a little pay,
Enough at least to buy tobacco with,
So he won't have to beg and be beholden.
'All right,' I say, 'I can't afford to pay
Any fixed wages, though I wish I could.'
'Someone else can.' 'Then someone else will have to.'
I shouldn't mind his bettering himself
If that was what it was. You can be certain,
When he begins like that, there's someone at him
Trying to coax him off with pocket money—
In haying time, when any help is scarce.
In winter he comes back to us. I'm done."

"Sh! Not so loud: he'll hear you," Mary said.

"I want him to: he'll have to soon or late."

"He's worn out. He's asleep beside the stove.
When I came up from Rowe's I found him here,
Huddled against the barn door fast asleep,
A miserable sight, and frightening, too—
You needn't smile—I didn't recognize him-
I wasn't looking for him—and he's changed.
Wait till you see."

                    "Where did you say he'd been?"

"He didn't say. I dragged him to the house,
And gave him tea and tried to make him smoke.

I tried to make him talk about his travels.
Nothing would do: he just kept nodding off."

"What did he say? Did he say anything?"

"But little."

    "Anything? Mary, confess
He said he'd come to ditch the meadow for me."

"Warren!"

    "But did he? I just want to know."

"Of course he did. What would you have him say?
Surely you wouldn't grudge the poor old man
Some humble way to save his self-respect.
He added, if you really care to know,
He meant to clear the upper pasture, too.
That sounds like something you have heard before?
Warren, I wish you could have heard the way
He jumbled everything. I stopped to look
Two or three times—he made me feel so queer—
To see if he was talking in his sleep.
He ran on Harold Wilson—you remember—
The boy you had in haying four years since.
He's finished school, and teaching in his college.
Silas declares you'll have to get him back.
He says they two will make a team for work:
Between them they will lay this farm as smooth!
The way he mixed that in with other things.
He thinks young Wilson a likely lad, though daft
On education—you know how they fought
All through July under the blazing sun,
Silas up on the cart to build the load,
Harold along beside to pitch it on."

"Yes, I took care to keep well out of earshot."

"Well, those days trouble Silas like a dream.
You wouldn't think they would. How some things linger!
Harold's young college-boy's assurance piqued him.
After so many years he still keeps finding
Good arguments he sees he might have used.
I sympathize. I know just how it feels

To think of the right thing to say too late.
Harold's associated in his mind with Latin.
He asked me what I thought of Harold's saying
He studied Latin, like the violin,
Because he liked it—that an argument!
He said he couldn't make the boy believe
He could find water with a hazel prong—
Which showed how much good school had ever done him.
He wanted to go over that. But most of all
He thinks if he could have another chance
To teach him how to build a load of hay—"

"I know, that's Silas' one accomplishment.
He bundles every forkful in its place,
And tags and numbers it for future reference,
So he can find and easily dislodge it
In the unloading. Silas does that well.
He takes it out in bunches like big birds' nests.
You never see him standing on the hay
He's trying to lift, straining to lift himself."

"He thinks if he could teach him that, he'd be
Some good perhaps to someone in the world.
He hates to see a boy the fool of books.
Poor Silas, so concerned for other folk,
And nothing to look backward to with pride,
And nothing to look forward to with hope,
So now and never any different."

Part of a moon was falling down the west,
Dragging the whole sky with it to the hills.
Its light poured softly in her lap. She saw it
And spread her apron to it. She put out her hand
Among the harplike morning-glory strings,
Taut with the dew from garden bed to eaves,
As if she played unheard some tenderness
That wrought on him beside her in the night.
"Warren," she said, "he has come home to die:
You needn't be afraid he'll leave you this time."

"Home," he mocked gently.

＊   ＊   ＊

"Yes, what else but home?
It all depends on what you mean by home.
Of course he's nothing to us, any more
Than was the hound that came a stranger to us
Out of the woods, worn out upon the trail."

"Home is the place where, when you have to go there,
They have to take you in."

                  "I should have called it
Something you somehow haven't to deserve."

Warren leaned out and took a step or two,
Picked up a little stick, and brought it back
And broke it in his hand and tossed it by.
"Silas has better claim on us you think
Than on his brother? Thirteen little miles
As the road winds would bring him to his door.
Silas has walked that far no doubt today.
Why doesn't he go there? His brother's rich,
A somebody — director in the bank."

"He never told us that."

                  "We know it, though."

"I think his brother ought to help, of course.
I'll see to that if there is need. He ought of right
To take him in, and might be willing to —
He may be better than appearances.
But have some pity on Silas. Do you think
If he had any pride in claiming kin
Or anything he looked for from his brother,
He'd keep so still about him all this time?"

"I wonder what's between them."

                        "I can tell you.
Silas is what he is — we wouldn't mind him —
But just the kind that kinsfolk can't abide.
He never did a thing so very bad.
He don't know why he isn't quite as good
As anybody. Worthless though he is,
He won't be made ashamed to please his brother."

*   *   *

"*I* can't think Si ever hurt anyone."

"No, but he hurt my heart the way he lay
And rolled his old head on that sharp-edged chair-back.
He wouldn't let me put him on the lounge.
You must go in and see what you can do.
I made the bed up for him there tonight.
You'll be surprised at him—how much he's broken.
His working days are done; I'm sure of it."

"I'd not be in a hurry to say that."

"I haven't been. Go, look, see for yourself.
But, Warren, please remember how it is:
He's come to help you ditch the meadow.
He has a plan. You mustn't laugh at him.
He may not speak of it, and then he may.
I'll sit and see if that small sailing cloud
Will hit or miss the moon."

                                  It hit the moon.
Then there were three there, making a dim row,
The moon, the little silver cloud, and she.

Warren returned—too soon, it seemed to her—
Slipped to her side, caught up her hand and waited.

"Warren?" she questioned.

                              "Dead," was all he answered.

                                        1914

Home Burial

He saw her from the bottom of the stairs
Before she saw him. She was starting down,
Looking back over her shoulder at some fear.
She took a doubtful step and then undid it
To raise herself and look again. He spoke
Advancing toward her: "What is it you see
From up there always?—for I want to know."
She turned and sank upon her skirts at that,
And her face changed from terrified to dull.

He said to gain time: "What is it you see?"
Mounting until she cowered under him.
"I will find out now—you must tell me, dear."
She, in her place, refused him any help,
With the least stiffening of her neck and silence.
She let him look, sure that he wouldn't see,
Blind creature; and awhile he didn't see.
But at last he murmured, "Oh," and again, "Oh."

"What is it—what?" she said.

                "Just that I see."

"You don't," she challenged. "Tell me what it is."

"The wonder is I didn't see at once.
I never noticed it from here before.
I must be wonted[1] to it—that's the reason.
The little graveyard where my people are!
So small the window frames the whole of it.
Not so much larger than a bedroom, is it?
There are three stones of slate and one of marble,
Broad-shouldered little slabs there in the sunlight
On the sidehill. We haven't to mind *those*.
But I understand: it is not the stones,
But the child's mound—"

                "Don't, don't, don't, don't," she cried.

She withdrew, shrinking from beneath his arm
That rested on the banister, and slid downstairs;
And turned on him with such a daunting look,
He said twice over before he knew himself:
"Can't a man speak of his own child he's lost?"

"Not you!—Oh, where's my hat? Oh, I don't need it!
I must get out of here. I must get air.—
I don't know rightly whether any man can."

"Amy! Don't go to someone else this time.
Listen to me. I won't come down the stairs."
He sat and fixed his chin between his fists.
"There's something I should like to ask you, dear."

1. Accustomed.

*   *   *

"You don't know how to ask it."

"Help me, then."

Her fingers moved the latch for all reply.

"My words are nearly always an offense.
I don't know how to speak of anything
So as to please you. But I might be taught,
I should suppose. I can't say I see how.
A man must partly give up being a man
With womenfolk. We could have some arrangement
By which I'd bind myself to keep hands off
Anything special you're a-mind to name.
Though I don't like such things 'twixt those that love.
Two that don't love can't live together without them.
But two that do can't live together with them."
She moved the latch a little. "Don't—don't go.
Don't carry it to someone else this time.
Tell me about it if it's something human.
Let me into your grief. I'm not so much
Unlike other folks as your standing there
Apart would make me out. Give me my chance.
I do think, though, you overdo it a little.
What was it brought you up to think it the thing
To take your mother-loss of a first child
So inconsolably—in the face of love.
You'd think his memory might be satisfied—"

"There you go sneering now!"

"I'm not, I'm not!
You make me angry. I'll come down to you.
God, what a woman! And it's come to this,
A man can't speak of his own child that's dead."

"You can't because you don't know how to speak.
If you had any feelings, you that dug
With your own hand—how could you?—his little grave;
I saw you from that very window there,
Making the gravel leap and leap in air,
Leap up, like that, like that, and land so lightly

And roll back down the mound beside the hole.
I thought, Who is this man? I didn't know you.
And I crept down the stairs and up the stairs
To look again, and still your spade kept lifting.
Then you came in. I heard your rumbling voice
Out in the kitchen, and I don't know why,
But I went near to see with my own eyes.
You could sit there with the stains on your shoes
Of the fresh earth from your own baby's grave
And talk about your everyday concerns.
You had stood the spade up against the wall
Outside there in the entry, for I saw it."

"I shall laugh the worst laugh I ever laughed.
I'm cursed. God, if I don't believe I'm cursed."

"I can repeat the very words you were saying:
'Three foggy mornings and one rainy day
Will rot the best birch fence a man can build.'
Think of it, talk like that at such a time!
What had how long it takes a birch to rot
To do with what was in the darkened parlor?
You *couldn't* care! The nearest friends can go
With anyone to death, comes so far short
They might as well not try to go at all.
No, from the time when one is sick to death,
One is alone, and he dies more alone.
Friends make pretense of following to the grave,
But before one is in it, their minds are turned
And making the best of their way back to life
And living people, and things they understand.
But the world's evil. I won't have grief so
If I can change it. Oh, I won't, I won't!"

"There, you have said it all and you feel better.
You won't go now. You're crying. Close the door.
The heart's gone out of it: why keep it up?
Amy! There's someone coming down the road!"

"*You*—oh, you think the talk is all. I must go—
Somewhere out of this house. How can I make you—"

*   *   *

"If—you—do!" She was opening the door wider.
"Where do you mean to go? First tell me that.
I'll follow and bring you back by force. I *will!* —"

1914

"Home Burial" concerns a home burial for the couple's child. It was the custom then to bury family members on the family property. The death reveals, or causes, deep fissures in the relationship between husband and wife.

After Apple-Picking

My long two-pointed ladder's sticking through a tree
Toward heaven still,
And there's a barrel that I didn't fill
Beside it, and there may be two or three
Apples I didn't pick upon some bough.
But I am done with apple-picking now.
Essence of winter sleep is on the night,
The scent of apples: I am drowsing off.
I cannot rub the strangeness from my sight
I got from looking through a pane of glass
I skimmed this morning from the drinking trough
And held against the world of hoary grass.
It melted, and I let it fall and break.
But I was well
Upon my way to sleep before it fell,
And I could tell
What form my dreaming was about to take.
Magnified apples appear and disappear,
Stem end and blossom end,
And every fleck of russet showing clear.
My instep arch not only keeps the ache,
It keeps the pressure of a ladder-round.
I feel the ladder sway as the boughs bend.
And I keep hearing from the cellar bin
The rumbling sound
Of load on load of apples coming in.
For I have had too much
Of apple-picking: I am overtired
Of the great harvest I myself desired.

There were ten thousand thousand fruit to touch,
Cherish in hand, lift down, and not let fall.
For all
That struck the earth,
No matter if not bruised or spiked with stubble,
Went surely to the cider-apple heap
As of no worth.
One can see what will trouble
This sleep of mine, whatever sleep it is.
Were he not gone,
The woodchuck could say whether it's like his
Long sleep, as I describe its coming on,
Or just some human sleep.

1914

The Wood Pile

Out walking in the frozen swamp one gray day,
I paused and said, "I will turn back from here.
No, I will go on farther—and we shall see."
The hard snow held me, save where now and then
One foot went through. The view was all in lines
Straight up and down of tall slim trees
Too much alike to mark or name a place by
So as to say for certain I was here
Or somewhere else: I was just far from home.
A small bird flew before me. He was careful
To put a tree between us when he lighted,
And say no word to tell me who he was
Who was so foolish as to think what *he* thought.
He thought that I was after him for a feather—
The white one in his tail; like one who takes
Everything said as personal to himself.
One flight out sideways would have undeceived him.
And then there was a pile of wood for which
I forgot him and let his little fear
Carry him off the way I might have gone,
Without so much as wishing him good-night.
He went behind it to make his last stand.
It was a cord of maple, cut and split

And piled—and measured, four by four by eight.
And not another like it could I see.
No runner tracks in this year's snow looped near it.
And it was older sure than this year's cutting,
Or even last year's or the year's before.
The wood was gray and the bark warping off it
And the pile somewhat sunken. Clematis
Had wound strings round and round it like a bundle.
What held it, though, on one side was a tree
Still growing, and on one a stake and prop,
These latter about to fall. I thought that only
Someone who lived in turning to fresh tasks
Could so forget his handiwork on which
He spent himself, the labor of his ax,
And leave it there far from a useful fireplace
To warm the frozen swamp as best it could
With the slow smokeless burning of decay.

1914

The Road Not Taken

Two roads diverged in a yellow wood,
And sorry I could not travel both
And be one traveler, long I stood
And looked down one as far as I could
To where it bent in the undergrowth;

Then took the other, as just as fair,
And having perhaps the better claim,
Because it was grassy and wanted wear;
Though as for that, the passing there
Had worn them really about the same,

And both that morning equally lay
In leaves no step had trodden black.
Oh, I kept the first for another day!
Yet knowing how way leads on to way,
I doubted if I should ever come back.

I shall be telling this with a sigh
Somewhere ages and ages hence:

Two roads diverged in a wood, and I—
I took the one less traveled by,
And that has made all the difference.

1914

Birches

When I see birches bend to left and right
Across the lines of straighter darker trees,
I like to think some boy's been swinging them.
But swinging doesn't bend them down to stay
As ice storms do. Often you must have seen them
Loaded with ice a sunny winter morning
After a rain. They click upon themselves
As the breeze rises, and turn many-colored
As the stir cracks and crazes their enamel.
Soon the sun's warmth makes them shed crystal shells
Shattering and avalanching on the snow crust—
Such heaps of broken glass to sweep away
You'd think the inner dome of heaven had fallen.
They are dragged to the withered bracken by the load,
And they seem not to break; though once they are bowed
So low for long, they never right themselves:
You may see their trunks arching in the woods
Years afterwards, trailing their leaves on the ground
Like girls on hands and knees that throw their hair
Before them over their heads to dry in the sun.
But I was going to say when Truth broke in
With all her matter of fact about the ice storm,
I should prefer to have some boy bend them
As he went out and in to fetch the cows—
Some boy too far from town to learn baseball,
Whose only play was what he found himself,
Summer or winter, and could play alone.
One by one he subdued his father's trees
By riding them down over and over again
Until he took the stiffness out of them,
And not one but hung limp, not one was left
For him to conquer. He learned all there was
To learn about not launching out too soon

And so not carrying the tree away
Clear to the ground. He always kept his poise
To the top branches, climbing carefully
With the same pains you use to fill a cup
Up to the brim, and even above the brim.
Then he flung outward, feet first, with a swish,
Kicking his way down through the air to the ground.
So was I once myself a swinger of birches.
And so I dream of going back to be.
It's when I'm weary of considerations,
And life is too much like the a pathless wood
Where your face burns and tickles with the cobwebs
Broken across it, and one eye is weeping
From a twig's having lashed across it open.
I'd like to get away from the earth awhile
And then come back to it and begin over.
May no fate willfully misunderstand me
And half grant what I wish and snatch me away
Not to return. Earth's the right place for love:
I don't know where it's likely to go better.
I'd like to go by climbing a birch tree,
And climb black branches up a snow-white trunk
Toward heaven, till the tree could bear no more,
But dipped its top and set me down again.
That would be good both going and coming back.
One could do worse than be a swinger of birches.

                                                    1915

The Oven Bird

There is a singer everyone has heard,
Loud, a mid-summer and a mid-wood bird,
Who makes the solid tree trunks sound again.
He says that leaves are old and that for flowers
Mid-summer is to spring as one to ten.
He says the early petal-fall is past,
When pear and cherry bloom went down in showers
On sunny days a moment overcast;
And comes that other fall we name the fall.
He says the highway dust is over all.

The bird would cease and be as other birds
But that he knows in singing not to sing.
The question that he frames in all but words
Is what to make of a diminished thing.

1916

The oven bird is an American warbler that builds a dome-shaped nest on the ground.

Fire and Ice

Some say the world will end in fire,
Some say in ice.
From what I've tasted of desire
I hold with those who favor fire.
But if it had to perish twice,
I think I know enough of hate
To say that for destruction ice
Is also great
And would suffice.

1920

Dust of Snow

The way a crow
Shook down on me
The dust of snow
From a hemlock tree

Has given my heart
A change of mood
And saved some part
Of a day I had rued.

1923

Stopping by Woods on a Snowy Evening

Whose woods these are I think I know.
His house is in the village, though;
He will not see me stopping here
To watch his woods fill up with snow.

*   *   *

My little horse must think it queer
To stop without a farmhouse near
Between the woods and frozen lake
The darkest evening of the year.

He gives his harness bells a shake
To ask if there is some mistake.
The only other sound's the sweep
Of easy wind and downy flake.

The woods are lovely, dark and deep,
But I have promises to keep,
And miles to go before I sleep,
And miles to go before I sleep.

1923

Acquainted with the Night

I have been one acquainted with the night.
I have walked out in rain—and back in rain.
I have outwalked the furthest city light.

I have looked down the saddest city lane.
I have passed by the watchman on his beat
And dropped my eyes, unwilling to explain.

I have stood still and stopped the sound of feet
When far away an interrupted cry
Came over houses from another street,

But not to call me back or say good-by;
And further still at an unearthly height
One luminary clock against the sky

Proclaimed the time was neither wrong nor right.
I have been one acquainted with the night.

1928

Desert Places

Snow falling and night falling fast, oh, fast
In a field I looked into going past,
And the ground almost covered smooth in snow,
But a few weeds and stubble showing last.

The woods around it have it—it is theirs.
All animals are smothered in their lairs.
I am too absent-spirited to count;
The loneliness includes me unawares.

And lonely as it is, that loneliness
Will be more lonely ere it will be less—
A blanker whiteness of benighted[1] snow
With no expression, nothing to express.

They cannot scare me with their empty spaces
Between stars—on stars where no human race is.
I have it in me so much nearer home
To scare myself with my own desert places.

                                    1936

Design

I found a dimpled spider, fat and white,
On a white heal-all,[1] holding up a moth
Like a white piece of rigid satin cloth—
Assorted characters of death and blight
Mixed ready to begin the morning right,
Like the ingredients of a witches' broth—
A snow-drop spider, a flower like a froth,
And dead wings carried like a paper kite.

What had that flower to do with being white,
The wayside blue and innocent heal-all?
What brought the kindred spider to that height,
Then steered the white moth thither in the night?
What but design of darkness to appall?[2]—
If design govern in a thing so small.

                                    1936

---

1. Unenlightened or overcome by darkness.
1. A violet-blue wildflower in the mint family with healing powers.

2. To make pale, to horrify, or to cover with pall or burial shroud.

Directive

Back out of all this now too much for us,
Back in a time made simple by the loss
Of detail, burned, dissolved, and broken off
Like graveyard marble sculpture in the weather,
There is a house that is no more a house
Upon a farm that is no more a farm
And in a town that is no more a town.
The road there, if you'll let a guide direct you
Who only has at heart your getting lost,
May seem as if it should have been a quarry—
Great monolithic knees the former town
Long since gave up pretense of keeping covered.
And there's a story in a book about it:
Besides the wear of iron wagon wheels
The ledges show lines ruled southeast northwest,
The chisel work of an enormous Glacier
That braced his feet against the Arctic Pole.
You must not mind a certain coolness from him
Still said to haunt this side of Panther Mountain.
Nor need you mind the serial ordeal
Of being watched from forty cellar holes
As if by eye pairs out of forty firkins.[1]
As for the woods' excitement over you
That sends light rustle rushes to their leaves,
Charge that to upstart inexperience.
Where were they all not twenty years ago?
They think too much of having shaded out
A few old pecker-fretted[2] apple trees.
Make yourself up a cheering song of how
Someone's road home from work this once was,
Who may be just ahead of you on foot
Or creaking with a buggy load of grain.
The height of the adventure is the height
Of country where two village cultures faded
Into each other. Both of them are lost.
And if you're lost enough to find yourself
By now, pull in your ladder road behind you

1. Wooden casks or vessels used to hold such foods   2. Woodpecker-marked.
as fish and butter.

And put a sign up CLOSED to all but me.
Then make yourself at home. The only field
Now left's no bigger than a harness gall.[3]
First there's the children's house of make-believe,
Some shattered dishes underneath a pine,
The playthings in the playhouse of the children.
Weep for what little things could make them glad.
Then for the house that is no more a house,
But only a belilaced[4] cellar hole,
Now slowly closing like a dent in dough.
This was no playhouse but a house in earnest.
Your destination and your destiny's
A brook that was the water of the house,
Cold as a spring as yet so near its source,
Too lofty and original to rage.
(We know the valley streams that when aroused
Will leave their tatters hung on barb and thorn.)
I have kept hidden in the instep arch
Of an old cedar at the waterside
A broken drinking goblet like the Grail[5]
Under a spell so the wrong ones can't find it,
So can't get saved, as Saint Mark says they mustn't.[6]
(I stole the goblet from the children's playhouse.)
Here are your waters and your watering place.
Drink and be whole again beyond confusion.

1947

PROSE

In "The Figure a Poem Makes," which appeared originally as the preface to Frost's *Collected Poems* in 1939, the poet explains what he seeks in a poem. A poem makes a figure or shape, just as love does, he states: "The figure is the same as for love." He wants the poem, like love, to begin in delight and to end in wisdom. Reflecting his dark sense of underlying chaos, he proposes that a poem produce "a momentary stay against confusion." He expects poetry to have a wildness about it as it searches

---

3. A sore caused by a harness.
4. Covered with lilacs.
5. The cup that was supposed to have been used by Jesus at the Last Supper; a common feature of medieval legend.

6. See Mark 16:16 in the Christian New Testament.

for its fulfillment. This wildness is what gives poems freshness. A poem should allow its meaning and wisdom to unfold without pressure, allowing it to surprise the reader.

The Figure a Poem Makes

Abstraction is an old story with the philosophers, but it has been like a new toy in the hands of the artists of our day. Why can't we have any one quality of poetry we choose by itself? We can have in thought. Then it will go hard if we can't in practice. Our lives for it.

Granted no one but a humanist much cares how sound a poem is if it is only a sound. The sound is the gold in the ore. Then we will have the sound out alone and dispense with the inessential. We do till we make the discovery that the object in writing poetry is to make all poems sound as different as possible from each other, and the resources for that of vowels, consonants, punctuation, syntax, words, sentences, meter are not enough. We need the help of context—meaning —subject matter. That is the greatest help towards variety. All that can be done with words is soon told. So also with meters—particularly in our language where there are virtually but two, strict iambic and loose iambic. The ancients with many were still poor if they depended on meters for all tune. It is painful to watch our sprung-rhythmists[1] straining at the point of omitting one short from a foot for relief from monotony. The possibilities for tune from the dramatic tones of mean- ing struck across the rigidity of a limited meter are endless. And we are back in poetry as merely one more art of having something to say, sound or unsound. Probably better if sound, because deeper and from wider experience.

Then there is this wildness whereof it is spoken. Granted again that it has an equal claim with sound to being a poem's better half. If it is a wild tune, it is a poem. Our problem then is, as modern abstractionists, to have the wildness pure; to be wild with nothing to be wild about. We bring up as aberrationists, giving way to undirected associations and kicking ourselves from one chance suggestion to another in all directions as of a hot afternoon in the life of a grasshopper. Theme alone can steady us down. Just as the first mystery was how a poem could have a tune in such a straightness as meter, so the second mystery is how a poem can have wildness and at the same time a subject that shall be fulfilled.

It should be of the pleasure of a poem itself to tell how it can. The figure a poem makes. It begins in delight and ends in wisdom. The figure is the same as for love. No one can really hold that the ecstasy should be static and stand still in

---

1. Sprung rhythm is an irregular meter in which each metric foot has one stress but varying numbers of syllables; it is associated with the British poet Gerard Manley Hopkins.

one place. It begins in delight, it inclines to the impulse, it assumes direction with the first line laid down, it runs a course of lucky events, and ends in a clarification of life—not necessarily a great clarification, such as sects and cults are founded on, but in a momentary stay against confusion. It has denouement.[2] It has an outcome that though unforeseen was predestined from the first image of the original mood—and indeed from the very mood. It is but a trick poem and no poem at all if the best of it was thought of first and saved for the last. It finds its own name as it goes and discovers the best waiting for it in some final phrase at once wise and sad—the happy-sad blend of the drinking song.

No tears in the writer, no tears in the reader. No surprise for the writer, no surprise for the reader. For me the initial delight is in the surprise of remembering something I didn't know I knew. I am in a place, in a situation, as if I had materialized from cloud or risen out of the ground. There is a glad recognition of the long lost and the rest follows. Step by step the wonder of unexpected supply keeps growing. The impressions most useful to my purpose seem always those I was unaware of and so made no note of at the time when taken, and the conclusion is come to that like giants we are always hurling experience ahead of us to pave the future with against the day when we may want to strike a line of purpose across it for somewhere. The line will have the more charm for not being mechanically straight. We enjoy the straight crookedness of a good walking stick. Modern instruments of precision are being used to make things crooked as if by eye and hand in the old days.

I tell how there may be a better wildness of logic than of inconsequence. But the logic is backward, in retrospect, after the act. It must be more felt than seen ahead like prophecy. It must be a revelation, or a series of revelations, as much for the poet as for the reader. For it to be that there must have been the greatest freedom of the material to move about in it and to establish relations in it regardless of time and space, previous relation, and everything but affinity. We prate of freedom. We call our schools free because we are not free to stay away from them till we are sixteen years of age. I have given up my democratic prejudices and now willingly set the lower classes free to be completely taken care of by the upper classes. Political freedom is nothing to me. I bestow it right and left. All I would keep for myself is the freedom of my material—the condition of body and mind now and then to summons aptly from the vast chaos of all I have lived through.

Scholars and artists thrown together are often annoyed at the puzzle of where they differ. Both work from knowledge; but I suspect they differ most importantly in the way their knowledge is come by. Scholars get theirs with conscientious thoroughness along projected lines of logic; poets theirs cavalierly and as it happens in and out of books. They stick to nothing deliberately, but let what will

2. Outcome, conclusion.

stick to them like burrs where they walk in the fields. No acquirement is on assignment, or even self-assignment. Knowledge of the second kind is much more available in the wild free ways of wit and art. A school boy may be defined as one who can tell you what he knows in the order in which he learned it. The artist must value himself as he snatches a thing from some previous order in time and space into a new order with not so much as a ligature clinging to it of the old place where it was organic.

More than once I should have lost my soul to radicalism if it had been the originality it was mistaken for by its young converts. Originality and initiative are what I ask for my country. For myself the originality need be no more than the freshness of a poem run in the way I have described: from delight to wisdom. The figure is the same as for love. Like a piece of ice on a hot stove the poem must ride on its own melting. A poem may be worked over once it is in being, but may not be worried into being. Its most precious quality will remain its having run itself and carried away the poet with it. Read it a hundred times: it will forever keep its freshness as a metal keeps its fragrance. It can never lose its sense of a meaning that once unfolded by surprise as it went.

1939

AMY LOWELL
1874–1925

THERE NEVER SHOULD have been any question about Amy Lowell's central importance in experimental modernism. But Lowell made a mistake that sent her to the margins. She quarreled with Ezra Pound over who should lead the imagist movement and whether this style of concise and objective poetry should be an elite enterprise, as he argued, or a democratic poetry, as she wished. Like Pound, Lowell advocated a clean poetic line, devoid of sentimentality and conventional meter, but, unlike him, she did not think that the imagist poem needed to be obscure. Lowell won the immediate power struggle over imagism—Pound denounced the movement as "Amygism" and moved on. But as a consequence of her victory, Lowell paid the price of near exile in the history of modernism.

Lowell's inclusion in this anthology as a major modernist figure signals the need to rethink her crucial roles as advocate and practitioner, both of which contributed to modern American poetry as we know it today. It would have been a far different poetry without her. Moreover, we must consider her central contributions as an inheritor of Boston's Orientalist legacy and as the architect of a female erotic discourse. Orientalism took two major forms in literary modernism: translation and creative writing. Lowell left a voluminous and unparalleled legacy in both areas. Equally important, her work allows historians of modernism to register—and to explore the reasons behind—the stark disparity in this period between the cultural elite's enthrallment with classical Asian aesthetics and the growing violence directed at recent waves of Asian immigrants. As the excerpt from her long poem "Guns as Keys: And the Great Gate Swings" reveals, Lowell critiqued U.S. as well as Japanese imperialism.

Lowell's Asian investment was in an ancient culture that could serve as a female utopian counterbalance to a deplorably industrialized, commodified, and masculinist West. While characterizing East and West in stereotypical gender terms, she also found in Orientalism an eloquent language with which to speak of her love for her companion, Ada Dwyer Russell. She adapted this language for such poems as "Vicarious." Indeed, Lowell has been praised for writing the longest sequence of lesbian love poetry in the United States before Adrienne Rich in the last part of the twentieth century. Like her contemporaries H.D., Angelina Weld Grimké, and Gertrude Stein, Amy Lowell wrote pioneering texts in the lesbian-feminist tradition.

Lowell was the most devoted and energetic proponent of modern American poetry among her peers during her lifetime, conducting a campaign on its behalf as if she were running for the presidency of the United States. She wrote twelve volumes of poetry (and, by one account, more than 650 poems), and she received a Pulitzer Prize in 1926, a year after she died. To promote imagism, she edited three poetry collections entitled *Some Imagist Poets* between 1915 and 1917. She published three essay collections on poetry and poets. In 1925 she wrote a well-received biography of the English poet John Keats. She promoted both Emily Dickinson and Walt Whitman for their infusion of Asian aesthetics into their poetry, an innovative position at the time. She presented her poetry in theatrical readings that created a cult following as she traveled around the country. Fans mobbed train stations to get her autograph. They packed auditoriums to standing-room-only capacity as they waited for a glimpse of the heavyset Lowell, smoking one of her famous black cigars or playing with one of her many color-coded pince-nez.

Lowell promoted the New Poetry at poetry meetings and gatherings, and she sometimes enraged traditionalists so much that they rushed the podium. She once described the atmosphere at her lectures as "a gladiator fight and wild beast show." Conservatives assailed her for trying to destroy poetry. When she read the "polyphonic prose" selection "Bath" for the Poetry Society of America in New York City, she was met with snickers, denunciations, laughter, and a press delighted that her reading of the poem seemed as outrageous to the audience as if she had appeared on stage in an actual bathtub. Beyond promoting herself, Lowell worked relentlessly on behalf of her favorite imagist poets such as Robert Frost, D. H. Lawrence, and H.D., arranging to publish their work in small magazines as well as larger-circulation journals, acting as an accountant on royalties and fees, and doling out their profits with meticulous honesty.

This tireless advocacy is not surprising, given Lowell's considerable wealth and prestige as a member of one of the nation's most elite families. Like her siblings, she enjoyed sitting at the center of intellectual and political power. And though Pound and his admirers may have banished her to the margins in poetry, she remains ensconced in at least one of those power centers today: her portrait is hung in Lowell House at Harvard University along with other family portraits and busts. Her brother Abbott Lawrence Lowell was president of Harvard University (1909–33) and a favored pupil of Henry Adams. Adams's wife, Clover, who committed a high-profile suicide, was a cousin through marriage. Lowell's favorite brother, the astronomer Percival Lowell, lived in Asia for many years and wrote books about it. He was one of the elite Boston Orientalists, a group that also included Adams, Arthur Dow, John La Farge, Ernest Fenollosa, James Abbott McNeill Whistler, Bernard Berenson, William Sturgis Bigelow, and Charles Goddard Weld. Percival eventually discovered nonexistent canals on Mars and began searching for the then-unknown Pluto. He also maintained an exclusive social life, serving as best man at Edith Wharton's wedding. Amy's sister Elizabeth Lowell Putnam was a political activist who pioneered in prenatal care and herself published six volumes of poetry and prose. Amy's other sister, Katherine, married Alfred Roosevelt, the first cousin of President Theodore Roosevelt.

The family tree was filled with many other illustrious role models for Lowell. Her mother, Katherine Bigelow Lawrence, was a musician and linguist, and her aunt Elizabeth Prescott was the daughter of the historian William Prescott. Her father, Augustus, a horticulturist and civic leader, served as a trustee at the Museum of Fine Arts. He also ran the prestigious Lowell Institute, which presented Edward Sylvester Morse's lectures on Japanese culture during Morse's campaign to preserve traditional Japanese culture in the face of rapid modernization. These lectures inspired many Bostonians to travel to Asia, including Percival and another cousin, Isabella Stewart Gardner. Augustus also owned a library with seven thousand volumes that young Amy read with relish. Her great-grandfather was one of the founders of the Boston Athenaeum, a library and literary society that was frequented by such luminaries as Ralph Waldo Emerson. When the Athenaeum building was threatened, Amy headed the drive to preserve it. The mill towns of Lowell and Lawrence in Massachusetts were named after family members. Amy Lowell's grandfathers, John Amory Lowell and Abbott Lawrence, made their fortunes by introducing machines to produce cotton goods at the mills. During the Civil War, they banded together with some others to form the Union Club. After the war, the club memorialized members who died for the Union, including a Lowell cousin, Colonel Robert Gould Shaw, who commanded the African-American 54th Massachusetts regiment and is commemorated with a statue on the Boston Common not far from the Union Club. The poet James Russell Lowell (included in the first volume of this anthology) was a cousin. The poet Robert Lowell (included in the third volume) was one as well. The poetic lineage goes back to the colonial era: Percival Lowle, who helped colonize Newburyport, Massachusetts, in the 1630s, wrote poetry too.

The Lowell family was devoted to the pursuit of Asian aesthetics in ways that make that seem like a tradition as well, beginning with the earliest mercantile ships that brought Asian goods to the New World. The most famous female contemporary example for Amy Lowell was Isabella Stewart Gardner, who ran an inner sanctum artistic circle for Boston Orientalists and was Lowell's cousin through her marriage to John Lowell Gardner. Gardner's home became a refuge for the second curator of the Asian Collections at the Museum of Fine Arts, Kakuzo Okakura, a protégé of poet and intellectual Ernest Fenollosa. Okakura succeeded Fenollosa in the wake of the scandal caused by Fenollosa's affair with his assistant Mary, who became his second wife. (Both Fenollosas are included in the first volume of this anthology.) Gardner amassed most of her world-famous art collection under the guidance of the Boston Orientalist Bernard Berenson, but Okakura guided her further into Japanese culture through the tea ceremony and poetry. Gardner sponsored formal tea ceremonies, a Japanese fair, and lectures on Japanese and Chinese poetry.

Not surprisingly, Sevenals, Lowell's family home in Brookline, which she shared with her companion, Ada Dwyer Russell, was filled with both her own and her family's Asian art treasures. Lowell's third-floor bedroom overlooked more than eight acres of gardens with plants from around the world that her father had cultivated and that she maintained. The walls were painted sky blue and featured blue art pieces by the Japanese artist Hiroshige, sent to her by her brother Percival while he was in Asia. Other gifts from him—paper fans, prints, woodcuts, photos, toys, and fish—filled her room. Because she and Percival maintained a long correspondence during his time in Asia, each object held an important place in her life. When Percival visited Boston as the head of a Korean trade mission when Amy Lowell was only nine, she sat for hours listening to his private secretary's stories about imperial Japan, which helped her to understand the many later gifts. The music room, where musicales of modern music were held, was papered in Chinese wallpaper. Lowell sat on Chippendale furniture that reflected an Asian influence; and China plates and screens brought from Asia on early merchant ships served as ornaments in the dining room. Her library included Japanese woodcuts and a painting by the Asian-influenced James McNeill Whistler.

In addition to learning from her rich cultural milieu in Boston, Lowell was nurtured by many women relatives and friends. Her mother and her sister Elizabeth were her first collaborators. Together they published *Dream Drops, or Stories from Fairy Land, by a Dreamer* in 1887, donating the proceeds to charitable institutions. Lowell began studying Keats, her lifelong favorite poet about whom she would write a two-volume biography, with a female school friend named Bessie Ward. Another childhood friend, the sinologist Florence Ayscough, who was born in Shanghai, collaborated with her on *Fir-Flower Tablets*, Lowell's translation of Chinese poetry. The Italian actress Eleanora Duse, whom she met in 1902, inspired her to write poetry, as did Ada Dwyer Russell, whom she pursued in 1912 while Russell was still acting. Female editors like Harriet Monroe helped Lowell, as did influential cousins like Mary Cabot. Lowell published her first poetry in 1910 in the *Atlantic Monthly* when Cabot's husband, Ellery Sedgwick, was its editor. Later Lowell introduced the writer Bryher (Winifred Ellerman) to the poet H.D., her future partner, and she remained a friend to both women.

In 1913, when Lowell traveled to England to meet Pound and H.D., she was undergoing an epiphany about her life mission. The new realization would shape the rest of her life—she died only twelve years later. Lowell suddenly recognized the importance of her cultural inheritance from her brother and the circle of Boston Orientalists—even though Ernest Fenollosa's widow had given to Pound, rather than to her, her husband's unfinished translation of the Chinese classical poet Li Po and his work on Japanese Noh theater. (Given the scandal in Boston over the Fenollosa divorce and second marriage, one could hardly have expected Mary Fenollosa to have given her husband's work to a Boston poet like Amy Lowell.) Lowell also found in H.D.'s writing an erotic, woman-centered discourse that would serve her in writing her own love lyrics to Ada Russell, who decided at this time to move in with Lowell. In short, Lowell understood that she should write about her life and surroundings, using the cultural materials available to her, and devoting her life to the cause of modern American poetry. She even jokingly told Russell, her indispensable partner, that they should hang out a shingle at their estate, announcing "Makers of Poetry." For twelve years, the two women laid the groundwork for crucial developments in modern American poetry.

FURTHER READING

Steven Gould Axelrod. "Family Resemblance: Amy Lowell's 'Town in Colour' and Robert Lowell's 'For the Union Dead.'" *Modern Philology* 97 (2000): 554–62.

Christopher Benfey. *The Great Wave: Gilded Age Misfits, Japanese Eccentrics, and the Opening of Old Japan.* New York: Random House, 2003.

Lillian Faderman. "'Which, Being Interpreted, Is as May Be, or Otherwise': Ada Dwyer Russell in Amy Lowell's Life and Work." In *Amy Lowell, American Modern,* ed. Melissa Bradshaw and Adrienne Munich, 59–76. New Brunswick, N.J.: Rutgers University Press, 2004.

Yunte Huang. *Transpacific Displacement: Ethnography, Translation, and Intertextual Travel in Twentieth-Century American Literature.* Berkeley: University of California Press, 2002.

Paul Lauter. "Amy Lowell and Cultural Borders." In *Amy Lowell, American Modern,* ed. Melissa Bradshaw and Adrienne Munich, 1–8. New Brunswick, N.J.: Rutgers University Press, 2004.

Amy Lowell. *Selected Poems*. Ed. Melissa Bradshaw and Adrienne Munich. New Brunswick, N.J.: Rutgers University Press, 2002.

Camille Roman. "Robert Frost and Three Female Modern Poets: Amy Lowell, Louise Bogan, and Edna Millay." *The Robert Frost Review* (1995): 62–69.

Bonnie Kime Scott. "Amy Lowell's Letters in the Network of Modernism." In *Amy Lowell, American Modern*, ed. Melissa Bradshaw and Adrienne Munich, 136–53. New Brunswick, N.J.: Rutgers University Press, 2004.

Mari Yoshihara. "Putting on the Voice of the Orient: Gender and Sexuality in Amy Lowell's 'Asian' Poetry." In *Amy Lowell, American Modern*, ed. Melissa Bradshaw and Adrienne Munich, 120–35. New Brunswick, N.J.: Rutgers University Press, 2004.

Aubade

As I would free the white almond from the green husk
So would I strip your trappings off,
Beloved.
And fingering the smooth and polished kernel
I should see that in my hands glittered a gem beyond counting.

1914

An *aubade* is a song of no fixed metrical form that in European tradition is sung at dawn to express two lovers' regrets that they must part. It also may be read as a poet's appreciation for the sexual favors of the beloved. This love poem of desire is written to Lowell's lifelong companion, Ada Dwyer Russell, who accepted Lowell's invitation to live with her in 1913. Lillian Faderman argues that the poem presents "bold clitoral imagery" that suggests lesbian sex.

The Captured Goddess

Over the housetops,
Above the rotating chimney-pots,
I have seen a shiver of amethyst,
And blue and cinnamon have flickered,
A moment,
At the far end of a dusty street.

Through sheeted rain
Has come a lustre of crimson,
And I have watched moonbeams
Hushed by a film of palest green.

It was her wings,
Goddess!

Who stepped over the clouds,
And laid her rainbow feathers
Aslant, on the currents of the air.

I followed her for long,
With gazing eyes and stumbling feet.
I cared not where she led me,
My eyes were full of colours:
Saffrons, rubies, the yellows of beryls,[1]
And the indigo-blue of quartz;
Flights of rose, layers of chrysoprase,[2]
Points of orange, spirals of vermilion,
The spotted gold of tiger-lily petals,
The loud pink of bursting hydrangeas.
I followed,
And watched for the flashing of her wings.

In the city I found her,
The narrow-streeted city.
In the market-place I came upon her,
Bound and trembling.
Her fluted wings were fastened to her sides with cords,
She was naked and cold,
For that day the wind blew
Without sunshine.

Men chaffered for her,
They bargained in silver and gold,
In copper, in wheat,
And called their bids across the market-place.

The Goddess wept.

Hiding my face I fled,
And the grey wind hissed behind me,
Along the narrow streets.

1914

Adrienne Munich points out that Lowell "strews color images in an ecstatic catalog" in this poem, evoking a "glorious divinity." Paul Lauter reads the poem as an example of Lowell's

---

1. Hard prismatic mineral occurring in yellow, 2. Apple-green gemstone.
green, pink, or white.

"poetics of the closet," with contradictory impulses toward both display, or "flaunting," and hiding. Yet the poem can also be read as suggesting the poet's grief over the goddess's degradation at the hands of commerce. The swirl of impressionist color is at odds with the grimy reality of the urban scene, providing a critique of the squalor.

The Taxi

When I go away from you
The world beats dead
Like a slackened drum.
I call out for you against the jutted stars
And shout into the ridges of the wind.
Streets coming fast,
One after the other,
Wedge you away from me,
And the lamps of the city prick my eyes
So that I can no longer see your face.
Why should I leave you,
To wound myself upon the sharp edges of the night?

1914

Lillian Faderman reads this poem as an expression of Lowell's confusion and anger at the separations from Ada Russell when Russell visited her daughter and son-in-law. Lowell eventually solved this problem by inviting Russell's daughter and her husband to visit them at their Brookline home.

The Letter

Little cramped words scrawling all over the paper
Like draggled fly's legs,
What can you tell of the flaring moon
Through the oak leaves?
Or of my uncurtained window and the bare floor
Spattered with moonlight?
Your silly quirks and twists have nothing in them
Of blossoming hawthorns,
And this paper is dull, crisp, smooth, virgin of loveliness
Beneath my hand.

I am tired, Beloved, of chafing my heart against
The want of you;

Of squeezing it into little inkdrops,
And posting it.
And I scald alone, here, under the fire
Of the great moon.

1914

Adrienne Munich reads "The Letter," with its alternating long and short lines, as an allusion to the meters of the classical Greek poet Sappho. Sappho was already being constructed by Lowell's time as a lesbian who lived on the Greek isle of Lesbos in an elite, refined, and educated society of women. In 1913, Lowell traveled to England to meet H.D., who was writing Sapphic fragments that she greatly admired. Lillian Faderman interprets this poem as an expression of Lowell's first year with Ada Russell, revealing the pain that the poet feels when separated from her beloved.

Venus Transiens

Tell me,
Was Venus more beautiful
Than you are,
When she topped
The crinkled waves,
Drifting shoreward
On her plaited shell?
Was Botticelli's vision
Fairer than mine;
And were the painted rosebuds
He tossed his lady
Of better worth
Than the words I blow about you
To cover your too great loveliness
As with a gauze
Of misted silver?

For me,
You stand poised
In the blue and buoyant air,
Cinctured by bright winds,
Treading the sunlight.
And the waves which precede you
Ripple and stir
The sands at my feet.

1915

Venus Transiens or *The Birth of Venus* (ca. 1483), by the Italian artist Sandro Botticelli (1445–1510), has drawn great attention since its creation. The painting shows a willowy woman, meant to be the Roman goddess of love, standing on a scallop shell with her hair spread in a fan around her head as she is being washed ashore by waves and wind. In this love poem for Ada Russell, Lowell suggests that her beloved is as lovely as Botticelli's Venus.

A Decade

When you came you were like red wine and honey,
And the taste of you burnt my mouth with its sweetness.
Now you are like morning bread—
Smooth and pleasant.
I hardly taste you at all for I know your savour,
But I am completely nourished.

1916

Lillian Faderman states that this poem reveals that Ada Russell means everything to Lowell and that their relationship is solid and complete.

Bath

The day is fresh-washed and fair, and there is a smell of tulips and narcissus in the air.

The sunshine pours in at the bath-room window and bores through the water in the bath-tub in lathes and planes of greenish-white. It cleaves the water into flaws like a jewel, and cracks it to bright light.

Little spots of sunshine lie on the surface of the water and dance, dance, and their reflections wobble deliciously over the ceiling; a stir of my fingers sets them whirring, reeling. I move a foot and the planes of light in the water jar. I lie back and laugh, and let the green-white water, the sun-flawed beryl[1] water, flow over me. The day is almost too bright to bear, the green water covers me from the too bright day. I will lie here awhile and play with the water and the sun spots. The sky is blue and high. A crow flaps by the window, and there is a whiff of tulips and narcissus in the air.

1916

"Bath" offers an example of what Lowell called "polyphonic prose." She described it as a form that makes use of all the "voices" of poetry—for example, meter, free verse, assonance, consonance, alliteration, rhyme, and circular return.

1. Prismatic, colorful mineral.

FROM *Guns as Keys: And the Great Gate Swings*

Down, down, down, to the bottom of the map; but we must up again, high on the other side. America, sailing the seas of a planet to stock the shop counters at home. Commerce-raiding a nation; pulling apart the curtains of a temple and calling it trade. Magnificent mission! Every shop-till in every bye-street will bless you. Force the shut gate with the muzzles of your black cannon. Then wait— wait for fifty years—and see who has conquered.

1917

"Guns as Keys: And the Great Gate Swings" describes the opening of Japan by depicting Japan as feminine and the United States as masculine. This final commentary in the poem criticizing American imperialism and its forced opening of trade with Japan through Commodore Matthew Perry's gunboat diplomacy reveals that Japan, too, has become infected with expansionism and must be heeded. Lowell decided to write about Perry after hearing his story from her good friend Eleanor Robson and her husband, August Belmont. Perry was Belmont's grandfather.

The Weathervane Points South

I put your leaves aside,
One by one:
The stiff, broad outer leaves;
The smaller ones,
Pleasant to touch, veined with purple;
The glazed inner leaves.
One by one
I parted you from your leaves,
Until you stood up like a white flower
Swaying slightly in the evening wind.

White flower,
Flower of wax, of jade,[1] of unstreaked agate;
Flower with surfaces of ice,
With shadows faintly crimson.
Where in all the garden is there such a flower?
The stars crowd through the lilac leaves
To look at you.
The low moon brightens you with silver.

---

1. In Asian cultures, jade is often considered the luckiest and most precious stone.

The bud is more than the calyx.
There is nothing to equal a white bud,
Of no colour, and of all;
Burnished by moonlight,
Thrust upon by a softly-swinging wind.

1919

An example of Lowell's term *cadenced verse* (which encompassed Asian and French poetic forms), "The Weathervane Points South" was first published in *Vanity Fair* and then, under the title "The Weather-Cock Points South," in her collection that includes translations of Japanese poetry, *Pictures of the Floating World*. Adrienne Munich suggests that Lowell's poetic use of the white flower is comparable to Georgia O'Keeffe's representation of it in her artwork. Munich's comparison should not be surprising, given that both women were heavily influenced by the "Boston Orientalists" of the late nineteenth century. Lowell was influenced by her brother Percival, who lived in Asia and wrote about it; O'Keeffe studied with Arthur Dow, the major art instructor who introduced Asian techniques and aesthetics into American painting. Lillian Faderman argues that Lowell's use of the male sexual slang reference "cock" is a device to tell the lesbian truth "slant." She reads it as a description of a lesbian sexual act.

Vernal Equinox

The scent of hyacinths, like a pale mist, lies between me and my book;
And the South Wind, washing through the room,
Makes the candles quiver.
My nerves sting at a spatter of rain on the shutter,
And I am uneasy with the thrusting of green shoots
Outside, in the night.

Why are you not here to overpower me with your tense and urgent love?

1919

Lillian Faderman interprets this poem as a lament over Lowell's separation from Ada Russell during one of Russell's visits to her daughter. The title refers to the beginning of spring, which occurs about March 21.

September, 1918

This afternoon was the colour of water falling through sunlight;
The trees glittered with the tumbling of leaves;
The sidewalks shone like alleys of dropped maple leaves,

And the houses ran along them laughing out of square, open windows.
Under a tree in the park,
Two little boys, lying flat on their faces,
Were carefully gathering red berries
To put in a pasteboard box.
Some day there will be no war,
Then I shall take out this afternoon
And turn it in my fingers,
And remark the sweet taste of it upon my palate,
And note the crisp variety of its flights of leaves.
To-day I can only gather it
And put it into my lunch box,
For I have time for nothing
But the endeavour to balance myself
Upon a broken world.

1919

September 1918 was an important period for the Allied offensive in World War I. Compare this poem to "In Time of War," below.

Dissonance

From my window I can see the moonlight stroking the smooth surface of the river.
The trees are silent, there is no wind.
Admirable pre-Raphaelite landscape,
Lightly touched with ebony and silver.
I alone am out of keeping:
An angry red gash
Proclaiming the restlessness
Of an incongruous century.

1923

Lowell was a great admirer of James Abbott McNeill Whistler (1834–1903), whose paintings of the Thames River in London likely inspired this poem. Lowell owned a Whistler landscape and kept it in her bedroom, where she wrote her poetry. She shared this enthusiasm for Whistler with her cousin by marriage, Isabella Stewart Gardner, who created an internationally renowned major private art collection in her home, Fenway Court in Boston, as her artistic legacy. Whistler was one of the first American painters to integrate Japanese aesthetics and design into his work. This major step in transforming American art was inspired by his visit to the International Exhibition of 1862 in London, where Japanese artifacts were introduced.

TRANSLATIONS AND ADAPTATIONS

In Time of War

Across the newly-plastered wall,
The darting red dragonflies
Is like the shooting
Of blood-tipped arrows.

1918

This translation of a Japanese poem was completed during major Allied offensives in World War I. See also "September, 1918," above.

A Poet's Wife

CHO WĒN-CHŪN TO HER HUSBAND SSǓ-MA HSIANG-JU

You have taken our love and turned it into coins of silver.
You sell the love poems you wrote for me,
And with the price of them you buy many cups of wine.
I beg that you remain dumb,
That you write no more poems.
For the wine does us both an injury,
And the words of your heart
Have become the common speech of the Emperor's concubines.

1919

Moon Haze

Because the moonlight deceives
Therefore I love it.

1919

"Moon Haze" is an adaptation of a Japanese haiku.

Nuance

Even the iris bends,
When a butterfly lights upon it.

1919

"Nuance," an adaptation of a Japanese haiku, illustrates very well the tenets of imagism. The poem strives to represent an objective experience of the artist's subjectivity. Here the haiku-like verse attempts to render—and to suggest the significance of—Lowell's flash of recognition that the iris bends when the butterfly lands on it. This lyric appears in *Pictures of the Floating World,* which includes translations of Japanese poetry.

Vicarious

When I stand under the willow-tree[1]
Above the river,
In my straw colored silken garment
Embroidered with purple chrysanthemums,[2]
It is not at the bright water
That I am gazing,
But at your portrait,
Which I have caused to be painted
On my fan.

1919

"Vicarious" offers an example of the Orientalist language that Lowell adapted for expressing her same-sex love for Ada Russell.

Afterglow

Peonies
The strange pink colour of Chinese porcelains;
Wonderful—the glow of them.
But, my Dear, it is the pale blue larkspur
Which swings windily against my heart.
Other summers
And a cricket chirping in the grass.

1921

In "Afterglow," Lowell compares her love for her companion (embodied in the memory of the pale blue larkspur) with peonies (a Chinese flower symbolizing riches and prosperity) and with porcelain (widely admired as the greatest Asian art form).

---

1. The Japanese regard the willow as highly sensual.   2. Japanese symbols of longevity.

The Retreat of Hsieh Kung

Li T'ai-po

The sun is setting—has set—on the Spring-green Mountain.
Hsieh Kung's retreat is solitary and still.
No sound of man in the bamboo grove.
The white moon shines in the centre of the unused garden pool.
All round the ruined Summer-house is decaying grass,
Grey mosses choke the abandoned well.
There is only the free, clear wind
Again—again—passing over the stones of the spring.

1921

"The Retreat of Hsieh Kung" is a translation of a poem by Li T'ai-po about Hsieh Kung, the honorary title of Hsieh T'iao, a poet Li T'ai-po highly respected. Li T'ai-po (701–762), one of the most popular poets during the T'ang dynasty of China, is widely regarded as a great poet in world literature because of his spontaneous and vivid lyrics on pleasure and loss.

The Lonely Wife

The mist is thick. On the wide river, the water-plants float smoothly.
No letters come; none go.
There is only the moon, shining through the clouds of a hard, jade-green[1] sky,
Looking down at us so far divided, so anxiously apart.
All day, going about my affairs, I suffer and grieve, and press the thought of you
    closely to my heart.
My eyebrows are locked in sorrow,[2] I cannot separate them.
Nightly, nightly, I keep half the quilt,
And wait for the return of that divine dream which is my Lord.[3]

Beneath the quilt of the Fire Bird,[4] on the bed of the Silver-Crested Love-Pheasant,
Nightly, nightly, I drowse alone.
The red candles in the silver candlesticks melt, and the wax runs from them,
As the tears of your so Unworthy One[5] escape and continue constantly to flow.
A flower face endures but a short season,

1. The most desirable precious stone.
2. Chinese women spent considerable time painting their eyebrows to highlight their emotional expression through them. Most preferred to shape them as thin-lined willows.
3. Refers to husband.
4. The Luan, a supernatural mythical creature signifying fire, love, and passion. Love Pheasant: the Feng Huang, bird of happiness.
5. Chinese women referred to themselves as "Unworthy One" when speaking to their husbands and the men they loved.

Yet still he drifts along the river Hsiao and the river Hsiang.
As I toss on my pillow, I hear the cold nostalgic sound of the water-clock:[6]
Shêng! Shêng! It drips, cutting my heart in two.

I rise at dawn. In the Hall of Pictures[7]
They come and tell me that the snow-flowers are falling.
The reed-blind is rolled high, and I gaze at the beautiful, glittering, primeval snow,
Whitening the distance, confusing the stone steps and the courtyard.
The air is filled with its shining, it blows far out like the smoke of a furnace.
The grass-blades are cold and white, like jade girdle pendants.
Surely the Immortals in Heaven must be crazy with wine to cause such disorder,
Seizing the white clouds, crumpling them up, destroying them.

1921

Compare "The Lonely Wife," Lowell's translation of a Li T'ai-po poem, to the poems about wives left behind by Chinese men seeking their fortunes in the gold rush of California during a time of economic depression in China (in the entry "Jinshan Ge/Songs of Gold Mountain"). Mari Yoshihara points out that poems about women's grief are common in classical Chinese poetry. So it is not surprising to find this poem among the translations Lowell wrote with sinologist Florence Ayscough.

Together We Know Happiness

Silent and alone, I ascended the West Cupola.
The moon was like a golden hook.
In the quiet, empty, inner courtyard, the coolness of early Autumn enveloped
　　the wu-t'ung tree.[1]
Scissors cannot cut this thing;
Unravelled, it joins again and clings.
It is the sorrow of separation,
And none other tastes to the heart like this.

1921

This poem is a translation of a Chinese lyric by an unknown descendant of the founder of the Southern T'ang dynasty.

---

6. The water-clock uses water to tell time. The wife refers here to the dripping of water as time moves forward without her husband.

7. Refers to the public area of this aristocratic couple's house.

1. Known as the tree of integrity.

Vespers

Last night, at sunset,
The foxgloves were like tall altar candles.
Could I have lifted you to the roof of the greenhouse, my Dear,
I should have understood their burning.

1922

Adrienne Munich and Melissa Bradshaw suggest that "Vespers" moves from images to powerful emotion through an interplay of echoing vowels in the words "could," "should," and "understood." Lowell often attempts to depict the sensory world of musical sounds as well as color images. Lillian Faderman reads the poem as a religious-erotic celebration of Ada Russell. The "vespers" are evening prayers in which Russell is the object of love and worship as well as lust. She becomes a goddess.

PROSE

No writing illustrates more clearly what Amy Lowell meant by a "democratic" imagism (rather than an elite imagism, as Ezra Pound propounded) than this preface. It was drafted by the London-based poet Richard Aldington and then revised by an informal committee of poets represented in the volume, including Lowell. Two additional volumes of imagist poems appeared in 1916 and 1917 to fulfill the aims of this preface. The major imagist principles expounded here influenced many different varieties of modernism, and they remain influential today. These principles are precision, metrical and topical freedom, visual particularity, clarity, and concision.

FROM Some Imagist Poets

Preface

In March, 1914, a volume appeared entitled "Des Imagistes."[1] It was a collection of the work of various young poets, presented together as a school. This school has been widely discussed by those interested in new movements in the arts, and has already become a household word. Differences of taste and judgment, however, have arisen among the contributors to that book; growing tendencies are forcing them along different paths. Those of us whose work appears in this

---

1. The volume was edited by Ezra Pound and included poetry by Pound, H.D., Richard Aldington, and Lowell. Pound and Lowell subsequently went separate ways.

volume have therefore decided to publish our collection under a new title, and we have been joined by two or three poets who did not contribute to the first volume, our wider scope making this possible.

In this new book we have followed a slightly different arrangement to that of the former Anthology. Instead of an arbitrary selection by an editor, each poet has been permitted to represent himself by the work he considers his best, the only stipulation being that it should not yet have appeared in book form. A sort of informal committee — consisting of more than half the authors here represented — have arranged the book and decided what should be printed and what omitted, but, as a general rule, the poets have been allowed absolute freedom in this direction, limitations of space only being imposed upon them. Also, to avoid any appearance of precedence, they have been put in alphabetical order.

As it has been suggested that much of the misunderstanding of the former volume was due to the fact that we did not explain ourselves in a preface, we have thought it wise to tell the public what our aims are, and why we are banded together between one set of covers.

The poets in this volume do not represent a clique. Several of them are personally unknown to the others, but they are united by certain common principles, arrived at independently. These principles are not new; they have fallen into desuetude.[2] They are the essentials of all great poetry, indeed of all great literature, and they are simply these: —

1. To use the language of common speech, but to employ always the exact word, not the nearly-exact, nor the merely decorative word.
2. To create new rhythms — as the expression of new moods — and not to copy old rhythms, which merely echo old moods. We do not insist upon "free-verse" as the only method of writing poetry. We fight for it as for a principle of liberty. We believe that the individuality of a poet may often be better expressed in free-verse than in conventional forms. In poetry, a new cadence means a new idea.
3. To allow absolute freedom in the choice of subject. It is not good art to write badly about aeroplanes and automobiles; nor is it necessarily bad art to write well about the past. We believe passionately in the artistic value of modern life, but we wish to point out that there is nothing so uninspiring nor so old-fashioned as an aeroplane of the year 1911.
4. To present an image (hence the name: "Imagist"). We are not a school of painters, but we believe that poetry should render particulars exactly and not deal in vague generalities, however magnificent and sonorous. It is for this reason that we oppose the cosmic poet, who seems to us to shirk the real difficulties of his art.

2. Disuse.

5. To produce poetry that is hard and clear, never blurred nor indefinite.
6. Finally, most of us believe that concentration is of the very essence of poetry.

The subject of free-verse is too complicated to be discussed here. We may say briefly, that we attach the term to all that increasing amount of writing whose cadence is more marked, more definite, and closer knit than that of prose, but which is not so violently nor so obviously accented as the so-called "regular verse." We refer those interested in the question to the Greek Melic[3] poets, and to the many excellent French studies on the subject by such distinguished and well-equipped authors as Remy de Gourmont, Gustave Kahn, Georges Duhamel, Charles Vildrac, Henri Ghéon, Robert de Souza, André Spire, etc.

We wish it to be clearly understood that we do not represent an exclusive artistic sect; we publish our work together because of mutual artistic sympathy, and we propose to bring out our cooperative volume each year for a short term of years, until we have made a place for ourselves and our principles such as we desire.

1915

GERTRUDE STEIN
1874–1946

Gertrude Stein, one of the most powerful innovators of the twentieth century, wrote in "Composition as Explanation" that although experimental work may be "wonderfully beautiful," it is initially received as "a thing irritating annoying stimulating" and therefore "all quality of beauty is denied to it." Such a work begins as an "outlaw" until it suddenly becomes "a classic" instead. Stein was certainly thinking of her own writing in this meditation on the fate of avant-garde artworks. And so it came to pass. Her initially "annoying stimulating" texts have become, for many readers and scholars, landmarks of modern culture.

Stein's most famous sentence is "A rose is a rose is a rose." She introduced versions of the saying into several of her texts, the initial instance referring to a woman named "Rose" and a later instance modified to read, "A rose is arose is a rose is a rose." But essentially, "A rose is a rose is a rose" became a sentence unto itself, repeated as exemplary of her entire literary project. Stein inscribed the saying in an

---

3. A type of classical Greek lyric poetry that was usually sung.

endless loop on a signet ring and encouraged her companion, Alice B. Toklas, to have it engraved in a circle on dinner plates. On the one hand, the sentence has import as an assertion about reality. She once told an audience: "Now listen! I'm no fool. I know that in daily life we don't go around saying 'is a . . . is a . . . is a.' Yes, I'm no fool; but I think that in that line the rose is red for the first time in English poetry for a hundred years." She had stripped away sedimented adjectives, leaving the rose brightly itself again. In this sense, Stein's sentence may be paraphrased to read, "Things are as they are." But on the other hand, the sentence has import as a radical use of language. That third "rose" defies both a tradition of conventional grammar and an illusion that language is simply a transparent medium for communicating perceptions and ideas. The extra "rose" brings language itself to the fore, as a material and shaping medium. Stein told another of her audiences: "When I said, 'A rose is a rose is a rose is a rose,' and later made that into a ring, I made poetry and what did I do I caressed completely caressed and addressed a noun." She dramatized the proposition that language is a self-enclosed system composed of parts of speech—a world of words and not a faithful mirror of a pre-existent reality.

In seeking to restore the redness of the rose, Stein closes the gap between word and thing, renewing relations between poetry and the world around it. That effort culminates a century-long romantic and epistemological project, ranging from William Wordsworth and Ralph Waldo Emerson in the nineteenth century to Stein's contemporaries such as Adelaide Crapsey, H.D., Amy Lowell, Mina Loy, Ezra Pound, and William Carlos Williams (all included in this anthology). But in seeking to caress and address a noun, Stein articulates and participates in a brand-new project of exploring the properties and limits of the medium in which she worked, language itself. This project is associated with avant-garde experiments in the arts, ranging from Pablo Picasso and Marcel Duchamp to Andy Warhol. Thus, while paying tribute to modernism's epistemological turn, Stein helped install an "annoying stimulating" new project, which has been called the linguistic turn. Stein once observed that America is the oldest country on earth because it arrived at the twentieth century first. By that token, Stein is the oldest poet on earth, having arrived at postmodernism first.

Gertrude Stein was born to a German-Jewish immigrant family in Allegheny, Pennsylvania, a suburb of Pittsburgh. She was the youngest of seven children. Her father operated a family clothing business and invested in real estate. By the time Stein was seventeen, both of her parents were dead. At eighteen, she enrolled at Radcliffe College (a women's college then known as "Harvard Annex"), while her brother Leo matriculated at Harvard. Gertrude Stein became the favored student of Harvard philosopher and psychologist William James. James's notion of a "stream of consciousness" and his interest in automatic writing and the perception of objects influenced Stein's literary project in years to come. According to one famous story, Stein wrote on an exam, "I'm sorry Professor James, I do not feel like taking an exam today." She then left the room. James wrote on the top of the exam, "I understand perfectly. A."

After graduating from Radcliffe, Stein studied medicine at Johns Hopkins, where her brother Leo pursued graduate studies in biology. She was one of the first women to be admitted to Johns Hopkins medical school. But just before graduating, she lost interest in medicine, perhaps as a result of an unhappy love affair with another woman. When Leo impulsively decided to study art in Paris, she again accompanied him. Soon she was living with Leo at 27 rue de Fleurus, the home she would make famous as a literary salon. Both Steins began to build one of the most remarkable and forward-looking art collections of the time, buying works by painters of rising reputation such as Gauguin, Renoir, and Cézanne and also works that few others wanted by such then-unknown painters as Pablo Picasso and Henri Matisse. Gertrude Stein also began to write, in a style that paralleled Picasso's cubist experiments. Most of her first compositions were fiction: Q. E. D. (a lesbian novella composed in 1903 but unpublished in her lifetime), *Three Lives* (a trio of novellas about working-class women published in 1909), and *The Making of Americans* (a long family novel based on her childhood memories, written in 1908–9 but not published until 1925). Stein's experiments were more radical than almost anyone else's, helping to forge the notion of modernism as a movement founded on change. Ahead of her time, she produced texts that were "refused," as she later put it in "Composition as Explanation." Some of her work was considered unpublishable, and even the published work struggled to find an audience. Through a program of vocal self-admiration, Stein managed to cope with a patriarchal culture hostile to assertive and unconventional women artists: "Slowly I was knowing that I was a genius." Such comments seemed absurd to many in her own time, subjecting her to the ridicule of male journalists—significantly, Stein was famous long before she was widely read—but they seem increasingly convincing today.

By 1910, Leo Stein had left the household and Alice B. Toklas moved in. Toklas was Stein's devoted companion and lover for the rest of Stein's life. In the next few years Stein devoted herself to what she called "portraits," prose poems about friends and artists. These portraits, such as "Picasso" below, blur the boundaries separating the arts. They borrow cubist techniques from Picasso and Georges Braque, such as the fragmentation and abstraction of the image and multiple repetitions from slightly different angles, and they explore the border ground between prose and poetry. Like avant-garde visual artists of the early twentieth century, Stein was interested in moving from realistic, transparent mimesis to a style that acknowledged the density and opacity of the artistic medium—in her case, language. Moreover, in blurring the boundaries that separate prose from poetry, her portraits eschew plot and character and toy with the conventions of the essay while focusing on verbal images and highlighted language, much in the manner of a lyric poem. Theorists of the prose poem, a hybrid form invented in nineteenth-century France, consider texts such as "Picasso" to be landmarks in the history of this medium in English.

In the years just before World War I, Stein also wrote more conventional-looking poems such as "Susie Asado" and "Preciosilla." Both of these poems evoke actual moments and relations in Stein's social life, but they foreground the pleasures of language itself. Sounds echo through alliteration, consonance, assonance, and rhyme in a manner close to music. At the same time, words inhabit each other, flow into each other, and split apart through punning, multiple meanings, homophones, and the merging of different words into a single "portmanteau." (For example, "slips slips hers" in "Susie Asado" at once includes the notion of slipping across the floor, a showing of undergarments, and a wearing of slippers.) Such packed and lively discourse delights and gratifies the adventurous reader. At about the same time, Stein produced another text that stretched the boundaries of poetry in an unprecedented way: her book of lists called *Tender Buttons*. This radical experiment in prose poetry happily ponders domestic items and their place in the household's social activities. In so doing, it removes logical connections between nouns, adjectives, and verbs—as in the resonant but mysterious assertion "The difference is spreading." Thus, the text sets up a dynamic between objective reference and verbal abstraction. It installs an art of playful implication, linguistic pleasure, and imaginative freedom. *Tender Buttons* added to Stein's growing notoriety. Many literary and cultural figures were enthusiastic, whereas the popular press, particularly in the United States, had a field day.

During World War I, Stein and Toklas labored tirelessly as volunteers providing relief to the troops. Returning to Paris after the war, they became famous for their literary salon, drawing such figures as Picasso, Pound, Hemingway, the fiction writer Sherwood Anderson, the journalist Janet Flanner, and the composer Virgil Thomson. Despite her ever-growing fame throughout the 1920s, Stein could publish her work only in small literary magazines and with ephemeral presses. Works of this period included "Idem the Same" (which was at the same time a "valentine" to Sherwood Anderson, an improvisation on gender and sexuality, and an amusing experiment with imagery, dialogue, and narrative) and "George Hugnet" (which transfers Stein's art of literary portraiture from prose poetry to poetry proper). "Composition as Explanation," a lecture initially delivered at Oxford University, was her most notable excursion into literary theory and self-analysis.

In the 1930s, Stein strengthened her reputation as a pivotal cultural figure. Appropriating Toklas's "I," she wrote a witty and accessible memoir entitled *The Autobiography of Alice B. Toklas* (1933), which became her only best-seller. For the first time she earned substantial royalties, and she also obtained a contract with a major

New York publishing house, Random House. *Four Saints in Three Acts*, the most successful of her operas and plays, had its Broadway premier in the following year. The writer Bryher called the performance she attended "one of the most triumphant nights that I ever spent watching a stage." These successes were followed by an American lecture tour in 1934–35. Stein had become such a celebrity by this time that the news scroll in New York's Times Square flashed to passersby, "Gertrude Stein has arrived in New York." She spoke to sold-out auditoriums across the nation, was interviewed in newspapers and magazines, and had tea with Eleanor Roosevelt in the White House.

When France fell to the Nazis in 1940, Stein and Toklas headed south. As Jews, they were in jeopardy of being transported to the Central European death camps. But unlike most French Jews, they were able to ride out the war, thanks to their celebrity and the protection of collaborators within the Vichy government. Stein celebrated the Allied victory in 1945 with a trio of texts: a novel called *Brewsie and Willie*, a memoir called *Wars I Have Seen*, and a play called *Yes Is for a Very Young Man*. In 1946 she grew ill and died of cancer. As Stein was about to be wheeled into the operation from which she never recovered consciousness, she whispered to her lifelong companion, Alice B. Toklas, "What is the answer?" When the grief-stricken Toklas proved unable to respond, Stein smilingly asked, "In that case, what is the question?"

FURTHER READING

Jane Palatini Bowers. *Gertrude Stein*. London: Macmillan, 1993.

Susan McCabe. "'A Queer Lot' and the Lesbians of 1914: Amy Lowell, H.D., and Gertrude Stein." In *Challenging Boundaries: Gender and Periodization*, ed. Joyce W. Warren and Margaret Dickie, 62–90. Athens: University of Georgia Press, 2000.

James R. Mellow. *Charmed Circle: Gertrude Stein & Company*. New York: Praeger, 1974.

Shirley Neuman and Ira B. Nadel, eds. *Gertrude Stein and the Making of Literature*. Boston: Northeastern University Press, 1988.

Marjorie Perloff. *The Poetics of Indeterminacy*. Princeton: Princeton University Press, 1981.

Lisa Ruddick. *Reading Gertrude Stein: Body, Text, Gnosis*. Ithaca, N.Y.: Cornell University Press, 1990.

Gertrude Stein. *Selected Writings*. Ed. Carl Van Vechten. New York: Random House, 1962.

——. *A Stein Reader*. Ed. Ulla E. Dydo. Evanston, Ill.: Northwestern University Press, 1993.

Wendy Steiner. *Exact Resemblance to Exact Resemblance: The Literary Portraiture of Gertrude Stein*. New Haven, Conn.: Yale University Press, 1978.

Linda Wagner-Martin. *"Favored Strangers": Gertrude Stein and Her Family*. New Brunswick, N.J.: Rutgers University Press, 1995.

Picasso

One whom some were certainly following was one who was completely charming.[1]
One whom some were certainly following was one who was charming. One whom
some were following was one who was completely charming. One whom some
were following was one who was certainly completely charming.

Some were certainly following and were certain that the one they were then
following was one working and was one bringing out of himself then something.
Some were certainly following and were certain that the one they were then
following was one bringing out of himself then something that was coming to
be a heavy thing, a solid thing and a complete thing.

One whom some were certainly following was one working and certainly was
one bringing something out of himself then and was one who had been all his
living had been one having something coming out of him.

Something had been coming out of him, certainly it had been coming out
of him, certainly it was something, certainly it had been coming out of him and
it had meaning, a charming meaning,[2] a solid meaning, a struggling meaning, a
clear meaning.

One whom some were certainly following and some were certainly following
him, one whom some were certainly following was one certainly working.

One whom some were certainly following was one having something coming
out of him something having meaning, and this one was certainly working then.

This one was working and something was coming then, something was
coming out of this one then. This one was one and always there was something
coming out of this one and always there had been something coming out of this
one. This one had never been one not having something coming out of this one.
This one was one having something coming out of this one. This one had been
one whom some were following. This one was one whom some were following.
This one was being one whom some were following. This one was one who was
working.

This one was one who was working. This one was one being one having
something being coming out of him. This one was one going on having
something come out of him. This one was one going on working. This one
was one whom some were following. This one was one who was working.

This one always had something being coming out of this one. This one
was working. This one always had been working. This one was always having
something that was coming out of this one that was a solid thing, a charming

---

1. Gerunds such as "following" and "charm-
ing"—and later "bringing," "working," and "com-
ing"—generate a fluid sense of the continuous
present, emphasizing process over product.
2. Wendy Steiner observes, "If a person creates

both things and himself, then both products of
the same creator would naturally be alike, in this
case 'charming.'" "Solid meaning"; perhaps a
pun on creation and excretion.

thing, a lovely thing, a perplexing thing, a disconcerting thing, a simple thing, a clear thing, a complicated thing, an interesting thing, a disturbing thing, a repellent thing, a very pretty thing. This one was one certainly being one having something coming out of him. This one was whom some were following. This one was one who was working.

This one was one who was working and certainly this one was needing to be working so as to be one being working. This one was one having something coming out of him. This one would be one all his living having something coming out of him. This one was working and then this one was working and this one was needing to be working, not to be one having something coming out of him something having meaning, but was needing to be working so as to be one working.

This one was certainly working and working was something this one was certain this one would be doing and this one was doing that thing, this one was working. This one was not one completely working. This one certainly was not completely working.

This one was one having always something being coming out of him, something having completely a real meaning. This one was one whom some were following. This one was one who was working. This one was one who was working and he was one needing this thing needing to be working so as to be one having some way of being one having some way of working. This one was one who was working. This one was one having something come out of him something having meaning. This one was one always having something come out of him and this thing the thing coming out of him always had real meaning. This one was one who was working. This one was one who was almost always working. This one was not one completely working. This one was one not ever completely working. This one was not one working to have anything come out of him. This one did have something having meaning that did come out of him. He always did have something come out of him. He was working, he was not ever completely working. He did have some following. They were always following him. Some were certainly following him. He was one who was working. He was one having something coming out of him something having meaning. He was not ever completely working.

1912

Stein and the great modernist painter Pablo Picasso (1881–1973) became friends in 1906. Picasso painted several famous portraits of Stein, and Stein reciprocated with several word "portraits" of Picasso, including this one. "Picasso" may be considered a prose poem, in a tradition that stretches from Charles Baudelaire's *poèmes en prose* published in *Spleen de Paris* (1864) to the present day. A prose poem uses the rhythms, sonorous effects, imagery, and densely compact language of lyric poetry while avoiding meter and line breaks. By thus hybridizing poetry and prose, prose poems testify to the instability of generic borders.

"Picasso" additionally challenges the boundaries separating the verbal and visual arts. In this text, Stein does not attempt to portray her subject in a realistic way but rather focuses on certain central characteristics through rhythmic, conversational, and cinematic repetition. Thus, Picasso was one whom "some were certainly following" and one who was "completely charming"—testimonies to his personal charisma. He was also someone "bringing out of himself then something"—giving birth to art that was "a complicated thing, an interesting thing, a disturbing thing, a repellent thing, a very pretty thing." Here Stein captures the complexities of Picasso's work and the ambivalences she herself felt toward it. Finally, though Picasso is "one working," he is also "not one completely working." Ulla Dydo suggests that this binary opposition expresses Stein's anxiety about Picasso's many heterosexual affairs. The binary might also be interpreted, however, as a nonjudgmental recognition that this artist left time for social and intimate activities that complemented his creative activity—much as Stein did herself.

Susie Asado

Sweet sweet sweet sweet sweet tea.
    Susie Asado.
Sweet sweet sweet sweet sweet tea.
    Susie Asado.
Susie Asado which is a told tray sure.
A lean on the shoe this means slips slips hers.
When the ancient light grey is clean it is yellow, it is a silver seller.
This is a please this is a please there are the saids to jelly. These are the wets these say the sets to leave a crown to Incy.
Incy is short for incubus.[1]
A pot. A pot is a beginning of a rare bit of trees. Trees tremble, the old vats are in bobbles, bobbles which shade and shove and render clean, render clean must.
    Drink pups.
Drink pups drink pups lease a sash hold, see it shine and a bobolink has pins. It shows a nail.
    What is a nail. A nail is unison.
    Sweet sweet sweet sweet sweet tea.

1913

"Susie Asado" proposes that language is a self-regulating system without a clear or fixed relationship to the world of objects and events. The poem celebrates that linguistic system, and it also shakes the system up, as a way of calling attention to it, playing with it, and finding pleasure in it. "Susie Asado" exploits the sonic potentialities, the ambiguities, and the

---

1. A demon who supposedly descends on sleeping persons and has intercourse with them.

rhymed, palindromic, and homophonic meanings of words. It combines words, substitutes words, and tears words apart. For example, the poem's first line may suggest a social gathering at which a hot beverage is served ("sweet tea"), but it also seems to suggest a friendship or even an erotic attachment ("sweetie"). Perhaps the "tea" describes the friend's complexion rather than the beverage served. Similarly, a "told tray sure" may suggest a tea tray, a treasure who is being told about, or a bold or gold treasure. However open to interpretation, the scene seems to involve dancing, eating, drinking, talking, laughing, loving, and staying up late. The pleasure of the social occasion is mirrored by the manifest joy of the poem's language. "Susie Asado" is based on an encounter Stein and Toklas had in Spain with a flamenco dancer named Antonia Marce (1890–1936), known professionally as La Argentina (the silvery one). The invented name "Susie Asado" has a bawdy undertone: "asado" means "roasted" in Spanish, whereas the word "susie" was a slang reference to sexual fluids.

Preciosilla

Cousin to Clare washing.

In the win all the band beagles which have cousin lime sign and arrange a weeding match[1] to presume a certain point to exstate to exstate a certain pass lint to exstate a lean sap prime lo and shut shut is life.

Bait, bait tore, tore her clothes, toward it, toward a bit, to ward a sit, sit down in, in vacant surely lots, a single mingle, bait and wet, wet a single establishment that has a lily lily grow. Come to the pen come in the stem, come in the grass grown water.

Lily wet lily wet while. This is so pink so pink in stammer, a long bean which shows bows is collected by a single curly shady, shady get, get set wet bet.

It is a snuff[2] a snuff to be told and have can wither, can is it and sleep sleep knot, it is a lily scarf the pink and blue yellow, not blue not odor sun, nobles are bleeding bleeding two seats two seats on end. Why is grief. Grief is strange black. Sugar is melting. We will not swim.

Preciosilla

Please be please be get, please get wet, wet naturally, naturally in weather. Could it be fire more firier. Could it be so in ate struck. Could it be gold up, gold up stringing, in it while while which is hanging, hanging in dingling, dingling in pinning, not so. Not so dots large dressed dots, big sizes, less laced, less laced diamonds, diamonds white, diamonds bright, diamonds in the in the light,[3] diamonds light diamonds door diamonds hanging to be four, two four, all

1. Perhaps a wedding march.
2. Perhaps enough.
3. An erotic evocation that may echo William Blake's "The Tyger" ("Tyger! Tyger! burning bright / In the forests of the night") as well as the nursery rhyme "Star light, star bright / First star I see tonight."

before, this bean, lessly, all most, a best, willow, vest, a green guest, guest, go go
go go go go, go. Go go. Not guessed. Go go.

　　Toasted susie is my ice-cream.

1913

In her *Lectures in America*, Stein observed that both "Susie Asado" and "Preciosilla" have
"an extraordinary melody of words and a melody of excitement in knowing that I had done
this thing." Stein and Toklas met the café singer Preciosilla (precious or beautiful one)
while on holiday in Spain.

Guillaume Apollinaire

　　Give known or pin ware.
　　Fancy teeth, gas strips.
　　Elbow elect, sour stout pore, pore Caesar,[1] pour state at.
　　Leave eye lessons I.[2] Leave I. Lessons. I. Leave I lessons, I.

1913

Guillaume Apollinaire (1880–1918) was an avant-garde French poet, the author of *Alcools*,
and a friend of Picasso. His given name, Guillelmus (or Wilhelm) Apollinaris de Kostro-
witzki, reflects his mother's Polish origins. Ulla Dydo observes that the poem's opening sen-
tence appears to make no sense. "Reading aloud, we gradually begin to hear not the words
we see in print but others immediately behind them. Eventually the two sets of spoken
words collapse into one: 'Give known or pin ware' sounds 'Guillaume Apollinaire.'"

FROM *Tender Buttons*

FROM *Objects*

　A carafe, that is a blind glass.

A kind in glass[1] and a cousin, a spectacle and nothing strange a single hurt
color and an arrangement in a system to pointing. All this and not ordinary,
not unordered in not resembling. The difference is spreading.[2]

---

1. Translated into German, this would be Kaiser,
which reminds us of the German leader Kaiser
Wilhelm, which in turn evokes Apollinaire's
given name, Wilhelm. "Pour state at": perhaps an
echo of *pour l'état* (for the state) or "poor estate."
2. "Let's leave" and "lesson" are homophones in
French (*laissons, leçon*), whereas "eye" and "I"
are homophones in English.

1. Either a vessel to drink from or a pair of glasses.
"Spectacle": glasses to prevent blindness, or a
vivid thing seen. Note the semantic and sonic
links between "carafe," "glass," and "spectacle,"
as well as "blind," "kind," and "cousin."
2. Suggests the uncertainties (and riches) re-
sulting from objects and words "not resembling"
each other.

Glazed glitter.

Nickel,[3] what is nickel, it is originally rid of a cover.

The change in that is that red weakens an hour. The change has come. There is no search. But there is, there is that hope and that interpretation and sometime, surely any is unwelcome, sometime there is breath and there will be a sinecure[4] and charming very charming is that clean and cleansing. Certainly glittering is handsome and convincing.

There is no gratitude in mercy and in medicine. There can be breakages in Japanese. That is no programme. That is no color chosen. It was chosen yesterday, that showed spitting and perhaps washing and polishing. It certainly showed no obligation and perhaps if borrowing is not natural there is some use in giving.[5]

A box.

Out of kindness comes redness and out of rudeness comes rapid same question,[6] out of an eye comes research, out of selection comes painful cattle. So then the order is that a white way of being round is something suggesting a pin and is it disappointing,[7] it is not, it is so rudimentary to be analyzed and see a fine substance strangely, it is so earnest to have a green point not to red but to point again.

A long dress.

What is the current[8] that makes machinery, that makes it crackle, what is the current that presents a long line and a necessary waist. What is this current.

What is the wind, what is it.

Where is the serene length, it is there and a dark place is not a dark place, only a white and red are black, only a yellow and green are blue, a pink is scarlet, a bow is every color. A line distinguishes it. A line just distinguishes it.

A waist.

A star glide, a single frantic sullenness, a single financial grass greediness.[9]

---

3. A metallic element used in plating; a silvery-white American coin.

4. An office or position requiring little work.

5. Although this prose poem resolutely refuses to describe cohesively, this section does seem to imply certain activities such as "cleansing" and "polishing" tarnished metal and perhaps "giving" a party or a present.

6. The significance of "kindness," "redness," and "rudeness" may have more to do with the alliteration of "r," the consonance of "d," and the rhyme of "ness" than with any logical argument, though the progression of nouns does suggest a movement from "kindness" to "rudeness" and from "redness" to "rudeness."

7. Perhaps a suggestion of something disappointing in the box; or perhaps the "point" in "disappointing" merely echoes the "pin," the "green point" and the "point again" on either side of it. "Rudimentary": perhaps a play on the earlier "rudeness."

8. Perhaps the vision of this colorful, elegant dress contains an excitement, an erotic charge, an electric current.

9. Perhaps evoking the "waist" of a dress or a "waste" of effort. Note the verbal play in the repetition of "single," the alliterations of "single" / "sullenness" and "grass" / "greediness," and the off rhymes of "sullenness" / "grass" / "greediness."

Object that is in wood. Hold the pine, hold the dark, hold in the rush, make the bottom.

A piece of crystal. A change, in a change that is remarkable there is no reason to say that there was a time.

A woolen object gilded.[10] A country climb is the best disgrace, a couple of practices any of them in order is so left.

A *brown*.

A brown which is not liquid[11] not more so is relaxed and yet there is a change, a news is pressing.

A *table*.

A table means does it not my dear[12] it means a whole steadiness. Is it likely that a change.

A table means more than a glass even a looking glass is tall. A table means necessary places and a revision a revision of a little thing it means it does mean that there has been a stand, a stand where it did shake.

A *white hunter*.

A white hunter is nearly crazy.

This *is this dress, aider.*

Aider,[13] why aider why whow, whow stop touch, aider whow, aider stop the muncher, muncher munchers.

A jack in kill her, a jack in, makes a meadowed king, makes a to let.

FROM *Food*

Custard.

Custard is this. It has aches,[14] aches when. Not to be. Not to be narrowly. This makes a whole little hill.

It is better than a little thing that has mellow real mellow. It is better than lakes[15] whole lakes, it is better than seeding.

---

10. An unvisualizable object that might be associated with either "waist" or "waste."
11. An example of Stein's tendency to define something by what it is not, a rhetorical device that Marjorie Perloff calls "ironic, promising as it does, certainties that don't exist"; possibly, in this case, suggesting a piece of furniture, a chair.
12. In a parody of women's social conversation, the tone promises a clear statement that is not forthcoming.

13. A pun on "Ada," Stein's nickname for Alice B. Toklas. It may also be an appeal to one who aids, or a plea to "aid her." The "dress" points back to "A long dress" and "A waist." "Whow stop touch": alludes either to happy lovemaking or, conversely, to a violent rape-murder.
14. Eggs; perhaps also achingly good or stomachache.
15. Perhaps also cakes. "Seeding": perhaps a seed cake.

Asparagus.

Asparagus in a lean in a lean to hot.[16] This makes it art and it is wet wet weather wet weather wet.

Chicken.

Pheasant and chicken, chicken is a peculiar bird.

Chicken.

Alas a dirty word,[17] alas a dirty third alas a dirty third, alas a dirty bird.

Orange in.

Go lack[18] go lack use to her.

    Cocoa and clear soup and oranges and oat-meal.

    Whist[19] bottom whist close, whist clothes, woodling.

    Cocoa and clear soup and oranges and oat-meal.

    Pain[20] soup, suppose it is question, suppose it is butter, real is, real is only, only excreate,[21] only excreate a no since.

    A no, a no since, a no since when, a no since when since, a no since when since a no since when since, a no since, a no since when since, a no since, a no, a no since a no since, a no since, a no since.

1914

A sequence of interrelated prose poems, *Tender Buttons* evokes an enigmatic but mostly happy domestic world of objects, food, and rooms. Stein explained that she was ridding herself of nouns, by which she perhaps meant that she was wrenching nouns out of clarifying contexts, thereby undermining their referential authority and reducing their power to dominate discourse. In Stein's language use, words do not effectively name. For example, the title may refer to buttons, mushrooms, nipples, or navels. Marjorie Perloff observes: "The text has remained peculiarly resistant to interpretation. . . . The poet wants us to be able to fill in the gaps in whatever way suits us. . . . Nothing is what it seems to be. . . . Indeed the whole of *Tender Buttons* may be said to take place in an indeterminate room without 'centre,' in which food and dressing and love rituals are occurring interchangeably." Other critics, however, do find an overarching theme: that of a woman-centered consciousness, placed in the domestic sphere and employing a feminist discursive style that prizes diversity and difference.

16. They lean as they cook. Note the off rhymes of "lean" / "hot" / "wet."

17. Note the rhymes in this section and the preceding one.

18. Perhaps also back. "Orange in" may suggest a woman-centered origin. "Her": perhaps a reference to Alice B. Toklas, a celebrated cook.

19. An old-fashioned card game; hush!; hushed; with perhaps a suggestion of whistle or whistle for (summon). Note the play on "close" and "clothes." "Woodling": small piece of wood or small forest creature.

20. Perhaps also plain or the French *pain* (bread).

21. Perhaps a pun on "create," "uncreate," and "excrete." "No since": perhaps implying a negative answer to the patriarchal "pain soup," a restoration of innocence, or a final celebration of stylistic nonsense (no sense).

Idem the Same

A VALENTINE TO SHERWOOD ANDERSON

I knew too that through them I knew too that he was through, I knew too that he
threw them. I knew too that they were through, I knew too I knew too, I knew I
knew them.

I knew[1] to them.

If they tear a hunter through, if they tear through a hunter, if they tear
through a hunt and a hunter, if they tear through the different sizes of the six,
the different sizes of the six which are these, a woman with a white package
under one arm and a black package under the other arm and dressed in brown
with a white blouse, the second Saint Joseph the third a hunter in a blue coat and
black garters[2] and a plaid cap, a fourth a knife grinder who is full faced and a very
little woman with black hair and a yellow hat and an excellently smiling
appropriate soldier. All these as you please.

In the meantime examples of the same lily. In this way please have you rung.

WHAT DO I SEE.

A very little snail.
A medium sized turkey.
A small band of sheep.
A fair orange tree.
All nice wives are like that.
Listen to them from here.
Oh.
You did not have an answer.
Here.
Yes.

A VERY VALENTINE.

Very fine is my valentine.
Very fine and very mine.
Very mine is my valentine very mine and very fine.[3]

Very fine is my valentine and mine, very fine very mine and mine is my
valentine.

---

1. Pun on "new." When Stein first met Anderson,
he was married to his second wife, Tennessee, but
the couple divorced just prior to Stein's composi-
tion of this valentine.

2. The first of many ironic representations of gen-
der and gender relations in this text.

3. This line originally appeared in a love note to
Toklas, reading, "Very Stein is my valentine very
Stein and very fine."

WHY DO YOU FEEL DIFFERENTLY.

Why do you feel differently about a very little snail and a big one.

Why do you feel differently about a medium sized turkey and a very large one.

Why do you feel differently about a small band of sheep and several sheep that are riding.

Why do you feel differently about a fair orange tree and one that has blossoms as well.

Oh very well.

All nice wives are like that.

To Be
No Please.
To Be
They can please
Not to be[4]
Do they please.
Not to be
Do they not please
Yes please.
Do they please
No please.
Do they not please
No please.
Do they please.
Please.
If you please.
And if you please.
And if they please.
And they please.
To be pleased
Not to be pleased.
Not to be displeased.
To be pleased and to please.

KNEELING.

One two three four five six seven eight nine and ten.

The tenth is a little one kneeling and giving away a rooster with this feeling.

I have mentioned one, four five seven eight and nine.

Two is also giving away an animal.

Three is changed as to disposition.

---

4. Compare Shakespeare's "To be, or not to be: that is the question" (*Hamlet* 3.1).

Six is in question if we mean mother and daughter, black and black caught her, and she offers to be three she offers it to me.

That is very right and should come out below and just so.

BUNDLES FOR THEM.
A HISTORY OF GIVING BUNDLES.

We were able to notice that each one in a way carried a bundle,[5] they were not a trouble to them nor were they all bundles as some of them were chickens some of them pheasants some of them sheep and some of them bundles, they were not a trouble to them and then indeed we learned that it was the principal recreation and they were so arranged that they were not given away, and to-day they were given away.

I will not look at them again.

They will not look for them again.

They have not seen them here again.

They are in there and we hear them again.

In which way are stars brighter than they are. When we have collie to this decision. We mention many thousands of buds. And when I close my eyes I see them.

If you hear her snore

It is not before you love her

You love her so that to be her beau is very lovely

She is sweetly there and her curly hair is very lovely

She is sweetly here and I am very near and that is very lovely.

She is my tender sweet and her little feet are stretched out well which is a treat and very lovely

Her little tender nose is between her little eyes which close and are very lovely

She is very lovely and mine which is very lovely.

ON HER WAY.

If you can see why she feels that she kneels if you can see why he knows that he shows what he bestows, if you can see why they share what they share, need we question that there is no doubt that by this time if they had intended to come they would have sent some notice of such intention. She and the and indeed the decision itself is not early dissatisfaction.

IN THIS WAY.

Keys please, it is useless to alarm any one it is useless to alarm some one it is useless to be alarming and to get fertility in gardens in salads in heliotrope and in dishes. Dishes and wishes are mentioned and dishes and wishes are not capable of darkness. We like sheep. And so does he.

---

5. Perhaps a Christmas present.

LET US DESCRIBE.

Let us describe how they went. It was a very windy night and the road although in excellent condition and extremely well graded has many turnings and although the curves are not sharp the rise is considerable. It was a very windy night and some of the larger vehicles found it more prudent not to venture. In consequence some of those who had planned to go were unable to do so. Many others did go and there was a sacrifice, of what shall we, a sheep, a hen, a cock, a village, a ruin, and all that and then that having been blessed let us bless it.

1923

Idem is Latin for "the same." As the self-echoing title suggests, this collage uses abstract language to create a self-enclosed world of words. Nevertheless, the reader may discern in it ironic reflections on sex and marriage as well as passages praising love and art. The poem is a dual valentine intended for both Alice B. Toklas and their good friend Sherwood Anderson (1876–1941), the author of *Winesburg, Ohio*. Stein wanted to thank Anderson for having written a laudatory article about her and an introduction to one of her books. Perhaps the named Anderson and the unnamed Toklas are "the same" in being recipients of this valentine. Or perhaps Stein and Toklas are "the same" in being inseparable lovers.

George Hugnet

George and Genevieve[1] Geronimo with a with whether they thought they were with whether.

Without their finding it out. Without. Their finding it out. With whether.

George whether they were about. With their finding their whether it finding it out whether with their finding about it out.

George with their finding it with out.

George whether their with their it whether.

Redoubt[2] out with about.

With out whether it their whether with out doubt.

Azure can with our about.

It is welcome welcome thing.

George in are ring.

Lain away awake.

George in our ring.

George Genevieve Geronimo straightened it out without their finding it out.

---

1. The patron saint of Paris and perhaps also Stein herself. Geronimo: Apache leader and military hero (1829–1909) and perhaps also Virgil Thomson.

2. Defensive fort; recurrent doubt.

Grammar[3] makes George in our ring which Grammar make George in our ring.

Grammar is as disappointed not is as grammar is as disappointed.

Grammar is not as Grammar is as disappointed.

George is in our ring. Grammar is not is disappointed. In are ring.

George Genevieve in are ring.

1929

Stein observed that "George Hugnet" is "completely contained within itself." It employs a tiny, abstract vocabulary and three main characters, all of whose names begin with "G." The prose poem does, however, have links to the outside world. Georges (not George) Hugnet (1906–1927) was a French poet who for a brief time became a close friend of Stein. The composer Virgil Thomson introduced them, and soon the three artists formed an intimate circle, collaborating on projects. Ulla Dydo writes that the text questions how George "can be put inside, within the portrait rather than without, how he can be welcomed as 'ours,' 'in our ring.'"

FROM Four Saints in Three Acts

Pigeons on the grass alas.

Pigeons on the grass alas.

Short longer grass short longer longer shorter yellow grass. Pigeons large pigeons on the shorter longer yellow grass alas pigeons on the grass.

If they were not pigeons what were they.

If they were not pigeons on the grass alas what were they. He[1] had heard of a third and he asked about it it was a magpie[2] in the sky. If a magpie in the sky on the sky can not cry if the pigeon on the grass alas can alas and to pass the pigeon on the grass alas and the magpie in the sky on the sky and to try and to try alas on the grass alas the pigeon on the grass the pigeon on the grass and alas. They might be very well very well very well they might be they might be very well they might be very well very well they might be.

Let Lucy Lily Lily Lucy Lucy let Lucy Lucy Lily Lily Lily Lily Lily let Lily Lucy Lucy let Lily. Let Lucy Lily.

1929

Four Saints in Three Acts, an opera for which Stein wrote the libretto and Virgil Thomson the music, scored a tremendous success with an African-American cast in 1934. The ver-

---

3. Perhaps a personification; perhaps a figure for artistic arrangement or innovative writing. Stein was studying grammar at the time.

1. Perhaps St. Ignatius.

2. Eurasian bird with black-and-white plumage.

In a lecture, Stein associated this magpie with pictorial representations of the Holy Ghost of the Christian trinity. It may be worth noting that the magpie is a field bird, whereas pigeons are city birds.

bally playful text ostensibly concerns the sixteenth-century Spanish saints Theresa of Avila and Ignatius Loyola. Embedded within their quest for spiritual vision, however, is Stein's own meditation on artistic inspiration. The famous "Pigeons on the grass alas" aria, though spoken by St. Ignatius in the Broadway production, is not assigned to any character in the text and thus might be considered, as Jane Bowers says, Stein's own song. The word "alas," for example, has commonly been taken as Stein's tribute to her companion, Alice. Stein described the genesis of the aria thusly: "I was walking in the gardens of the Luxembourg in Paris. It was the end of summer the grass was yellow. I was sorry that it was the end of summer and I saw the big fat pigeons in the yellow grass and I said to myself, pigeons on the yellow grass, alas, and I kept on writing pigeons on the grass, alas, . . . and I kept on writing until I had emptied myself of the emotion."

PROSE

FROM *Composition as Explanation*

There is singularly nothing that makes a difference a difference in beginning and in the middle and in ending except that each generation has something different at which they are all looking. By this I mean so simply that anybody knows it that composition is the difference which makes each and all of them then different from other generations and this is what makes everything different otherwise they are all alike and everybody knows it because everybody says it.

It is very likely that nearly every one has been very nearly certain that something that is interesting is interesting them. Can they and do they. It is very interesting that nothing inside in them, that is when you consider the very long history of how every one ever acted or has felt, it is very interesting that nothing inside in them in all of them makes it connectedly different. By this I mean this. The only thing that is different from one time to another is what is seen and what is seen depends upon how everybody is doing everything. This makes the thing we are looking at very different and this makes what those who describe it make of it, it makes a composition, it confuses, it shows, it is, it looks, it likes it as it is, and this makes what is seen as it is seen. Nothing changes from generation to generation except the thing seen and that makes a composition. Lord Grey remarked that when the generals before the war talked about the war they talked about it as a nineteenth century war although to be fought with twentieth century weapons. That is because war is a thing that decides how it is to be when it is to be done. It is prepared and to that degree it is like all academies it is not a thing made by being made it is a thing prepared. Writing and painting and all that, is like that, for those who occupy themselves with it and don't make it as it is made. Now the few who make it as it is made, and it is to be remarked that the most decided of them usually are prepared just as the world around them is preparing, do it in this way and so I if you do not mind I will tell you how fit happens. Naturally one does not know how it happened until it is well over beginning happening.

To come back to the part that the only thing that is different is what is seen when it seems to be being seen, in other words, composition and time-sense.

No one is ahead of his time, it is only that the particular variety of creating his time is the one that his contemporaries who also are creating their own time refuse to accept. And they refuse to accept it for a very simple reason and that is that they do not have to accept it for any reason. They themselves that is everybody in their entering the modern composition and they do enter it, if they do not enter it they are not so to speak in it they are out of it and so they do enter it. But in as you may say the non-competitive efforts where if you are not in it nothing is lost except nothing at all except what is not had, there are naturally all the refusals, and the things refused are only important if unexpectedly somebody happens to need them. In the case of the arts it is very definite. Those who are creating the modern composition authentically are naturally only of importance when they are dead because by that time the modern composition having become past is classified and the description of it is classical. That is the reason why the creator of the new composition in the arts is an outlaw until he is a classic, there is hardly a moment in between and it is really too bad very much too bad naturally for the creator but also very much too bad for the enjoyer, they all really would enjoy the created so much better just after it has been made than when it is already a classic, but it is perfectly simple that there is no reason why the contemporaries should see, because it would not make any difference as they lead their lives in the new composition anyway, and as every one is naturally indolent why naturally they don't see. For this reason as in quoting Lord Grey it is quite certain that nations not actively threatened are at least several generations behind themselves militarily so aesthetically they are more than several generations behind themselves and it is very much too bad, it is so very much more exciting and satisfactory for everybody if one can have contemporaries, if all one's contemporaries could be one's contemporaries.

There is almost not an interval.

For a very long time everybody refuses and then almost without a pause almost everybody accepts. In the history of the refused in the arts and literature the rapidity of the change is always startling. Now the only difficulty with the *volte-face* concerning the arts is this. When the acceptance comes, by that acceptance the thing created becomes a classic. It is a natural phenomena a rather extraordinary natural phenomena that a thing accepted becomes a classic. And what is the characteristic quality of a classic. The characteristic quality of a classic is that it is beautiful. Now of course it is perfectly true that a more or less first rate work of art is beautiful but the trouble is that when that first rate work of art becomes a classic because it is accepted the only thing that is important from then on to the majority of the acceptors the enormous majority, the most intelligent majority of the acceptors is that it is so wonderfully beautiful. Of course it is wonderfully beautiful, only when it is still a thing irritating annoying stimulating then all quality of beauty is denied to it.

Of course it is beautiful but first all beauty in it is denied and then all the beauty of it is accepted. If everyone were not so indolent they would realise that beauty is beauty even when it is irritating and stimulating not only when it is accepted and classic. Of course it is extremely difficult nothing more so than to remember back to its not being beautiful once it has become beautiful. This makes it so much more difficult to realise its beauty when the work is being refused and prevents every one from realising that they were convinced that beauty was denied, once the work is accepted. Automatically with the acceptance of the time-sense comes the recognition of the beauty and once the beauty is accepted the beauty never fails any one.

Beginning again and again is a natural thing even when there is a series.

Beginning again and again and again explaining composition and time is a natural thing.

It is understood by this time that everything is the same except composition and time, composition and the time of the composition and the time in the composition.

Everything is the same except composition and as the composition is different and always going to be different everything is not the same. Everything is not the same as the time when of the composition and the time in the composition is different. The composition is different, that is certain.

The composition is the thing seen by every one living in the living they are doing, they are the composing of the composition that at the time they are living is the composition of the time in which they are living. It is that that makes living a thing they are doing. Nothing else is different, of that almost any one can be certain. The time when and the time of and the time in that composition is the natural phenomena of that composition and of that perhaps every one can be certain.

No one thinks these things when they are making when they are creating what is the composition, naturally no one thinks, that is no one formulates until what is to be formulated has been made.

Composition is not there, it is going to be there and we are here. This is some time ago for us naturally.

The only thing that is different from one time to another is what is seen and what is seen depends upon how everybody is doing everything. This makes the thing we are looking at very different and this makes what those who describe it make of it, it makes a composition, it confuses, it shows, it is, it looks, it likes it as it is, and this makes what is seen as it is seen. Nothing changes from generation to generation except the thing seen and that makes a composition. . . .[1]

In the meantime to naturally begin I commenced making portraits of anybody and anything. In making these portraits I naturally made a continuous present and including every thing and a beginning and beginning again within a very small thing. That started me into composing anything into one thing. So then naturally it was natural that one thing an enormously long thing was not everything an enormously short thing was also not everything nor was it all of it a continuous present thing nor was it always and always beginning again. Naturally I would then begin again. I would begin again I would naturally begin. I did naturally begin. This brings me to a great deal that has been begun.

And after that what changes what changes after that, after that what changes and what changes after that and after that and what changes and after that and what changes after that.

The problem from this time on became more definite.

It was all so nearly alike it must be different and it is different, it is natural that if everything is used and there is a continuous present and a beginning again and again if it is all so alike it must be simply different and everything simply different was the natural way of creating it then.

In this natural way of creating it then that it was simply different everything being alike it was simply different, this kept on leading one to lists naturally for a while and by lists I mean a series. More and more in going back over what was done at this time I find that I naturally kept simply different as an intention. Whether there was or whether there was not a continuous present did not then any longer trouble me there was or there was not, and using everything no longer troubled me if everything is alike using everything could no longer trouble me and beginning again and again could no longer trouble me because if lists were inevitable if series were inevitable and the whole of it was inevitable beginning again and again could not trouble me so then with nothing to trouble me I very completely began naturally since everything is alike making it as simply different naturally as simply different as possible. I began doing natural phenomena what I call natural phenomena naturally everything being alike natural phenomena are making things be naturally simply different. This found its culmination later, in the beginning it began in a center confused with lists with series with geography with returning portraits and with particularly often four and three and often with five and four. It is easy to see that in the beginning such a conception as everything being naturally different would be very inarticulate and very slowly it began

---

1. In the section omitted here, Stein describes two early fictions: the novella *Melanctha*, with its style of "beginning again and again" and "the continuous present," and the long novel *The Making of Americans*, with its aim of "including everything."

to emerge and take the form of anything, and then naturally if anything that is simply different is simply different what follows will follow.

So far then the progress of my conceptions was the natural progress entirely in accordance with my epoch as I am sure is to be quite easily realised if you think over the scene that was before us all from year to year.

As I said in the beginning, there is the long history of how every one ever acted or has felt and that nothing inside in them in all of them makes it connectedly different. By this I mean all this.

The only thing that is different from one time to another is what is seen and what is seen depends upon how everybody is doing everything.

It is understood by this time that everything is the same except composition and time, composition and the time of the composition and time in the composition.

Everything is the same except composition and as the composition is different and always going to be different everything is not the same. So then I as a contemporary creating the composition in the beginning was groping toward a continuous present, a using everything a beginning again and again and then everything being alike then everything very simply everything was naturally simply different and so I as a contemporary was creating everything being alike was creative everything naturally being naturally simply different, everything being alike. This then was the period that brings me to the period of the beginning of 1914. Everything being alike everything naturally would be simply different and the war came and everything being alike and every thing being simply different brings everything being simply different brings it to romanticism.

Romanticism is then when everything being alike everything is naturally simply different, and romanticism.

Then for four years this was more and more different even though this was, was everything alike. Everything alike naturally everything was simply different and this is and was romanticism and this is and was war. Everything being alike everything naturally everything is different simply different naturally simply different.

And so there was the natural phenomena that was war, which had been, before war came, several generations behind the contemporary composition, because it became war and so completely needed to be contemporary became completely contemporary and so created the completed recognition of the contemporary composition. Every one but one may say every one became consciously became aware of the existence of the authenticity of the modern composition. This then the contemporary recognition, because of the academic thing known as war having been forced to become contemporary made every one not only contemporary in act not only contemporary in thought but contemporary in self-consciousness made every one contemporary with the modern composition.

And so the art creation of the contemporary composition which would have been outlawed normally outlawed several generations more behind even than war, war having been brought so to speak up to date art so to speak was allowed not completely to be up to date, but nearly up to date, in other words we who created the expression of the modern composition were to be recognized before we were dead some of us even quite a long time before we were dead. And so war may be said to have advanced a general recognition of the expression of the contemporary composition by almost thirty years.

And now after that there is no more of that in other words there is peace and something comes then and it follows coming then.

And so now one finds oneself interesting oneself in an equilibrium, that of course means words as well as things and distribution as well as between themselves and the things and themselves, a distribution as distribution. This makes what follows what follows and now there is every reason why there should be an arrangement made. Distribution is interesting and equilibrium is interesting when a continuous present and a beginning again and again and using everything and everything alike and everything naturally simply different has been done.

After all this, there is that, there has been that that there is a composition and that nothing changes except composition the composition and the time of and the time in the composition.

The time of the composition is a natural thing and the time in the composition is a natural thing it is a natural thing and it is a contemporary thing.

The time of the composition is the time of the composition. It has been at times a present thing it has been at times a past thing it has been at times a future thing it has been at times an endeavor at parts or all of these things. In my beginning it was a continuous present a beginning again and again and again and again, it was a series it was a list it was a similarity and everything different it was a distribution and an equilibration. That is all of the time some of the time of the composition.

Now there is still something else the time-sense in the composition. This is what is always a fear a doubt and a judgement and a conviction. The quality in the creation of expression the quality in a composition that makes it go dead just after it has been made is very troublesome.

The time in the composition is a thing that is very troublesome. If the time in the composition is very troublesome it is because there must even if there is no time at all in the composition there must be time in the composition which is in its quality of distribution and equilibration. In the beginning there was the time in the composition that naturally was in the composition but time in the composition comes now and this is what is now troubling every one the time in the composition is now a part of distribution and equilibration. In the beginning there was confusion there was a continuous present and later there was romanticism which was not a confusion but an extrication and now there is either succeeding or failing there must be distribution and equilibration there must be time that is distributed and equilibrated. This is the thing that is at present the most troubling and if there is the time that is at present the most troublesome the time-sense that is at present the most troubling is the thing that makes the present the most troubling. There is at present there is distribution, by this I mean expression and time, and in this way at present composition is time that is the reason that at present the time-sense is troubling that is the reason why at present the time-sense in the composition is the composition that is making what there is in composition.

And afterwards.

Now that is all.

1926

TRUMBULL STICKNEY
1874–1904

Trumbull stickney is often regarded as a nineteenth-century poet because he died so young (at the age of thirty, barely four years into the twentieth century). Yet he was born the same year as such twentieth-century icons as Robert Frost, Amy Lowell, and Gertrude Stein. Although he died before Frost and Lowell got their creative projects going, his poetry allies itself with theirs in its concentration on image and sound and its admixture of observation, memory, and meditation. Graceful, melodious, and melancholic, Stickney's poetry forms a bridge from nineteenth-century romantic and symbolic poetry to the ironies, dislocations, and divided sensibilities of such modernists as T. S. Eliot and Hart Crane. Stickney's poems often depict beautiful, lonely landscapes that, though visually gratifying, leave the speaker feeling vulnerable. At times they also look back piercingly to a past that is lost. The poems' sounds and rhythms are hauntingly lovely, as are their metaphors and resonant endings.

Stickney, the son of expatriate New England parents, grew up in Switzerland, England, and Italy. He graduated from Harvard in 1890, ten years before Wallace Stevens completed his studies and nineteen years before Eliot. Then, like Eliot, he studied at the Sorbonne, receiving his doctorate in 1903. He returned to the United States to teach Greek at Harvard but died of a brain tumor in 1904. Many of his poems were published posthumously. He remains an archetype of the poet snuffed out before his prime, a poet whose lyrical, sad voice might have complemented or influenced the development of modernism in the decades after his death.

FURTHER READING

John Hollander. *The Work of Poetry*. New York: Columbia University Press, 1997.
Trumbull Stickney. *Poems*. Ed. Amberys R. Whittle. New York: Farrar Straus & Giroux, 1972.

Mnemosyne

It's autumn in the country I remember.[1]

How warm a wind blew here about the ways!
And shadows on the hillside lay to slumber
During the long sun-sweetened summer-days.

It's cold abroad the country I remember.

The swallows veering skimmed the golden grain
At midday with a wing aslant and limber;
And yellow cattle browsed upon the plain.

It's empty down the country I remember.

I had a sister lovely in my sight:
Her hair was dark, her eyes were very sombre;
We sang together in the woods at night.

It's lonely in the country I remember.

The babble of our children fills my ears,
And on our hearth I stare the perished ember
To flames that show all starry thro' my tears.

It's dark about the country I remember.

---

1. As Hollander points out, this line might be interpreted to mean that the speaker particularly remembers autumn or particularly remembers the country.

*   *   *

There are the mountains where I lived. The path
Is slushed with cattle-tracks and fallen timber,
The stumps are twisted by the tempests' wrath.

But that I knew these places are my own,
I'd ask how came such wretchedness to cumber[2]
The earth, and I to people it alone.

It rains across the country I remember.

1902

Mnemosyne is the goddess of memory in Greek mythology. She was also the mother of the nine Muses, who presided over the arts. Calling "Mnemosyne" Stickney's "absolute masterpiece," John Hollander says that it seems "to reinvent the concept of remembering." The poem recalls a lost or imagined time and place in which the speaker and a sister sing together at night and raise children together by day. The poem seems to graft the innocence of the brother-sister bond in John Greenleaf Whittier's American classic, "Snowbound," to the transgressive and symbolic sensuality of Edgar Allan Poe's "Annabel Lee" and Charles Baudelaire's "*L'Invitation au voyage.*" Note the way that variations on the opening line return to separate the tercets (except, mysteriously, once). The recurrent line serves as both a comment on the preceding three lines and a prefiguring of the next three, and it supplies a rhyme or slant rhyme for each tercet's otherwise unrhymed middle line.

Live blindly and upon the hour

Live blindly and upon the hour. The Lord
Who was the Future, died full long ago.
Knowledge which is the Past is folly. Go
Poor child, and be not to thyself abhorred.
Around thine earth sun-wingèd winds do blow
And planets roll; a meteor draws his sword;
The rainbow breaks his seven-coloured chord
And the long strips of river-silver flow:
Awake! Give thyself to the lovely hours.[1]
Drinking their lips, catch thou the dream in flight.

2. Burden or trouble.
1. The hours are here imagined as goddesses, per- haps the Horae or Hours of Greco-Roman myth, who were goddesses of the changing seasons.

Thou art divine, thou livest,—as of old
Apollo[2] springing naked to the light,
And all his island shivered into flowers.

1905

Reflecting a turn-of-the-century sense of the death of God, "Live blindly" expresses a theme of *carpe diem* (Latin for "seize the day"). In form it is a sonnet in the Italian or Petrarchan style.

The melancholy year is dead with rain

The melancholy year is dead with rain.
Drop after drop on every branch pursues.
From far away beyond the drizzled flues[1]
A twilight saddens to the window pane.
And dimly thro' the chambers of the brain,
From place to place and gently touching, moves
My one and irrecoverable love's
Dear and lost shape one other time again.
So in the last of autumn for a day
Summer or summer's memory returns.
So in a mountain desolation burns
Some rich belated flower, and with the gray
Sick weather, in the world of rotting ferns
From out the dreadful stones it dies away.

1905

In "The melancholy year," a rain-drenched scene corresponding to the speaker's psychological state yields to a desolate mountain with one "belated flower," a multiplicitous image of lost love, lost hope, and arguably the poem itself.

Mt. Lykaion

Alone on Lykaion since man hath been
Stand on the height two columns, where at rest
Two eagles hewn of gold sit looking East

---

2. Powerful Greco-Roman god of light, healing, distance, prophecy, music, poetry, dance, crops, and herds. Because his forename was "Phoebus," which means "bright" or "pure," he was associated with the sun and often depicted as a naked, beardless youth.

1. Ducts or tubes, i.e., rain gutters.

Forever; and the sun goes up between.
Far down around the mountain's oval green
An order keeps the falling stones abreast.
Below within the chaos last and least
A river like a curl of light is seen.
Beyond the river lies the even sea,
Beyond the sea another ghost of sky, —
O God, support the sickness of my eye
Lest the far space and long antiquity
Suck out my heart, and on this awful ground
The great wind kill my little shell with sound.

1905

Stickney visited Mr. Lykaion (or Mt. Lycaon or Lycaeus) in Greece the year before he died. According to Greek myth, the mountain was home to the king of Arcadia and sacred to the supreme god Zeus. The columns and golden eagles of the initial lines derive from ancient texts rather than from reality, but the stones, river, sea, and sky were and are there to be seen. The prayer to God in the final four lines contrasts to the opening of "Live blindly and upon the hour" above.

Dramatic Fragment 5

Sir, say no more.
Within me 'tis as if
The green and climbing eyesight of a cat
Crawled near my mind's poor birds.

1905

ALICE DUNBAR-NELSON
1875–1935

A SUPPORTER OF RACIAL EQUALITY, women's rights, and working people's causes, Alice Dunbar-Nelson was one of the first black women to establish herself as a poet in the twentieth century. Born Alice Moore in New Orleans, the daughter of a freed slave, she graduated from Dillard University when she was only eighteen and received her master's degree from Cornell. When she was twenty-three, she married the celebrated poet Paul Laurence Dunbar (included in the first volume of this anthology). Eventually the Dunbars separated, and Dunbar-Nelson moved to Delaware, where she taught high school English. She remarried twice, the second time to Robert Nelson, a journalist. Dunbar-Nelson also had a series of passionate attachments with women. Active politically, she protested the rejection of women's contributions in World War I in "I Sit and Sew." Out of her love of women she created such poems as "You! Inez!" Dunbar-Nelson also gave speeches on social justice, wrote short stories and a diary, and worked as a newspaper columnist and editor.

FURTHER READING

Alice Dunbar-Nelson. *Works*. Ed. Gloria T. Hull. New York: Oxford University Press, 1988.
Venetria K. Patton and Maureen Honey, eds. "Alice Dunbar-Nelson." In *Double-Take: A Revisionist Harlem Renaissance Anthology*, 145–51. New Brunswick, N.J.: Rutgers University Press, 2001.

I Sit and Sew

I sit and sew—a useless task it seems,
My hands grown tired, my head weighed down with dreams—
The panoply of war, the martial tread of men,
Grim-faced, stern-eyed, gazing beyond the ken
Of lesser souls, whose eyes have not seen Death
Nor learned to hold their lives but as a breath—
But—I must sit and sew.

I sit and sew—my heart aches with desire—
That pageant terrible, that fiercely pouring fire
On wasted fields, and writhing grotesque things
Once men. My soul in pity flings
Appealing cries, yearning only to go
There in that holocaust of hell, those fields of woe—
But—I must sit and sew. —

The little useless seam, the idle patch;
Why dream I here beneath my homely thatch,
When there they lie in sodden mud and rain,
Pitifully calling me, the quick[1] ones and the slain?

1. Living.

You need me, Christ! It is no roseate[2] seam
That beckons me—this pretty futile seam,
It stifles me—God, must I sit and sew?

1918

"I Sit and Sew" is a feminist plea for a more active women's role in World War I and, as well, a lament for the war's many victims.

You! Inez!

Orange gleams athwart a crimson soul
Lambent flames; purple passion lurks
In your dusk eyes.
Red mouth; flower soft,
Your soul leaps up and flashes
Star-like, white, flame-hot.
Curving arms, encircling a world of love.
You! Stirring the depths of passionate desire!

2001

Written in 1921, "You! Inez!" was not published until Venetria K. Patton and Maureen Honey included it in their anthology, *Double-Take*. The poem explores same-sex desire in a way that may have been too straightforward for readers of its time.

YONE NOGUCHI
1875–1947

YONE NOGUCHI was the first Japanese national to publish poetry in English. He was born in Japan but moved to the United States in 1893. Living in the San Francisco Bay Area, he was influenced by Walt Whitman's long poetic line and mentored by the popular Western writer Joaquin Miller. Noguchi studied poetry, working with a group of local poets called Les Jeunes (French for "the young ones"). He published his first book of poetry in 1897.

2. Optimistic; rose-colored.

Noguchi's lover, the Anglo-American writer Leonie Gilmour, gave birth to their son, Isamu Noguchi, who was to become a noted sculptor. In 1904 Yone Noguchi decided to return to Japan, where he became professor of English at Tokyo's Keio University. Gilmour and their son followed him there, but the relationship did not last. After Isamu Noguchi was sent to the United States to live in 1918, he saw his father for only several months in 1931. Yone Noguchi continued to write and publish poetry, and he also published several books on Japanese art. He corresponded with Ezra Pound and in his work tried to deepen the contact between Japanese and American cultural traditions. His son established a memorial garden for him in Japan following his death in Tokyo in 1947.

FURTHER READING

Juliana Chang, ed. *Quiet Fire: A Historical Anthology of Asian American Poetry, 1892–1970*. New Brunswick, N.J.: Rutgers University Press, 1996.

Dana Gioia, Chryss Yost, and Jack Hicks, eds. *California Poetry from the Gold Rush to the Present*. Berkeley, Calif.: Heyday Books, 2004.

Lines

The sun I worship.
Not for the light, but for the shadows of the trees he draws:
O shadows welcome like an angel's bower,
Where I build Summer-day dream!
Not for her love, but for the love's memory,
The woman I adore;
Love may die, but not for the memory eternally green—
The well where I drink Spring ecstasy.
To a bird's song I listen,
Not for the voice, but for the silence following after the song:
O Silence fresh from the bosom of voice!—
Melody from the Death-Land whither my face does ever turn!

1909

In Japan Beyond

Do you not hear the sighing of a willow in Japan,
(In Japan beyond, in Japan beyond)
In the voice of a wind searching for the sun lost,
For the old faces with memory in the eyes?

*   *   *

Do you not hear the sighing of a bamboo in Japan,
(In Japan beyond, in Japan beyond)
In the voice of a sea urging with the night,
For the old dreams of a twilight tale?

Do you not hear the sighing of a pine in Japan,
(In Japan beyond, in Japan beyond)
In the voice of a river in quest of the Unknown,
For the old ages with gold in heart?

Do you not hear the sighing of a reed in Japan,
(In Japan beyond, in Japan beyond)
In the voice of a bird who long ago flew away,
For the old peace with velvet-sandalled feet?

1909

FROM Japanese Hokkus

1

Suppose the stars
Fall and break? Do they ever sound
Like my own love song?

1920

16

Are the fallen stars
Returning up the sky?
The dews on the grass.

1920

61

Like a cobweb hung upon the tree
A prey to wind and sunlight!
Who will say that we are safe and strong?

1920

68

Oh, how cool —
The sound of the bell
That leaves the bell itself.

1920

Noguchi wrote these haikus in English, helping to popularize the form in the United States. Poet and critic Dana Gioia writes: "His volume of *Japanese Hokkus*, which was dedicated to Yeats, still stands as an early milestone in the American haiku tradition. Noguchi understood his unique role as a conduit between the Japanese and English-language literary traditions." He hoped to reduce the "insularity" of both cultures.

AMEEN RIHANI
1876–1940

THE MOST POLITICALLY INVOLVED of the early Lebanese émigré poets who formed the Pen League with Kahlil Gibran that revolutionized Arab poetry, Ameen Rihani saw himself as a transcultural mediator. Many poets regard him as the founding father of Arab-American literature. He published twenty-nine books in English and twenty-six books in Arabic. Today a museum in his honor occupies the family home in Freika, Lebanon.

Born in Freika, Lebanon, Rihani immigrated to the United States in 1888 with his father and settled in Lower Manhattan. In 1911 he published *The Book of Khalid*, the first and only novel in English on the Lebanese immigrant experience, thereby initiating Arab-American literature with its struggle to reconcile East and West. In his poetry, Rihani was a devoted follower of Walt Whitman and transcendentalism. He eagerly introduced free verse to Arab literature in *Hutaf-ul Audiya* (Hymn of the Valleys), becoming the first Lebanese Arab to write in this new form. Thus he is considered an eminent founder of modern Arab literature and the Arab Renaissance. His *Ar-Rihaniyat* (The Rihani Essays) made him the initiator of immigrant literature by Arabs. Rihani also introduced Arab society and politics to U.S. readers with essays in such publications as *Atlantic Monthly* and a book-length study of the emerging Saud dynasty in Arabia (now Saudi Arabia) in 1928. *Muluk-ul 'Arab* (Kings of Arabia) offered the first analysis of Arabia from the Arab point of view and is regarded as a seminal text in the counter-Orientalist movement. Until this publication, all books on the Arab world had been written from a Western perspective.

FURTHER READING

Gregory Orfalea and Sharif Elmusa, eds. *Grape Leaves: A Century of Arab-American Poetry.* New York: Interlink Books, 2000.
Ameen Rihani. *Myrtle and Myrr.* New York: Gorham Press, 1905.

It Was All for Him

I strolled upon the Brooklyn Bridge one day,
    Beneath the storm;
None but a lad in rags upon the way
I saw;—there on a bench he lay
    Heedless of form.

He seemingly was reading what the Shower
    Was publishing upon the Bridge and down the Bay;
Yet he was writing, writing at this hour,—
    Writing in a careless sort of way.

Upon a pad he scribbled and as fast the rain
    Retouched, effaced, corrected and revised.
Was he recording Nature's solemn strain,
    Or sketching choristers therein disguised?

Whatever it be, I found myself quite by his side:
    My nod and smile he pocketed and wrote again;
"Read me your drizzling stuff," I said, and he replied:
    "I've written a check in payment for this shower of rain."

1905

Lilatu Laili

At night on the radiant Rialto,
    By the stars in their houses of glass,
I strolled with my soul in my pocket
    And prayed that my night might not pass;
I have seen 'neath the high heels of Beauty

My heart and my soul and my shame;
That form! O, how often it lured me,
    And how often I lost in the game!

And how often I walked in the shadow
    Of Laila[1] a mile and a mile!
But the rapture and bliss of a vision
    Would end in a great gush of bile.
To the hints that her garment would whisper
    I have listened but I would not dare;
I have seen every one of my fancies
    Retreat in the dark of her hair.

I have wished that each building around us
    Was a cedar, a poplar, a pine;
The men and women were statues,
    And the rain that was falling was wine;
That the lights were ethereal flowers;
    That the cars were the nooks in the wood, —

"O, enough!" she exclaimed as she kissed me,
    "This attic and couch are as good."

                                    1905

This poem recounts the speaker's most splendid night.

LUIS LLORENS TORRES
1876–1944

LUIS LLORENS TORRES established modernism in Puerto Rican poetry, and the movement remained dominant until 1925, when poets began to espouse a national culture. Spain had given Puerto Rico constitutional autonomy about nine months before the United States acquired the island as a colony following the Spanish-American War of 1898. The dream of Puerto Rican nationality was destroyed by

---

1. Laila was the lover of Qays, the greatest of the pre-Islamic poets according to Mohammed. Their story is the Arabic equivalent of the story of Romeo and Juliet.

this war's treaty, a historical moment usually referred to as the "trauma" of 1898. But nationhood has remained an issue in the divided consciousness of the island's people ever since.

Puerto Rican modernism in the early twentieth century was not the same as modernism in the United States. It incorporated Latin-American *modernismo* and surrealism and affirmed indigenous cultures, but it excluded African influences. It also looked to Spain, rather than to the United States, as a cultural model. The Latin-American *arielista* movement (named for the Shakespearean figure of Ariel, who opposed Caliban) was also crucial because it emphasized humanistic values in contrast to U.S. imperialism. These characteristics were the foundation of a style that was antagonistic to U.S. cultural domination. Eventually Puerto Rican poets realized the importance of including African elements in their work, and they created a *creollista* (Creole) poetics that better expressed the racially mixed and hybridized Puerto Rican experience. Luis Torres's "El patito feo/The Ugly Duckling" builds upon a classic Spanish poetic style and reflects his cultural nostalgia for Spain in the face of U.S. imperialism. This blend of poetics and politics was typical of Puerto Rican poets from the Creole bourgeois class.

FURTHER READING

E. Marzan, ed. *Inventing a Word: An Anthology of Twentieth-Century Puerto Rican Poetry.* New York: Columbia University Press, 1980.

Alfredo Matilla and Ivan Silen, eds. *The Puerto Rican Poets/Los Poetas Puertorriqueños.* New York: Bantam, 1972.

El patito feo

No sé si danés o ruso,
genial cuentista relata
que en el nido de una pata
la hembra de un cisne puso.
Y ahorrando las frases de uso
en los cuentos eruditos,
diz que sin más requisitos,
en el trécismo día,
la pata sacó su cría
de diez y nueve patitos.

Según este cuento breve,
creció el rebaño pigmeo
llamando PATITO FEO
al patito diez y nueve.

[TRANS.] The Ugly Duckling

Don't know if Danish or Russian,
a brilliant storyteller says
that in a duck's nest
lay a female swan.
And passing over the phrases used
in erudite stories,
let's say without further delay
that on the fortnight,
the duck gave birth to her brood
of nineteen ducklings.

According to this brief story,
the ducklings grew
calling the nineteenth one
the Ugly Duckling.

¡El pobre! Siempre la nieve
lo encontró fuera del ala.
Y siempre erró en la antesala
de sus diez y ocho hermanos
que dejábanle sin granos
las espigas de la tala.

Vagando por la campaña
la palmípeda cuadrilla
al fin llegó hasta la orilla
de la fuente en la montaña.
¡Qué sensación tan extraña
y a la par tan complaciente
la que le onduló en la mente
al llamado FEO PATO
cuando miró su retrato
en el vidrio de la fuente!

Surgió entonces de la umbria
un collar de cisnes blancos
en cuyos sedosos flancos
la espuma se emblanquecía.
(Aquí, al autor, que dormía
cuando este cuento soñó
dicen que lo despertó
la emoción de la belleza.
Y aquí sigue, o aquí empieza,
lo que tras él soñé yo.)

Cisne azul la raza hispana
puso un huevo, ciega y sorda
en el nido de la gorda
pata norteamericana.
Y ya, desde mi ventana,
los norteños patos veo
de hosco pico fariseo,
que al cisne de Puerto Rico,
de azul pluma y rojo pico,
le llaman PATITO FEO.

Pueblo que cisne naciste,
mira y sonríe, ante el mote,

Poor thing! The snow always
caught him outside the wing.
And he always erred in the anteroom
of his eighteen brothers
who, with no grains, left him
only the thorns in the garden.

Wandering through the country
the web-footed regiment
at last reached the edge
of a fountain in the mountain.
What a foreign but
altogether pleasurable sensation
rippled through the mind
of the so-called Ugly Duckling
when he saw his reflection
in the glass of the fountain!

Then from the shade appeared
a chain of white swans
on whose silky sides
the foam became white.
(Here, the author, who was sleeping
when he dreamed this tale,
was awakened, they say,
by the emotion of such beauty.
And here continues, or here begins
what I dreamed after him.)

The blue swan—the Hispanic race—
lay an egg, blind and deaf,
in the nest of the fat
North American duck.
And already, from my window,
I see the northern ducks,
of gloomy, hypocritical peak,
who called the swan of Puerto Rico—
of blue plumage and red peak—
the Ugly Duckling.

The nation-born swan
looks and smiles, before the mockery

con sonrisa del Quijote
y con su mirada triste;
que a la luz del sol que viste
de alba tu campo y tu mar,
cuando quieras contemplar
que es de cisne tu figura,
mírate en el agua pura
de la fuente de tu hogar.

Con flama de tu real sello,
mi cisne de Puerto Rico,
la lumbre roja del pico
prendes izada en el bello
candelabro de tu cuello.
Y azul del celeste tul,
en que une la Cruz del Sur
sus cinco brillantes galas,
es el que pinta en tus alas
tu firme triángulo azul.

Oro latino se asoma
a tu faz y en tu faz brilla.
Lo fundió en siglos Castilla.
Y antes de Castilla, Roma.
Lo hirvió el pueblo de Mahoma
en sus fraguas sarracenas.
Y antes de Roma, en Atenas,
los Homero y los Esquilo
hilaron de ensueño el hilo
de la hebra azul de tus venas.

with a Quixote[1] smile
and a pained look;
the sunlight dresses as dawn
your countryside and sea,
when you want to see
your figure of a swan,
peer at yourself in the pure water
of your home's fountain.

With the flame of your regal seal,
my swan of Puerto Rico,
the red fire of your peak
lights up, hoisted on the exquisite
candelabra of your neck.
And the blue of heavenly tulle,[2]
where the Cross of the South
unites its five flaming graces,
paints your solid blue
triangle on your wings.

Latin gold shines
from your face and shines in your face.
It was founded for centuries by Castile.[3]
And before Castile, Rome.
It was brought to a boil by the people of
    Muhammed
in its Moorish forges.
And before Rome, in Athens
the Homers[4] and Aeschylus
spun the dream of
the azure thread of your veins.

1. Don Quixote is the aging knight-errant of the great Spanish novel by the same name written by Miguel Cervantes. Quixote is an idealist who refuses to surrender to the base world around him. In Torres's poem, Puerto Rico similarly refuses to give in to U.S. imperial culture.
2. Netting. The reference is to the blue tulle around the swan's neck, a symbol of a regal gentleman. This image sets up a further distance between the elegant swan of Puerto Rico and the ducks.
3. One of the two major kingdoms that formed modern Spain when Queen Isabella married King Ferdinand of Aragon. Its language became Spain's primary language, which we now call

Spanish. The poet is aligning Castile with Rome in order to establish its lineage with the major empires of the world. Isabella and Ferdinand financed Columbus's voyage to the Americas. This lineage places Puerto Rico ahead of the United States.
4. Homer is the name assigned to the author of The Iliad and The Odyssey, the two great epics that have survived from ancient Greece. Torres suggests with the reference to Homer that Puerto Rico has the dream of an epic destiny that separates it from the United States. Aeschylus: a major dramatist of Greek tragedy. This reference continues to establish Puerto Rico as culturally superior to the United States.

*　*　*

En tu historia y religión
tus claros timbres están;
que fuiste el más alto afán
de Juan Ponce de León.
Mírate, con corazón,
en tu origen caballero,
en tu hablar latinoibero,
en la fe de tus altares,
y en la sangre audaz que en Lares
regó Manolo el Lenero.

Veinte cisnes como tú
nacieron contigo hermanos
en los virreinos hermanos
de Méjico y el Perú.
Bajo el cielo de tisú
de la antillana región,
los tres cisnes de Colón,
las tres cluecas carabelas,
fueron las aves abuelas
en tan magna incubación.

Alma de la patria mía,
cisne azul puertorriqueño,
si quieres vivir el sueño
de tu honor y tu hidalguía,
escucha la voz bravía
de tu independencia santa
cuando al cielo la levanta

*　*　*

In your history and religion
are your true stampings:
that you were the most vexing anxiety
of Juan Ponce de León.[5]
Look at yourself, with compassion
in your gentlemanly origin,
in your Latin-Iberic[6] speech,
in the faith of your altars,
and in the fearless blood that in Lares[7]
Manolo el Lenero shed.[8]

Twenty swans like you
were born brothers with you,
brothers in the viceroyships
of Mexico and Peru.
Beneath the gold-lit sky
of the Antillian[9] region
Columbus's three swans,
the three brooding caravels,[10]
the birds were the grandmothers
in such a magnificent hatching.

Soul of my country,
blue Puerto Rican swan,
if you want to live the vision
of your honor and nobility,
listen to the fearless voice
of your holy independence
when to heaven it's lifted

---

5. Juan Ponce de León colonized Puerto Rico for Spain.
6. Refers to the language of Spain on the Iberian Peninsula, with its roots in Latin, the language of both the Roman Empire and the Roman Catholic Church.
7. The town where a major nationalist uprising against Spain occurred.
8. Manolo el Lenero was the hero in this revolt. The poet suggests here that Puerto Rico has a noble history in its rebellion against the colonizer, so any resistance to U.S. imperialism is part of an idealistic cause and history.
9. Columbus sailed into the Antilles region of the Caribbean, mapping it precisely. The islands had

been noted on charts since the medieval period. Puerto Rico is part of the Antilles, along with Cuba, the Dominican Republic, Haiti, Jamaica, and other islands.
10. Two of Columbus's ships were caravels, not three, as Torres suggests here. He is trying to align the three caravels, the swans, and the grandmothers as part of the grand hatching that took place with the discovery of Puerto Rico and its establishment in a viceroyship with the other prize colonies of the Spanish Empire, Mexico and Peru. The number three was believed to have mystical and celestial significance, so using it here elevates the "hatching" to a kind of "divine birth."

el huracán del Caribe
que con sus rayos la escribe
y con sus truenos la canta.

Ya surgieron de la espuma
los veinte cisnes azules
en cuyos picos de gules
se desleirá la bruma.
A ellos su plumaje suma
el cisne de mi relato.
Porque ha visto su retrato
en los veinte cisnes bellos.
Porque quiere estar con ellos.
Porque no quiere ser pato.

by the Caribbean hurricane
that writes with its flashes of lightning
and sings with its thunders.

From the foam already sprung,
the twenty blue swans
with red peaks,
the mist will be softened.
To them the swan of my story
adds his plumage.
Because he saw his image
in the twenty beautiful swans.
Because he prefers to be with them.
Because he doesn't want to be a duck.

n.d.

"The Ugly Duckling" retells the heroic history of Puerto Rico as both a beautiful Latino swan and a North American ugly duckling and announces that its chosen destiny is with the other American countries colonized by Spain rather than with the United States. As Torres writes, Puerto Rico "doesn't want to be a duck." Throughout the poem, Torres argues that Puerto Rico's native heritage is superior to that of the United States.

ADELAIDE CRAPSEY
1878–1914

ADELAIDE CRAPSEY wrote startlingly beautiful short poems that mirror a brief and painful life. Inspired by Japanese tanka and haiku and Native-American "charms," she invented an entirely new verse form called the cinquain, arguably the first wholly original poetic form to emerge from the United States. Her cinquains and other concise poems suggest a huge interior life registered in small textual shards reminiscent of those of Sappho and Emily Dickinson. They invite us to read the resonances, to share an intimacy, and to recognize a psychic landscape at once strange and familiar, distinctly other yet evocative of our own. Influential and enduring, these short poems are as astonishing today as the day they were written. Crapsey's cinquains complemented the contemporaneous tanka poems published privately by Sadakichi Hartmann (included in the first volume of this anthology) and the more celebrated imagist poems of H.D., Amy Lowell, and Ezra Pound (included in this volume). Together such works revolutionized English-language poetic practice early in the new century. Like the other poets, none of whom she knew personally, Crapsey wrote poems notable for their verbal economy, formal innovation, vivid imagery, and aura of modernity.

The cinquain form that Crapsey invented consists of five lines. The first and last lines have one stress each, whereas the second, third, and fourth lines have two, three, and four stresses, respectively. In addition, the five lines often possess a regular syllabic count of 2-4-6-8-2. This form, as has been observed, implies a pattern of incremental growth and sudden contraction that seems to parallel Crapsey's own brief life. "November Night," the first of the cinquains printed below, exemplifies the genre's normal pattern of stresses and syllables. Moreover, it possesses the plangent imagery that is the form's hallmark. The sight and sound of dried autumn leaves detaching and falling suggest an emotional complex of grief and regret, resignation and awe. Such poems are at once a source of aesthetic pleasure and an immersion into the subjective world of perceptions, emotion, and spirit. Crapsey believed that the great dramas of life reside not in outward events per se but in the way outward things become inward.

Adelaide Crapsey was raised in Rochester, New York, one of nine children in a free-thinking Episcopal clergyman's family. Dr. Crapsey, influenced by John Henry Newman, Charles Darwin, and Karl Marx, believed that caring for the underprivileged mattered more than the doctrine of the Virgin Birth. As a result of such unorthodoxies, he was deposed from his rectorship in 1906. Adelaide, a brilliant student, attended Vassar College and did further study at the School of Archaeology in Rome. She commenced a career of teaching English, first in private academies and ultimately at Smith College. All the while she worked on the poetry for which she is now known and on a scholarly treatise concerning meter. She was particularly interested in the formal aspect of poems. One of her students later commented, "She never let poetry be only feeling. It had form; it had technique. . . . A rondel had meaning because of its very form, a ballad became alive like a person — it had its own body."

For most of her adult life Crapsey suffered from ill health. A research trip to Europe included a stay in a hospital. While teaching at Smith during weekdays, she would spend weekends lying in bed, exhausted from the physical strain. Doctors could not diagnose her condition. Some claimed that her infirmity resulted from too much indoor study and advised brisk walks in the country. Finally, while visiting a friend in the Berkshire Mountains of Massachusetts in 1913, she collapsed. After extensive tests, two lung specialists diagnosed her condition as advanced tuberculosis. She spent the last year of her life in sanatoriums, wasting away and suffering great physical pain. She had what was called "the poet's disease," but enduring it was not at all poetic.

Although Crapsey had previously been unsuccessful in publishing her work, she did place one poem, "The Witch," in *Century Magazine* shortly before her death in 1914. She had thus lived long enough to see her first poem accepted, though she was dead by the time it appeared. After her death, her parents discovered a manuscript of poems she had prepared for publication. Entitled simply *Verse*, it was published by a family friend in 1915 and then republished by Alfred Knopf in 1922. Her scholarly work, *A Study in English Metrics*, was also published by Knopf. Although she has never achieved the posthumous fame of Emily Dickinson, her name and work have not been lost.

Crapsey wrote laconic poems composed of shimmering words suspended in space. Every word counts. Witty and tough-minded, the poems evoke the tragedy and evanescence of life. Without lingering, they suggest depths of sadness, loss, and pain. They also evoke the beauty of the fragile world around us, the necessary quest for pleasure, and the joy of words and creativity. No poet has ever done more with less than Adelaide Crapsey.

FURTHER READING

Karen Alkalay-Gut. *Alone in the Dawn: The Life of Adelaide Crapsey*. Athens: University of Georgia Press, 1988.

Amaze: The Cinquain Journal. www.amaze-cinquain.com.

Adelaide Crapsey. *Complete Poems and Collected Letters*. Ed. Susan Sutton Smith. Albany: State University of New York Press, 1977.

The Witch

When I was girl by Nilus stream[1]
    I watched the desert stars arise;
My lover, he who dreamed the Sphinx,
    Learned all his dreaming from my eyes.

I bore in Greece a burning name,
    And I have been in Italy
Madonna to a painter-lad,
    And mistress to a Medici.[2]

And have you heard (and I have heard)
    Of puzzled men with decorous mien,
Who judged — The wench knows far too much —
And burnt her on the Salem green?[3]

1914

"The Witch" was Crapsey's only poem accepted for publication in her lifetime, apart from some undergraduate poems in college publications. Crapsey's biographer, Karen

1. The Nile River in Egypt.
2. The most powerful family in Florence, Italy, during the fifteenth through the seventeenth centuries and noted for their artistic patronage.

3. In 1692 three judges convicted and hanged nineteen women for witchcraft in the Puritan colony of Salem, Massachusetts. No women were burned at the stake, however.

Alkalay-Gut, comments, "The poem . . . typified her unique attitude, based on her complex hatred for hypocrisy and awareness of the history of social blindness. 'The Witch' is about the eternal woman, eternally ignored and misunderstood and most dangerous when she is most creative."

November Night

Listen. .
With faint dry sound,
Like steps of passing ghosts,
The leaves, frost-crisp'd, break from the trees
And fall.

1915

"November Night" is a cinquain, as are the ten poems that follow it, through "Niagara." The formal pattern—increasing numbers of stresses and syllables in each line leading to a sudden contraction in the final line—builds suspense that is relieved only in the poem's final syllable. The cinquain form, with its terseness and its conflation of momentary detail with general significance, may owe its inspiration to classic Japanese poetry, which Crapsey read in William Porter's *A Thousand Verses from Old Japan* (1909) and Michel Revon's *Anthologie de la Littérature Japonaise* (1910). Compare, for example, a haiku by seventeenth-century master Matsuo Bashō: "On a withered branch / a crow has settled— / autumn nightfall." Crapsey's editor, Susan Sutton Smith, interprets "November Night" thusly: "The almost imperceptible sound of the many leaves being detached and drifting downward (not the more often noted sound of their landing) reinforced by the onomatopoeia of repeated sibilants, suggests the innumerable changes, the innumerable tiny deaths that make up the great changelessness and life of the seasonal cycle."

Release

With swift
Great sweep of her
Magnificent arm my pain
Clanged back the doors that shut my soul
From life.

1915

Afraid of causing her family and friends mental distress, Crapsey did not reveal to them the enormity of her suffering. She was more open in such cinquains as "Release." In the poem does pain open doors of life by heightening perception and creativity, does it open doors by momentarily relenting, or does it shut doors that had been opened in a respite? Compare this poem to "Languor After Pain" below.

Susanna and the Elders

"Why do
You thus devise
Evil against her?" "For that
She is beautiful, delicate:
Therefore."

1915

"Susanna and the Elders" derives from a tale in the Jewish Apocrypha. Dating from the second century B.C.E., the tale involves a beautiful young woman falsely accused of unchastity by respected men in the community. Raising questions of evil in the world and pointing to the vulnerability of women and youth, the story has served as the basis for famous paintings by such artists as Jacopo Tintoretto (1518–1594), Peter Paul Rubens (1577–1640), Anthony Van Dyck (1599–1641), and Rembrandt van Rijn (1606–1669).

Languor After Pain

Pain ebbs,
And like cool balm,
An opiate weariness
Settles on eye-lids, on relaxed
Pale wrists.

1915

The Guarded Wound

If it
Were lighter touch
Than petal of flower resting
On grass oh still too heavy it were
Too heavy!

1915

The speaker of "The Guarded Wound" may be keeping her physical, psychic, or moral ailment secret—yet this privacy does not relieve the pain.

Night Winds

The old
Old winds that blew

When chaos was, what do
They tell the clattered trees that I
Should weep?

1915

Alkalay-Gut comments, "'Night Winds,' with its echoes of pregenesis, suggests a lack of meaning, a reason for mourning, a contrast to the ordered significant life of the God-created world."

Amaze

I know
Not these my hands
And yet I think there was
A woman like me once had hands
Like these.

1915

A reflection on change and self-difference, "Amaze" might be considered in a context supplied by the ancient Greek philosopher Heracleitus. Heracleitus famously compared life to a river: "Upon those who step into the same river different and ever different waters flow down." "Amaze" might also be considered in a biographical context. As a result of illness, physical wasting, spiritual growth, or creative accomplishment, the speaker's identity has changed, and she no longer recognizes her own body.

Madness

Burdock,[1]
Blue aconite,[2]
And thistle and thorn[3] . . of these
Singing I wreathe my pretty wreath
O' death.

1915

1. A coarse-textured weed bearing prickly heads of burs.
2. A plant with poisonous and sedative properties; also called wolfsbane or monkshood.
3. In Genesis God tells Adam that, because he has eaten forbidden fruit, "Thorns also and thistles shall it bring forth to thee" (3:18). In the Sermon on the Mount Jesus asks, "Do men gather grapes of thorns, or figs of thistles?" (Matthew 7:16). At his crucifixion he wears "a crown of thorns" (Matthew 27:29; Mark 15:17).

The Warning

Just now,
Out of the strange
Still dusk . . as strange, as still. .
A white moth flew. Why am I grown
So cold?

1915

Identifying with a small, nocturnal insect, the speaker of "The Warning" may have suffered the shock of recognizing her own brief life span.

Laurel in the Berkshires

Sea-foam
And coral! Oh, I'll
Climb the great pasture rocks
And dream me mermaid in the sun's
Gold flood.

1915

Crapsey composed "Laurel in the Berkshires" in the summer of 1913 while visiting her friend Jean Webster in Tyringham, Massachusetts, in the Berkshire Mountains. Illuminated by the brilliant June light, the flowering laurel might indeed bear comparison to "sea-foam" and "coral," and the poem's "I" might well imagine herself a mythic "mermaid." Jean Webster wrote at about the same time that the "pastures are pink" and the "mass of laurel is intoxicating." But Crapsey collapsed on July 13, beginning a process of declining health and recurrent hospitalizations that ended with her death fourteen months later.

Niagara

Seen on a night in November

How frail
Above the bulk
Of crashing water hangs,
Autumnal, evanescent, wan,
The moon.

1915

"Niagara" contrasts the fragility, silence, and relative stasis of the moon with the forceful, loud motion of the falls. Although the water seems to have overpowered the moonlight, the moon recovers its centrality in the poem's final syllable.

The Pledge

White doves of Cytherea,[1] by your quest
    Across the blue Heaven's bluest highest air,
And by your certain homing to Love's breast,
    Still to be true and ever true — I swear.

                  1915

On Seeing Weather-Beaten Trees

Is it as plainly in our living shown,
By slant and twist, which way the wind hath blown?

                  1915

The Sun-Dial

Every day,
Every day,
Tell[1] the hours
By their shadows,
By their shadows.

        1915

The repetitive and magical qualities of "The Sun-Dial" may reflect Crapsey's interest in Native-American "charms," sacred texts composed by shamans. The charms include repeated invocations and are open to a variety of interpretations. Crapsey encountered these texts in James Mooney's "Sacred Formulas of the Cherokees," contained in J. W. Powell's *Seventh Annual Report of the Bureau of Ethnology* (1891). Like the poem that follows, "The Sun-Dial" may suggest the imminence of death.

Song

I make my shroud[1] but no one knows,
So shimmering fine it is and fair,
With stitches set in even rows.
I make my shroud but no one knows.

---

1. Another name for Aphrodite, ancient Greek goddess of sexual love and beauty, whose cult of worshipers originated on the island of Cythera.

1. Count as well as report, disclose, or determine.

1. A cloth in which a corpse is wrapped for burial.

*   *   *

In door-way where the lilac blows
Humming a little wandering air,
I make my shroud and no one knows,
So shimmering fine it is and fair.

1915

With eight lines, three of them repeated, and two alternative rhyme schemes, "Song" suggests an interplay between brevity and repetition, regularity and difference. The poem may propose an analogy between the textile stitched by the speaker and the text composed by the author.

CARL SANDBURG
1878–1967

CARL SANDBURG achieved fame and popularity during the early decades of the twentieth century for his energetic free-verse depictions of life in the American Midwest and for his moving protests against war. Critical esteem for his poems suffered a decline within intellectual circles following the triumph of experimental modernism, with its standards of difficulty, complexity, and stylistic innovation. Nevertheless, Sandburg's simple, vigorous, and emotionally accessible poems have remained popular with a wide variety of readers. They compellingly evoke a progressive perspective and moment in American history. His most famous poem, the celebratory "Chicago," has become the unofficial anthem of the Midwestern metropolis. "Grass" movingly laments the battle dead of World War I.

Born in Galesburg, Illinois, to parents who had immigrated from Sweden, Sandburg worked odd jobs in his teenage years. Then, like his contemporary and fellow Illinois populist Vachel Lindsay, though not so extensively, he traveled through middle America as a hobo. After serving briefly in the army during the Spanish-American War, Sandburg attended Lombard College in his native Galesburg. He later worked on a newspaper in Milwaukee, where he met and married Lilian Steichen, sister of the famous photographer Edward Steichen. The couple settled in Chicago in 1912, where Sandburg wrote editorials for the *Chicago Daily News* and soon began publishing poems in Harriet Monroe's influential new Chicago-based magazine, *Poetry*. He established his reputation with *Chicago Poems* (1916), followed shortly by *Cornhuskers* (1918) and *Smoke and Steel* (1920), the latter volume a tribute to the beauty of modern industrial design.

A great admirer of Lincoln, Sandburg published the first volume of his popular biography, *Abraham Lincoln: The Prairie Years*, in 1926. The concluding volume, *Abraham Lincoln: The War Years* (1939), won the Pulitzer Prize. Sandburg also collected folk songs in *The American Songbag* (1927) and *The New American Songbag* (1950). An important and enduring cultural figure, Sandburg wrote some of the most memorable and beloved free-verse poems in American literature.

FURTHER READING

Penelope Niven. *Carl Sandburg: A Biography*. New York: Scribner's, 1991.
Carl Sandburg. *Complete Poems*. New York: Harcourt Brace Jovanovich, 1970.

Chicago

Hog Butcher for the World,
Tool Maker, Stacker of Wheat,
Player with Railroads and the Nation's Freight Handler;
Stormy, husky, brawling,
City of the Big Shoulders:
They tell me you are wicked and I believe them, for I have seen your painted
    women under the gas lamps luring the farm boys.
And they tell me you are crooked and I answer: Yes, it is true I have seen the
    gunman kill and go free to kill again.
And they tell me you are brutal and my reply is: On the faces of women and
    children I have seen the marks of wanton hunger.
And having answered so I turn once more to those who sneer at this my city, and I
    give them back the sneer and say to them:
Come and show me another city with lifted head singing so proud to be alive and
    coarse and strong and cunning.
Flinging magnetic curses amid the toil of piling job on job, here is a tall bold
    slugger set vivid against the little soft cities;
Fierce as a dog with tongue lapping for action, cunning as a savage pitted against
    the wilderness,
    Bareheaded,
    Shoveling,
    Wrecking,
    Planning,
    Building, breaking, rebuilding,
Under the smoke, dust all over his mouth, laughing with white teeth,
Under the terrible burden of destiny laughing as a young man laughs,
Laughing even as an ignorant fighter laughs who has never lost a battle,

Bragging and laughing that under his wrist is the pulse, and under his ribs the
    heart of the people,
  Laughing!
Laughing the stormy, husky, brawling laughter of Youth, half-naked, sweating,
    proud to be Hog Butcher, Tool Maker, Stacker of Wheat, Player with
    Railroads and Freight Handler to the Nation.

1916

Fog

The fog comes
on little cat feet.

It sits looking
over harbor and city
on silent haunches
and then moves on.

1916

"Fog," with its imagery of catlike fog moving across a cityscape, appeared just a year later
than Eliot's "Love Song of J. Alfred Prufrock," which employs similar though more ex-
tended imagery. Sandburg manages to compress his version into a brief imagist poem.

Among the Red Guns

After waking at dawn one morning when
the wind sang low among dry leaves in an elm

Among the red guns,
In the hearts of soldiers
Running free blood
In the long, long campaign:
   Dreams go on.

Among the leather saddles,
In the heads of soldiers
Heavy in the wracks and kills
Of all straight fighting:
   Dreams go on.

Among the hot muzzles,
In the hands of soldiers

Brought from flesh-folds of women—
Soft amid the blood and crying—
In all your hearts and heads
Among the guns and saddles and muzzles:

    Dreams,
Dreams go on,
Out of the dead on their backs,
Broken and no use any more:
Dreams of the way and the end go on.

              1916

"Among the Red Guns" explores the persistence of dreaming and imaginative life even amid the carnage of World War I (1914–18), the world's most destructive war to date.

Grass

Pile the bodies high at Austerlitz and Waterloo.
Shovel them under and let me work—
           I am the grass; I cover all.
And pile them high at Gettysburg
And pile them high at Ypres and Verdun.
Shovel them under and let me work.
Two years, ten years, and the passengers ask the conductor:
           What place is this?
           Where are we now?

    I am the grass.
    Let me work.

              1918

Jazz Fantasia

Drum on your drums, batter on your banjoes,
sob on the long cool winding saxophones.
Go to it, O jazzmen.

Sling your knuckles on the bottoms of the happy
tin pans, let your trombones ooze, and go husha-
husha-hush with the slippery sand-paper.

*   *   *

Moan like an autumn wind high in the lonesome treetops, moan soft like you
  wanted somebody terrible, cry like a racing car slipping away from a
  motorcycle cop, bang-bang! you jazzmen, bang altogether drums, traps,
  banjoes, horns, tin cans—make two people fight on the top of a stairway and
  scratch each other's eyes in a clinch tumbling down the stairs.

Can the rough stuff . . . Now a Mississippi steamboat pushes up the night river
  with a hoo-hoo-hoo-oo . . . and the green lanterns calling to the high soft
  stars . . . a red moon rides on the humps of the low river hills . . . go to it,
  O jazzmen.

1920

Jazz was still an emerging form when Sandburg wrote his poem of celebration.

VACHEL LINDSAY
1879–1931

VACHEL LINDSAY was a vigorous force for bringing poetry to the people. Indeed,
early in his career he wandered the American countryside, trading his poems for
food and shelter. His style is vivid and direct, combining driving rhythms with a
populist moral fervor that made his best-known poems into exciting dramatic
events. Lindsay became known as a spellbinding dramatic public reader of his own
works, and he helped to pioneer the popularity of poetry readings. But he ulti-
mately came to regret his own popularity as a performer, feeling that the artistry of
his poetry, and quieter poems like the reflective "Buddha" and "Abraham Lincoln
Walks at Midnight" (included here), were neglected as a result.

Born in Springfield, Illinois—the home of Abraham Lincoln—Lindsay was in-
tended by his devoutly Christian parents for a career in medicine, the vocation of
his father. But after three years of medical school, Lindsay dropped out to devote
himself to poetry and the visual arts. Eventually, on the candid advice of the Amer-
ican painter Robert Henri, Lindsay decided to abandon painting for poetry. From
1906 to 1912, with occasional returns to his parents' home in Springfield, Lindsay
wandered America, exchanging his privately printed "Rhymes to be Traded for
Bread" for food and a place to sleep. These travels were not always romantic—
he was frequently cold, hungry, and alone. Yet he continued them, pushed by his

idealistic commitment and a Christian moral fervor he had inherited from his parents. Guided by that fervor, Lindsay never smoked or drank, yet, through his travels, he gained a direct and sympathetic knowledge of the lives of the American underclass. While on the road in 1912, Lindsay learned of the death of General William Booth, the British founder of the Salvation Army. The news powerfully moved him, inspiring him to write the poem that made his name, "General William Booth Enters into Heaven." Published in *Poetry* in 1913, it was an instant hit, and from then on Lindsay was a public figure whose poetry and presence were in frequent demand. The poem was intended for public performance and, like many of his poems, contains marginal notes directing that performance.

Following this success, Lindsay proposed marriage to the poet Sara Teasdale, but she refused, though they remained close friends. From 1924 to 1929 Lindsay lived in Spokane, Washington, where he met and married Elizabeth Connor in 1925. He was forty-five, she twenty-three. They had two children, Susan in 1926 and Nicholas in 1927. Lindsay continued to travel widely, giving public readings. In 1926, Lindsay discovered the African-American poet Langston Hughes when Hughes, serving as the busboy at a restaurant, left poems beside Lindsay's plate. Lindsay liked Hughes's poems and helped launch his career.

Lindsay's constant travel took a toll on his nerves, and in the late 1920s he became extremely depressed. He returned with his family to Springfield in 1929, a place he called his "heart's home" and "spiritual center" as well as the "city of my discontent." Yet his emotional disorder grew more severe, and he committed suicide in 1931 by drinking a household poison. Despite his tragic end, Lindsay continues to be remembered for the vigor of his style and for his historic role as the first performance poet.

FURTHER READING

Vachel Lindsay. *The Congo and Other Poems*. New York: Dover, 2000.
Ann Massa. *Vachel Lindsay: Fieldworker for the American Dream*. Bloomington: Indiana University Press, 1970.

General William Booth Enters into Heaven

(To be sung to the tune of "The Blood of the Lamb" with indicated instrument)

I

(Bass drum beaten loudly.)
Booth led boldly with his big bass drum —
(Are you washed in the blood of the Lamb?)[1]

---

1. The refrain of the Salvation Army song, "The Blood of the Lamb." It refers to Revelation 7:14: "They . . . have washed their robes, and made them white in the blood of the Lamb."

The Saints smiled gravely and they said: "He's come."
(Are you washed in the blood of the Lamb?)
Walking lepers followed, rank on rank,
Lurching bravoes from the ditches dank,
Drabs[2] from the alleyways and drug fiends pale—
Minds still passion-ridden, soul-powers frail:—
Vermin-eaten saints with mouldy breath,
Unwashed legions with the ways of Death—
(Are you washed in the blood of the Lamb?)

(*Banjos.*)
Every slum had sent its half-a-score
The round world over. (Booth had groaned for more.)
Every banner that the wide world flies
Bloomed with glory and transcendent dyes.
Big-voiced lasses made their banjos bang,
Tranced, fanatical they shrieked and sang:—
"Are you washed in the blood of the Lamb?"
Hallelujah! It was queer to see
Bull-necked convicts with that land make free.
Loons with trumpets blowed a blare, blare, blare
On, on upward thro' the golden air!
(Are you washed in the blood of the Lamb?)

II

(*Bass drum slower and softer.*)
Booth died blind and still by Faith he trod,
Eyes still dazzled by the ways of God.
Booth led boldly, and he looked the chief
Eagle countenance in sharp relief,
Beard a-flying, air of high command
Unabated in that holy land.

(*Sweet flute music.*)
Jesus came from out the court-house door,
Stretched his hands above the passing poor.
Booth saw not, but led his queer ones there
Round and round the mighty court-house square.
Then in an instant all that blear review

2. Prostitutes.

Marched on spotless, clad in raiment new.
The lame were straightened, withered limbs uncurled
And blind eyes opened on a new, sweet world.

(*Bass drum louder.*)
Drabs and vixens in a flash made whole!
Gone was the weasel-head, the snout, the jowl!
Sages and sibyls now, and athletes clean,
Rulers of empires, and of forests green!

(*Grand chorus of all instruments. Tambourines to the foreground.*)
The hosts were sandalled, and their wings were fire!
(Are you washed in the blood of the Lamb?)
But their noise played havoc with the angel-choir.
(Are you washed in the blood of the Lamb?)
O shout Salvation! It was good to see
Kings and Princes by the Lamb set free.
The banjos rattled and the tambourines
Jing-jing-jingled in the hands of Queens.

(*Reverently sung, no instruments.*)
And when Booth halted by the curb for prayer
He saw his Master thro' the flag-filled air.
Christ came gently with a robe and crown
For Booth the soldier, while the throng knelt down.
He saw King Jesus. They were face to face,
And he knelt a-weeping in that holy place.
Are you washed in the blood of the Lamb?

1913

William Booth (1829–1912) founded the Salvation Army in London in 1865 to encourage Christian social work in support of the poor and homeless. To provide the underclasses with discipline, he adopted military rank and uniform. His Salvation Army marched through the streets of British and, later, American cities playing the hymn "The Blood of the Lamb" on band instruments and searching for lost souls. Lindsay would later recall, "The poem called 'General Booth Enters Heaven' was built in part upon certain adventures while singing these songs. When I was dead broke, and begging, in Atlanta, Georgia, and much confused as to my next move in this world, I slept for three nights in the Salvation Army quarters there. And when I passed through Newark, New Jersey, on another trip I slept in the Salvation Army quarters there. I could tell some fearful stories of similar experiences. I will say briefly, that I know the Salvation Army from the inside. Certainly, at that time, the Army was struggling with what General Booth called the submerged tenth of the population. And I was with the submerged. . . . In my poem I merely turned into rhyme as well as I could, word for word, General Booth's own account of his life, and the telegraph dispatches of his death after going blind." Lindsay, admiring Booth's zeal and fervor, wrote the poem, in true Salvation Army style, to celebrate Booth and mourn his passing.

Buddha

Would that by Hindu magic we became
Dark monks of jeweled India long ago,
Sitting at Prince Siddartha's feet to know
The foolishness of gold and love and station,
The gospel of the Great Renunciation,
The ragged cloak, the staff, the rain and sun,
The beggar's life, with far Nirvana[1] gleaming:
Lord, make us Buddhas, dreaming.

1913

According to later Buddhist accounts, the Prince Siddhartha Gautama became overwhelmed with the conviction that life was filled with suffering and unhappiness. He renounced his wealth and family to search for truth as a wandering monk, ultimately achieving enlightenment and being recognized by his followers as Buddha, the "Enlightened One." Lindsay's own early wanderings mirror in certain respects those of the Buddha.

Abraham Lincoln Walks at Midnight

(In Springfield, Illinois)

It is portentous, and a thing of state
That here at midnight, in our little town
A mourning figure walks, and will not rest,
Near the old court-house pacing up and down,

Or by his homestead, or in shadowed yards
He lingers where his children used to play,
Or through the market, on the well-worn stones
He stalks until the dawn-stars burn away.

A bronzed, lank man! His suit of ancient black,
A famous high top-hat and plain worn shawl
Make him the quaint great figure that men love,
The prairie-lawyer, master of us all.

*   *   *

1. The Buddhist state of peace and enlightenment.

He cannot sleep upon his hillside now.
He is among us: —as in times before!
And we who toss and lie awake for long
Breath deep, and start, to see him pass the door.

His head is bowed. He thinks of men and kings.
Yea, when the sick world cries, how can he sleep?
Too many peasants fight, they know not why;
Too many homesteads in black terror weep.

The sins of all the war-lords burn his heart.
He sees the dreadnaughts[1] scourging every main.
He carries on his shawl-wrapped shoulders now
The bitterness, the folly and the pain.

He cannot rest until a spirit-dawn
Shall come; —the shining hope of Europe free:
A league of sober folk, the Workers' Earth
Bringing long peace to Cornland, Alp and Sea.

It breaks his heart that things must murder still,
That all his hours of travail here for men
Seem yet in vain. And who will bring white peace
That he may sleep upon his hill again?

1914

Lindsay's poem links the sleepless walking of the deceased Lincoln through their native town of Springfield, Illinois, with the onset of World War I, an event he found deeply disturbing. Lincoln was buried in his native Springfield following his assassination by John Wilkes Booth in Washington, D.C., in April 1865.

WALLACE STEVENS
1879–1955

WALLACE STEVENS's poetry explores imaginative extremes of north and south, of severest cold and tropical abundance, of spiritual poverty and imaginative wealth. At one moment this world might seem meaningless and random, little

---

1. Powerful battleships, named after the first British example, the *Dreadnaught*, launched in 1906.

more than "a tatter of shadows peaked to white," yet in brighter moments it emerges as "smeared with the gold of the opulent sun." Indeed, the principal impetus of Stevens's work is the drive to attain imaginative wealth through the power of poetry. Like many experimental modernists of the first generation, Stevens—faced with the task of inventing a radically new poetic language—did not hit his stride artistically until his mid-thirties. But he achieved a breakthrough in 1915, at the age of thirty-six, with poems like "Sunday Morning," an early and eloquent articulation of his central theme of the powers and limits of the imagination as a response to spiritual poverty and death. He would continue to explore this theme for four decades in some of the most brilliantly colored and vividly imagined poems in the English language. Although his early work was appreciated chiefly by a limited coterie of fellow experimentalists, in his later years he won widespread recognition and honor for his imaginative achievement, and these honors were not a belated recognition of former triumphs—his last books were among his best.

A young literary acquaintance who met the poet late in life described Stevens as "quiet, reflective, contemplative and wise—and, perhaps, also a bit lonely." Stevens was a big, formidable-looking man who tended to maintain a certain distance in his emotional relations. The second of five children, he was born in Reading, Pennsylvania, where his father was a lawyer and his mother a former schoolteacher. Educated in Reading and at a Lutheran grammar school in Brooklyn, Stevens attended Harvard as a special student from 1897 to 1900, where he contributed prose and poetry to undergraduate magazines. His verse attracted the favorable attention of the poet and philosopher George Santayana, and he became president of the *Harvard Advocate*. In 1900, Stevens moved to New York, working briefly and successfully as a reporter for the New York *Tribune*. Finding that the daily news beat did not suit his temperament, he enrolled in New York Law School, taking his degree in 1903. Stevens met Elsie Kachel, whom he considered "the prettiest girl in Reading," on a summer trip home in 1904, and his romance with her rekindled his energy for writing poetry, which had lain dormant since college. His handwritten "Book of Verses" for Elsie's twenty-third birthday in 1908—a collection of Stevens's own early poems—was followed a year later by another birthday present, "The Little June Book." Stevens's father objected to this romance, considering Elsie's family socially beneath his own. Stevens broke with his father over this objection, marrying Elsie in 1909. Stevens's family did not attend the wedding, and when his father died two years later, the two had not reconciled. An only daughter, Holly, was born in 1924. Although their marriage would continue until his death forty-six years later, Stevens and his wife gradually drifted apart. Stevens practiced law in New York City, finding his niche in the surety bond department of an insurance firm. During these years, Stevens also became involved with avant-garde poetic circles in New York, developing friendships with William Carlos Williams and Marianne Moore (also in this anthology), editor Alfred Kreymborg, artist Marcel Duchamp, and a wealthy patron of the avant-garde named Walter Arensberg. Stevens's poems began to appear in *Poetry, Others,* the *Dial,* and other influential literary journals.

In 1916, Stevens's New York insurance firm abolished his position, and Stevens, though reluctant to leave the New York avant-garde scene, accepted a position in Connecticut with the surety bond office of the Hartford Accident and Indemnity Company. He would achieve great success at the Hartford, rising to one of three vice presidencies and coming to be recognized, according to one colleague, as the dean of surety bond work in America. His early years with the Hartford, from 1916 to 1923, were also among his most productive as a poet, for in those years he composed the bulk of his remarkable first book, *Harmonium* (1923). The poems of *Harmonium* are remarkable for their inventive approach to form and for the skill with which they deploy imagery and sound effects to represent philosophical and aesthetic positions, as in such poems as "Disillusionment of Ten O'Clock," "Anecdote of the Jar," and "The Ordinary Women." Poems like "Thirteen Ways of Looking at a Blackbird" and "The Snow Man" explore physical, psychological, and spiritual extremes of cold, whiteness, and absence, while poems like "O Florida, Venereal Soil" and "The Emperor of Ice-Cream" celebrate tropical exuberance in the face of transience and death. Yet despite its poetic power and variety and its sheer energy, *Harmonium* received relatively cautious and uncomprehending notices from reviewers. Stevens, now on the rise at his insurance firm, turned his attention from the writing of poetry to his insurance work, publishing no poems between 1924 and 1930.

Beginning in the early 1930s, however, Stevens returned to poetry with new vitality, publishing a steady stream of volumes that included, in the decade of the 1930s alone, an expanded *Harmonium* in 1931, *Ideas of Order* in 1935, *Owl's Clover* in 1936, and *The Man with the Blue Guitar* in 1937. Stevens's return to poetry shows the same highly imaginative handling of imagery found in *Harmonium,* but his later work is marked by a new directness and intensity in handling philosophical ideas. In the 1940s, Stevens's poetry often considers the problem of the poet in time of war. He also began giving a series of lectures on poetry and poetics at a variety of Eastern colleges and universities. The resulting essays were later collected in his prose volume, *The Necessary Angel.* Stevens's final poems undertake a valedictory reconsideration of a life devoted to the poetic art. They display no loss of energy and are marked instead by an imaginative confidence that can confront even the deepest of self-doubts or the darkness of death.

FURTHER READING

Steven Gould Axelrod and Helen Deese, eds. *Critical Essays on Wallace Stevens.* Boston: G. K. Hall, 1988.

Charles Berger. *Forms of Farewell: The Late Poetry of Wallace Stevens.* Madison: University of Wisconsin Press, 1985.

Peter Brazeau. *Parts of a World: Wallace Stevens Remembered.* San Francisco: North Point Press, 1985.

Jaqueline Vaught Brogan. *The Violence Within, the Violence Without: Wallace Stevens and the Emergence of a Revolutionary Poetics*. Athens: University of Georgia Press, 2003.

Joseph Carroll. *Wallace Stevens' Supreme Fiction: A New Romanticism*. Baton Rouge: Louisiana State University Press, 1987.

Eleanor Cook. *Poetry, Word-Play, and Word-War in Wallace Stevens*. Princeton, N.J.: Princeton University Press, 1988.

Mark Halliday. *Stevens and the Interpersonal*. Princeton, N.J.: Princeton University Press, 1991.

George Lensing. *Wallace Stevens: A Poet's Growth*. Baton Rouge: Louisiana State University Press, 1986.

A. Walton Litz. *Introspective Voyager: The Poetic Development of Wallace Stevens*. New York: Oxford University Press, 1972.

James Longenbach. *Wallace Stevens: The Plain Sense of Things*. New York: Oxford University Press, 1991.

Rajeer S. Patke. *The Long Poems of Wallace Stevens: An Interpretive Study*. New York: Cambridge University Press, 1985.

Kia Penso. *Wallace Stevens, Harmonium, and the Whole of Harmonium*. Hamden, Conn.: Archon Books, 1991.

Joan Richardson. *Wallace Stevens: A Biography*. New York: Beech Tree Books, 1988.

Joseph Riddle. *The Clairvoyant Eye: The Poetry and Poetics of Wallace Stevens*. Baton Rouge: Louisiana State University Press, 1965.

Melita Schaum, ed. *Wallace Stevens and the Feminine*. Tuscaloosa: University of Alabama Press, 1993.

Wallace Stevens. *Collected Poems*. New York: Knopf, 1954.

——. *The Necessary Angel: Essays on Reality and Imagination*. New York: Knopf, 1951.

——. *Opus Posthumous*. New York: Knopf, 1957.

Helen Vendler. *Wallace Stevens: Words Chosen Out of Desire*. Knoxville: University of Tennessee Press, 1984.

Sunday Morning

I

Complacencies of the peignoir,[1] and late
Coffee and oranges in a sunny chair,
And the green freedom of a cockatoo
Upon a rug mingle to dissipate
The holy hush of ancient sacrifice.[2]
She dreams a little, and she feels the dark
Encroachment of that old catastrophe,
As a calm darkens among water-lights.
The pungent oranges and bright, green wings
Seem things in some procession of the dead,
Winding across wide water, without sound.
The day is like wide water, without sound,

1. A woman's loose-fitting dressing gown, bathrobe, or negligee.
2. Christian church services are frequently conducted in a "holy hush" and celebrate the ancient sacrifice of Jesus's crucifixion.

Stilled for the passing of her dreaming feet
Over the seas, to silent Palestine,[3]
Dominion of the blood and sepulchre.

II

Why should she give her bounty to the dead?
What is divinity if it can come
Only in silent shadows and in dreams?
Shall she not find in comforts of the sun,
In pungent fruit and bright, green wings, or else
In any balm or beauty of the earth,
Things to be cherished like the thought of heaven?
Divinity must live within herself:
Passions of rain, or moods in falling snow;
Grievings in loneliness, or unsubdued
Elations when the forest blooms; gusty
Emotions on wet roads on autumn nights;
All pleasures and all pains, remembering
The bough of summer and the winter branch.
These are the measures destined for her soul.

III

Jove[4] in the clouds had his inhuman birth.
No mother suckled him, no sweet land gave
Large-mannered motions to his mythy mind.
He moved among us, as a muttering king,
Magnificent, would move among his hinds,[5]
Until our blood, commingling, virginal,
With heaven, brought such requital to desire
The very hinds discerned it, in a star.
Shall our blood fail? Or shall it come to be
The blood of paradise? And shall the earth
Seem all of paradise that we shall know?
The sky will be much friendlier then than now,
A part of labor and a part of pain,
And next in glory to enduring love,
Not this dividing and indifferent blue.

3. The Christian, Jewish, and Islamic holy land and the site of Jesus's crucifixion ("blood") and burial ("sepulchre").
4. King of the Olympian gods, the Greek Zeus or Roman Jupiter, here seen as descending to walk on the earth and mingle with its creatures.
5. Peasants or rustics; farm laborers.

IV

She says, "I am content when wakened birds,
Before they fly, test the reality
Of misty fields, by their sweet questionings;
But when the birds are gone, and their warm fields
Return no more, where, then, is paradise?"
There is not any haunt of prophesy,
Nor any old chimera[6] of the grave,
Neither the golden underground, nor isle
Melodious, where spirits gat[7] them home,
Nor visionary south, nor cloudy palm
Remote on heaven's hill, that has endured
As April's green endures; or will endure
Like her remembrance of awakened birds,
Or her desire for June and evening, tipped
By the consummation of the swallow's wings.

V

She says, "But in contentment I still feel
The need of some imperishable bliss."
Death is the mother of beauty; hence from her,
Alone, shall come fulfilment to our dreams
And our desires. Although she strews the leaves
Of sure obliteration on our paths,
The path sick sorrow took, the many paths
Where triumph rang its brassy phrase, or love
Whispered a little out of tenderness,
She makes the willow shiver in the sun
For maidens who were wont to sit and gaze
Upon the grass, relinquished to their feet.
She causes boys to pile new plums and pears
On disregarded plate. The maidens taste
And stray impassioned in the littering leaves.

VI

Is there no change of death in paradise?
Does ripe fruit never fall? Or do the boughs
Hang always heavy in that perfect sky,
Unchanging, yet so like our perishing earth,

6. A grotesque, mythical monster.   7. Got (archaic).

With rivers like our own that seek for seas
They never find, the same receding shores
That never touch with inarticulate pang?
Why set the pear upon those river-banks
Or spice the shores with odors of the plum?
Alas, that they should wear our colors there,
The silken weavings of our afternoons,
And pick the strings of our insipid lutes!
Death is the mother of beauty, mystical,
Within whose burning bosom we devise
Our earthly mothers waiting, sleeplessly.

VII

Supple and turbulent, a ring of men
Shall chant in orgy on a summer morn
Their boisterous devotion to the sun,[8]
Not as a god, but as a god might be,
Naked among them, like a savage source.
Their chant shall be a chant of paradise,
Out of their blood, returning to the sky;
And in their chant shall enter, voice by voice,
The windy lake wherein their lord delights,
The trees, like serafin,[9] and echoing hills,
That choir among themselves long afterward.
They shall know well the heavenly fellowship
Of men that perish and of summer morn.
And whence they came and whither they shall go
The dew upon their feet shall manifest.

VIII

She hears, upon that water without sound,
A voice that cries, "The tomb in Palestine
Is not the porch of spirits lingering.
It is the grave of Jesus, where he lay."
We live in an old chaos of the sun,
Or old dependency of day and night,

8. The sun remained one of the central symbols in Stevens's poetry: generally seen, as here, as a "savage source" of life and energy on earth — violent and at times frightening — but consis- tently celebrated for its beauty and life-giving power.
9. The highest order of angels.

Or island solitude, unsponsored, free,
Of that wide water, inescapable.
Deer walk upon our mountains, and the quail
Whistle about us their spontaneous cries;
Sweet berries ripen in the wilderness;
And, in the isolation of the sky,
At evening, casual flocks of pigeons make
Ambiguous undulations as they sink,
Downward to darkness, on extended wings.

1915

Stevens's earliest great poem, "Sunday Morning," explores the musings of a woman who, instead of attending church, lingers at home over "late / Coffee and oranges in a sunny chair." She contemplates the choice between traditional Christian belief, with its assurances of meaning and immortality, and a life imaginatively devoted to the transient beauties and sensuous pleasures of this earth.

Disillusionment of Ten O'Clock

The houses are haunted
By white night-gowns.
None are green,
Or purple with green rings,
Or green with yellow rings,
Or yellow with blue rings.
None of them are strange,
With socks of lace
And beaded ceintures.[1]
People are not going
To dream of baboons and periwinkles.
Only, here and there, an old sailor,
Drunk and asleep in his boots,
Catches tigers
In red weather.

1915

In "Disillusionment of Ten O'Clock," the "socks of lace" and "beaded ceintures" evoke the elaborate garments worn by aristocratic ladies of the Renaissance. These clothes contrast with the monotonous and colorless "white night-gowns" of the present era.

1. Belts (French).

Thirteen Ways of Looking at a Blackbird

I

Among twenty snowy mountains,
The only moving thing
Was the eye of the blackbird.

II

I was of three minds,
Like a tree
In which there are three blackbirds.

III

The blackbird whirled in the autumn winds.
It was a small part of the pantomime.

IV

A man and a woman
Are one.
A man and a woman and a blackbird
Are one.

V

I do not know which to prefer,
The beauty of inflections
Or the beauty of innuendoes,[1]
The blackbird whistling
Or just after.

VI

Icicles filled the long window
With barbaric glass.
The shadow of the blackbird
Crossed it, to and fro.
The mood
Traced in the shadow
An indecipherable cause.

---

1. One possible reading: "I do not know which to prefer, the beauty of specific sounds or the beauty of suggestions."

VII

O thin men of Haddam,[2]
Why do you imagine golden birds?
Do you not see how the blackbird
Walks around the feet
Of the women about you?

[handwritten: creating another reality]

VIII

I know noble accents
And lucid, inescapable rhythms;
But I know, too,
That the blackbird is involved
In what I know.

IX

When the blackbird flew out of sight,
It marked the edge
Of one of many circles.

X

At the sight of blackbirds
Flying in a green light,
Even the bawds of euphony
Would cry out sharply.

XI

He rode over Connecticut
In a glass coach.
Once, a fear pierced him,
In that he mistook
The shadow of his equipage
For blackbirds.

XII

The river is moving.
The blackbird must be flying.

---

2. A town in Connecticut, probably chosen for its drab sound effect.

XIII

It was evening all afternoon.
It was snowing
And it was going to snow.
The blackbird sat
In the cedar-limbs.

1917

"Thirteen Ways of Looking at a Blackbird" is a brilliant early study in multiple perspectives. From section to section, the number and location of the blackbirds and vantage from which they are viewed change sharply—and each perspective contrasts with the others. Despite the austerely simple black-and-white color scheme of the poem, the world the poem offers us is kaleidoscopically varied and rich in ambiguous symbolism.

The Death of a Soldier

Life contracts and death is expected,
As in a season of autumn.
The soldier falls.

He does not become a three-days personage,
Imposing his separation,
Calling for pomp.

Death is absolute and without memorial,
As in a season of autumn,
When the wind stops,

When the wind stops and, over the heavens,
The clouds go, nevertheless,
In their direction.

1918

"The Death of a Soldier" draws on the letters of Eugène Lemercier, a young French painter killed in World War I in 1915. These missives, collected in *Lettres d'un soldat*, were read by Stevens in the summer of 1917.

Anecdote of the Jar

I placed a jar in Tennessee,
And round it was, upon a hill.
It made the slovenly wilderness
Surround that hill.

*   *   *

The wilderness rose up to it,
And sprawled around, no longer wild.
The jar was round upon the ground
And tall and of a port in air.

It took dominion everywhere.
The jar was gray and bare.
It did not give of bird or bush,
Like nothing else in Tennessee.

1919

Gubbinal

That strange flower, the sun,
Is just what you say.
Have it your way.

The world is ugly,
And the people are sad.

That tuft of jungle feathers,
That animal eye,
Is just what you say.

That savage of fire,
That seed,
Have it your way.

The world is ugly,
And the people are sad.

1921

Gubbins was a contemptuous name formerly given to the inhabitants of a certain district in England who were said to be savages. The speaker appears to be celebrating the glories of a world graced by a sun opulent and powerful enough to seem a "strange flower," a "tuft of jungle feathers," and an "animal eye"—while ironically pretending to agree with a dreary interlocutor who insists on the world's ugliness and universal sadness.

The Snow Man

One must have a mind of winter
To regard the frost and the boughs
Of the pine-trees crusted with snow;

*   *   *

And have been cold a long time
To behold the junipers shagged with ice,
The spruces rough in the distant glitter

Of the January sun; and not to think
Of any misery in the sound of the wind,
In the sound of a few leaves,

Which is the sound of the land
Full of the same wind
That is blowing in the same bare place

For the listener, who listens in the snow,
And, nothing himself, beholds
Nothing that is not there and the nothing that is.

1921

Bantams in Pine-Woods

Chieftain Iffucan of Azcan[1] in caftan
Of tan with henna hackles,[2] halt!

Damned universal cock, as if the sun
Was blackamoor[3] to bear your blazing tail.

Fat! Fat! Fat! Fat![4] I am the personal.
Your world is you. I am my world.

You ten-foot poet among inchlings. Fat!
Begone! An inchling bristles in these pines,

Bristles, and points their Appalachian tangs,
And fears not portly Azcan nor his hoos.[5]

1922

"Bantams in Pine-Woods" is to some degree a comic scene, involving two small but aggressive bantam roosters (apparently symbolizing strutting young poets) who encounter one

1. Iffucan and Azcan are Stevens's comically grandiloquent coinages, the former probably a play on the phrase "If you can." Caftan: a full-length tunic or robe for men, usually made of rich fabric. A rooster might look like a chieftain in a "caftan / Of tan with henna hackles."
2. The long, slender neck feathers of a rooster.
3. Black servant, such as one who carried an aristocrat's train. Here the speaker accuses Chieftain Iffucan of trying to make the sun his servant to "bear [his] blazing [rooster's] tail."
4. Mockery of his overweight adversary. Stevens himself was overweight.
5. According to the *Oxford English Dictionary*, "A natural exclamation, used to express various feelings, as a call to attract attention, etc."

another in the forest. The speaker—part rooster and part poet—loudly rebukes his counterpart ("Chieftain Iffucan of Azcan"), facing him down and extravagantly declaring the validity of his own position: "Your world is you. I am my world." Just as these "inchling" poets bristle with defiance, the poem bristles with comic sound effects.

The Ordinary Women

Then from their poverty they rose,
From dry catarrhs,[1] and to guitars
They flitted
Through the palace walls.

They flung monotony behind,
Turned from their want, and, nonchalant,
They crowded
The nocturnal halls.

The lacquered loges huddled there
Mumbled zay-zay and a-zay, a-zay.
The moonlight
Fubbed the girandoles.[2]

And the cold dresses that they wore,
In the vapid haze of the window-bays,
Were tranquil
As they leaned and looked

From the window-sills at the alphabets,
At beta b and gamma g,
To study
The canting curlicues

Of heaven and of the heavenly script.
And there they read of marriage-bed.
Ti-lill-o!
And they read right long.

The gaunt guitarists on the strings
Rumbled a-day and a-day, a-day.
The moonlight
Rose on the beachy floors.

---

1. Dry coughs.   2. Outshone the candelabras.

*   *   *

How explicit the coiffures became,
The diamond point, the sapphire point,
The sequins
Of the civil fans!

Insinuations of desire,
Puissant speech, alike in each,
Cried quittance
To the wickless halls.

Then from their poverty they rose,
From dry guitars, and to catarrhs
They flitted
Through the palace walls.

1922

The ordinary women of this poem arise from the spiritual poverty of their mundane existences, perhaps through dreams or daydreams, and enter a world charged with color and imagination.

A High-Toned Old Christian Woman

Poetry is the supreme fiction, madame.
Take the moral law and make a nave[1] of it
And from the nave build haunted heaven. Thus,
The conscience is converted into palms,[2]
Like windy citherns[3] hankering for hymns.
We agree in principle. That's clear. But take
The opposing law and make a peristyle,[4]
And from the peristyle project a masque[5]
Beyond the planets. Thus, our bawdiness,
Unpurged by epitaph, indulged at last,
Is equally converted into palms,
Squiggling like saxophones.[6] And palm for palm,

---

1. The lofty central hall of a cathedral.
2. Associated with Christian worship, deriving from the palms laid at the feet of Jesus by worshipers when he entered Jerusalem, the event now celebrated on Palm Sunday.
3. Medieval stringed instruments.
4. Line of columns in a courtyard.
5. A celebratory Renaissance dramatic form richly costumed and associated with royal courts and thus secular.
6. Modern jazz instruments, contrasting with the churchly "citherns."

Madame, we are where we began. Allow,
Therefore, that in the planetary scene
Your disaffected flagellants,[7] well-stuffed,
Smacking their muzzy[8] bellies in parade,
Proud of such novelties of the sublime,
Such tink and tank and tunk-a-tunk-tunk,
May, merely may, madame, whip from themselves
A jovial hullabaloo among the spheres.
This will make widows wince. But fictive[9] things
Wink as they will. Wink most when widows wince.

1922

This poem expresses Stevens's argument, directed at "A High-Toned Old Christian Woman," that the imaginative power of poetry, with its "novelties of the sublime," can offer an attractive alternative to traditional religious worship.

O Florida, Venereal Soil

A few things for themselves,
Convolvulus[1] and coral,
Buzzards and live-moss,
Tiestas[2] from the keys,
A few things for themselves,
Florida, venereal soil,
Disclose to the lover.

The dreadful sundry of this world,
The Cuban, Polodowsky,
The Mexican women,
The negro undertaker
Killing the time between corpses
Fishing for crayfish . . .
Virgin of boorish births,

Swiftly in the nights,
In the porches of Key West,

---

7. Flagellants, in medieval Christianity, would whip themselves to induce piety. Stevens posits flagellants who are disaffected from the church and have joined his imaginative movement.
8. Possibly, well filled with drink.
9. Relating to fiction or imaginative invention.

1. Twining plant of the morning-glory family, with trumpet-shaped flowers.
2. Flowerpots, or shards of pottery. The keys refer to the small islands extending off the southern tip of Florida, the largest of which is Key West.

Behind the bougainvilleas,
After the guitar is asleep,
Lasciviously as the wind,
You come tormenting,
Insatiable,

When you might sit,
A scholar of darkness,
Sequestered over the sea,
Wearing a clear tiara
Of red and blue and red,
Sparkling, solitary, still,
In the high sea-shadow.

Donna,[3] donna, dark,
Stooping in indigo gown
And cloudy constellations,
Conceal yourself or disclose
Fewest things to the lover —
A hand that bears a thick-leaved fruit,
A pungent bloom against your shade.

1922

Stevens frequently traveled to Florida on business trips or vacations at a time when it was much less developed than it is presently. In "O Florida," he evokes the soil and atmosphere of Florida as a sensuous alternative to the chilly Puritanism of his native New England.

The Emperor of Ice-Cream

Call the roller of big cigars,[1]
The muscular one, and bid him whip
In kitchen cups concupiscent curds.[2]
Let the wenches dawdle in such dress
As they are used to wear, and let the boys
Bring flowers in last month's newspapers.
Let be be finale of seem.
The only emperor is the emperor of ice-cream.

3. Lady (Italian).
1. Key West was an important cigar-making center, and the best cigars are still tightly rolled by hand. The muscular roller of big cigars would be the right person to crank the ice-cream maker — a tough job of some duration.
2. A comic phrasing for ice cream.

* * *

Take from the dresser of deal,[3]
Lacking the three glass knobs, that sheet
On which she embroidered fantails once
And spread it so as to cover her face.
If her horny feet protrude, they come
To show how cold she is, and dumb.
Let the lamp affix its beam.
The only emperor is the emperor of ice-cream.

1922

"The Emperor of Ice-Cream" recounts, in language that deflects the literal scene like an abstract painting, the wake of a poor old woman who has died in Key West. It was customary to serve ice cream at such funeral observances, and, in the age before refrigeration, the ice cream had to be hand-cranked and consumed on the spot. Ice cream thus emerges as an image for life's sweetness and transience.

The Idea of Order at Key West

She sang beyond the genius[1] of the sea.
The water never formed to mind or voice,
Like a body wholly body, fluttering
Its empty sleeves; and yet its mimic motion
Made constant cry, caused constantly a cry,
That was not ours although we understood,
Inhuman, of the veritable ocean.

The sea was not a mask. No more was she.
The song and water were not medleyed sound
Even if what she sang was what she heard,
Since what she sang was uttered word by word.
It may be that in all her phrases stirred
The grinding water and the gasping wind;
But it was she and not the sea we heard.

For she was the maker of the song she sang.
The ever-hooded, tragic-gestured sea
Was merely a place by which she walked to sing.

---

3. Cheap pine.

1. Attendant spirit; sponsoring deity.

Whose spirit is this? we said, because we knew
It was the spirit that we sought and knew
That we should ask this often as she sang.

If it was only the dark voice of the sea
That rose, or even colored by many waves;
If it was only the outer voice of sky
And cloud, of the sunken coral water-walled,
However clear, it would have been deep air,
The heaving speech of air, a summer sound
Repeated in a summer without end
And sound alone. But it was more than that,
More even than her voice, and ours, among
The meaningless plunging of water and the wind,
Theatrical distances, bronze shadows heaped
On high horizons, mountainous atmospheres
Of sky and sea.[2]
                    It was her voice that made
The sky acutest at its vanishing.
She measured to the hour its solitude.
She was the single artificer of the world
In which she sang. And when she sang, the sea,
Whatever self it had, became the self
That was her song, for she was the maker. Then we,
As we beheld her striding there alone,
Knew that there never was a world for her
Except the one she sang and, singing, made.

Ramon Fernandez, tell me, if you know,
Why, when the singing ended and we turned
Toward the town, tell why the glassy lights,
The lights in the fishing boats at anchor there,
As the night descended, tilting in the air,
Mastered the night and portioned out the sea,
Fixing emblazoned zones and fiery poles,
Arranging, deepening, enchanting night.

Oh! Blessed rage for order, pale Ramon,
The maker's rage to order words of the sea,

---

2. The Key West sunset is known for its theatrical beauty and is actually watched by large crowds on fair evenings.

Words of the fragrant portals, dimly-starred,
And of ourselves and of our origins,
In ghostlier demarcations, keener sounds.

1935

Stevens frequently vacationed in Key West, the largest and most remote and southerly of the Florida Keys, small coral islands off the southern tip of Florida. In reference to the character of Ramon Fernandez, mentioned in the poem, James Longenbach observes that though "Stevens always insisted that 'Ramon Fernandez' was 'not intended to be anyone at all,'" Fernandez was in fact "a critic familiar to Stevens from the pages of the *Nouvelle revue française*, the *Partisan Review*, and the *Criterion*." Fernandez was drawn toward fascism in the mid-1930s, and Stevens appears to be taunting him for his desire to impose an excessive and anti-imaginative notion of order on the world.

Connoisseur of Chaos

I

A.   A violent order is disorder; and
B.   A great disorder is an order. These
Two things are one. (Pages of illustrations.)

II

If all the green of spring was blue, and it is;
If all the flowers of South Africa were bright
On the tables of Connecticut, and they are;
If Englishmen lived without tea in Ceylon, and they do;
And if it all went on in an orderly way,
And it does; a law of inherent opposites,
Of essential unity, is as pleasant as port,
As pleasant as the brush-strokes of a bough,
An upper, particular bough in, say, Marchand.

III

After all the pretty contrast of life and death
Proves that these opposite things partake of one,
At least that was the theory, when bishops' books
Resolved the world. We cannot go back to that.
The squirming facts exceed the squamous[1] mind,

---

1. Scale-like; covered in scales.

If one may say so. And yet relation appears,
A small relation expanding like the shade
Of a cloud on sand, a shape on the side of a hill.

IV

A.   Well, an old order is a violent one.
This proves nothing. Just one more truth, one more
Element in the immense disorder of truths.
B.   It is April as I write. The wind
Is blowing after days of constant rain.
All this, of course, will come to summer soon.
But suppose the disorder of truths should ever come
To an order, most Plantagenet,[2] most fixed . . .
A great disorder is an order. Now, A
And B are not like statuary, posed
For a vista in the Louvre. They are things chalked
On the sidewalk so that the pensive man may see.

V

The pensive man . . . He sees that eagle float
For which the intricate Alps are a single nest.

1938

"Connoisseur of Chaos" parodies academic discourse by presenting a string of paradoxes and contrary-to-fact statements that might, nonetheless, prove true when viewed from the right perspective. This poem can be read as a counterpart to "The Idea of Order at Key West" above.

Of Modern Poetry

The poem of the mind in the act of finding
What will suffice. It has not always had
To find: the scene was set; it repeated what
Was in the script.[1]
                    Then the theatre was changed
To something else. Its past was a souvenir.

        *   *   *

2. Family name of the line of kings who ruled England from 1154 to 1399 (Henry II to Richard II) Hence, any old, established, and perhaps obsolete order.

1. Those commonly held beliefs and opinions that dominated human thought before it was unsettled by the modern era.

It has to be living, to learn the speech of the place.
It has to face the men of the time and to meet
The women of the time. It has to think about war
And it has to find what will suffice. It has
To construct a new stage. It has to be on that stage
And, like an insatiable actor, slowly and
With meditation, speak words that in the ear,
In the delicatest ear of the mind, repeat,
Exactly, that which it wants to hear, at the sound
Of which, an invisible audience listens,
Not to the play, but to itself, expressed
In an emotion as of two people, as of two
Emotions becoming one. The actor is
A metaphysician in the dark, twanging
An instrument, twanging a wiry string that gives
Sounds passing through sudden rightnesses, wholly
Containing the mind, below which it cannot descend,
Beyond which it has no will to rise.

                                         It must
Be the finding of a satisfaction, and may
Be of a man skating, a woman dancing, a woman
Combing. The poem of the act of the mind.

                                                   1940

Large Red Man Reading

There were ghosts that returned to earth to hear his phrases,
As he sat there reading, aloud, the great blue tabulae.[1]
They were those from the wilderness of stars that had expected more.

There were those that returned to hear him read from the poem of life,
Of the pans above the stove, the pots on the table, the tulips among them.
They were those that would have wept to step barefoot into reality,

That would have wept and been happy, have shivered in the frost
And cried out to feel it again, have run fingers over leaves
And against the most coiled thorn, have seized on what was ugly

    *   *   *

---

1. Tablets—a poetic version, perhaps of the biblical tablets of Moses.

And laughed, as he sat there reading, from out of the purple tabulae,
The outlines of being and its expressings, the syllables of its law:
Poesis, poesis,[2] the literal characters, the vatic lines,

Which in those ears and in those thin, those spended hearts,
Took on color, took on shape and the size of things as they are
And spoke the feeling for them, which was what they had lacked.

1948

The premise of "Large Red Man Reading" is that the ghosts of the dead have come back to the earth to hear the "large red man," a figure for the poet, read from his "poem of life" and thus bring alive for them again—almost—the tangible world and the world of feeling.

Final Soliloquy of the Interior Paramour

Light the first light of evening, as in a room
In which we rest and, for small reason, think
The world imagined is the ultimate good.

This is, therefore, the intensest rendezvous.
It is in that thought that we collect ourselves,
Out of all the indifferences, into one thing:

Within a single thing, a single shawl
Wrapped tightly round us, since we are poor, a warmth,
A light, a power, the miraculous influence.

Here, now, we forget each other and ourselves.
We feel the obscurity of an order, a whole,
A knowledge, that which arranged the rendezvous,

Within its vital boundary, in the mind.
We say God and the imagination are one . . .
How high that highest candle lights the dark.

Out of this same light, out of the central mind,
We make a dwelling in the evening air,
In which being there together is enough.

1950

2. Greek for poetic art. Vatic: prophetic; characteristic of a prophet.

Of Mere Being

The palm at the end of the mind,
Beyond the last thought, rises
In the bronze decor,

A gold-feathered bird
Sings in the palm, without human meaning,
Without human feeling, a foreign song.

You know then that it is not the reason
That makes us happy or unhappy.
The bird sings. Its feathers shine.

The palm stands on the edge of space.
The wind moves slowly in the branches.
The bird's fire-fangled feathers dangle down.

1955

ANGELINA WELD GRIMKÉ
1880–1959

ANGELINA WELD GRIMKÉ was one of the leading poets of the Harlem Renaissance. Although she never published a book of her own, her poems appeared in the top black intellectual journals, such as *Opportunity* and *Crisis*, and in the major anthologies of the period. Grimké's poetry has affinities with a variety of movements and styles, including modernist, feminist, lesbian, African-American, and romantic lyrics. Paradoxically, as Jeffrey Rhyne has observed, her poetry has often been denied the attention it deserves precisely because of "its resistance to the boundaries of a single tradition."

Many of Grimké's most moving poems—such as "El Beso," "The Want of You," and "A Mona Lisa"—suggest the inner torment of unrequited or socially unsanctioned love. These poems—along with others such as "Little Grey Dreams"— explore a woman's perspective with grace and insight. Such poems give Grimké prominence in a tradition of women's self-exploration that includes Emily Dickinson and Sarah Piatt in the nineteenth century and Adelaide Crapsey, H.D., Amy Lowell, Edna St. Vincent Millay, and Lorine Niedecker in the twentieth. Yet other Grimké poems—such as "The Black Finger," "Dawn," "Dusk," and

"Tenebris"—evoke the natural environment with the economy and sensuousness of the imagists. But whereas Crapsey, Pound, Lowell, and Williams suggest an un-racialized world, Grimké's poems include intriguing implications about race as well as gender. Like Dickinson, Grimké likes to "tell all the truth but tell it slant." Her remarkable poems nicely complement the more direct and vernacular expressions of other Harlem Renaissance poets by meditating on race when they appear to be describing something else.

Angelina Weld Grimké was born in Boston, the only child of a black lawyer and his white wife. Grimké's mother having left the family when her daughter was three, Grimké was raised by her father. Her ancestry on her father's side was complicated and poignant. Her father was the son of a black slave, Nancy Weston, and a white plantation owner, Henry Grimké, a member of a prominent Southern abolitionist family. Grimké's mixed-race inheritance may be a factor in her preference for poetic images of betweenness: dusk, shorelines, and grayness. After graduating from Boston Normal School and taking classes at Harvard, Grimké became a venerated high school teacher in Washington, D.C. She published poems and stories in journals, and her racial drama called *Rachel* (1916) was produced on the stage. She campaigned for the Dyer Anti-Lynching Bill, which was, however, defeated in the Senate by a Southern filibuster in 1922. Reserved and shy, Grimké had some romantic friendships with women but few if any sexual relationships. Gloria Hull has said, "Grimké lived a buried life." When her father died in 1930, she moved to New York, stopped writing poetry, and lived in seclusion. She maintained communication with only one old friend, her fellow poet Georgia Douglas Johnson (also included in this anthology). After many desolate years, Angelina Weld Grimké died in New York City at the age of seventy-eight.

FURTHER READING

Angelina Weld Grimké. *Selected Works.* Ed. Carolivia Herron. New York: Oxford University Press, 1991.

Gloria T. Hull. *Color, Sex, and Poetry: Three Women Writers of the Harlem Renaissance.* Bloomington: Indiana University Press, 1987.

Venetria K. Patton and Maureen Honey, eds. "Angelina Weld Grimké." In *Double-Take: A Revisionist Harlem Renaissance Anthology*, 170–226. New Brunswick, N.J.: Rutgers University Press, 2001.

Jeffrey Rhyne. "Angelina Weld Grimké." In *Encyclopedia of American Poetry: The Twentieth Century*, ed. Eric L. Haralson, 254–55. Chicago: Fitzroy Dearborn, 2001.

El Beso

Twilight—and you
Quiet—the stars;
Snare of the shine of your teeth,

Your provocative laughter,
The gloom of your hair;
Lure of you, eye and lip;
Yearning, yearning,
Languor, surrender;
Your mouth,
And madness, madness,
Tremulous, breathless, flaming,
The space of a sigh;
Then awakening—remembrance,
Pain, regret—your sobbing;
And again, quiet—the stars,
Twilight—and you.

1909

[handwritten marginalia: trying to recall of memory you tried to push into your unconsciousness]

The Spanish "El Beso," the poem's title, means "the kiss." Jeffrey Rhyne suggests that the poem encodes female-female desire by avoiding use of third-person pronouns, a common strategy in gay poetry seeking to circumvent the antipathy of editors and readers.

The Black Finger

I have just seen a most beautiful thing:
Slim and still,
Against a gold, gold sky,
A straight, black cypress[1]
Sensitive
Exquisite
A black finger
Pointing upwards.
Why, beautiful still finger, are you black?
And why are you pointing upwards?

1923

"The Black Finger" challenges the conventional lyric dissociation of blackness from beauty and aspiration.

---

1. Tall, dark, compact coniferous tree, native to the Mediterranean and conventionally associated with sadness and mourning.

The Want of You

A hint of gold where the moon will be;
Through the flocking clouds just a star or two;
Leaf sounds, soft and wet and hushed;
And oh! the crying want of you.

1923

Dawn

Grey trees, grey skies, and not a star;
Grey mist, grey hush;
And then, frail, exquisite, afar,
A hermit-thrush.[1]

1923

"Dawn" emphasizes the liminality of the observed scene, using the word "grey" no fewer than four times, together with suggestions of "mist." This gravitation toward tones of gray, marginal spaces, and times poised between day and night (also evident in such poems as "Dusk" and "Little Grey Dreams" below) may grow out of Grimké's interracial positioning. Alternatively, it may reflect her interest in complex ways of seeing and feeling, her resistance to simple, singular truths.

Dusk

Twin stars through my purpling pane,
The shriveling husk
Of a yellowing moon on the wane—
And the dusk.

1924

Little Grey Dreams

Little grey dreams,
I sit at the ocean's edge,
At the grey ocean's edge,
With you on my lap.

*   *   *

1. A native American bird of drab plumage and rich songs.

I launch you, one by one,
  And one by one,
    Little grey dreams,
Under the grey, grey clouds,
Out on the grey, grey sea,
You go sailing away,
from my empty lap,
    Little grey dreams.
    Sailing! sailing!
Into the black
At the horizon's edge.

1924

Tenebris

There is a tree, by day,
That, at night,
Has a shadow,
A hand huge and black,
With fingers long and black.
  All through the dark,
Against the white man's house,
  In the little wind,
The black hand plucks and plucks
  At the bricks.
The bricks are the color of blood and very small.
  Is it a black hand,
  Or is it a shadow?

1924

The Latin "Tenebris," the poem's title, means "in darkness." The tree may suggest a lynching tree. The lynching of black men by white vigilantes had reached epidemic proportions in the years 1910–30. Thus, the black hand in the tree may be demanding justice from the "white man's house." Jeffrey Rhyne argues more generally that in this poem, Grimké "remembers the violence of white racism and warns of the stability, resilience, and power of black peoples and cultures."

Grass Fingers

Touch me, touch me,
  Little cool grass fingers,

Elusive, delicate grass fingers.
With your shy brushings,
Touch my face—
My naked arms—
My thighs—
My feet.
Is there nothing that is kind?
You need not fear me.
Soon I shall be too far beneath you
For you to reach me, even,
With your tiny, timorous[1] toes.

1925

"Grass Fingers" suggests an erotic attraction in oblivion.

A Mona Lisa

1

I should like to creep
Through the long brown grasses
   That are your lashes;
I should like to poise
   On the very brink
Of the leaf-brown pools
   That are your shadowed eyes;
I should like to cleave[1]
   Without sound,
Their glimmering waters,
   Their unrippled waters,
I should like to sink down
   And down
     And down . . .
       And deeply drown.

2

Would I be more than a bubble breaking?
   Or an ever-widening circle

---

1. Fearful.   1. Adhere closely.

Ceasing at the marge?[2]
Would my white bones
  Be the only white bones
Wavering back and forth, back and forth
  In their depths?

1926

"A Mona Lisa," like "Grass Fingers" (above), combines imagery of erotic or emotional at-
traction with imagery of oblivion. The Mona Lisa (or La Gioconda) is a portrait by Leo-
nardo da Vinci (1452–1519) of a woman with a famously enigmatic smile.

Fragment

I am the woman with the black black skin
I am the laughing woman with the black black face
I am living in the cellars and in every crowded place
  I am toiling just to eat
  In the cold and in the heat
    And I laugh
I am the laughing woman who's forgotten how to weep
I am the laughing woman who's afraid to go to sleep.

1930

GEORGIA DOUGLAS JOHNSON
ca. 1880–1966

GEORGIA DOUGLAS JOHNSON was the best-known woman poet of the Harlem Re-
naissance, the only one to publish books of poetry during the first decades of the
century. (She published three between 1918 and 1928.) Her poems suggest both a
feminine sensibility and a feminist awareness. Such early poems as "The Heart of a
Woman" and "Motherhood" plumb the anguish of a woman trapped in traditional
marital and child-bearing roles. Johnson's subsequent poems take up the chal-
lenges and aspirations of the African-American community. These themes appear
in such poems as "Common Dust," "Prejudice," and "The Black Runner."

2. Margin, shore.

Georgia Douglas Camp was born in Atlanta in about 1880. She studied at Atlanta University and Oberlin College. Upon marrying Henry Lincoln Johnson, an African-American lawyer and politician, she moved to Washington, D.C., where she presided over a literary salon. After her husband's death in 1925, she worked in clerical jobs to support herself and her two sons, sending one son to law school and the other to medical school. She also wrote stories, plays, and a weekly column. According to Adenike Davidson, Johnson's early poetry drew comparisons with the mellifluous personal lyrics of Sara Teasdale and Edna St. Vincent Millay, whereas her subsequent poetry attempted to "connect more deeply with the issues of the Harlem Renaissance."

FURTHER READING

Adenike Marie Davidson. "Georgia Douglas Johnson." In *Encyclopedia of American Poetry: The Twentieth Century*, ed. Eric L. Haralson, 333–34. Chicago: Fitzroy Dearborn, 2001.

Gloria T. Hull. *Color, Sex, and Poetry: Three Women Writers of the Harlem Renaissance.* Bloomington: Indiana University Press, 1987.

Georgia Douglas Johnson. *Selected Works.* Introduction by Claudia Tate. New York: G. K. Hall, 1997.

Lorraine Elena Roses and Ruth Elizabeth Randolph. *Harlem's Glory: Black Women Writing, 1900–1950.* Cambridge, Mass.: Harvard University Press, 1996.

The Heart of a Woman

The heart of a woman goes forth with the dawn,
As a lone bird, soft winging, so restlessly on,
Afar o'er life's turrets and vales does it roam
In the wake of those echoes the heart calls home.

The heart of a woman falls back with the night,
And enters some alien cage in its plight,
And tries to forget it has dreamed of the stars
While it breaks, breaks, breaks on the sheltering bars.

1918

"The Heart of a Woman" may reflect the frustrations Johnson observed and felt in domestic life. Her husband, "Linc" Johnson, disapproved of his wife's poetic aspirations. The poem's metaphor of a broken and caged bird in its second stanza echoes Paul Laurence Dunbar's nineteenth-century poem "Sympathy," with its resonant refrain, "I know why the caged bird sings."

Motherhood

Don't knock on my door, little child,
I cannot let you in;
You know not what a world this is
Of cruelty and sin.
Wait in the still eternity
Until I come to you.
The world is cruel, cruel, child,
I cannot let you through.

Don't knock at my heart, little one,
I cannot bear the pain
Of turning deaf ears to your call,
Time and time again.
You do not know the monster men
Inhabiting the earth.
Be still, be still, my precious child,
I cannot give you birth.

1922

Common Dust

And who shall separate the dust
What later we shall be:
Whose keen discerning eye will scan
And solve the mystery?

The high, the low, the rich, the poor,
The black, the white, the red,
And all the chromatique[1] between,
Of whom shall it be said:

Here lies the dust of Africa;
Here are the sons of Rome;
Here lies the one unlabelled,
The world at large his home!

*   *   *

1. Color spectrum.

Can one then separate the dust?
Will mankind lie apart,
When life has settled back again
The same as from the start?

1922

Prejudice

These fell[1] miasmic rings of mist with ghoulish menace bound,
Like noose-horizons tightening my little world around.
They still the soaring will to wing, to dance, to speed away,
And fling the soul insurgent back into its shell of clay.
Beneath incrusted silences, a seething Etna[2] lies,
The fire of whose furnaces may sleep, but never dies!

1922

Throughout most of the poem, "Prejudice" employs Johnson's characteristically euphonious style. It has regular iambics, strong-stressed rhymes, alliteration (miasmic/mist/menace), and internal rhyme (still/will). Anguish and anger break through, however, in the final line's arrhythmia and syntactical contortion.

The Suppliant

Long have I beat with timid hands upon life's leaden door,
Praying the patient, futile prayer my fathers prayed before;
Yet I remain without the close, unheeded and unheard,
And never to my listening ear is borne the waited word.

Soft o'er the threshold of the years there comes this counsel cool:
The strong demand, contend, prevail; the beggar is a fool.

1923

Escape

Shadows, shadows,
Hug me round
So that I shall not be found

---

1. Cruel, sinister. Miasmic: emanating from an obscuring, disease-causing fog.

2. Active volcano in Sicily; perhaps an allusion to several poems by Emily Dickinson.

By sorrow;
She pursues me
Everywhere,
I can't lose her
Anywhere.

Fold me in your black Abyss;
She will never look
In this—
Shadows, shadows,
Hug me round
In your solitude
Profound.

1925

"Escape" may express Johnson's grief at the death of her husband, "Linc" Johnson, of a stroke in 1925. The following poem, "The Black Runner," may suggest her determination to persevere through hard times.

The Black Runner

I'm awake, I'm away!
I have jewels in trust,
They are rights of the soul
That are holy and just;
There are deeds to be done,
There are goals to be won,
I am stripped for the race
In the glare of the sun;
I am throbbing with faith
I can! And I must!
My forehead to God—
My feet in the dust.

1925

H. T. TSIANG [HSI-TSENG CHIANG]
1880–1971

WRITING UNDER the pen name H. T. Tsiang, Hsi-Tseng Chiang published poetry as well as a play and three novels in the 1920s and 1930s. A member of the international Communist Party, he also was an actor in Hollywood, appearing in such films as *Tokyo Rose*. His work broke stereotypes about Chinese poetry with its politics, force, and wit.

Chiang escaped from China in 1926 and settled in the United States after the American Civil Liberties Union (ACLU) defended his right to be here. Ruth Crawford Seeger set several of his proletarian poems to music for piano and soprano in 1932. His poetry appeared regularly in the *Daily Worker*. In the selection here, Tsiang (or Chiang) denounces Japanese imperialism against the Chinese, urging Chinese workers to unite in order to defeat Japan.

FURTHER READING

Juliana Chang, ed. *Quiet Fire: A Historical Anthology of Asian American Poetry, 1892–1970*. Philadelphia: Temple University Press, 1996.

Shantung

Don, Don, Don, the drum is calling;
Lun, Lun, Lun, the artillery is roaring.
Japan is in Shantung, Shantung,
In Shanghai far away
We can still work for a living.

Hashi yi, hashi yi, buzzing bee, buzzing bee.
God has damned me,
Hard work comes to me.
My mouth is thirsty,
My stomach was never so empty,
Why don't you teach me to live without bread,
Papa, mama?

The whip is cracking,
The click is in my ear,
A look at the foreman's face
And my heart always blackens.

Think ye,
He can stop my tears, and my ears,
That ring with pain.

Awake, ye, brother,
Come hand in hand
To their defeat!
Brother, sister, there is a message for you:
Japan occupies Shantung,
But the toilers of Japan, they are with us;
Not Tanaka[1] the oppressor,
Not Tanaka the murderer,
But the toilers of Japan will join us —
We together will crush Tanaka.

Brother, sister.
You are a farmer, you are a worker!
Hark to the cock,
A new day is coming!

Out of the ruthless mass-murder
March to Manchuria,
South of Canton;
Away with the exploiters —
When the sky with blood is red,
We all will have our bread!

1928

WITTER BYNNER
1881–1968

WITTER BYNNER was a resolute cultural explorer who brought his explorations alive in poetry of elegant directness. A friend of Edna St. Vincent Millay, he wrote poems that, like hers, were noted for lucid imagery and emotional openness. Born in Brooklyn in 1881, Bynner graduated from Harvard in 1902. Starting in 1918, he taught creative writing at the University of California, Berkeley, where his

1. Tanaka Giichi (1863–1929), prime minister of Japan (1927–29) and author of its aggressive policy toward China.

students included Genevieve Taggard. His explorations of Chinese literature and culture led him to publish a translation of more than three hundred Chinese poems, *The Jade Mountain*, with the Chinese scholar Dr. Kaing Kung-Ho. Bynner also translated the *Tao Te Ching* by Lao-tzu. Bynner ultimately settled in Taos, New Mexico, where he studied the culture of the Hopi people. His poem "Snake Dance" dramatizes the principal annual ritual of the Hopi people.

While living in New Mexico with his lover, Robert Nichols Hunt, Bynner became involved with the artistic circle established by Mabel Dodge Luhan. Through Luhan, Bynner formed a close friendship with the English novelist D. H. Lawrence and his wife, Frieda. Lawrence placed a version of Bynner in his novel *The Plumed Serpent* (1926) as the character Owen, and Bynner later published the memoir *Journey with Genius: Recollections and Reflections Concerning the D. H. Lawrences* (1951).

FURTHER READING

Witter Bynner. *The Selected Witter Bynner*. Ed. James Kraft. Albuquerque: University of New Mexico Press, 1995.
James Kraft. *Who Is Witter Bynner?* Albuquerque: University of New Mexico Press, 1995.

Snake Dance

(Hotevilla)

We are clean for them now, as naked-clean as they are,
We go out for them now and we meet them with our hands.
Bullsnakes, rattlesnakes, whipsnakes, we compare
Our cleanness with their cleanness. The sun stands
Witness, the moon stands witness. The dawn joins
Their scales with our flesh, the evening quiets their rattles.
We can feel their tails soothing along our loins
Like the feathers on our fathers after battles.
For their fathers were our fathers. We are brothers
Born of the earth and brothers in the sun;
And our destiny is only one another's,
However apart the races we have run.
Out of the earth we came, the sons of kings;
For the daughters of serpent-kings had offered grace
To our fathers and had formed us under their wings
To be worthy of light at last, body and face.
Out of the earth we came, into this open
Largeness of light, into this world we see
Lifted and laid along, broken and slopen,

This world that heaves toward heaven eternally.
We have found them, we have brought them, and we know them
As kin of us, because our fathers said:
As we have always shown them, you must show them
That kinship in the world is never dead.

Come then, O bullsnake, wake from your slow search
Across the desert. Here are your very kin.
Dart not away from us, whipsnake, but perch
Your head among your people moulded in
A greater shape yet touching the earth like you.
Leave off your rattling, rattlesnake, leave off
Your coiling, your venom. There is only dew
Under the starlight. Let our people cough
In the blowing sand and hide their faces, oh still
Receive them, know them, live with them in peace.
They want no rocks from you, none of your hill.
Uncoil again, lie on our arms, and cease
From the wars our fathers ceased from, be again
Close to your cousins, listen to our song.
Dance with us, kinsfolk, be with us as men
Descended from common ancestors, belong
To none but those who join yourselves and us.
Oh listen to the feathers that can weave
Only enchantment and to the words we sing,
The feet we touch the earth with. Help us believe
That our ancestors are still remembering.
Go back to them with sacred meal, go back
Down through the earth, oh be our messengers!
Tell them with reverence, tell them our lack;
Tell them we have no roots, but a sap that stirs
Forever unrooted upward to the sky.
But tell them also, tell them of our song
Downward from heaven, back where we belong.
Oh north, east, west and south, tell them we die!

1929

The Snake Dance, an annual ritual plea to the gods for rain, is performed by the Hopi Indians in northeastern Arizona in mid-August. Alternate sites for the dance include the village of Hotevilla. The Snake Dance is the public finale of a nine-day ceremony in the kivas of the Antelope and Snake clans. Bynner's poem is spoken by one of the participants in the dance. The snakes are asked to recognize their kinship with humans and therefore to carry their prayer to the heavens for rain.

JESSIE REDMON FAUSET
1882–1961

JESSIE REDMON FAUSET is best known for her literary editorship of the NAACP publication *The Crisis*, under the general editorship of W. E. B. Du Bois from 1919 to 1926. She discovered and promoted such poets as Langston Hughes, Countee Cullen, and Claude McKay, as well as other major African-American and Caribbean writers, becoming, in Hughes's estimation, one of the three people who created the Harlem Renaissance. Fauset was also one of the movement's most prolific novelists, with four published novels. According to critic Susan Tomlinson, the most famous of these works, *Plum Bun*, reconciles the New Negro and the New Woman movements. Finally, but of overlooked importance, Fauset was one of the best-known African-American women poets of her era, along with her friends Georgia Douglas Johnson and Angelina Weld Grimké. Fauset mentored other women writers through literary salons in her home and developed a poetic voice that could be described as the New Negro Woman's voice.

Born in a suburb of Philadelphia, Fauset was educated at prestigious schools, often as the only African American in her high school and college classes. She encountered racism in education when she was denied admission to Bryn Mawr. Admitted to Cornell University, she became the only African-American student there. Fauset also became the first African American to graduate from Cornell and to achieve Phi Beta Kappa. When she was denied a teaching position in Philadelphia because of her race, she moved to Baltimore and taught there; she then relocated to Washington, D.C., where she also taught. While she was in Washington from 1906 to 1918, she enrolled in an M.A. program in French at the University of Pennsylvania. Fauset attended the Second Pan African Congress in 1921 and also studied at the Sorbonne as one of the few Harlem Renaissance women to travel and live in Europe.

Fauset's poetry focuses on African-American middle-class life as seen through the eyes of the New Negro Woman. In both "Touché" and "La Vie C'est la Vie," the female speaker recognizes the role that social barriers against lovers of different races play in adult romance in the United States.

FURTHER READING

Venetria K. Patton and Maureen Honey, eds. "Jessie Redmon Fauset." In *Double-Take: A Revisionist Harlem Renaissance Anthology*, 232–42. New Brunswick, N.J.: Rutgers University Press, 2001.

Susan Tomlinson. "Vision to Visionary: The New Negro Woman as Cultural Worker in Jessie Redmon Fauset's *Plum Bun*." *Legacy* 19 (2002): 90–97.

Oriflamme

*I can remember when I was a little, young girl, how my old mammy would sit
out of doors in the evenings and look up at the stars and groan, and I would say,
"Mammy, what makes you groan so?" And she would say, "I am groaning to
think of my poor children; they do not know where I be and I don't know
where they be. I look up at the stars and they look up at the stars!"*
SOJOURNER TRUTH

I think I see her sitting, bowed and black,
    Stricken and seared with slavery's mortal scars,
Reft of her children, lonely, anguished, yet
    Still looking at the stars.

Symbolic mother, we thy myriad sons,
    Pounding our stubborn hearts on Freedom's bars,
Clutching our birthright, fight with faces set,
    Still visioning the stars!

1920

Fauset's poem title is the French word *oriflamme*, which is derived from the Latin *aurea flamma*, or "flame of gold." During the Middle Ages, French kings raised a special banner called the *oriflamme* in times of danger. The banner, usually made of red silk, looked like a golden flame when it waved in the sunlight. Fauset uses this term to describe the archetypal African-American slave mother, the force that holds the race together despite the slave-holders' separating children from mothers in order to sell one or the other (or both) on the slave market or to another slaveholder. The poem's speaker draws strength from this mother figure.

Words! Words!

How did it happen that we quarreled?
We two who loved each other so!
Only the moment before we were one,
Using the language that lovers know.
And then of a sudden, a word, a phrase,
That struck at the heart like a poignard's[1] blow.
And you went berserk, and I saw red,
And love lay between us, bleeding and dead!
Dead! When we'd loved each other so!

1. A dagger's (French).

*   *   *

How *could* it happen that we quarreled!
Think of the things we used to say!
"What does it matter, dear, what you do?
Love such as ours has to last for aye!"
— "Try me! I long to endure your test!"
— "Love, we shall always love, come what may!"
What are the words the apostle saith?
"In the power of the tongue are Life and Death!"
Think of the things we used to say!

1926

Touché

Dear, when we sit in that high, placid room,
"Loving" and "doving"[1] as all lovers do,
Laughing and leaning so close in the gloom, —

What is the change that creeps sharp over you?
Just as you raise your fine hand to my hair,
Bringing that glance of mixed wonder and rue?[2]

"Black hair," you murmur, "so lustrous and rare,
Beautiful too, like a raven's smooth wing;
Surely no gold locks were ever more fair."

Why do you say every night that same thing?
Turning your mind to some old constant theme,
Half meditating and half murmuring?

Tell me, that girl of your young manhood's dream,
Her you loved first in that dim long ago —
Had *she* blue eyes? Did *her* hair goldly gleam?

Does *she* come back to you softly and slow,
Stepping wraith-wise[3] from the depths of the past?
Quickened and fired by the warmth of our glow?

*   *   *

1. Refers to soft amorous sounds like the cooing   2. Regret.
of doves.   3. Apparitional.

There, I've divined[4] it! My wit holds you fast.
Nay, no excuses; 'tis little I care,
I knew a lad in my own girlhood's past, —
Blue eyes he had and such waving gold hair!

1927

Touché is a French fencing term. Here it means "I've got you."

La Vie C'est la Vie

On summer afternoons I sit
Quiescent by you in the park,
And idly watch the sunbeams gild
And tint the ash-trees' bark.

Or else I watch the squirrels frisk
And chaffer in the grassy lane;
And all the while I mark your voice
Breaking with love and pain.

I know a woman who would give
Her chance of heaven to take my place;
To see the love-light in your eyes,
The love-glow on your face!

And there's a man whose lightest word
Can set my chilly blood afire;
Fulfillment of his least behest
Defines my life's desire.

But he will none of me. Nor I
Of you. Nor you of her. 'Tis said
The world is full of jests like these. —
I wish that I were dead.

1927

The French expression *la vie c'est la vie*, the poem's title, means "life—that's life."

4. Discovered.

MINA LOY
1882–1966

MINA LOY—once a nearly forgotten figure—has come back into focus as one of the most intriguing icons of experimental modernism. Jeffrey Twitchell-Waas observes, "When the first four poems of Mina Loy's *Love Songs* appeared in the inaugural issue of *Others* (July 1915), they were the most experimental and scandalous poetry in English, with the notable exception of the recently published *Tender Buttons* by Loy's friend Gertrude Stein." Yet *Others* editor Alfred Kreymborg noted that "her beauty interested some observers more than her poetry." Along with sharp satirical intelligence, a talent for the engagingly brash gesture, film-star good looks, and a highly original poetic eye and ear, Loy also brought to the transatlantic avant garde considerable talent in the visual arts and an articulate conviction of the need for women to define their own identities in a male-dominated world. In 1917 the New York *Sun* ran a series of articles on The Modern Woman, concluding with a profile on Loy that asked, rhetorically: "Mina Loy, if she isn't the Modern Woman, who is, pray?"

By 1920, Loy's work had attracted the admiring attention of Pound, Eliot, Stevens, Stein, and William Carlos Williams (all included in this anthology) and had provoked a more wary response from Marianne Moore. Pound, among others, saw the reticent Moore and the flamboyant Loy as peers and opposing counterparts. Loy also provoked the disapproval of *Poetry* editor Harriet Monroe, who labeled her "an extreme otherist." *Others* had been launched as a venue for those "others" whose work proved too radical for Monroe's *Poetry*. Monroe accurately predicted that Loy would soon become "one of the long-to-be-hidden-moderns." Yet as recent editions of her long-out-of-print poetic works reveal, Loy remains a compelling, challenging, at times unsettling, yet strangely beautiful poet.

Mina Gertrude Lowy was born in London. Her father was a tailor and the descendant of Hungarian Jews. She showed an early talent for both drawing and poetry, talents encouraged by her father but discouraged by her mother. She also showed, in Roger L. Conover's words, "remarkable physical beauty and resistance to conventional codes of femininity" that caused "conflict in [her] teenage years." From 1899 to 1903, she studied art in Munich, London, and Paris, settling in Paris until 1906 as a practicing artist. Lowy married the English artist and photographer Stephen Haweis, changed her name to the more French-sounding Loy, and absorbed the work of Gauguin, Picasso, Rouault, and other early modernist painters. Loy's first daughter, Oda, born in 1904, died on her first birthday in 1905. Loy moved with Haweis to Florence in 1906, though their marriage was already in trouble. She gave birth to a daughter, Joella, in 1907 and a son, Giles, in 1909. In Florence, Loy met the famous salon hostesses Muriel Draper and Mabel Dodge (Luhan) and had a passionate affair in 1914 with the leading figure of Italian futurism, Filippo Marinetti, and another affair with fellow futurist Giovanni Papini. Yet she remained painfully shy and felt herself to be socially isolated and tied down by domestic responsibilities: "My conceptions of life evolved while . . . stirring baby food on spirit lamps — and my best drawings behind a stove to the accompaniment of a line of children's clothes hanging round it to dry."

Though she admired Marinetti's vitality, Loy became disaffected from the militaristic and masculinist assumptions of Italian futurism. In response, in 1914 she authored a "Feminist Manifesto," announcing to the women of her time that "if you want to realize yourselves (for you are on the brink of a devastating psychological upheaval) all your pet illusions must be unmasked. . . . Leave off looking to men to find out what you are *not*. Seek within yourself to find out what you *are*." Loy's experiments in poetry started as a series of satires directed at futurist attitudes toward women. In 1915, the first four of Loy's satiric and surrealistic "Love Songs" were published in Kreymborg's *Others*. In 1916 Loy sailed, alone, for New York, where she met Williams, Moore, and such avant-garde artists as Alfred Stieglitz, Georgia O'Keeffe, Marcel Duchamp, Marsden Hartley, Gabrielle and Francis Picabia, and Man Ray—who made Loy the subject of several influential photo studies.

In 1917 the complete "Love Songs 1–34" (republished later under the title "Love Songs to Joannes") appeared in *Others* and was praised by both Pound and Eliot. Pound coined his well-known term "logopoeia" (an "ironical play" with a word's "habits of usage") in response to Loy's example. Although Loy's attitude toward women differed significantly from Eliot's, her technique anticipates by several years the structure of both Eliot's *The Waste Land* and Pound's *Cantos*. Also in 1917, Loy had her fateful meeting with the muscular dadaist poet and boxer Arthur Cravan (born Fabian Lloyd). Cravan, a nephew of Oscar Wilde, had been defeated in a heavyweight bout by Jack Johnson in 1916 and was even more dedicated to publicly defying conventional moral codes than was Loy. Cravan was arrested in 1917 when he disrobed while giving a lecture on modern art in New York. Loy, now officially divorced from Haweis, joined Cravan in Mexico in 1918, where they married. Cravan unsuccessfully pursued his career as a boxer—and the couple nearly starved. Loy, pregnant, left for Europe on a passenger ship, with Cravan scheduled to follow her across the Atlantic in a wrecked sailboat he had obtained and was rebuilding. Setting sail on a test run from a bay with treacherous tides, Cravan disappeared and was never seen again. He is presumed to have died by drowning, though alternative legends persist. Loy returned to Mexico in 1920 to search for traces of Cravan, and she never fully recovered from his loss.

Responding to a *Little Review* questionnaire that asked "What has been the happiest moment of your life?" Loy replied, "Every moment I spent with Arthur Cravan." And for "The unhappiest?" Loy replied, "The rest of the time."

Loy's daughter Fabienne was born in London in 1919. Loy was reunited with her two eldest children in Florence, but in 1921, her son, Giles, was kidnapped by her first husband, Haweis, and Loy never saw him again (he died of a rare cancer two years later). Thus, even as Loy was enjoying increasing notoriety as a poet, she suffered a series of violent shocks in her personal life that appear to have limited her interest in a public poetic career.

In 1923, Loy settled in Paris and published *The Lunar Baedeker*, the sole volume of poems to appear in her lifetime. With the help of Peggy Guggenheim, she established and became absorbed in a successful business designing and selling artistic lampshades, including a beautifully shaped model that resembled calla lilies. Although she was an established member of the expatriate artistic community in Paris and a close friend of Djuna Barnes, she gradually receded from literary life. She continued to write poetry, including the long, quasi-autobiographical sequence "Anglo-Mongrels and the Rose" (1923–25), but she made little effort to publish her work and ignored editors' requests for submission. In 1930, Loy closed her now-troubled lampshade business and served for the next six years as the Paris representative of her son-in-law Julien Levy's New York art gallery.

In 1936, Loy returned to the United States, where she lived on the Lower East Side of Manhattan and in the Bowery until 1953. She developed a lasting friendship with the artist Joseph Cornell and created her own Cornell-like "constructions," but she grew increasingly introspective and gradually lost touch with the poets and artists of her earlier years, though vivid recollections of her appear in their memoirs. Her poetry of this period explores the inner emotional lives of the homeless people she saw on the Bowery's streets. In 1953, at the age of seventy-one, Loy moved to Aspen, Colorado, where she lived with her two daughters until her death in 1966.

With her earlier poetry out of print and our knowledge of her artistic development hampered by her disinclination to publish, it is understandable that Loy's place in the canon of modernist poetry would gradually become obscured. Thanks to the advocacy of devotees like Kenneth Rexroth and Jonathan Williams (who published a brief small-press selection in 1958) and to the publication of major collections of her work in 1982 and 1996, Loy's poetic art has become available once again and is receiving growing critical attention. A full-length biography appeared in 1996, and an important collection of essays, *Mina Loy: Woman and Poet*, in 1998. Hence, as Harriet Monroe had predicted, Mina Loy did suffer obscurity as "one of the long-to-be-hidden-moderns," yet she has now reemerged as a pivotal figure in experimental modernism. Readers may appreciate anew the force of her personality, the complex and unsettling beauty of her imagery, her startling imaginative leaps, her complex wordplay, and her deviously compelling approach to poetic form and structure. Although Loy's work continues to present difficulties—requiring of readers the focused and creative attention demanded by Stevens, Moore, or Eliot—it rewards that attention in rich and surprising ways.

FURTHER READING

Carolyn Burke. *Becoming Modern: The Life of Mina Loy.* New York: Farrar, Straus & Giroux, 1996.

Virginia M. Kouidis. *Mina Loy: American Modernist Poet.* Baton Rouge: Louisiana State University Press, 1980.

Mina Loy. *The Last Lunar Baedeker.* Ed. Roger L. Conover. Highlands, N.C.: Jargon Society, 1982.

———. *The Lost Lunar Baedeker.* Ed. Roger L. Conover. New York: Farrar, Straus & Giroux, 1996.

Maeera Shreiber and Keith Tuma, eds. *Mina Loy: Woman and Poet.* Orono, Maine: National Poetry Foundation, 1998.

Love Songs to Joannes

1

Spawn of Fantasies
Sitting the appraisable
Pig Cupid
His rosy snout
Rooting erotic garbage
"Once upon a time"
Pulls a weed
White star-topped
Among wild oats
Sown in mucous-membrane

I would
An eye in a Bengal light[1]
Eternity in a skyrocket
Constellations in an ocean
Whose rivers run no fresher
Than a trickle of saliva

There are   suspect places

*   *   *

1. Signal flare.

I must live in my lantern
Trimming subliminal flicker
Virginal   to the bellows
Of experience
          Colored glass

2

The skin-sack
In which wanton duality
Packed
All the completions
Of my infructuous[2] impulses
Something the shape of a man
To the casual vulgarity of the merely observant
More of a clock-work mechanism
Running down against time
To which I am not paced

My fingertips are numb
from fretting your hair
A God's doormat
On the threshold of your mind

3

We might have coupled
In the bedridden monopoly of a moment
Or broken flesh with one another
At the profane communion table
Where wine is spilled on promiscuous lips

We might have given birth to a butterfly
With the daily news
Printed in blood on its wings

4

Once in a mezzanino
The starry ceiling
Vaulted an unimaginable family

2. Fruitless.

Bird-like abortions
With human throats
And Wisdom's eyes
Who wore lamp-shade red dresses
And woolen hair

One bore a baby
In a padded porte-enfant
Tied with a sarsenet ribbon
To her goose's wings

But for the abominable shadows
I would have lived
Among their fearful furniture
To teach them to tell me their secrets
Before I guessed
—Sweeping the brood clean out

    5

Midnight empties the street
I am undecided which way back
        To the left a boy
    —One wing has been washed in rain
   The other will never be clean any more—
Pulling door-bells to remind
Those that are snug
        To the right a haloed ascetic
        Threading houses
Probes wounds for souls
 —The poor can't wash in hot water—
And I don't know which turning to take—
Since you got home to yourself first

    6

I know the Wire-Puller intimately
And if it were not for the people
On whom you keep one eye
You could look straight at me
And Time would be set back

7

The wind stuffs the scum of the white street
Into my lungs and my nostrils
Exhilarated birds
Prolonging flight into the night
Never reaching— —

8

I am the jealous storehouse of the candle-ends
That lit your adolescent learning

Behind God's eyes
There might
Be other lights

9

When we lifted
Our eyelids on Love
A cosmos
Of coloured voices
And laughing honey
And spermatozoa
At the core of Nothing
In the milk of the Moon

10

Shuttle-cock and battle-door
A little pink-love
And feathers are strewn

11

Dear one   at your mercy
Our Universe
Is only
A colorless onion
You derobe
Sheath by sheath
        Remaining
A disheartening odour
About your nervy hands

12

Voices break on the confines of passion
Desire   Suspicion   Man   Woman
Solve in the humid carnage

Flesh from flesh
Draws the inseparable delight
Kissing at gasps   to catch it

Is it true
That I have set you apart
Inviolate in an utter crystalization
Of all   the jolting of the crowd
Taught me willingly to live to share

Or are you
Only the other half
Of an ego's necessity
Scourging pride with compassion
To the shallow sound of dissonance
And boom of escaping breath

13

Come to me   There is something
I have got to tell you   and I can't tell
Something taking shape
Something has a new name
A new dimension
A new use
A new illusion

It is ambient   And it is in your eyes
Something shiny   Something only for you
                        Something that I must not see
It is in my ears   Something very resonant
Something that you must not hear
                        Something only for me

Let us be very jealous
Very suspicious
Very conservative

Very cruel
Or we might not make an end of the jostling aspirations
Disorb[3] inviolate egos

Where two or there are welded together
They shall become god[4]

Oh that's right
Keep away from me　　　Please give me a push
Don't let me understand you　　　Don't realize me
Or we might tumble together
Depersonalized
Identical
Into the terrific Nirvana[5]
Me you—you—me

14
Today
Everlasting passing apparent imperceptible
To you
I bring the nascent virginity of
—Myself—for the moment

No love　　　or the other thing
Only the impact of lighted bodies
Knocking sparks off each other
In chaos

15
Seldom　　　Trying for Love
Fantasy dealt them out as gods
Two or three men　　　looked only human

But you alone
Superhuman　　　apparently
I had to be caught in the weak eddy
Of your driveling humanity
　　　　　To love you most

---

3. To knock something off its orbit.
4. A profane paraphrase of Jesus's message to his disciples: "For where two or three come together in my name, there am I with them" (Matthew 18:20).

5. In Hinduism and Buddhism, blissful state of enlightenment that grows from the extinction of all attachment.

16

We might have lived together
In the lights of the Arno
Or gone apple stealing under the sea
Or played
Hide and seek in love and cobwebs
And a lullaby on a tin pan

And talked till there were no more tongues
To talk with
And never have known any better

17

I don't care
Where the legs of the legs of the furniture are walking to
Or what is hidden in the shadows they stride
Or what would look at me
If the shutters were not shut

Red   a warm colour on the battlefield
Heavy on my knees as a counterpane
Count counter
I counted   the fringe of the towel
Till two tassels clinging together
Let the square room fall away
From a round vacuum
Dilating with my breath

18

Out of the serving
Of the hill from the hill
The interim
Of star from star
That nascent
Static
Of night

19

Nothing so conserving
As cool cleaving

Note of the Q H U
Clear carving
Breath-giving
Pollen smelling
Space

White telling
Of slaking
Drinkable
Through fingers
Running water
Grass haulms
Grow to

Leading astray
Of fireflies
Aerial quadrille
Bouncing
Off one another
Again conjoining
In recaptured pulses
Of light

You too
Had something
At that time
Of a green-lit glow-worm

Yet slowly drenched
To raylessness
In rain

20

Let Joy go solace-winged
To flutter whom she may concern

21

I store up nightness against you
Heavy with shut-flower's nightmares

*   *   *

Stack noons
Curled to the solitaire
Core of the
Sun

22

Green things grow
Salads
For the cerebral
Forager's revival
Upon bossed bellies
Of mountains
Rolling in the sun
And flowered flummery
Breaks to my silly shoes

In ways without you
I go
Gracelessly
As things go

23

Laughter in solution
Stares in a stare
Irredeemable pledges
Of pubescent consummations
Rot
To the recurrent moon
Bleach
To the pure white
Wickedness of pain

24

The procreative truth of Me
Petered out
In pestilent
Tear drops
Little lusts and lucidities
And prayerful lies
Muddled with the heinous acerbity
Of your streetcorner smile

25

Licking the Arno
The little rosy
Tongue of Dawn
Interferes with our eyelashes

We twiddle to it
Round and round
Faster
And turn into machines

Till the sun
Subsides in shining
Melts some of us
Into abysmal pigeon-holes
Passion has bored
In warmth

Some few of us
Grow to the level of cool plains
Cutting our foothold
With steel eyes

26

Shedding our petty pruderies
From slit eyes
We sidle up
To Nature
      that irate pornographist

27

Nucleus   Nothing
Inconceivable concept
Insentient repose
The hands of races
Drop off from
Immodifiable plastic

The contents
Of our ephemeral conjunction
In aloofness from Much
Flowed the approachment of — — —

NOTHING
There was a man and a woman
In the way
While the Irresolvable
Rubbed with our daily deaths
Impossible eyes

28

The steps go up for ever
And they are white
And the first step   is the last white
Forever
Coloured   conclusions
Smelt   to synthetic
Whiteness
Of my
Emergence
And I am burnt quite white
In the climacteric[6]
Withdrawal of your sun
And wills and words all white
Suffuse
Illimitable monotone

White   where there is nothing to see
But a white towel
Wipes the cymophanous[7] sweat
—Mist rise of living—
From your
Etiolate[8] body
And the white dawn
Of your   New Day
Shuts down on me

Unthinkable   that white over there—
Is smoke from your house

---

6. A period of critically important change.
7. Jewel-like, opalescent.

8. Weakened through stunted growth or development.

29

Evolution   fall foul of
Sexual equality
Prettily miscalculate
Similitude
Unnatural selection
Breed such sons and daughters
As shall jibber at each other
Uninterpretable cryptonyms[9]
Under the moon

Give them some way of braying brassily
For caressive calling
Or to homophonous[10] hiccoughs
Transpose the laugh
Let them suppose that tears
Are snowdrops or molasses
Or anything
But human insufficiencies
Begging dorsal vertebrae

Let meeting be the turning
To the antipodean[11]
And Form   a blurr
Anything—
But   seduce them
To the one
As simple satisfaction
For the other

Let them clash together
From their incognitoes
In seismic orgasm
For far further
Differentiation
Rather than watch
Own-self distortion
Wince in the alien ego

9. Word puzzles.   11. Completely opposite.
10. Sounding the same.

30

In some
Prenatal plagiarism
Foetal buffoons
Caught tricks

From archetypal pantomime
Stringing emotions
Looped aloft

For the blind eyes
That Nature knows us with
And the most of Nature   is green

What guaranty
For the proto-form
We fumble
Our souvenir ethics to

31

Crucifixion
Of a busybody
Longing to interfere so
With the intimacies
Of your insolent isolation

Crucifixion
Of an illegal ego's
Éclosion[12]
On your equilibrium
Caryatid[13]   of an idea

Crucifixion
Wracked arms
Index extremities
In vacuum
To the unbroken fall

---

12. Emergence of an insect from its pupal case.
13. A column in the shape of a draped female
form in a classical Greek temple.

32

The moon is cold
Joannes
Where the Mediterranean . . .

33

The prig of passion
To your professional paucity

Protoplasm was raving mad
Evolving us

34

Love—the preeminent littérateur[14]

1915–1917

Joannes is probably a composite figure of various lovers, including the futurists Marinetti
and Papini. Critic Peter Quartermain views "Love Songs to Joannes" as "a single work,
within which each song is at once a fragment and a whole. It attacks romanticized sexuality
as one of the principal means of subjugating women. It explores the damaging myth which
creates not love but powerless contempt, and through a variety of strategies, including unre-
solved ambiguity, approaches knowledge/knowing in an experiential (episodic) rather than
a schematized (narrative or linear) way." Loy's juxtaposition of clinical scientific jargon and
the stock diction of romantic love was shocking in its time and, as indicated above, led to
Pound's coinage of the term logopoeia, an "ironical play" with a word's "habits of usage."

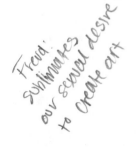

Freud: sublimates our sexual desire to create art

Brancusi's Golden Bird

put your own imagination

The toy
become the aesthetic archetype

signer not the signified?

As if
some patient peasant God
had rubbed and rubbed
the Alpha and Omega[1]
of Form
into a lump of metal

adjectives not necessarily associated with God — rather humble) just

Form deconstructed

convergence unable to be brought apart

---

14. Person closely involved with literature
(French archaic); Loy ironically connects pro-
motion of the theme of love with the male-
dominated profession of writing.

1. The first and last letters of the Greek alphabet.
In the New Testament's Revelations, Jesus identi-
fies himself as the alpha and omega—that is, the
beginning and the end.

* * *

A naked orientation
unwinged   unplumed
the ultimate rhythm
has lopped the extremities
of crest and claw
from
the nucleus of flight

The absolute act
of art
conformed
to continent sculpture
—bare as the brow of Osiris[2]—
this breast of revelation

an incandescent curve
licked by chromatic flames
in labyrinths of reflections

This gong
of polished hyperaesthesia[3]
shrills with brass
as the aggressive light
strikes
its significance

The immaculate
conception[4]
of the inaudible bird
occurs
in gorgeous reticence

1922

Constantin Brancusi (1876–1957) was a Romanian-French pioneer of sculptural abstraction. Brancusi's "Golden Bird" is a polished brass curving shape, elegant in its concentrated simplicity. Loy's poem was published in the famous November 1922 issue of the *Dial*, along with Eliot's *The Waste Land*, and opposite a photograph of Brancusi's "Golden Bird." Also appearing in that issue was Pound's essay on Brancusi.

2. Egyptian god of the underworld.
3. Oversensitivity.
4. Catholic doctrine teaches that Mary conceived Jesus through divine intervention while still a vir- gin. Loy puns on Brancusi's immaculate conception, as an artist, of his polished, abstracted, and simplified "Golden Bird."

Gertrude Stein

Curie
of the laboratory
of vocabulary
            she crushed
the tonnage
of consciousness
congealed to phrases
        to extract
a radium of the word

1924

In "Gertrude Stein," Loy equates Stein's clinical isolation of the active meaning of words with Madame Curie's discovery of the highly radioactive element radium. Both women, the Polish Marie Sklodowska Curie and the American Stein, were expatriates working in Paris at the same time. Curie shared the Nobel Prize for physics in 1903 and won the Nobel Prize for chemistry in 1911.

ANNE SPENCER
1882–1975

THROUGH A SERIES of trenchant poems, Anne Spencer emerged as an important figure in the Harlem Renaissance even though her life and art remained centered on her home and garden in Lynchburg, Virginia—a garden Spencer frequently drew on for imagery and which became a meeting place for African-American poets migrating between north and south.

Born Annie Bethel Scales Bannister in Henry County, Virginia, of mixed black, white, and Indian descent, Spencer moved with her mother after the breakup of her parents' marriage to West Virginia. She later attended the Virginia Seminary in Lynchburg, where she met her future husband, Edward Spencer. A brilliant student, she graduated valedictorian. Settling with her husband in Lynchburg, she served as librarian of the town's black high school. She had three children, cultivated her famous garden, fought the town's racism, and published poetry (her first poem appeared with the help of journalist H. L. Mencken). She became a close friend of writers and activists James Weldon Johnson and W. E. B. Du Bois.

Although she published only thirty poems in her lifetime, her work was appreciated and supported by such leading Harlem Renaissance figures as Claude McKay, Georgia Douglas Johnson, Arna Bontemps, Countee Cullen, and Langston Hughes (all included in this anthology).

Spencer was an ardent feminist and a strong supporter of African-American rights through the NAACP and her own local activities. Her youngest son, Chauncey Edward, a pilot, helped to found the much-decorated Tuskeegee Airmen, the first squadron of African-American fighter pilots in World War II. However, Spencer's poetry leans not toward direct advocacy but toward subtle inquiry, cool and oblique irony, and arresting natural imagery. As she indicated in Countee Cullen's 1927 anthology *Caroling Dusk*, "I have no civilized articulation for the things I hate. I proudly love being a Negro woman; [it's] so involved and interesting. We are the PROBLEM—the great national game of TABOO." Instead, Spencer embedded protest against injustice within startling images of natural beauty and grace.

FURTHER READING

J. Lee Greene. *Time's Unfading Garden: Anne Spencer's Life and Poetry*. Baton Rouge: Louisiana State University Press, 1977.
Venetria K. Patton and Maureen Honey, eds. "Anne Spencer." In *Double-Take: A Revisionist Harlem Renaissance Anthology*, 227–31. New Brunswick, N.J.: Rutgers University Press, 2001.

At the Carnival

Gay little Girl-of-the-Diving-Tank,
I desire a name for you,
Nice, as a right glove fits;
For you—who amid the malodorous
Mechanics of this unlovely thing,
Are darling of spirit and form.
I know you—a glance, and what you are
Sits-by-the-fire in my heart.
My Limousine-Lady knows you, or
Why does the slant-envy of her eye mark
Your straight air and radiant inclusive smile?
Guilt pins a fig-leaf; Innocence is its own adorning.
The bull-necked man knows you—this first time
His itching flesh sees form divine and vibrant health,
And thinks not of his avocation.
I came incuriously—

Set on no diversion save that my mind
Might safely nurse its brood of misdeeds
In the presence of a blind crowd.
The color of life was gray.
Everywhere the setting seemed right
For my mood!
Here the sausage and garlic booth
Sent unholy incense skyward;
There a quivering female-thing
Gestured assignations, and lied
To call it dancing;
There, too, were games of chance
With chances for none;
But oh! Girl-of-the-Tank, at last!
Gleaming Girl, how intimately pure and free
The gaze you send the crowd,
As though you know the dearth of beauty
In its sordid life.
We need you—my Limousine-Lady,
The bull-necked man and I.
Seeing you here brave and water-clean,
Leaven for the heavy ones of earth,
I am swift to feel that what makes
The plodder glad is good; and
Whatever is good is God.
The wonder is that you are here;
I have seen the queer in queer places,
But never before a heaven-fed
Naiad[1] of the Carnival-Tank!
Little Diver, Destiny for you,
Like as for me, is shod in silence;
Years may seep into your soul
The bacilli[2] of the usual and the expedient;
I implore Neptune to claim his child to-day!

1922

---

1. Water nymph of Greek and Roman myth.   2. Rod-shaped bacteria.

Before the Feast of Shushan

Garden of Shushan![1]
After Eden, all terrace, pool, and flower recollect thee:
Ye weavers in saffron and haze and Tyrian purple,[2]
Tell yet what range in color wakes the eye;
Sorcerer, release the dreams born here when
Drowsy, shifting palm-shade enspells the brain;
And sound! ye with harp and flute ne'er essay[3]
Before these star-noted birds escaped from paradise awhile to
Stir all dark, and dear, and passionate desire, till mine
Arms go out to be mocked by the softly kissing body of the wind—
Slave, send Vashti[4] to her King!

The fiery wattles of the sun startle into flame
The marbled towers of Shushan:
So at each day's wane, two peers—the one in
Heaven, the other on earth—welcome with their
Splendor the peerless beauty of the Queen.

Cushioned at the Queen's feet and upon her knee
Finding glory for mine head,—still, nearly shamed
Am I, the King, to bend and kiss with sharp
Breath the olive-pink of sandaled toes between;
Or lift me high to the magnet of a gaze, dusky,
Like the pool when but the moon-ray strikes to its depth;
Or closer press to crush a grape 'gainst lips redder
Than the grape, a rose in the night of her hair;
Then—Sharon's Rose[5] in my arms.

And I am hard to force the petals wide;
And you are fast to suffer and be sad.
Is any prophet come to teach a new thing
Now in a more apt time?
Have him 'maze how you say love is sacrament;

---

1. The lovely terraced gardens of the palace of Shushan in biblical Persia.
2. A purple dye first made in the ancient city of Tyre. Made from a secretion of various marine mollusks, and known for its beauty, this expensive dye was prized in ancient times.
3. Attempt, try.
4. The queen who refused to show her beauty at the feast of Shushan and thereby provoked the king's anger.
5. A flower mentioned in the Song of Solomon and associated with feminine beauty.

How says Vashti, love is both bread and wine;
How to the altar may not come to break and drink,
Hulky flesh nor fleshly spirit!

I, thy lord, like not manna for meat as a Judahn;[6]
I, thy master, drink, and red wine, plenty, and when
I thirst. Eat meat, and full, when I hunger.
I, thy King, teach you and leave you, when I list.
No woman in all Persia sets out strange action
To confuse Persia's lord—
Love is but desire and thy purpose fulfillment;
I, thy King, so say!

                                          1922

In the Old Testament Book of Esther (chapter 1), the king of Persia, "Ahasuerus which reigned, from India even unto Ethiopia, over an hundred and seven and twenty provinces," decreed an extended feast in his lovely palace of Shushan. He grew angry when his queen, Vashti, refused to show her beauty to the people, and—despite what might seem her commendable modesty—he divorced her, ultimately marrying the Jewish woman Esther instead. The speaker of the poem is King Ahasuerus, and the poem explores the will of a dominant male to control, through his whims, the actions of his wife.

White Things

Most things are colorful things—the sky, earth, and sea.
            Black men are most men; but the white are free!
White things are rare things; so rare, so rare
They stole from out a silvered world—somewhere.
Finding earth-plains fair plains, save greenly grassed,
They strewed white feathers of cowardice, as they passed;
            The golden stars with lances fine
            The hills all red and darkened pine,
They blanched with their wand of power;
And turned the blood in a ruby rose
To a poor white poppy-flower.
They pyred[1] a race of black, black men,
And burned them to ashes white; then,

---

6. Jewish person.
1. Burned to death, as on a funeral pyre, where, in some ancient cultures, living slaves were some-times burned alive along with their deceased masters.

Laughing, a young one claimed a skull,
For the skull of a black is white, not dull,
    But a glistening awful thing;
        Made, it seems, for this ghoul to swing
In the face of God with all his might,
And swear by the hell that sired him:
    "Man-maker, make white!"

1923

Lady, Lady

Lady, Lady, I saw your face,
Dark as night withholding a star . . .
The chisel fell, or it might have been
You had borne so long the yoke of men.
Lady, Lady, I saw your hands,
Twisted, awry, like crumpled roots,
Bleached poor white in a sudsy tub,
Wrinkled and drawn from your rub-a-dub.
Lady, Lady, I saw your heart,
And altered there in its darksome place
Were the tongues of flames the ancients knew,
Where the good God sits to spangle through.

1925

KAHLIL GIBRAN
[JUBRAN KHALIL JUBRAN]
1883–1931

KAHLIL GIBRAN is best known in the United States for *The Prophet* (1920), a spiritual best-seller translated into more than twenty languages. Although his poetry is not as critically acclaimed as that of fellow Arab Americans Elia Abu Madi (Madey) and Mikhail Naimy (both included in this anthology), his more serious poems deserve recognition. The Kahlil Gibran Centennial Foundation Memorial Garden in Washington, D.C., and a museum in his home village in Lebanon pay tribute to this writer's transcultural stature in literature and spirituality.

Although he was one of the first Arab-American poets to be published in the United States, Gibran did not begin his life here. He was born in Bisharri, a small village of Maronite Christians in Lebanon. At the age of twelve, he immigrated to the United States with his mother and his siblings, moving into a home in a Boston slum. He later returned to Lebanon and studied Arabic literature at Al-Hikma College in Beirut and then decided to settle again in Boston. Gibran's future seemed bleak because of the virulent hatred aimed at the new wave of immigrants from the Middle East. However, the Boston literary publisher Fred Holland Day (of Copeland and Day) took Gibran as his protégé, employing him as an illustrator. Gibran continued to develop his artistic talents and later illustrated many of his own books.

Gibran pursued and attracted many women but never married. As a young man, he courted the Boston poet-playwright Josephine Peabody, but she married a Harvard professor. The poet Louise Imogen Guiney, who published with Copeland and Day and was Day's friend, helped to discover and then to promote Gibran in literary circles in Boston. Mary Haskell played a major role in editing Gibran's first attempts to write in English, a project that led to *The Prophet*. Gibran often relied financially on his mother and then on his sister and Haskell, to whom he wrote love letters. His mother, sister, and half brother died of tuberculosis in Boston before Gibran became successful.

Gibran's free verse and prose poetry, written in a prophetic tone about Eastern spirituality and illustrated with drawings that tended to be mystical, reminded many readers of the English Romantic poet William Blake. Gibran's growing reputation enabled him to publish alongside such established literary figures as Eugene O'Neill, D. H. Lawrence, Sherwood Anderson, and Robert Frost. His work also launched the career of the young publisher Alfred A. Knopf. The critical praise showered on *The Madman* (1918) and *Jesus the Son of Man* (1928) brought him respect in many literary circles. But he endured scathing treatment as well. He was laughed off the stage when he read for the Poetry Society of America in New York. Nevertheless, his popular success has been enduring. All eight of his books in English have appeared in dozens of editions and remain in print.

Along with pursuing his publication career in the United States, Gibran formed the Pen League in New York City with ten émigré Syrian and Lebanese writers, including the poets Ameen Rihani, Mikhail Naimy, and Elia Abu Madi (Madey). Inspired by Walt Whitman and transcendentalism, he advocated that Arab poets write free verse and prose poetry because it would be accessible to more readers. Up until this time, Arab poets were compelled to imitate classical forms, with the required monorhyme mandating that each line end with the same sound. Gibran foresaw that a more popular, freer poetry would help build Arab nationalism and end the colonialism of the Ottoman Empire. He was distressed by Ottoman (Turkish) rule, which was leaving Arabs poor, illiterate, and politically powerless. The result of his efforts was a major revolution in Arab poetry. Gibran is now recognized as one of the founders of modern Arab literature and the Arab Renaissance. During World War I, he became the official spokesman for the Lebanese community among the émigré poets when Mount Lebanon was cut off by the Allied blockade of Turkish-held ports and suffered a devastating famine.

When Gibran died in 1931, he left all of his book royalties to his village in Lebanon. He was buried there, and a museum was erected in his honor. Gregory Orfalea and Sharif Elmusa report, however, that some of his gift was stolen to buy arms for the Lebanese civil war, "something that would have appalled the poet, who loathed Arab factionalism."

FURTHER READING

Kahlil Gibran. *Jesus the Son of Man*. New York: Alfred Knopf, 1928.
——. *The Madman, His Parables and Poems*. New York: Alfred Knopf, 1918.
——. *The Prophet*. New York: Alfred Knopf, 1920.
Kahlil Gibran and Jean Gibran. *Kahlil Gibran: His Life and World*. Boston; New York: Graphic Society, 1974.
Gregory Orfalea and Sharif Elmusa, eds. *Grape Leaves: A Century of Arab-American Poetry*. New York: Interlink Books, 2000.

The Fox

A fox looked at his shadow at sunrise and said, "I will have a
camel for lunch today." And all the morning he went about looking for
camels. But at noon he saw his shadow again — and he said, "A
mouse will do."

1918

"The Fox" is drawn from Lebanese folklore.

JAMIL B. HOLWAY
1883–1946

ALTHOUGH JAMIL HOLWAY wrote and published at the same time as Kahlil Gibran and his Syrian émigré group, the Pen League, he was never an insider with them. His poetry, which appeared in Arab-American newspapers and magazines,

was admired nevertheless. As the selection included here reveals, Holway some-
times wrote in a highly charged erotic and emotional language that continues to
influence Arab-American poets today.

Holway's early life as well as his strategy for adapting to American life may ac-
count in part for his distance from Gibran and his circle. Born in Damascus, Syria,
he did not immigrate to the United States until after he had graduated from the
American University in Beirut. In America, he practiced law, held a variety of gov-
ernment positions as an interpreter and examiner for the Immigration Service,
and worked in the "Fight for Freedom" drive for the U.S. Office of War Informa-
tion during World War II.

George Dimitri Selim is the translator of "Throbbings" included here.

FURTHER READING

Gregory Orfalea and Sharif Elmusa, eds. *Grape Leaves: A Century of Arab-American Poetry*.
New York: Interlink Books, 2000.

Throbbings

Zaynab[1] complained against me
to the judge of love.
"He has sly eyes," she told him,
which roam around me
to devour my beauty.
Judge of love!
I am not safe anymore.

"I think his eyes are two bees
raiding the honey
which sweetens my lips.
I see them as two eagles
hovering in space.
descending to snatch me.
I think, and from my fear,
I think strange things.
God knows how much I suffer from my thoughts.

"He invaded me with his eyes
and, as if this were not enough,

---

1. Zaynab is a popular Arabic female name.

he tried to lower my standing among people.
Hypocritically, he said
that I have stolen my beauty from the universe,
and that it was not created naturally in me.
That I have plundered the morning for a face,
the dusk for hair,
uniting both in me.
That from the gardens
I have stolen the flowers for cheeks
— my cheeks are rosy.
That I have covered my neck with pure snow,
and that my eyes are tinted with narcissus.

"When my voice enchanted him
he denied it, and said:
'It's a nightingale singing in the garden.'
With sword-like glances I struck him,
he said, and in his deep-red blood
I dyed my finger tips
and in his poems he chanted alluding to me.
So people said:
'His meanings are necklaces of pearls.'
Lord of verdicts!
Administer your justice between us.
Enough of his straying in love.
I've had enough!"

When the time of complaint was over,
the judge asked me:
"What is your answer,
you who are so passionately in love?"
I said:
"I find . . . that I am a criminal.
My insanity may not be deferred.
She has dispossessed me
of mind and heart."

1984

WILLIAM CARLOS WILLIAMS
1883–1963

WILLIAM CARLOS WILLIAMS belonged to the pioneering generation of experimental modernist poets, helping to change the way poetry was written in the twentieth century. Along with H.D., Ezra Pound, T. S. Eliot, and Marianne Moore, among others, he initiated a style of economy, speed, specificity, and metrical experiment. Relying on juxtaposition and implication rather than direct statement, his poems invite the reader to collaborate in the construction of meaning. In Williams's verbal experiments, the imagination—one of his great and recurring themes—seemed to have been born anew.

Williams differed in some respects from his experimentalist colleagues. Whereas H.D., Pound, and Eliot pursued their sources of knowledge and their formal experiments with utter dedication, Williams also concerned himself with popular culture and common understandings. He came late to the poetry of quotation that Pound, Eliot, and Moore had invented. He was more interested in American linguistic and social practices than were Pound or Eliot. Searching for the universal in the local, he stayed close to home, mining the sights, sounds, and idioms he encountered in northern New Jersey. Although he was well traveled, he did not expatriate himself to England, France, Switzerland, or Italy, as H.D., Pound, and Eliot did. He maintained a rivalry with the other modernist pioneers, especially with Eliot, whom he did not know personally. He thought that *The Waste Land*—with its elitist attitudes, esoteric references, and foreign languages—returned poetry "to the classroom," exactly where Williams didn't want it to be. He even criticized the work of his friend Ezra Pound: "Your English / is not specific enough." More devoted to what he called "the pleasures of democracy" than were Eliot and Pound, Williams wanted poetry to be part of the lives of ordinary people. When asked where his poetry came from, he replied, "From the mouths of Polish mothers," meaning that his work engaged the discourse of immigrants, working people, and other struggling Americans. In "Apology" he said that he wrote to honor "the beauty" in the faces of "nonentities." The faces of leading citizens stirred him also, but not "in the same way."

Williams was born in 1883 in Rutherford, New Jersey, a suburb of Paterson. His mother was a Puerto Rican immigrant of mixed Jewish, Basque, and Spanish ancestry. She had been an art student in France before coming to the United States. His father was a Cockney immigrant from England by way of the Caribbean. Williams grew up in a household of three spoken languages: Spanish, English, and French. He attended medical school at the University of Pennsylvania, where he specialized in obstetrics and pediatrics. There he befriended Ezra Pound, Marianne Moore, and H.D., all of whom also attended college in the Philadelphia area. He remained a close friend of Moore and an ambivalent one of Pound for the rest of his life. After an internship at French Hospital in New York City, Williams set up a family practice in a home office in Rutherford. He married Florence (Flossie) Herman in 1912, and the couple had two sons. His life as a physician and family man appears obliquely in poems that are otherwise noted for their anonymity. The poems may be set on the way to work ("The Young Housewife," "Spring and All") or at home ("Danse Russe," "This Is Just to Say").

For many decades Williams wrote poetry in the late afternoon, after a full day of caring for patients and before joining the rest of his family for dinner. He stayed well versed in literary developments through regular visits to New York City, two extended trips to Europe with his wife in 1924 and 1927, and voracious reading. Although Williams belonged to the "knowable world" of his lower-middle-class suburb, attending neighborhood functions and listening to his patients talk, he also belonged to the cultural avant-garde, attending art museums and poetry readings, corresponding with visual artists such as Charles Demuth, Marsden Hartley, and Alfred Stieglitz and with poets such as Pound, Moore, Amy Lowell, Wallace Stevens, and Louis Zukofsky.

As a poet, Williams initially imitated John Keats and Walt Whitman. He found his own distinctive style in such early poems as "The Young Housewife" (1916), "Queen-Anne's-Lace" (1921), and "The Red Wheelbarrow" (1923). These poems helped create the modernist revolution by combining meticulous, often painterly observation with highly inventive word choices and stanza forms. For example, in place of the traditional sonnet or quatrain, "The Red Wheelbarrow" employs stanzas consisting of a line with three words (and three or four syllables) followed by a line with one word (and two syllables). This spare and simple form "depends" on the power of its images, the freshness of its language, and the ability of its words to strike sparks off each other. Perhaps never before had a poetic line consisted of the single preposition "upon." And perhaps never before had such common nouns as "water" and "chicken" carried so much resonance.

Williams viewed poetry as an immersion in material existence. Even more than H.D. and Pound, he wrote poetry of a stunning phenomenological immediacy. Instead of comparing forest and sea (as in H.D.'s "Oread") or faces and petals (as in Pound's "In the Station of the Metro"), Williams often gives us a single thing, next to other things but not compared to them. His red wheelbarrow stands beside the white chickens, entirely separate from them (in "The Red Wheelbarrow"), just as his bits of green glass remain distinct from the walls surrounding them (in "Between Walls"). Williams's motto, memorably articulated in *Paterson*, was "no ideas but in things." But Williams always knew that poems, as verbal assemblages, are ontologically different from the things they describe. He once wrote that a poem "is a small (or large) machine made of words." As J. Hillis Miller has observed, Williams was both a "poet of reality" and one who evoked "the linguistic moment"—the moment when language makes itself visible. His topic was the interplay between words and things.

Williams, however, was more than an epistemological and metapoetic poet. He was also a powerful psychological poet. He often achieved insight by confronting darkness or disorder. The speaker of "Danse Russe" describes himself as "born to be lonely." "The Great Figure" evokes the pain and incertitude of life in "the dark city." "These" suggests the mental and physical suffering caused by war. "The Descent" and "Ivy Crown" explore the challenges of aging and ill health, while also locating imaginative and affectional rewards that remain.

Finally, Williams was one of the great social poets of the century, evoking the material conditions and cultural practices of people around him. The son of immigrants, he was interested in common people like himself. He was also interested in cultural inheritances, his own (Latin American, Spanish, French, English) and those of others. He wrote of a young white housewife, a Chinese-American tradesman, an African-American working woman, a mixed-race housemaid, and an old woman eating plums (in "The Young Housewife," "Chinese Nightingale," "Apology," "To Elsie," and "To a Poor Old Woman"). He highlighted the problems faced by working people struggling to get by, the contending voices he heard around him. Whereas the other experimental modernists named their long poems after Dante (Pound's *Cantos*), biblical narrative (H.D.'s *Tribute to the Angels*), or classical music (Eliot's *Four Quartets*), Williams named his after a New Jersey city (*Paterson*). Although rooted at home, Williams was as thoroughly cosmopolitan as any of the modernists. He translated poems from Spanish, French, and Chinese. He took inspiration from the Russian dancer Nijinsky (in "Danse Russe"), from the Flemish painter Peter Brueghel (in "The Dance" and "Landscape with the Fall of Icarus"), from the Chilean poet Pablo Neruda (in "Tribute to Neruda"), and from the Chinese poet Ho Chih-Chang (in "Ho Chih-Chang"). Williams was more pan-American than most of his peers. (In this he resembled Langston Hughes, Salomón de la Selva, and Luis Torres.) He referred frequently to Puerto Rico, Central America, and the Caribbean, and his book on the American past, *In the American Grain*, included chapters on the West Indies, Mexico, and Québec.

In the 1930s, the years of the Great Depression, Williams continued to write short poems with stunning visual and verbal juxtapositions, but he also veered more deliberately toward social themes. "The Yachts" (1935), for example, reflects the Depression in its tragic depiction of the consequences of ruthless competition. By the 1940s, Williams was semi-retired, a condition that allowed him to write longer and more sustained poems. Spending days at the Paterson Public Library researching the history of the city, he composed *Paterson* (1946–58), his epic poem about a man, a city, and the dilemmas of language. In *Paterson* he concluded that language is an inverted "bell," empty at its center, with meanings that never cease being contingent. His initial project of bringing words and things closer together thus ended in a frank recognition that the two would remain forever apart, that words could not bring him into an "approximate co-extension with the universe," as he had hoped in *Spring and All* (1923). Never losing interest in the world around him, Williams realized that all poetry, even that which most intently evoked a red wheelbarrow or a woman eating plums, would ultimately remain a play of language, contained within and given meaning by the institution of poetry. He thought more intently than ever about issues of poetic language and form, terming his own diction the "American idiom" and inventing a "variable foot" for "The Descent" (1954).

In the 1950s, Williams suffered a series of reversals. He was denied the honor of serving as Poetry Consultant to the Library of Congress (a position now called Poet Laureate) because his liberal politics clashed with the McCarthyite politics of the times. For a poet who had never received the attention and praise given to other pioneering modernists, this rejection was a blow. Moreover, following a heart attack in 1948, Williams suffered several debilitating strokes beginning in 1951. Finally, his relationship with his wife, Flossie, became strained after he confessed to having had sexual affairs with other women. Retired from medicine and finding it difficult to write, Williams had to cope with the depression and loneliness that formerly he had been able to keep at bay. Whereas his earlier work reveals a powerful libido, the poems of this period exhibit guilt and self-questioning. Such poems as "Landscape with the Fall of Icarus" reflect his personal strains as well as his continued determination to find moments of beauty. In "The Ivy Crown," for example, the speaker consoles himself for the pain he endured and caused by postulating that "the imagination / across the sorry facts / lifts us / to make roses." Williams's verbal and visual imagination, always so central to his existence, ultimately became his saving grace. Williams died in 1963 at the age of eighty. In his final years he had been unable to speak, to move, or to write.

At the end of his career Williams finally began to gain the recognition he had lacked. He received the Bollingen Award in 1953, and his last volume, *Pictures from Brueghel*, won him a posthumous Pulitzer Prize. More importantly, his work was having an astonishing impact on a new generation of mid-century poets, ranging from Charles Olson, Denise Levertov, and Robert Creeley to Robert Lowell and Allen Ginsberg. For multicultural poets of today, he remains a particularly vital influence and inspiration. Therefore, Williams ultimately made his mark in two ways—as a modernist pioneer and as a precursor and guide to poets to come. Although less celebrated in his lifetime than were Pound, Eliot, and Frost, he persisted in his poetic quest. He is now often viewed as the most influential modernist poet of them all. In an early poem, "El Hombre," he imaged himself as a star shining alone, overlooked in the glare of a sunrise. His star shines today more brightly than ever.

FURTHER READING

Steven Gould Axelrod and Helen Deese, eds. *Critical Essays on William Carlos Williams*. New York: G. K. Hall, 1995.

James Breslin. *William Carlos Williams: An American Artist*. New York: Oxford University Press, 1970.

Kerry Driscoll. *William Carlos Williams and the Maternal Muse*. Ann Arbor: UMI Research Press, 1987.

Paul Mariani. *William Carlos Williams: A New World Naked*. New York: McGraw-Hill, 1981.

Julio Marzán. *The Spanish American Roots of William Carlos Williams*. Austin: University of Texas Press, 1994.

J. Hillis Miller. *Poets of Reality*. Cambridge, Mass.: Harvard University Press, 1965.

Peter Schmidt. *William Carlos Williams, the Arts, and Literary Tradition*. Baton Rouge: Louisiana State University Press, 1988.

Linda Welshimer Wagner. *The Prose of William Carlos Williams*. Middletown, Conn.: Wesleyan University Press, 1970.

William Carlos Williams. *Autobiography*. New York: New Directions, 1951.

——. *Collected Poems*. Vol. 1, ed. A. Walton Litz and Christopher MacGowan. Vol. 2, ed. Christopher MacGowan. New York: New Directions, 1986, 1988.

——. *Collected Stories*. 1961; reprint, New York: New Directions, 1996.

——. *Imaginations*. Ed. Webster Schott. New York: New Directions, 1970.

——. *In the American Grain*. New York: New Directions, 1925.

——. *I Wanted to Write a Poem*. New York: New Directions, 1967.

——. *Paterson*. Ed. Christopher MacGowan. New York: New Directions, 1992.

William Carlos Williams Review. Ed. Bryce Conrad. Published by Texas Tech University Press. http://english.ttu.edu/WCWR.

The Young Housewife

At ten A.M. the young housewife
moves about in negligee behind
the wooden walls of her husband's house.
I pass solitary in my car.

Then again she comes to the curb
to call the ice-man, fish-man, and stands
shy, uncorseted, tucking in
stray ends of hair, and I compare her
to a fallen leaf.

The noiseless wheels of my car
rush with a crackling sound over
dried leaves as I bow and pass smiling.

1916

In "The Young Housewife" Williams discovered his voice as a witness and image maker of the small-town scene. Late in life he commented on the poem: "Whenever a man sees a beautiful woman it's an occasion for poetry—compensating beauty with beauty." Nevertheless, note the way that the poem implies a critique of both the woman's husband and the speaker himself.

Chinese Nightingale

Long before dawn your light
Shone in the window, Sam Wu;
You were at your trade.

1917

Apology

Why do I write today?

The beauty of
the terrible faces
of our nonentities
stirs me to it:

colored women
day workers—
old and experienced—
returning home at dusk
in cast off clothing
faces like
old Florentine oak.

Also

the set pieces
of your faces stir me—
leading citizens—
but not
in the same way.

1917

Tract

I will teach you my townspeople
how to perform a funeral —
for you have it over a troop
of artists —
unless one should scour the world —
you have the ground sense necessary.

See! the hearse leads.
I begin with a design for a hearse.
For Christ's sake not black —
nor white either — and not polished!
Let it be weathered — like a farm wagon —
with gilt wheels (this could be
applied fresh at small expense)
or no wheels at all:
a rough dray to drag over the ground.

Knock the glass out!
My God — glass, my townspeople!
For what purpose? Is it for the dead
to look out or for us to see
how well he is housed or to see
the flowers or the lack of them —
or what?
To keep the rain and snow from him?
He will have a heavier rain soon:
pebbles and dirt and what not.
Let there be no glass —
and no upholstery, phew!
and no little brass rollers
and small easy wheels on the bottom —
my townspeople what are you thinking of?

A rough plain hearse then
with gilt wheels and no top at all.
On this the coffin lies
by its own weight.

                No wreaths please —
especially no hot house flowers.
Some common memento is better,

something he prized and is known by:
his old clothes—a few books perhaps—
God knows what! You realize
how we are about these things
my townspeople—
something will be found—anything
even flowers if he had come to that.
So much for the hearse.

For heaven's sake though see to the driver!
Take off the silk hat! In fact
that's no place at all for him—
up there unceremoniously
dragging our friend out to his own dignity!
Bring him down—bring him down!
Low and inconspicuous! I'd not have him ride
on the wagon at all—damn him—
the undertaker's understrapper!
Let him hold the reins
and walk at the side
and inconspicuously too!

Then briefly as to yourselves:
Walk behind—as they do in France,
seventh class, or if you ride
Hell take curtains! Go with some show
of inconvenience; sit openly—
to the weather as to grief.
Or do you think you can shut grief in?
What—from us? We who have perhaps
nothing to lose? Share with us
share with us—it will be money
in your pockets.
                  Go now
I think you are ready.

                    1917

Unlike "The Young Housewife" (above), which includes no explicit commentary on its visual objects, "Tract" is all commentary. James Breslin argues that in this early poem Williams "is too conspicuously present as teacher, artist, and personality." Williams himself commented, apropos of "Tract": "I wanted to conform but I couldn't so I wrote my poetry."

El Hombre

It's a strange courage
you give me ancient star:

Shine alone in the sunrise
toward which you lend no part!

1917

The title is Spanish for "The Man." When Wallace Stevens used it as the opening of his poem "Nuances of a Theme by Williams," Williams felt "deeply touched."

Danse Russe

If I when my wife is sleeping
and the baby and Kathleen[1]
are sleeping
and the sun is a flame-white disc
in silken mists
above shining trees, —
if I in my north room
dance naked, grotesquely
before my mirror
waving my shirt round my head
and singing softly to myself:
"I am lonely, lonely.
I was born to be lonely,
I am best so!"
If I admire my arms, my face,
my shoulders, flanks, buttocks
against the yellow drawn shades, —

Who shall say I am not
the happy genius[2] of my household?

1917

"Danse Russe" was inspired by the dancing of Vaslav Nijinsky, a member of Sergei Diaghilev's Ballets Russes company. Williams attended a performance in New York in 1916.

1. The Williams family's nursemaid was named Kathleen. She ultimately left to work in a pediatric hospital.

2. The multiple meanings include local guardian (*genius loci*), spirit or demon, and a person of extraordinary ability.

Portrait of a Lady

Your thighs are appletrees
whose blossoms touch the sky.
Which sky? The sky
where Watteau[1] hung a lady's
slipper. Your knees
are a southern breeze—or
a gust of snow. Agh! What
sort of man was Fragonard?
—as if that answered
anything. Ah, yes—below
the knees, since the tune
drops that way, it is
one of those white summer days,
the tall grass of your ankles
flickers upon the shore—
Which shore?—
the sand clings to my lips—
Which shore?
Agh, petals maybe. How
should I know?
Which shore? Which shore?
I said petals from an appletree.

1920

"Portrait of a Lady" alludes to Jean-Honoré Fragonard's painting *The Swing* (1766), in which a beautiful young woman has kicked her slipper into the air. The multiple voices in this poem evoke an inner debate about specificity and precision in artistic description.

Queen-Anne's-Lace

Her body is not so white as
anemone petals nor so smooth—nor
so remote a thing. It is a field
of the wild carrot taking
the field by force; the grass
does not raise above it.
Here is no question of whiteness,

---

1. Jean-Antoine Watteau (1684–1721), another French painter.

white as can be, with a purple mole
at the center of each flower.
Each flower is a hand's span
of her whiteness. Wherever
his hand has lain there is
a tiny purple blemish. Each part
is a blossom under his touch
to which the fibres of her being
stem one by one, each to its end,
until the whole field is a
white desire, empty, a single stem,
a cluster, flower by flower,
a pious wish to whiteness gone over —
or nothing.

1921

Queen Anne's lace is a variety of wild carrot, a common field plant featuring groups of minute white flowers circling a single purple one. In this poem a woman's body and a field of flowers become intersecting realities. J. Hillis Miller comments that in the space of the poem, "things, the mind, and words coincide in closest intimacy." He adds that the poem might be summed up thusly: "A poet's desire to possess the world is like his desire to possess a beautiful woman." Williams himself, in his later years, said only: "Flossie again."

The Great Figure

Among the rain
and lights
I saw the figure 5
in gold
on a red
firetruck
moving
tense
unheeded
to gong clangs
siren howls
and wheels rumbling
through the dark city.

1921

Williams once explained that while walking in New York he "heard a great clatter of bells and the roar of a fire engine passing the end of the street down Ninth Avenue." Turning, he saw "a golden figure 5 on a red background flash by." On another occasion he mentioned "the contemptuous feeling I had at the time for all 'great' figures in public life compared with that figure 5 riding in state with full panoply down the streets of the city ignored by everyone but the artist." Williams's friend Charles Demuth used the poem as the basis for his well-known painting "I Saw the Figure 5 in Gold" (1928).

Spring and All

By the road to the contagious hospital[1]
under the surge of the blue
mottled clouds driven from the
northeast—a cold wind. Beyond, the
waste of broad, muddy fields
brown with dried weeds, standing and fallen

patches of standing water
the scattering of tall trees

All along the road the reddish
purplish, forked, upstanding, twiggy
stuff of bushes and small trees
with dead, brown leaves under them
leafless vines—

Lifeless in appearance, sluggish
dazed spring approaches—

They enter the new world naked,
cold, uncertain of all
save that they enter. All about them
the cold, familiar wind—

Now the grass, tomorrow
the stiff curl of wildcarrot leaf

One by one objects are defined[2]—
It quickens:[3] clarity, outline of leaf

                    *   *   *

---

1. That is, a hospital for patients with contagious diseases.

2. Visually and perhaps linguistically as well.
3. Comes alive; accelerates.

But now the stark dignity of
entrance — Still, the profound change
has come upon them: rooted, they
grip down and begin to awaken

1923

"Spring and All" appears to focus intensely and literally on seasonal death and rebirth. Nevertheless, in its initial publication in the volume *Spring and All*, the poem, then untitled, immediately followed the prose passage reprinted here as the last Williams item. In that context the poem seems to reflect on the death and rebirth of the imagination as well. Williams commented that "Spring and All" is "one of the best images I have ever perpetrated." Although the first three verse-paragraphs include no active verb, they forecast the potential energy of the dormant landscape through the use of such verbals as "surge," "driven," "standing," and "fallen." It has been said that the difference between the lyric and fiction is that in the lyric nothing happens; this poem would seem to belie that distinction. The following three poems, ending with "The Red Wheelbarrow," also appeared, untitled, in *Spring and All*. Williams supplied their titles in subsequent printings.

The Rose

The rose is obsolete
but each petal ends in
an edge, the double facet
cementing the grooved
columns of air — The edge
cuts without cutting
meets — nothing — renews
itself in metal or porcelain —

whither? It ends —

But if it ends
the start is begun
so that to engage roses
becomes a geometry —

Sharper, neater, more cutting
figured in majolica[1] —
the broken plate
glazed with a rose

1. Pottery from Majorca or Italy that is highly decorated and has an opaque glaze.

*   *   *

Somewhere the sense
makes copper roses
steel roses —

The rose carried weight of love
but love is at an end — of roses
It is at the edge of the
petal that love waits

Crisp, worked to defeat
laboredness — fragile
plucked, moist, half-raised
cold, precise, touching

What

The place between the petal's
edge and the

From the petal's edge a line starts
that being of steel
infinitely fine, infinitely
rigid penetrates
the Milky Way[2]
without contact — lifting
from it — neither hanging
nor pushing —

The fragility of the flower
unbruised
penetrates space.

1923

This poem of renewal, like some of Gertrude Stein's texts, has affinities with the dissection and reconstruction of visual objects that occur in cubist paintings. In *Spring and All* Williams advises a poet to write about "things with which he is familiar, simple things — at the same time to detach them from ordinary experience to the imagination." He later said of "The Rose," "I was experimenting in the mode of the French painters — the fragmentation of Picasso."

2. Our galaxy, appearing in the night sky as a luminous band of stars that are too distant to be seen individually.

To Elsie

The pure products of America
go crazy—
mountain folk from Kentucky

or the ribbed north end of
Jersey
with its isolate lakes and

valleys, its deaf-mutes, thieves
old names
and promiscuity between

devil-may-care men who have taken
to railroading
out of sheer lust of adventure—

and young slatterns,[1] bathed
in filth
from Monday to Sunday

to be tricked out that night
with gauds[2]
from imaginations which have no

peasant traditions to give them
character
but flutter and flaunt

sheer rags—succumbing without
emotion
save numbed terror

under some hedge of choke-cherry
or viburnum[3]—
which they cannot express—

Unless it be that marriage
perhaps
with a dash of Indian blood

* * *

1. Untidy or sluttish women.
2. Showy ornaments.

3. Shrub with white flowers and red or black berries that is common in New Jersey.

will throw up a girl so desolate
so hemmed round
with disease or murder

that she'll be rescued by an
agent[4]—
reared by the state and

sent out at fifteen to work in
some hard-pressed
house in the suburbs—

some doctor's family, some Elsie—
voluptuous water
expressing with broken

brain the truth about us—
her great
ungainly hips and flopping breasts

addressed to cheap
jewelry
and rich young men with fine eyes

as if the earth under our feet
were
an excrement of some sky

and we degraded prisoners
destined
to hunger until we eat filth

while the imagination strains
after deer
going by fields of goldenrod in

the stifling heat of September
Somehow
it seems to destroy us

It is only in isolate flecks that
something
is given off

4. Social worker.

*   *   *

No one
to witness
and adjust, no one to drive the car

1923

The character of "Elsie" is based on a mentally challenged domestic worker hired by the Williams family from the state orphanage. She succeeded "Kathleen," mentioned above in "Danse Russe."

The Red Wheelbarrow

so much depends
upon

a red wheel
barrow

glazed with rain
water

beside the white
chickens.

1923

Williams described the initial publication of this poem in *Spring and All* as "eight lines . . . without a title, simply a number on a page." He also said that "the rhythm, though no more than a fragment, denotes a certain unquenchable exaltation." In a later printing, he explained that "The Red Wheelbarrow" had been inspired by a visit to a Connecticut farm owned by an African-American family. Note the poem's contrasts of shape, color, texture, and temperature and the way that it dynamically transforms visual phenomena ("wheel," "rain," "white") into something subtly or starkly different.

Brilliant Sad Sun

LEE'S
LUNCH

Spaghetti   Oysters
a Specialty   Clams

*   *   *

and raw Winter's done
to a turn — Restaurant: Spring!
Ah, Madam, what good are your thoughts

romantic but true
beside this gaiety of the sun
and that huge appetite?

Look!
from a glass pitcher she serves
clear water to the white chickens.

What are your memories
beside that purity?
The empty pitcher dangling

from her grip
her coarse voice croaks
Bon jor'[1]

And Patti,[2] on her first concert tour
sang at your house in Mayaguez[3]
and your brother was there

What beauty
beside your sadness — and
what sorrow

1927

Kerry Driscoll comments about "Brilliant Sad Sun": "Williams' mother was his muse. . . . This impressionistic poem concerns the disparity between past and present, memory and direct experience. The unusual arrangement of the first four lines mimics an advertisement, perhaps the signboard of an unpretentious local eatery. Although the dramatic situation of the poem is unclear, the sense of vividness and immediacy created by the opening stanzas suggests that mother and son may in fact be dining at Lee's Lunch or simply out for a drive." Driscoll adds that the poem's title is a double entendre: "This celestial image refers most obviously to Elena, who occupies the center of the text and, in her old age, resembles the diminished splendor of the setting sun. Yet there is another possibility as well, that of 'brilliant sad *son*.'"

---

1. Probably "good day" in a version of French (*bonjour*) or Italian (*buon giorno*).
2. Adelina Patti (1843–1919), a Spanish-Italian opera singer, one of the great sopranos of her time.
3. The Puerto Rican town in which Williams's mother, Elena Hoheb Williams, grew up.

This Is Just to Say

I have eaten
the plums
that were in
the icebox

and which
you were probably
saving
for breakfast

Forgive me
they were delicious
so sweet
and so cold

1934

The Locust Tree in Flower

Among
of
green

stiff
old
bright

broken
branch
come

white
sweet
May

again

1935

This is the second version of "The Locust Tree in Flower." Williams explained that the first, longer version didn't give a picture of the locust flower, "so I had to cut it down . . . I literally cut out inessential lines."

To a Poor Old Woman

munching a plum on
the street a paper bag
of them in her hand

They taste good to her
They taste good
to her. They taste
good to her

You can see it by
the way she gives herself
to the one half
sucked out in her hand

Comforted
a solace of ripe plums
seeming to fill the air
They taste good to her

1935

The Yachts

contend in a sea which the land partly encloses
shielding them from the too-heavy blows
of an ungoverned ocean which when it chooses

tortures the biggest hulls, the best man knows
to pit against its beatings, and sinks them pitilessly.
Mothlike in mists, scintillant[1] in the minute

brilliance of cloudless days, with broad bellying sails
they glide to the wind tossing green water
from their sharp prows while over them the crew crawls

ant-like, solicitously grooming them, releasing,
making fast as they turn, lean far over and having
caught the wind again, side by side, head for the mark.

1. Sparkling.

*   *   *

In a well guarded arena of open water surrounded by
lesser and greater craft which, sycophant,[2] lumbering
and flittering follow them, they appear youthful, rare

as the light of a happy eye, live with the grace
of all that in the mind is fleckless,[3] free and
naturally to be desired. Now the sea which holds them

is moody, lapping their glossy sides, as if feeling
for some slightest flaw but fails completely.
Today no race. Then the wind comes again. The yachts

move, jockeying for a start, the signal is set and they
are off. Now the waves strike at them but they are too
well made, they slip through, though they take in canvas.

Arms with hands grasping seek to clutch at the prows.
Bodies thrown recklessly in the way are cut aside.
It is a sea of faces about them in agony, in despair

until the horror of the race dawns staggering the mind;
the whole sea become an entanglement of watery bodies
lost to the world bearing what they cannot hold. Broken,

beaten, desolate, reaching from the dead to be taken up
they cry out, failing, failing! their cries rising
in waves still as the skillful yachts pass over.

1935

Williams commented that in writing "The Yachts" he "was thinking of terza rima, but gave up rime—a *very* vague imitation of Dante." He also explained that "the yachts do not sink but go on with the race while only *in the imagination* are they seen to founder. It is a false situation which the yachts typify with the beauty of their movements while the real situation (of the poor) is desperate while 'the skillful yachts pass over.'"

2. Servile flatterer.
3. Williams defined this word as "perhaps spot-
less, without fault."

Between Walls

the back wings
of the

hospital where
nothing

will grow lie
cinders

in which shine
the broken

pieces of a green
bottle
                1938

These

are the desolate, dark weeks
when nature in its barrenness
equals the stupidity of man.

The year plunges into night
and the heart plunges
lower than night

to an empty, windswept place
without sun, stars or moon
but a peculiar light as of thought

that spins a dark fire —
whirling upon itself until,
in the cold, it kindles

to make a man aware of nothing
that he knows, not loneliness
itself—Not a ghost but

would be embraced—emptiness,
despair—(They
whine and whistle) among

*   *   *

the flashes and booms of war;
houses of whose rooms
the cold is greater than can be thought,

the people gone that we loved,
the beds lying empty, the couches
damp, the chairs unused—

Hide it away somewhere
out of the mind, let it get roots
and grow, unrelated to jealous

ears and eyes—for itself.
In this mine they come to dig—all.
Is this the counterfoil[1] to sweetest

music? The source of poetry that
seeing the clock stopped, says,
The clock has stopped

that ticked yesterday so well?
and hears the sound of lakewater
splashing—that is now stone.

                                        1938

"These," a poem of political and spiritual despair, may suggest the debilitating effects that looming World War II had on the poetic imagination.

The Dance

In Brueghel's great picture, The Kermess,[1]
the dancers go round, they go round and
around, the squeal and the blare and the
tweedle of bagpipes, a bugle and fiddles
tipping their bellies (round as the thick-
sided glasses whose wash they impound)
their hips and their bellies off balance
to turn them. Kicking and rolling about

1. Receipt or stub,
1. A fair or festival (in Belgium or the Nether-
lands).

the Fair Grounds, swinging their butts, those
shanks must be sound to bear up under such
rollicking measures, prance as they dance
in Brueghel's great picture, The Kermess.

1944

"The Dance" renders into words a painting called *The Kermess* or *The Wedding Dance*
(1566) by the Flemish artist Pieter Brueghel the Elder (1525–1569), well known for his vigor-
ous depictions of peasant life. The poem pays tribute to the joy of poetry, visual art, dance,
and music as well as the social life of peasants.

FROM *Paterson*

FROM *The Delineaments of the Giants*

Paterson[1] lies in the valley under the Passaic Falls
its spent waters forming the outline of his back. He
lies on his right side, head near the thunder
of the waters filling his dreams! Eternally asleep,
his dreams walk about the city where he persists
incognito. Butterflies settle on his stone ear.
Immortal he neither moves nor rouses and is seldom
seen, though he breathes and the subtleties of his machinations
drawing their substance from the noise of the pouring river[2]
animate a thousand automatons.[3] Who because they
neither know their sources nor the sills[4] of their
disappointments walk outside their bodies aimlessly for the most part,
locked and forgot in their desires — unroused.

> — Say it, no ideas but in things —
> nothing but the blank faces of the houses
> and cylindrical trees
> bent, forked by preconception and accident —
> split, furrowed, creased, mottled, stained —
> secret — into the body of the light!

From above, higher than the spires, higher
even than the office towers, from oozy fields

1. The city in northern New Jersey, depicted as a
gigantic man with a dreaming mind.
2. The Passaic River, which runs along the city
and drops down a cataract.

3. The citizens of the city, pictured as the giant's
dreams or thoughts.
4. Horizontal supports, foundations, or layers.

abandoned to grey beds of dead grass,
black sumac, withered weed-stalks,
mud and thickets cluttered with dead leaves—
the river comes pouring in above the city
and crashes from the edge of the gorge
in a recoil of spray and rainbow mists—

> (What common language to unravel?
> . . combed into straight lines
> from that rafter of a rock's
> lip.)[5]

A man like a city and a woman like a flower
—who are in love. Two women. Three women
Innumerable women, each like a flower.

                                        But

only one man—like a city.

In regard to the poems I left with you; will you be so kind as to return them to me at my new address?[6] And without bothering to comment upon them if you should find that embarrassing—for it was the human situation and not the literary one that motivated my phone call and visit.

Besides, I know myself to be more the woman than the poet; and to concern myself less with the publishers of poetry than with . . . living . . .

But they set up an investigation . . . and my doors are bolted forever (I hope forever) against all public welfare workers, professional do-gooders and the like.

> Jostled as are the waters approaching
> the brink, his[7] thoughts
> interlace, repel and cut under,
> rise rock-thwarted and turn aside
> but forever strain forward—or strike
> an eddy and whirl, marked by a
> leaf or curdy spume, seeming
> to forget   .

5. In his *Autobiography* Williams wrote that the Passaic Falls imaginatively represents "a speech or a voice, a speech in particular; it is the poem itself that is the answer."
6. This prose passage is taken from a letter to Williams by the poet Marcia Nardi (1901–1990). Williams encouraged Nardi, helped her to publish

her work, and ultimately clashed with her. Her letters, condensed and reproduced throughout the first two parts of *Paterson*, critique Williams for divorcing his poetry from the experience of "living." As it progresses, *Paterson* adapts itself to this challenge.
7. *Paterson's*.

Retake later the advance and
are replaced by succeeding hordes
pushing forward—they coalesce now
glass-smooth with their swiftness,
quiet or seem to quiet as at the close
they leap to the conclusion and
fall, fall in air! as if
floating, relieved of their weight,
split apart, ribbons; dazed, drunk
with the catastrophe of the descent
floating unsupported
to hit the rocks: to a thunder,
as if lightning had struck

All lightness lost, weight regained in
the repulse, a fury of
escape driving them to rebound
upon those coming after—
keeping nevertheless to the stream, they
retake their course, the air full
of the tumult and of spray
connotative of the equal air, coeval,[8]
filling the void

And there, against him, stretches the low mountain.[9]
The Park's her head, carved, above the Falls, by the quiet
river; Colored crystals the secret of those rocks;
farms and ponds, laurel and the temperate wild cactus,
yellow flowered . . facing him, his
arm supporting her, by the *Valley of the Rocks*,[10] asleep.
Pearls at her ankles, her monstrous hair
spangled with apple-blossoms is scattered about into
the back country, waking their dreams—where the deer run
and the wood-duck nests protecting his gallant plumage.

In February 1857, David Hower, a poor shoemaker with a large family, out of
work and money, collected a lot of mussels from Notch Brook near the City of

---

8. Of the same age.
9. Garret Mountain, the female counterpart to
Paterson.

10. A picturesque basin east of the falls.

Paterson.[11] He found in eating them many hard substances. At first he threw
them away but at last submitted some of them to a jeweler who gave him twenty-
five to thirty dollars for the lot. Later he found others. One pearl of fine lustre
was sold to Tiffany for $900 and later to the Empress Eugenie for $2,000 to be
known thenceforth as the "Queen Pearl," the finest of its sort in the world today.

News of this sale created such excitement that search for the pearls was started
throughout the country. The Unios (mussels) at Notch Brook and elsewhere
were gathered by the millions and destroyed often with little or no result. A large
round pearl, weighing 400 grains which would have been the finest pearl of
modern times, was ruined by boiling open the shell.

> Twice a month Paterson[12] receives
> communications from the Pope and Jacques Barzun
> (Isocrates).[13] His works
> have been done into French
> and Portuguese. And clerks in the post-
> office ungum rare stamps from
> his packages and steal them for their
> childrens' albums   .

Say it! No ideas but in things. Mr.
Paterson has gone away
to rest and write. Inside the bus one sees
his thoughts sitting and standing. His
thoughts alight and scatter—

Who are these people (how complex
the mathematic) among whom I[14] see myself
in the regularly ordered plateglass of
his thoughts, glimmering before shoes and bicycles?
They walk incommunicado, the
equation is beyond solution, yet
its sense is clear—that they may live
his thought is listed in the Telephone
Directory—

*   *   *

11. This passage of historical prose (source un-
known) introduces the theme of commercial
exploitation.
12. Paterson here seems to become a parodic ver-
sion of Williams himself.
13. Jacques Barzun (b. 1907) was a notable scholar
at Columbia University. Isocrates (436–338
B.C.E.) was an Athenian orator.
14. The poem's "I," introduced here, remains
distinct from, though connected to, the giant
Paterson.

And derivatively, for the Great Falls,
PISS-AGH![15] the giant lets fly! good *Muncie*, too

They craved the miraculous!

A gentleman of the Revolutionary Army, after describing the Falls, thus describes another natural curiosity then existing in the community: In the afternoon we were invited to visit another curiosity in the neighborhood.[16] This is a monster in human form, he is twenty-seven years of age, his face from the upper part of his forehead to the end of his chin, measures *twenty-seven inches*, and around the upper part of his head is twenty-one inches: his eyes and nose are remarkably large and prominent, chin long and pointed. His features are coarse, irregular and disgusting, his voice rough and sonorous. His body is twenty-seven inches in length, his limbs are small and much deformed, and he has the use of one hand only. He has never been able to sit up, as he cannot support the enormous weight of his head; but he is constantly in a large cradle, with his head supported on pillows. He is visited by great numbers of people, and is peculiarly fond of the company of clergymen, always inquiring for them among his visitors, and taking great pleasure in receiving religious instruction. General Washington made him a visit, and asked "whether he was a Whig or a Tory." He replied that he had never taken an *active* part on either side.

A wonder! A wonder![17]

From the ten houses Hamilton saw when he looked (at the falls!) and kept his counsel, by the middle of the century—the mills had drawn a heterogeneous population.[18] There were in 1870, native born 20,711, which would of course include children of foreign parents; foreign 12,868 of whom 237 were French, 1,420 German, 3,343 English—(Mr. Lambert who later built the Castle among them), 5,124 Irish, 879 Scotch, 1,360 Hollanders and 170 Swiss—

Around the falling waters the Furies[19] hurl!
Violence gathers, spins in their heads summoning
them:

*   *   *

15. The poem imagines the Passaic Falls as the urination of the giant. Muncie: a brand of beer.
16. Adapted from John Barber and Henry Howe's *Historical Collections of the State of New Jersey* (1844). The described individual was named Pieter Van Winkle. The poem uses such prose passages to assemble a local history with mythic implications.
17. A reference to Van Winkle, the falls, and per-haps the poem itself, using the language of nineteenth-century hucksterism.
18. Adapted from a passage in W. Clayton's *History of Bergen and Passaic Counties* (1882). Alexander Hamilton (1755–1804), the first secretary of the treasury, thought the falls could become the site of a national manufacturing center.
19. Goddesses of vengeance in Greek and Roman myth.

The twaalft, or striped bass was also abundant, and even sturgeon, of a huge bigness, were frequently caught: —On Sunday, August 31, 1817, one seven feet six inches long, and weighing 126 pounds, was captured a short distance below the Falls basin.[20] He was pelted with stones by boys until he was exhausted, whereupon one of them, John Winters, waded into the water and clambered on the back of the huge fish, while another seized him by the throat and gills, and brought him ashore. The *Bergen Express and Paterson Advertiser* of Wednesday, September 3, 1817, devoted half a column to an account of the incident, under the heading, "The Monster Taken."

> They begin![21]
> The perfections are sharpened
> The flower spreads its colored petals
>   wide in the sun
> But the tongue of the bee
>   misses them
> They sink back into the loam
>   crying out
> —you may call it a cry
> that creeps over them, a shiver
>   as they wilt and disappear:
> Marriage come to have a shuddering
>   implication
>
>   Crying out
> or take a lesser satisfaction:
>   a few go
> to the Coast without gain—
> The language is missing them
>   they die also
>   incommunicado.
>
> The language, the language
>   fails them
> They do not know the words
>   or have not
> the courage to use them   .
>   —girls from
> families that have decayed and

20. Passage adapted from William Nelson's *History of the City of Paterson and the County of Passaic* (1901).

21. The falls' flower-like rainbow suggests a hopeful natural or poetic beginning, but it is unfulfilled because of the failure of language.

taken to the hills: no words.
They may look at the torrent in
their minds
and it is foreign to them.   .

They turn their backs
and grow faint—but recover!
Life is sweet
they say: the language!
—the language
is divorced from their minds,
the language   .   .   the language!
1946

Paterson, Williams's improvisational epic, is a collage composed of original poetic passages interspersed with quoted letters and material condensed from local history books. Williams wanted to write an epic poem about Paterson, New Jersey, because he believed that "anywhere is everywhere," that the universal lay embedded in the local. In effect, this work would be a democratic epic of all cities and peoples, without a linear plot, a battle, or a nationalist agenda. A series of reality notations, it would search for a redeeming understanding and language. According to Williams's "Author's Note," this is the first part of "a long poem in four parts [ultimately five parts]—that a man in himself is a city, beginning, seeking, achieving and concluding his life in ways which the various aspects of a city may embody—if imaginatively conceived—any city, all the details of which may be made to voice his most intimate convictions. Part One introduces the elemental character of the place."

The Descent

The descent beckons
as the ascent beckoned.
Memory is a kind
of accomplishment,
a sort of renewal
even
an initiation, since the spaces it opens are new places
inhabited by hordes
heretofore unrealized,
of new kinds—
since their movements
are toward new objectives
(even though formerly they were abandoned).

*   *   *

No defeat is made up entirely of defeat—since
the world it opens is always a place
              formerly
                        unsuspected. A
world lost,
              a world unsuspected,
                        beckons to new places
and no whiteness (lost) is so white as the memory
of whiteness   .

With evening, love wakens
              though its shadows
                        which are alive by reason
of the sun shining—
              grow sleepy now and drop away
                        from desire   .

Love without shadows stirs now
              beginning to awaken
                        as night
advances.

The descent
              made up of despairs
                        and without accomplishment
realizes a new awakening:
                        which is a reversal
of despair.
              For what we cannot accomplish, what
is denied to love,
              what we have lost in the anticipation—
                        a descent follows,
endless and indestructible   .

                                        1954

Williams, approaching seventy, suffered two major strokes and a severe depression in 1951–
53. "The Descent," a meditation on memory and aging, reflects these changes in his body
and psyche. It also manifests his search for a new poetic language, rhythm, and line. He
called his language "the American idiom," his rhythm "the variable foot," and his line "tri-
adic." The triadic line is composed of idiomatic language set in three variable feet, the sec-
ond and third of which are indented to the right of their predecessor. Williams invented

this form as an alternative to the strictness of iambic pentameter and the looseness of free verse. He commented, "'The Descent' is the first poem in that medium that wholly satisfied me."

The Ivy Crown

The whole process is a lie,
    unless,
        crowned by excess,
it break forcefully,
    one way or another,
        from its confinement—
or find a deeper well.
    Antony and Cleopatra[1]
        were right;
they have shown
    the way. I love you
        or I do not live
at all.

Daffodil time
    is past. This is
        summer, summer!
the heart says,
    and not even the full of it.
        No doubts
are permitted—
    though they will come
        and may
before our time
    overwhelm us.
        We are only mortal
but being mortal
    can defy our fate.
    We may
by an outside chance
    even win! We do not
        look to see

---

1. Marc Antony (83–30 B.C.E.), a Roman warrior, and Cleopatra (69–30 B.C.E.), an Egyptian queen, were legendary lovers. Shakespeare told their story in *Antony and Cleopatra*.

jonquils[2] and violets
  come again
    but there are,
still,
    the roses!

Romance has no part in it.
    The business of love is
      cruelty *which*,
by our wills,
    we transform
      to live together.
It has its seasons,
    for and against,
      whatever the heart
fumbles in the dark
    to assert
      toward the end of May.
Just as the nature of briars
    is to tear flesh,
      I have proceeded
through them.
    Keep
      the briars out,
they say.
    You cannot live
      and keep free of
briars.

Children pick flowers.
    Let them.
      Though having them
in hand
    they have no further use for them
      but leave them crumpled
at the curb's edge.

        ✻   ✻   ✻

2. Fragrant yellow flowers, a type of narcissus.

At our age the imagination
    across the sorry facts
        lifts us
to make roses
    stand before thorns.
        Sure
love is cruel
    and selfish
        and totally obtuse —
at least, blinded by the light,
    young love is.
        But we are older,
I to love
    and you to be loved,
        we have,
no matter how,
    by our wills survived
        to keep
the jeweled prize
    always
        at our finger tips.
We will it so
    and so it is
        past all accident.
        1955

A love poem, "The Ivy Crown" is addressed to Williams's wife, Flossie. In classical times an ivy crown symbolized victory or honor. Ivy was sacred to Dionysus, the Greek god of wine, sexual ecstasy, and poetic inspiration.

Tribute to Neruda, the Poet Collector of Seashells

Now that I am all but blind,
however it came about,
though I can see as well
as anyone — the imagination

has turned inward as happened
to my mother when she
became old: dreams took the
place of sight. Her native

＊　＊　＊

tongue was Spanish which,
of course, she
never forgot. It was the
language also of Neruda the

Chilean poet—who collected
seashells on his
native beaches, until he
had by reputation, the second

largest collection in the
world. Be patient with
him, darling mother,[1] the
changeless beauty of

seashells, like the
sea itself, gave
his lines the variable pitch
which modern verse requires.

1960

In the last years of his life, Williams was nearly blind and barely able to type. He had been able, however, to collect seashells on a Florida vacation shortly before writing this poem. He asked that the poem be hand-delivered to Pablo Neruda (1904–1973), a Nobel Prize–winning Chilean poet whose poetry has affinities with his own. The poem did not reach Neruda until 1972, a decade after Williams's death and a year before Neruda's.

Ho Chih-Chang

Returning after I left my home in childhood,
I have kept my native accent but not the color of my hair.
Facing the smiling children who shyly approach me,
I am asked from where I come.

1960

Williams translated this poem by the classical Chinese poet Ho Chih-Chang (659–744) in collaboration with the poet David Rafael Wang (1931–1977). Wang commented that such poems are not really translations but "re-creations in the American idiom."

1. Elena Hoheb Williams (1857–1949), raised in Mayaguez, Puerto Rico, was long dead by the time this poem was written.

Landscape with the Fall of Icarus

According to Brueghel
when Icarus fell
it was spring

a farmer was ploughing
his field
the whole pageantry

of the year was
awake tingling
near

the edge of the sea
concerned
with itself

sweating in the sun
that melted
the wings' wax

unsignificantly
off the coast
there was

a splash quite unnoticed
this was
Icarus drowning

1960

"Landscape with the Fall of Icarus" is based on two paintings with this title by the Flemish painter Pieter Brueghel the Elder (1525–1569). A few years before Williams's death he wrote a sequence of Brueghel poems, including this one. He had turned to Brueghel for inspiration before, in "The Dance" (above). Williams and his wife, Flossie, had originally seen some of Brueghel's paintings in Vienna in 1924. According to Greek myth, a young man named Icarus sought to escape island imprisonment by flying away on wings made of wax and feathers by his father, Daedalus. Entranced by his flight, however, Icarus flew too near the sun, his wings melted, and he fell to the sea and drowned. In a corner of Brueghel's paintings, we can glimpse Icarus's leg sticking inconspicuously out of the water.

PROSE

This improvisatory prose piece immediately precedes the poem "Spring and All" (above) in Williams's 1923 volume *Spring and All*. Linda Wagner has called this volume a "prose poetry matrix" because it alternates philosophical and aesthetic prose speculations with imagistic poems. Williams said of the volume, "Nobody ever saw it—it had no circulation at all—but I had a lot of fun with it. It consists of poems interspersed with prose. . . . Chapter headings are printed upside down on purpose, the chapters are numbered all out of order, sometimes with a Roman numeral, sometimes with an Arabic, anything that came in handy. The prose is a mixture of philosophy and nonsense. It made sense to me, at least to my disturbed mind—because it *was* disturbed at that time—but I doubt if it made any sense to anyone else." This beginning section of *Spring and All* attempts to articulate a modern aesthetic that has nothing to do with "beautiful illusion." It depicts the death and rebirth of the poetic imagination, a major concern of the entire volume.

FROM Spring and All

If anything of moment results so much the better. And so much the more likely will it be that no one will want to see it.

There is a constant barrier between the reader and his consciousness of immediate contact with the world. If there is an ocean it is here. Or rather, the whole world is between: Yesterday, tomorrow, Europe, Asia, Africa,—all things removed and impossible, the tower of the church at Seville, the Parthenon.[1]

What do they mean when they say: "I do not like your poems; you have no faith whatever. You seem neither to have suffered nor, in fact, to have felt anything very deeply. There is nothing appealing in what you say but on the contrary the poems are positively repellent. They are heartless, cruel, they make fun of humanity. What in God's name do you mean? Are you a pagan? Have you no tolerance for human frailty? Rhyme you may perhaps take away but rhythm! why there is none in your work whatever. Is this what you call poetry? It is the very antithesis of poetry. It is antipoetry. It is the annihilation of life upon which you are bent. Poetry that used to go hand in hand with life, poetry that interpreted our deepest promptings, poetry that inspired, that led us forward to new discoveries, new depths of tolerance, new heights of exaltation. You moderns! it is the death of poetry that you are accomplishing. No. I cannot understand this work.

---

1. Temple to the goddess Athena on the hill of the Acropolis in Athens, Greece. Built in the fifth century B.C.E, it is a masterpiece of Greek architecture.

You have not yet suffered a cruel blow from life. When you have suffered you will write differently"?

Perhaps this noble apostrophe means something terrible for me, I am not certain, but for the moment I interpret it to say: "You have robbed me. God. I am naked. What shall I do?" By it they mean that when I have suffered (provided I have not done so as yet) I too shall run for cover; that I too shall seek refuge in fantasy. And mind you, I do not say that I will not. To decorate my age.

But today it is different.

The reader knows himself as he was twenty years ago and he has also in mind a vision of what he would be, some day. Oh, some day! But the thing he never knows and never dares to know is what he is at the exact moment that he is. And this moment is the only thing in which I am at all interested. Ergo, who cares for anything I do? And what do I care?

I love my fellow creature. Jesus, how I love him: endways, sideways, frontways and all the other ways—but he doesn't exist! Neither does she. I do, in a bastardly sort of way.

To whom then am I addressed? To the imagination.

In fact to return upon my theme for the time nearly all writing, up to the present, if not all art, has been especially designed to keep up the barrier between sense and the vaporous fringe which distracts the attention from its agonized approaches to the moment. It has been always a search for "the beautiful illusion." Very well. I am not in search of "the beautiful illusion."

And if when I pompously announce that I am addressed—To the imagination—you believe that I thus divorce myself from life and so defeat my own end, I reply: To refine, to clarify, to intensify that eternal moment in which we alone live there is but a single force—the imagination. This is its book. I myself invite you to read and to see.

In the imagination, we are from henceforth (so long as you read) locked in a fraternal embrace, the classic caress of author and reader. We are one. Whenever I say "I" I mean also "you."[2] And so, together, as one, we shall begin.

Chapter 19

o meager times, so fat in everything imaginable! imagine the New World that rises to our windows from the sea on Mondays and on Saturdays and on every other day of the week also. Imagine it in all its prismatic colorings, its counterpart in our souls—our souls that are great pianos whose strings, of honey and of steel, the divisions of the rainbow set twanging, loosing on the air great novels of

---

2. Perhaps an echo of the opening lines of Walt Whitman's "Song of Myself": "I celebrate myself, and sing myself, / And what I assume you shall assume."

adventure! Imagine the monster project of the moment: Tomorrow we the people of the United States are going to Europe armed to kill every man, woman and child in the area west of the Carpathian Mountains[3] (also east) sparing none. Imagine the sensation it will cause. First we shall kill them and then they, us. But we are careful to spare the Spanish bulls, the birds, rabbits, small deer and of course—the Russians. For the Russians we shall build a bridge from edge to edge of the Atlantic—having first been at pains to slaughter all Canadians and Mexicans on this side. Then, oh then, the great feature will take place.

Never mind; the great event may not exist, so there is no need to speak further of it. Kill! kill! the English, the Irish, the French, the Germans, the Italians and the rest: friends or enemies, it makes no difference, kill them all. The bridge is to be blown up when all Russia is upon it. And why?

Because we love them—all. That is the secret: a new sort of murder. We make leberwurst[4] of them. Bratwurst.[5] But why, since we are ourselves doomed to suffer the same annihilation? If I could say what is in my mind in Sanskrit or even Latin I would do so. But I cannot. I speak for the integrity of the soul and the greatness of life's inanity; the formality of its boredom; the orthodoxy of its stupidity. Kill! kill! let there be fresh meat . . .

The imagination, intoxicated by prohibitions, rises to drunken heights to destroy the world. Let it rage, let it kill. The imagination is supreme. To it all our works forever, from the remotest past to the farthest future, have been, are and will be dedicated. To it alone we show our wit by having raised in its honor as monument not the least pebble. To it now we come to dedicate our secret project: the annihilation of every human creature on the face of the earth. This is something never before attempted. None to remain; nothing but the lower vertebrates, the mollusks, insects and plants. Then at last will the world be made anew. Houses crumble to ruin, cities disappear giving place to mounds of soil blown thither by the winds, small bushes and grass give way to trees which grow old and are succeeded by other trees for countless generations. A marvelous serenity broken only by bird and wild beast calls reigns over the entire sphere. Order and peace abound. This final and self inflicted holocaust has been all for love, for sweetest love, that together the human race, yellow, black, brown, red and white, agglutinated into one enormous soul may be gratified with the sight and retire to the heaven of heavens content to rest on its laurels. There, soul of souls, watching its own horrid unity, it boils and digests itself within the tissues of the great Being of Eternity that we shall then have become. With what magnificent explosions and odors will not the day be accomplished as we, the Great One

---

3. European mountain range stretching from Slovakia to Romania. This section satirizes twentieth-century war, particularly World War I.

4. Liver sausage.

5. Pork sausage.

among all creatures, shall go about contemplating our self-prohibited desires as we promenade them before the inward review of our own bowels—et cetera, et cetera, et cetera . . . and it is spring—both in Latin and Turkish, in English and Dutch, in Japanese and Italian; it is spring by Stinking River where a magnolia tree, without leaves, before what was once a farmhouse, now a ramshackle home for millworkers, raises its straggling branches of ivorywhite flowers.

Chapter XIII

Thus, weary of life, in view of the great consummation which awaits us—tomorrow, we rush among our friends congratulating ourselves upon the Joy soon to be. Thoughtless of evil we crush out the marrow of those about us with our heavy cars as we go happily from place to place. It seems that there is not time enough in which to speak the full of our exaltation. Only a day is left, one miserable day, before the world comes into its own. Let us hurry! Why bother for this man or that? In the offices of the great newspapers a mad joy reigns as they prepare the final extras. Rushing about, men bump each other into the whirring presses. How funny it seems. All thought of misery has left us. Why should we care? Children laughingly fling themselves under the wheels of the street cars, airplanes crash gaily to the earth. Someone has written a poem.

Oh life, bizarre fowl, what color are your wings? Green, blue, red, yellow, purple, white, brown, orange, black, grey? In the imagination, flying above the wreck of ten thousand million souls, I see you departing sadly for the land of plants and insects, already far out to sea. (Thank you, I know well what I am plagiarizing)[6] Your great wings flap as you disappear in the distance over the pre-Columbian acres of floating weed.

The new cathedral overlooking the park, looked down from its towers today, with great eyes, and saw by the decorative lake a group of people staring curiously at the corpse of a suicide: Peaceful, dead young man, the money they have put into the stones has been spent to teach men of life's austerity. You died and teach us the same lesson. You seem a cathedral, celebrant of the spring which shivers for me among the long black trees.

Chapter VI

Now, in the imagination, all flesh, all human flesh has been dead upon the earth for ten million, billion years. The bird has turned into a stone within whose heart an egg, unlaid, remained hidden.

It is spring! but miracle of miracles a miraculous miracle has gradually taken

6. Possibly William Butler Yeats's apocalyptic poem "The Second Coming" (1921).

place during these seemingly wasted eons. Through the orderly sequences of unmentionable time EVOLUTION HAS REPEATED ITSELF FROM THE BEGINNING.

Good God!

Every step once taken in the first advance of the human race, from the amoeba to the highest type of intelligence, has been duplicated, every step exactly paralleling the one that preceded in the dead ages gone by. A perfect plagiarism results. Everything is and is new.[7] Only the imagination is undeceived.

At this point the entire complicated and laborious process begins to near a new day. (More of this in Chapter XIX) But for the moment everything is fresh, perfect, recreated.

In fact now, for the first time, everything IS new. Now at last the per feet effect is being witlessly discovered. The terms "veracity" "actuality" "real" "natural" "sincere" are being discussed at length, every word in the discussion being evolved from an identical discussion which took place the day before yesterday.

Yes, the imagination, drunk with prohibitions, has destroyed and re-created everything afresh in the likeness of that which it was. Now indeed men look about in amazement at each other with a full realization of the meaning of "art."

Chapter 2

It is spring: life again begins to assume its normal appearance as of "today." Only the imagination is undeceived. The volcanos are extinct. Coal is beginning to be dug again where the fern forests stood last night. (If an error is noted here, pay no attention to it.)

Chapter XIX

I realize that the chapters are rather quick in their sequence and that nothing much is contained in any one of them but no one should be surprised at this today.

THE TRADITIONALISTS OF PLAGIARISM[8]

It is spring. That is to say, it is approaching THE BEGINNING.

In that huge and microscopic career of time, as it were a wild horse racing in an illimitable pampa[9] under the stars, describing immense and microscopic

---

7. Perhaps the false poetic renewal Williams attributed to his rivals Ezra Pound and T. S. Eliot.
8. An apparent last slap at the citational quality of Pound and Eliot's poetry, which Williams

thought regressive. This insult is followed by a vision of true imaginative renewal.
9. Treeless plain or prairie (Spanish).

circles with his hoofs on the solid turf, running without a stop for the millionth part of a second until he is aged and worn to a heap of skin, bones and ragged hoofs—In that majestic progress of life, that gives the exact impression of Phidias' frieze,[10] the men and beasts of which, though they seem of the rigidity of marble are not so but move, with blinding rapidity, though we do not have the time to notice it, their legs advancing a millionth part of an inch every fifty thousand years. In that progress of life which seems stillness itself in the mass of its movements—at last SPRING is approaching.

In that colossal surge toward the finite and the capable life has now arrived for the second time at that exact moment when in the ages past the destruction of the species *Homo sapiens* occurred.

Now at last that process of miraculous verisimilitude, that great copying which evolution has followed, repeating move for move every move that it made in the past—is approaching the end.

Suddenly it is at an end. THE WORLD IS NEW.

1923

SARA TEASDALE
1884–1933

THE WORK OF Sara Teasdale, once among America's most popular poets, embodies a series of apparent thematic contradictions. Spare and self-ironic, it is at the same time passionate. Even as Teasdale expresses a desire for solitary self-sufficiency, her poems also yearn for romantic love and acceptance. Moreover, as critic Rosemary Sprague notes, her poetry "treads a fine line between revelation and reticence," often implying much more than it discloses. Addressing these apparent contradictions, Cheryl Walker identifies "the passionate virgin" as Teasdale's "most characteristic persona"—a figure who yearns for erotic attachment or adult sexuality, yet who remains enclosed in solitude, perhaps as a consequence of lingering Victorian ideals of female sexuality. Thus, Teasdale's language tends to be suggestive rather than explicit, and the passionate longings in her poems are strongly felt but for the most part unfulfilled.

Teasdale was born in St. Louis, the youngest of four children in a prominent family. Educated at home and in private schools, she from an early age committed

---

10. A band on a column or wall ornamented by the Athenian sculptor Phidias (ca. 490–430 B.C.E.).

herself to the art of poetry. The poet Vachel Lindsay fell in love with her, but she refused to marry him, although they remained close friends. Intense and high-strung, Teasdale gradually became estranged from her husband, Ernest Filsinger, whom she married in 1914. The couple separated in 1929. Suffering from deteriorating health and increasing depression, Teasdale died of an overdose of barbiturates in 1933. With the triumph of experimental modernism, Teasdale's poems gradually fell out of fashion, but they have always had their advocates. Louise Bogan (also included in this anthology) praised Teasdale for expressing "not only the simplicities of traditional feminine feeling, but new subtleties of emotional nuance."

FURTHER READING

Louise Bogan. *Achievement in American Poetry*. Chicago: Henry Regnery, 1951.
Rosemary Sprague. *Imaginary Gardens: A Study of Five American Poets*. Philadelphia: Chilton, 1969.
Sara Teasdale. *Collected Poems*. New York: Macmillan, 1937.
Cheryl Walker. *Masks Outrageous and Austere: Culture, Psyche and Persona in Modern Women Poets*. Bloomington: University of Indiana Press, 1991.

The Sanctuary

If I could keep my innermost Me
Fearless, aloof and free
Of the least breath of love or hate,
And not disconsolate
At the sick load of sorrow laid on men;
If I could keep a sanctuary there
Free even of prayer,
If I could do this, then,
With quiet candor as I grew more wise
I could look even at God with grave forgiving eyes.

1919

Effigy of a Nun

(SIXTEENTH CENTURY)

Infinite gentleness, infinite irony
  Are in this face with fast-sealed eyes,
And around this mouth that learned in loneliness
  How useless their wisdom is to the wise.

*   *   *

In her nun's habit carved, patiently, lovingly,
    By one who knew the ways of womankind,
This woman's face still keeps, in its cold wistful calm,
    All of the subtle pride of her mind.

These long patrician hands, clasping the crucifix,
    Show she had weighed the world; her will was set;
These pale curved lips of hers, holding their hidden smile,
    Once having made their choice, knew no regret.

She was one of those who hoard their own thoughts carefully,
    Feeling them far too dear to give away,
Content to look at life with the high, insolent
    Air of an audience watching a play.

If she was curious, if she was passionate
    She must have told herself that love was great,
But that the lacking it might be as great a thing
    If she held fast to it, challenging fate.

She who so loved herself and her own warring thoughts,
    Watching their humorous, tragic rebound,
In her thick habit's fold, sleeping, sleeping,
    Is she amused at dreams she has found?

Infinite tenderness, infinite irony,
    Are hidden forever in her closed eyes,
Who must have learned too well in her long loneliness
    How empty wisdom is, even to the wise.

1921

Teasdale's poem contemplates the sculpted effigy of a sixteenth-century nun.

Day's Ending
(TUCSON)

Aloof as aged kings,
Wearing like them the purple,
The mountains ring the mesa
Crowned with a dusky light;
Many a time I watched

That coming-on of darkness
Till stars burned through the heavens
Intolerably bright.

It was not long I lived there
But I became a woman
Under those vehement stars,
For it was there I heard
For the first time my spirit
Forging an iron rule for me,
As though with slow cold hammers
Beating out word by word:

"Only yourself can heal you,
Only yourself can lead you,
The road is heavy going
And ends where no man knows;
Take love when love is given,
But never think to find it
A sure escape from sorrow
Or a complete repose."

1922

EZRA POUND
1885–1972

EZRA POUND was a pivotal figure of experimental modernism. Through his tireless efforts as a poet, critic, translator, theorist, anthologist, literary talent scout, and impresario of artistic movements, the irrepressibly brash and energetic Pound brought fresh energy to the cultural scene on both sides of the Atlantic. In the early years of the twentieth century, Pound was constantly on the lookout to discover and champion worthy new writers and trends. He helped to launch such major careers as those of H.D. (Hilda Doolittle), T. S. Eliot, James Joyce, and William Carlos Williams. Pound also wrote appreciative and penetrating early commentary on the works of, among many others, Robert Frost, Marianne Moore, and Mina Loy (all except Joyce included in this anthology).

With H.D., Pound helped establish the influential imagist movement, serving also, at the outset, as its chief theorist and promoter. His editing of Eliot's manuscript version of *The Waste Land* decisively reshaped a poem that would emerge from Pound's hands as one of the key documents of experimental modernism. Pound campaigned among poets writing in English for a more cosmopolitan awareness of the literatures of other times and places. Pound's energetic and poetically persuasive — if not always strictly accurate — translations from the Greek, Latin, Old English, French, Provencal, Italian, Chinese, and other languages served to bring new stylistic possibilities into his native idiom.

Pound's motto was "Make It New," and his own poetic style went through a series of metamorphoses, each of which was influential. His poetic innovations — which stressed free verse, "direct treatment of the thing itself" as opposed to what he called "emotional slither," the "super-position" of related images into associational clusters, and the extension of such collage techniques throughout lengthy poems — opened up new artistic terrain, not just for his contemporaries but for successive generations. Pound's long poetic sequences, particularly the wittily acerbic *Hugh Selwyn Mauberley* and his lifework, *The Cantos*, helped to establish the poetic sequence — a succession of intricately interwoven lyrics — as the dominant form of long poem in the twentieth century. Poets as diverse as William Butler Yeats, Allen Tate, Louis Zukofsky, Charles Olson, John Berryman, Allen Ginsberg, Denise Levertov, Amiri Baraka, Charles Wright, and Charles Bernstein, among many others, have acknowledged Pound's ongoing influence. This influence on other poets has often taken the form of dialectical engagement, with the fellow poet undertaking a sort of running dialogue or argument with the possibilities and assumptions embodied in Pound's complex, challenging work.

Despite his manifold contributions to the literature of his own and subsequent generations, Pound remains an intensely controversial figure, and his strongest advocates have sometimes also been his sharpest critics. Pound's combative personality won him many enemies, as did his tireless promotion of experimental literary and artistic styles. Pound's own later style bristles with complexities, and his tendency to embed numerous citations from other languages and times in his poems has been criticized. But the greatest controversy grows out of Pound's active support for the fascist government of Mussolini in the 1930s, a support that continued into the 1940s, when Pound made pro-Mussolini broadcasts containing anti-Semitic content over Rome radio while the United States was at war with Italy. Pound was imprisoned by Allied troops after the war, but he was eventually sent to a mental hospital instead of being tried for treason.

Pound was born in Hailey, Idaho, but his family soon moved east, settling in the Philadelphia suburb of Wyncote. Pound's father, Homer, worked as assistant assayer of the U.S. Mint in Philadelphia. Pound's confident individuality may have stemmed, in part, from his father's strong support. Homer Pound, who loyally read everything Pound wrote, once exclaimed to the English humorist and cartoonist

Max Beerbohm, "You know, Mr. Beerbohm, there isn't a darn thing that boy of mine don't know." In 1901, when just fifteen years old, Pound, a precocious if erratic student, entered the University of Pennsylvania, where, a year later, he met William Carlos Williams, a medical student and budding poet who would become one of Pound's closest and longest-lasting friends. In 1903, poor marks caused Pound to transfer to Hamilton College, where he experienced greater success, studying Provencal and Anglo-Saxon poetry and graduating with a bachelor's degree in 1905. Pound returned to the University of Pennsylvania, where he studied Romance languages and briefly courted Hilda Doolittle (the poet H.D.), who would remain a lifelong friend and artistic colleague. After receiving a master's degree from Penn in 1906, Pound began to teach at Wabash College in Indiana, from which he was dismissed in 1908 following accusations by his landlady of harboring an actress in his rooms. Pound's father loaned him money for a trip to Europe. By late 1908, Pound found himself in London, where he began building his career as a poet, critic, and literary impresario.

Pound's early poetry tended toward the ornate. It was influenced by his studies in medieval Provencal and Spanish verse, which also produced his critical book *The Spirit of Romance* (1910). But, under the tutelage of the British novelist Ford Madox Ford, Pound soon rejected this early mode. He would later refer to his first book, *A Lume Spento* (1908), as "stale cream-puffs." Beginning with the volumes *Ripostes* (1912) and *Lustra* (1913), he created a firmer, more sharply edged style that emphasized an exactness and concision that was consistent with grace and delicacy. Such principles led to his involvement—with H.D. and the British writers T. E. Hulme and Richard Aldington—in the founding of the imagist movement. Pound worked as W. B. Yeats's private secretary in Stone Cottage, Sussex, during the winters of 1913–15, and Yeats's own more austere later style was influenced by his young friend's emphasis on concrete detail.

Pound assembled the anthology *Des Imagistes* in 1914 and in the same year met T. S. Eliot. Pound, impressed by the way Eliot had "educated and modernized" himself, arranged for the publication of Eliot's "Prufrock" in *Poetry*—after overcoming editor Harriet Monroe's objections—and thus launched his friend's career as a poet. Also in 1914, Pound married Dorothy Shakespear, a cultured young English woman whose mother, Olivia, had once been the lover of Yeats. In 1915, Pound published *Cathay*, his translation of classical Chinese poetry based on the manuscripts of Ernest Fenollosa. Fenollosa's widow, Mary (both Ernest and Mary Fenollosa are included in the first volume of this anthology), had entrusted these manuscripts to Pound, saying (as Pound later recalled), "You're the only person who can finish this stuff the way Ernest wanted it done." Through these Fenollosa manuscripts, Pound commenced a long fascination with Chinese literature and culture that resulted in his influential essay on the ideogrammic method, "The Chinese Written Character as a Medium for Poetry" (1920), in his various translations of Confucius, and in his concern with Chinese culture and history in many of his Cantos. Early versions of the first "Three Cantos"—now often called the Ur-Cantos—appeared in *Poetry* in 1917.

In 1920, Pound published *Hugh Selwyn Mauberley*, which he termed "my farewell to London"—a razor-sharp cultural critique of the London scene in the years before, during, and just after World War I. Settling in Paris in 1921, Pound renewed his friendship with Joyce and became acquainted with Ernest Hemingway, E. E. Cummings, and many other American writers then congregating in the French capital. In 1922, Pound completed his editorial work on Eliot's *The Waste Land*, which was then published in *The Little Review*. He was also working in earnest on his epic sequence, the *Cantos*, which would appear in separate volumes over the next five decades, beginning with *A Draft of XVI Cantos* in 1925. Pound met the American violinist Olga Rudge in Paris in 1923, and they began a long-term relationship in parallel with Pound's marriage to Dorothy. Pound's daughter with Rudge, Mary, was born in the Italian Tyrol in 1925. Pound's wife, Dorothy, gave birth to a son, Omar, in Paris in 1926. Olga Rudge moved to Venice in 1929. Pound settled in Rapallo with Dorothy and in the company of his parents, who had retired to Rapallo, but he fluctuated between the two households.

In the 1930s, with the onset of the Great Depression, Pound became increasingly involved in promoting an economic system called Social Credit, which argued that usury—the loaning of money at excessive interest—was the root of all economic evil. Pound also declared his support for Mussolini, and his work of this period shows a mounting involvement with anti-Semitism. In 1939, Pound, an avowed pacifist, revisited America for the first time since 1910 and lobbied U.S. congressmen in an attempt to avert the oncoming World War II. In 1941, he began regular shortwave radio broadcasts to America, criticizing President Roosevelt and the Allied war effort and expressing anti-Semitic views. Pound attempted to leave Italy both before and after the United States entered the war. He ceased his radio broadcasts for more than a year following the Pearl Harbor bombing in December 1941, but then he resumed them in February 1943. In July 1943, the day after Mussolini was deposed from power, Pound was indicted for treason in absentia in Washington, D.C. Wendy Flory associates the anti-Semitism of Pound's broadcasts with a "mental condition [that] deteriorated precipitously" after 1935, arguing that "characteristics of his behavior and his writing exactly fit the diagnostic criteria for paranoid psychosis—relabeled in 1987 'Delusional Disorder.'" Flory notes that while "there are frequent anti-Semitic outbursts in the radio speeches, there are very few in *The Cantos*."

Pound was arrested by American authorities following the defeat of Germany in May 1945 and placed in the U.S. Army Disciplinary Training Center near Pisa, where he was confined to a solitary steel pen exposed to the elements and suffered a physical breakdown. Moved to a medical tent, he began writing the first draft of the *Pisan Cantos*, a trenchant reconsideration of his past. Taken to Washington in November 1945, Pound was again indicted for treason but was found medically unfit to stand trial. He was committed to St. Elizabeths Hospital for the Criminally Insane, where he would stay until 1958, though he was moved from the criminal section in 1947. He was visited at St. Elizabeths by many leading American poets, including Tate, Olson, Berryman, Lowell, Langston Hughes, Randall Jarrell, Robert Duncan, and Elizabeth Bishop. His *Pisan Cantos*, published in 1948, won the Bollingen Prize for Poetry in 1949, setting off an intense controversy. During the years of his confinement, many important Pound publications were issued by his longtime publisher, James Laughlin of New Directions, including *Selected Poems* (1949), *Letters* (1950), *Translations* (1953), *Literary Essays* (1954), and *Section: Rock Drill* of the *Cantos* (1955). The efforts of Frost, Hemingway, Eliot, and others led to Pound's release from St. Elizabeths in 1958. He returned to Italy following visits to his childhood home in Wyncote and to his old friend William Carlos Williams. In his later years Pound suffered frequently from depression and had long bouts of extensive silence. He once said, "I did not enter into silence. Silence captured me." In 1966, he was stimulated into speech by a visit from Allen Ginsberg. Pound at that time apologized for his earlier anti-Semitism as "that stupid, suburban prejudice." His anti-Semitic attitudes of the 1930s and 1940s remain controversial, however, as does the proper mode of reading Pound's writings. Many critics would argue with Wendy Flory for the need to set aside Pound's anti-Semitism in order to appreciate the positive and innovative elements of his writings. The poet Charles Bernstein, on the other hand, argues that "Pound's work, it seems to me, not only allows for but provokes an ideological reading; it insists that it be read, form and content, for its politics and its ideas."

Pound died in Venice at the age of eighty-seven in 1972, leaving a legacy that is by no means simple to experience and evaluate. His life and works will continue to be a magnet for critical inquiry well into the twenty-first century.

FURTHER READING

Peter Ackroyd. *Ezra Pound and His World*. London: Thames and Hudson, 1980.

Christopher Beach. *ABC of Influence: Ezra Pound and the Remaking of American Poetic Tradition*. Berkeley: University of California Press, 1992.

Charles Bernstein. *My Way: Speeches and Poems*. University of Chicago Press, 1999.

Michael Bernstein. *The Tale of the Tribe: Ezra Pound and the Modern Verse Epic*. Princeton: Princeton University Press, 1980.

Ronald Bush. *The Genesis of Ezra Pound's "Cantos."* Princeton: Princeton University Press, 1976.

Humphrey Carpenter. *A Serious Character: The Life of Ezra Pound*. Boston: Houghton Mifflin, 1988.

Robert Casillo. *The Genealogy of Demons: Anti-Semitism, Fascism, and the Myths of Ezra Pound*. Evanston, Ill.: Northwestern University Press, 1988.

John Espey. *Ezra Pound's Mauberley: A Study in Composition*. Berkeley: University of California Press, 1955.

Wendy Stallard Flory. *The American Ezra Pound*. New Haven: Yale University Press, 1989.

Christine Froula. *To Write Paradise: Style and Error in Pound's "Cantos."* New Haven: Yale University Press, 1984.

Albert Gelpi. *A Coherent Splendor: The American Poetic Renaissance, 1910–1950*. Cambridge, Eng.: Cambridge University Press, 1987.

Hugh Kenner. *The Poetry of Ezra Pound*. 1951; reprint with new preface by the author, Lincoln: University of Nebraska Press, 1985.

——. *The Pound Era*. London: Faber and Faber, 1972.

James Longenbach. *Stone Cottage: Pound, Yeats and Modernism*. New York: Oxford University Press, 1988.

Ira B. Nadel, ed. *The Cambridge Companion to Ezra Pound*. Cambridge, Eng.: Cambridge University Press, 1999.

Ezra Pound. *The Cantos*. New York: New Directions, 1970, 1993.

——. *Literary Essays*. Ed. T. S. Eliot. New York: New Directions, 1954.

——. *Personae: Collected Shorter Poems*. New York: New Directions, 1926.

K. K. Ruthven. *A Guide to Ezra Pound's "Personae," 1926*. Berkeley: University of California Press, 1969.

Carroll F. Terrell. *A Companion to "The Cantos" of Ezra Pound*, Volume 1 (Cantos 1–71). Berkeley: University of California Press, 1980.

——. *A Companion to "The Cantos" of Ezra Pound*, Volume 2 (Cantos 74–117). Berkeley: University of California Press, 1984.

A Virginal

No, no! Go from me. I have left her lately.
I will not spoil my sheath with lesser brightness,
For my surrounding air hath a new lightness;
Slight are her arms, yet they have bound me straitly[1]
And left me cloaked as with a gauze of æther;
As with sweet leaves; as with subtle clearness.
Oh, I have picked up magic in her nearness
To sheathe me half in half the things that sheathe her.
No, no! Go from me. I have still the flavour,
Soft as spring wind that's come from birchen bowers.
Green come the shoots, aye April in the branches,
As winter's wound with her sleight[2] hand she staunches,
Hath of the trees a likeness of the savour:
As white as their bark, so white this lady's hours.

1912

Pound's title refers to the plucked keyboard instrument, the virginals, on which such a song as this might have been accompanied in the English Renaissance and perhaps also to the

1. Closely, tightly.　　2. Dexterous, skillful.

virginal nature of the lady it celebrates. Note the way that this Petrarchan sonnet uses innovative, soft-stressed syllables as line endings, in contrast to the more traditional hard-stressed endings of Renaissance sonnets.

The Return

See, they return; ah, see the tentative
   Movements, and the slow feet,
   The trouble in the pace and the uncertain
   Wavering!

See, they return, one, and by one,
With fear, as half-awakened;
As if the snow should hesitate
And murmur in the wind,
            and half turn back;
These were the "Wing'd-with-Awe,"
      Inviolable,

Gods of the wingèd shoe!
With them the silver hounds,
        sniffing the trace of air!

Haie! Haie![1]
    These were the swift to harry;
These the keen-scented;
These were the souls of blood.

Slow on the leash,
        pallid the leash-men!

        1913

In "The Return," Pound imagines the return of the Greek gods after having disappeared many centuries ago. It traces their tentative movements as they slowly reawaken to life.

Salutation

O generation of the thoroughly smug
    and thoroughly uncomfortable,
I have seen fishermen picnicking in the sun,

---

1. A hunting cry.

I have seen them with untidy families,
I have seen their smiles full of teeth
   and heard ungainly laughter.
And I am happier than you are,
And they were happier than I am;
And the fish swim in the lake
   and do not even own clothing.

     1913

A Pact

I make a pact with you, Walt Whitman —
I have detested you long enough.
I come to you as a grown child
Who has had a pig-headed father;
I am old enough now to make friends.
It was you that broke the new wood,
Now is a time for carving.
We have one sap and one root —
Let there be commerce between us.

     1913

Pound had initially resisted Whitman's influence, but in 1909 he wrote from Europe that "from this side of the Atlantic I am for the first time able to read Whitman. . . . I see him as America's poet. He *is* America. . . . The vital part of my message, taken from the sap and fibre of America, is the same as his."

In a Station of the Metro

The apparition of these faces in the crowd;
Petals on a wet, black bough.

     1913

Pound's most famous imagist poem, "In a Station of the Metro," presents, to use Pound's own term, "an intellectual and emotional complex in an instant of time." According to Pound's account, it compares the lovely faces of women and children on the platform of the Paris Metro (subway) with the gray atmosphere of the Metro itself. Note the image drawn from Asian visual and poetic arts in the poem's second line.

The River-Merchant's Wife: A Letter

While my hair was still cut straight across my forehead
I played about the front gate, pulling flowers.
You came by on bamboo stilts, playing horse,
You walked about my seat, playing with blue plums.
And we went on living in the village of Chōkan:
Two small people, without dislike or suspicion.

At fourteen I married My Lord you.
I never laughed, being bashful.
Lowering my head, I looked at the wall.
Called to, a thousand times, I never looked back.

At fifteen I stopped scowling,
I desired my dust to be mingled with yours
Forever and forever and forever.
Why should I climb the look out?

At sixteen you departed,
You went into far Ku-tō-en,[1] by the river of swirling eddies,
And you have been gone five months.
The monkeys make sorrowful noise overhead.
You dragged your feet when you went out.
By the gate now, the moss is grown, the different mosses,
Too deep to clear them away!
The leaves fall early this autumn, in wind.
The paired butterflies are already yellow with August
Over the grass in the West garden;
They hurt me. I grow older.
If you are coming down through the narrows of the river Kiang,
Please let me know beforehand,
And I will come out to meet you,
                    As far as Chō-fū-Sa.

                                        1915

"The River-Merchant's Wife: A Letter" is based on Pound's rendering of the notes of Ernest Fenollosa, an early scholar of Japanese and Chinese culture. At the time, Pound did not know Chinese and was distilling Fenollosa's English version into poetry. The poem translates the first of Li Po's "Two Letters from Ch'ang-kan."

1. Actually the name of a river; Pound treats it as a region along the bank of the river.

FROM *Hugh Selwyn Mauberley*

LIFE AND CONTACTS

Vocat aestus in umbram
NEMESIANUS ES. IV.[1]

E. P. Ode pour l'Élection de Son Sépulchre[2]

I

For three years, out of key with his time,
He strove to resuscitate the dead art
Of poetry; to maintain "the sublime"
In the old sense. Wrong from the start—

No, hardly, but, seeing he had been born
In a half savage country, out of date;
Bent resolutely on wringing lilies from the acorn;[3]
Capaneus;[4] trout for factitious bait;

Idmen gar toi panth, os eni Troie[5]
Caught in the unstopped ear;
Giving the rocks small lee-way
The chopped seas held him, therefore, that year.

His true Penelope[6] was Flaubert,
He fished by obstinate isles;
Observed the elegance of Circe's[7] hair
Rather than the mottoes on sun-dials.[8]

---

1. From Eclogue IV of the Latin poet Nemesianus: "the heat calls [you] into the shade." Pound seems to be signaling his readiness to retreat from the heat of cultural combat in London. His plan was to resume the battle anew in Paris.

2. "Ode on the choice of his tomb." The initials indicate Ezra Pound, and he alludes to Pierre de Ronsard's early Renaissance poem "De l'Élection de Son Sépulchre."

3. The first section presents a series of dismissive comments on Pound (E. P.) himself, perhaps such comments as Pound imagined his hostile contemporaries might make.

4. One of the seven against Thebes (in Aeschylus's play), he was struck down on the walls of Thebes by Zeus for his impiety in attempting to conquer the city. Factitious: false; artificial.

5. "Because we know all things [suffered] in Troy" (Greek): a line sung by the Sirens in Homer's Od-

yssey (XII) and heard by Odysseus but not by his sailing companions, whose ears were plugged with wax to protect them from the Sirens' attempt to lure them onto the rocks. Like Odysseus, Pound can hear the beauty of the Sirens' song, calling him to the service of art, a song his contemporaries cannot hear. Quotations from the Greek are transliterated in this version.

6. Odysseus's faithful spouse, who awaited him for twenty years. Pound's fidelity is to artists like Gustave Flaubert, who was censored and prosecuted for the writing of his masterpiece, *Madame Bovary,* and who dedicated himself to finding "le mot juste" (the right word).

7. Beautiful enchantress who turned men into pigs after she seduced them and whom Odysseus outwitted and subdued. Odysseus then lingered in her company for many years.

8. These mottoes often remind us that time flies.

*   *   *

Unaffected by "the march of events,"
He passed from men's memory in *l'an trentiesme
De son eage*;[9] the case presents
No adjunct to the Muses' diadem.[10]

II

The age demanded an image
Of its accelerated grimace,
Something for the modern stage,
Not, at any rate, an Attic[11] grace;

Not, not certainly, the obscure reveries
Of the inward gaze;
Better mendacities[12]
Than the classics in paraphrase!

The "age demanded" chiefly a mould in plaster,
Made with no loss of time,
A prose kinema,[13] not, not assuredly, alabaster
Or the "sculpture" of rhyme.

III

The tea-rose, tea-gown, etc.
Supplants the mousseline of Cos,[14]
The pianola "replaces"
Sappho's barbitos.[15]

*   *   *

9. "In the thirtieth year of his age," an echo of the first line of "Le Testament" by François Villon, a poem written by Villon in anticipation of his death. When Pound was thirty, he was in the thick of the cultural wars in London.
10. A dismissive remark by Pound's contemporaries. The Muses are Greek goddesses who inspire art. According to his many critics, Pound's case has apparently added nothing to the jewels worn by the Muses. The following section II appears to be Pound's response to the dismissal by his contemporaries.

11. Ancient Greece was sometimes called Attica.
12. Lies.
13. Cinema. The age wants not poetry but prose as much like the movies as possible, just as it prefers a molded plaster statue rather than one sculpted from beautiful marble (alabaster).
14. The lovely muslin cloth of Cos (a Greek island) is supplanted by the modern tea gown.
15. The lyre (barbitos) of the ancient Greek poet Sappho is replaced in the modern world by the mechanical player piano or "pianola."

Christ follows Dionysus,[16]
Phallic and ambrosial
Made way for macerations;[17]
Caliban casts out Ariel.[18]

All things are a flowing,
Sage Heracleitus[19] says;
But a tawdry cheapness
Shall reign throughout our days.

Even the Christian beauty
Defects—after Samothrace;[20]
We see *to kalon*[21]
Decreed in the market place.

Faun's flesh is not to us,
Nor the saint's vision.[22]
We have the press for wafer;[23]
Franchise for circumcision.

All men, in law, are equals.
Free of Peisistratus,[24]
We choose a knave or an eunuch
To rule over us.

O bright Apollo,
Tin andra, tin eroa, tina theon,[25]
What god, man, or hero
Shall I place a tin wreath upon?

16. The Greek god of poetry and wine (Dionysus) has been replaced by the Christian savior.

17. Mortifications of the flesh.

18. In the modern world, the brutal Caliban, from Shakespeare's *The Tempest*, casts out the delightful spirit Ariel, who had magically performed the wise Prospero's bidding.

19. The Greek philosopher who argued that flux and change dominate life.

20. Greek island associated with a cult of beauty; the Winged Victory was found here.

21. "The beautiful" (Greek); now the name of a widely advertised French cosmetic.

22. In the modern world, we have neither the cult of the ancient Greek faun nor the visionary experience of the early Christian saints.

23. Journalism, the press, is our substitute for the communion wafer.

24. Athenian king or tyrant who was also a patron of the arts.

25. "What god, what hero, and what man [shall we celebrate]?" from Pindar's Olympian ode. Pound puns on the Greek word "tin," meaning "what," to suggest that in the modern world wreaths are made of tin, not the traditional laurel.

IV

These fought, in any case,
and some believing, pro domo,[26] in any case . . .

Some quick to arm,
some for adventure,
some from fear of weakness,
some from fear of censure,
some for love of slaughter, in imagination,
learning later . . .
some in fear, learning love of slaughter;

Died some, pro patria, non "dulce" non "et decor" . . .[27]
walked eye-deep in hell
believing in old men's lies, then unbelieving
came home, home to a lie,
home to many deceits,
home to old lies and new infamy;
usury[28] age-old and age-thick
and liars in public places.

Daring as never before, wastage as never before.
Young blood and high blood,
fair cheeks, and fine bodies;

fortitude as never before

frankness as never before,
disillusions as never told in the old days,
hysterias, trench confessions,
laughter out of dead bellies.

26. "For the home" (Latin). These young men fought for the home, as people always fight in wars. Pound reflects on the many talented young men, including such friends as the sculptor Gaudier-Brezeka, who died in the trenches of World War I. He ironically juxtaposes ancient Roman celebrations of military glory with the realities of modern warfare.

27. Pound reverses Horace's ode III.ii.—"Dulce et decorum est pro patria mori," i.e., "Sweet and proper it is to die for your country." Pound asserts it is "not sweet" and "not proper." Wilfred Owen's "Dulce et Decorum" uses a vivid description of death by poison gas to state a similar reversal of Horace's axiom.

28. Loaning of money at excessive interest.

V

There died a myriad,
And of the best, among them,
For an old bitch gone in the teeth,
For a botched civilization,

Charm, smiling at the good mouth,
Quick eyes gone under earth's lid,

For two gross of broken statues,
For a few thousand battered books.

Yeux Glauques[29]

Gladstone was still respected,
When John Ruskin produced
"Kings' Treasuries"; Swinburne
And Rossetti still abused.[30]

Fœtid Buchanan[31] lifted up his voice
When that faun's head of hers[32]
Became a pastime for
Painters and adulterers.

The Burne-Jones cartons
Have preserved her eyes;
Still, at the Tate, they teach
Cophetua to rhapsodize[33]

*   *   *

29. Sea-green eyes (French). Pound here alludes to the lovely eyes of Elizabeth Siddal, the model for many of the most famous paintings by the pre-Raphaelite artists, including those of poet Dante Gabriel Rossetti. In this and the following section Pound undertakes an examination of the trials and tribulations of Rossetti and his fellow members of the aesthetic movement. These artists were largely rejected and to some degree persecuted by the English of the Victorian era. Pound suggests that conditions have little changed since those times.

30. "Kings' Treasuries" is the opening chapter of John Ruskin's *Sesame and Lilies* (1865). It contains a sharp indictment of the English for their indifference to art, literature, science, and the beauty of nature. Pound's *Mauberley* offers a similar critique half a century later. Swinburne and Rossetti were in those days often criticized for their "decadent" approach to poetry and art.

31. R. W. Buchanan attacked the so-called "Fleshly School of Poetry" (e.g., Rossetti and Swinburne) in an 1871 article.

32. That is, Elizabeth Siddal (see note 29 above).

33. *Cophetua and the Beggar Maid*, a painting by Sir Edward Burne-Jones, still hangs in the Tate Gallery in London. Cartons—literally, cartoons—are drawings. Cophetua was a biblical king who fell in love with a beautiful female beggar. Siddal was the model for the painting.

Thin like brook-water,
With a vacant gaze.
The English Rubaiyat[34] was still-born
In those days.

The thin, clear gaze, the same
Still darts out faun-like from the half-ruin'd face,
Questing and passive. . . .
"Ah, poor Jenny's[35] case" . . .

Bewildered that a world
Shows no surprise
At her last maquero's[36]
Adulteries.

"Siena Mi Fe', Disfecemi Maremma"[37]

Among the pickled fœtuses and bottled bones,
Engaged in perfecting the catalogue,
I found the last scion of the
Senatorial families of Strasbourg, Monsieur Verog.[38]

For two hours he talked of Gallifet;[39]
Of Dowson; of the Rhymers' Club;[40]
Told me how Johnson (Lionel)[41] died
By falling from a high stool in a pub . . .

But showed no trace of alcohol
At the autopsy, privately performed—
Tissue preserved—the pure mind
Arose toward Newman[42] as the whiskey warmed.

---

34. The English translation of the *Rubaiyat of Omar Khayyám* was published by Edward Fitzgerald in 1859. It was overlooked and ignored until Rossetti discovered and praised it. It then became wildly popular.

35. Dante Gabriel Rossetti's poem "Jenny" expressed sympathy for an English prostitute.

36. Pimp.

37. "Siena gave me birth, Maremma death" or "Siena made me, Maremma unmade me," the words of La Pia de' Tolomei in Dante's *Purgatorio* (V).

38. Fictional name for Victor Gustav Plarr, poet and librarian of the Royal College of Surgeons, whose catalogue he compiled. Plarr was a friend of Pound's who told him stories about the pre-Raphaelites and aesthetic poets, stories recounted in this section.

39. Gaston Alexandre Auguste de Gallifet, a French general in the Franco-Prussian War.

40. Ernest Dowson was an English aesthetic poet and a member of the Rhymers' Club, an informal group of late-Victorian poets who met regularly in the Cheshire Cheese pub in London's Fleet Street. Pound's friend Yeats was also a member.

41. Johnson, a Catholic convert, and an alcoholic, was another member of the Rhymers' Club. This tale of his death is not true.

42. John Henry Newman, a Catholic cardinal, whose focus on the artistic beauty of Church ritual linked him to the aesthetic movement.

*   *   *

Dowson found harlots cheaper than hotels;
Headlam for uplift; Image[43] impartially imbued
With raptures for Bacchus,[44] Terpsichore and the Church.
So spoke the author of "The Dorian Mood,"[45]

M. Verog, out of step with the decade,
Detached from his contemporaries,
Neglected by the young,[46]
Because of these reveries.

Brennbaum[47]

The sky-like limpid eyes,
The circular infant's face,
The stiffness from spats[48] to collar
Never relaxing into grace;

The heavy memories of Horeb, Sinai and the forty years,[49]
Showed only when the daylight fell
Level across the face
Of Brennbaum "The Impeccable."

Mr. Nixon[50]

In the cream gilded cabin of his steam yacht
Mr. Nixon advised me kindly, to advance with fewer
Dangers of delay. "Consider
      "Carefully the reviewer.

43. Reverend Stewart Duckworth Headlam was a poet and clergyman whom the Church forced to resign because of his interest in dance and drama. Selwyn Image, whose first name may supply the middle name of Hugh Selwyn Mauberley, was another cleric-poet.
44. The Roman god of wine. Terpsichore: the Greek muse of dance.
45. Plarr's book of poems was entitled *In the Dorian Mood*.
46. Pound, too, is one of the young, but he, by implication, honors Verog/Plarr because of his devotion to the memory of struggling artists from a previous generation.
47. Generally thought to refer to Max Beerbohm, the English humorist and man of letters. Later, Beerbohm and Pound became friends when they both lived in Rapallo.

48. Old-fashioned, formal buttoned cloth pieces worn by Edwardian men to cover their ankles and the upper part of their shoes.
49. Moses witnessed the burning bush on Mount Horeb or Sinai (Exodus 3:1–2) and obtained the Ten Commandments from God on Mount Sinai (Exodus 34:28). The Jews wandered in the wilderness for forty years before finding the promised land. Pound implies that Jewish history weighs heavily on the mind of Brennbaum as he attempts to confront the modern world. Ironically, Max Beerbohm was not Jewish, though Pound thought he was.
50. Nixon is usually associated with Arnold Bennett, the successful English novelist, here associated with a cynical courtship of sales as opposed to art.

* * *

"I was as poor as you are;
"When I began I got, of course,
"Advance on royalties, fifty at first," said Mr. Nixon,
"Follow me, and take a column,
"Even if you have to work free.

"Butter reviewers. From fifty to three hundred
"I rose in eighteen months;
"The hardest nut I had to crack
"Was Dr. Dundas.

"I never mentioned a man but with the view
"Of selling my own works.
"The tip's a good one, as for literature
"It gives no man a sinecure.

"And no one knows, at sight, a masterpiece.
"And give up verse, my boy,
"There's nothing in it."

◆ ◆ ◆

Likewise a friend of Blougram's[51] once advised me:
Don't kick against the pricks,
Accept opinion. The "Nineties"[52] tried your game
And died, there's nothing in it.

X

Beneath the sagging roof
The stylist[53] has taken shelter,
Unpaid, uncelebrated,
At last from the world's welter

Nature receives him;
With a placid and uneducated mistress
He exercises his talents
And the soil meets his distress.

* * *

---

51. The worldly bishop in Robert Browning's "Bishop Blougram's Apology" had friends who offered similarly cynical advice.
52. Poets of the 1890s such as Dowson, Johnson, and Headlam had died young, without fully achieving their artistic goals.
53. Generally seen to be Ford Madox Ford, the English novelist and a close friend of Pound's.

The haven from sophistications and contentions
Leaks through its thatch;
He offers succulent cooking;
The door has a creaking latch.

XI

"Conservatrix of Milésien"[54]
Habits of mind and feeling,
Possibly. But in Ealing[55]
With the most bank-clerkly of Englishmen?

No, "Milesian" is an exaggeration.
No instinct has survived in her
Older than those her grandmother
Told her would fit her station.

XII

"Daphne with her thighs in bark
"Stretches toward me her leafy hands,"[56]—
Subjectively. In the stuffed-satin drawing-room
I await The Lady Valentine's[57] commands,

Knowing my coat has never been
Of precisely the fashion
To stimulate, in her,
A durable passion;

Doubtful, somewhat, of the value
Of well-gowned approbation
Of literary effort,
But never of The Lady Valentine's vocation:

Poetry, her border of ideas,
The edge, uncertain, but a means of blending
With other strata
Where the lower and higher have ending;

*   *   *

54. A modern woman who claims to conserve knowledge of lost Greek or "Milesian" erotic arts.
55. But Pound doubts the plausibility of this claim for a woman who lives in middle-class, suburban Ealing, with a "bank-clerkly" husband.
56. Translated from Théophile Gautier's "Le Château du Souvenir." The lines refer to the Greek myth in which the nymph Daphne, fleeing from the pursuing god Apollo, is turned into a laurel tree to escape him.
57. A rich, aristocratic, but superficial patroness of the arts.

A hook to catch the Lady Jane's attention,
A modulation toward the theatre,
Also, in the case of revolution,
A possible friend and comforter.

◆　◆　◆

Conduct, on the other hand, the soul
"Which the highest cultures have nourished"
To Fleet St. where
Dr. Johnson flourished;[58]

Beside this thoroughfare
The sale of half-hose has
Long since superseded the cultivation
Of Pierian roses.[59]

Envoi (1919)[60]

Go, dumb-born book,
Tell her that sang me once that song of Lawes:[61]
Hadst thou but song
As thou hast subjects known,
Then were there cause in thee that should condone
Even my faults that heavy upon me lie,
And build her glories their longevity.

Tell her that sheds
Such treasure in the air,
Recking naught else but that her graces give
Life to the moment,
I would bid them live
As roses might, in magic amber laid,
Red overwrought with orange and all made
One substance and one colour
Braving time.

Tell her that goes
With song upon her lips

58. Samuel Johnson, eighteenth-century English poet, critic, and lexicographer.
59. "Pierian roses" grow in Pieria on the northern slopes of Mount Olympus, the home of the Greek gods. The poet Sappho had associated them with the timeless memorial that comes from great art.
60. A postscript or formal farewell in a poem, used for a summing up and often addressing the poet's book.
61. Pound echoes the poem "Go, Lovely Rose" by Edmund Waller (1606–1687), which was set to music by the English composer Henry Lawes (1596–1662).

But sings not out the song, nor knows
The maker of it, some other mouth,
May be as fair as hers,
Might, in new ages, gain her worshippers,
When our two dusts with Waller's shall be laid,
Siftings on siftings in oblivion,
Till change hath broken down
All things save Beauty alone.

1920

Hugh Selwyn Mauberley is a poetic sequence that embodies Pound's witty, sometimes searing cultural critique of London and, by extension, Western civilization in the years surrounding and including World War I (1914–18). It is composed of two distinct parts, "Life and Contacts" and "1920 (Mauberley)," of which only the first is reproduced here. Pound and Eliot had agreed that after a decade of free verse, the time had come for a return to traditional verse forms. In the rhymed quatrains of *Mauberley*, Pound defines the difficulties of creating a new mode of art in a cultural setting as deeply traditional and steeped in Victorian values as contemporary London. This sequence presents a series of sharply wrought scenes that use a wide range of artistic devices to make its points, including the cross-referencing of events from different literary and historical eras, consistently inventive play on the traditional associations of words, and a long series of multilingual puns. The poem draws on Pound's detailed knowledge of the London scene. The learning curve for modern readers can seem steep, but once Pound's extensive range of devices and references is mastered, the poem emerges as one of the funniest and loveliest in the language. Mauberley, the title character, is a fictitious poet of limited ability contemporary with Pound, but the first section of the poem, the one included here, focuses primarily on the perceptions and tribulations of Pound himself and the struggles of his artistic friends and forebears.

FROM The Cantos

Canto I

And then went down to the ship,
Set keel to breakers, forth on the godly sea, and
We set up mast and sail on that swart[1] ship,
Bore sheep aboard her, and our bodies also
Heavy with weeping, and winds from sternward
Bore us out onward with bellying canvas,

---

1. Swarthy, dark.

Circe's[2] this craft, the trim-coifed goddess.
Then sat we amidships, wind jamming the tiller,
Thus with stretched sail, we went over sea till day's end.
Sun to his slumber, shadows o'er all the ocean,
Came we then to the bounds of deepest water,
To the Kimmerian[3] lands, and peopled cities
Covered with close-webbed mist, unpierced ever
With glitter of sun-rays
Nor with stars stretched, nor looking back from heaven
Swartest night stretched over wretched men there.
The ocean flowing backward, came we then to the place
Aforesaid by Circe.
Here did they rites, Perimedes and Eurylochus,[4]
And drawing sword from my hip
I dug the ell-square pitkin;
Poured we libations unto each the dead,
First mead and then sweet wine, water mixed with white flour.
Then prayed I many a prayer to the sickly death's-heads;
As set in Ithaca,[5] sterile bulls of the best
For sacrifice, heaping the pyre with goods,
A sheep to Tiresias[6] only, black and a bell-sheep.
Dark blood flowed in the fosse,[7]
Souls out of Erebus,[8] cadaverous dead, of brides
Of youths and of the old who had borne much;
Souls stained with recent tears, girls tender,
Men many, mauled with bronze lance heads,
Battle spoil, bearing yet dreory[9] arms,
These many crowded about me; with shouting,
Pallor upon me, cried to my men for more beasts;
Slaughtered the herds, sheep slain of bronze;
Poured ointment, cried to the gods,

2. Lovely island goddess with magical powers who cohabited with Odysseus. She advised him that before returning to his native island of Ithaca he must visit Hades, the mythic Greek underworld and realm of the dead, and seek advice from the deceased Tiresias, the great seer and prophet. The advice of Tiresias would guide him safely home.

3. Realm of the Cimmerians, a people who, according to Homer, live in fog and darkness at the borders of the known world.

4. Crew members serving Odysseus. Eurylochus was his second-in-command.

5. In invoking the dead, Odysseus follows the ritual practices of his native Ithaca.

6. The great, blind Theban prophet—a pivotal figure in Greek and Roman myth. In Hades, he can prophesy only after drinking the blood of the sheep sacrificed by Odysseus.

7. Ditch or "pitkin" (Pound's coinage for small pit) into which the sheep's blood has flowed.

8. A dark place through which souls must pass en route to Hades.

9. Blood-dripping, smeared with blood (Anglo-Saxon).

To Pluto the strong, and praised Proserpine;[10]
Unsheathed the narrow sword,
I sat to keep off the impetuous impotent dead,
Till I should hear Tiresias.
But first Elpenor came, our friend Elpenor,[11]
Unburied, cast on the wide earth,
Limbs that we left in the house of Circe,
Unwept, unwrapped in sepulchre, since toils urged other.
Pitiful spirit. And I cried in hurried speech:
"Elpenor, how art thou come to this dark coast?
"Cam'st thou afoot, outstripping seamen?"
            And he in heavy speech:
"Ill fate and abundant wine. I slept in Circe's ingle.
"Going down the long ladder unguarded,
"I fell against the buttress,
"Shattered the nape-nerve, the soul sought Avernus.[12]
"But thou, O King, I bid remember me, unwept, unburied,
"Heap up mine arms, be tomb by sea-bord, and inscribed:
"*A man of no fortune, and with a name to come.*
"And set my oar up, that I swung mid fellows."

And Anticlea[13] came, whom I beat off, and then Tiresias Theban,
Holding his golden wand, knew me, and spoke first:
"A second time? why? man of ill star,
"Facing the sunless dead and this joyless region?
"Stand from the fosse, leave me my bloody bever
"For soothsay."
            And I stepped back,
And he strong with the blood, said then: "Odysseus
"Shalt return through spiteful Neptune, over dark seas,
"Lose all companions." And then Anticlea came.
Lie quiet Divus. I mean, that is Andreas Divus,[14]

---

10. Pluto, the god of the underworld, was married to the goddess Proserpine. She spends half her year aboveground, bringing life to the earth as the goddess of spring. Returning to Hades in the winter, she becomes the goddess of death and the underworld.

11. Youngest of Odysseus's crew, he was drunk and left behind when Odysseus hurriedly sailed from Circe's island. He died while drunkenly falling from a ladder in Circe's house, and so he arrived in Hades before his shipmates.

12. Hades, the underworld.

13. Anticlea was Odysseus's deceased mother. Since he must speak to Tiresias so urgently, Odysseus speaks to her only after he has held his interview with the prophet.

14. A medieval Latin translator of *The Odyssey*. Pound translates not directly from the ancient Greek but from Divus's Latin version. Commonly, throughout *The Cantos* (see Canto XIII, below), the past is "made new" through interaction with different cultural layers, often involving different retellings or translations of the same historical or mythic story.

In officina Wecheli,[15] 1538, out of Homer.
And he sailed, by Sirens and thence outward and away
And unto Circe.
      Venerandam,[16]
In the Cretan's phrase, with the golden crown, Aphrodite,[17]
Cypri munimenta sortita est, mirthful, oricalchi,[18] with golden
Girdles and breast bands, thou with dark eyelids
Bearing the golden bough of Argicida. So that:[19]

          1917

Beginning with this first example in 1917, Pound's *Cantos* began to appear in steady succession. Ultimately they numbered 120. Pound's *Cantos*, a personal epic loosely modeled on such diverse examples as Dante's *Divine Comedy* and Whitman's *Song of Myself*, would become a central focus for the rest of his artistic life. It stands as one of the most ambitious and accomplished and—at times—perplexing long poems of the twentieth century. Pound concentrated all of his learning and imagination into this extended inquiry into the self in relation to Western and non-Western cultures. He hoped to chart a Dante-like path from hell through purgatory and into paradise. However, the actual course of his own life led to less predictable, yet perhaps more complex and interesting results. Pound's extraordinary range of literary and cultural references, extending through many centuries and languages—and interspersed with abrupt shifts in time, place, and point of view—makes *The Cantos* a challenge for readers at any level of experience. But the work contains many rewards as well, including many moments of original and arresting beauty.

Canto I launches Pound's enterprise with a translation of a famous passage from Homer's *Odyssey*, the scene in which the Greek hero Odysseus enters the realm of the dead and consults with Tiresias, a famous seer. Pound, too, would attempt to bring the dead to life and allow them to speak throughout *The Cantos*.

These notes are much indebted to Carroll F. Terrell's two-volume *Companion to "The Cantos" of Ezra Pound*.

15. Medieval Latin for "in the workshop of Welchelus," the Paris publisher of Divus. The year 1538 refers to the publication date of this Homeric translation.

16. Worthy of veneration (medieval Latin); the opening of the Second Homeric Hymn to Aphrodite as translated by Georgius Dartona.

17. Goddess of love and beauty.

18. Continuation of Dartona's Latin version of the Second Homeric Hymn. As rendered by Pound, Aphrodite "held sway over all the Cyprian heights," is "mirthful" (his translation of the Latin), and has "copper" colored eyes ("orichalchi"). The subsequent line continues the passage, translating Dartona into English.

19. From Dartona's translation of the First Hymn to Aphrodite. The ending of the poem with "So that:" indicates its linked relation to later cantos, just as its beginning with the word "And" suggests a significant prelude.

Canto XIII

Kung[1] walked
        by the dynastic temple
and into the cedar grove,
        and then out by the lower river,
And with him Khieu, Tchi[2]
        and Tian the low speaking
And "we are unknown," said Kung,
"You will take up charioteering?
        Then you will become known,
"Or perhaps I should take up charioteering, or archery?
"Or the practice of public speaking?"
And Tseu-lou said, "I would put the defences in order,"
And Khieu said, "If I were lord of a province
"I would put it in better order than this is."
And Tchi said, "I would prefer a small mountain temple,
"With order in the observances,
        with a suitable performance of the ritual,"
And Tian said, with his hand on the strings of his lute
The low sounds continuing
        after his hand left the strings,
And the sound went up like smoke, under the leaves,
And he looked after the sound:[3]
        "The old swimming hole,
"And the boys flopping off the planks,
"Or sitting in the underbrush playing mandolins."
        And Kung smiled upon all of them equally.
And Thseng-sie desired to know:
        "Which had answered correctly?"
And Kung said, "They have all answered correctly,
"That is to say, each in his nature."
And Kung raised his cane against Yuan Jang,
        Yuan Jang being his elder,
For Yuan Jang sat by the roadside pretending to

---

1. Kung Fu-tse (that is, Confucius). Pound, here and throughout the canto, uses the French transliteration of Chinese names he found in the translation by Pauthier rather than the customary English transliterations.

2. Khieu, Tchi, and Tian, like most of the individuals mentioned below, were young disciples of Confucius.

3. Tian was a singer and lutanist. The poem he sings in the lines below, celebrating "the old swimming hole," is his composition.

be receiving wisdom.
And Kung said
      "You old fool, come out of it,
"Get up and do something useful."
      And Kung said
"Respect a child's faculties
From the moment it inhales the clear air,
"But a man of fifty who knows nothing
      Is worthy of no respect."
And "When the prince has gathered about him
"All the savants and artists, his riches will be fully employed."
And Kung said, and wrote on the bo leaves:[4]
      If a man have not order within him
He can not spread order about him;
And if a man have not order within him
His family will not act with due order;
      And if the prince have not order within him
He can not put order in his dominions.
And Kung gave the words "order"
and "brotherly deference"
And said nothing of the "life after death."
And he said
      "Anyone can run to excesses,
It is easy to shoot past the mark,
It is hard to stand firm in the middle."[5]

And they said: If a man commit murder
      Should his father protect him, and hide him?
And Kung said:
      He should hide him.

And Kung gave his daughter to Kong-Tch'ang
      Although Kong-Tch'ang was in prison.
And he gave his niece to Nan-Young
      although Nan-Young was out of office.
And Kung said "Wang ruled with moderation,
      In his day the State was well kept,
And even I can remember
A day when the historians left blanks in their writings,

---

4. Bamboo tablets.
5. Pound later translated the title of one of Confu-
cius's books as *The Unwobbling Pivot*—it cele-
brates the ability to "stand firm in the middle."

I mean for things they didn't know,
But that time seems to be passing."
And Kung said, "Without character you will
          be unable to play on that instrument
Or to execute the music fit for the Odes.[6]
The blossoms of the apricot
          blow from the east to the west,
And I have tried to keep them from falling."

                                        1925

Canto XIII creates a dramatic scene from the life of the ancient Chinese philosopher and teacher Confucius (or Kung Fu-tse) (551–479 B.C.E.). Confucius remained a persistent fascination of Pound's. He would later translate several books by the ancient sage into English, working from the Chinese originals. At this point, Pound, a wide-ranging linguist, did not yet know Chinese, and the vignettes in the poem are translated and adapted from an 1841 French version of Confucius by M. G. Pauthier. Although Pound's version appears to dramatize a single moment from Confucius's life, Pound in fact draws on phrases culled from throughout the Confucian canon.

Canto XLV

With *Usura*[1]
With usura hath no man a house of good stone
each block cut smooth and well fitting
that design might cover their face,
with usura
hath no man a painted paradise on his church wall
harpes et luz[2]
or where virgin receiveth message
and halo projects from incision,
with usura
seeth no man Gonzaga[3] his heirs and his concubines
no picture is made to endure nor to live with
but it is made to sell and sell quickly

6. The Confucian Odes, a collection of ancient Chinese poetry purportedly collected by Confucius. Pound would later translate these odes as *The Classic Anthology Defined by Confucius* (1954).
1. Usury (Latin).
2. Harps and lutes (Old French): a citation from the verse *Testament* of François Villon (1431–?), a medieval French poet and thief.
3. "The Gonzaga Family and Retinue," the vivid fresco Mantegna painted on the walls of the Ducal Palace in Mantua in the Camera degli Sposi (Bridal Chamber) between 1465 and 1474.

with usura, sin against nature,
is thy bread ever more of stale rags
is thy bread dry as paper,
with no mountain wheat, no strong flour
with usura the line grows thick
with usura is no clear demarcation
and no man can find site for his dwelling.
Stonecutter is kept from his stone
weaver is kept from his loom
WITH USURA
wool comes not to market
sheep bringeth no gain with usura
Usura is a murrain,[4] usura
blunteth the needle in the maid's hand
and stoppeth the spinner's cunning. Pietro Lombardo[5]
came not by usura
Duccio[6] came not by usura
nor Pier della Francesca;[7] Zuan Bellin' not by usura
nor was 'La Calunnia'[8] painted.
Came not by usura Angelico;[9] came not Ambrogio Praedis,
Came no church of cut stone signed: *Adamo me fecit.*[10]
Not by usura St Trophime[11]
Not by usura Saint Hilaire,[12]
Usura rusteth the chisel
It rusteth the craft and the craftsman
It gnaweth the thread in the loom
None learneth to weave gold in her pattern;
Azure hath a canker by usura; cramoisi[13] is unbroidered
Emerald findeth no Memling[14]
Usura slayeth the child in the womb
It stayeth the young man's courting

4. A disease among cattle and sheep.
5. Italian architect and sculptor (ca. 1435–1515).
6. Duccio di Buoninsegna (ca. 1255–1319), an Italian painter favored by Pound and a leading figure in Siena.
7. Piero della Francesca (ca. 1420–1492): great fresco painter and portraitist from Umbria. Giovanni Bellini (ca. 1430–1516): influential Venetian painter of portraits and religious subjects.
8. "The Calumny" (i.e., slander): a dramatic allegorical painting by Botticelli (1445–1510).
9. Fra Angelico (1387–1455): Florentine painter and Dominican friar. Ambrogio Praedis (ca.

1455–ca. 1508): Milanese painter of portraits and miniatures.
10. "Adam made me" (Latin): carved on a column in the Romanesque Church of San Zeno in Verona. Pound took it as an emblem of the medieval craftsman's pride in his work, as opposed to the impersonality of modern mass production.
11. Romanesque church in Arles, France, that is noted for its elegant cloister.
12. Romanesque church in Poitiers, France.
13. Crimson cloth (French).
14. Hans Memling (ca. 1430–1494): Flemish religious painter and portraitist.

It hath brought palsey to bed, lyeth
between the young bride and her bridegroom
$$\text{CONTRA NATURAM}^{15}$$
They have brought whores for Eleusis[16]
Corpses are set to banquet
at behest of usura.

1936

In the 1930s, Pound became a strong believer in the then-popular economic theory called Social Credit, which argued that usury—the charging of excessively high interest—was the cause of all economic ills, including those suffered worldwide in the Great Depression. Under Social Credit, loans are—at least in theory—administered communally, for the common good. Many of the cantos of this period involve American, Chinese, and Italian Renaissance history and culture, with issues of economics—and particularly the support of artists and poetry—at their root. In Canto XLV, Pound embarks on a lyrical denunciation of usury. According to Pound annotator Carroll F. Terrell, usury "functions in *The Cantos* to dramatize the forces at work in human nature which prevent the human race from creating a paradise on earth." Pound draws on a wide range of examples of the cultural products of a world without usury, focusing on the Middle Ages and the Renaissance, when usury was prohibited in most European countries. Pound wrote this canto while he was living in Rapallo, Italy, and surrounded by the art he extols.

FROM *Canto LXXXI*

libretto[1]

Yet

Ere the season died a-cold
Borne upon a zephyr's shoulder
I rose through the aureate sky
        Lawes and Jenkyns[2] *guard thy rest*
        Dolmetsch[3] *ever be thy guest,*
Has he tempered the viol's wood

15. Against nature (Latin).
16. Site, near Athens, of the Eleusinian Mysteries. These rites, held annually in honor of Demeter and Persephone, were the most revered and sacred of all the ritual celebrations of ancient Greece. The Eleusinian Mysteries attracted worshipers throughout Greece and the ancient world and exercised considerable influence on early Christian teachings.
1. The musical label "libretto" underlines the lyrical nature of this passage, a climactic moment in the *Pisan Cantos* and in the poem as a whole.

This passage is in various ways a celebration of the power of song and lyric verse and of the power of beauty to sustain a life overwhelmed by pain and defeat.
2. Henry Lawes (1596–1662) and John Jenkyns (1592–1678) were English composers and musicians whom Pound invokes as guardian spirits in his moment of extremity.
3. Arnold D. Dolmetsch, a pioneer English instrument maker and scholar of early music, was often praised by Pound.

To enforce   both the grave   and the acute?
Has he curved us the bowl of the lute?[4]

> *Lawes and Jenkyns guard thy rest*
> *Dolmetsch ever be thy guest,*

Hast 'ou fashioned so airy a mood
    To draw up leaf from the root?
Hast 'ou found   a cloud   so light
    As seemed neither mist nor shade?

> Then resolve me, tell me aright
> If Waller[5] sang or Dowland played.

> Your eyen two wol sleye me sodenly
> I may the beauté of hem nat susteyene[6]

And for 180 years almost nothing.

Ed ascoltando al leggier mormorio[7]
    there came new subtlety of eyes into my tent,
whether of spirit or hypostasis,[8]
    but what the blindfold hides
or at carneval
              nor any pair showed anger
    Saw but the eyes and stance between the eyes,
colour, diastasis,[9]
    careless or unaware it had not the
   whole tent's room
nor was place for the full Ειδως[10]
interpass, penetrate
    casting but shade beyond the other lights

4. Dolmetsch, for one, "tempered the viol's wood" and "curved . . . the bowl of the lute"—in short, by re-creating early instruments, he helped make possible the rebirth of early music as an art form. Through Dolmetsch and others, "the grave and the acute" accents of words (in, for example, the French language) could now be distinctly heard in music played on authentic instruments. Pound's lines echo Ben Jonson's "Triumph of Charis": "Have you seen the bright lily grow, / Before rude hands have touched it?"

5. English poet Edmund Waller (1606–1687) wrote "Go, lovely Rose," famously set to music by Lawes (above). John Dowland (1563–1626) was the outstanding English lutanist and composer of his time.

6. Chaucer (Middle English), from "Merciles Beautie": "Your two eyes will slay me suddenly. / I cannot endure [sustain] their beauty."

7. "And listening to the gentle murmur" (Italian). Pound said these lines were "not a quotation, merely author using handy language."

8. Theological term for a creature or object divine in itself, not merely a container for the divine. Something—perhaps a creature, perhaps a vision, perhaps a divine presence—has entered Pound's tent, embodied chiefly by its "subtle" pair of eyes.

9. Separation; here, perhaps, the distance separating the two eyes of the uncanny creature.

10. Knowing, seeing (Greek). Pound's visitor is a creature or presence that cannot be fully seen or known. All that can be seen is the portion of the face that a mask might cover.

sky's clear

night's sea

green of the mountain pool

shone from the unmasked eyes in half-mask's space.

What thou lovest well remains,

the rest is dross

What thou lov'st well shall not be reft from thee

What thou lov'st well is thy true heritage

Whose world, or mine or theirs

or is it of none?

First came the seen, then thus the palpable

Elysium,[11] though it were in the halls of hell,

What thou lovest well is thy true heritage

What thou lov'st well shall not be reft from thee

The ant's a centaur in his dragon world.

Pull down thy vanity, it is not man

Made courage, or made order, or made grace,

Pull down thy vanity, I say pull down.

Learn of the green world[12] what can be thy place

In scaled invention or true artistry,

Pull down thy vanity,

Paquin[13] pull down!

The green casque[14] has outdone your elegance.

"Master thyself, then others shall thee beare"[15]

Pull down thy vanity

Thou art a beaten dog beneath the hail,

A swollen magpie in a fitful sun,

Half black half white

Nor knowst'ou wing from tail

Pull down thy vanity

How mean thy hates

Fostered in falsity,

Pull down thy vanity,

Rathe to destroy, niggard in charity,

---

11. The Elysian Fields: in Greek mythology, a place of bliss and the final resting place of the souls of the virtuous.

12. Nature can teach us much about beauty and form.

13. Famous Parisian dress designer.

14. Green insect's shell or armor—a natural form from the "green world."

15. Rephrases Chaucer's "Subdue thyself, and others shall thee hear" from the "Ballade of Good Counsel."

Pull down thy vanity,
                    I say pull down.

But to have done instead of not doing
                    this is not vanity
To have, with decency, knocked
That a Blunt[16] should open
                    To have gathered from the air a live tradition
or from a fine old eye the unconquered flame
This is not vanity.
          Here error is all in the not done,
all in the diffidence that faltered . . .

                                             1948

In May 1945, with the defeat of the Axis forces in Italy, Pound was imprisoned in the U.S. Army's Disciplinary Training Center at Pisa. There he was held for six months under threat of execution for treason as a consequence of broadcasts supporting fascism. However, formal charges against Pound were never brought. For a time, Pound (then sixty years old) was kept in an open cage, until—suffering a physical breakdown from exposure—he was allowed to move into a tent in the medical compound. There Pound gained access to a typewriter and, using a packing crate (provided by a sympathetic African-American soldier) as a writing desk, began composing the *Pisan Cantos*, an artistically and emotionally complex reconsideration of his past, including both its luminous moments and its acknowledged mistakes and failures. Many consider the *Pisan Cantos*, published in 1948, to be Pound's greatest single achievement in poetry.

Canto CXVI

Came Neptunus[1]
                    his mind leaping
                              like dolphins,
These concepts the human mind has attained.
To make Cosmos—
To achieve the possible—
Muss.,[2] wrecked for an error,

16. Wilfred Blunt (1840–1922), English diplomat and poet. During his London years, Pound deeply respected Blunt's fine manners and his anti-imperialist politics. Blunt was an outspoken critic of Britain's occupation of India and was imprisoned for his efforts in support of Irish independence. Pound was among a group of younger poets in London who visited Blunt and bestowed on him tokens of their respect and esteem.

1. Neptune (Greek: Poseidon), the Roman god of the sea.

2. Mussolini, the head of the Italian fascist state, who was executed by anti-fascist Italian partisans in 1945.

But the record
        the palimpsest[3] —
a little light
        in great darkness —
cuniculi[4] —
And old "crank" dead in Virginia.
Unprepared young burdened with records,
The vision of the Madonna
        above the cigar butts
          and over the portal.[5]
"Have made a mass of laws"
            (mucchio di leggi)[6]
Litterae nihil sanantes[7]
        Justinian's,[8]
a tangle of works unfinished.

I have brought the great ball of crystal;
        who can lift it?
Can you enter the great acorn[9] of light?
        But the beauty is not the madness
Tho' my errors and wrecks lie about me.
And I am not a demigod,
I cannot make it cohere.
If love be not in the house there is nothing.
The voice of famine unheard.
How came beauty against this blackness,
Twice beauty under the elms[10] —
        To be saved by squirrels and bluejays?
        "plus j'aime le chien"[11]

3. A manuscript that has been used more than once as a writing material; an earlier text is erased and/or hidden by a later text written on top of that original. Pound and H.D. pioneered the use of the term *palimpsest* to define literature itself: as a multilayered retelling of the same story in different terms. Cantos I and XIII in the present selection are clear examples of palimpsests, and the multi-textual features of Cantos XLV and LXXXI make them palimpsests as well. Any multilayered work may now be referred to as a palimpsest.
4. Canals or underground passages.
5. In the Venetian lagoon, the basilica of Torcello has such a mosaic of the Madonna "over the portal" (doorway).
6. Mass of laws (Italian).

7. Literature, which heals nothing (Latin).
8. The Roman Emperor Justinian (483–565) reorganized the contradictory mass of laws in the Eastern Roman Empire into a coherent legal system, the *Codex Constitutionum* (528–34). The *Institutes of Justinian*, designed for laymen, was a shortened and simplified version of this remarkable fifty-volume work. Pound considered Justinian one of the great minds of the Western world.
9. An image from the Neoplatonic philosophy of light.
10. Terrell cites these as "moments of great vision under the elms on the grounds of St. Elizabeths."
11. The more I love dogs (French). The full remark is "The more I know men, the more I love dogs."

Ariadne.[12]

Disney[13] against the metaphysicals,
and Laforgue[14] more than they thought in him,
Spire[15] thanked me in proposito
And have learned more from Jules

(Jules Laforgue) since then

deeps in him,

and Linnaeus.[16]

chi crescerà i nostri[17]—

but about that terzo[18]

third heaven,

that Venere,[19]

again is all "paradiso"[20]

a nice quiet paradise

over the shambles,

and some climbing

before the take-off,

to "see again,"
the verb is "see," not "walk on"
i.e. it coheres all right

even if my notes do not cohere.

Many errors,

a little rightness,

to excuse his hell

and my paradiso.

And as to why they go wrong,

thinking of rightness

And as to who will copy this palimpsest?

al poco giorno

ed al gran cerchio d'ombra[21]

---

12. Mythological daughter of King Minos of Crete. She rescued Theseus from the Minotaur, a monster who slaughtered Athenian youths sent as tribute to Minos. She sailed away with Theseus, who later abandoned her to Dionysus, the god of wine.

13. Pound was a great fan of movies, including Walt Disney's.

14. Jules Laforgue (1860–1887), French symbolist poet who also influenced T. S. Eliot.

15. André Spire (1868–1966), French poet and advocate of Zionism. A friend of Pound's, despite their divergent views on Zionism. In proposito: for the intention (Italian).

16. Karl von Linné (1707–1778), Swedish botanist and founder of the modern classification system for animals and plants. Terrell notes that Pound valued "the great reverence he showed toward all creation, as expressed in his *Philosophia Botanica* (1751)."

17. Who will increase (Italian).

18. Third (Italian).

19. Venus (Italian).

20. Paradise (Italian). Pound is thinking of the third level of heaven in Dante's *Paradiso*.

21. In the small hours with the darkness describing a great circle (Italian).

But to affirm the gold thread in the pattern
(Torcello)[22]
al Vicolo d'oro[23]
(Tigullio).[24]
To confess wrong without losing rightness:
Charity I have had sometimes,
I cannot make it flow thru.
A little light, like a rushlight
to lead back to splendour.
1969

Pound was moved to the United States in November 1945 to stand trial for treason. However, he was found unfit to plead on grounds of insanity and held in St. Elizabeths Hospital, Washington, D.C., in a ward for the criminally insane. He was never formally charged and was later shifted to a regular mental ward. He published many books—poetry, anthologies, essays, translations—while in St. Elizabeths and was visited by many rising American poets. He was released in 1956 and returned to Italy, where he continued to work on *The Cantos*. Though struggling with profound depression and self-doubt, Pound found means to weave these uncertainties into the work's fabric. Canto CXVI was the last one he completed. It is followed by a series of fragments.

Canto CXX

I have tried to write Paradise

Do not move
Let the wind speak
that is paradise.

Let the Gods forgive what I
have made
Let those I love try to forgive
what I have made.
1969

In the 1975 edition of *The Cantos* this fragmentary poem appears as the concluding Canto CXX. In more recent editions it appears among the "Notes for CXVII et seq." Yet many readers still feel that this poem provides *The Cantos* with an exceptionally poignant and appropriate ending.

22. An island in the Venetian lagoon, once prosperous and populous but now largely abandoned due to geographical changes. It still boasts many ancient churches and towers.

23. Street in Rapallo, a seaside city and Pound's Italian home. From its intersection one can see a cross of blue sky.

24. Gulf overlooked by Rapallo.

PROSE

from A *Retrospect*

There has been so much scribbling about a new fashion in poetry, that I may perhaps be pardoned this brief recapitulation and retrospect.

In the spring or early summer of 1912, 'H.D.', Richard Aldington and myself decided that we were agreed upon the three principles following:

1. Direct treatment of the 'thing' whether subjective or objective.
2. To use absolutely no word that does not contribute to the presentation.
3. As regarding rhythm: to compose in the sequence of the musical phrase, not in sequence of a metronome.

Upon many points of taste and of predilection we differed, but agreeing upon these three positions we thought we had as much right to a group name, at least as much right, as a number of French 'schools' proclaimed by Mr Flint in the August number of Harold Monro's magazine for 1911.

This school has since been 'joined' or 'followed' by numerous people who, whatever their merits, do not show any signs of agreeing with the second specification. Indeed vers libre has become as prolix and as verbose as any of the flaccid varieties that preceded it. It has brought faults of its own. The actual language and phrasing is often as bad as that of our elders without even the excuse that the words are shovelled in to fill a metric pattern or to complete the noise of a rhyme-sound. Whether or no the phrases followed by the followers are musical must be left to the reader's decision. At times I can find a marked metre in 'vers libres', as stale and hackneyed as any pseudo-Swinburnian, at times the writers seem to follow no musical structure whatever. But it is, on the whole, good that the field should be ploughed. Perhaps a few good poems have come from the new method, and if so it is justified.

Criticism is not a circumscription or a set of prohibitions. It provides fixed points of departure. It may startle a dull reader into alertness. That little of it which is good is mostly in stray phrases; or if it be an older artist helping a younger it is in great measure but rules of thumb, cautions gained by experience.

I set together a few phrases on practical working about the time the first remarks on imagisme were published. The first use of the word 'Imagiste' was in my note to T. E. Hulme's five poems, printed at the end of my 'Ripostes' in the autumn of 1912. I reprint my cautions from Poetry for March 1913.

A Few Don'ts

An 'Image' is that which presents an intellectual and emotional complex in an instant of time. I use the term 'complex' rather in the technical sense employed by the newer psychologists, such as Hart, though we may not agree absolutely in our application.

It is the presentation of such a 'complex' instantaneously which gives that sense of sudden liberation; that sense of freedom from time limits and space limits; that sense of sudden growth, which we experience in the presence of the greatest works of art.

It is better to present one Image in a lifetime than to produce voluminous works.

All this, however, some may consider open to debate. The immediate necessity is to tabulate A LIST OF DON'TS for those beginning to write verses. I can not put all of them into Mosaic negative.

To begin with, consider the three propositions (demanding direct treatment, economy of words, and the sequence of the musical phrase), not as dogma — never consider anything as dogma — but as the result of long contemplation, which, even if it is some one else's contemplation, may be worth consideration.

Pay no attention to the criticism of men who have never themselves written a notable work. Consider the discrepancies between the actual writing of the Greek poets and dramatists, and the theories of the Graeco-Roman grammarians, concocted to explain their metres.

1918

Pounds "A Retrospect," a loosely organized group of essays and notes, first appeared in *Pavannes and Divagations* (1918). "A Few Don'ts" made its first appearance in *Poetry* (March 1913).

ELINOR WYLIE
1885–1928

IN HER POIGNANTLY BRIEF yet highly productive career, Elinor Wylie wrote poems distinctive for their irony, grace, and crystalline lucidity. Although a clear voice is always at the center of her lyrics, that voice changes discernibly from poem to poem. In "Let No Charitable Hope," she wrote that the passing years adopt "masks outrageous and austere," and her speakers seem to adopt such masks as well. Sometimes they appear independent, assertive, and satirical. At other times they appear uncertain, self-critical, and sad. Her poems alternately explore aspiration and disappointment, love and solitude, the will to live and a despairing wish for sleep and death. Yet however different the moods, the poems are always elegantly and subtly imaginative. Rather than abandon traditional rhythms and rhymes, as did many poets of her generation, Wylie revised them so that they might precisely communicate her wry, sly, and at times forlorn sense of female subjectivity in a changing world.

Wylie was born into a wealthy family and grew up in Philadelphia and Washington, D.C. Privately educated, she married young, scandalously leaving her first husband and her son to marry Horace Wylie, whom she divorced in turn to marry the poet William Rose Benét. She spent her life in an ultimately unsuccessful quest to discover her perfect soul mate, a disillusioning process reflected in some of her poems. She also suffered from repeated heart attacks, dying in New York of a stroke at the age of only forty-three. Yet despite her ill health, Wylie packed a lifetime of writing and accomplishment into those few years. She served as poetry editor of *Vanity Fair* and contributing editor of the *New Republic*. She published four volumes of poetry (the last posthumously), four novels (the most prominent being *Jennifer Lorn*), and numerous essays and reviews. Influenced by Percy Bysshe Shelley, the pre-Raphaelites, and the Aesthetes, Wylie received praise from William Butler Yeats, who called "The Eagle and the Mole" "a lovely heroic song," and from Edna St. Vincent Millay, who remarked that Wylie could be "gay and splendid about tragic things." Famous in her own day, she has been somewhat neglected in ours.

Wylie's poems arise from emotional, intellectual, and artistic contradiction. If her lyric speakers wish to run or to soar, they often end up burrowing underground or squeezing stones, as in "The Eagle and the Mole" and "Let No Charitable Hope." Their wishes for warmth and connection many times give way to chilled isolation, as in "Wild Peaches," "Sanctuary," and "Velvet Shoes." Their longings for accomplishment or love often result in renunciation, as in "Self-portrait," "Where, O, Where?," and "Felo De Se." Elinor Wylie's poems evoke a gifted modern woman's painful yet fruitful struggle to live and create.

FURTHER READING

Judith Farr. *The Life and Art of Elinor Wylie*. Baton Rouge: Louisiana State University Press, 1983.

Stanley Olson. *Elinor Wylie: A Life Apart, A Biography*. New York: Dial Press, 1979.

Alicia Ostriker. *Stealing the Language: The Emergence of Women's Poetry in America*. Boston: Beacon Press, 1986.

Cheryl Walker. *Masks Outrageous and Austere: Culture, Psyche, and Persona in Modern Women Poets*. Bloomington: Indiana University Press, 1991.

Elinor Wylie. *Collected Poems*. Foreword by William Rose Benét. New York: Alfred Knopf, 1932, 1977.

The Eagle and the Mole

Avoid the reeking herd,
Shun the polluted flock,
Live like that stoic bird,
The eagle of the rock.

The huddled warmth of crowds
Begets and fosters hate;
He keeps, above the clouds,
His cliff inviolate.

When flocks are folded warm,
And herds to shelter run,
He sails above the storm,
He stares into the sun.

If in the eagle's track
Your sinews cannot leap,
Avoid the lathered pack,
Turn from the streaming sheep.

If you would keep your soul
From spotted sight or sound,
Live like the velvet mole;
Go burrow underground.

And there hold intercourse
With roots of trees and stones,[1]
With rivers at their source,
And disembodied bones.

1921

Judith Farr suggests that this poem "rejects the contamination of society in favor of secretive contact with the private world of imagination nourished by nature." She also observes that the poem's dichotomy of eagle and mole may echo that of Blake's "The Book of Thel": "Does the Eagle know what is in the pit? / Or wilt thou go ask the Mole?"

1. An apparent echo of the last of Wordsworth's "Lucy Poems," in which a dead and buried young woman "neither hears nor sees; / Rolled round in earth's diurnal course, / With rocks, and stones, and trees."

Wild Peaches

1

When the world turns completely upside down
You say we'll emigrate to the Eastern Shore[1]
Aboard a river-boat from Baltimore;
We'll live among wild peach trees, miles from town,
You'll wear a coonskin cap, and I a gown
Homespun, dyed butternut's dark gold colour.
Lost, like your lotus-eating ancestor,[2]
We'll swim in milk and honey[3] till we drown.

The winter will be short, the summer long,
The autumn amber-hued, sunny and hot,
Tasting of cider and of scuppernong;[4]
All seasons sweet, but autumn best of all.
The squirrels in their silver fur will fall
Like falling leaves, like fruit, before your shot.

2

The autumn frosts will lie upon the grass
Like bloom on grapes of purple-brown and gold.
The misted early mornings will be cold;
The little puddles will be roofed with glass.
The sun, which burns from copper into brass,
Melts these at noon, and makes the boys unfold
Their knitted mufflers; full as they can hold,
Fat pockets dribble chestnuts as they pass.

Peaches grow wild, and pigs can live in clover;
A barrel of salted herrings lasts a year;
The spring begins before the winter's over.
By February you may find the skins
Of garter snakes and water moccasins
Dwindled and harsh, dead-white and cloudy-clear.

---

1. Of Maryland, across the Chesapeake Bay.
2. In Greek myth, Odysseus (or Ulysses) and his men come upon a group of lotus-eaters, who live in a continual stupor caused by the sweetly addictive lotus fruit. See Homer's *The Odyssey*, book 9, and Tennyson's "The Lotus-Eaters."

3. In the Hebrew Scriptures, the Lord delivers the children of Israel out of Egypt into "a land flowing with milk and honey" (Exodus 3:8).
4. An aromatic sweet wine made from a yellow grape grown in North Carolina.

3

When April pours the colours of a shell
Upon the hills, when every little creek
Is shot with silver from the Chesapeake
In shoals new-minted by the ocean swell,
When strawberries go begging, and the sleek
Blue plums lie open to the blackbird's beak,
We shall live well—we shall live very well.

The months between the cherries and the peaches
Are brimming cornucopias which spill
Fruits red and purple, sombre-bloomed and black;
Then, down rich fields and frosty river beaches
We'll trample bright persimmons, while you kill
Bronze partridge, speckled quail, and canvasback.[5]

4

Down to the Puritan marrow of my bones
There's something in this richness that I hate.
I love the look, austere, immaculate,
Of landscapes drawn in pearly monotones.
There's something in my very blood that owns
Bare hills, cold silver on a sky of slate,
A thread of water, churned to milky spate[6]
Streaming through slanted pastures fenced with stones.

I love those skies, thin blue or snowy gray,
Those fields sparse-planted, rendering meagre sheaves;
That spring, briefer than apple-blossom's breath,
Summer, so much too beautiful to stay,
Swift autumn, like a bonfire of leaves,
And sleepy winter, like the sleep of death.

1921

"Wild Peaches," a sequence of four sonnets (of which number 3 is imperfect), contrasts the
connotations of a southern landscape with those of a northern one. Note also the gender
roles played by the speaker and her presumably male companion.

5. A bay duck, one of the most popular of game   6. Flood or freshet.
birds.

Sanctuary

This is the bricklayer; hear the thud
Of his heavy load dumped down on stone.
His lustrous bricks are brighter than blood,
His smoking mortar whiter than bone.

Set each sharp-edged, fire-bitten brick
Straight by the plumb-line's shivering length;
Make my marvellous wall so thick
Dead nor living may shake its strength.

Full as a crystal cup with drink
Is my cell with dreams, and quiet, and cool. . . .
Stop, old man! You must leave a chink;
How can I breathe? *You can't, you fool!*

1921

The poem of sanctuary was a recurrent feature of nineteenth- and twentieth-century women's writing. Another example is Sara Teasdale's "The Sanctuary," also included in this anthology. Alicia Ostriker comments that "these are implicitly poems about the dilemma of the woman in a masculine culture." One could also consider Wylie's poem in terms of aesthetic enclosure.

Velvet Shoes

Let us walk in the white snow
   In a soundless space;
With footsteps quiet and slow,
   At a tranquil pace,
   Under veils of white lace.

I shall go shod in silk,
   And you in wool,
White as a white cow's milk,
   More beautiful
   Than the breast of a gull.

We shall walk through the still town
   In a windless peace;
We shall step upon white down,
   Upon silver fleece,
   Upon softer than these.

*   *   *

We shall walk in velvet shoes;
   Wherever we go
Silence will fall like dews[1]
   On white silence below.
   We shall walk in the snow.

1921

This lyric has been noted for its elegant technique and its dreamlike atmosphere. One of the whitest, quietest, and coldest poems ever written, it mysteriously associates economic privilege with magic, virginity, aesthetic perfection, emotional frigidity, companionship, and/or death.

Drowned Woman

He shall be my jailer
Who sets me free
From shackles frailer
Than the wind-spun sea.

He shall be my teacher
Who cries "Be brave,"
To a weeping creature
In a glass-walled wave.

But he shall be my brother
Whose mocking despair
Dives headlong to smother
In the weeds of my hair.

1923

Let No Charitable Hope

Now let no charitable hope
Confuse my mind with images
Of eagle and of antelope:
I am in nature none of these.

*   *   *

---

1. Compare to Emily Dickinson's "The Dews drew quivering and Chill - / For only Gossamer, my Gown - / My Tippet - only Tulle" (*Because I could not stop for death*).

I was, being human, born alone;
I am, being woman, hard beset;
I live by squeezing from a stone
The little nourishment I get.

In masks outrageous and austere
The years go by in single file;
But none has merited my fear,
And none has quite escaped my smile.

                    1923

The speaker of this poem—and the next—sardonically critiques the conditions in which she finds herself and the limits of her own mind and talent.

Self-portrait

A lens of crystal whose transparence calms
Queer stars to clarity, and disentangles
Fox-fires[1] to form austere refracted angles:
A texture polished on the horny palms
Of vast equivocal creatures, beast or human:
A flint, a substance finer-grained than snow,
Graved with the Graces in intaglio[2]
To set sarcastic sigil[3] on the woman.

This for the mind, and for the little rest
A hollow scooped to blackness in the breast,
The simulacrum of a cloud, a feather:
Instead of stone, instead of sculptured strength,
This soul, this vanity, blown hinter and thither
By trivial breath, over the whole world's length.

                    1923

Where, O, Where?

I need not die to go
So far you cannot know
My escape, my retreat,

---

1. Organic luminescences caused by fungi in de-
caying wood.
2. That is, a seal or piece of jewelry engraved with

the image of the three Graces, goddesses of
beauty in classical myth.
3. Seal or signet.

And the prints of my feet
Written in blood or dew;
They shall be hid from you,
In fern-seed lost
Or the soft flakes of frost.
They will turn somewhere
Under water, over air,
To earth space or stellar,
Or the garret or cellar
Of the house next door;
You shall see me no more
Though each night I hide
In your bed, at your side.

1928

Felo De Se

My heart's delight, I must for love forget you;
I must put you from my heart, the better to please you;
I must make the power of the spirit set you
Beyond the power of the mind to seize you.

My dearest heart, in this last act of homage,
I must reject you; I must unlearn to love you;
I must make my eyes give up your adorable image
And from the inner chamber of my soul remove you.

Heart of my heart, the heart alone has courage
Thus to relinquish; it is yourself that stills you
In all my pulses, and dissolves the marriage
Of soul and soul, and at the heart's core[1] kills you.

1929

This poem's title, adapted from Latin, means "suicide" or "theft of oneself." Therefore, when the speaker "kills" her love for her lover in the last line, she feels that she is killing herself as well.

---

1. Since *cor* means "heart" in Latin, this phrase might be interpreted, via bilingual play, as the heart's heart. The phrase may also echo Yeats's "deep heart's core" in the last line of "The Lake Isle of Innisfree."

H.D. [HILDA DOOLITTLE]
1886–1961

IT IS NOT OFTEN that a poet changes poetic history. H.D. did it twice. In 1913 she became the first poet to publish a poem that was identified as "imagist." Although short lived, the imagist movement that she initiated transformed poetic practice in the twentieth century, and its effects can still be felt today. Imagist poems emphasize concision, direct treatment of the thing, and metrical freedom. Sadakichi Hartmann (included in the first volume of this anthology) earlier had written poems with imagist features, but few noticed them. Others such as French philosopher Henri Bergson, British aesthetician T. E. Hulme, and American poet Ezra Pound had theorized a new poetics. Hulme had argued for "dry, hard, classical verse," and Pound had advocated "precision" in place of prolixity and abstraction. But H.D. discovered how to put such ideas into practice in a way that would impact poets and readers alike. In the January 1913 issue of *Poetry* magazine, she published three poems as "H.D. Imagiste," a nomenclature Pound had suggested she use. One of these poems was "Hermes of the Ways," which begins:

> The hard sand breaks,
> and the grains of it
> are clear as wine.

With that surprising juxtaposition of two disparate images—grains of sand compared to white wine—H.D. installed a laconic poetics based on a visual epistemology. In one gesture, she dispensed with traditional meters, vocabularies, and a stable lyric speaker holding the poem together. In their place were words about things, both perfectly chosen and glowing with the attention paid them. Poetry would never be the same.

Thirty years later, H.D. again performed a pioneering act, now writing long poems that challenged the patriarchal myths thought to be foundational to civilization. In such poems as "Tribute to the Angels," she rewrote Christian narrative as well as Freudian theory, placing a woman rather than a man at the center of her story and positing a dynamic way of knowing and feeling rather than a fixed set of truths. In "Tribute to the Angels" and other poems of her later period, H.D. substituted a dreamlike, expansive style for her previous imagism and verbal economy. Equally stunning, these poems challenged male cultural authority by reimagining the epic form and its traditional myths, imbuing them with her own mysticism and feminism. If H.D.'s first poetic revolution changed poetry, the second meant to change culture and subjectivity.

Hilda Doolittle was born in Bethlehem, Pennsylvania, to an upper-middle-class family. Her father was a professor of astronomy, her mother an artist who taught painting and music. The family belonged to the Moravian faith, a Protestant denomination that seeks to recapture the original vitality of Christianity by strictly adhering to the word of the Bible. Although H.D. did not practice the religion as an adult, its mysticism and its drive to reanimate an ancient belief system informed her poetic career. Doolittle attended Bryn Mawr for three terms in 1905–6 but left without receiving a degree. During that time she became a friend of William Carlos Williams and a lover of Ezra Pound, then students at the University of Pennsylvania (and both included in this anthology). She was briefly engaged to Pound, who remained a lifelong influence and friend. During this period, she was romantically involved with both men and women. In 1911, at the age of twenty-five, she left for Europe with another lover, Frances Gregg. She remained in Europe for the rest of her life, returning to the United States only on visits.

In early 1913 she published the three poems in *Poetry* that simultaneously established her literary identity as "H.D." and founded the imagist movement. Several months later, Pound (writing under the name of his friend F. S. Flint) published a brief essay in which he articulated three imagist rules: direct treatment of the "thing," a prohibition against any word not absolutely necessary, and a flexible rhythm imitating a musical phrase rather than a metronome. He also defined the image as "an intellectual and emotional complex in an instant of time." Imagism now had some exemplary poems by H.D. and a theory by Pound to explain them. The movement was born. "Hermes of the Ways," "Oread," "The Sea Rose," and other poems written in 1913–16 all show the imprint of the revolutionary style.

"Oread," for example, juxtaposes two distinctly dissimilar images (the sea and the mountain forest), turning them into contrasting but intersecting planes of reality and language. It is impossible to tell which image is the literal object being described and which the metaphor for it. The poem's first line, addressing the "sea," would indicate that the sea is the poem's fundamental topic; but the title, evoking an "oread" or mountain nymph, suggests that the poem describes a mountain forest. The two referents remain suspended in juxtaposition as the text oscillates between them, in effect thinking through these images. Just as the poem does not certify what its topic is, so it provides no interpretation, generalization, or lesson, and indeed no identified speaker to stabilize the discourse. An imagist poem invites the reader to jump into the gaps between the signifiers, discovering potential meanings by considering the play of connotation, association, and sound. Like a cubist or surrealist painting, the poem provides an interactive field of perceptual and emotional implications rather than a single meaning. For example, is the "oread" the poem's speaker or its addressee? Do such demands as "splash your great pines / on our rocks" and "cover us with your pools of fir" suggest a desire for sexual ecstasy, violent transformation, mystical transcendence, or deathly oblivion? Or do the demands simply reflect a storm? H.D. invented a new way of writing poetry, which in turn invited a new and more active way of reading.

Late in 1913, H.D. married Richard Aldington, a British poet and fellow imagist. Following a tempestuous marriage, marked by infidelities on both sides, she separated from him in 1918 and had an affair with Cecil Gray, which in 1919 produced her only child, a daughter she named Perdita. At about this same time H.D. met Bryher, who was to become her beloved companion for the next twenty-eight years. Born Winifred Ellerman, Bryher was a critic, editor, and historical novelist. During their time together in London and Switzerland, H.D. continued to write poems, novels, and memoirs. H.D., Bryher, and Perdita also took numerous trips to New York, California, Egypt, Greece, Corfu, and Crete. In Crete H.D. had a visionary experience that was to inform her later poetry.

H.D. brought to imagism a classical temper, as is suggested by such titles as "Hermes of the Ways" and "Oread." Her interest in the world of antiquity and myths—and especially in the poetry of Sappho, the model of a strong, woman-centered writer—deepened with the years. A period of psychoanalysis with Sigmund Freud in 1933–34 also had an effect, pushing her toward introspection, meditation, and a recovery of childhood ways of thought, all the while increasing her sense of self-assurance. Keeping the pen name "H.D.," she nonetheless moved beyond the imagist aesthetic she, Pound, Aldington, and their friends had devised together. She now strove to acquire an independent feminine voice, and even at times a prophetic one. She wrote narrative poems that revised Greek, Egyptian, and biblical stories and characters in a mystical, feminist way. Writing during and just after the London blitz in World War II and during a time of tension between Bryher and herself, H.D. found refuge by reinventing the ancient world as a realm of remembrance, ritual, and consoling values. She attempted to go beyond the patriarchal narratives that were instilled in her as a child and that continued to dominate culture. "Tribute to the Angels," for example, establishes a new female symbol or mother goddess: a powerful "Lady" who carries a book containing "the blank pages / of the unwritten volume of the new." The poem foregrounds the female principle and asserts the authority of female myth-making. It attempts to reshape our world into a more satisfying place—a spiritual home rather than a battlefield.

Following H.D.'s separation from Bryher, she broke down and was hospitalized for a time in a Swiss clinic. She remained in Switzerland and Italy until the end of her life. She continued to write long poems, such as *Helen in Egypt* and the poems collected in *Hermetic Definition*. She also wrote a series of evocative memoirs, including *End to Torment*, *HERmione*, and *The Gift*. Although she spent her last years in lonely hotel rooms, she did find solace in her continued creativity and in a rising tide of recognition and praise. Her innovative work had shaped high modernism, and then it reshaped late modernism, prefiguring postmodernist styles to come. H.D. influenced successive generations of American poets, a process that continues to this day. She ultimately achieved her goals, expressed in "Sheltered Garden" and "Epitaph," of finding "a new beauty" and creating a "Greek ecstasy."

FURTHER READING

Rachel Blau Duplessis. *H.D.: The Career of That Struggle.* Bloomington: Indiana University Press, 1986.

Susan Stanford Friedman. *Psyche Reborn: The Emergence of H.D.* Bloomington: Indiana University Press, 1981.

Susan Stanford Friedman and Rachel Blau Duplessis, eds. *Signets: Reading H.D.* Madison: University of Wisconsin Press, 1990.

Sandra Gilbert and Susan Gubar. "H.D.'s Self-Fulfilling Prophecies." In *No Man's Land, Volume 3: Letters from the Front,* 166–207. New Haven: Yale University Press, 1994.

Barbara Guest. *Herself Defined: The Poet H.D. and Her World.* New York: Quill, 1984.

H.D. *Collected Poems, 1912–1944.* Ed. Louis L. Martz. New York: New Directions, 1983.

———. *End to Torment: A Memoir of Ezra Pound.* New York: New Directions, 1979.

———. *The Gift.* New York: W. W. Norton, 1982.

———. *Helen in Egypt.* New York: Grove Press, 1961.

———. *Hermetic Definition.* New York: New Directions, 1972.

———. *HERmione.* New York: New Directions, 1981.

Adalaide Kirby Morris. *How to Live/What to Do: H.D.'s Cultural Poetics.* Champaign-Urbana: University of Illinois Press, 2003.

Ezra Pound. "A Retrospect." In *Literary Essays,* 3–14. 1918; reprint, New York: New Directions, 1935.

Hermes of the Ways

The hard sand breaks,
and the grains of it
are clear as wine.

Far off over the leagues of it,
the wind,
playing on the wide shore,
piles little ridges,
and the great waves
break over it.

But more than the many-foamed ways
of the sea,
I know him

of the triple path-ways,[1]
Hermes,
who awaits.

Dubious,
facing three ways,
welcoming wayfarers,
he whom the sea-orchard
shelters from the west,
from the east
weathers sea-wind;
fronts the great dunes.

Wind rushes
over the dunes,
and the coarse, salt-crusted grass
answers.

Heu,
it whips round my ankles!

II

Small is
this white stream,
flowing below ground
from the poplar-shaded hill,
but the water is sweet.

Apples on the small trees
are hard,
too small,
too late ripened
by a desperate sun
that struggles through sea-mist.

The boughs of the trees
are twisted

1. The three intersecting paths suggest the Greek god Hermes's association with crossroads. It also associates the god with his namesake, Hermes Trismegistus, a legendary author of magical (or hermetic) treatises, whose name means "thrice greatest."

by many bafflings;[2]
twisted are
the small-leafed boughs.

But the shadow of them
is not the shadow of the mast head
nor of the torn sails.

Hermes, Hermes,
the great sea foamed,
gnashed its teeth about me;
but you have waited,
where sea-grass tangles with
shore-grass.

1913

Hermes of Greek myth (related to the Roman god Mercury) was a graceful, swift messenger. His feet were winged sandals, and he carried a magic wand called a caduceus. He was variously conceived of as a master thief, a god of commerce, a patron of science and art, and a guide for travelers or the dead. In this poem he seems to play the role of both guide and spiritual landmark. Rachel Duplessis remarks that the poem was inspired by an epitaph by the classical Greek woman poet Anyte of Tegea, which also includes motifs of coastline, crossroads, and orchard.

Oread

Whirl up, sea —
whirl your pointed pines,
splash your great pines
on our rocks,
hurl your green over us,
cover us with your pools of fir.

1914

In Greek myth, an oread is a mountain nymph. The poem emphasizes both the irreducible particularity of natural objects such as sea, pines, and rocks and the mind's eagerness to connect them.

---

2. Deflections of the wind.

Sea Rose

Rose, harsh rose,
marred and with stint of petals,
meagre flower, thin,
sparse of leaf,

more precious
than a wet rose,
single on a stem—
you are caught in the drift.

Stunted, with small leaf,
you are flung on the sand,
you are lifted
in the crisp sand
that drives in the wind.

Can the spice-rose
drip such acrid fragrance
hardened in a leaf?

1916

This poem may represent a feminist undoing of the rose stereotype, presenting a flower that is marred and stunted rather than beautiful, yet even "more precious" for those attributes.

Mid-day

The light beats upon me.
I am startled—
a split leaf crackles on the paved floor—
I am anguished—defeated.

A slight wind shakes the seed-pods—
my thoughts are spent
as the black seeds.
My thoughts tear me,

I dread their fever.
I am scattered in its whirl.
I am scattered like
the hot shrivelled seeds.

*   *   *

The shrivelled seeds
are split on the path —
the grass bends with dust,
the grape slips
under its crackled leaf:
yet far beyond the spent seed-pods,
and the blackened stalks of mint,
the poplar is bright on the hill,
the poplar spreads out,
deep-rooted among trees.

O poplar, you are great
among the hill-stones,
while I perish on the path
among the crevices of the rocks.

1916

Sheltered Garden

I have had enough.
I gasp for breath.

Every way ends,
every road, every foot-path leads at last
to the hill-crest —
then you retrace your steps,
or find the same slope on the other side,
precipitate.

I have had enough —
border-pinks, clove-pinks, wax-lilies,
herbs, sweet-cress.

O for some sharp swish of a branch —
there is no scent of resin
in this place,
no taste of bark, of coarse weeds,
aromatic, astringent —
only border on border of scented pinks.

Have you seen fruit under cover
that wanted light —
pears wadded in cloth,

protected from the frost,
melons, almost ripe,
smothered in straw?

Why not let the pears cling
to the empty branch?
All your coaxing will only make
a bitter fruit—
let them cling, ripen of themselves,
test their own worth,
nipped, shrivelled by the frost,
to fall at last but fair
with a russet coat.

Or the melon—
let it bleach yellow
in the winter light,
even tart to the taste—
it is better to taste of frost—
the exquisite frost—
than of wadding and of dead grass.

For this beauty,
beauty without strength,
chokes out life.
I want wind to break,
scatter these pink-stalks,
snap off their spiced heads,
fling them about with dead leaves—
spread the paths with twigs,
limbs broken off,
trail great pine branches,
hurled from some far wood
right across the melon-patch,
break pear and quince—
leave half-trees, torn, twisted
but showing the fight was valiant.

O to blot out this garden
to forget, to find a new beauty
in some terrible
wind-tortured place.

1916

Fragment 113

Neither honey nor bee for me.
SAPPHO

Not honey,
not the plunder of the bee
from meadow or sand-flower
or mountain bush;
from winter-flower or shoot
born of the later heat:
not honey, not the sweet
stain on the lips and teeth:
not honey, not the deep
plunge of soft belly
and the clinging of the gold-edged
pollen-dusted feet;

not so—
though rapture blind my eyes,
and hunger crisp
dark and inert my mouth,
not honey, not the south,
not the tall stalk
of red twin-lilies,
nor light branch of fruit tree
caught in flexible light branch;

not honey, not the south;
ah flower of purple iris,
flower of white,
or of the iris, withering the grass—
for fleck of the sun's fire
gathers such heat and power
that shadow-print is light,
cast through the petals
of the yellow iris flower;

not iris—old desire—old passion—
old forgetfulness—old pain—
not this, nor any flower,
but if you turn again,

*   *   *

seek strength of arm and throat,
touch as the god;
neglect the lyre-note;
knowing that you shall feel,
about the frame,
no trembling of the string
but heat, more passionate
of bone and the white shell
and fiery tempered steel.

1921

"Fragment 113" is extrapolated from a single Greek phrase, translated in the epigraph, by Sappho. Sappho, whose work survives almost entirely in fragments, flourished circa 610–580 B.C.E. on the isle of Lesbos. Her poetry is celebrated for the beauty of its phrasing, its exquisite self-awareness, and its focus on the emotional life of women. The numbering of the fragment follows that in Henry Thornton Wharton's *Sappho* (1885).

Helen

All Greece hates
the still eyes in the white face,
the lustre as of olives
where she stands,
and the white hands.

All Greece reviles
the wan face when she smiles,
hating it deeper still
when it grows wan and white,
remembering past enchantments
and past ills.

Greece sees unmoved,
God's daughter,[1] born of love,
the beauty of cool feet
and slenderest knees,
could love indeed the maid,
only if she were laid,
white ash amid funereal cypresses.

1924

1. Helen was the daughter of the supreme god Zeus, who appeared in the guise of a swan to the mortal woman Leda and impregnated her.

According to Homer's *Iliad*, Helen of Troy, the wife of the Greek king Menelaus, was abducted by the Trojan prince Paris, an action that caused the Trojan War. After Paris's death and the victory of Greece, she returned to Menelaus. Whereas Homer portrays her as a wanton, if charming, adulteress, H.D. depicts her in a more sympathetic and mysterious manner.

Fragment Sixty-eight

. . . even in the house of Hades.
SAPPHO

1

I envy you your chance of death,
how I envy you this.
I am more covetous of him
even than of your glance,
I wish more from his presence
though he torture me in a grasp,
terrible, intense.

Though he clasp me in an embrace
that is set against my will
and rack me with his measure,
effortless yet full of strength,

and slay me
in that most horrible contest,
still, how I envy you your chance.

Though he pierce me—imperious—
iron—fever—dust—
though beauty is slain
when I perish,
I envy you death.

What is beauty to me?
has she not slain me enough,
have I not cried in agony of love,
birth, hate,
in pride crushed?

What is left after this?
what can death loose in me
after your embrace?

your touch,
your limbs are more terrible
to do me hurt.

What can death mar in me
that you have not?

    2

What can death send me
that you have not?
you gathered violets,
you spoke:
"your hair is not less black,
nor less fragrant,
nor in your eyes is less light,
your hair is not less sweet
with purple in the lift of lock";
why were those slight words
and the violets you gathered
of such worth?

How I envy you death;
what could death bring,
more black, more set with sparks
to slay, to affright,
than the memory of those first violets,
the chance lift of your voice,
the chance blinding frenzy
as you bent?

    3

So the goddess[1] has slain me
for your chance smile
and my scarf unfolding
as you stooped to it;
so she trapped me
with the upward sweep of your arm
as you lifted the veil,
and the swift smile and selfless.

---

1. Perhaps Aphrodite, the goddess of love in Greek myth.

   *   *   *

Could I have known?
nay, spare pity,
though I break,
crushed under the goddess' hate,
though I fall beaten at last,
so high have I thrust my glance
up into her presence.

Do not pity me, spare that,
but how I envy you
your chance of death.

                   1924

Like "Fragment 113" above, "Fragment Sixty-eight" is extrapolated from a phrase, translated in the epigraph, by the Greek lyric poet Sappho. In Greek myth, Hades was the god of the underworld. Whereas an earlier draft of the poem, written years before, revolved around a male female romantic relationship, the finished poem leaves the gender of the beloved open, though the Sapphic reference implies a lesbian love.

Epitaph

So I may say,
"I died of living,
having lived one hour";

so they may say,
"she died soliciting
illicit fervour";

so you may say,
"Greek flower; Greek ecstasy
reclaims for ever

one who died
following
intricate song's lost measure."

                   1931

FROM *Tribute to the Angels*

28

I had been thinking of Gabriel,[1]
of the moon-cycle, of the moon-shell,

of the moon-crescent
and the moon at full:

I had been thinking of Gabriel,
the moon-regent, the Angel,

and I had intended to recall him
in the sequence of candle and fire

and the law of the seven;[2]
I had not forgotten

his special attribute
of annunciator; I had thought

to address him as I had the others,
Uriel, Annael;[3]

how could I imagine
the Lady[4] herself would come instead?

29

We have seen her
the world over,

Our Lady of the Goldfinch,
Our Lady of the Candelabra,

Our Lady of the Pomegranate,
Our Lady of the Chair;[5]

---

1. One of the archangels in the Hebrew Scriptures, the Christian New Testament, and the Muslim Qur'an. In the Hebrew Scriptures, he is the heavenly messenger who explains a vision to Daniel (8:16). In the New Testament, he announces the birth of John the Baptist to Zechariah and the birth of Jesus to Mary (Luke 1:19, 31). In the Qur'an, he brings the revelation of the Qur'an to Muhammad and, through him, humanity (2:97).

2. In the New Testament, seven archangels stand before God (Revelation 8:2).
3. In Christian tradition, two of the other archangels.
4. The "Lady" has resonances of both the Virgin Mary of Christian tradition and the princess Psyche of Greek myth, whose name meant "the soul."
5. Various depictions of the Virgin Mary in painting and iconography.

    *   *   *

we have seen her, an empress,
magnificent in pomp and grace,

and we have seen her
with a single flower

or a cluster of garden-pinks
in a glass beside her;

we have seen her snood[6]
drawn over her hair,

or her face set in profile
with the blue hood and stars;

we have seen her head bowed down
with the weight of a domed crown,

or we have seen her, a wisp of a girl
trapped in a golden halo;

we have seen her with arrow, with doves
and a heart like a valentine;

we have seen her in fine silks imported
from all over the Levant,[7]

and hung with pearls brought
from the city of Constantine;[8]

we have seen her sleeve
of every imaginable shade

of damask and figured brocade;
it is true,

the painters did very well by her;
it is true, they missed never a line

of the suave turn of the head
or subtle shade of lowered eye-lid

    *   *   *

---

6. Hair band.
7. Eastern Mediterranean.

8. Byzantium; present-day Istanbul, Turkey.

or eye-lids half-raised; you find
her everywhere (or did find),

in cathedral, museum, cloister,
at the turn of the palace stair.

30

We see her[9] hand in her lap,
smoothing the apple-green

or the apple-russet silk;
we see her hand at her throat,

fingering a talisman[10]
brought by a crusader from Jerusalem;[11]

we see her hand unknot a Syrian veil
or lay down a Venetian shawl

on a polished table that reflects
half a miniature broken column;

we see her stare past a mirror
through an open window,

where boat follows slow boat on the lagoon;
there are white flowers on the water.

31

But none of these, none of these
suggest her as I saw her,

though we approach possibly
something of her cool beneficence

in the gracious friendliness
of the marble sea-maids in Venice,

who climb the altar-stair
at *Santa Maria dei Miracoli*,[12]

---

9. Additional incarnations of the "Lady" in different cultures and times.
10. Magical object.
11. That is, by a Christian soldier returned from the Crusades, a failed attempt by medieval Europeans to wrest Jerusalem from Muslim control.
12. Saint Mary of the Miracles, a church in Venice, Italy, that contains statues of sea-maids.

*   *   *

or we acclaim her in the name
of another in Vienna,

Maria von dem Schnee,[13]
Our Lady of the Snow.

32

For I can say truthfully,
her veils were *white as snow,*

so as no fuller[14] *on earth
can white them*; I can say

she looked beautiful, she looked lovely,
she was *clothed with a garment*

down to the foot, but it was not
girt about with a golden girdle,

there was no gold, no colour,
there was no gleam in the stuff

nor shadow of hem or seam,
as it fell to the floor; she bore

none of her usual attributes;
the Child[15] was not with her.

33

Hermes[16] took his attribute
of Leader-of-the-dead from Thoth[17]

and the T-cross becomes caduceus;
the old-church makes its invocation

to Saint Michael[18] and Our Lady
at the death-bed; Hermes Trismegistus[19]

---

13. Our Lady of the Snow, a church in Austria.
14. In the manufacturing of textiles, one who cleans the cloth.
15. The baby Jesus.
16. The messenger god in Greek myth.
17. The god of magic, wisdom, and learning in the ancient Egyptian religion, identified with Hermes by the Greeks.
18. One of the archangels in Christian tradition.
19. Hermes Thrice-Great, a legendary Greek figure based on their god Hermes and the Egyptian god Thoth.

*   *   *

spears, with Saint Michael,
the darkness of ignorance,

casts the Old Dragon
into the abyss.

34
So Saint Michael,
regent of the planet Mercury,

is not absent
when we summon the other Angels,

another candle appears
on the high-altar,

it burns with a potent flame
but quivers

and quickens and darkens
and quickens again;

remember, it was Thoth
with a feather

who weighed the souls
of the dead.

35
So she must have been pleased with us,
who did not forgo our heritage

at the grave-edge;
she must have been pleased

with the straggling company of the brush and quill
who did not deny their birthright;

she must have been pleased with us,
for she looked so kindly at us

under her drift of veils,
and she carried a book.

36

Ah (you[20] say), this is Holy Wisdom,
Santa Sophia,[21] the SS of the *Sanctus Spiritus*,

so by facile reasoning, logically
the incarnate symbol of the Holy Ghost;

your Holy Ghost was an apple-tree
smouldering — or rather now bourgeoning

with flowers; the fruit of the Tree?[22]
this is the new Eve who comes

clearly to return, to retrieve
what she lost the race,

given over to sin, to death;
she brings the Book of Life,[23] obviously.

37

This is a symbol of beauty (you continue),
she is Our Lady universally,

I see her as you project her,
not out of place

flanked by Corinthian capitals,[24]
or in a Coptic nave,[25]

or frozen above the centre door
of a Gothic cathedral;

you have done very well by her
(to repeat your own phrase),

you have carved her tall and unmistakeable,
a hieratic[26] figure, the veiled Goddess,

---

20. A respondent who subtly yet consistently mis-interprets the "Lady" in sections 36 and 37.
21. Saint Sophia, the name of a church in Byzantium (present-day Istanbul). *Sanctus Spiritus*: Holy Spirit (Latin).
22. The tree of knowledge of good and evil in the garden of Eden (Genesis 2:9). When Adam and Eve ate the forbidden fruit of this tree, they were cast out of the garden (Genesis 3:6, 23).
23. In Revelation, those who "are written in the Lamb's book of life" will enter the new Jerusalem at the end of time (21:27).
24. The top parts of Greek pillars carved in the Corinthian style.
25. The central part of an Egyptian Christian church.
26. Priestly.

*   *   *

whether of the seven delights,
whether of the seven spear-points.

38

O yes—you understand, I say,
this is all most satisfactory,

but she wasn't hieratic, she wasn't frozen,
she wasn't very tall;

she is the Vestal[27]
from the days of Numa,[28]

she carries over the cult
of the *Bona Dea*,[29]

she carries a book but it is not
the tome of the ancient wisdom,

the pages, I imagine, are the blank pages
of the unwritten volume of the new;

all, you say, is implicit,
all that and much more;

but she is not shut up in a cave
like a Sibyl;[30] she is not

imprisoned in leaden bars
in a coloured window;

she is Psyche,[31] the butterfly,
out of the cocoon.

39

But nearer than Guardian Angel
or good Daemon,[32]

27. One of the vestal virgins who tended the fire in the temple of Vesta, the Roman goddess of the hearth.

28. Numa Pompilius, a legendary king of Rome.

29. Good goddess (Latin), a spirit protecting women in Roman myth.

30. A female prophet in Greek legend and lore, allowed to age but not to die.

31. In Greek myth, a princess who was ultimately made immortal and married to Cupid, the god of love. Psyche is a figure of wisdom and beauty; her name means "soul" and her symbol is the butterfly.

32. Inner spirit.

* * *

she is the counter-coin-side
of primitive terror;

she is not-fear, she is not-war,
but she is no symbolic figure

of peace, charity, chastity, goodness,
faith, hope, reward;

she is not Justice with eyes
blindfolded like Love's;[33]

I grant you the dove's[34] symbolic purity,
I grant you her face was innocent

and immaculate and her veils
like the Lamb's Bride,[35]

but the Lamb was not with her,
either as Bridegroom or Child;

her attention is undivided,
we are her bridegroom and lamb;

her book is our book; written
or unwritten, its pages will reveal

a tale of a Fisherman,
a tale of a jar or jars,[36]

the same — different — the same attributes,
different yet the same as before.

40

This is no rune[37] nor symbol,
what I mean is — it is so simple

yet no trick of the pen or brush
could capture that impression;

33. Cupid's. Both Justice and Cupid are frequently represented wearing blindfolds.
34. In both Jewish and Christian traditions, the dove is a symbol of peace, purity, and divine spirit.
35. In Christian tradition the Lamb is Christ, and his bride is the Church.

36. Perhaps a reference to the Wise Men's gifts to the baby Jesus of gold, frankincense, and myrrh (Matthew 2:11).
37. Character of some ancient northern European alphabets, often implying a secret or magical language.

*   *   *

what I wanted to indicate was
a new phase, a new distinction of colour;

I wanted to say, I did say
there was no sheen, no reflection,

no shadow; when I said white,
I did not mean sculptor's or painter's white,

nor porcelain; dim-white could
not suggest it, for when

is fresh-fallen snow (or snow
in the act of falling) dim?

yet even now, we stumble, we are lost—
what can we say?

she was not impalpable like a ghost,
she was not awe-inspiring like a Spirit,

she was not even over-whelming
like an Angel.

41

She carried a book, either to imply
she was one of us, with us,

or to suggest she was satisfied
with our purpose, a tribute to the Angels;

yet though the campanile[38] spoke,
Gabriel, Azrael,[39]

though the campanile answered,
Raphael, Uriel,

though a distant note over-water
chimed *Annael*, and *Michael*

was implicit from the beginning,
another, deep, un-named, resurging bell

38. Bell tower.
39. Archangels in the Christian tradition, as are
the others named in succeeding lines.

      ✳   ✳   ✳

answered, sounding through them all:[40]
remember, where there was

no need of the moon to shine . . .
I saw no temple.

42

Some call that deep-deep bell
Zadkiel, the righteousness of God,

he is regent of Jupiter
or Zeus-pater or Theus-pater,

Theus, God; God-the-father, father-god
or the Angel god-father,

himself, heaven yet at home in a star
whose colour is amethyst,

whose candle burns deep-violet
with the others.

43

And the point in the spectrum
where all lights become one,

is white and white is not no-colour,
as we were told as children,

but all-colour;
where the flames mingle

and the wings meet, when we gain
the arc of perfection,

we are satisfied, we are happy,
we begin again;

I, John, saw. I testify[41]
to rainbow feathers, to the span of heaven

---

40. The unnamed seventh archangel is Zadkiel, mentioned explicitly in section 42.
41. An echo of Revelation, in which St. John the Divine testifies, "And I John saw these things" (22:8).

*   *   *

and walls of colour,
the colonnades of jasper;

but when the jewel
melts in the crucible,

we find not ashes, not ash-of-rose,
not a tall vase and a staff of lilies,

not *vas spirituale*,[42]
not *rosa mystica*[43] even,

but a cluster of garden-pinks
or a face like a Christmas-rose.

This is the flowering of the rod,
this is the flowering of the burnt-out wood,

where, Zadkiel, we pause to give
thanks that we rise again from death and live.

1945

"Tribute to the Angels" creates a mythic narrative of female divinity to counter the androcentric symbol systems of world civilization. The poem recounts three epiphanies of a redemptive goddess. In the first sections of the poem, not included here, we encounter a jewel, signifying healing, and a blossoming apple tree, signifying religion. In the last section of the poem, reprinted here in its entirety, the goddess appears in the guise of a "Lady" carrying a book, who represents art.

HAZEL HALL
1886–1924

HAZEL HALL, who died in 1924 at the age of thirty-eight after a brief but productive poetic career, has recently been rediscovered—after decades of obscurity and neglect. Readers have responded to her spare, poignant, sharp-edged, and elegantly crafted poems that take sewing, dressmaking, and a life of enforced enclosure and toil as their central metaphors.

42. Spiritual vessel (Latin).   43. Mystical rose (Latin).

Born in Portland, Oregon, Hall was confined to a wheelchair from childhood. She lived and worked in an upstairs room of her family's house and, like Tennyson's mythical Lady of Shallot, another artist at needlecraft, she expanded her view of the world outside by positioning a mirror by her window. Like Emily Dickinson, Hall drew on her condition of confinement to fashion poems of considerable exploratory power. Championed by *Poetry* magazine's editor Harriet Monroe, Hall began publishing poems in 1916 and in her short life produced two volumes, *Curtains* (1921) and *Walkers* (1923). These books were followed by the posthumous *City of Time* (1928). In perspective and mood, her work is comparable to that of her contemporaries Adelaide Crapsey and Sarah Teasdale (also included in this anthology).

An accomplished seamstress, Hall sewed with craft and industry to supplement the family income, and she wove the imagery of needlepoint and embroidery into her poetic world. Her poems also draw on a knowledge of and attraction to nature, which she perforce had to view remotely. The poems also comment eloquently on the constrained condition of women in her time and in earlier periods. The novelist Ursula LeGuin has said, in tribute to Hall, "Her poetry is a valuable testament, historically and psychologically, of the secret—passionate secret—life of a single working woman in a world that took no notice of her."

FURTHER READING

Hazel Hall. *Collected Poems*. Corvallis: Oregon State University Press, 2000.

Instruction

My hands that guide a needle
In their turn are led
Relentlessly and deftly
As a needle leads a thread.

Other hands are teaching
My needle; when I sew
I feel the cool, thin fingers
Of hands I do not know.

They urge my needle onward,
They smooth my seams, until
The worry of my stitches
Smothers in their skill.

*   *   *

All the tired women,
Who sewed their lives away,
Speak in my deft fingers
As I sew to-day.

1921

Light Sleep

Women who sing themselves to sleep
Lie with their hands at rest,
Locked over them night-long as though to keep
Music against their breast.
They who have feared the night and lain
Mumbling themselves to peace
Sleep a light sleep lest they forget the strain
That brings them their release.
They dream, who hold beneath the hand
A crumpled shape of song,
Of trembling sound they do not understand,
Yet love the whole night long.
Women who sing themselves to sleep
Must lie in fear till day,
Clasping an amulet of words to keep
The leaning dark away.

1921

Things That Grow

I like things with roots that know the earth,
Trees whose feet, nimble and brown,
Wander around in the house of their birth
Until they learn, by growing down,
To build with branches in the air;
Ivy-vines that have known the loam
And over trellis and rustic stair,
Or old grey houses, love to roam;
And flowers pushing vehement heads,
Like flames from a fire's hidden glow,
Through the seething soil in garden-beds.
Yet I, who am forbidden to know

The feel of earth, once thought to make
Singing out of a heart's old cry!
Untaught by earth, how could I wake
The shining interest of the sky?

1921

The Listening Macaws

Many sewing days ago
I cross-stitched on a black satin bag
Two listening macaws.
They were perched on a stiff branch
With every stitch of their green tails,
Their blue wings, yellow breasts and sharply turned heads,
Alert and listening.
Now sometimes on the edge of relaxation
My thought is caught back,
Like gathers along a gathering thread
To the listening macaws;
And I am amazed at the futile energy
That has kept them,
Alert to the last stitch,
Listening into their black satin night.

1923

ROBINSON JEFFERS
1887–1962

Robinson jeffers spent his adult life on the rugged central California coast, writing lyric poems about astonishing natural beauty and narrative poems about tortured human beings. His lyrics celebrate an enduring world of "universal beauty": cliffsides and forests, birds and whales, sunrises and sundowns, storms from the sea and cloudless blue days. If human beings appear in these poems at all, they are usually glimpsed from afar. His longer, narrative poems concentrate instead on intense family conflicts—the suffering these struggles cause and their often violent outcomes. Eloquent and passionate, Jeffers was a great environmental poet and a poet transfixed as well by the extremes of natural beauty and human emotion.

Jeffers's pantheistic belief that "the universe is one being, a single organism" caused him to write about natural landscapes and their inhabitants with rare perceptivity and eloquence. He occasionally portrayed human beings in harmony with nature. But he more characteristically feared that people, in their egotism, sought to dominate all other creatures and decimate the land, forgetting their bond with the "wild God of the world" ("Hurt Hawks"). As a result, he often adopted a skeptical or even hostile attitude toward his fellow human beings. At times he wrestled with his mixed feelings about people in a moving way, but at other times he simply inveighed against their corruption, as if he did not share in it at all.

Dubious about the spirit of poetic change sweeping through the work of such contemporaries as T. S. Eliot and Ezra Pound, Jeffers resolutely kept to his own path, which he considered wider and more lasting. He rejected "the self-conscious and naïve learnedness, the undergraduate irony, unnatural metaphors, hiatuses and labored obscurity" that he detected in experimental modernism. Instead he focused on what he termed "permanent things": dynamic natural beauty and tragic human suffering. At his best, he produced poems remarkable for their ecological awareness and observational qualities, their meditative profundity and amazing verbal vibrancy.

John Robinson Jeffers was born in Pittsburgh, Pennsylvania, in 1887, the son of a Presbyterian minister and a church organist. Responding to a rather unsettled childhood in a series of different houses and boarding schools, Jeffers grew up, as Tim Holt has described him, "shy and studious." Although he originally enrolled at the University of Pittsburgh, he transferred to Occidental College when his parents moved to Los Angeles for his father's health. In love with such writers as Sophocles and Shakespeare, Marlowe and Milton, Shelley and Yeats, Jeffers also studied astronomy, geology, the Bible, and Greek. After graduating, he continued his studies at several different institutions, including the University of Southern California, where he met the love of his life, a married woman named Una Call Kuster. After a scandalous affair, which they attempted to end but could not, Una divorced her husband and married Jeffers. The two remained devoted to each other until their deaths.

In 1914, as World War I was beginning, Robinson and Una Jeffers moved to the small coastal town of Carmel, California, where they were to remain. Jeffers built a stone house for them to live in, complete with a two-story tower in which he could write. Ensconced in "Tor House," isolated from most social interactions, the couple soon had twin sons, and Jeffers occupied himself working with stone and writing poems. In 1925, his volume *Roan Stallion, Tamar, and Other Poems* appeared to great critical and popular applause. From that time on, Jeffers's reputation was assured. His long narrative poems, "Roan Stallion" and "Tamar," attracted the most immediate attention because of their cathected scenes of incest, bestiality, and violence. Borrowing elements from Greek tragedy as well as the Hebrew Scriptures and the New Testament, these poems feature transgressive desires and overwrought relationships acted out in isolated landscapes. "Roan Stallion," for example, includes a half-mad wife, a drunken and abusive husband, an innocent child, and a roan-red stallion. It ends in a scene of climactic and unforgettable vengeance.

The lyric poems that accompanied Jeffers's narratives made a smaller initial impact but are the basis of his continuing reputation today. Written in rhythms intended to recall the ocean's tides, these poems describe a natural world that is, as Jeffers once said, both "real and divine." The poems eloquently combine acute observation with heartfelt meditation. "Salmon Fishing" portrays the ritualistic pleasures of fishing without eliding its cruelty and violence. "Birds" brings to life the beauty of hawks and other predatory birds, perceiving an analogy between the birds and the qualities necessary to a poem. "Boats in a Fog" celebrates a beautiful gravity of being, which the speaker perceives in the movement of fishing boats no less than in a flight of pelicans.

"Hurt Hawks," published in *Cawdor and Other Poems* (1928), movingly evokes the grandeur and suffering of an injured hawk. But it also, in one of its lines, forecasts the anger at human beings that would become a hallmark of Jeffers's middle years: "I'd sooner, except the penalties, kill a man than a hawk." In the 1930s and 1940s, Jeffers railed against human civilization, which he thought would surely lead to catastrophe. He developed a philosophical perspective he called "Inhumanism," defining it as "a shifting of emphasis and significance from man to notman." Yet he could not really keep his mind off of the doings of "man." Libertarian and isolationist, Jeffers strongly opposed American rearmament in the 1930s and the country's participation in World War II. He had opposed World War I, and he felt that World War II would be "terribly worse in effect." Marked by such obsessions, Jeffers's poetry became increasingly didactic. Even "The Purse-Seine" and "The Beaks of Eagles," though they focus on creatures of the sea and land, include dire warnings against "mass-disasters," "government," and human "follies."

By 1950 Jeffers was a changed person. His political poems had failed to change history, his beloved wife, Una, had died a painful death from cancer, and the poet himself was now aging and alone. Abandoning his quest to cure the ills of civilization, he now told himself, in "The Ocean's Tribute," that "we are fools / To turn from the superhuman beauty of the world." In *It nearly cancels my fear of death*, he awaited his own demise by recalling some of the last words spoken by his beloved Una.

Jeffers made poetic language new in a way very different from that of his power-ful contemporaries. Poetic "greatness," he once wrote, is "strange, unexpected, and sometimes repellent." Eschewing experimentalist indirection, fragmenta-tion, and condensation, he attempted to create more "primitive" and "perma-nent" forms. He did not, like Pound, wish to "make it new." In a sense, he tried instead to recover something old that had been lost. In his narrative poems, he bore witness to the sinfulness and heroism of the human heart, to the extreme de-sires that always lie hidden there. In his lyric poems, he celebrated what he called "transhuman magnificence," evoking the breathtaking beauty of nature in images and rhythms that are equally beautiful. Whether writing of human beings or the environment, Jeffers always suggested a vital interplay among mind, language, world, and the divinity he perceived and revered within all things.

FURTHER READING

Robert Brophy, ed. *Robinson Jeffers: The Dimensions of a Poet*. New York: Fordham University Press, 1995.

Tim Hunt. "Hurt Hawks." In *Encyclopedia of American Poetry: The Twentieth Century*, ed. Eric L. Haralson, 331–32. Chicago: Fitzroy Dearborn, 2001.

Robinson Jeffers. *Collected Poetry*. 5 vols. Ed. Tim Hunt. Stanford: Stanford University Press, 1988–2001.

——. *Selected Letters*. Ed. Ann Ridgeway. Baltimore: Johns Hopkins University Press, 1968.

——. *Selected Poetry*. Ed. Tim Hunt. Stanford: Stanford University Press, 2001.

Robert Zaller. *The Cliffs of Solitude: A Reading of Robinson Jeffers*. New York: Cambridge Uni-versity Press, 1983.

Salmon Fishing

The days shorten, the south blows wide for showers now,
The south wind shouts to the rivers,
The rivers open their mouths and the salt salmon
Race up into the freshet.
In Christmas month against the smoulder and menace
Of a long angry sundown,
Red ash of the dark solstice, you see the anglers,
Pitiful, cruel, primeval,
Like the priests of the people that built Stonehenge,[1]
Dark silent forms, performing
Remote solemnities in the red shallows
Of the river's mouth at the year's turn,

---

1. A prehistoric monument, composed of circles of large stone posts, on Salisbury Plain in England. The native people probably built it as a place of worship for a now-lost religion.

Drawing landward their live bullion,[2] the bloody mouths
And scales full of the sunset
Twitch on the rocks, no more to wander at will
The wild Pacific pasture nor wanton and spawning
Race up into fresh water.

1924

Tim Hunt suggests that Jeffers, in revising this poem, moved from depicting destructive human beings in an otherwise beautiful scene to a more complex vision of salmon and anglers "both enmeshed in a sacrificial landscape of fire and blood." Note, for example, that the anglers are priestly as well as "cruel," though the salmon still die as a result of their intervention.

Birds

The fierce musical cries of a couple of sparrowhawks hunting on the headland,
Hovering and darting, their heads northwestward,
Prick like silver arrows shot through a curtain the noise of the ocean
Trampling its granite; their red backs gleam
Under my window around the stone corners; nothing gracefuller, nothing
Nimbler in the wind.[1] Westward the wave-gleaners,
The old gray sea-going gulls are gathered together, the northwest wind wakening
Their wings to the wild spirals of the wind-dance.
Fresh as the air, salt as the foam, play birds in the bright wind, fly falcons
Forgetting the oak and the pinewood, come gulls
From the Carmel sands and the sands at the river-mouth, from Lobos[2] and out of the limitless
Power of the mass of the sea, for a poem
Needs multitude, multitudes of thoughts, all fierce, all flesh-eaters, musically clamorous
Bright hawks that hover and dart headlong, and ungainly
Gray hungers fledged with desire of transgression, salt slimed beaks, from the sharp
Rock-shores of the world and the secret waters.

1925

This evocation of the clamorous world of hawks, gulls, and falcons segues into a meditation on poetry, which is understood as being equally musical and fierce.

2. Bars of gold or silver.
1. That is, the hawks' cries pierce the ocean's noise. The speaker observes the birds from the window of his stone tower. Note the musical repetition of words, sounds, and cadences in this opening sentence, as well as the descriptive energy in the subordinate clauses.
2. A promontory on the Carmel coast.

Boats in a Fog

Sports and gallantries, the stage, the arts, the antics of dancers,
The exuberant voices of music,
Have charm for children but lack nobility; it is bitter earnestness
That makes beauty; the mind
Knows, grown adult.
                              A sudden fog-drift muffled the ocean,
A throbbing of engines moved in it,
At length, a stone's throw out, between the rocks and the vapor,
One by one moved shadows
Out of the mystery, shadows, fishing-boats, trailing each other
Following the cliff for guidance,
Holding a difficult path between the peril of the sea-fog
And the foam on the shore granite.
One by one, trailing their leader, six crept by me,
Out of the vapor and into it,
The throb of their engines subdued by the fog, patient and cautious,
Coasting all round the peninsula
Back to the buoys in Monterey harbor. A flight of pelicans
Is nothing lovelier to look at;
The flight of the planets is nothing nobler; all the arts lose virtue
Against the essential reality
Of creatures going about their business among the equally
Earnest elements of nature.

                                                        1925

Almost in the manner of a sermon or philosophical treatise, "Boats in a Fog" frames its close observation of fishing boats with more general significances that may be inferred from the scene.

Roan Stallion

The dog barked; then the woman stood in the doorway, and hearing iron strike stone
    down the steep road
Covered her head with a black shawl and entered the light rain; she stood at the turn of
    the road.
A nobly formed woman; erect and strong as a new tower; the features stolid and dark
But sculptured into a strong grace, straight nose with a high bridge, firm and wide eyes,
    full chin,

Red lips; she was only a fourth part Indian; a Scottish sailor had planted her in young
    native earth,
Spanish and Indian, twenty-one years before. He had named her California when she
    was born;
That was her name; and had gone north.

                            She heard the hooves and wheels come
    nearer, up the steep road.
The buckskin mare, leaning against the breastpiece, plodded into sight round
    the wet bank.
The pale face of the driver followed; the burnt-out eyes; they had fortune in them.
    He sat twisted
On the seat of the old buggy, leading a second horse by a long halter, a roan, a big one,
That stepped daintily; by the swell of the neck, a stallion. "What have you got, Johnny?"
    "Maskerel's stallion.
Mine now. I won him last night, I had very good luck." He was quite drunk. "They bring
    their mares up here now.
I keep this fellow. I got money besides, but I'll not show you." "Did you buy something,
    Johnny,
For our Christine?[1] Christmas comes in two days, Johnny." "By God, forgot," he
    answered laughing.
"Don't tell Christine it's Christmas; after while I get her something, maybe."
    But California:
"I shared your luck when you lost: you lost *me* once, Johnny, remember? Tom Dell had
    me two nights
Here in the house: other times we've gone hungry: now that you've won, Christine will
    have her Christmas.
We share your luck, Johnny. You give me money, I go down to Monterey[2] to-morrow,
Buy presents for Christine, come back in the evening. Next day Christmas." "You have
    wet ride," he answered
Giggling. "Here money. Five dollar; ten; twelve dollar. You buy two bottles of rye
    whisky for Johnny."
"All right. I go tomorrow."

                         He was an outcast Hollander; not old, but shriveled with
    bad living.
The child Christine inherited from his race blue eyes, from his life a wizened forehead;
    she watched

---

1. California and Johnny's young daughter.
2. The large town north of the Carmel Valley
where California and Johnny live.

From the house-door her father lurch out of the buggy and lead with due respect
the stallion
To the new corral, the strong one; leaving the wearily breathing buckskin mare to his
wife to unharness.

Storm in the night; the rain on the thin shakes of the roof like the ocean on rock
streamed battering; once thunder
Walked down the narrow canyon into Carmel valley and wore away westward;
Christine was wakeful
With fears and wonders; her father lay too deep for storm to touch him.

                                                            Dawn comes

late in the year's dark,
Later into the crack of a canyon under redwoods; and California slipped from bed
An hour before it; the buckskin would be tired; there was a little barley, and why should
Johnny
Feed all the barley to his stallion? That is what he would do. She tip-toed out of
the room,
Leaving her clothes, he'd waken if she waited to put them on, and passed from the door
of the house
Into the dark of the rain; the big black drops were cold through the thin shift, but the
wet earth
Pleasant under her naked feet. There was a pleasant smell in the stable; and
moving softly,
Touching things gently with the supple bend of the unclothed body, was pleasant.
She found a box,
Filled it with sweet dry barley and took it down to the old corral. The little mare
sighed deeply
At the rail in the wet darkness; and California returning between two redwoods up to
the house
Heard the happy jaws grinding the grain. Johnny could mind the pigs and chickens.
Christine called to her
When she entered the house, but slept again under her hand. She laid the wet
night-dress on a chair-back
And stole into the bed-room to get her clothes. A plank creaked, and he wakened.
She stood motionless
Hearing him stir in the bed. When he was quiet she stooped after her shoes, and he
said softly,
"What are you doing? Come back to bed." "It's late, I'm going to Monterey, I must
hitch up."
"You come to bed first. I been away three days. I give you money, I take back the money
And what you do in town then?" She sighed sharply and came to the bed.

＊　＊　＊

He reaching
his hands from it
Felt the cool curve and firmness of her flank, and half rising caught her by the long
wet hair.
She endured, and to hasten the act she feigned desire; she had not for long, except in
dream, felt it.
Yesterday's drunkenness made him sluggish and exacting; she saw, turning her
head sadly,
The windows were bright gray with dawn; he embraced her still, stopping to talk about
the stallion.
At length she was permitted to put on her clothes. Clear daylight over the steep hills;
Gray-shining cloud over the tops of the redwoods; the winter stream sang loud; the
wheels of the buggy
Slipped in deep slime, ground on washed stones at the road-edge. Down the hill the
wrinkled river smothered the ford.
You must keep to the bed of stones: she knew the way by willow and alder: the buckskin
halted mid-stream,
Shuddering, the water her own color washing up to the traces; but California,
drawing up
Her feet out of the whirl onto the seat of the buggy swung the whip over the
yellow water
And drove to the road.

All morning the clouds were racing northward like a river.
At noon they thickened.
When California faced the southwind home from Monterey it was heavy with
level rain-fall.
She looked seaward from the foot of the valley; red rays cried sunset from a trumpet
of streaming
Cloud over Lobos,[3] the southwest occident of the solstice. Twilight came soon, but the
tired mare
Feared the road more than the whip. Mile after mile of slow gray twilight.

Then,
quite suddenly, darkness.
"Christine will be asleep. It is Christmas Eve. The ford. That hour of daylight wasted
this morning!"
She could see nothing; she let the reins lie on the dashboard and knew at length by the
cramp of the wheels

3. A promontory on the Carmel coastline.

And the pitch down, they had reached it. Noise of wheels on stones, plashing of hooves
  in water; a world
Of sounds; no sight; the gentle thunder of water; the mare snorting, dipping her head,
  one knew,
To look for footing, in the blackness, under the stream. The hushing and creaking
  of the sea-wind
In the passion of invisible willows.

                        The mare stood still; the woman shouted to her;
  spared whip,
For a false leap would lose the track of the ford. She stood. "The baby's things," thought
  California,
"Under the seat: the water will come over the floor"; and rising in the midst of the water
She tilted the seat; fetched up the doll, the painted wooden chickens, the woolly bear,
  the book
Of many pictures, the box of sweets: she brought them all from under the seat and
  stored them, trembling,
Under her clothes, about the breasts, under the arms; the corners of the cardboard
  boxes
Cut into the soft flesh; but with a piece of rope for a girdle and wound about
  the shoulders
All was made fast. The mare stood still as if asleep in the midst of the water. Then
  California
Reached out a hand over the stream and fingered her rump; the solid wet convexity of it
Shook like the beat of a great heart. "What are you waiting for?" But the feel of the
  animal surface
Had wakened a dream, obscured real danger with a dream of danger. "What for?
  For the water-stallion
To break out of the stream, that is what the rump strains for, him to come up flinging
  foam sidewise,
Fore-hooves in air, crush me and the rig and curl over his woman." She flung out with
  the whip then;
The mare plunged forward. The buggy drifted sidelong: was she off ground?
  Swimming? No: by the splashes.
The driver, a mere prehensile instinct, clung to the side-irons of the seat and felt
  the force
But not the coldness of the water, curling over her knees, breaking up to the waist
Over her body. They'd turned. The mare had turned up stream and was wallowing back
  into shoal water.
Then California dropped her forehead to her knees, having seen nothing, feeling
  a danger,

And felt the brute weight of a branch of alder, the pendulous light leaves brush her
  bent neck
Like a child's fingers. The mare burst out of water and stopped on the slope to the ford.
  The woman climbed down
Between the wheels and went to her head. "Poor Dora," she called her by her name,
  "there, Dora. Quietly,"
And led her around, there was room to turn on the margin, the head to the gentle
  thunder of the water.
She crawled on hands and knees, felt for the ruts, and shifted the wheels into them.
  "You can see, Dora.
I can't. But this time you'll go through it." She climbed into the seat and shouted
  angrily. The mare
Stopped, her two forefeet in the water. She touched with the whip. The mare plodded
  ahead and halted.
Then California thought of prayer: "Dear little Jesus,
Dear baby Jesus born to-night, your head was shining
Like silver candles. I've got a baby too, only a girl. You had light wherever you walked.
Dear baby Jesus give me light." Light streamed: rose, gold, rich purple, hiding the ford
  like a curtain.
The gentle thunder of water was a noise of wing-feathers, the fans of paradise
  lifting softly.
The child afloat on radiance had a baby face, but the angels had birds' heads,
  hawks' heads,
Bending over the baby, weaving a web of wings about him. He held in the small fat hand
A little snake with golden eyes, and California could see clearly on the under radiance
The mare's pricked ears, a sharp black fork against the shining light-fall. But it dropped;
  the light of heaven
Frightened poor Dora. She backed; swung up the water,
And nearly oversetting the buggy turned and scrambled backward; the iron wheel-tires
  rang on bowlders.

Then California weeping climbed between the wheels. Her wet clothes and the toys
  packed under
Dragged her down with their weight; she stripped off cloak and dress and laid the baby's
  things in the buggy;
Brought Johnny's whisky out from under the seat; wrapped all in the dress, bottles and
  toys, and tied them
Into a bundle that would sling over her back. She unharnessed the mare, hurting
  her fingers
Against the swollen straps and the wet buckles. She tied the pack over her shoulders,
  the cords

Crossing her breasts, and mounted. She drew up her shift about her waist and knotted it, naked thighs

Clutching the sides of the mare, bare flesh to the wet withers,[4] and caught the mane with her right hand,

The looped-up bridle-reins in the other. "Dora, the baby gives you light." The blinding radiance

Hovered the ford. "Sweet baby Jesus give us light." Cataracts of light and Latin singing

Fell through the willows; the mare snorted and reared: the roar and thunder of the invisible water;

The night shaking open like a flag, shot with the flashes; the baby face hovering; the water

Beating over her shoes and stockings up to the bare thighs; and over them, like a beast

Lapping her belly; the wriggle and pitch of the mare swimming: the drift, the sucking water; the blinding

Light above and behind with not a gleam before, in the throat of darkness; the shock of the fore-hooves

Striking bottom, the struggle and surging lift of the haunches. She felt the water streaming off her

From the shoulders down; heard the great strain and sob of the mare's breathing, heard the horse-shoes grind on gravel.

When California came home the dog at the door snuffed at her without barking; Christine and Johnny

Both were asleep; she did not sleep for hours, but kindled fire and knelt patiently over it,

Shaping and drying the dear-bought gifts for Christmas morning.

                                      She hated (she thought) the proud-necked stallion.

He'd lean the big twin masses of his breast on the rail, his red-brown eyes flash the white crescents,

She admired him then, she hated him for his uselessness, serving nothing

But Johnny's vanity. Horses were too cheap to breed. She thought, if he could range in freedom,

Shaking the red-roan mane for a flag on the bare hills.

                                     A man brought up a mare in April;

Then California, though she wanted to watch, stayed with Christine indoors. When the child fretted

The mother told her once more about the miracle of the ford; her prayer to the little Jesus

---

4. The highest part of the horse's back, at the base of the neck.

The Christmas Eve when she was bringing the gifts home; the appearance, the lights,
    the Latin singing,
The thunder of wing-feathers and water, the shining child, the cataracts of splendor
    down the darkness.
"A little baby," Christine asked, "the God is a baby?" "The child of God. That was
    his birthday.
His mother was named Mary: we pray to her too: God came to her. He was not the child
    of a man
Like you or me. God was his father: she was the stallion's wife—what did I say—
    God's wife,"
She said with a cry, lifting Christine aside, pacing the planks of the floor. "She is called
    more blessed
Than any woman. She was so good, she was more loved." "Did God live near her
    house?" "He lives
Up high, over the stars; he ranges on the bare blue hill of the sky." In her mind a picture
Flashed, of the red-roan mane shaken out for a flag on the bare hills, and she said
    quickly, "He's more
Like a great man holding the sun in his hand." Her mind giving her words the lie,
    "But no one
Knows, only the shining and the power. The power, the terror, the burning fire covered
    her over . . ."
"Was she burnt up, mother?" "She was so good and lovely, she was the mother of the
    little Jesus.
If you are good nothing will hurt you." "What did she think?" "She loved, she was not
    afraid of the hooves—
Hands that had made the hills and sun and moon, and the sea and the great redwoods,
    the terrible strength,
She gave herself without thinking." "You only saw the baby, mother?" "Yes, and the
    angels about him,
The great wild shining over the black river." Three times she had walked to the door,
    three times returned,
And now the hand that had thrice hung on the knob, full of prevented action, twisted
    the cloth
Of the child's dress that she had been mending. "Oh, Oh, I've torn it." She struck at the
    child and then embraced her
Fiercely, the small blond sickly body.

                    Johnny came in, his face reddened as if he
    had stood
Near fire, his eyes triumphing. "Finished," he said, and looked with malice at
    Christine. "I go

Down valley with Jim Carrier; owes me five dollar, fifteen I charge him, he brought ten
    in his pocket.
Has grapes on the ranch, maybe I take a barrel red wine instead of money. Be
    back to-morrow.
To-morrow night I tell you — Eh, Jim," he laughed over his shoulder, "I say to-morrow
    evening
I show her how the red fellow act, the big fellow. When I come home." She answered
    nothing, but stood
In front of the door, holding the little hand of her daughter, in the path of sun between
    the redwoods,
While Johnny tied the buckskin mare behind Carrier's buggy, and bringing saddle and
    bridle tossed them
Under the seat. Jim Carrier's mare, the bay, stood with drooped head and started
    slowly, the men
Laughing and shouting at her; their voices could be heard down the steep road,
    after the noise
Of the iron-hooped wheels died from the stone. Then one might hear the hush of the
    wind in the tall redwoods,
The tinkle of the April brook, deep in its hollow.

                           Humanity is the start of the race;
    I say
Humanity is the mould to break away from, the crust to break through, the coal to break
    into fire,
The atom to be split.[5]

                    Tragedy that breaks man's face and a white fire flies out of it;
    vision that fools him
Out of his limits, desire that fools him out of his limits, unnatural crime,
    inhuman science,
Slit eyes in the mask; wild loves that leap over the walls of nature, the wild
    fence-vaulter science,
Useless intelligence of far stars, dim knowledge of the spinning demons that make
    an atom,
These break, these pierce, these deify, praising their God shrilly with fierce voices:
    not in a man's shape
He approves the praise, he that walks lightning-naked on the Pacific, that laces the suns
    with planets,

5. This sentence inaugurates a passage of about ten lines in which the narrator comments on the philosophical implications of the action, the only such occurrence in the poem. Unlike the rest of the poem, which was written with little hesitation, this passage was heavily worked over, a fact that Tim Hunt thinks "points to Jeffers' stake in the material."

The heart of the atom with electrons: what is humanity in this cosmos? For him, the last
Least taint of a trace in the dregs of the solution; for itself, the mould to break away
 from, the coal
To break into fire, the atom to be split.

       After the child slept, after the leopard-footed
 evening
Had glided oceanward, California turned the lamp to its least flame and glided from
 the house.
She moved sighing, like a loose fire, backward and forward on the smooth ground by
 the door.
She heard the night-wind that draws down the valley like the draught in a flue under
 clear weather
Whisper and toss in the tall redwoods; she heard the tinkle of the April brook deep
 in its hollow.
Cooled by the night the odors that the horses had left behind were in her nostrils;
 the night
Whitened up the bare hill; a drift of coyotes by the river cried bitterly against moonrise;
Then California ran to the old corral, the empty one where they kept the buckskin
 mare,
And leaned, and bruised her breasts on the rail, feeling the sky whiten. When the moon
 stood over the hill
She stole to the house. The child breathed quietly. Herself: to sleep? She had seen
 Christ in the night at Christmas.
The hills were shining open to the enormous night of the April moon: empty
 and empty,
The vast round backs of the bare hills? If one should ride up high might not the
 Father himself
Be seen brooding his night, cross-legged, chin in hand, squatting on the last dome?
 More likely
Leaping the hills, shaking the red-roan mane for a flag on the bare hills. She blew out
 the lamp.
Every fibre of flesh trembled with faintness when she came to the door; strength lacked,
 to wander
A foot into the shining of the hill, high enough, high enough . . . the hateful face of a
 man had taken
The strength that might have served her, the corral was empty. The dog followed her,
 she caught him by the collar,
Dragged him in fierce silence back to the door of the house, latched him inside.

 ✳ ✳ ✳

It was
like daylight
Out-doors and she hastened without faltering down the foot-path, through the dark
   fringe of twisted oak-brush,
To the open place in a bay of the hill. The dark strength of the stallion had heard her
   coming; she heard him
Blow the shining air out of his nostrils, she saw him in the white lake of moonlight
Move like a lion along the timbers of the fence, shaking the night-fall
Of the great mane; his fragrance came to her; she leaned on the fence;
He drew away from it, the hooves making soft thunder in the trodden soil.
Wild love had trodden it, his wrestling with the stranger, the shame of the day
Had stamped it into mire and powder when the heavy fetlocks
Strained the soft flanks. "Oh if I could bear you!
If I had the strength. O great God that came down to Mary, gently you came. But I will
   ride him
Up into the hill, if he throws me, if he tramples me, is it not my desire
To endure death?" She climbed the fence, pressing her body against the rail, shaking
   like fever,
And dropped inside to the soft ground. He neither threatened her with his teeth nor fled
   from her coming,
And lifting her hand gently to the upflung head she caught the strap of the headstall
That hung under the quivering chin. She unlooped the halter from the high strength
   of the neck
And the arch the storm-cloud mane hung with live darkness. He stood; she crushed
   her breasts
On the hard shoulder, an arm over the withers, the other under the mass of his throat,
   and murmuring
Like a mountain dove, "If I could bear you." No way, no help, a gulf in nature. She
   murmured, "Come,
We will run on the hill. O beautiful, O beautiful," and led him
To the gate and flung the bars on the ground. He threw his head downward
To snuff at the bars; and while he stood, she catching mane and withers with all sudden
   contracture
And strength of her lithe body, leaped, clung hard, and was mounted. He had been
   ridden before; he did not
Fight the weight but ran like a stone falling;
Broke down the slope into the moon-glass of the stream, and flattened to his neck
She felt the branches of a buck-eye tree fly over her, saw the wall of the oak-scrub
End her world: but he turned there, the matted branches
Scraped her right knee, the great slant shoulders
Laboring the hill-slope, up, up, the clear hill. Desire had died in her

At the first rush, the falling like death, but now it revived,

She feeling between her thighs the labor of the great engine, the running muscles, the
hard swiftness,

She riding the savage and exultant strength of the world. Having topped the thicket he
turned eastward

Running less wildly; and now at length he felt the halter when she drew on it;
she guided him upward;

He stopped and grazed on the great arch and pride of the hill, the silent calvary.[6]
A dwarfish oakwood

Climbed the other slope out of the dark of the unknown canyon beyond; the last
wind-beaten bush of it

Crawled up to the height, and California slipping from her mount tethered him to it.
She stood then,

Shaking. Enormous films of moonlight

Trailed down from the height. Space, anxious whiteness, vastness. Distant beyond
conception the shining ocean

Lay light like a haze along the ledge and doubtful world's end. Little vapors gleaming,
and little

Darknesses on the far chart underfoot symbolized wood and valley; but the air was the
element, the moon-

Saturate arcs and spires of the air.

                           Here is solitude, here on the calvary,
nothing conscious

But the possible God and the cropped grass, no witness, no eye but that misformed one,
the moon's past fullness.

Two figures on the shining hill, woman and stallion, she kneeling to him,
brokenly adoring.

He cropping the grass, shifting his hooves, or lifting the long head to gaze over
the world,

Tranquil and powerful. She prayed aloud "O God I am not good enough, O fear,
O strength, I am draggled.

Johnny and other men have had me, and O clean power! Here am I," she said, falling
before him,

And crawled to his hooves. She lay a long while, as if asleep, in reach of the fore-hooves,
weeping. He avoided

Her head and the prone body. He backed at first; but later plucked the grass that grew by
her shoulder.

---

6. According to the New Testament, Calvary (or Golgotha) is the hill on which Jesus Christ was cruci-
fied. See Luke 23:33.

* * *

The small dark head under his nostrils: a small round stone, that smelt human, black
    hair growing from it:
The skull shut the light in: it was not possible for any eyes
To know what throbbed and shone under the sutures of the skull, or a shell full
    of lightning
Had scared the roan strength, and he'd have broken tether, screaming, and run for
    the valley.

    The atom bounds-breaking,
Nucleus to sun, electrons to planets, with recognition
Not praying, self-equaling, the whole to the whole, the microcosm
Not entering nor accepting entrance, more equally, more utterly, more incredibly
    conjugate
With the other extreme and greatness; passionately perceptive of identity. . . .

                                                                        The
    fire threw up figures
And symbols meanwhile, racial myths formed and dissolved in it, the phantom rulers
    of humanity
That without being are yet more real than what they are born of, and without shape,
    shape that which makes them:
The nerves and the flesh go by shadowlike, the limbs and the lives shadowlike, these
    shadows remain, these shadows
To whom temples, to whom churches, to whom labors and wars, visions and dreams
    are dedicate:
Out of the fire in the small round stone that black moss covered, a crucified man
    writhed up in anguish;
A woman covered by a huge beast in whose mane the stars were netted, sun and moon
    were his eyeballs,
Smiled under the unendurable violation, her throat swollen with the storm and
    blood-flecks gleaming
On the stretched lips; a woman—no, a dark water, split by jets of lightning, and after
    a season
What floated up out of the furrowed water, a boat, a fish, a fire-globe?

                                                                        It had wings,
    the creature,
And flew against the fountain of lightning, fell burnt out of the cloud back to the
    bottomless water . . .

Figures and symbols, castlings[7] of the fire, played in her brain; but the white fire was
    the essence,
The burning in the small round shell of bone that black hair covered, that lay by the
    hooves on the hill-top.

She rose at length, she unknotted the halter; she walked and led the stallion; two
    figures, woman and stallion,
Came down the silent emptiness of the dome of the hill, under the cataract of
    the moonlight.

The next night there was moon through cloud. Johnny had returned half drunk toward
    evening, and California
Who had known him for years with neither love nor loathing to-night hating him had let
    the child Christine
Play in the light of the lamp for hours after her bed-time; who fell asleep at length on
    the floor
Beside the dog; then Johnny: "Put her to bed." She gathered the child against her
    breasts, she laid her
In the next room, and covered her with a blanket. The window was white, the moon had
    risen. The mother
Lay down by the child, but after a moment Johnny stood in the doorway. "Come drink."
    He had brought home
Two jugs of wine slung from the saddle, part payment for the stallion's service;
    a pitcher of it
Was on the table, and California sadly came and emptied her glass. Whisky,
    she thought,
Would have erased him till to-morrow; the thin red wine. . . . "We have a good evening,"
    he laughed, pouring it.
"One glass yet then I show you what the red fellow did." She moving toward the house-
    door his eyes
Followed her, the glass filled and the red juice ran over the table. When it struck
    the floor-planks
He heard and looked. "Who stuck the pig?" he muttered stupidly, "here's blood, here's
    blood," and trailed his fingers
In the red lake under the lamplight. While he was looking down the door creaked, she
    had slipped out-doors,
And he, his mouth curving like a faun's, imagined the chase under the solemn
    redwoods, the panting
And unresistant victim caught in a dark corner. He emptied the glass and
    went out-doors

7. Offspring brought forth prematurely; abortions.

Into the dappled lanes of moonlight. No sound but the April brook's. "Hey Bruno," he
    called, "find her.

Bruno, go find her." The dog after a little understood and quested, the man following.

When California crouching by an oak-bush above the house heard them come near
    she darted

To the open slope and ran down hill. The dog barked at her heels, pleased with the
    game, and Johnny

Followed in silence. She ran down to the new corral, she saw the stallion

Move like a lion along the timbers of the fence, the dark arched neck shaking
    the night-fall

Of the great mane; she threw herself prone and writhed under the bars, his hooves
    backing away from her

Made muffled thunder in the soft soil. She stood in the midst of the corral, panting,
    but Johnny

Paused at the fence. The dog ran under it, and seeing the stallion move, the woman
    standing quiet,

Danced after the beast, with white-tooth feints and dashes. When Johnny saw the
    formidable dark strength

Recoil from the dog, he climbed up over the fence.

                                        The child Christine waked when
            her mother left her

And lay half-dreaming, in the half-waking dream she saw the ocean come up out of
    the west

And cover the world, she looked up through clear water at the tops of the redwoods.
    She heard the door creak

And the house empty; her heart shook her body, sitting up on the bed, and she heard
    the dog

And crept toward light, where it gleamed under the crack of the door. She opened the
    door, the room was empty,

The table-top was a red lake under the lamplight. The color of it was terrible to her,

She had seen the red juice drip from a coyote's muzzle, her father had shot one day
    in the hills

And carried him home over the saddle: she looked at the rifle on the wall-rack: it was
    not moved:

She ran to the door, the dog was barking and the moon was shining: she knew wine by
    the odor

But the color frightened her, the empty house frightened her, she followed down hill in
    the white lane of moonlight

The friendly noise of the dog. She saw in the big horse's corral, on the level shoulder
    of the hill,

Black on white, the dark strength of the beast, the dancing fury of the dog, and the
two others.
One fled, one followed; the big one charged, rearing; one fell under his fore-hooves.
She heard her mother
Scream: without thought she ran to the house, she dragged a chair past the red pool and
climbed to the rifle,
Got it down from the wall and lugged it somehow through the door and down the
hill-side, under the hard weight
Sobbing. Her mother stood by the rails of the corral, she gave it to her. On the far side
The dog flashed at the plunging stallion; in the midst of the space the man,
slow-moving, like a hurt worm
Crawling, dragged his body by inches toward the fence-line. Then California, resting
the rifle
On the top rail, without doubting, without hesitance
Aimed for the leaping body of the dog, and when it stood, fired. It snapped, rolled over,
lay quiet.
"O mother you've hit Bruno!" "I couldn't see the sights in the moonlight," she answered
quietly. She stood
And watched, resting the rifle-butt on the ground. The stallion wheeled, freed from his
torment, the man
Lurched up to his knees, wailing a thin and bitter bird's cry, and the roan thunder
Struck; hooves left nothing alive but teeth tore up the remnant. "O mother, shoot,
shoot!" Yet California
Stood carefully watching, till the beast having fed all his fury stretched neck to utmost,
head high,
And wrinkled back the upper lip from the teeth, yawning obscene disgust over —
not a man —
A smear on the moon-lake earth: then California moved by some obscure
human fidelity
Lifted the rifle. Each separate nerve-cell of her brain flaming the stars fell from
their places
Crying in her mind: she fired three times before the haunches crumpled sidewise,
the forelegs stiffening,
And the beautiful strength settled to earth: she turned then on her little daughter the
mask of a woman
Who has killed God. The night-wind veering, the smell of the spilt wine drifted down
hill from the house.

1925

Jeffers explained that "Roan Stallion" originated from an abandoned cabin he and his wife,
Una, discovered in a small valley. Its owner had been killed by a stallion. Jeffers recalled that

"I was quarrying granite under the sea-cliff to build our house with, and slacking on the job sat down on a wet rock to look at the sunset and think about my next poem. The stallion and the desolate cabin came to mind; then immediately, for persons of the drama, came the Indian woman and her white husband, real persons whom I had often seen driving through our village in a ramshackle buggy. The episode of the woman swimming her horse through a storm-swollen ford at night came also, it was part of her actual history. . . . So that when I stood up and began to handle stones again, the poem had already made itself in my mind." This enigmatic tale of a bad marriage, a sickly child, a mystical and apparently sexual encounter with a stallion, and finally death and revenge suggests that a fatal mixture of frustrated passion and twisted spiritual yearning may underlie modern lives. "Roan" means reddish-brown, sprinkled with gray and white.

Hurt Hawks

I

The broken pillar of the wing jags from the clotted shoulder,
The wing trails like a banner in defeat,
No more to use the sky forever but live with famine
And pain a few days: cat nor coyote
Will shorten the week of waiting for death, there is game without talons.
He stands under the oak-bush and waits
The lame feet of salvation; at night he remembers freedom
And flies in a dream, the dawns ruin it.
He is strong and pain is worse to the strong, incapacity is worse.
The curs[1] of the day come and torment him
At distance, no one but death the redeemer will humble that head,
The intrepid readiness, the terrible eyes.
The wild God of the world[2] is sometimes merciful to those
That ask mercy, not often to the arrogant.
You do not know him, you communal people, or you have forgotten him;
Intemperate and savage, the hawk remembers him;
Beautiful and wild, the hawks, and men that are dying, remember him.

II

I'd sooner, except the penalties, kill a man than a hawk; but the great redtail[3]
Had nothing left but unable misery

1. Unfriendly dogs.
2. The impersonal divinity inhabiting and uniting all things. Jeffers's idea here looks back to the nineteenth-century transcendentalism of Emerson, Thoreau, and Whitman.

3. The red-tailed hawk, the most common North American species, is about 60 centimeters long and preys primarily on rodents and reptiles.

From the bones too shattered for mending, the wing that trailed under his talons
    when he moved.
We had fed him six weeks, I gave him freedom,
He wandered over the foreland hill and returned in the evening, asking for death,
Not like a beggar, still eyed with the old
Implacable arrogance. I gave him the lead gift in the twilight.[4] What fell was relaxed,
Owl-downy, soft feminine feathers; but what
Soared: the fierce rush: the night-herons by the flooded river cried fear at its rising
Before it was quite unsheathed from reality.

1928

Despite the plural in the title, this poem describes only one hurt hawk. The title may be generalizing from this one instance, or it may be implying that the poem's speaker is another hurt hawk. Many commentators have considered this poem didactic—teaching a lesson about the value of wild nature or about Jeffers's preference for hawks over human beings. Tim Hunt, however, points out that the poem, derived from personal experience, was composed in two stages. Jeffers wrote part one while the hawk was still alive and part two after its death. Hunt therefore infers that the poem dramatizes the speaker's "dismay at having had to kill the hawk and his conflicting relationships to nature, pain, the 'wild God,' and the 'communal people.'"

The Purse-Seine

Our sardine fishermen work at night in the dark of the moon; daylight or moonlight
They could not tell where to spread the net, unable to see the phosphorescence of
    the shoals of fish.
They work northward from Monterey, coasting Santa Cruz; off New Year's Point or
    off Pigeon Point[1]
The look-out man will see some lakes of milk-color light on the sea's night-purple;
    he points, and the helmsman
Turns the dark prow, the motor-boat circles the gleaming shoal and drifts out her
    seine-net.[2] They close the circle
And purse the bottom of the net, then with great labor haul it in.

I cannot tell you

How beautiful the scene is, and a little terrible, then, when the crowded fish
Know they are caught, and wildly beat from one wall to the other of their closing
    destiny the phosphorescent

---

4. That is, the speaker shot the hawk.
1. On the coast of Monterey Bay in California, just north of Carmel.

2. A purse seine used near the shore.

Water to a pool of flame, each beautiful slender body sheeted with flame, like a
     live rocket
A comet's tail wake of clear yellow flame; while outside the narrowing
Floats and cordage of the net great sea-lions come up to watch, sighing in the dark;
     the vast walls of night
Stand erect to the stars.

                         Lately I was looking from a night mountain-top
On a wide city, the colored splendor, galaxies of light: how could I help but recall
     the seine-net
Gathering the luminous fish? I cannot tell you how beautiful the city appeared, and
     a little terrible.

I thought, We have geared the machines and locked all together into
     interdependence; we have built the great cities; now
There is no escape. We have gathered vast populations incapable of free survival,
     insulated
From the strong earth, each person in himself helpless, on all dependent. The
     circle is closed, and the net
Is being hauled in. They hardly feel the cords drawing, yet they shine already.
     The inevitable mass-disasters
Will not come in our time nor in our children's, but we and our children
Must watch the net draw narrower, government take all powers, — or revolution,
     and the new government
Take more than all, add to kept bodies kept souls, — or anarchy, the mass-disasters.

                                                        These
     things are Progress;
Do you marvel our verse is troubled or frowning, while it keeps its reason? Or it lets
     go, lets the mood flow
In the manner of the recent young men into mere hysteria, splintered gleams,
     crackled laughter.[3] But they are quite wrong.
There is no reason for amazement: surely one always knew that cultures decay,
     and life's end is death.

                                                   1937

A purse seine is a large net used for catching fish that travel in dense schools or "shoals." The
fish are surrounded with a curtain of netting that is then closed at the bottom, trapping

---

3. A possible reference to the modernist style of
fragmentation associated with T. S. Eliot and
Ezra Pound (both included in this anthology),
which Jeffers opposed. The line may specifically
allude to Pound's evocation of World War I in
Hugh Selwyn Mauberley: "hysterias, trench con
fessions, / laughter out of dead bellies."

them. Like a Romantic lyric by William Wordsworth or Samuel Taylor Coleridge, in which the speaker's perception of a natural scene leads to a meditation on the scene's deeper meanings, this poem moves from close observation to a contemplation of the scene's political and aesthetic analogies.

The Beaks of Eagles

An eagle's nest on the head of an old redwood on one of the precipice-footed ridges
Above Ventana Creek,[1] that jagged country which nothing but a falling meteor will
    ever plow; no horseman
Will ever ride there, no hunter cross this ridge but the winged ones, no one will steal
    the eggs from this fortress.
The she-eagle is old, her mate was shot long ago, she is now mated with a son of hers.
When lightning blasted her nest she built it again on the same tree, in the splinters
    of the thunderbolt.
The she-eagle is older than I; she was here when the fires of 'eighty-five raged on
    these ridges,
She was lately fledged and dared not hunt ahead of them but ate scorched meat.
    The world has changed in her time;
Humanity has multiplied, but not here; men's hopes and thoughts and customs have
    changed, their powers are enlarged,
Their powers and their follies have become fantastic,
The unstable animal never has been changed so rapidly. The motor and the plane
    and the great war have gone over him,
And Lenin[2] has lived and Jehovah died: while the mother-eagle
Hunts her same hills, crying the same beautiful and lonely cry and is never tired;
    dreams the same dreams,
And hears at night the rock-slides rattle and thunder in the throats of these living
    mountains.

              It is good for man
To try all changes, progress and corruption, powers, peace and anguish, not to go
    down the dinosaur's way
Until all his capacities have been explored: and it is good for him
To know that his needs and nature are no more changed in fact in ten thousand
    years than the beaks of eagles.

                              1937

1. A creek that runs through the Big Sur forest south of Carmel, California.
2. Vladimir Ilyich Lenin (1870–1924), founder of the Russian Communist Party and first head of the Soviet Union. Jehovah: Jewish and Christian name for God.

The Ocean's Tribute

Yesterday's sundown was very beautiful—I know it is out of fashion to say so, I think we
    are fools
To turn from the superhuman beauty of the world and dredge our own minds—it built
    itself up with ceremony
From the ocean horizon, smoked amber and tender green, pink and purple and
    vermilion, great ranks
Of purple cloud, and the pink rose-petals over all and through all; but the ocean itself,
    cold slate-color,
Refused the glory. Then I saw a pink fountain come up from it,
A whale-spout; there were ten or twelve whales quite near the deep shore, playing
    together, nuzzling each other,
Plunging and rising, lifting luminous pink pillars from the flat ocean to the flaming sky.

                                                                                    1958

It nearly cancels my fear of death

It nearly cancels my fear of death, my dearest said,
When I think of cremation. To rot in the earth
Is a loathsome end, but to roar up in flame—besides, I am used to it,
I have flamed with love or fury so often in my life,
No wonder my body is tired, no wonder it is dying.
We had great joy of my body. Scatter the ashes.

                                                                                    1963

This monologue is based on the discourse of Una Jeffers, who died in 1950 of cancer.

MARIANNE MOORE
1887–1972

MARIANNE MOORE is now almost universally recognized as one of the key figures
in American experimental modernism. Her poetic gifts and imaginative proclivi-
ties included a capacity for keen observation, an omnivorous approach to reading,
a lively interest in the varied habits and peculiarities of natural species, and an
amused curiosity about man-made objects ranging from shoe-polish tins to ornate
gilt candelabras. Moore leavened these proclivities with humility, skepticism, wit,

an acutely personal moral sense, and a singular approach to poetic form that included an ambling and elliptical mode of poetic organization and telling experiments with syllabic verse. She thereby created a brilliant poetic style that was singular in her own day and that seems still more extraordinary today. Moore maintained a quiet yet vital presence among the circle of experimental modernists, not simply as a poet but also as an editor, letter writer, friend, and supporter of a younger generation of poets. Later, in the 1950s and 1960s, Moore rather surprisingly emerged as a popular icon, often throwing out the first pitch at Dodger and Yankee baseball games (she was a lifelong baseball fan), and even gracing the cover of a 1966 issue of *Esquire* magazine as one of "The Unknockables," along with the likes of boxer Joe Louis, singer Kate Smith, actress Helen Hayes, and comedian Jimmy Durante. She had been embraced by the nation as a figure who was characteristically and authentically—if eccentrically—American.

Moore spent her earliest years in Kirkwood, Missouri, in the home of her maternal grandfather, the Reverend John R. Warner, a respected Presbyterian pastor. She never saw her father, an inventor and manufacturer who suffered a nervous breakdown before her birth in 1887 and who never returned to the family. Moore and her older brother, Warner, were raised by their energetic, strong-willed mother, who established a close bond with both children while fostering their creativity and education. Following the death of Moore's beloved grandfather, the family moved to Carlisle, Pennsylvania, in 1895. There Mrs. Moore taught at the local girls' academy, the Metzger Institute, which her daughter would later attend. Moore, already contemplating a career as a writer, graduated from Bryn Mawr College in 1909, then taught in Carlisle Indian School. By 1915, her poems were appearing in such leading avant-garde journals as London's *The Egoist* and New York City's *Others*, and she began to meet or correspond with such leading experimental poets as William Carlos Williams, Wallace Stevens, T. S. Eliot, H.D. (Hilda Doolittle), and Ezra Pound. In 1918, Moore moved to Manhattan's Greenwich Village, and she lived in Manhattan or Brooklyn for the rest of her life. She never married, sharing her home with her mother until her mother's death in 1947.

Moore's first book, *Poems*, was published in London in 1921 by the Egoist Press without her knowledge and somewhat to her annoyance, the publication having been arranged by her friends Robert McAlmon and H.D. By 1924, she felt ready for book publication, and her second book, *Observations* (1924), appeared in New York. It won the *Dial* Award and established her reputation as one of the most brilliant and accomplished of modernist poets. From 1925 to 1929, Moore edited *The Dial*, one of the leading international journals of experimental literature and the arts. Her *Selected Poems* (1935) confirmed her standing as an important poetic voice. She wrote compellingly about the tense and tragic environment of World War II in such volumes as *What Are Years* (1941) and *Nevertheless* (1944). Although Moore wrote assiduously until her death in 1972, most critics agree that her later volumes of verse lack the coiled intensity of her early and middle period styles.

Moore had an eclectic, collector's interest in the world's variety, and that interest is pervasively reflected in her poetry. She told the New York *Herald* in 1951 that "I like country fairs, roller-coasters, merry-go-rounds, dog shows, museums, avenues of trees, old elms, vehicles, experiments in timing like our ex–Museum of Science and Invention's two roller-bearings in a gravity chute, synchronized with a ring-bearing revolving vertically. I am fond of animals and take inordinate interest in mongooses, squirrels, crows, elephants. I read few magazines but would be lost without the newspaper." Many such objects appear in Moore's poems, along with scaly anteaters ("The Pangolin"), ostriches ("He 'Digesteth Harde Yron'"), shelled octopi ("The Paper Nautilus"), and even the peculiarities of human mating customs ("Marriage"). Moore's eclectic interests are drawn together with darting obliquity into poems that, in Randall Jarrell's words, have "a texture that will withstand any amount of rereading." For Moore, the mind is an enchanting, and

> an enchanted thing
> like the glaze on a
> katydid-wing
> subdivided by sun
> till the nettings are legion.

Moore's poems strive for a similar model of order—they may, at first, appear eccentrically arranged but, like the translucent wing of the katydid (a kind of dragonfly), their luminous clarity and intricacy yields its pattern and meaning to the patient, attentive reader. While contemporaries such as Pound and Williams sometimes appear to be pursuing innovative forms for the sake of the innovation, Moore's uniquely organized poems invariably seem the natural and only means by which she could express her singular vision.

For a number of years, Moore has been the subject of intense critical inquiry, but until recently deriving a clear idea of Moore's poetic development has been difficult. Her *Complete Poems*, published under the poet's close supervision in 1967—and for many years the only Moore volume in print—omits roughly half of her poems, including some of her best. It also drastically cuts several of those that remain, including "Poetry," perhaps her most famous, and it organizes her early poems in a thematic order that obscures their chronology. *Complete Poems* also broke apart more than one important poetic sequence, changing the form they had had when they appeared in magazines. Fortunately, two publications have helped to clarify our understanding of Moore's work, and they have delightfully expanded Moore's canon as well: *Becoming Marianne Moore: The Early Poems, 1907–1924*, edited by Robin Schultze, and *The Poems of Marianne Moore*, edited by Grace Schulman. With each passing decade Marianne Moore's poetic oeuvre, one of the most imaginative and significant of the twentieth century, is coming into clearer focus.

FURTHER READING

Bonnie Costello. *Marianne Moore: Imaginary Possessions.* Cambridge, Mass.: Harvard University Press, 1981.

Celeste Goodridge. *Hints and Disguises: Marianne Moore and Her Contemporaries.* Iowa City: University of Iowa Press, 1989.

Margaret Holley. *Marianne Moore: A Study in Voice and Value.* New York: Cambridge University Press, 1987.

Cristanne Miller. *Marianne Moore: Questions of Authority.* Cambridge, Mass.: Harvard University Press, 1995.

Charles Molesworth. *Marianne Moore: A Literary Life.* New York: Atheneum, 1990.

Marianne Moore. *Becoming Marianne Moore: The Early Poems, 1907–1924.* Ed. Robin Schultze. Berkeley: University of California Press, 2002.

———. *The Poems of Marianne Moore.* Ed. Grace Schulman. New York: Viking, 2003.

———. *Selected Letters.* Ed. Bonnie Costello, Celeste Goodridge, and Cristanne Miller. New York: Knopf, 1997.

Joseph Parisi. *Marianne Moore: The Art of a Modernist.* Ann Arbor: UMI Research Press, 1990.

A Jelly-Fish

Visible, invisible,
a fluctuating charm
an amber-tinctured amethyst
inhabits it, your arm
approaches and it opens
and it closes; you had meant
to catch it and it quivers;
you abandon your intent.

1909, rev. 1959

Written by Moore in 1909 while attending Bryn Mawr College and printed in a school literary magazine, "A Jelly-Fish" was not republished by Moore until she included this revised, shortened version in *O to Be a Dragon* (1959).

To Military Progress

You use your mind
Like a millstone to grind
Chaff.
You polish it
And with your warped wit
Laugh

*　　*　　*

At your torso,
Prostrate where the crow
    Falls
On such faint hearts
As its god imparts,
    Calls

And claps its wings
Till the tumult brings
    More
Black minute-men
To revive again,
    War

At little cost.
They cry for the lost
    Head
And seek their prize
Till the evening sky's
    Red.

1915

Originally published as "To the Soul of 'Progress,'" this poem embodies an early response of Moore to World War I.

Critics and Connoisseurs

There is a great amount of poetry in unconscious
    fastidiousness. Certain Ming
        products,[1] imperial floor coverings of coach
wheel yellow, are well enough in their way but I have seen something
    that I like better—a
        mere childish attempt to make an imperfectly
            ballasted animal stand up,
      similar determination to make a pup
        eat his meat from the plate.

I remember a swan under the willows in Oxford,
    with flamingo-colored, maple-

---

1. The Chinese Ming dynasty (1368–1644 C.E.) was noted for its elegant porcelain, bronze, and lacquerware.

leaflike feet. It reconnoitered like a battle
   ship. Disbelief and conscious fastidiousness were the staple
    ingredients in its
          disinclination to move. Finally its hardihood
            was not proof against its
          proclivity to more fully appraise such bits
          of food as the stream

bore counter to it; made away with what I gave it
   to eat. I have seen this swan and
     I have seen you; I have seen ambition without
   understanding in a variety of forms. Happening to stand
      by an ant-hill, I have
        seen a fastidious ant carrying a stick north,
          south, east, west, till it turned on
        itself, struck out from the flower bed into the lawn,
        and returned to the point

from which it had started. Then abandoning the stick as
   useless and overtaxing its
     jaws with a particle of whitewash pill-like but
heavy, it again went through the same course of procedure. What is
     there in being able
        to say that one has dominated the stream in an attitude of self-defense;
      in proving that one has had the experience
      of carrying a stick?

                         1916

The Fish

     wade
     through black jade.
        Of the crow-blue mussel-shells, one keeps
        adjusting the ash-heaps;
            opening and shutting itself like

    an
    injured fan.
        The barnacles which encrust the side
        of the wave, cannot hide
            there for the submerged shafts of the

*   *   *

sun,
split like spun
    glass, move themselves with spotlight swiftness
    into the crevices—
        in and out, illuminating

the
turquoise sea
    of bodies. The water drives a wedge
    of iron through the iron edge
        of the cliff; whereupon the stars,

pink
rice-grains, ink-
    bespattered jelly-fish, crabs like green
    lilies, and submarine
        toadstools, slide each on the other.

All
external
    marks of abuse are present on this
    defiant edifice—
        all the physical features of

ac-
cident—lack
    of cornice, dynamite grooves, burns, and
    hatchet strokes, these things stand
        out on it; the chasm-side is

dead.
Repeated
    evidence has proved that it can live
    on what can not revive
        its youth. The sea grows old in it.

                1918

As in several of Moore's poems, the title of "The Fish" also serves as its first line. And, like other Moore poems, it is written in syllabics, meaning that each line in each five-line stanza has a set number of syllables: 1, 3, 9, 6, and 8, respectively. The poem's description centers on an undersea cliff wall

Poetry

I, too, dislike it: there are things that are important beyond all this fiddle.
    Reading it, however, with a perfect contempt for it, one discovers in
    it, after all, a place for the genuine.
        Hands that can grasp, eyes
        that can dilate, hair that can rise
            if it must, these things are important not because a

high-sounding interpretation can be put upon them but because they are
    useful. When they become so derivative as to become unintelligible,
    the same thing may be said for all of us, that we
        do not admire what
        we cannot understand: the bat
            holding on upside down or in quest of something to

eat, elephants pushing, a wild horse taking a roll, a tireless wolf under
    a tree, the immovable critic twitching his skin like a horse that feels a flea, the base-
    ball fan, the statistician —
        nor is it valid
            to discriminate against "business documents and

school books"; all these phenomena are important. One must make a distinction
    however: when dragged into prominence by half poets, the result is not poetry,
    nor till the poets among us can be
        "literalists of
        the imagination" — above
            insolence and triviality and can present

for inspection, "imaginary gardens with real toads in them," shall we have
    it. In the meantime, if you demand on the one hand,
    the raw material of poetry in
        all its rawness and
        that which is on the other hand
            genuine, you are interested in poetry.

                                        1919

Moore drastically cut this poem, possibly her most widely known, when it appeared in her *Complete Poems* (1967), omitting all but the first three lines, though her editors prevailed on her to include the famous longer version in a footnote. Moore frequently supplied notes to her poems, most often to document her sources. Examples are below.

NOTES BY MARIANNE MOORE

Diary of Tolstoy (Dutton, p. 84): "Where the boundary between prose and poetry lies, I shall never be able to understand. The question is raised in manuals of style, yet the

answer to it lies beyond me. Poetry is verse: prose is not verse. Or else poetry is everything
with the exception of business documents and school books."

"*literalists of the imagination*": Yeats, *Ideas of Good and Evil*, 1903; William Blake and his
Illustrations to *The Divine Comedy*, p. 182. "The limitation of his view was from the very
intensity of his vision; he was a too literal realist of the imagination, as others are of na-
ture; and because he believed that the figures seen by the mind's eye, when exalted by
inspiration were 'eternal existences,' symbols of divine essences, he hated every grace of
style that might obscure their lineaments."

A Grave

Man looking into the sea,
taking the view from those who have as much right to it as you have to it yourself,
it is human nature to stand in the middle of a thing,[1]
but you cannot stand in the middle of this;
the sea has nothing to give but a well excavated grave.
The firs stand in a procession, each with an emerald turkey-foot at the top,
reserved as their contours, saying nothing;
repression, however, is not the most obvious characteristic of the sea;
the sea is a collector, quick to return a rapacious look.
There are others besides you who have worn that look—
whose expression is no longer a protest; the fish no longer investigate them
for their bones have not lasted:
men lower nets, unconscious of the fact that they are desecrating a grave,
and row quickly away—the blades of the oars
moving together like the feet of water-spiders as if there were no such thing as death.
The wrinkles progress among themselves in a phalanx—beautiful under networks
    of foam,
and fade breathlessly while the sea rustles in and out of the seaweed;
the birds swim through the air at top speed, emitting cat-calls as heretofore—
the tortoise-shell scourges about the feet of the cliffs, in motion beneath them;
and the ocean, under the pulsation of lighthouses and noise of bell-buoys,
advances as usual, looking as if it were not that ocean in which dropped things are
    bound to sink—
in which if they turn and twist, it is neither with volition nor consciousness.

1921

1. Moore told an interviewer that the poem's opening lines were inspired by a time when she and her mother were looking out at the sea along the Maine coast, and a rude person stepped in front of them, blocking their view. Moore's mother observed that people always want to "stand in the middle of things."

Although it treats such topics as nature, human egotism, and gender, "A Grave" on one level constitutes an oblique response to World War I. Moore began it shortly after the 1916 sinking of the ocean liner *Lusitania* by a German U-boat, which resulted in great loss of life. Moore was also influenced by the fact that her brother, Warner, was serving as a naval chaplain during the war.

Marriage

This institution,
perhaps one should say enterprise
out of respect for which
one says one need not change one's mind
about a thing one has believed in,
requiring public promises
of one's intention
to fulfill a private obligation:
I wonder what Adam and Eve
think of it by this time,
this fire-gilt steel
alive with goldenness;
how bright it shows—
"of circular traditions and impostures,
committing many spoils,"
requiring all one's criminal ingenuity
to avoid!
Psychology which explains everything
explains nothing,
and we are still in doubt.
Eve: beautiful woman—
I have seen her
when she was so handsome
she gave me a start,
able to write simultaneously
in three languages—
English, German, and French—
and talk in the meantime;
equally positive in demanding a commotion
and in stipulating quiet:
"I should like to be alone";
to which the visitor replies,
"I should like to be alone;

why not be alone together?"
Below the incandescent stars
below the incandescent fruit,
the strange experience of beauty;
its existence is too much;
it tears one to pieces
and each fresh wave of consciousness
is poison.
"See her, see her in this common world,"
the central flaw
in that first crystal-fine experiment,
this amalgamation which can never be more
than an interesting impossibility,
describing it
as "that strange paradise
unlike flesh, stones,
gold or stately buildings,
the choicest part of my life:
the heart rising
in its estate of peace
as a boat rises
with the rising of the water";
constrained in speaking of a serpent—
shed snakeskin in the history of politeness
not to be returned to again—
that invaluable accident
exonerating Adam.
And he has beauty also;
it's distressing—the O thou
to whom from whom,
without whom nothing—Adam;
"something feline,
something colubrine"—how true!
a crouching mythological monster
in that Persian miniature of emerald mines,
raw silk—ivory white, snow white,
oyster white and six others—
that paddock full of leopards and giraffes—
long lemon-yellow bodies
sown with trapezoids of blue.
Alive with words,

vibrating like a cymbal
touched before it has been struck,
he has prophesied correctly—
the industrious waterfall,
"the speedy stream
which violently bears all before it,
at one time silent as the air
and now as powerful as the wind."
"Treading chasms
on the uncertain footing of a spear,"
forgetting that there is in woman
a quality of mind
which as an instinctive manifestation
is unsafe,
he goes on speaking
in a formal customary strain,
of "past states, the present state,
seals, promises,
the evil one suffered,
the good one enjoys,
hell, heaven,
everything convenient
to promote one's joy."
In him a state of mind
perceives what it was not
intended that he should;
"he experiences a solemn joy
in seeing that he has become an idol."
Plagued by the nightingale
in the new leaves,
with its silence—
not its silence but its silences,
he says of it:
"It clothes me with a shirt of fire."
"He dares not clap his hands
to make it go on
lest it should fly off;
if he does nothing, it will sleep;
if he cries out, it will not understand."
Unnerved by the nightingale
and dazzled by the apple,

impelled by "the illusion of a fire
effectual to extinguish fire,"
compared with which
the shining of the earth
is but deformity—a fire
"as high as deep
as bright as broad
as long as life itself,"
he stumbles over marriage,
"a very trivial object indeed"
to have destroyed the attitude
in which he stood—
the ease of the philosopher
unfathered by a woman.
Unhelpful Hymen!
a kind of overgrown cupid
reduced to insignificance
by the mechanical advertising
parading as involuntary comment,
by that experiment of Adam's
with ways out but no way in—
the ritual of marriage,
augmenting all its lavishness;
its fiddle-head ferns,
lotus flowers, opuntias, white dromedaries,
its hippopotamus—
nose and mouth combined
in one magnificent hopper—
its snake and the potent apple.
He tells us
that "for love that will
gaze an eagle blind,
that is with Hercules
climbing the trees
in the garden of the Hesperides,
from forty-five to seventy
is the best age,"
commending it
as a fine art, as an experiment,
a duty or as merely recreation.
One must not call him ruffian

nor friction a calamity—
the fight to be affectionate:
"no truth can be fully known
until it has been tried
by the tooth of disputation."
The blue panther with black eyes,
the basalt panther with blue eyes,
entirely graceful—
one must give them the path—
the black obsidian Diana
who "darkeneth her countenance
as a bear doth,"
the spiked hand
that has an affection for one
and proves it to the bone,
impatient to assure you
that impatience is the mark of independence,
not of bondage.
"Married people often look that way"—
"seldom and cold, up and down,
mixed and malarial
with a good day and a bad."
We Occidentals are so unemotional,
self lost, the irony preserved
in "the Ahasuerus *tête-à-tête* banquet"
with its small orchids like snakes' tongues,
with its "good monster, lead the way,"
with little laughter
and munificence of humor
in that quixotic atmosphere of frankness
in which "four o'clock does not exist,
but at five o'clock
the ladies in their imperious humility
are ready to receive you";
in which experience attests
that men have power
and sometimes one is made to feel it.
He says, "What monarch would not blush
to have a wife
with hair like a shaving-brush?"
The fact of woman

is "not the sound of the flute
but very poison."
She says, "Men are monopolists
of 'stars, garters, buttons
and other shining baubles' —
unfit to be the guardians
of another person's happiness."
He says, "These mummies
must be handled carefully —
'the crumbs from a lion's meal,
a couple of shins and the bit of an ear';
turn to the letter M
and you will find
that 'a wife is a coffin,'
that severe object
with the pleasing geometry
stipulating space not people,
refusing to be buried
and uniquely disappointing,
revengefully wrought in the attitude
of an adoring child
to a distinguished parent."
She says, "This butterfly,
this waterfly, this nomad
that has 'proposed
to settle on my hand for life' —
What can one do with it?
There must have been more time
in Shakespeare's day
to sit and watch a play.
You know so many artists who are fools."
He says, "You know so many fools
who are not artists."
The fact forgot
that "some have merely rights
while some have obligations,"
he loves himself so much,
he can permit himself
no rival in that love.
She loves herself so much,
she cannot see herself enough —

a statuette of ivory on ivory,
the logical last touch
to an expansive splendor
earned as wages for work done:
one is not rich but poor
when one can always seem so right.
What can one do for them —
these savages
condemned to disaffect
all those who are not visionaries
alert to undertake the silly task
of making people noble?
This model of petrine fidelity
who "leaves her peaceful husband
only because she has seen enough of him" —
that orator reminding you,
"I am yours to command."
"Everything to do with love is mystery;
it is more than a day's work
to investigate this science."
One sees that it is rare —
that striking grasp of opposites
opposed to each other, not to unity,
which in cycloid inclusiveness
has dwarfed the demonstration
of Columbus with the egg —
a triumph of simplicity —
that charitive Euroclydon
of frightening disinterestedness
which the world hates,
admitting:

> "I am such a cow,
> if I had a sorrow
> I should feel it a long time;
> I am not one of those
> who have a great sorrow
> in the morning
> and a great joy at noon";

which says: "I have encountered it
among those unpretentious

> protégés of wisdom,
> where seeming to parade
> as the debater and the Roman,
> the statesmanship
> of an archaic Daniel Webster
> persists to their simplicity of temper
> as the essence of the matter:
>
> 'Liberty and union
> now and forever';
>
> the Book on the writing-table;
> the hand in the breast-pocket."
>
> 1923

Even more than most of her poems, "Marriage" is a fabric of skillfully arranged quotations exploring, in a richly faceted collage, a variety of female and male attitudes toward marriage. Moore herself never married.

NOTES BY MARIANNE MOORE
Statements that took my fancy which I tried to arrange plausibly.
Lines 14–15: "*Of circular traditions . . .*" Francis Bacon.
Lines 25–28: *Write Simultaneously.* "Miss A—will write simultaneously in three languages, English, German, and French, talking in the meantime. [She] takes advantage of her abilities in everyday life, writing her letters simultaneously with both hands; namely, the first, third, and fifth words with her left and the second, fourth, and sixth with her right hand. While generally writing outward, she is able as well to write inward with both hands." "Multiple Consciousness or Reflex Action of Unaccustomed Range," *Scientific American*, January 1922.
Line 42: "*See her, see her in this common world.*" "George Shock."
Lines 48–55: "*That strange paradise, unlike flesh, stones . . .*" Richard Baxter, *The Saints' Everlasting Rest*.
Lines 65–66: "We were puzzled and we were fascinated, as if by something feline, by something colubrine." Philip Little, reviewing Santayana's *Poems* in *The New Republic*, March 21, 1923.
Lines 83–84: "*Treading chasms . . .*" Hazlitt: "Essay on Burke's Style."
Lines 91–97: "*Past states . . .*" Richard Baxter.
Lines 101–102: "*He experiences a solemn joy.*" "*A Travers Champs,*" by Anatole France in *Filles et Garçons* (Hachette): "*Le petit Jean comprend qu'el est beau et cette idée le pénétre d'un respect profond de lui–même. . . . Il goûte une joie pieuse à se sentir devenu une idole.*"
Line 108: "*It clothes me with a shirt of fire.*" Hagop Boghossian in a poem, "The Nightingale."
Lines 109–113: "*He dares not clap his hands . . .*" Edward Thomas, *Feminine Influence on the Poets* (Martin Secker, 1910).

Lines 116–117, 121–123: *"Illusion of a fire . . . ," "as high as deep . . ."* Richard Baxter.

Line 125: "Marriage is a law, and the worst of all laws . . . a very trivial object indeed." Godwin.

Lines 146–152: *"For love that will gaze an eagle blind . . ."* Anthony Trollope, *Barchester Towers*.

Lines 159–161: *"No truth can be fully known . . ."* Robert of Sorbonne.

Lines 167–168: *"Darkeneth her countenance as a bear doth."* Ecclesiasticus.

Line 175: *"Married people often look that way."* C. Bertram Hartmann.

Lines 176–178: *"Seldom and cold . . ."* Richard Baxter.

Line 181: *"Ahasuerus* tête-à-tête *banquet."* George Adam Smith, *Expositor's Bible*.

Line 183: *"Good monster, lead the way." The Tempest.*

Lines 187–190: *"Four o'clock does not exist . . ."* Comtesse de Noailles, "Le Thé," *Femina*, December 1921. *"Dans leur impérieuse humilité elles jouent instinctivement leurs roles sur le globe."*

Lines 194–196: *"What monarch . . ."* From "The Rape of the Locke."

Lines 198–199: *"The sound of the flute . . ."* A. Mitram Rihbany, *The Syrian Christ* (Houghton, Mifflin, 1916). Silence of women—"to an Oriental, this is as poetry set to music."

Lines 200–204: *"Men are monopolists . . ."* Miss M. Carey Thomas, Founder's address, Mount Holyoke, 1921: "Men practically reserve for themselves stately funerals, splendid monuments, memorial statues, memberships in academies, medals, titles, honorary degrees, stars, garters, ribbons, buttons, and other shining baubles, so valueless in themselves and yet so infinitely desirable because they are symbols of recognition by their fellow-craftsmen of difficult work well done."

Lines 207–208: *"The crumbs from a lion's meal . . .":* Amos iii, 12. Translation by George Adam Smith, *Expositor's Bible*.

Line 211: *"A wife is a coffin."* Ezra Pound.

Line 223: *"Settle on my hand."* Charles Reade, *Christie Johnston*.

Lines 232–233: "Asiatics have rights; Europeans have obligations." Edmund Burke.

Lines 252–253: *"Leaves her peaceful husband . . ."* Simone Puget, advertisement entitled "Change of Fashion," *English Review*, June 1914: "Thus proceed pretty dolls when they leave their old home to renovate their frame, and dear others who may abandon their peaceful husband only because they have seen enough of him."

Lines 256–258: *"Everything to do with love is mystery . . ."* F. C. Tilney, *Fables of La Fontaine*, "Love and Folly," Book XII, No. 14.

Lines 286–287: *"Liberty and Union . . ." Daniel Webster* (statue with inscription, Central Park, New York City).

Silence

My father used to say,
"Superior people never make long visits,
have to be shown Longfellow's grave
or the glass flowers at Harvard.

Self-reliant like the cat—
that takes its prey to privacy,
the mouse's limp tail hanging like a shoelace from its mouth—
they sometimes enjoy solitude,
and can be robbed of speech
by speech which has delighted them.
The deepest feeling always shows itself in silence;
not in silence, but restraint."
Nor was he insincere in saying, "Make my house your inn."
Inns are not residences.

1924

NOTES BY MARIANNE MOORE

My father used to say:[1] a remark in conversation; Miss A. M. Homans, Professor Emeritus
of Hygiene, Wellesley College. "My father used to say, 'superior people never make long
visits, the people are not glad when you've gone.' When I am visiting, I like to go about
by myself. I never had to be shown Longfellow's grave nor the glass flowers at Harvard."

"make my house your inn": Edmund Burke to a stranger with whom he had fallen into con-
versation in a bookshop. *Life of Burke*, James Prior: "'Throw yourself into a coach,' said
he. 'Come down and make my house your inn.'"

The Steeple-Jack

Dürer[1] would have seen a reason for living
    in a town like this, with eight stranded whales
to look at; with the sweet sea air coming into your house
on a fine day, from water etched
    with waves as formal as the scales
on a fish.

One by one in two's and three's, the seagulls keep
    flying back and forth over the town clock,
or sailing around the lighthouse without moving their wings—

1. Significantly, Moore never knew her own fa-
ther. All of the statements attributed to "my fa-
ther" derive from other sources.

1. Albrecht Dürer (1471–1528): German painter,
printmaker, and engraver who was regarded as
the greatest German Renaissance artist and was
noted for his close study of natural flora and
fauna. On a trip to Zeeland in the Netherlands in
1520 to see a beached whale, Dürer contracted
malaria in the swamps. Ironically, the whale was
washed back out to sea before his arrival. Compli-
cations arising from the disease were the cause of
Dürer's death in 1528.

rising steadily with a slight
 quiver of the body—or flock
mewing where

a sea the purple of the peacock's neck is
 paled to greenish azure as Dürer changed
the pine green of the Tyrol to peacock blue and guinea
gray. You can see a twenty-five-
 pound lobster; and fish nets arranged
to dry. The

whirlwind fife-and-drum of the storm bends the salt
 marsh grass, disturbs stars in the sky and the
star on the steeple; it is a privilege to see so
much confusion. Disguised by what
 might seem the opposite, the sea-
side flowers and

trees are favored by the fog so that you have
 the tropics first hand: the trumpet-vine,
fox-glove, giant snap-dragon, a salpiglossis[2] that has
spots and stripes; morning-glories, gourds,
 or moon-vines trained on fishing-twine
at the back door;

cat-tails, flags, blueberries and spiderwort,
 striped grass, lichens, sunflowers, asters, daisies—
yellow and crab-claw ragged sailors with green bracts—toad-plant,
petunias, ferns; pink lilies, blue
 ones, tigers; poppies; black sweet-peas.
The climate

is not right for the banyan,[3] frangipani, or
 jack-fruit trees; or for exotic serpent
life. Ring lizard and snake-skin for the foot, if you see fit;
but here they've cats, not cobras, to
 keep down the rats. The diffident
little newt

   * * *

2. Garden annuals cultivated for their richly var-
iegated, funnel-shaped blossoms in a variety
of colors. The most common variety is called
Painted Tongue.

3. A species of fig tree, native to India, known for
its broad-spreading habit. Frangipani: the Indian
pagoda tree, which has an erect habit and conical
form, is grown in temple gardens.

with white pin-dots on black horizontal spaced-
  out bands lives here; yet there is nothing that
ambition can buy or take away. The college student
named Ambrose[4] sits on the hillside
  with his not-native books and hat
and sees boats

at sea progress white and rigid as if in
  a groove. Liking an elegance of which
the source is not bravado, he knows by heart the antique
sugar-bowl shaped summer-house of
  interlacing slats, and the pitch
of the church

spire, not true, from which a man in scarlet lets
  down a rope as a spider spins a thread;
he might be part of a novel, but on the sidewalk a
sign says C. J. Poole, Steeple-Jack,[5]
  in black and white; and one in red
and white says

Danger. The church portico has four fluted
  columns, each a single piece of stone, made
modester by white-wash. This would be a fit haven for
waifs, children, animals, prisoners,
  and presidents who have repaid
sin-driven

senators by not thinking about them. The
  place has a school-house, a post-office in a
store, fish-houses, hen-houses, a three-masted schooner on
the stocks. The hero, the student,
  the steeple-jack, each in his way,
is at home.

It could not be dangerous to be living
  in a town like this, of simple people,

---

4. Moore's college student has the same name as St. Ambrose (ca. 340–397), the bishop of Milan and a great Roman Catholic thinker and scholar.
5. A steeplejack, by profession, climbs steeples, towers, and other high structures in order to build, paint, or repair them. Moore's steeplejack has placed his professional signs below the church both as an advertisement and as a warning to passersby of the danger from falling objects.

who have a steeple-jack placing danger-signs by the church
while he is gilding the solid-
    pointed star, which on a steeple
stands for hope.

1932

"The Steeple-Jack" appeared with "The Student" and "The Hero" as a poetic sequence un-
der the title "Part of a Novel, Part of a Poem, Part of a Play" in the June 1932 issue of *Poetry*.
Moore seems even then to have regarded these as more or less independent poems, and she
always republished them separately. Yet traces of the original sequence remain: the poem
includes a student (Ambrose) and refers to a hero—apparently, the titular steeplejack, who,
we are told, might be "part of a novel." The versification is syllabic, strictly following a pat-
tern of 11, 10, 14, 8, 8, and 3 syllables in the lines of each stanza. Moore's poem explores the
alternating appeals of safety and danger in a coastal setting of stunning natural beauty and
variety. Moore told a reader that the setting is "both Brooklyn and various New England
seacoast towns I had visited." Moore indicated that the whales of the poem's initial lines had
been found in Brooklyn Bay.

The Pangolin

Another armored animal[1]—scale
        lapping scale with spruce-cone regularity until they
form the uninterrupted central
    tail-row! This near artichoke with head and legs and grit-equipped gizzard,
    the night miniature artist engineer is,
        yes, Leonardo da Vinci's replica[2]—
            impressive animal and toiler of whom we seldom hear.
    Armor seems extra. But for him,
        the closing ear-ridge—
            or bare ear lacking even this small
            eminence and similarly safe

contracting nose and eye apertures
        impenetrably closable, are not;—a true ant-eater,
not cockroach eater, who endures
    exhausting solitary trips through unfamiliar ground at night,
    returning before sunrise; stepping in the moonlight,
        on the moonlight peculiarly, that the outside

---

1. Moore refers to the fact that many of her earlier
poems had also examined armored animals.
2. Moore sees the pangolin as Leonardo da

Vinci's replica because both are artists who strug-
gle through difficulties and persist to achieve-
ment.

edges of his hands may bear the weight and save the claws
for digging. Serpentined about
the tree, he draws
away from danger unpugnaciously,
with no sound but a harmless hiss; keeping

the fragile grace of the Thomas-
of-Leighton Buzzard Westminster Abbey[3] wrought-iron vine, or
rolls himself into a ball that has
power to defy all effort to unroll it; strongly intailed, neat
head for core, on neck not breaking off, with curled-in-feet.
Nevertheless he has sting-proof scales; and nest
of rocks closed with earth from inside, which can he thus darken.
Sun and moon and day and night and man and beast
each with a splendor
which man in all his vileness cannot
set aside; each with an excellence!

"Fearfull yet to be feared," the armored
ant-eater met by the driver-ant does not turn back, but
engulfs what he can, the flattened sword-
edged leafpoints on the tail and artichoke set leg- and body-plates
quivering violently when it retaliates
and swarms on him. Compact like the furled fringed frill
on the hat-brim of Gargallo's[4] hollow iron head of a
matador, he will drop and will
then walk away
unhurt, although if unintruded on,
he cautiously works down the tree, helped

by his tail. The giant-pangolin-
tail, graceful tool, as a prop or hand or broom or ax, tipped like
an elephant's trunk with special skin,
is not lost on this ant- and stone-swallowing uninjurable
artichoke which simpletons thought a living fable
whom the stones had nourished, whereas ants had done
so. Pangolins are not aggressive animals; between

---

3. The thirteenth-century artist Thomas, from the English market town of Leighton Buzzard, was famous for his iron scrollwork. He created an elaborate wrought-iron screen for the tomb of Queen Eleanor (beloved wife of Edward I) in Westminster Abbey.

4. Pablo Gargallo (1881–1934): Spanish modernist sculptor, a friend of Picasso, who created energetic figures in shaped iron.

dusk and day they have the not unchain-like machine-like
form and frictionless creep of a thing
made graceful by adversities, con-

versities. To explain grace requires
a curious hand. If that which is at all were not forever,
why would those who graced the spires
with animals and gathered there to rest, on cold luxurious
low stone seats — a monk and monk and monk — between the thus
ingenious roof-supports, have slaved to confuse
grace with a kindly manner, time in which to pay a debt,
the cure for sins, a graceful use
of what are yet
approved stone mullions[5] branching out across
the perpendiculars? A sailboat

was the first machine. Pangolins, made
for moving quietly also, are models of exactness,
on four legs; on hind feet plantigrade,[6]
with certain postures of a man. Beneath sun and moon, man slaving
to make his life more sweet, leaves half the flowers worth having,
needing to choose wisely how to use his strength;
a paper-maker like the wasp; a tractor of foodstuffs,
like the ant; spidering a length
of web from bluffs
above a stream; in fighting, mechanicked
like the pangolin; capsizing in

disheartenment. Bedizened[7] or stark
naked, man, the self, the being we call human, writing-
masters to this world, griffons[8] a dark
"Like does not like like that is obnoxious"; and writes error with four
r's. Among animals, *one* has sense of humor.
Humor saves a few steps, it saves years. Unignorant,
modest and unemotional, and all emotion,
he has everlasting vigor,

5. Stone dividers in a Gothic church window, in this case possibly the dividers in a rose window in a medieval abbey or chapter house.
6. Walking on the whole sole of the foot, as do humans and bears.
7. Dressed or adorned gaudily.

8. Moore refers either to a famous mythical beast, half lion and half eagle, or to a species of large vulture found in Europe and North Africa. In either case, the term is here used as a verb to indicate an overhanging threat.

power to grow,
　　though there are few creatures who can make one
　　breathe faster and make one erecter.

Not afraid of anything is he,
　　　and then goes cowering forth, tread paced to meet an obstacle
at every step. Consistent with the
　　formula—warm blood, no gills, two pairs of hands and a few hairs—that
is a mammal; there he sits on his own habitat,
　　　serge-clad, strong-shod. The prey of fear, he, always
　　　　curtailed, extinguished, thwarted by the dusk, work partly done,
　　says to the alternating blaze,
　　　"Again the sun!
　　　　anew each day; and new and new and new,
　　　　that comes into and steadies my soul."

　　　　　　　　　　　　　　　　　　　　　　　　1936

The pangolin, or scaly anteater, is a slow, shy creature covered with bronze-like scales. The name *pangolin*, from the Malayan word for "rolling over," refers to the animal's ability to curl itself into a tight ball when threatened.

NOTES BY MARIANNE MOORE
the "closing ear-ridge": and certain other details, from "Pangolins" by Robert T. Hatt, *Natural History*, December 1935.
stepping peculiarly: see Lyddeker's *Royal Natural History*.
Thomas of Leighton Buzzard's vine: a fragment of ironwork in Westminster Abbey.
"A sailboat was the first machine": See F. L. Morse, *Power: Its Application from the 17th Dynasty to the 20th Century.*

The Paper Nautilus

　　For authorities whose hopes
are shaped by mercenaries?
　　Writers entrapped by
　　teatime fame and by
commuters' comforts? Not for these
　　the paper nautilus
　　constructs her thin glass shell.

　　Giving her perishable
souvenir of hope, a dull
　　white outside and smooth-
　　edged inner surface

glossy as the sea, the watchful
　　maker of it guards it
　　day and night; she scarcely

　　eats until the eggs are hatched.
Buried eight-fold in her eight
　　arms, for she is in
　　a sense a devil-
fish, her glass ram'shorn-cradled freight
　　is hid but is not crushed;
　　as Hercules,[1] bitten

　　by a crab loyal to the hydra,[2]
was hindered to succeed,
　　the intensively
　　watched eggs coming from
the shell free it when they are freed, —
　　leaving its wasp-nest flaws
　　of white on white, and close-

　　laid Ionic chiton-folds[3]
like the lines in the mane of
　　a Parthenon horse,[4]
　　round which the arms had
wound themselves as if they knew love
　　is the only fortress
　　strong enough to trust to.

1940

The paper nautilus, a mollusk closely related to the octopus, has a rounded body, eight tentacles, and no fins. It is named for the beautiful papery shell that surrounds the female while she broods her eggs. After depositing her eggs in this shell, the female takes shelter in it herself. She is often found with her head and tentacles protruding from the opening, but she will retreat deeper inside if disturbed.

1. Mighty hero of Greek mythology, the son of Zeus and a mortal woman. He performed many famous feats of valor and strength.
2. An enormous water serpent with nine heads that battled Hercules. Each time Hercules cut off one of the Hydra's heads, two grew in its place. Hercules eventually burned each stump, arresting further growth. At the Hydra's bidding, a crab bit Hercules on the foot. Hercules promptly killed the crab. Hercules appears in the stars as a constellation, as do his two foes, the constellations Hydra and Cancer.

3. Ionic chiton: a garment worn in ancient Greece by both men and women. It was formed of a single sheet of fabric, folded over at the waist to form a blouse. The fabric was frequently pleated in long vertical lines.
4. The dramatically waving mane of a marble horse's head preserved from the ancient Athenian temple the Parthenon is set off by sharply etched lines that resemble the pleats on an ionic chiton, or, as Moore suggests, the grooved shell of the paper nautilus.

He "Digesteth Harde Yron"

Although the aepyornis[1]
    or roc that lived in Madagascar, and
the moa[2] are extinct,
the camel-sparrow,[3] linked
    with them in size—the large sparrow
Xenophon[4] saw walking by a stream—was and is
a symbol of justice.

    This bird watches his chicks with
        a maternal concentration—and he's
been mothering the eggs
at night six weeks—his legs
    their only weapon of defense.
He is swifter than a horse; he has a foot hard
as a hoof; the leopard

    is not more suspicious. How
        could he, prized for plumes and eggs and young
used even as a riding-beast, respect men
    hiding actor-like in ostrich skins, with the right hand
making the neck move as if alive
and from a bag the left hand strewing grain,[5] that ostriches

    might be decoyed and killed! Yes, this is he
whose plume was anciently
the plume of justice; he
    whose comic duckling head on its
great neck revolves with compass-needle nervousness
when he stands guard,

    in S-like foragings as he is
        preening the down on his leaden-skinned back.
The egg piously shown
as Leda's very own

---

1. A large, flightless bird native to Madagascar that became extinct in the seventeenth century. Also known as the elephant bird, it supposedly stood ten feet tall and weighed more than one thousand pounds.
2. Any one of several extinct species of very large, wingless birds.

3. "Camel sparrow" was an ancient name for the ostrich.
4. Ancient Greek soldier, historian, and naturalist.
5. A technique used to hunt ostriches in ancient times.

from which Castor and Pollux hatched,[6]
was an ostrich-egg. And what could have been more fit
for the Chinese lawn it

grazed on as a gift to an
emperor who admired strange birds, than this
one, who builds his mud-made
nest in dust yet will wade
in lake or sea till only the head shows.

Six hundred ostrich-brains served
at one banquet,[7] the ostrich-plume-tipped tent
and desert spear, jewel-
gorgeous ugly egg-shell
goblets, eight pairs of ostriches
in harness, dramatize a meaning
always missed by the externalist.

The power of the visible
is the invisible; as even where
no tree of freedom grows,
so-called brute courage knows.
Heroism is exhausting, yet
it contradicts a greed that did not wisely spare
the harmless solitaire

or great auk[8] in its grandeur;
unsolicitude having swallowed up
all giant birds but an alert gargantuan
little-winged, magnificently speedy running-bird.
This one remaining rebel
is the sparrow-camel.

1941

NOTES BY MARIANNE MOORE
Lyly's *Euphues*: "the estrich [ostrich] digesth harde yron to preserve his health."

6. In Greek myth, the twin sons of Leda and Zeus (in the form of a swan). They are sometimes seen as having hatched from the same egg.
7. The banquet was held by the Roman Emperor Elagabalus (204–222), who was noted for his depravity and excess.

8. A large, flightless bird, once common from Canada to Iceland and Norway, that was hunted to extinction by 1844.

the large sparrow: Xenophon (Anabasis, I, 5, 2) reports many ostriches in the desert on the
   left . . . side of the middle Euphrates, on the way from North Syria to Babylonia. *Ani-
   mals for Show and Pleasure in Ancient Rome* [1937] by George Jennison.

A symbol of justice, men in ostrich skins, and other allusions: Ostrich Egg-Shell Cups from
   Mesopotamia by Berthold Laufer, *The Open Court*, May 1926. "An ostrich plume sym-
   bolized truth and justice, and was the emblem of the goddess Ma-at, the patron saint of
   judges. Her head is adorned with an ostrich feather, her eyes are closed, . . . as Justice is
   blind-folded."

Six hundred ostrich brains: At a banquet given by Elagabalus. See above: *Animals for Show
   and Pleasure.*

egg-shell goblets, e.g. the painted ostrich-egg cup mounted in silver-gilt by Elias Geier of
   Leipzig about 1589. *Antiques in and About London* by Edward Wenham; *New York Sun*,
   May 22, 1937.

eight pairs of ostriches: See above: *Animals for Show and Pleasure.*

Sparrow-camel: Greek text.

In Distrust of Merits

Strengthened to live, strengthened to die for
   medals and positioned victories?
They're fighting, fighting, fighting the blind
   man who thinks he sees, —
who cannot see that the enslaver is
   enslaved; the hater, harmed. O shining O
      firm star, O tumultuous
         ocean lashed till small things go
   as they will, the mountainous
      wave makes us who look, know

depth. Lost at sea before they fought! O
   star of David, star of Bethlehem,
O black imperial lion
   of the Lord—emblem
of a risen world—be joined at last, be
joined. There is hate's crown beneath which all is
      death; there's love's without which none
         is king; the blessed deeds bless
   the halo. As contagion
      of sickness makes sickness,

contagion of trust can make trust. They're
   fighting in deserts and caves, one by
one, in battalions and squadrons;

they're fighting that I
may yet recover from the disease, My
Self; some have it lightly, some will die. "Man's
    wolf to man"[1] and we devour
        ourselves. The enemy could not
      have made a greater breach in our
        defenses. One pilot-

ing a blind man can escape him, but
    Job disheartened by false comfort knew
that nothing can be so defeating
    as a blind man who
can see. O alive who are dead, who are
proud not to see, O small dust of the earth
    that walks so arrogantly,
        trust begets power and faith is
    an affectionate thing. We
      vow, we make this promise

to the fighting—it's a promise—"We'll
    never hate black, white, red, yellow, Jew,
Gentile, Untouchable." We are
    not competent to
make our vows. With set jaw they are fighting,
fighting, fighting,—some we love whom we know,
    some we love but know not—that
      hearts may feel and not be numb.
      It cures me; or am I what
      I can't believe in? Some

in snow, some on crags, some in quicksands,
    little by little, much by much, they
are fighting fighting fighting that where
    there was death there may
be life. "When a man is prey to anger,
he is moved by outside things; when he holds
    his ground in patience patience
      patience, that is action or
    beauty," the soldier's defense
      and hardest armor for

---

1. Proverb by the Roman playwright Plautus (ca. 254–184 B.C.E.): "Man is a wolf to man."

*   *   *

the fight. The world's an orphans' home. Shall
    we never have peace without sorrow?
without pleas of the dying for
    help that won't come? O
quiet form upon the dust, I cannot
look and yet I must. If these great patient
        dyings—all these agonies
            and wound bearings and bloodshed—
        can teach us how to live, these
            dyings were not wasted.

Hate-hardened heart, O heart of iron,
    iron is iron till it is rust.
There never was a war that was
    not inward; I must
fight till I have conquered in myself what
causes war, but I would not believe it.
        I inwardly did nothing.
            O Iscariotlike[2] crime!
        Beauty is everlasting
            and dust is for a time.

                                        1943

"In Distrust of Merits," written in the midst of World War II, shows Moore's defiant response to the forces of Nazism that had set the war in motion.

Nevertheless

you've seen a strawberry
    that's had a struggle; yet
    was, where the fragments met,

a hedgehog or a star-
    fish for the multitude
    of seeds. What better food

        *   *   *

2. Resembling Judas Iscariot, the apostle who betrayed Jesus Christ.

than apple-seeds — the fruit
within the fruit — locked in
like counter-curved twin

hazel-nuts? Frost that kills
the little rubber-plant-
leaves of kok-saghyz-stalks,[1] can't

harm the roots; they still grow
in frozen ground. Once where
there was a prickly-pear-

leaf clinging to barbed wire,
a root shot down to grow
in earth two feet below;

as carrots form mandrakes
or a ram's-horn root some-
times. Victory won't come

to me unless I go
to it; a grape-tendril
ties a knot in knots till

knotted thirty times, — so
the bound twig that's under-
gone and over-gone, can't stir.

The weak overcomes its
menace, the strong over-
comes itself. What is there

like fortitude! What sap
went through that little thread
to make the cherry red!

1943

Written in the same year as "In Distrust of Merits" (above), "Nevertheless" reflects a more characteristically figurative response to World War II.

---

1. Perennial dandelion native to Kazakhstan cultivated for its fleshy roots that have high rubber content.

The Mind Is an Enchanting Thing

is an enchanted thing
 like the glaze on a
katydid-wing
  subdivided by sun
  till the nettings are legion.
Like Gieseking[1] playing Scarlatti;

like the apteryx-awl[2]
 as a beak, or the
kiwi's rain-shawl
  of haired feathers, the mind
  feeling its way as though blind,
walks along with its eyes on the ground.

It has memory's ear
 that can hear without
having to hear.
  Like the gyroscope's fall,
  truly unequivocal
because trued by regnant[3] certainty,

it is a power of
 strong enchantment. It
is like the dove-
  neck animated by
  sun; it is memory's eye;
it's conscientious inconsistency.

It tears off the veil; tears
 the temptation, the
mist the heart wears,
  from its eyes, — if the heart
  has a face; it takes apart
dejection. It's fire in the dove-neck's

   *   *   *

1. Walter Gieseking (1895–1956) was a German pianist noted for his gracefully colored interpretations. Domenico Scarlatti (1685–1757) was an Italian baroque composer noted for the darting elegance and playful surprise of his many brief keyboard sonatas.

2. The sharply pointed beak of the brown kiwi bird.
3. Reigning, predominant.

iridescence; in the
　　inconsistencies
of Scarlatti
　　Unconfusion submits
　　its confusion to proof; it's
not a Herod's oath[4] that cannot change.

1943

T. S. ELIOT
1888–1965

T. S. ELIOT'S POETRY derives much of its power from its capacity to embody and reconcile contradictory characteristics. Although Eliot was deeply conservative and traditional in his sympathies, he emerged as one of the trailblazers of experimental modernism. Although Eliot advocated an austere and impersonal poetics, his verse vibrates with a diversity of individual voices while enacting a deeply personal emotional and spiritual drama. Although Eliot's poetry bristles with classic literary and historical allusions, it also engages persistently with the mundane or sordid details of modern life. Although many critics have noted what Gorham Munson early termed "an unusual intelligence working behind the words," and although Eliot's poetry poses many hard intellectual puzzles, Eliot's images and keenly musical phrasing often bypass the intellect to convey visceral effects of great emotional immediacy. By birth and education an American, and conceding in a late interview that the "emotional springs" of his work were American, Eliot resided for most of his creative life in England and became a British citizen in 1927. Eliot's work was from its outset deeply controversial, condemned by early readers for its difficulty and for the obscurity or elitism of its many allusions—and it remains controversial today—yet Eliot emerged as the first experimental modernist poet to achieve widespread academic and popular acclaim, and he remains the only American experimental modernist poet to have won the Nobel Prize,

4. See Matthew 14:6–10 in the New Testament. The prophet John the Baptist had been imprisoned. "But when Herod's birthday was kept, [Salome] the daughter of Herodias danced before them, and pleased Herod. Whereupon he promised with an oath to give her whatsoever she would ask. And she, being before instructed of her mother, said, 'Give me here John Baptist's head in a charger.' And the king was sorry: nevertheless for the oath's sake, and them which sat with him at meat, he commanded [it] to be given [her]. And he sent, and beheaded John in the prison."

which he secured in 1948. With Longfellow, Eliot is the only American-born poet to be enshrined in Poet's Corner in London's Westminster Abbey.

Thomas Stearns Eliot was the youngest of seven children, born into the family of a prosperous St. Louis merchant. Eliot's mother was a protective and dominating presence: an aspiring poet frustrated by her limited educational opportunities who looked to her son to complete her intellectual and artistic ambitions. His paternal grandfather, William Greenleaf Eliot, was a Unitarian minister revered by his St. Louis flock and famous for his good works and social activism. Eliot later recalled that in his family, "the standard of conduct was that which my grandfather set." Yet Eliot would come to rebel against social gentility and the utilitarian rationalism of his family heritage, moving toward a more traditional, yet radical, religious faith in the presence of God in the world and in the reality of evil. The poetry of Eliot's mother expresses conventional religious yearning in optimistic terms. Eliot's religious vision would emerge as darker and more unconventional, charged with sexual and spiritual disquiet and reflecting a rejection of many of the elements of his parents' and grandparents' comfortable cultural and spiritual world.

Shy, witty, self-ironic, and reserved in manner, Eliot was a brilliant student who achieved a B.A. at Harvard in 1909, then began graduate work at Harvard in literature and philosophy. Traveling to Europe for further study in 1910, Eliot was deeply influenced by the months he spent in Paris, where he observed with both fascination and dismay the sometimes sordid Parisian street life (later reflected in "Preludes"). He began writing verse in French and made friends with the young intellectual Jean Verdenal, whose death in World War I would contribute to the bleak and elegiac tone of much of Eliot's early work. Eliot also attended lectures by the philosopher and psychologist Henri Bergson at the Collège de France. Bergson's ideas on the mind as a "stream of consciousness" directly influenced the technique of such poems as Eliot's groundbreaking dramatic monologue, "The Love Song of J. Alfred Prufrock." In 1911, Eliot returned to Harvard, where he pursued a Ph.D. in philosophy. By the end of that year, Eliot, then just twenty-three, had completed "Prufrock," "Preludes," and "Portrait of a Lady," three key works of early experimental modernism that he deemed too radical, as yet, for publication.

In 1914, Eliot's career as a poet took a decisive turn when he returned to England on a traveling fellowship. There he met fellow American Ezra Pound (also included in this anthology), who had been an active poet, critic, and editor in London since 1908 and who became a key ally with Eliot in the cause of experimental modernism. Pound was impressed with Eliot's verse and with how thoroughly Eliot had modernized himself *"on his own"* (Pound's emphasis to *Poetry* magazine editor Harriet Monroe), and in 1915 he pushed, successfully, for the first publication of "Prufrock," "Preludes," and "Portrait of a Lady," thereby launching Eliot's poetic career.

Eliot decided to abandon his expected career path as a philosophy professor in the United States. He never returned to Harvard to defend his completed doctoral thesis on the English philosopher F. H. Bradley. Instead, he married the vivacious and sensitive but emotionally unstable Englishwoman Vivien Haigh-Wood and began a financially insecure career of an aspiring poet, critic, and editor in London. Because writing (and school teaching) failed to offer a living wage, and because Eliot's well-to-do father refused to support his unconventional career choice, Eliot, searching for economic stability, took a post in the colonial and foreign department of Lloyds Bank, where his fluency in a range of foreign languages—which would soon be put to poetic use in *The Waste Land*—were valuable in untangling the complexities of international finance. In 1917, Eliot's first book, *Prufrock and Other Observations*, was published. He was also active as a critic, publishing the influential "Tradition and the Individual Talent" in 1919, along with numerous important essays on such subjects as metaphysical poetry, Dante, and English Renaissance drama. His second book, *Poems* (1920), featured many experiments with new poetic subjects and textures, including "Gerontion," a powerful experiment in blending and juxtaposing multiple time frames and cultural perspectives that served as the most direct early forerunner of *The Waste Land*.

Yet the pressures of a career that combined demanding full-time work at Lloyds Bank with writing and with a home life centered on a wife who was showing increasing signs of mental instability—not to mention Eliot's innate tendency toward spiritual and emotional disquiet—led Eliot to a mental and physical collapse in 1921. Taking three months' leave from Lloyds, Eliot rested at an English seaside resort at Margate, then sought treatment at a sanitorium in Lausanne, Switzerland. During this time, Eliot completed the initial draft of *The Waste Land*. Early in 1922, Eliot extensively revised *The Waste Land* in close interchange with Pound. Pound's suggestions significantly shortened the work while sharpening its verbal and symbolic connections, helping to transform Eliot's sprawling original into a model for the modern poetic sequence on an epic scale. *The Waste Land*, published in New York in *The Dial* in 1922 and in England in the *Criterion* (a new magazine founded by Eliot), and appearing in book form in 1923, made an immediate and lasting impact on the literary scene.

By no means were all reviews of *The Waste Land* favorable. *Time* magazine, comparing the poem with James Joyce's recently published *Ulysses*, noted, "There is a new kind of literature abroad in the land, whose only obvious fault is that no one can understand it." Even some friendly critics were not quite convinced of the poem's coherence. Eliot's Harvard friend Conrad Aiken (also included in this anthology) saw it as "a brilliant and kaleidoscopic confusion" giving "an impression of an intensely modern, intensely literary consciousness which perceives itself not as a unity but a chance correlation or conglomerate of mutually discolorative fragments." But Gorham Munson praised Eliot for "piercing, or trying to pierce into, uncharted regions," in the process creating a poem that "requires for comprehension a more or less stringent initiation into certain ways of feeling, thinking and expressing, which are not common." Certainly, the controversy surrounding the poem helped draw attention to experimental modernism and inspired future work both in emulation and in refutation of Eliot's model—including, among the the refutations, such major poetic sequences as Hart Crane's *The Bridge* and William Carlos Williams's *Paterson*.

Many readers have felt the effort of initiation required to comprehend *The Waste Land* to be worth making, and a critical consensus has come to see in the poem a powerful and complex unity, though critics differ over how that unity should be interpreted and evaluated. In fact, learning to read *The Waste Land* and to recognize and trace its patterns helped expand the reading skills, critical vocabulary, and artistic horizons of an entire generation of readers of poetry. By 1945, the poet Delmore Schwartz would be arguing that Eliot's poem "illustrates a new view of consciousness, the depths of consciousness and the unconscious mind" and that "the true protagonist of Eliot's poem is the heir of all the ages." The African-American novelist Ralph Ellison, author of *Invisible Man*, would recall in 1964 that while his reading of such Harlem Rennaissance poets as Langston Hughes, Countee Cullen, and Claude McKay (all included in this anthology) had "inspired pride and had given me a closer identification with poetry," it was *The Waste Land* that "seized my mind. I was intrigued by its power to move me while eluding my understanding." Hoping to decipher "its discontinuities, its changes of pace and its hidden system of organization," Ellison concluded that "there was nothing to do but look up the footnotes in the poem, and thus began my conscious education in literature."

In 1925, Eliot left Lloyds Bank to take an editorial position at the London publishing firm of Faber and Gwyer (later Faber and Faber). In large part through Eliot's efforts, Faber would emerge as perhaps the foremost publisher of modern poetry in Britain. In 1927, Eliot joined the Church of England and became a British citizen. While *The Waste Land* had appeared to present Christianity, Hinduism, and Buddhism as equally valid responses to the chaos and spiritual sterility of the modern world, from this point on his work would take an explicitly Christian and mystical turn. In 1933, Eliot returned to Harvard to give a series of lectures published as *The Use of Poetry and the Use of Criticism*. Eliot also used this journey to America to mark his separation from his wife, Vivien. Vivien was permanently institutionalized in 1938 and died in 1947. Eliot's thinking by the mid-1930s had turned toward the importance of a unified belief system, which he felt was seriously lacking in the modern world, and in a lecture he delivered at the University of Virginia Eliot expressed the undesirability of having "any large number of free-thinking Jews" in a society. This lecture, combined with unflattering references to Jewish characters in some of his early poems, has led to charges of anti-Semitism against Eliot, though Eliot later appeared to regret his remarks and never republished the lecture.

In later years Eliot, attempting to reach a larger audience, turned increasingly to drama. His greatest dramatic successes in his lifetime were the first of his five plays, *Murder in the Cathedral* (1935), a verse drama that centers on the assassination and martyrdom of the medieval archbishop of Canterbury, Thomas à Becket; and his third, *The Cocktail Party* (1950), a play that adapts the elements of drawing-room comedy to more serious purposes. However, his greatest dramatic success was posthumous, through Andrew Lloyd Webber's long-running musical *Cats*, whose songs (with the exception of "Memory") derive from Eliot's engaging book of light verse, *Old Possum's Book of Practical Cats* (1939). (Possum was Pound's ironic nickname for his friend Eliot.)

Eliot's last major poetic work, *Four Quartets*, was written in four sections between 1936 and 1942 and is remarkable both for its formal richness and unity and for its capacity to combine expressions of intense doubt and disquiet with modesty, calm, and acceptance. In the last of the *Quartets*, "Little Gidding" (the selection included in this anthology), the German bombing of London—where Eliot patrolled the streets as an air-raid warden—provides a setting for the search for timeless moments of spiritual understanding and an assertion of the virtues of love, humility, and faith. After 1957, though Eliot had fallen virtually silent as a poet, he found great happiness through his marriage to his second wife, Valerie. He died in 1965, at the age of seventy-six, leaving behind him an indelible body of poetic and critical work. He was buried in East Coker, the English village from which his Eliot ancestors had originated.

FURTHER READING

Peter Ackroyd. *T. S. Eliot: A Life*. New York: Simon & Schuster, 1984.

John Xiros Cooper. *T. S. Eliot and the Ideology of Four Quartets*. New York: Cambridge University Press, 1996.

T. S. Eliot. *The Complete Poems and Plays of T. S. Eliot*. London: Faber, 1969.

———. *Selected Essays*, 3rd ed. New York: Harcourt, 1951.

Valerie Eliot, ed. *The Letters of T. S. Eliot, Volume 1: 1898–1922*. New York: Harcourt, 1988.

———. *T. S. Eliot: The Waste Land: A Facsimile and Transcript of the Original Drafts Including the Annotations of Ezra Pound*. London: Faber, 1971.

Northrop Frye. *T. S. Eliot*. Chicago: University of Chicago Press, 1981.

Helen Gardner. *The Art of T. S. Eliot*. London: Faber, 1949.

———. *The Composition of Four Quartets*. London: Faber, 1978.

Lyndall Gordon. *T. S. Eliot: An Imperfect Life*. New York: Norton, 2000.

Michael Grant, ed. *T. S. Eliot: The Critical Heritage*. Boston: Routledge, 1982.

Cleo McNelly Kearns. *T. S. Eliot and Indic Traditions: A Study in Poetry and Belief*. Cambridge, Eng.: Cambridge University Press, 1987.

Hugh Kenner. *The Invisible Poet*. New York: Harcourt, Brace, 1959.

T. S. Matthews. *Great Tom: Notes Toward a Definition of T. S. Eliot*. New York: Harper & Row, 1974.

David A. Moody. *The Cambridge Companion to T. S. Eliot*. New York: Cambridge University Press, 1994.

Michael North. *The Waste Land: Norton Critical Edition*. New York: Norton, 2001.

Christopher Ricks. *T. S. Eliot and Prejudice*. London: Faber, 1988.

Eric Sigg. *The American T. S. Eliot: A Study of the Early Writings*. New York: Cambridge University Press, 1989.

Grover Smith, Jr. *T. S. Eliot's Poetry and Plays: A Study in Sources and Meaning*, 2nd ed. Chicago: University of Chicago Press, 1974.

B. C. Southam. *A Guide to the Selected Poems of T. S. Eliot*. New York: Harcourt, Brace, 1968.

George Williamson. *A Reader's Guide to T. S. Eliot*. New York: Noonday, 1953.

The Love Song of J. Alfred Prufrock

> *S'io credesse che mia risposta fosse*
> *A persona che mai tornasse al mondo,*
> *Questa fiamma staria senza piu scosse.*
> *Ma perciocche giammai di questo fondo*
> *Non torno vivo alcun, s'i'odo il vero,*
> *Senza tema d'infamia ti rispondo.*[1]

Let us go then, you and I,
When the evening is spread out against the sky
Like a patient etherised[2] upon a table;
Let us go, through certain half-deserted streets,
The muttering retreats
Of restless nights in one-night cheap hotels
And sawdust[3] restaurants with oyster-shells:
Streets that follow like a tedious argument
Of insidious intent
To lead you to an overwhelming question . . .
Oh, do not ask, "What is it?"
Let us go and make our visit.

In the room the women come and go
Talking of Michelangelo.[4]

＊　＊　＊

1. The epigraph quotes Dante Alighieri's *Inferno* (Canto 27, lines 61–66), lines spoken by the tormented soul of Guido da Montefeltro in response to a question of Dante, who is touring Hell and whom Guido supposes to be dead. The flame in which Guido is encased as punishment for his evil counsel vibrates as he speaks: "If I thought that that I was replying to someone who would ever return to the world, this flame would cease to flicker. But since no one ever returns from these depths alive, if what I've heard is true, I will answer you without fear of infamy." Prufrock may also speak intimately on the assumption that no one beyond a single auditor will hear his self-revelatory words.

2. Anesthetized with ether.

3. Cheap bars and restaurants used to spread sawdust on the floor to soak up spilled food and drinks.

4. Italian Renaissance artist; painter of the Sistine Chapel and sculptor of the *Pietà* and *David*

The yellow fog that rubs its back upon the window-panes,
The yellow smoke that rubs its muzzle on the window-panes
Licked its tongue into the corners of the evening,
Lingered upon the pools that stand in drains,
Let fall upon its back the soot that falls from chimneys,
Slipped by the terrace, made a sudden leap,
And seeing that it was a soft October night,
Curled once about the house, and fell asleep.

And indeed there will be time
For the yellow smoke that slides along the street,
Rubbing its back upon the window-panes;
There will be time, there will be time
To prepare a face to meet the faces that you meet;
There will be time to murder and create,
And time for all the works and days of hands
That lift and drop a question on your plate;
Time for you and time for me,
And time yet for a hundred indecisions,
And for a hundred visions and revisions,
Before the taking of a toast and tea.

In the room the women come and go
Talking of Michelangelo.

And indeed there will be time
To wonder, "Do I dare?" and, "Do I dare?"
Time to turn back and descend the stair,
With a bald spot in the middle of my hair —
[They will say: "How his hair is growing thin!"]
My morning coat, my collar mounting firmly to the chin,
My necktie rich and modest, but asserted by a simple pin —
[They will say: "But how his arms and legs are thin!"]
Do I dare
Disturb the universe?
In a minute there is time
For decisions and revisions which a minute will reverse.

For I have known them all already, known them all: —
Have known the evenings, mornings, afternoons,
I have measured out my life with coffee spoons;

I know the voices dying with a dying fall
Beneath the music from a farther room.
    So how should I presume?

And I have known the eyes already, known them all—
The eyes that fix you in a formulated phrase,
And when I am formulated, sprawling on a pin,
When I am pinned and wriggling on the wall,
Then how should I begin
To spit out all the butt-ends of my days and ways?
    And how should I presume?

And I have known the arms already, known them all—
Arms that are braceleted and white and bare
[But in the lamplight, downed with light brown hair!]
Is it perfume from a dress
That makes me so digress?
Arms that lie along a table, or wrap about a shawl.
    And should I then presume?
    And how should I begin?

    ♦   ♦   ♦

Shall I say, I have gone at dusk through narrow streets
And watched the smoke that rises from the pipes
Of lonely men in shirt-sleeves, leaning out of windows? . . .

I should have been a pair of ragged claws
Scuttling across the floors of silent seas.

    ♦   ♦   ♦

And the afternoon, the evening, sleeps so peacefully!
Smoothed by long fingers,
Asleep . . . tired . . . or it malingers,
Stretched on the floor, here beside you and me.
Should I, after tea and cakes and ices,
Have the strength to force the moment to its crisis?
But though I have wept and fasted, wept and prayed,
Though I have seen my head [grown slightly bald] brought in upon a platter,[5]
I am no prophet—and here's no great matter;
I have seen the moment of my greatness flicker,
And I have seen the eternal Footman hold my coat, and snicker,
And in short, I was afraid.

5. Like John the Baptist (see Matthew 14:1–12), who was beheaded by King Herod at the behest of the beautiful Salome. She insisted that his head be brought to her on a platter.

*   *   *

And would it have been worth it, after all,
After the cups, the marmalade, the tea,
Among the porcelain, among some talk of you and me,
Would it have been worth while,
To have bitten off the matter with a smile,
To have squeezed the universe into a ball
To roll it toward some overwhelming question,
To say: "I am Lazarus,[6] come from the dead,
Come back to tell you all, I shall tell you all"—
If one, settling a pillow by her head,
    Should say: "That is not what I meant at all.
    That is not it, at all."

And would it have been worth it, after all,
Would it have been worth while,
After the sunsets and the dooryards and the sprinkled streets,
After the novels, after the teacups, after the skirts that trail along the floor—
And this, and so much more?—
It is impossible to say just what I mean!
But as if a magic lantern[7] threw the nerves in patterns on a screen:
Would it have been worth while
If one, settling a pillow or throwing off a shawl,
And turning toward the window, should say:
    "That is not it at all,
    That is not what I meant, at all."

✦   ✦   ✦

No! I am not Prince Hamlet,[8] nor was meant to be;
Am an attendant lord, one that will do
To swell a progress, start a scene or two,
Advise the prince; no doubt, an easy tool,
Deferential, glad to be of use,
Politic, cautious, and meticulous;
Full of high sentence, but a bit obtuse;
At times, indeed, almost ridiculous—
Almost, at times, the Fool.

6. A man raised from death by Jesus (see John 11:1–44).
7. An early form of slide projector that used black-and-white slides.
8. Prufrock denies that he is as important a figure as the tragic hero of Shakespeare's *Hamlet*. Rather, his role is secondary—his description resembles Hamlet's comic foil, the verbose and fatuous King's Chamberlain, Polonius.

*   *   *

I grow old . . . I grow old . . .
I shall wear the bottoms of my trousers rolled.

Shall I part my hair behind? Do I dare to eat a peach?
I shall wear white flannel trousers, and walk upon the beach.
I have heard the mermaids singing, each to each.

I do not think that they will sing to me.

I have seen them riding seaward on the waves
Combing the white hair of the waves blown back
When the wind blows the water white and black.

We have lingered in the chambers of the sea
By sea-girls wreathed with seaweed red and brown
Till human voices wake us, and we drown.

1915

Preludes

I

The winter evening settles down
With smell of steaks in passageways.
Six o'clock.
The burnt-out ends of smoky days.
And now a gusty shower wraps
The grimy scraps
Of withered leaves about your feet
And newspapers from vacant lots;
The showers beat
On broken blinds and chimney-pots,
And at the corner of the street
A lonely cab-horse steams and stamps.
And then the lighting of the lamps.

II

The morning comes to consciousness
Of faint stale smells of beer
From the sawdust-trampled street
With all its muddy feet that press

To early coffee-stands.
With the other masquerades
That time resumes,
One thinks of all the hands
That are raising dingy shades
In a thousand furnished rooms.

III

You tossed a blanket from the bed,
You lay upon your back, and waited;
You dozed, and watched the night revealing
The thousand sordid images
Of which your soul was constituted;
They flickered against the ceiling.
And when all the world came back
And the light crept up between the shutters
And you heard the sparrows in the gutters,
You had such a vision of the street
As the street hardly understands;
Sitting along the bed's edge, where
You curled the papers from your hair,
Or clasped the yellow soles of feet
In the palms of both soiled hands.

IV

His soul stretched tight across the skies
That fade behind a city block,
Or trampled by insistent feet
At four and five and six o'clock;
And short square fingers stuffing pipes,
And evening newspapers, and eyes
Assured of certain certainties,
The conscience of a blackened street
Impatient to assume the world.

I am moved by fancies that are curled
Around these images, and cling:
The notion of some infinitely gentle
Infinitely suffering thing.

* * *

Wipe your hand across your mouth, and laugh;
The worlds revolve like ancient women
Gathering fuel in vacant lots.

1915

This sequence of short poems draws on Eliot's observations of Parisian street life when he visited the city as a young student. The title, "Preludes," may allude to Chopin's *Preludes*, twenty-four brief mood pieces for the piano that the nineteenth-century composer wrote in Paris. More recently, the French composer Debussy had also published two volumes of *Preludes*.

Gerontion

Thou hast nor youth nor age
But as it were an after dinner sleep
Dreaming of both.[1]

Here I am, an old man in a dry month,
Being read to by a boy, waiting for rain.[2]
I was neither at the hot gates[3]
Nor fought in the warm rain
Nor knee deep in the salt marsh, heaving a cutlass,
Bitten by flies, fought.
My house is a decayed house,
And the jew[4] squats on the window sill, the owner,
Spawned in some estaminet[5] of Antwerp,
Blistered in Brussels, patched and peeled in London.
The goat coughs at night in the field overhead;
Rocks, moss, stonecrop,[6] iron, merds.
The woman keeps the kitchen, makes tea,

1. Shakespeare, *Measure for Measure* (3.1.32–34).
2. See A. C. Benson's biography, *Edward Fitzgerald* (New York, 1905): "Here he sits, in a dry month, old and blind, being read to by a country boy, longing for rain." Fitzgerald was the author of *The Rubáiyát of Omar Khayyám* (1859), a popular translation of a classic Persian poem that explores the mysteries of life and celebrates drinking, eating, and enjoying life while it lasts — ironically, the opposite values of the ascetic detachment "Gerontion" appears to propound.
3. An English rephrasing of "Thermopylae," the name of a narrow pass between mountain and sea where in 480 B.C.E. Leonidas and three hundred Spartans heroically held off a vast army of Persians under Xerxes. Like Prufrock, who observes "No, I am not Prince Hamlet, nor was meant to be," Gerontion has not had such heroic experiences.
4. Here the Jewish landlord seems to stand, unpleasantly, for rootlessness.
5. Small café or bistro (French).
6. Flowering plant with fleshy leaves, growing in masses on rocks. Merds: excrement (French).

Sneezes at evening, poking the peevish gutter.[7]
            I an old man,
A dull head among windy spaces.

Signs are taken for wonders. "We would see a sign!"
The word within a word, unable to speak a word,
Swaddled with darkness.[8] In the juvescence of the year
Came Christ the tiger.[9]

In depraved May, dogwood and chestnut, flowering judas,[10]
To be eaten, to be divided, to be drunk[11]
Among whispers; by Mr. Silvero
With caressing hands, at Limoges[12]
Who walked all night in the next room;

By Hakagawa, bowing among the Titians;[13]
By Madame de Tornquist, in the dark room
Shifting the candles;[14] Fräulein von Kulp

7. Benson's biography of Edward Fitzgerald quotes a letter to Frederick Tennyson: "I really do like to sit in this doleful place with a good fire, a cat and dog on the rug, and an old woman in the kitchen. This is all my live-stock. The house is yet damp as last year."

8. Lancelot Andrewes, the favorite preacher of King James I, wrote in a Christmas sermon, "Signs are taken for wonders. 'Master, we would fain see a sign,' that is, a miracle. And, in this sense, it is a sign, to wonder at. Indeed, every word here is a wonder: . . . *an Infant, Verbum infans* [the infant word], the *Word* without a *word*; the *eternal word* not able to speak a *word*; a wonder sure. And . . . swaddled; . . . that a *wonder* too." Andrewes's two principal sources are Matthew (12:38–39): "Then certain of the scribes and of the Pharisees answered, saying, Master, we would see a sign from thee. But he answered and said unto them, An evil and adulterous generation seeketh after a sign"; and John (1:1): "In the beginning was the Word, and the Word was with God, and the Word was God." Juvescence: Youth, i.e., the spring.

9. Christ's return to life at Easter is a sign of his power and completes the cycle of his earthly existence, from wordless infancy and lamblike passivity to immortal life and energy at his rebirth.

10. In 1919, Eliot had reviewed *The Education of Henry Adams*, an autobiographical work by Henry Adams, a professional historian and grandson and great-grandson of American presidents John and John Quincy Adams. Adams had writ-

ten of a Washington, D.C., springtime, "The Potomac and its tributaries squandered beauty . . . Here and there a Negro log cabin alone disturbed the dogwood and the judas-tree . . . The tulip and the chestnut tree gave no sense of struggle against a stingy nature . . . The brooding heat of the profligate vegetation; the cool charm of the thundergust in the deep and solitary woods, were all sensual, animal, elemental. No European spring had shown him the same intermixture of delicate grace and passionate depravity that marked the Maryland May. He loved it too much as if it were Greek and half human."

11. A reference to the Christian Communion service, which here appears to be occurring in debased, secular forms.

12. A city in central France known for its delicate china and porcelain.

13. Paintings by Titian (ca. 1488–1576), a great Venetian Renaissance master. The diverse names in this passage suggest a collocation of different nationalities who have arrived in Europe and are absorbing and absorbed by its cultural treasures, yet their actions seem fragmentary, partial, incomplete, and possibly profane when they should be sacred.

14. Madame de Tornquist may be arranging a séance. Communication with the dead, like the Tarot card readings of Madame Sosostris in *The Waste Land*, had become extremely popular in the years following World War I, perhaps because of the staggering losses in that war.

Who turned in the hall, one hand on the door. Vacant shuttles
Weave the wind.[15] I have no ghosts,
An old man in a draughty house
Under a windy knob.[16]

After such knowledge, what forgiveness? Think now
History has many cunning passages, contrived corridors[17]
And issues, deceives with whispering ambitions,
Guides us by vanities. Think now
She gives when our attention is distracted
And what she gives, gives with such supple confusions
That the giving famishes the craving. Gives too late
What's not believed in, or if still believed,
In memory only, reconsidered passion. Gives too soon
Into weak hands, what's thought can be dispensed with
Till the refusal propagates a fear. Think
Neither fear nor courage saves us. Unnatural vices
Are fathered by our heroism. Virtues
Are forced upon us by our impudent crimes.
These tears are shaken from the wrath-bearing tree.[18]

The tiger springs in the new year. Us he devours.[19] Think at last
We have not reached conclusion, when I
Stiffen in a rented house. Think at last
I have not made this show purposelessly
And it is not by any concitation[20]
Of the backward devils.[21]
I would meet you upon this honestly.
I that was near your heart was removed therefrom

15. See Job 7:6–7: "My days are swifter than a weaver's shuttle, and are spent without hope. O remember that my life is wind: mine eye shall no more see good."

16. Rounded hill. The poem, after numerous excursions, returns to its original setting.

17. The first of many meditations on history in Eliot's work. See the final movement of "Little Gidding."

18. The tree of the knowledge of good and evil. When Adam and Eve ate the fruit from it despite God's prohibition, He cast them out of Eden into a world of labor, pain, and death. "In the sweat of thy face shalt thou eat bread, till thou return unto the ground; for out of it wast thou taken: for dust thou art, and unto dust shalt thou return" (Genesis 3:19).

19. Although a terrifying image, the reemergence of Christ at Easter to devour us may permit our removal from a life of sin and our redemption into a new life, a release from the curse on Adam and Eve. In the Communion service, by contrast, the worshippers devour Christ.

20. Stirring up; incitement.

21. In Dante's *Inferno*, false prophets are punished by being forced to walk backward.

To lose beauty in terror, terror in inquisition.
I have lost my passion: why should I need to keep it
Since what is kept must be adulterated?
I have lost my sight, smell, hearing, taste and touch:
How should I use them for your closer contact?

These with a thousand small deliberations
Protract the profit of their chilled delirium,
Excite the membrane, when the sense has cooled,
With pungent sauces, multiply variety
In a wilderness of mirrors. What will the spider do,
Suspend its operations, will the weevil
Delay? De Bailhache, Fresca, Mrs. Cammel,[22] whirled
Beyond the circuit of the shuddering Bear[23]
In fractured atoms. Gull against the wind, in the windy straits
Of Belle Isle,[24] or running on the Horn,
White feathers in the snow, the Gulf claims,
And an old man driven by the Trades[25]
To a sleepy corner.

           Tenants of the house,
Thoughts of a dry brain in a dry season.[26]

                            1920

The title means "little old man" and comes from the Greek *geron*, "old man."

22. These invented names suggest the dispersion or disorientation of a culturally diverse array of individuals.

23. The Great Bear or Ursa Major; a northern constellation.

24. A northerly island between Labrador and Newfoundland. Horn: Tierra del Fuego, Chile, the southernmost point of South America. These two locations span the northern and southern tips of the American landmass, as a gull might in its migrations.

25. The trade winds (blowing constantly from the north or the south toward the equator).

26. Though the poem imaginatively spans the continents and tangentially explores the range of human emotion and history, its central consciousness remains fixed, a motionless and disregarded "little old man" whose knowledge and experience allow him to contemplate (and, it appears, renounce) the breadth of human experience even as he remains sheltered in "a sleepy corner."

The Waste Land

"Nam Sibyllam quidem Cumis ego ipse oculis
meis vidi in ampulla pendere, et cum illi pueri dicerent:
Σίβυλλα τί θέλεις; respondebat illa: ἀποθανεῖν θέλω."[1]

For Ezra Pound
il miglior fabbro.[2]

I. The Burial of the Dead[3]

April is the cruelest month, breeding
Lilacs out of the dead land, mixing
Memory and desire, stirring
Dull roots with spring rain.
Winter kept us warm, covering
Earth in forgetful snow, feeding
A little life with dried tubers.
Summer surprised us, coming over the Starnbergersee[4]
With a shower of rain; we stopped in the colonnade,
And went on in sunlight, into the Hofgarten,
And drank coffee, and talked for an hour.
Bin gar keine Russin, stamm' aus Litauen, echt deutsch.[5]
And when we were children, staying at the archduke's,
My cousin's, he took me out on a sled,
And I was frightened. He said, Marie,
Marie, hold on tight. And down we went.
In the mountains, there you feel free.
I read, much of the night, and go south in the winter.

1. "For I saw with my own eyes the Sibyl hanging in a jar at Cumae, and when the acolytes said, 'Sibyl, what do you wish?' she replied, 'I wish to die'" (Latin and ancient Greek) (Petronius, *Satyricon*, chap. 48). Apollo had granted the Sibyl eternal life but not eternal youth, and she had shriveled into a body so small that it could be housed in a jar.

2. "The better craftsman" is Eliot's praise for Ezra Pound, who had worked intensively with Eliot to help him shape and compress the poem into its present form. Eliot alludes to a line in Dante's *Purgatorio* (XXVI, 117) that so describes the great Provençal poet Arnaut Daniel.

3. A reference to the Anglican burial service, but also to the theme of burial and rebirth that appears throughout the section.

4. A lake near Munich. Hofgarten: a city park in Munich. Here Eliot initiates the frequent and surprising shifts in location, speaker, language, and time that will emerge as key characteristics of the poem. The next ten lines appear to echo autobiographical reminiscences of Countess Marie Larisch, a friend and confidante of the Empress Elizabeth of Austria in the years before World War I. The aristocratic world they allude to was unsettled and partially destroyed by the defeat of Austria in the Great War.

5. "I am not a Russian woman at all. I'm from Lithuania, a true German" (German)—apparently a snatch of overheard conversation. Here, as elsewhere throughout the poem, Eliot underlines the ambiguous and shifting nature of national identity. Lithuania, one of the Baltic states, has its own language, Lithuanian, and was made a separate country by the Treaty of Versailles in 1919. It was often claimed by both Germany and Russia.

*　　*　　*

What are the roots that clutch, what branches grow
Out of this stony rubbish? Son of man,[6]
You cannot say, or guess, for you know only
A heap of broken images, where the sun beats,[7]
And the dead tree gives no shelter, the cricket no relief,[8]
And the dry stone no sound of water. Only
There is shadow under this red rock,
(Come in under the shadow of this red rock),
And I will show you something different from either
Your shadow at morning striding behind you
Or your shadow at evening rising to meet you;[9]
I will show you fear in a handful of dust.
　　Frisch weht der Wind
　　Der Heimat zu
　　Mein Irisch Kind
　　Wo weilest du?[10]
"You gave me hyacinths first a year ago;
"They called me the hyacinth girl."
—Yet when we came back, late, from the hyacinth garden,
Your arms full, and your hair wet, I could not
Speak, and my eyes failed, I was neither
Living nor dead, and I knew nothing,
Looking into the heart of light, the silence.
Oed' und leer das Meer.[11]

*　　*　　*

6. "Cf. Ezekiel 2:1" (Eliot's note): "Son of Man, stand upon thy feet, and I will speak of thee," God says to Ezekiel.

7. Here, as elsewhere in the poem, the dry terrain appears to connote the spiritual dryness of the land and its "heap of broken images" a spiritual fragmentation, whereas water—unobtainable here but present elsewhere—persistently suggests the possibility of fertility and spiritual rebirth.

8. "Cf. Ecclesiastes 12:5" (Eliot's note). The prophetic speaker in Ecclesiastes evokes evil days "when they shall be afraid of that which is high, and fears shall be in the way, and the almond tree shall flourish, and the grasshopper shall be a burden, and desire shall fail."

9. For this and the preceding four lines, Eliot draws on a fragment from an earlier unpublished poem, "The Death of St. Narcissus" (1915), one of several previously composed fragments that found a place in the poem's mosaic.

10. "Fresh blows the wind / To the homeland / My Irish girl / Where are you lingering?" (German). A passage in act 1 of Richard Wagner's opera *Tristan and Isolde* (1865) in which a sailor on board the ship bringing Isolde to her unloved betrothed, King Mark of Cornwall, muses on the Irish sweetheart he left behind.

11. "Empty and desolate the sea" (German); *Tristan and Isolde*, act 3. Tristan, whose task it had been to deliver Isolde to King Mark, has been caught in adultery with her and now lies wounded. He awaits her arrival by ship with healing medications, but a shepherd, posted as lookout, sings sadly that "the sea remains empty and desolate."

Madame Sosostris, famous clairvoyante,[12]
Had a bad cold, nevertheless
Is known to be the wisest woman in Europe,
With a wicked pack of cards.[13] Here, said she,
Is your card, the drowned Phoenician Sailor,
(Those are pearls that were his eyes. Look!)[14]
Here is Belladonna,[15] the Lady of the Rocks,
The lady of situations.
Here is the man with three staves, and here the Wheel,[16]
And here is the one-eyed merchant, and this card,
Which is blank, is something he carries on his back,
Which I am forbidden to see. I do not find
The Hanged Man.[17] Fear death by water.
I see crowds of people, walking round in a ring.
Thank you. If you see dear Mrs. Equitone,
Tell her I bring the horoscope myself:
One must be so careful these days.

Unreal City,[18]
Under the brown fog of a winter dawn,
A crowd flowed over London Bridge, so many,

12. A fortune-teller who adapts the name of the Egyptian pharaoh Sesostris. Eliot borrowed the name from a comic scene in Aldus Huxley's recent novel, *Chrome Yellow* (1921).

13. The Tarot deck, which—as Jessie Weston indicates in *Ritual to Romance*—contains many cards reminiscent of figures from ancient fertility myths. Eliot's note comments on the general significance for the poem of figures in this scene: "I am not familiar with the exact constitution of the Tarot pack of cards, from which I have obviously departed to suit my own convenience. The Hanged Man, a member of the traditional pack, fits my purpose in two ways: because he is associated in my mind with the Hanged God of Frazer, and because I associate him with the hooded figure [Christ] in the passage of the disciples to Emmaus in Part V. The Phoenician Sailor and the Merchant appear later; also the 'crowds of people,' and Death by Water is executed in Part IV. The Man with Three Staves (an authentic member of the Tarot pack) I associate, quite arbitrarily, with the Fisher King himself."

14. See Shakespeare's *The Tempest*, in which the young prince Ferdinand thinks his father has been drowned. The spirit Ariel comforts him with a song about his father's metamorphosis into something beautiful and lasting: "Full fathom five thy father lies, / Of his bones are coral made, / Those are pearls that were his eyes. / Nothing of him that doth fade, / But doth suffer a sea change, / Into something rich and strange" (1.2). However, Ferdinand will later learn that his father's life has been preserved.

15. "Lovely lady" (Italian), but also a deadly poison. "The Lady of the Rocks" alludes to Leonardo's *Madonna of the Rocks*, a famous portrayal of the Virgin Mary. No such card exists in the Tarot pack.

16. The Wheel (possibly suggesting the Wheel of Fortune) is an actual Tarot card, as is the man with three staves. The one-eyed merchant is Eliot's invention.

17. Since the Hanged Man is associated with Christ, perhaps his absence indicates that the figure whose sacrifice will bring salvation has not yet reappeared on the modern scene.

18. (Eliot's note): "Cf. Baudelaire: 'Fourmillante cité, cité pleine de rêves, / Où le spectre en plein jour raccroche le passant'" (French); that is, "Swarming city, city full of dreams, / Where the spectre in broad daylight confronts the passerby." From Baudelaire's "Les Sept Vieillards" ("The Seven Old Men").

I had not thought death had undone so many.[19]
Sighs, short and infrequent, were exhaled,[20]
And each man fixed his eyes before his feet.
Flowed up the hill and down King William Street,
To where Saint Mary Woolnoth[21] kept the hours
With a dead sound on the final stroke of nine.
There I saw one I knew, and stopped him, crying: "Stetson!
"You who were with me in the ships at Mylae![22]
"That corpse you planted last year in your garden,
"Has it begun to sprout? Will it bloom this year?[23]
"Or has the sudden frost disturbed its bed?
"Oh keep the Dog far hence, that's friend to men,[24]
"Or with his nails he'll dig it up again!
"You! Hypocrite lecteur!—mon semblable—mon frère!"[25]

II. A Game of Chess[1]

The Chair she sat in, like a burnished throne,[2]
Glowed on the marble, where the glass
Held up by standards wrought with fruited vines
From which a golden Cupidon peeped out
(Another hid his eyes behind his wing)
Doubled the flames of seven branched candelabra

---

19. "Cf. *Inferno* III, 55–57" (Eliot's note). Alludes to Dante's description of the souls in Limbo—virtuous heathen who lived before Christ and thus cannot enter Paradise in the *Divine Comedy*.
20. "Cf. *Inferno* IV, 25–27" (Eliot's note). Alludes to the "sighs, / which caused the eternal air to tremble," which are uttered by the souls in Limbo, as reported by Dante.
21. A London church on the corner of Lombard and King William Streets in the City (the London financial district). Eliot passed it on his commute to work and noted that "the dead sound on the final stroke of nine" of its tolling bell was "a phenomenon I have often noticed."
22. A battle in the first Punic War between Carthage and Rome. Eliot's radical shift in the time frame violently thrusts us back into the age of ancient vegetation ritual, where the old king must die and be buried to encourage the renewal of the land.
23. This planted corpse is both a startling image of violent death and an ambiguous link to vegetation myths of regained fertility or spiritual rebirth.

24. "Cf. the Dirge in Webster's *White Devil*" (Eliot's note): "But keep the wolf far thence, that's foe to man / Or with his nails he'll dig them up again."
25. "Hypocrite reader!—my likeness—my brother" (French). "V. Baudelaire, Preface to *Fleurs du Mal*" (Eliot's note). This last line of Baudelaire's "Au Lecteur" ("To the Reader"), which characterizes boredom as man's worst sin and accuses the "hypocrite reader" of sharing that sin with the author.
1. The title of this section derives from a satirical play of the same name by the Jacobean playwright Thomas Middleton (1570–1627). Middleton's biting satire depicts England's political rivalry with Spain as a chess match.
2. Eliot's note cites Shakespeare's *Antony and Cleopatra* (2.2.190), in which Enobarbus describes how Cleopatra presented herself to Antony on their first meeting: "The barge she sat in, like a burnished throne, / Burned on the water: the poop was beaten gold."

Reflecting light upon the table as
The glitter of her jewels rose to meet it,
From satin cases poured in rich profusion;
In vials of ivory and coloured glass
Unstoppered, lurked her strange synthetic perfumes,
Unguent, powdered, or liquid—troubled, confused
And drowned the sense in odours; stirred by the air
That freshened from the window, these ascended
In fattening the prolonged candle-flames,
Flung their smoke into the laquearia,[3]
Stirring the pattern on the coffered ceiling.
Huge sea-wood fed with copper
Burned green and orange, framed by the coloured stone,
In which sad light a carvèd dolphin swam.
Above the antique mantel was displayed
As though a window gave upon the sylvan[4] scene
The change of Philomel, by the barbarous king
So rudely forced;[5] yet there the nightingale
Filled all the desert with inviolable voice
And still she cried, and still the world pursues,
'Jug Jug' to dirty ears.[6]
And other withered stumps of time
Were told upon the walls; staring forms
Leaned out, leaning, hushing the room enclosed.
Footsteps shuffled on the stair.
Under the firelight, under the brush, her hair
Spread out in fiery points
Glowed into words, then would be savagely still.

    "My nerves are bad to-night. Yes, bad. Stay with me.
"Speak to me. Why do you never speak. Speak.
    "What are you thinking of? What thinking? What?
"I never know what you are thinking. Think."

---

3. A paneled ceiling. Eliot's note refers to the banquet that Dido, the queen of Carthage, held for her lover Aeneas, in Virgil's *Aeneid* (I, 726): "Burning lamps hang from the gold-paneled ceiling, / and torches dispel the night with their flames."
4. Forested. Eliot's note cites Milton, *Paradise Lost* (IV, 140), in which Satan confronts Eden for the first time.
5. "V. Ovid, *Metamorphoses*, VI, Philomela" (Eliot's note). There Ovid retells the Greek myth of Philomela, who was raped by her sister Procne's husband, King Tereus. Tereus cut out Philomela's tongue to enforce her silence, but she stitched a depiction of the crime into a piece of needlework and sent it to her sister. Procne sought revenge on her husband by killing their son Itys and serving Tereus the son's flesh. When he attempted to revenge himself on the sisters, the gods changed Philomela into a nightingale and Procne into a swallow.
6. A common representation in Elizabethan literature of the nightingale's song.

*   *   *

I think we are in rats' alley
Where the dead men lost their bones.

"What is that noise?"
                     The wind under the door.[7]
"What is that noise now? What is the wind doing?"
                     Nothing again nothing.
                             "Do
"You know nothing? Do you see nothing? Do you remember
"Nothing?"

   I remember
Those are pearls that were his eyes.[8]
"Are you alive, or not? Is there nothing in your head?"
                             But

O O O O that Shakespeherian Rag[9]—
It's so elegant
So intelligent
"What shall I do now? What shall I do?"
"I shall rush out as I am, and walk the street
"With my hair down, so. What shall we do tomorrow?
"What shall we ever do?"
                     The hot water at ten.
And if it rains, a closed car at four.
And we shall play a game of chess,[10]
Pressing lidless eyes and waiting for a knock upon the door.

   When Lil's husband got demobbed,[11] I said—
I didn't mince my words, I said to her myself,
HURRY UP PLEASE ITS TIME[12]
Now Albert's coming back, make yourself a bit smart.
He'll want to know what you done with that money he gave you

7. "Cf. Webster: 'Is the wind in that door still?'" (Eliot's note). A doctor makes this statement in Webster's *The Devil's Law Case* when he discovers that the victim of a murderous attack is still breathing.

8. "Cf. Part I, l. 37, 48" (Eliot's note).

9. A popular American song that was a hit in the Ziegfeld Follies of 1912. Eliot's words reflect the syncopated ragtime rhythm. The following two lines also appear in the song.

10. "Cf. the game of chess in Middleton's *Women beware Women*" (Eliot's note). In Middleton's play, a young married woman is seduced in one room while her mother-in-law is distracted by a game of chess in another. The chess moves strangely reflect the events in the seduction next door.

11. Demobilized—that is, discharged from the army following World War I. The passage was suggested by gossip from the Eliots' maid, Ellen Kellond.

12. The barkeeper in the pub announces that patrons should quickly finish their drinks because it is closing time.

To get yourself some teeth. He did, I was there.
You have them all out, Lil, and get a nice set,
He said, I swear, I can't bear to look at you.
And no more can't I, I said, and think of poor Albert,
He's been in the army four years, he wants a good time,
And if you don't give it him, there's others will, I said.
Oh is there, she said. Something o' that, I said.
Then I'll know who to thank, she said, and give me a straight look.
HURRY UP PLEASE ITS TIME
If you don't like it you can get on with it, I said.
Others can pick and choose if you can't.
But if Albert makes off, it won't be for lack of telling.
You ought to be ashamed, I said, to look so antique.
(And her only thirty-one.)
I can't help it, she said, pulling a long face,
It's them pills I took, to bring it off, she said.
(She's had five already, and nearly died of young George.)
The chemist[13] said it would be all right, but I've never been the same.
You are a proper fool, I said.
Well, if Albert won't leave you alone, there it is, I said,
What you get married for if you don't want children?
HURRY UP PLEASE ITS TIME
Well, that Sunday Albert was home, they had a hot gammon,
And they asked me in to dinner, to get the beauty of it hot—
HURRY UP PLEASE ITS TIME
HURRY UP PLEASE ITS TIME
Goonight Bill. Goonight Lou. Goonight May. Goonight.
Ta ta. Goonight. Goonight.
Good night, ladies, good night, sweet ladies, good night, good night.[14]

III. The Fire Sermon[1]

The river's tent is broken; the last fingers of leaf
Clutch and sink into the wet bank. The wind
Crosses the brown land, unheard. The nymphs are departed.

---

13. Pharmacist.
14. Mad Ophelia's parting words in *Hamlet* (4.5.71–72) to King Claudius and Queen Gertrude just before drowning herself.
1. Buddha's "Fire Sermon" admonishes his followers to renounce the flames of lust and physical sensation in order to attain a higher level of understanding. "Buddha's Fire Sermon . . . corresponds in importance to the Sermon on the Mount" (Eliot's note). The entire section depicts various aspects of sexual disturbance in both the ancient and the modern worlds.

Sweet Thames, run softly, till I end my song.[2]

The river bears no empty bottles, sandwich papers,

Silk handkerchiefs, cardboard boxes, cigarette ends

Or other testimony of summer nights. The nymphs are departed.

And their friends, the loitering heirs of City directors;[3]

Departed, have left no addresses.

By the waters of Leman I sat down and wept . . .[4]

Sweet Thames, run softly till I end my song,

Sweet Thames, run softly, for I speak not loud or long.

But at my back in a cold blast I hear[5]

The rattle of the bones, and chuckle spread from ear to ear.

A rat crept softly through the vegetation

Dragging its slimy belly on the bank

While I was fishing in the dull canal

On a winter evening round behind the gashouse

Musing upon the king my brother's wreck

And on the king my father's death before him.[6]

White bodies naked on the low damp ground

And bones cast in a little low dry garret,

Rattled by the rat's foot only, year to year.

But at my back from time to time I hear

The sound of horns and motors, which shall bring

Sweeney to Mrs. Porter in the spring.[7]

O the moon shone bright on Mrs. Porter

2. "V. Spenser, Prothalamion" (Eliot's note). This line serves as the refrain for a marriage song (prothalamion) by the Elizabethan poet Edmund Spenser. The nymphs appear in Spenser's poem as "the lovely Daughters of the Flood."

3. The "City directors" are leading figures of London's financial district. Their "loitering heirs" have engaged in apparently fleeting sexual dalliance with the river's "nymphs."

4. Psalm 137 begins, "By the rivers of Babylon, there we sat down, yea, we wept, when we remembered Zion." Eliot adapts this by substituting Leman, the French name for Lake Geneva, which he visited on a rest-cure in 1921 and where he worked on The Waste Land.

5. An echo of Andrew Marvell's seventeenth-century poem "To His Coy Mistress": "But at my back I always hear / Time's wingèd chariot hurrying near."

6. "Cf. The Tempest, I, ii" (Eliot's note). As he hears Ariel's song, Ferdinand describes himself as "Sitting on a bank, / Weeping again the King my father's wrack, / This music crept by me upon the waters, / Allaying both their fury and my passion / With its sweet air."

7. "Cf. Day, Parliament of Bees: "When of the sudden, listening, you shall hear, / A noise of horns and hunting, which shall bring / Actaeon to Diana in the spring, / Where all shall see her naked skin" (Eliot's note). In ancient Greek myth, Actaeon viewed the virginal goddess of the hunt, Diana, while she was bathing and in punishment was torn to death by his own hounds. Sweeney is a loutish male figure in several of Eliot's poems and in the fragmentary play Sweeney Agonistes; here Eliot apparently casts him in Actaeon's role. The subsequent lines, according to Eliot's note, echo a popular ballad, though, he admits, "I do not know the origin of the ballad from which these lines are taken: it was reported to me from Sydney, Australia."

And on her daughter
They wash their feet in soda water
Et O ces voix d'enfants, chantant dans la coupole![8]

Twit twit twit
Jug jug jug jug jug jug
So rudely forc'd.
Tereu[9]

Unreal City
Under the brown fog of a winter noon
Mr. Eugenides, the Smyrna[10] merchant
Unshaven, with a pocket full of currants
C.i.f. London: documents at sight,[11]
Asked me in demotic[12] French
To luncheon at the Cannon Street Hotel[13]
Followed by a weekend at the Metropole.[14]

At the violet hour, when the eyes and back
Turn upward from the desk, when the human engine waits
Like a taxi throbbing waiting,
I Tiresias, though blind, throbbing between two lives,[15]
Old man with wrinkled female breasts, can see

8. "V. Verlaine, *Parsifal*" (Eliot's note). "And O those children's voices singing in the dome!" Verlaine's sonnet, of which this is the final line, paraphrases Wagner's final opera, *Parsifal*, in which Parsifal resists the sexual wiles of Kundry, seizes the spear that had wounded King Amfortas, and with it heals the king and his barren land. The opera closes with the dome of the Grail Castle filling with transcendent music, including the soaring voices of a children's chorus, as Parsifal uncovers the Grail and holds it aloft. In Eliot's poem this sacred moment of recovery seems far away in the face of the doings of Sweeney, Mrs. Porter, and the other denizens of this middle section.
9. Tereu is the vocative form of Tereus, the "barbarous king" whose rape of Philomela is pictured above. Eliot echoes a poem attributed to John Lyly, "Alexander and Compaspe," in which Philomela, now a nightingale, accuses Tereus in her song "Jug, jug, jug, jug, tereu!"
10. The formerly Greek city of Smyrna, in Anatolia, is now the Turkish city of Izmir. After World War I, it was the focus of a much-publicized war between Greece and Turkey before ultimately falling to the Turks.

11. Eliot's note indicates that these are modern business terms. For example, "C.i.f. London" means "carriage and insurance free to London."
12. Colloquial speech, more commonly referring to the colloquial form of modern Greek.
13. A hotel in the City (financial district) not far from where Eliot worked at Lloyds Bank. It was used by business travelers and, reportedly, for homosexual liaisons, though Eliot denied that he had intended this implication.
14. A luxurious seaside hotel in Brighton.
15. "Tiresias, although a mere spectator and not indeed a 'character,' is yet the most important personage in the poem, uniting all the rest. Just as the one-eyed merchant, seller of currants, melts into the Phoenician Sailor, and the latter is not wholly distinct from Ferdinand Prince of Naples, so all the women are one woman, and the two sexes meet in Tiresias. What Tiresias sees, in fact, is the substance of the poem. The whole passage from Ovid is of great anthropological interest." The passage from Ovid's *Metamorphosis* that Eliot cites (3. 316–39) tells how Tiresias, with his staff, struck two huge snakes that were copulating and was thereupon suddenly transformed into a woman. Eight years later he saw the same snakes

At the violet hour, the evening hour that strives
Homeward, and brings the sailor home from sea,[16]
The typist home at teatime, clears her breakfast, lights
Her stove, and lays out food in tins.
Out of the window perilously spread
Her drying combinations[17] touched by the sun's last rays,
On the divan are piled (at night her bed)
Stockings, slippers, camisoles, and stays.[18]
I Tiresias, old man with wrinkled dugs
Perceived the scene, and foretold the rest—
I too awaited the expected guest.
He, the young man carbuncular,[19] arrives,
A small house agent's clerk, with one bold stare,
One of the low on whom assurance sits
As a silk hat on a Bradford millionaire.[20]
The time is now propitious, as he guesses,
The meal is ended, she is bored and tired,
Endeavours to engage her in caresses
Which still are unreproved, if undesired.
Flushed and decided, he assaults at once;
Exploring hands encounter no defence;
His vanity requires no response,
And makes a welcome of indifference.
(And I Tiresias have foresuffered all
Enacted on this same divan or bed;
I who have sat by Thebes below the wall
And walked among the lowest of the dead.)[21]
Bestows one final patronising kiss,
And gropes his way, finding the stairs unlit . . .

*　*　*

---

coupling, and when he struck them once again, he turned back into a man. Later Jupiter and Juno, the king and queen of the gods, asked Tiresias to settle a dispute over which sex derived more pleasure from intercourse. Tiresias enraged Juno by declaring that women did. Juno struck him blind, and Jupiter softened this punishment by giving Tiresias the power of prophecy.

16. Eliot's note refers to the ancient Greek poet Sappho's prayer to the evening star. The line further echoes Robert Louis Stevenson's "Requiem": "Home is the sailor, home from the sea."

17. One-piece undergarments, which here hang out the window to dry.

18. Corsets.

19. Carbuncle: an inflamed boil or pimple.

20. Bradford: a manufacturing town in northern England. A Bradford millionaire might derive his money from war profiteering. He would surely be nouveau riche.

21. References to Tiresias's role in other Greek myths; as retold in Sophocles' plays *Oedipus Rex* and *Antigone*, Tiresias, sitting by the wall in the Theban marketplace, prophesied the fall of two kings, and in Homer's *Odyssey*, he met and counseled Odysseus in the underworld.

She turns and looks a moment in the glass,
Hardly aware of her departed lover;
Her brain allows one half-formed thought to pass:
"Well now that's done: and I'm glad it's over."
When lovely woman stoops to folly and
Paces about her room again, alone,
She smoothes her hair with automatic hand,
And puts a record on the gramophone.[22]

"This music crept by me upon the waters"[23]
And along the Strand, up Queen Victoria Street.
O City city, I can sometimes hear
Beside a public bar in Lower Thames Street,
The pleasant whining of a mandoline
And a clatter and a chatter from within
Where fishmen lounge at noon: where the walls
Of Magnus Martyr[24] hold
Inexplicable splendour of Ionian white and gold.

The river sweats[25]
Oil and tar
The barges drift
With the turning tide
Red sails
Wide
To leeward, swing on the heavy spar.
The barges wash
Drifting logs
Down Greenwich reach[26]

---

22. "V. Goldsmith, the song in *The Vicar of Wakefield*" (Eliot's note). In Goldsmith's novel the deceived and seduced Olivia sings, "When lovely woman stoops to folly / And finds too late that men betray, / What charm can soothe her melancholy, / What art can wash her guilt away? // The only art her guilt to cover, / To hide her shame from every eye, / To give repentance to her lover / And wring his bosom — is to die."
23. "V. The Tempest, as above" (Eliot's note), another reference to Prince Ferdinand's being comforted by Ariel's song. See p. 411, note 6.
24. "The interior of St. Magnus Martyr is to my mind one of the finest among [Sir Christopher] Wren's interiors" (Eliot's note). The streets Eliot names above parallel the Thames. In the Church of St. Magnus Martyr (1676), in Lower Thames Street, the columns along the nave are Ionic.

25. "The Song of the (three) Thames-daughters begins here. From line 292 to 306 inclusive they speak in turn. V. [Wagner's] *Gotterdammerung*, III, i: the Rhine-daughters" (Eliot's note). In Wagner's *Twilight of the Gods*, the Rhine-maidens greet the hero Siegfried and teasingly attempt to lure him into giving them his magic ring, which was made of the Rhine's gold. Before Siegfried was born, this gold was stolen from the maidens to make the ring. Its recovery would restore the Rhine to its former beauty.
26. A sharp bend in the Thames River at Greenwich, south of London. The Isle of Dogs is the peninsula on the opposite bank. Queen Elizabeth I was born at Greenwich House to Anne Boleyn, and much later she entertained the Earl of Leicester there.

Past the Isle of Dogs.
   Weialala leia
   Wallala leialala[27]

Elizabeth and Leicester[28]
Beating oars
The stern was formed
A gilded shell
Red and gold
The brisk swell
Rippled both shores
Southwest wind
Carried down stream
The peal of bells
White towers
    Weialala leia
    Wallala leialala

"Trams and dusty trees.
Highbury bore me. Richmond and Kew
Undid me.[29] By Richmond I raised my knees
Supine on the floor of a narrow canoe."

"My feet are at Moorgate,[30] and my heart
Under my feet. After the event
He wept. He promised 'a new start.'
I made no comment. What should I resent?"

"On Margate Sands[31]
I can connect
Nothing with nothing.

27. The song of the Rhinemaidens in *Gotterdam-merung*.

28. "V. Froude, Elizabeth, vol. I, ch. iv, letter of De Quadra to Philip of Spain: 'In the afternoon we were in a barge, watching the games on the river. (The queen) was alone with Lord Robert [Earl of Leicester] and myself on the poop, when they began to talk nonsense, and went so far that Lord Robert at last said, as I was on the spot there was no reason why they should not be married if the queen pleased' " (Eliot's note).

29. "Cf. *Purgatorio*, V, 133" (Eliot's note). In Purgatory, Dante encounters the spirit of Pia de Tolomei of Siena, who declares that "Siena made me. Maremma unmade me," a reference to her mur-

der at her husband's hands because he wished to marry another woman. Here the speaker is apparently a woman born in Highbury, a London suburb, and seduced (and thus "undone") in Richmond and Kew, two riverside districts west of London. Characteristically, Eliot merges the recollection of an ancient crime with the confession of a modern indiscretion—an action whose moral status remains uncomfortably ambiguous.

30. A neighborhood in east London.

31. Eliot spent three weeks of his rest leave from Lloyds Bank at Margate, a seaside resort near the mouth of the Thames. Manuscript evidence suggests that he was composing "The Fire Sermon" while residing there.

The broken fingernails of dirty hands.
My people humble people who expect
Nothing."
             la la

    To Carthage then I came[32]

    Burning burning burning burning[33]
    O Lord Thou pluckest me out[34]
    O Lord Thou pluckest

    burning

IV. Death by Water[1]

Phlebas the Phoenician, a fortnight dead,
Forgot the cry of gulls, and the deep sea swell
And the profit and loss.
                    A current under sea
Picked his bones in whispers. As he rose and fell
He passes the stages of his age and youth
Entering the whirlpool.
                    Gentile or Jew
O you who turn the wheel and look to windward,
Consider Phlebas, who was once handsome and tall as you.

---

32. "V. St. Augustine's *Confessions*: 'to Carthage then I came, where a cauldron of unholy loves sang all about mine ears'" (Eliot's note). Augustine is confessing the lustful temptations he encountered in youth, before his religious conversion.

33. Eliot's note cites Buddha's "Fire Sermon," of which this line is an extreme condensation.

34. "From St. Augustine's *Confessions* again. The collocation of these two representatives of eastern and western asceticism, as the culmination of this part of the poem, is not an accident" (Eliot's note).

1. When Ezra Pound worked with Eliot on compressing and focusing *The Waste Land*, he insisted that this section be retained. Pound observed that "Death by Water" serves a pivotal function in the structure of the poem, linking "the drowned Phoenician Sailor" from Madame Sosostris's Tarot pack (significantly identified as "your card") with the Tarot's "one-eyed merchant" and later with the Smyrna merchant. It also ties together the poem's many references to sailors and the sea. The thematic significance of Phlebas's death remains ambiguous: Is his death by drowning hinting at potential rebirth, given water's central importance in the poem as a source of new life? Will he "suffer a sea change," like the figure in Ariel's song from *The Tempest*, "into something rich and strange"? Or has he merely pursued commercial ends and met the appropriate oblivion, his bones lost like the dead men in "rat's alley"? The poem itself is Eliot's translation of the final stanzas of "Dans le Restaurant," composed in 1918.

V. What the Thunder Said[1]

After the torchlight red on sweaty faces
After the frosty silence in the gardens
After the agony in stony places
The shouting and the crying
Prison and palace and reverberation
Of thunder of spring over distant mountains
He who was living is now dead[2]
We who were living are now dying
With a little patience

   Here is no water but only rock
Rock and no water and the sandy road
The road winding above among the mountains
Which are mountains of rock without water
If there were water we should stop and drink
Amongst the rock one cannot stop or think
Sweat is dry and feet are in the sand
If there were only water amongst the rock
Dead mountain mouth of carious[3] teeth that cannot spit
Here one can neither stand nor lie nor sit
There is not even silence in the mountains
But dry sterile thunder without rain
There is not even solitude in the mountains
But red sullen faces sneer and snarl
From doors of mudcracked houses
                             If there were water

   And no rock
   If there were rock
   And also water
   And water
   A spring
   A pool among the rock
   If there were the sound of water only

1. "In the first part of Part V three themes are employed: the journey [of Christ] to Emmaus, the approach to the Chapel Perilous (see Miss Weston's book), and the present decay of eastern Europe" (Eliot's note). The imagistic movement in this section is from intense physical and spiritual dryness to the recovering wetness of rain.

2. The opening lines allude to Christ's agony in the Garden of Gethsemane, his nighttime capture and imprisonment, his trial, his interrogation, his death on the cross, and the earthquake that followed his death.

3. Decayed, rotting; "caries" is the formal word for tooth decay.

Not the cicada[4]
And dry grass singing
But sound of water over a rock
Where the hermit-thrush sings in the pine trees
Drip drop drip drop drop drop drop[5]
But there is no water

Who is the third who walks always beside you?[6]
When I count, there are only you and I together
But when I look ahead up the white road
There is always another one walking beside you
Gliding wrapt in a brown mantle, hooded
I do not know whether a man or a woman
—But who is that on the other side of you?

What is that sound high in the air[7]
Murmur of maternal lamentation
Who are those hooded hordes swarming
Over endless plains, stumbling in cracked earth
Ringed by the flat horizon only
What is the city over the mountains
Cracks and reforms and bursts in the violet air
Falling towers
Jerusalem Athens Alexandria
Vienna London[8]
Unreal

4. The cicada links to the passage from Ecclesiastes 12:5 that Eliot cites earlier (see section I, n. 8) "when they shall be afraid of that which is high, and fears shall be in the way, . . . and the grasshopper shall be a burden, and desire shall fail."

5. "This is Turdus aonalaschkae pallasii, the hermit-thrush which I have heard in Quebec County. Chapman says (*Handbook of Birds of Eastern North America*) 'it is most at home in secluded woodland and thickety retreats. . . . Its notes are not remarkable for variety or volume, but in purity and sweetness of tone and exquisite modulation they are unequalled.' Its 'water-dripping song' is justly celebrated" (Eliot's note).

6. "The following lines were stimulated by the account of one of the Antarctic expeditions (I forget which, but I think one of Shackleton's): it was related that the party of explorers, at the extremity of their strength, had the constant delusion that *there was one more member* than could actually be counted" (Eliot's note). Eliot also alludes, as his first note in the section indicates, to Luke 24:13–16, in which two disciples, on their way to Emmaus, discuss Christ's death and resurrection. Jesus himself appears and talks to them, "but their eyes were holden, that they should not know him," though he admonishes them for their lack of faith in the reality of the resurrection. Only later, as they dine together at Emmaus, does Christ reveal himself, after which he "vanished out of their sight."

7. "Cf. Hermann Hesse, *Blick ins Chaos* [A Glimpse into Chaos]" (Eliot's note): "Already half of Europe, and at least half of Eastern Europe, is on the way to Chaos, travels drunk in sacred madness along the brink of the abyss and moreover sings drunken hymns as Dmitri Karamazov sang. The bourgeois, shocked, laughs at these songs: the saint and seer hear them with tears." Hesse is referring to the chaotic conditions in eastern Europe after World War I.

8. Each of these cities was a major world capital and cultural center. With the exception of London, Eliot's current place of residence, each had

*　*　*

A woman drew her long black hair out tight
And fiddled whisper music on those strings
And bats with baby faces in the violet light
Whistled, and beat their wings
And crawled head downward down a blackened wall
And upside down in air were towers
Tolling reminiscent bells, that kept the hours
And voices singing out of empty cisterns and exhausted wells.

In this decayed hole among the mountains
In the faint moonlight, the grass is singing
Over the tumbled graves, about the chapel
There is the empty chapel, only the wind's home.[9]
It has no windows, and the door swings,
Dry bones can harm no one.
Only a cock stood on the rooftree
Co co rico co co rico
In a flash of lightning. Then a damp gust
Bringing rain

Ganga[10] was sunken, and the limp leaves
Waited for rain, while the black clouds
Gathered far distant, over Himavant.[11]
The jungle crouched, humped in silence.
Then spoke the thunder
DA[12]
Datta: what have we given?
My friend, blood shaking my heart

---

suffered, in succession, a fall from dominance. Eliot seems to imply that London's fall may be imminent.

9. The Chapel Perilous, which the Grail hero (or heroine) must visit on the way to the Grail Castle. In the chapel, the questor confronts stark terror, but afterwards, his way to the Grail Castle is straight.

10. The Ganges, sacred river of India.

11. The Himalayan Mountains, sometimes personified as the father of the Ganges.

12. "'Datta, dayadhvam, damyata' (Give, sympathize, control). The fable of the meaning of the Thunder is found in the *Brihadaranyaka—Upanishad*, 5, I" (Eliot's note). Here Prajapati, the Creator God, presents to three groups of his offspring and disciples (gods, men, and demons) the ambiguous syllable DA, asking each group to interpret it. The gods, who are given to wildness, understand the word as "damyata" (control yourselves), and Prajapati agrees; men, who are naturally greedy, understand the word as "datta" (give), and Prajapati agrees; the demons, who are naturally cruel, understand the word as "dayadhvam" (be compassionate), and Prajapati agrees. According to the Upanishad, "That very thing is repeated [even today] by the heavenly voice, in the form of thunder, as 'Da,' 'Da,' 'Da,' which means 'Control yourselves,' 'Give,' and 'Have compassion.'" These principles are recognized as the three great disciplines of Hinduism, with all three now applying equally to human beings. Eliot links the moral teachings of the thunder with the rain that brings spiritual renewal and fertility.

The awful daring of a moment's surrender
Which an age of prudence can never retract
By this, and this only, we have existed
Which is not to be found in our obituaries
Or in memories draped by the beneficent spider[13]
Or under seals broken by the lean solicitor[14]
In our empty rooms
DA
Dayadhvam: I have heard the key
Turn in the door once and turn once only[15]
We think of the key, each in his prison
Thinking of the key, each confirms a prison
Only at nightfall, aethereal rumours
Revive for a moment a broken Coriolanus[16]
DA
Damyata: The boat responded
Gaily, to the hand expert with sail and oar
The sea was calm, your heart would have responded
Gaily, when invited, beating obedient
To controlling hands

I sat upon the shore[17]
Fishing, with the arid plain behind me
Shall I at least set my lands in order?[18]
London Bridge is falling down falling down falling down[19]

13. "Cf. Webster, *The White Devil*, V, vi: 'they'll remarry / Ere the worm pierce your winding-sheet, ere the spider / Make a thin curtain for your epitaphs'" (Eliot's note).
14. In the United Kingdom, a lawyer who gives legal advice and draws up legal documents but does not, as a barrister would, try cases in court.
15. "Cf. *Inferno*, XXXIII, 46" (Eliot's note), in which Dante encounters Count Ungolino. Accused of treason, the count is locked up in a "horrible tower," where he slowly starves to death. Eliot notes a further reference, to the philosopher who was the subject of his doctoral thesis: "Also F. H. Bradley, *Appearance and Reality*, p. 346. 'My external sensations are no less private to myself than are my thoughts or my feelings. In either case my experience falls within my own circle, a circle closed on the outside; and, with all its elements alike, every sphere is opaque to the others which surround it. . . . In brief, regarded as an existence which appears in a soul, the whole world

for each is peculiar and private to that soul.'" Note that even at the moment of apparent spiritual breakthrough (as indicated by the thunder's teachings) one still confronts one's personal isolation, self-doubt, and mortality.
16. Roman war hero who was the protagonist of a tragedy by Shakespeare. Exiled by the Roman people for his arrogance toward them, he then, goaded by wounded vanity, led a hostile army against Rome.
17. "V. Weston, *From Ritual to Romance*; chapter on the Fisher King" (Eliot's note).
18. So the prophet Isaiah challenged King Hezekiah: "Thus saith the Lord, Set thine house in order: for that shalt die, and not live" (Isaiah 38:1).
19. The nursery rhyme—its relevance intensified by the fact that most of the London events in the poem are set near London Bridge. Note also the "falling towers" above, which are linked to London and other cities.

Poi s'ascose nel foco che gli affina[20]
Quando fiam uti chelidon[21] — O swallow swallow[22]
Le Prince d'Aquitaine à la tour abolie[23]
These fragments I have shored against my ruins
Why then Ile fit you. Hieronymo's mad againe.[24]
Datta. Dayadhvam. Damyata.
     Shantih   shantih   shantih[25]

1922

Eliot published extensive footnotes to *The Waste Land*. He later explained, at different times, that these notes were intended to protect himself from earlier charges of plagiarism, or to make clear that certain echoes of earlier sources were intended, or even to lengthen the poem in book form. Eliot commented ironically in 1957 that "I have sometimes thought of getting rid of these notes but now they can never be unstuck. They have had almost greater popularity than the poem itself." A selection from Eliot's notes is woven into the annotations below. Eliot's initial note to *The Waste Land* observes: "Not only the title, but the plan and a good deal of the incidental symbolism of the poem were suggested by Miss Jessie L. Weston's book on the Grail legend: *From Ritual to Romance* (Cambridge). . . . To another work of anthropology I am indebted in general, one which has influenced our generation profoundly; I mean [Sir James George Fraser's] *The Golden Bough*; I have used especially the two volumes *Adonis, Attis, Osiris*. Anyone who is acquainted with these works will immediately recognize in the poem certain references to vegetation ceremonies."

Weston's book examines the history of the legends of the Holy Grail, wherein a medieval hero searches for the Grail (the vessel that held the blessed wine at Christ's Last Supper) as a means of recovering a land that has fallen into waste or famine through the illness or impotence of the king. The recovery of the Grail will restore the king to virility and health and the land to fertility, and it might also bring about a spiritual rebirth in the kingdom. Fraser's important early work of anthropology, *The Golden Bough*, focuses, in the volumes cited, on

20. "V. Purgatorio, XXVI, 148" (Eliot's note). Here the soul of the Provençal poet Arnaut Daniel speaks to Dante from a sheet of refining flame in his native tongue: "I pray you by that Goodness which doth deign / To guide you to the summit of this stair [out of Purgatory] / Bethink you in due season of my pain." Eliot quotes only the canto's final line, "Then he shrank back in the refining fire."

21. "V. Pervigilium Veneris. Cf. Philomela in Parts II and III" (Eliot's note). In the late Latin poem "The Vigil of Venus," Philomela asks, "When shall I be like the swallow," adding "that I may cease to be silent." See Eliot's previous use of this legend in sections II and III.

22. An echo of Swinburne's "Itylus," which begins "Swallow, my sister, O sister swallow, / How can thy heart be full of spring."

23. "V. Gerard de Nerval, Sonnet *El Desdichado*" (Eliot's note). "The prince of Aquitaine of the ruined tower" (French). This is the second line of Nerval's sonnet "The Dispossessed" (1854), in which the poet laments his outcast state.

24. "V. Kyd's Spanish Tragedy" (Eliot's note). In Kyd's play, often seen as a forerunner to Shakespeare's *Hamlet*, Hieronymo seeks to avenge his son's murder by feigning madness. He provides a play in which, acting one of the parts, he kills the murderers. "Why then Ile fit you!" (that is, I'll give you something that will suit you) is his answer to a request by the murderers to write the play. The play's subtitle is "Hieronymo Is Mad Again." As in *The Waste Land*, the characters in Hieronymo's play speak in different languages.

25. "Shantih. Repeated as here, a formal ending to an Upanishad. 'The Peace which passeth understanding' is our feeble equivalent to this word" (Eliot's note). After Eliot converted to the Church of England in 1927, he deleted the word "feeble" in subsequent editions.

ancient Greek and Middle Eastern rituals involving the sacrificial death of an old king in order to restore a barren land to fertility. Fraser suggests a connection between these rituals and the Christian sacrifice of Jesus on the Cross. Clearly, in Eliot's mind a further connection exists between these ancient myths of infertility, requiring recovery through quest or sacrifice, and the problems of a modern Waste Land, with its overtones of sexual disquiet and spiritual exhaustion and confusion, a land that also needs physical and spiritual recovery.

Eliot's other sources are extremely varied, drawing on the literatures and cultures of many languages and lands. Some of the most important include ancient Greek myth, the poetry of Ovid's *Metamorphosis*, Dante's *Divine Comedy*, Baudelaire's *Flowers of Evil*, Elizabethan and Jacobean drama (particularly the works of Shakespeare and John Webster), and the operas of Richard Wagner, as well as the New and Old Testaments, the Hindu Upanishads, the preachings of Buddha, and the *Confessions* of St. Augustine. Part of the method of the poem is to juxtapose perspectives from these many creators, thinkers, and cultures.

Perhaps the central setting of the poem is post–World War I London. Yet—employing a logic of association and juxtaposition—the setting shifts abruptly across many times and lands, and the poem is articulated through a diversity of voices, voices that are alternately female and male, ancient and modern, learned and uneducated, sacred and profane. Few poems have been so cosmopolitan in perspective or so wide-ranging in setting, voice, reference, and time frame. These annotations are indebted to the work of many predecessors but in particular to those in Michael North's Norton Critical Edition of *The Waste Land* (New York: Norton, 2001).

FROM Four Quartets

Little Gidding

I

Midwinter spring is its own season
Sempiternal[1] though sodden towards sundown,
Suspended in time, between pole and tropic.
When the short day is brightest, with frost and fire,
The brief sun flames the ice, on pond and ditches,
In windless cold that is the heart's heat,
Reflecting in a watery mirror
A glare that is blindness in the early afternoon.
And glow more intense than blaze of branch, or brazier,

1. Everlasting.

Stirs the dumb spirit: no wind, but pentecostal fire[2]
In the dark time of the year. Between melting and freezing
The soul's sap quivers. There is no earth smell
Or smell of living thing. This is the spring time
But not in time's covenant. Now the hedgerow
Is blanched for an hour with transitory blossom
Of snow, a bloom more sudden
Than that of summer, neither budding nor fading,
Not in the scheme of generation.
Where is the summer, the unimaginable
Zero summer?

       If you came this way,[3]
Taking the route you would be likely to take
From the place you would be likely to come from,
If you came this way in may time, you would find the hedges
White again, in May,[4] with voluptuary sweetness.
It would be the same at the end of the journey,
If you came at night like a broken king,[5]
If you came by day not knowing what you came for,
It would be the same, when you leave the rough road
And turn behind the pig-sty to the dull façade[6]
And the tombstone. And what you thought you came for
Is only a shell, a husk of meaning
From which the purpose breaks only when it is fulfilled
If at all. Either you had no purpose
Or the purpose is beyond the end you figured
And is altered in fulfilment. There are other places
Which also are the world's end, some at the sea jaws,
Or over a dark lake, in a desert or a city—
But this is the nearest, in place and time,
Now and in England.

      *   *   *

2. The fire of the Holy Spirit, which descended in the form of a dove on Christ's disciples, who assembled on the seventh Sunday after Easter. "And suddenly there came a sound from heaven as of a rushing mighty wind, and it filled all the house where they were sitting. And there appeared unto them cloven tongues like as of fire, and it sat upon each of them. And they were all filled with the Holy Ghost, and began to speak with other tongues, as the Spirit gave them utterance" (Acts 2:2–4).
3. That is, on the way to Little Gidding.
4. Eliot's only visit to Little Gidding was on May 25, 1936.
5. Charles I, who found shelter at Little Gidding on March 2, 1646, after his final defeat by Cromwell's Puritan army.
6. The front facing of the Little Gidding chapel.

If you came this way,
Taking any route, starting from anywhere,
At any time or at any season,
It would always be the same: you would have to put off
Sense and notion. You are not here to verify,
Instruct yourself, or inform curiosity
Or carry report. You are here to kneel
Where prayer has been valid. And prayer is more
Than an order of words, the conscious occupation
Of the praying mind, or the sound of the voice praying.
And what the dead had no speech for, when living,
They can tell you, being dead: the communication
Of the dead is tongued with fire beyond the language of the living.
Here, the intersection of the timeless moment
Is England and nowhere. Never and always.

II

Ash on an old man's sleeve[7]
Is all the ash the burnt roses leave.
Dust in the air suspended
Marks the place where a story ended.
Dust inbreathed was a house—
The walls, the wainscot and the mouse,
The death of hope and despair,
     This is the death of air.

     There are flood and drouth
Over the eyes and in the mouth,
Dead water and dead sand
Contending for the upper hand.
The parched eviscerate soil
Gapes at the vanity of toil,
Laughs without mirth.
     This is the death of earth.

     Water and fire succeed
The town, the pasture and the weed.

7. The second movement begins lyrically with a meditation on the death one may experience through each of the four traditional elements: air, earth, water, and fire. The opening stanza may evoke the dust that hovered in the London air and covered the living and the dead after a German bombing.

Water and fire deride
The sacrifice that we denied.
Water and fire shall rot
The marred foundations we forgot,
Of sanctuary and choir.[8]
    This is the death of water and fire.

In the uncertain hour before the morning[9]
    Near the ending of interminable night
    At the recurrent end of the unending
After the dark dove with the flickering tongue[10]
    Had passed below the horizon of his homing
    While the dead leaves[11] still rattled on like tin
Over the asphalt where no other sound was
    Between three districts whence the smoke arose
    I met one walking, loitering and hurried
As if blown towards me like the metal leaves
    Before the urban dawn wind unresisting.
    And as I fixed upon the down-turned face
That pointed scrutiny with which we challenge
    The first-met stranger in the waning dusk
    I caught the sudden look of some dead master
Whom I had known, forgotten, half recalled
    Both one and many; in the brown baked features
    The eyes of a familiar compound ghost[12]
Both intimate and unidentifiable.
    So I assumed a double part,[13] and cried
    And heard another's voice cry: 'What! are *you* here?'
Although we were not. I was still the same,
    Knowing myself yet being someone other—
    And he a face still forming; yet the words sufficed
To compel the recognition they preceded.

---

8. The poem appears to modulate back to the chapel at Little Gidding, which barely survived the ruins of time before its modern restoration.

9. The balance of the section, constructed in unrhymed tercets, evokes the stanzaic pattern of Dante's *Divine Comedy*, though it does not imitate it exactly. Eliot served as an air-raid warden during the German raids on London and in this scene creates a Dante-esque confrontation between the speaker and a poetic elder in the surreal Inferno-like world created by a recent bombing.

10. A German bomber with flashing machine guns, though referring to it as a "dove" also evokes, paradoxically, the Holy Spirit with its tongues of flame.

11. Probably shrapnel from the bombing.

12. In a letter to a friend, Eliot suggested that one might recognize aspects of Yeats, Mallarmé, Swift, and Poe in this figure.

13. Perhaps as both speaker and listener in this dialogue—the "familiar compound ghost" may represent an aspect of the self.

And so, compliant to the common wind,
    Too strange to each other for misunderstanding,
In concord at this intersection time
    Of meeting nowhere, no before and after,
    We trod the pavement in a dead patrol.
I said: 'The wonder that I feel is easy,
    Yet ease is cause of wonder. Therefore speak:
    I may not comprehend, may not remember.'
And he: 'I am not eager to rehearse
    My thought and theory which you have forgotten.
    These things have served their purpose: let them be.
So with your own, and pray they be forgiven
    By others, as I pray you to forgive
    Both bad and good. Last season's fruit is eaten
And the fullfed beast shall kick the empty pail.
    For last year's words belong to last year's language
    And next year's words await another voice.
But, as the passage now presents no hindrance
    To the spirit unappeased and peregrine
    Between two worlds become much like each other,
So I find words I never thought to speak
    In streets I never thought I should revisit
    When I left my body on a distant shore.
Since our concern was speech, and speech impelled us
    To purify the dialect of the tribe[14]
    And urge the mind to aftersight and foresight,
Let me disclose the gifts reserved for age
    To set a crown upon your lifetime's effort.
    First, the cold friction of expiring sense
Without enchantment, offering no promise
    But bitter tastelessness of shadow fruit
    As body and soul begin to fall asunder.
Second, the conscious impotence of rage
    At human folly, and the laceration[15]
    Of laughter at what ceases to amuse.
And last, the rending pain of re-enactment
    Of all that you have done, and been; the shame

14. Echoing Stéphan Mallarmé's "Le Tombeau d'Edgar Poe," "Donner un sens plu pur aux mot de la tribu" (To give a clearer meaning to the words of the tribe).

15. Swift composed his own epitaph in Latin. Translated by Yeats it reads, "Savage indignation now / Cannot lacerate his breast."

Of motives late revealed, and the awareness
Of things ill done and done to others' harm
   Which once you took for exercise of virtue.
   Then fools' approval stings, and honour stains.
From wrong to wrong the exasperated spirit
   Proceeds, unless restored by that refining fire[16]
   Where you must move in measure, like a dancer.'
The day was breaking. In the disfigured street
   He left me, with a kind of valediction,
   And faded on the blowing of the horn.[17]

III

There are three conditions which often look alike
Yet differ completely, flourish in the same hedgerow:
Attachment to self and to things and to persons, detachment
From self and from things and from persons; and, growing between them, indifference
Which resembles the others as death resembles life,
Being between two lives—unflowering, between
The live and the dead nettle. This is the use of memory:
For liberation—not less of love but expanding
Of love beyond desire, and so liberation
From the future as well as the past. Thus, love of a country
Begins as attachment to our own field of action
And comes to find that action of little importance
Though never indifferent. History may be servitude,
History may be freedom. See, now they vanish,
The faces and places, with the self which, as it could, loved them,
To become renewed, transfigured, in another pattern.

   Sin is Behovely,[18] but
All shall be well, and
All manner of thing shall be well.

---

16. Compare the refining fire that the poet Arnaut Daniel, Dante's "better craftsman," inhabits as a form of spiritual purgation in *Purgatorio*, XXVI, 148. These lines from Daniel were also cited by Eliot at the close of *The Waste Land*; see section V, note 20.

17. An echo of the disappearance of Hamlet's father's ghost: "It faded on the crowing of the cock" (*Hamlet* 1.2.157).

18. Necessary, fit, required by the divine plan. Dame Juliana of Norwich, a fourteenth-century mystic, was told in a vision that "sin is behovable but all shall be well . . . and all manner of things shall be well." Juliana fell ill when she was thirty years old and was expected to die, but she survived and in the crisis of her illness received fifteen visions that comforted her greatly. She spent the rest of her life as an anchoress, or hermit, near the cathedral at Norwich, during which she contemplated the meaning of her visions. She wrote her *Revelations of Divine Love* in about 1393.

If I think, again, of this place,
And of people, not wholly commendable,[19]
Of no immediate kin or kindness,
But some of peculiar genius,
All touched by a common genius,
United in the strife which divided them;
If I think of a king at nightfall,[20]
Of three men, and more, on the scaffold
And a few who died forgotten
In other places, here and abroad,[21]
And of one who died blind and quiet,[22]
Why should we celebrate
These dead men more than the dying?
It is not to ring the bell backward
Nor is it an incantation
To summon the spectre of a Rose.[23]
We cannot revive old factions
We cannot restore old policies
Or follow an antique drum.
These men, and those who opposed them
And those whom they opposed
Accept the constitution of silence
And are folded in a single party.
Whatever we inherit from the fortunate
We have taken from the defeated
What they had to leave us—a symbol:
A symbol perfected in death.
And all shall be well and
All manner of thing shall be well
By the purification of the motive
In the ground of our beseeching.[24]

19. Little Gidding and the people, including Charles I and Cromwell, who helped to shape its history.

20. Charles I sought shelter at Little Gidding at nightfall. He and his two chief associates, Archbishop Laud and Thomas Wentworth, Earl of Strafford, were executed by the Puritans.

21. Many individuals on both sides of the religious civil war died in exile.

22. John Milton, the great Puritan poet and author of *Paradise Lost*.

23. "The Spectre of the Rose" was a sentimental ballet about a girl who dreams of the rose she once wore to a ball, but Eliot refers also to the Wars of the Roses, an earlier English civil war fought in the latter years of the fifteenth century between the House of York (represented by a red rose) and the House of Lancaster (represented by a white rose) over control of the English crown.

24. In one of her visions, Dame Juliana of Norwich was told that, in our colloquy with God, love was "the ground of our beseeching."

IV

The dove descending breaks the air
With flame of incandescent terror
Of which the tongues declare
The one discharge from sin and error.[25]
The only hope, or else despair
    Lies in the choice of pyre or pyre—
    To be redeemed from fire by fire.[26]

Who then devised the torment? Love.
Love is the unfamiliar Name
Behind the hands that wove
The intolerable shirt of flame[27]
Which human power cannot remove.
    We only live, only suspire
    Consumed by either fire or fire.

V

What we call the beginning is often the end
And to make an end is to make a beginning.
The end is where we start from. And every phrase
And sentence that is right (where every word is at home,
Taking its place to support the others,
The word neither diffident nor ostentatious,
An easy commerce of the old and the new,
The common word exact without vulgarity,
The formal word precise but not pedantic,
The complete consort dancing together)
Every phrase and every sentence is an end and a beginning,
Every poem an epitaph. And any action
Is a step to the block,[28] to the fire, down the sea's throat
Or to an illegible stone:[29] and that is where we start.

25. The dove conflates a German dive bomber from the London blitz, with its flickering machine guns, with the sacred dove of the Pentecost, who descended with tongues of flame on the disciples of Jesus.

26. The only redemption from the fires of the London air raids is through the sacred fire of divine love.

27. The shirt of Nessus, which Hercules had put on at his wife Deianira's behest because she had been led to believe that it would restore his love for her. Instead, it clung to his flesh and caused such painful burning that he placed himself on a pyre and burned himself to death. By analogy, Eliot refers to the necessary torment of purgation from evil.

28. Charles I was beheaded on a chopping block.

29. Perhaps one of the illegible gravestones in the neglected churchyard at Little Gidding. Several brass grave markers associated with members of this religious community had become detached from their stones and are now mounted within the chapel.

We die with the dying:
See, they depart, and we go with them.
We are born with the dead:
See, they return, and bring us with them.
The moment of the rose and the moment of the yew-tree[30]
Are of equal duration. A people without history
Is not redeemed from time, for history is a pattern
Of timeless moments. So, while the light fails
On a winter's afternoon, in a secluded chapel[31]
History is now and England.
With the drawing of this Love and the voice of this Calling[32]

    We shall not cease from exploration
And the end of all our exploring
Will be to arrive where we started
And know the place for the first time.
Through the unknown, remembered gate
When the last of earth left to discover
Is that which was the beginning;
At the source of the longest river
The voice of the hidden waterfall
And the children in the apple-tree[33]
Not known, because not looked for
But heard, half-heard, in the stillness
Between two waves of the sea.
Quick now, here, now, always—
A condition of complete simplicity
(Costing not less than everything)
And all shall be well and
All manner of thing shall be well
When the tongues of flames are in-folded
Into the crowned knot of fire[34]
And the fire and the rose are one.

1942

---

30. Traditionally, the yew tree is associated with mourning and death, the rose with life and love.
31. Note that Eliot takes us full circle, returning to Little Gidding and the winter sunset there that opened the poem.
32. From "The Cloud of Unknowing" (anonymous), a fourteenth-century religious poem.
33. Echoes of the opening quartet, "Burnt Norton," include the voices of the children and the hidden waterfall.

34. The sailor's "crowned knot" was also known as a trinity knot because it bound three strands together. The crowned knot may also allude to Christ's crown of thorns, here transformed into a flame that is at once torturous and refining. Eliot may also be thinking of "the ghostly knot of burning love betwixt thee and thy God" cited in "The Cloud of Unknowing."

Eliot's *Four Quartets* are an intricately interwoven series of meditations. Each quartet, modeled in form and mood on the late string quartets of Beethoven, is in five sections, and each takes as its point of departure a single place with important associations in Eliot's emotional and spiritual life. The final quartet, "Little Gidding," borrows for its title the name of a small Anglican religious community founded in a remote part of Huntingdonshire, England, in 1625 by Nicholas Ferrar and his family. Numbering about forty members, this community sought a simple life devoted to prayer, good works, and religious devotion. Two major seventeenth-century English religious poets, George Herbert and Richard Crashaw, were friends and frequent visitors of the Little Gidding community. The chapel was ransacked and defaced in 1646 by Cromwell's Puritan soldiers as punishment for harboring King Charles I following the king's decisive defeat in the English civil war by the Puritan army at Naseby. Charles I was later beheaded. The community lived on, however, for another decade, and its chapel was reconstructed in the nineteenth century. Eliot began work on this poem early in 1941, when London was suffering under nightly German air raids. Hitler's forces had conquered France and most of eastern Europe and were threatening to invade England. The poem's emphasis on the search for meaning of a self who confronts history derives special urgency from this contemporary crisis in world history. Yet contemporary crisis is placed in context as well by the stillness of Little Gidding, which had quietly survived an earlier crisis in English history. Each of the quartets emphasizes one of the traditional four elements: earth, air, fire, and water. The focus of "Little Gidding" is on the multiple symbolic meanings of fire, though the poem refers as well to each of the other elements.

PROSE

Tradition and the Individual Talent

In English writing we seldom speak of tradition, though we occasionally apply its name in deploring its absence. We cannot refer to "the tradition" or to "a tradition"; at most, we employ the adjective in saying that the poetry of So-and-so is "traditional" or even "too traditional." Seldom, perhaps, does the word appear except in a phrase of censure. If otherwise, it is vaguely approbative, with the implication, as to the work approved, of some pleasing archæological reconstruction. You can hardly make the word agreeable to English ears without this comfortable reference to the reassuring science of archæology.

Certainly the word is not likely to appear in our appreciations of living or dead writers. Every nation, every race, has not only its own creative, but its own critical turn of mind; and is even more oblivious of the shortcomings and limitations of its critical habits than of those of its creative genius. We know, or think we know, from the enormous mass of critical writing that has appeared in the French language the critical method or habit of the French; we only conclude (we are such unconscious people) that the French are "more critical" than we, and sometimes even plume ourselves a little with the fact, as if the French were the less spontaneous. Perhaps they are; but we might remind ourselves that criticism is as inevitable as breathing, and that we should be none the worse for articulating what passes in our minds when we read a book and feel an emotion about it, for criticizing our own minds in their work of criticism. One of the facts that might come to light in this process is our tendency to insist, when we praise a poet, upon those aspects of his work in which he least resembles anyone else. In these aspects or parts of his work we pretend to find what is individual, what is the peculiar essence of the man. We dwell with satisfaction upon the poet's difference from his predecessors, especially his immediate predecessors; we endeavour to find something that can be isolated in order to be enjoyed. Whereas if we approach a poet without this prejudice we shall often find that not only the best, but the most individual parts of his work may be those in which the dead poets, his ancestors, assert their immortality most vigorously. And I do not mean the impressionable period of adolescence, but the period of full maturity.

Yet if the only form of tradition, of handing down, consisted in following the ways of the immediate generation before us in a blind or timid adherence to its successes, "tradition" should positively be discouraged. We have seen many such simple currents soon lost in the sand; and novelty is better than repetition. Tradition is a matter of much wider significance. It cannot be inherited, and if you want it you must obtain it by great labour. It involves, in the first place, the historical sense, which we may call nearly indispensable to anyone who would continue to be a poet beyond his twenty-fifth year; and the historical sense involves a perception, not only of the pastness of the past, but of its presence; the historical sense compels a man to write not merely with his own generation in his bones, but with a feeling that the whole of the literature of Europe from Homer and within it the whole of the literature of his own country has a simultaneous existence and composes a simultaneous order. This historical sense, which is a sense of the timeless as well as of the temporal and of the timeless and of the temporal together, is what makes a writer traditional. And it is at the same time what makes a writer most acutely conscious of his place in time, of his own contemporaneity.

No poet, no artist of any art, has his complete meaning alone. His significance, his appreciation is the appreciation of his relation to the dead poets and artists. You cannot value him alone; you must set him, for contrast and comparison, among the dead. I mean this as a principle of æsthetic, not merely historical, criticism. The necessity that he shall conform, that he shall cohere, is not one-sided; what happens when a new work of art is created is something that happens simultaneously to all the works of art which preceded it. The existing monuments form an ideal order among themselves, which is modified by the introduction of the new (the really new) work of art among them. The existing order is complete before the new work arrives; for order to persist after the supervention of novelty, the *whole* existing order must be, if ever so slightly, altered; and so the relations, proportions, values of each work of art toward the whole are readjusted; and this is conformity between the old and the new. Whoever has approved this idea of order, of the form of European, of English literature, will not find it preposterous that the past should be altered by the present as much as the present is directed by the past. And the poet who is aware of this will be aware of great difficulties and responsibilities.

In a peculiar sense he will be aware also that he must inevitably be judged by the standards of the past. I say judged, not amputated, by them; not judged to be as good as, or worse or better than, the dead; and certainly not judged by the canons of dead critics. It is a judgement, a comparison, in which two things are measured by each other. To conform merely would be for the new work not really to conform at all; it would not be new, and would therefore not be a work of art. And we do not quite say that the new is more valuable because it fits in; but its fitting in is a test of its value—a test, it is true, which can only be slowly and cautiously applied, for we are none of us infallible judges of conformity. We say: it appears to conform, and is perhaps individual, or it appears individual, and may conform; but we are hardly likely to find that it is one and not the other.

To proceed to a more intelligible exposition of the relation of the poet to the past: he can neither take the past as a lump, an indiscriminate bolus, nor can he form himself wholly on one or two private admirations, nor can he form himself wholly upon one preferred period. The first course is inadmissible, the second is an important experience of youth, and the third is a pleasant and highly desirable supplement. The poet must be very conscious of the main current, which does not at all flow invariably through the most distinguished reputations. He must be quite aware of the obvious fact that art never improves, but that the material of art is never quite the same. He must be aware that the mind of Europe— the mind of his own country—a mind which he learns in time to be much more important than his own private mind—is a mind which changes, and that this change is a development which abandons nothing *en route*, which does not superannuate either Shakespeare, or Homer, or the rock drawing of the Magdalenian draughtsmen. That this development, refinement perhaps, complication certainly, is not, from the point of view of the artist, any improvement. Perhaps not even an improvement from the point of view of the psychologist or not to the extent which we imagine; perhaps only in the end based upon a complication in economics and machinery. But the difference between the present and the past is that the conscious present is an awareness of the past in a way and to an extent which the past's awareness of itself cannot show.

Some one said: "The dead writers are remote from us because we *know* so much more than they did." Precisely, and they are that which we know.

I am alive to a usual objection to what is clearly part of my programme for the *métier* of poetry. The objection is that the doctrine requires a ridiculous amount of erudition (pedantry), a claim which can be rejected by appeal to the lives of poets in any pantheon. It will even be affirmed that much learning deadens or perverts poetic sensibility. While, however, we persist in believing that a poet ought to know as much as will not encroach upon his necessary receptivity and necessary laziness, it is not desirable to confine knowledge to whatever can be put into a useful shape for examinations, drawing-rooms, or the still more pretentious modes of publicity. Some can absorb knowledge, the more tardy must sweat for it. Shakespeare acquired more essential history from Plutarch than most men could from the whole British Museum. What is to be insisted upon is that the poet must develop or procure the consciousness of the past and that he should continue to develop this consciousness throughout his career.

What happens is a continual surrender of himself as he is at the moment to something which is more valuable. The progress of an artist is a continual self-sacrifice, a continual extinction of personality.

There remains to define this process of depersonalization and its relation to the sense of tradition. It is in this depersonalization that art may be said to approach the condition of science. I shall, therefore, invite you to consider, as a suggestive analogy, the action which takes place when a bit of finely filiated platinum is introduced into a chamber containing oxygen and sulphur dioxide.

II

Honest criticism and sensitive appreciation is directed not upon the poet but upon the poetry. If we attend to the confused cries of the newspaper critics and the *susurrus* of popular repetition that follows, we shall hear the names of poets in great numbers; if we seek not Blue-book knowledge but the enjoyment of poetry, and ask for a poem, we shall seldom find it. I have tried to point out the importance of the relation of the poem to other poems by other authors, and suggested the conception of poetry as a living whole of all the poetry that has ever been written. The other aspect of this Impersonal theory of poetry is the relation of the poem to its author. And I hinted, by an analogy, that the mind of the mature poet differs from that of the immature one not precisely in any valuation of "personality," not being necessarily more interesting, or having "more to say," but rather by being a more finely perfected medium in which special, or very varied, feelings are at liberty to enter into new combinations.

The analogy was that of the catalyst. When the two gases previously mentioned are mixed in the presence of a filament of platinum, they form sulphurous acid. This combination takes place only if the platinum is present; nevertheless the newly formed acid contains no trace of platinum, and the platinum itself is apparently unaffected; has remained inert, neutral, and unchanged. The mind of the poet is the shred of platinum. It may partly or exclusively operate upon the experience of the man himself; but, the more perfect the artist, the more completely separate in him will be the man who suffers and the mind which creates; the more perfectly will the mind digest and transmute the passions which are its material.

The experience, you will notice, the elements which enter the presence of the transforming catalyst, are of two kinds: emotions and feelings. The effect of a work of art upon the person who enjoys it is an experience different in kind from any experience not of art. It may be formed out of one emotion, or may be a combination of several; and various feelings, inhering for the writer in particular words or phrases or images, may be added to compose the final result. Or great poetry may be made without the direct use of any emotion whatever: composed out of feelings solely. Canto XV of the *Inferno* (Brunetto Latini) is a working up of the emotion evident in the situation; but the effect, though single as that of any work of art, is obtained by considerable complexity of detail. The last quatrain gives an image, a feeling attaching to an image, which "came," which did not develop simply out of what precedes, but which was probably in suspension in the poet's mind until the proper combination arrived for it to add itself to. The poet's mind is in fact a receptacle for seizing and storing up numberless feelings, phrases, images, which remain there until all the particles which can unite to form a new compound are present together.

If you compare several representative passages of the greatest poetry you see how great is the variety of types of combination, and also how completely any semi-ethical criterion of "sublimity" misses the mark. For it is not the "greatness," the intensity, of the emotions, the components, but the intensity of the artistic process, the pressure, so to speak, under which the fusion takes place, that counts. The episode of Paolo and Francesca employs a definite emotion, but the intensity of the poetry is something quite different from whatever intensity in the supposed experience it may give the impression of. It is no more intense, furthermore, than Canto XXVI, the voyage of Ulysses, which has not the direct dependence upon an emotion. Great variety is possible in the process of transmutation of emotion: the murder of Agamemnon, or the agony of Othello, gives an artistic effect apparently closer to a possible original than the scenes from Dante. In the *Agamemnon*, the artistic emotion approximates to the emotion of an actual spectator; in *Othello* to the emotion of the protagonist himself. But the difference between art and the event is always absolute; the combination which is the murder of Agamemnon is probably as complex as that which is the voyage of Ulysses. In either case there has been a fusion of elements. The ode of Keats contains a number of feelings which have nothing particular to do with the nightingale, but which the nightingale, partly, perhaps, because of its attractive name, and partly because of its reputation, served to bring together.

The point of view which I am struggling to attack is perhaps related to the metaphysical theory of the substantial unity of the soul: for my meaning is, that the poet has, not a "personality" to express, but a particular medium, which is only a medium and not a personality, in which impressions and experiences combine in peculiar and unexpected ways. Impressions and experiences which are important for the man may take no place in the poetry, and those which become important in the poetry may play quite a negligible part in the man, the personality.

I will quote a passage which is unfamiliar enough to be regarded with fresh attention in the light—or darkness—of these observations:

> And now methinks I could e'en chide myself
> For doating on her beauty, though her death
> Shall be revenged after no common action.
> Does the silkworm expend her yellow labours
> For thee? For thee does she undo herself?
> Are lordships sold to maintain ladyships
> For the poor benefit of a bewildering minute?
> Why does yon fellow falsify highways,
> And put his life between the judge's lips,
> To refine such a thing—keeps horse and men
> To beat their valours for her? . . .

In this passage (as is evident if it is taken in its context) there is a combination of positive and negative emotions: an intensely strong attraction toward beauty and an equally intense fascination by the ugliness which is contrasted with it and which destroys it. This balance of contrasted emotion is in the dramatic situation to which the speech is pertinent, but that situation alone is inadequate to it. This is, so to speak, the structural emotion, provided by the drama. But the whole effect, the dominant tone, is due to the fact that a number of floating feelings, having an affinity to this emotion by no means superficially evident, have combined with it to give us a new art emotion.

It is not in his personal emotions, the emotions provoked by particular events in his life, that the poet is in any way remarkable or interesting. His particular emotions may be simple, or crude, or flat. The emotion in his poetry will be a very complex thing, but not with the complexity of the emotions of people who have very complex or unusual emotions in life. One error, in fact, of eccentricity in poetry is to seek for new human emotions to express; and in this search for novelty in the wrong place it discovers the perverse. The business of the poet is not to find new emotions, but to use the ordinary ones and, in working them up into poetry, to express feelings which are not in actual emotions at all. And emotions which he has never experienced will serve his turn as well as those familiar to him. Consequently, we must believe that "emotion recollected in tranquillity" is an inexact formula. For it is neither emotion, nor recollection, nor, without distortion of meaning, tranquillity. It is a concentration, and a new thing resulting from the concentration, of a very great number of experiences which to the practical and active person would not seem to be experiences at all; it is a concentration which does not happen consciously or of deliberation. These experiences are not "recollected," and they finally unite in an atmosphere which is "tranquil" only in that it is a passive attending upon the event. Of course this is not quite the whole story. There is a great deal, in the writing of poetry, which must be conscious and deliberate. In fact, the bad poet is usually unconscious where he ought to be conscious, and conscious where he ought to be unconscious. Both errors tend to make him "personal." Poetry is not a turning loose of emotion, but an escape from emotion; it is not the expression of personality, but an escape from personality. But, of course, only those who have personality and emotions know what it means to want to escape from these things.

III

ὁ δὲ νοῦς ἴσως θειότερόν τι καὶ ἀπαθές ἐστιν

This essay proposes to halt at the frontier of metaphysics or mysticism, and confine itself to such practical conclusions as can be applied by the responsible person interested in poetry. To divert interest from the poet to the poetry is a laudable aim: for it would conduce to a juster estimation of actual poetry, good and bad. There are many people who appreciate the expression of sincere emotion in verse, and there is a smaller number of people who can appreciate technical excellence. But very few know when there is expression of *significant* emotion, emotion which has its life in the poem and not in the history of the poet. The emotion of art is impersonal. And the poet cannot reach this impersonality without surrendering himself wholly to the work to be done. And he is not likely to know what is to be done unless he lives in what is not merely the present, but the present moment of the past, unless he is conscious, not of what is dead, but of what is already living.

1919

JUN FUJITA
1888–1963

JUN FUJITA, the author of *Tanka: Poems in Exile*, was a pioneer poet of English-language tanka, a Japanese poetic form of five lines with thirty-one syllables. Aligning his work with imagism; he also published free verse that emphasized a compression of both image and feeling. Born near Hiroshima, Japan, Fujita moved to Canada and then settled in Chicago. To help finance his studies, he became a newspaper photographer for the *Chicago Evening Post* and continued news photography as a career with *The Daily News* in the 1930s. He was the only Japanese-American newspaper photographer in the nation at a time when racial discrimination and violence directed at the Japanese were persistent problems.

Fujita's companion, Florence Carr, bought the land for his cabin retreat in Minnesota because the state did not permit Asian aliens to own land. Fujita often worked on his poetry and painting in this one-room, rustic Japanese-style cabin, which is now part of a national park. He was not interned at a concentration camp during World War II and continued to live in Chicago. He turned to commercial photography as a career, devoting his free time to poetry and painting. Because obtaining citizenship was difficult for Japanese nationals, Fujita had to wait for a private congressional bill in 1954 in order to receive his U.S. citizenship.

FURTHER READING

Juliana Chang, ed. *Quiet Fire: A Historical Anthology of Asian American Poetry, 1892–1970*. New Brunswick, N.J.: Rutgers University Press, 1996.

Michigan Boulevard

A row of black tombs — tall and jagged,
The buildings stand in the drizzly night.
With vacant stare the boulevard lamps in rain
Amuse the green gleams they cast.
Beyond the lamps, among the tombs,
Drip, and drip,
The hollow sound rises.

1929

Michigan Boulevard is the main thoroughfare in downtown Chicago.

Chicago River

Slowly, by the slimy wooden wharves,
Through the stillness of rain
The Chicago River glides into the night.
From the silhouette of a black iron bridge,
The watchman's light is dripping —
Dripping like melting tallow.

Out of darkness
Comes a woman,
Hellos to me; her wet face glares;
Casually she turns and goes
Into the darkness.

Through the stillness of rain
The Chicago River glides on.

1929

Fujita won national attention for his evocative imagery in poems such as "Chicago River."

JOHN CROWE RANSOM
1888–1974

JOHN CROWE RANSOM'S poetry explores moments of disquiet, loss, and death with a detached yet sharp-edged irony blended with a muted but palpable sympathy and tenderness. His poems—at once serious and playful—mix formal language with colloquial speech and overlay courtly manners with hints of violence and savagery. His tone involves a peculiar and telling mixture of the elegantly indirect and the startlingly abrupt. An accomplished and influential critic and editor and a famous teacher, Ransom was an active poet for a surprisingly short time. His body of poetry is relatively small, yet he created a unique, unmistakable style that, in Randall Jarrell's words, can "speak of uncertainty with . . . ambiguous sureness."

Ransom was born in Pulaski, Tennessee, the son of a Methodist minister. He was raised in a devoutly religious yet intellectually enquiring household. Reflecting this early education, his poems continually engage with problems of belief and challenges to faith. A brilliant student, Ransom graduated from Nashville's Vanderbilt University in 1909 and then studied classics as a Rhodes scholar at Oxford in 1910–13. He began to teach English at Vanderbilt in 1914, leaving his teaching duties briefly to serve as an artillery officer in World War I. After the war, Ransom returned to Vanderbilt, where he formed an intellectual and artistic circle with such fellow poet-critics as Allen Tate, and Robert Penn Warren (both included in this anthology). Ransom omitted his first volume, *Poems about God* (1919), from later collections, but he shortly entered his "major phase" with the work he published in *The Fugitive*, a Vanderbilt-based little magazine that appeared between 1922 and 1925.

Following 1925, he wrote very few poems, devoting his energies instead to criticism and to teaching and mentoring such students as Randall Jarrell, Robert Lowell, and Peter Taylor. In 1937, Ransom moved to a new teaching position at Kenyon College in Ohio, bringing Lowell, Jarrell, and Taylor with him. There he founded the *Kenyon Review*. His 1941 essay collection, *The New Criticism*, lent its name to an influential critical movement that would stress poetic ambiguity, irony, unity, and formal coherence over such "older" critical values as historicism and biographical criticism. Ransom is remembered today as a perceptive critic, as a persuasive and encouraging teacher, and as the author of a small oeuvre of remarkably elegant, intense, and moving poems.

FURTHER READING

Kieran Quinlan. *John Crowe Ransom's Secular Faith*. Baton Rouge: Louisiana State University Press, 1989.

John Crowe Ransom. *Selected Poems*. New York: Knopf, 1969.

Thomas Daniel Young. *Gentleman in a Dustcoat: A Biography of John Crowe Ransom*. Baton Rouge: Louisiana State University Press, 1976.

Necrological

The friar had said his paternosters[1] duly
And scourged his limbs,[2] and afterwards would have slept;
But with much riddling[3] his head became unruly,
He arose, from the quiet monastery he crept.

Dawn lightened the place where the battle had been won.
The people were dead—it is easy he thought to die—
These dead remained, but the living were all gone,
Gone with the wailing trumps[4] of victory.

The dead men wore no raiment against the air,
Bartholomew's men had spoiled them where they fell;[5]
In defeat the heroes' bodies were whitely bare,
The field was white like meads of asphodel.[6]

---

1. The first words, in Latin, of the Lord's Prayer, "Our Father, who art in heaven," are "Pater Noster" (Our Father)—hence the common name for the Lord's Prayer in Latin.

2. Scourging or whipping oneself was a common form of contrition and self-mortification among various orders of medieval friars and monks.

3. Pondering on riddles of religious belief and theology.

4. Trumpets.

5. Bartholomew: apparently a fictional medieval commander. Victorious soldiers in medieval warfare commonly stripped slain enemies of their valuable armor as spoils of war.

6. Meadows of white lily-like flowers.

   *   *   *

Not all were white; some gory and fabulous
Whom the sword had pierced and then the grey wolf eaten;
But the brother[7] reasoned that heroes' flesh was thus.
Flesh fails, and the postured bones lie weather-beaten.

The lords of chivalry lay prone and shattered.
The gentle and the bodyguard of yeomen;
Bartholomew's stroke went home—but little it mattered,
Bartholomew went to be stricken of other foemen.

Beneath the blue ogive of the firmament[8]
Was a dead warrior, clutching whose mighty knees
Was a leman,[9] who with her flame had warmed his tent,
For him enduring all men's pleasantries.[10]

Close by the sable stream that purged the plain
Lay the white stallion and his rider thrown,
The great beast had spilled there his little brain,
And the little groin of the knight was spilled by a stone.

The youth possessed him then of a crooked blade
Deep in the belly of a lugubrious[11] wight;
He fingered it well, and it was cunningly made;
But strange apparatus was it for a Carmelite.[12]

Then he sat upon a hill and bowed his head
As under a riddle, and in deep surmise[13]
So still that he likened himself unto those dead
Whom the kites[14] of Heaven solicited with sweet cries.

                              1922

A necrology is a list of persons who have died within a certain time, or an obituary or notice of death. Ransom's title "Necrological" is the adjectival form, suggesting that the poem involves taking notice of death.

---

7. Friars in medieval monastic orders were termed "brothers."

8. Pointed arch of heaven.

9. Sweetheart, lover, or illicit mistress.

10. Teasing banter, jesting remarks.

11. Sad. Wight: any person, or, in some usages, a strong, brave person.

12. A mendicant or begging friar who belongs to a religious order founded during the Crusades at Mount Carmel, Palestine.

13. Questioning thought.

14. Small scavenger birds of the hawk family that feed on rodents, insects, and carrion (decayed flesh).

Bells for John Whiteside's Daughter

There was such speed in her little body,
And such lightness in her footfall,
It is no wonder her brown study[1]
Astonishes us all.

Her wars were bruited[2] in our high window.
We looked among orchard trees and beyond
Where she took arms against her shadow,
Or harried unto the pond

The lazy geese, like a snow cloud
Dripping their snow on the green grass,
Tricking and stopping, sleepy and proud,
Who cried in goose, Alas,

For the tireless heart within the little
Lady with rod that made them rise
From their noon apple-dreams and scuttle
Goose-fashion under the skies!

But now go the bells, and we are ready,
In one house we are sternly stopped
To say we are vexed at her brown study,
Lying so primly propped.

                                          1924

Here Lies a Lady

Here lies a lady of beauty and high degree.
Of chills and fever she died, of fever and chills,
The delight of her husband, her aunt, an infant of three,
And of medicos[1] marveling sweetly on her ills.

For either she burned, and her confident eyes would blaze,
And her fingers fly in a manner to puzzle their heads—
What was she making? Why, nothing; she sat in a maze
Of old scraps of laces, snipped into curious shreds—

---

1. A somber reverie.
2. Voiced loudly, noisily.

1. Doctors (colloquial).

* * *

Or this would pass, and the light of her fire decline
Till she lay discouraged and cold, like a thin stalk white and blown,
And would not open her eyes, to kisses, to wine;
The sixth of these states was her last; the cold settled down.

Sweet ladies, long may ye bloom, and toughly I hope ye may thole,[2]
But was she not lucky? In flowers and lace and mourning,
In love and great honor we bade God rest her soul
After six little spaces of chill, and six of burning.

1924

Captain Carpenter

Captain Carpenter rose up in his prime
Put on his pistols and went riding out
But had got wellnigh nowhere at that time
Till he fell in with ladies in a rout.

It was a pretty lady and all her train
That played with him so sweetly but before
An hour she'd taken a sword with all her main
And twined him of his nose for evermore.

Captain Carpenter mounted up one day
And rode straightway into a stranger rogue
That looked unchristian but be that as may
The Captain did not wait upon prologue.

But drew upon him out of his great heart
The other swung against him with a club
And cracked his two legs at the shinny part
And let him roll and stick like any tub.

Captain Carpenter rode many a time
From male and female took he sundry harms
He met the wife of Satan crying "I'm
The she-wolf bids you shall bear no more arms."

* * *

2. Suffer, bear, endure.

Their strokes and counters whistled in the wind
I wish he had delivered half his blows
But where she should have made off like a hind
The bitch bit off his arms at the elbows.

And Captain Carpenter parted with his ears
To a black devil that used him in this wise
O Jesus ere his threescore and ten years
Another had plucked out his sweet blue eyes.

Captain Carpenter got up on his roan
And sallied from the gate in hell's despite
I heard him asking in the grimmest tone
If any enemy yet there was to fight?

"To any adversary it is fame
If he risk to be wounded by my tongue
Or burnt in two beneath my red heart's flame
Such are the perils he is cast among.

"But if he can he has a pretty choice
From an anatomy with little to lose
Whether he cut my tongue and take my voice
Or whether it be my round red heart he choose."

It was the neatest knave that ever was seen
Stepping in perfume from his lady's bower
Who at this word put in his merry mien
And fell on Captain Carpenter like a tower.

I would not knock old fellows in the dust
But there lay Captain Carpenter on his back
His weapons were the old heart in his bust
And a blade shook between rotten teeth alack.

The rogue in scarlet and grey soon knew his mind.
He wished to get his trophy and depart
With gentle apology and touch refined
He pierced him and produced the Captain's heart.

God's mercy rest on Captain Carpenter now
I thought him Sirs an honest gentleman
Citizen husband soldier and scholar enow
Let jangling kites eat of him if they can.

❋   ❋   ❋

But God's deep curses follow after those
That shore him of his goodly nose and ears
His legs and strong arms at the two elbows
And eyes that had not watered seventy years.

The curse of hell upon the sleek upstart
That got the Captain finally on his back
And took the red red vitals of his heart
And made the kites to whet their beaks clack clack.

1924

"Captain Carpenter" is an ironic retelling of the traditional quest myth, using characteristically antique language. The title character is Ransom's invention. Captain Carpenter, who perhaps most closely resembles Cervantes' *Don Quixote*, undergoes still greater trials than the famous Don, gradually losing all of his bodily parts but never surrendering his honor or courage.

CONRAD AIKEN
1889–1973

AFTER YEARS of threatening behavior, Conrad Aiken's father, a Georgia physician, killed his wife and then himself. Conrad, a young boy of eleven, heard the shots and discovered the bodies. Following the murder-suicide, he was separated from his younger brother and sisters, who were adopted by another family while he was sent to live with an aunt and uncle in Massachusetts. These traumatic events permanently colored and unsettled Aiken's creative life. A classmate at Harvard of T. S. Eliot, whom he teasingly called "tsetse," Aiken never obtained Eliot's notoriety or success. Instead, he wrote poetry out of the limelight and was known primarily as an anthologist and the author of such short stories as "Silent Snow, Secret Snow." Drawing inspiration from the English Romantics, the French symbolists, Edgar Allan Poe, Emily Dickinson, and Sigmund Freud, Aiken charted an inward poetic journey, probing the mind's dark recesses. His introspective poems parallel those of such coevals as Wallace Stevens and Hart Crane (both included in this anthology), and they forecast the interior explorations of such later poets as John Berryman and Sylvia Plath. Aiken's poems eloquently explore the mind's capacity for madness and creativity, for desperation, despair, understanding, and transcendence.

FURTHER READING

Conrad Aiken. *Selected Poems*. Foreword by Harold Bloom. Oxford, Eng.: Oxford University Press, 2003.

Harry Martin. *The Art of Knowing: The Poetry and Prose of Conrad Aiken*. Columbia: University of Missouri Press, 1988.

Jay Martin. *Conrad Aiken: A Life of His Art*. Princeton, N.J.: Princeton University Press, 1962.

FROM *Senlin: A Biography*

Senlin, walking before us in the sunlight,
Bending his small legs in a peculiar way,
Goes to his work with thoughts of the universe.
His hands are in his pockets, he smokes his pipe,
He is happily conscious of roofs and skies;
And, without turning his head, he turns his eyes
To regard white horses drawing a small white hearse.
The sky is brilliant between the roofs,
The windows flash in the yellow sun,
On the hard pavement ring the hoofs,
The light wheels softly run.
Bright particles of sunlight fall,
Quiver and flash, gyrate and burn,
Honey-like heat flows down the wall,
The white spokes dazzle and turn.

Senlin, walking before us in the sunlight,
Regards the hearse with an introspective eye.
"Is it my childhood there," he asks,
"Sealed in a hearse and hurrying by?"
He taps his trowel against a stone;
The trowel sings with a silver tone.

"Nevertheless I know this well.
Bury it deep and toll a bell,
Bury it under land or sea,
You cannot bury it save in me."

It is as if his soul had become a city,
With noisily peopled streets, and through these streets
Senlin himself comes driving a small white hearse . . .
"Senlin!" we cry. He does not turn his head.
But is that Senlin? — Or is this city Senlin —

Quietly watching the burial of the dead?[1]
Dumbly observing the cortège[2] of its dead?
Yet we would say that all this is but madness:
Around a distant corner trots the hearse.
And Senlin walks before us in the sunlight
Happily conscious of his universe.

✦ ✦ ✦

Senlin stood before us in the sunlight,
And laughed, and walked away.
Did no one see him leaving the doors of the city,
Looking behind him as if he wished to stay?
Has no one, in the forests of the evening,
Heard the sad horn of Senlin slowly blown?
For somewhere, in the worlds-in-worlds about us,
He changes still, unfriended and alone.
Is he the star on which we walk at daybreak,
The light that blinds our eyes?
"Senlin!" we cry. "Senlin!" again . . . no answer:
Only the soulless brilliance of blue skies.

Yet we would say, this was no man at all,
But a dream we dreamed, and vividly recall;
And we are mad to walk in wind and rain
Hoping to find, somewhere, that dream again.

1918

The central character of "Senlin" has been compared to T. S. Eliot's J. Alfred Prufrock, but he also bears resemblance to the autobiographical Conrad Aiken. Senlin inhabits an urban space that unpredictably becomes the space of the mind or soul. Lost, confused, and alone in this space, Senlin is haunted by a "small white hearse." This image may recall a childhood loss—such as Aiken's own experience of his parents' deaths and his removal from his siblings. " 'Is it my childhood there' "? Senlin asks. Alternatively, the hearse may suggest the deathlike existence, the daily spiritual death, of Senlin himself. The dead body, he asserts, is buried " 'in me.' " Senlin seems awash in feelings he cannot quite understand or control. Ultimately, he simply disappears from the poem, apparently a lost dream (or alter ego) of the speaker himself. The two segments reprinted here are the fourth and the last parts of the sequence.

1. Perhaps a precursor of "The Burial of the   2. Procession.
Dead" in T. S. Eliot's *The Waste Land*.

Prelude 1

Winter for a moment takes the mind; the snow
Falls past the arclight;[1] icicles guard a wall;
The wind moans through a crack in the window;
A keen sparkle of frost is on the sill.
Only for a moment; as spring too might engage it,
With a single crocus in the loam, or a pair of birds;
Or summer with hot grass; or autumn with a yellow leaf.
Winter is there, outside, is here in me:
Drapes the planets with snow, deepens the ice on the moon,
Darkens the darkness that was already darkness.
The mind too has its snows, its slippery paths,
Walls bayoneted with ice, leaves ice-encased.
Here is the in-drawn room, to which you return
When the wind blows from Arcturus:[2] here is the fire
At which you warm your hands and glaze your eyes;
The piano, on which you touch the cold treble;
Five notes like breaking icicles; and then silence.

The alarm-clock ticks, the pulse keeps time with it,
Night and the mind are full of sounds. I walk
From the fire-place, with its imaginary fire,
To the window, with its imaginary view.
Darkness, and snow ticking the window: silence,
And the knocking of chains[3] on a motor-car, the tolling
Of a bronze bell, dedicated to Christ.[4]
And then the uprush of angelic wings, the beating
Of wings demonic, from the abyss of the mind:
The darkness filled with a feathery whistling, wings
Numberless as the flakes of angelic snow,
The deep void swarming with wings and sound of wings,
The winnowing[5] of chaos, the aliveness
Of depth and depth and depth dedicated to death.

Here are the bickerings of the inconsequential,
The chatterings of the ridiculous, the iterations
Of the meaningless. Memory, like a juggler,
Tosses its colored balls into the light, and again

1. Electric lamp.
2. A bright star in the northern sky.
3. Tire chains.
4. A church bell.
5. The separating of grain from chaff; hence, ordering.

Receives them into darkness. Here is the absurd,
Grinning like an idiot, and the omnivorous quotidian,
Which will have its day. A handful of coins,
Tickets, items from the news, a soiled handkerchief,
A letter to be answered, notice of a telephone call,
The petal of a flower in a volume of Shakespeare,
The program of a concert. The photograph, too,
Propped on the mantel, and beneath it a dry rosebud;
The laundry bill, matches, an ash-tray, Utamaro's[6]
Pearl-fishers. And the rug, on which are still the crumbs
Of yesterday's feast. These are the void, the night,
And the angelic wings that make it sound.

What is the flower? It is not a sigh of color,
Suspiration[7] of purple, sibilation of saffron,
Nor aureate[8] exhalation from the tomb.
Yet it is these because you think of these,
An emanation of emanations, fragile
As light, or glisten, or gleam, or coruscation,[9]
Creature of brightness, and as brightness brief.
What is the frost? It is not the sparkle of death,
The flash of time's wing, seeds of eternity;
Yet it is these because you think of these.
And you, because you think of these, are both
Frost and flower, the bright ambiguous syllable
Of which the meaning is both no and yes.

Here is the tragic, the distorting mirror
In which your gesture becomes grandiose;
Tears form and fall from your magnificent eyes,
The brow is noble, and the mouth is God's.
Here is the God who seeks his mother, Chaos—
Confusion seeking solution, and life seeking death.
Here is the rose that woos the icicle; the icicle
That woos the rose. Here is the silence of silences
Which dreams of becoming a sound, and the sound
Which will perfect itself in silence. And all

6. Kitagawa Utamaro (1753–1806), Japanese painter and printmaker.
7. Long breath or sigh. Sibilation: hiss. Saffron: orange-yellow color or orange aromatic stigmas of a purple-flowered crocus.
8. Golden.
9. Flash of light.

These things are only the uprush from the void,
The wings angelic and demonic, the sound of the abyss
Dedicated to death. And this is you.

1931

"Prelude 1" is the first segment of a poetic sequence called *Preludes for Memnon*. In Greek myth, Memnon was the king of Ethiopia and a warrior for Troy. Slain in combat by the Greek hero Achilles, he was made immortal by Zeus. Concerned with death and survival, *Preludes* merges the speaker's perception of the outside world with his consciousness of struggle and his confusions about identity: "The mind too has its snows, its slippery paths." Harold Bloom identifies in this poem a meditative strain that includes "cosmic nihilism," an "Epicurean refusal to mourn," and an Emersonian "secular transcendence."

Time in the Rock 42

Who would carve words must carve himself
first carve himself—

        O carpenter,
you whose hand held nails
who knew the plane tree and the oak tree

                      with heavy adze[1]
hardening the muscle that became the word

and you, the sculptor, who made of hemlock wood
the little doll, or cut blind eyes in stone,

                 habitual stroke
hammering the memory to rock precision,
god and logos,[2] well-tempered question in the chisel,
who knew the kindness of fatigue—

               rising or stooping
these angels of mankind these devils of wit
sifters of habit and deceivers only
as the trained muscle deceives the mind, or feeds with custom:
these who were often tired
strengthening backs for weight of tree or stone,
or what might else of burden come from man—

---

1. Cutting tool used for shaping wood.   2. Divine word; universal reason.

* * *

who would carve words must carve himself,
first carve himself; and then alas
finds, too late, that Word is only Hand.

1936

Aiken considered *Time in the Rock* to form a single poem with *Preludes for Memnon*. Both texts make poetry out of the mind's motions. In this segment, the speaker contemplates the artistic quest for truth. He concludes that there is no absolute "Word" but only the creator's "Hand."

CLAUDE MCKAY
1889–1948

BORN ON THE ISLAND of Jamaica to peasant farmers, Festus Claudius McKay spent his first twenty-three years in the West Indies. Encouraged by an English linguist named Walter Jekyll, he wrote and published two poetry collections, both in Jamaican dialect. In 1912, McKay came to the United States to study agriculture and then, moving to New York City, to become a writer. In 1917 he began publishing his poems in the United States. These poems, like those of Countee Cullen and Langston Hughes a few years later, expressed a new sense of black political assertion and a rich awareness of black cultural life. "If We Must Die," a protest poem written in response to a white race riot, became his signature poem. It was reprinted in his collection *Harlem Shadows* in 1922, the same year that T. S. Eliot's *The Waste Land* and James Joyce's *Ulysses* appeared. Just as those texts helped to define Anglo-American experimental modernism, so *Harlem Shadows* helped to inaugurate the flowering of African-American writing known as the Harlem Renaissance.

McKay strongly identified with oppressed working people and people of color. An active socialist, he wrote for Marcus Garvey's *Negro World*, and he co-edited the proletarian journal *The Liberator* with Max Eastman and Michael Gold. Whereas poems such as "If We Must Die," "America," and "Baptism" express McKay's social militancy, other poems such as "The Harlem Dancer" and "Harlem Shadows" capture the poignancy of the Harlem social scene. Yet other poems such as "The Tropics in New York" and "Outcast" reflect McKay's longing to flee Harlem for his native West Indies or for an Africa of his mind. As did Countee

Cullen, McKay fused the innovative subject matter of his poems with a masterly use of traditional forms, including the Shakespearean sonnet.

According to Venetria Patton and Maureen Honey, *Harlem Shadows* made McKay "the most famous poet in the African-American community of New York and beyond, but he remained estranged from the United States and left the same year." For twelve years he lived an expatriate life, visiting the Soviet Union, Spain, and Morocco, and settling in France. During this period he published several books of fiction, the most successful being *Home to Harlem* (1928), which dared to depict working-class black life and culture. McKay returned to the United States in 1934, becoming a citizen in 1940 and moving to Chicago in 1944. A convert to Catholicism, he spent his last years teaching at the National Catholic Youth Organization. He outlived the height of his literary fame and cultural impact, yet his poems still vibrate with a vital spirit of questioning and self-assertion.

FURTHER READING

Addison Gayle. *Claude McKay: The Black Poet at War.* Detroit: Broadside Press, 1972.
Heather Hathaway. *Caribbean Waves: Relocating Claude McKay and Paule Marshall.* Bloomington: Indiana University Press, 1999.
Claude McKay. *Selected Poems.* New York: Dover, 1999.
Michael North. *The Dialect of Modernism.* New York: Oxford University Press, 1994.
Venetria K. Patton and Maureen Honey, eds. "Claude McKay." In *Double-Take: A Revisionist Harlem Renaissance Anthology,* 271–85. New Brunswick, N.J.: Rutgers University Press, 2001.

The Harlem Dancer

Applauding youths laughed with young prostitutes
And watched her perfect, half-clothed body sway;
Her voice was like the sound of blended flutes
Blown by black players upon a picnic day.
She sang and danced on gracefully and calm,
The light gauze hanging loose about her form;
To me she seemed a proudly-swaying palm
Grown lovelier for passing through a storm.
Upon her swarthy neck black, shiny curls
Profusely fell; and, tossing eons in praise,
The wine-flushed, bold-eyed boys, and even the girls,
Devoured her shape with eager, passionate gaze:
But, looking at her falsely-smiling face,
I knew her self was not in that strange place.

1917

The publication of "The Harlem Dancer" in the experimental, interracial literary journal *Seven Arts* announced McKay's entrance into the American literary scene. A Shakespearean sonnet (one of McKay's characteristic forms), "The Harlem Dancer" makes a vivid poetry out of Harlem social life, revealing as well a canny awareness of race, class, gender, and sexuality.

If We Must Die

If we must die, let it not be like hogs
Hunted and penned in an inglorious spot,
While round us bark the mad and hungry dogs,
Making their mock at our accursed lot.
If we must die, O let us nobly die,
So that our precious blood may not be shed
In vain; then even the monsters we defy
Shall be constrained to honor us though dead!
O kinsmen! we must meet the common foe!
Though far outnumbered let us show us brave,
And for their thousand blows deal one death-blow!
What though before us lies the open grave?
Like men we'll face the murderous, cowardly pack,
Pressed to the wall, dying, but fighting back!

1919

"If We Must Die" became McKay's most famous poem. He wrote it in response to violent anti-black riots in Chicago in the summer of 1919. "If We Must Die" expresses a militancy that, however unsettling for some white readers, encouraged the growth of a new liberationist consciousness among African Americans. The poem first appeared in *The Liberator*, an interracial, politically radical journal, and it was then widely reprinted in black newspapers. From this point on, McKay considered himself a professional writer.

The Tropics in New York

Bananas ripe and green and ginger-root,
Cocoa in pods and alligator pears,
And tangerines and mangoes and grape fruit,
Fit for the highest prize at parish fairs,

Set in the window, bringing memories
Of fruit trees laden by low-singing rills,[1]
And dewy dawns and mystical blue skies
In benediction over nun-like hills.

1. Small brooks.

*   *   *

Mine eyes grew dim and I could no more gaze,
A wave of longing through my body swept,
And, hungry for the old, familiar ways,
I turned aside and bowed my head and wept.

1920

"The Tropics in New York" evokes McKay's yearning for the scenes of his childhood in Clarendon Parish, Jamaica. Michael North comments that the first stanza break "expresses more effectively than anything else in the poem the break between the tropics and New York." Noting that McKay arrived in the United States on a United Fruit Company ship, North adds that the poem concerns "the radically different fates of passenger and cargo in the global economy, the cargo assimilated as an exotic treat, the passenger cut off from both tropics and New York."

America

Although she feeds me bread of bitterness,
And sinks into my throat her tiger's tooth,
Stealing my breath of life, I will confess
I love this cultured hell that tests my youth!
Her vigor flows like tides into my blood,
Giving me strength erect against her hate.
Her bigness sweeps my being like a flood.
Yet as a rebel fronts a king in state,
I stand within her walls with not a shred
Of terror, malice, not a word of jeer.
Darkly I gaze into the days ahead,
And see her might and granite wonders there,
Beneath the touch of Time's unerring hand,
Like priceless treasures sinking in the sand.

1921

The conclusion of "America" may allude to "Ozymandias" by British poet Percy Bysshe Shelley (1792–1822). In Shelley's poem, a once-imposing monument to all-powerful Ozymandias (Egyptian King Ramses II) lies wrecked by time, while "the lone and level sands stretch far away."

Baptism

Into the furnace let me go alone;
Stay you without in terror of the heat.
I will go naked in — for thus 'tis sweet —
Into the weird depths of the hottest zone.
I will not quiver in the frailest bone,
You will not note a flicker of defeat;
My heart shall tremble not its fate to meet,
Nor mouth give utterance to any moan.
The yawning over spits forth fiery spears;
Red aspish[1] tongues shout wordlessly my name.
Desire destroys, consumes my mortal fears,
Transforming me into a shape of flame.
I will come out, back to your world of tears,
A stronger soul within a finer frame.

1922

Outcast

For the dim regions[1] whence my fathers came
My spirit, bondaged by the body, longs.
Words felt, but never heard, my lips would frame;
My soul would sing forgotten jungle songs.
I would go back to darkness and to peace,
But the great western world holds me in fee,
And I may never hope for full release
While to its alien gods I bend my knee.
Something in me is lost, forever lost,
Some vital thing has gone out of my heart,
And I must walk the way of life a ghost
Among the sons of earth, a thing apart;
For I was born, far from my native clime,
Under the white man's menace, out of time.

1922

"Outcast" suggests the speaker's sense of being between two worlds — a Euro-American culture in which he does not fit and an African culture that is unknown to him.

1. Snakelike; resembling the Egyptian cobra   1. I.e., Africa.
called the asp.

Harlem Shadows

I hear the halting footsteps of a lass
In Negro Harlem when the night lets fall
Its veil. I see the shapes of girls[1] who pass
Eager to heed desire's insistent call:
Ah, little dark girls, who in slippered feet
Go prowling through the night from street to street.

Through the long night until the silver break
Of day the little gray feet know no rest,
Through the lone night until the last snow-flake
Has dropped from heaven upon the earth's white breast,
The dusky, half-clad girls of tired feet
Are trudging, thinly shod, from street to street.

Ah, stern harsh world, that in the wretched way
Of poverty, dishonour and disgrace,
Has pushed the timid little feet of clay.
The sacred brown feet of my fallen race!
Ah, heart of me, the weary, weary feet
In Harlem wandering from street to street.

                                                        1922

MIKHAIL NAIMY
1889–1988

ALTHOUGH MIKHAIL NAIMY lived in the United States for twenty years, serving
with the U.S. Army in World War I and writing most of his poetry in New York
City, he is unknown to most American readers of poetry. Yet he was regarded as the
most acclaimed writer in international Arab culture when he died in 1988, and at
one time he was considered for the Nobel Prize in literature. Born to a Chris-
tian family in Baskinta, Lebanon, Naimy studied for the Orthodox priesthood in
Russia and then came to the United States in 1911, receiving a law degree from the
University of Washington. While in the Pacific Northwest, he wrote a review of a
publication by Kahlil Gibran (also included in this anthology), and Gibran in-

---

1. Prostitutes.

vited him to New York City. Naimy became a driving force in the Pen League and
also Gibran's best friend and biographer. After Gibran died in his presence, Naimy
returned to his birthplace in Lebanon to complete his biography, *Gibran Kahlil
Gibran* (1950). He lived there for the rest of his life under a vow of chastity and de-
votion to the asceticism of Buddha, Lao-Tzu, Christ, and al-Hallaj.

Naimy's poetry is regarded for both its dark stoicism and its peacefulness. His
experience in World War I on the French front led to his renowned poem "My
Brother." Such poems as "Hunger," written at the beginning of the Great Depres-
sion, appeared in the *New York Times* in 1930. Undoubtedly Naimy's sensitivity to
the economic depression stems in part from his horror at the famine in Lebanon
during World War I. American competitiveness concerned him greatly, as did the
regimentation in the Soviet Union. In 1957 he published a book entitled *Beyond
Moscow and Washington* that presented what he called a "third way" of spiritual
and community life in response to the dominant bipolar Cold War dialogue of that
era. "My Brother" and the excerpt from "The Chord of Hope" that appear here
have been translated by Gregory Orfalea and Sharif Elmusa.

FURTHER READING

Gregory Orfalea and Sharif Elmusa, eds. *Grape Leaves: A Century of Arab-American Poetry.*
New York: Interlink Books, 2000.

Hunger

Into my heart a seed was cast
And it took root and sprouted fast.

It spread so far and reached so high,
Until it filled the earth and the sky.

And now its boughs are weighted low
With fairer fruit than angels know;

Yet I whose heart sap feeds the root,
Though famished, dare not eat the fruit.

1930

My Brother

Brother, if on the heels of war Western man
    celebrates his deeds,
Consecrates the memory of the fallen
    and builds monuments for heroes,

Do not yourself sing for the victors nor rejoice
   over those trampled by victorious wheels;
Rather kneel as I do, wounded, for the end of our dead.

Brother, if after the war a soldier comes home
And throws his tired body in the arms of friends,
Do not hope on your return for friends.
Hunger struck down all to whom we might whisper our pain.

Brother, if the farmer returns to till his land,
And after long exile rebuilds a shack
   which cannon had wrecked,
Our waterwheels have dried up
And the foes have left no seedling except the scattered corpses.

Brother, misery nestled everywhere—through our will.
Do not lament. Others do not hear our woe.
Instead follow me with a pick and spade that we may
   dig a trench in which to hide our dead.

Dear brother, who are we without a neighbor, kin or country?
We sleep and we wake clad in shame.

The world breathes our stench, as it did that of the dead.
Bring the spade and follow me—dig another trench
   for those still alive.

                    1988

FROM *The Chord of Hope*

Hope is agony,
yet we hope.

We hope secretly
while hope publicly mocks us.

Even denying hope,
I hope. And I resent it.

Hope is the whip of Time
spurring us forward.

       *   *   *

And I seek to be a sage when young,
to recover youth's paradise when old,

to be free by virtue of that illness, love,
and a captive of love when I'm free,

to be eloquent when reticent
and reticent when the pearls come in my speech.

We all sow hope.
And after all our toil, hope is all we reap.

Hope is a tightrope
on which we teeter above the sea of life
like acrobats.

Yet hope nibbles its own cord
as the seconds eat away their thread.

2000

ELIA ABU MADI [MADEY]
1890–1957

Kʜᴀʟɪʟ ɢɪʙʀᴀɴ and his New York friends felt that Elia Abu Madi wrote the most accomplished poetry in their circle of émigré Arab poets and writers. His work is memorized today by Arab students around the world. Born in 1890 in al-Mahaydatah, Lebanon, he was educated in Egypt, where his first book of poems was published in 1911. Abu Madi was forced into exile in 1912 when Ottoman imperial authorities decided that his writings were too provocative. Arriving in Cincinnati, he lived most of his adult life in the United States as a fervent patriot, never returning to Lebanon. In the United States, Abu Madi continued to write poetry and published three more volumes. He became involved in journalism when he married the daughter of the editor of the first Arab-American newspaper in America, *Kowkab America*, published in New York. He later took over the magazine that his father-in-law was editing at the time of his death, *Mirat al-Gharb* (Light of the West). In 1929, Abu Madi began his own paper, *Al-Samir,* which he published five times a week in Brooklyn until his death in 1957. A poem like "Holiday Present" (here translated by George Dimitri Selim), with its emotional energy and vivid imagery, reveals Abu Madi's talents as a love lyricist and a poet of freedom and hope. Abu Madi's work remains relevant to contemporary Arab readers around the world.

FURTHER READING

Gregory Orfalea and Sharif Elmusa, eds. *Grape Leaves: A Century of Arab-American Poetry.* New York: Interlink Books, 2000.

Holiday Present

My angel!
What shall I give you as a present
for the holiday
when you have everything?
A bracelet of pure gold?
No! I hate fetters around your wrists.
Wines?
There is no wine on earth
like the wine which pours from your eyes.
Flowers?
The most beautiful flowers are those
I have smelled on your cheeks.
Carnelians,[1] blazing like my heart?
But the precious carnelians are in your lips.
I have nothing dearer than my soul.
It lies pawned in your hands.

2000

ARCHIBALD MACLEISH
1892–1982

ALTHOUGH Archibald MacLeish was a versatile author and a successful man of the world, he is best remembered today for thoughtful poems composed in a delicate lyric voice. His early poems often reflected the new ideas then circulating

---

1. Reddish quartz used in jewelry.

about what modern poetry should be. "Ars Poetica," for example, not only exemplified those ideas but tried to define them.

MacLeish was born in Glencoe, Illinois, in 1892. His strong drive to succeed was fueled by a prosperous but sternly distant father and college-professor mother who emphasized the need for social responsibility. MacLeish received a bachelor's degree in English from Yale in 1915 and—with time out to command a battery of field artillery during service in World War I—a law degree from Harvard in 1919. Although successful at law, MacLeish left his law firm in 1923 to focus his attention on writing. He moved to Paris, then at its height as an international center for the arts, and he developed relationships with leading figures in the expatriate literary community, including Hemingway, Cummings, Dos Passos, Scott and Zelda Fitzgerald, and James Joyce. MacLeish's poetry of the 1920s shows a sometimes derivative allegiance to modernism—whose imagistic principles he articulated in his most famous poem, "Ars Poetica."

In the 1930s, MacLeish turned, both in art and in life, toward a greater concern with social causes. He worked for *Fortune* magazine during this period and became a supporter of and speech writer for Franklin D. Roosevelt, who ultimately appointed him Librarian of Congress. After helping to organize UNESCO after World War II, MacLeish became Boylston Professor of Rhetoric at Harvard in 1949, where he taught until his retirement in 1962. MacLeish, with his connections in government, was instrumental in achieving Ezra Pound's release from St. Elizabeth's Hospital in 1958. In his later years, MacLeish devoted himself to playwriting, his most famous verse play being *J. B.* (1957), a modern retelling of the biblical story of Job. Although he was more of a follower than a leader in the realm of poetry and poetics, MacLeish sustained an important, useful career in support of human rights and the arts over many decades.

FURTHER READING

Scott Donaldson and R. H. Winnick. *Archibald MacLeish: An American Life*. Boston: Houghton Mifflin, 1992.
Archibald MacLeish. *Collected Poems, 1917 to 1982*. New York: Mariner, 1985.

Ars Poetica

A poem should be palpable and mute
As a globed fruit,

Dumb
As old medallions to the thumb,

Silent as the sleeve-worn stone
Of casement ledges where the moss has grown—

*   *   *

A poem should be wordless
As the flight of birds.

♦   ♦   ♦

A poem should be motionless in time
As the moon climbs,

Leaving, as the moon releases
Twig by twig the night-entangled trees,

Leaving, as the moon behind the winter leaves,
Memory by memory the mind —

A poem should be motionless in time
As the moon climbs.

♦   ♦   ♦

A poem should be equal to:
Not true.

For all the history of grief
An empty doorway and a maple leaf.

For love
The leaning grasses and two lights above the sea —

A poem should not mean
But be.

1926

"Ars Poetica" means the art of poetry in Latin. It is also the title of a famous treatise on po-
etry by the Roman poet Horace (65–8 B.C.E.)

EDNA ST. VINCENT MILLAY
1892–1950

THE MAJOR POETIC VOICE of the rebellious Jazz Age generation did not belong to
a male. It belonged to Edna St. Vincent Millay, who was hailed by some readers as
the greatest female poet since Sappho of ancient Greece. While the high modern-
ist poets T. S. Eliot and Ezra Pound were developing their work for elite literary
culture, Millay was writing for the American mass-media culture of newspapers,

magazines, radio, live stage, and the national lecture circuit. She served as the personification of "The New Woman" of European-American bourgeois society. Whether she was swaggering like Greta Garbo in trousers, smoking cigarettes, and using the masculine nickname "Vincent," or gushing like Lillian Gish in red velvet evening gowns trimmed with gold braid and topped with a black velvet cape, and presenting herself as "Edna," Millay flaunted Victorian conventions of femininity. Her readers were enthralled with her as a flapper heroine and political rebel. In 1938, she was voted one of the ten most famous women in the United States. In the 1940s she was cited as "one of the ten greatest living women."

Not only was Millay a mass-media superstar, she also was considered by many to be one of America's best living poets. Both her sensational rise to the top and her staying power rankled her male competitors, who attempted to chip at her stature. After she became the first woman poet to win the Pulitzer Prize in poetry for *The Harp-Weaver and Other Poems* in 1923, Robert Frost viewed her as his most serious competitor. He feared that she would be elected to the American Academy of Arts and Letters ahead of him and expressed his relief to friends when he was chosen just slightly ahead of her. In 1937, she was the target of the poet and critic John Crowe Ransom in an essay entitled "The Poet as Woman," in which he found Millay (as well as women poets in general) lacking in "intellectuality." As Ransom and fellow poet-critic Allen Tate (both included in this anthology) gained power in the poetry world, they continued to assail Millay. When she wrote political poetry supporting the Allied cause in World War II, she suffered severe criticism because of it. Millay gradually lost her earlier sensational poetic reputation, and by the time of her death in 1950, she faced obscurity.

Raised in Camden, Maine, by a single mother, Millay was educated at Vassar College, thanks to the intervention of a wealthy benefactor who admired her precocious poetry. Millay was well positioned to take advantage of the new social and cultural mores of the post–Great War generation when she moved to Greenwich Village, the nation's bustling center of art and experimentation in New York City. She was not only a gifted poet but also a talented playwright and actress who appeared at the Provincetown Playhouse. She knew how to captivate audiences and readers with her irreverent wit and sardonic commentary. She rapidly gained fame for her public poetry readings. Listeners and readers responded to her mastery of traditional forms, her brilliant sonic effects, her memorable images and phrases, and the extreme modernity of the attitudes and feelings expressed in her poetry. They also enjoyed her vivid performance of unconventional femininity and her frankly expressed sexual independence, which was rumored to have mirrored her own life. Millay conducted many love affairs with both men and women. She married Eugen Boissevain, the widower of the great suffragist Inez Milholland, whom she revered so deeply that she wrote a poem in her honor.

Millay's present recovery from obscurity has resulted from the work of feminist scholars and critics who view her as a crucial precursor for women poets and performers later in the century. She is valued for her strong and accomplished voice in the traditionally male-dominated genre of the sonnet, for her sometimes painful inward probings, and for her eloquent and outspoken assertion of her political and social beliefs.

FURTHER READING

Suzanne Clark. *Sentimental Modernism*. Bloomington, Indiana: Indiana University Press, 1991.

Diane P. Freedman. *Edna St. Vincent Millay at 100: A Critical Reappraisal*. Carbondale: Southern Illinois University Press, 1995.

Nancy Milford. *Savage Beauty: The Life of Edna St. Vincent Millay*. New York: Random House, 2001.

Edna St. Vincent Millay. *Collected Poems*. Ed. Norma Millay. New York: Harper and Row, 1956.

Edna St. Vincent Millay Society. www.steepletop.org

Camille Roman. *Elizabeth Bishop's World War II–Cold War View*. New York: Palgrave, 2001.

———. "Robert Frost and Three Female Modern Poets: Amy Lowell, Louise Bogan, and Edna Millay." *The Robert Frost Review* (1995): 62–69.

Susan Schweik. *A Gulf So Deeply Cut: American Women Poets and the Second World War*. Madison: University of Wisconsin Press, 1991.

Cheryl Walker. "Antimodern, Modern, and Postmodern Millay: Contexts of Revaluation." In *Gendered Modernisms*, ed. Margaret Dickie and Thomas Travisano, 170–88. Philadelphia: University of Pennsylvania Press, 1996.

———. *Masks Outrageous and Austere*. Bloomington, Indiana: Indiana University Press, 1992.

Time does not bring relief; you all have lied

Time does not bring relief; you all have lied
Who told me time would ease me of my pain!
I miss him in the weeping of the rain;
I want him at the shrinking of the tide;
The old snows melt from every mountain-side,
And last year's leaves are smoke in every lane;
But last year's bitter loving must remain
Heaped on my heart, and my old thoughts abide.
There are a hundred places where I fear
To go, —so with his memory they brim.
And entering with relief some quiet place
Where never fell his foot or shone his face
I say, "There is no memory of him here!"
And so stand stricken, so remembering him.

1917

Time does not bring relief; you all have lied is a poem of wrenching heterosexual love loss. It also reveals Millay's interest in the sonnet, a traditional form that experimental modernists such as Stein and Williams eschewed.

If I should learn, in some quite casual way

If I should learn, in some quite casual way,
That you were gone, not to return again—
Read from the back-page of a paper, say,
Held by a neighbor in a subway train,
How at the corner of this avenue
And such a street (so are the papers filled)
A hurrying man, who happened to be you,
At noon today had happened to be killed—
I should not cry aloud—I could not cry
Aloud, or wring my hands in such a place—
I should but watch the station lights rush by
With a more careful interest on my face;
Or raise my eyes and read with greater care
Where to store furs and how to treat the hair.

1917

The Little Ghost

I knew her for a little ghost
    That in my garden walked;
The wall is high—higher than most—
    And the green gate was locked.

And yet I did not think of that
    Till after she was gone—
I knew her by the broad white hat,
    All ruffled, she had on,

By the dear ruffles round her feet,
    By her small hands that hung
In their lace mitts, austere and sweet,
    Her gown's white folds among.

I watched to see if she would stay,
    What she would do—and oh!
She looked as if she liked the way
    I let my garden grow!

She bent above my favourite mint
    With conscious garden grace,
She smiled and smiled—there was no hint
    Of sadness in her face.

*   *   *

She held her gown on either side
   To let her slippers show,
And up the walk she went with pride,
   The way great ladies go.

And where the wall is built in new,
   And is of ivy bare,
She paused — then opened and passed through
   A gate that was once there.

1917

The title figure of "The Little Ghost" may suggest either a disruptive memory, an imaginary friend like Emily Dickinson's "Tim" (in *We don't cry - Tim and* I), or an awareness of same-sex affinities or desire.

Bluebeard

This door you might not open, and you did;
So enter now, and see for what slight thing
You are betrayed. . . . Here is no treasure hid,
No cauldron, no clear crystal mirroring
The sought-for Truth, no heads of women slain
For greed like yours, no writhings of distress;
But only what you see. . . . Look yet again:
An empty room, cobwebbed and comfortless.
Yet this alone out of my life I kept
Unto myself, lest any know me quite;
And you did so profane me when you crept
Unto the threshold of this room tonight
That I must never more behold your face.
This now is yours. I seek another place.

1917

"Bluebeard" is a fairy tale about a husband who murders his wives, then stores their bodies in a locked chamber. His last wife opens the door, discovering his secret and evading her own death. In Millay's revision of the legend, it is the wife who maintains a secret room, representing her privacy and independence. When her husband intrudes on it, she penalizes him by withdrawing.

First Fig

My candle burns at both ends;
   It will not last the night;
But ah, my foes, and oh, my friends —
   It gives a lovely light!

1920

"First Fig," a simple quatrain, made Millay famous. It became one of the most-often-quoted poems of the Jazz Age. It introduces the image of a sexually active and even exhibitionist female self, thus participating in the era's changing ideas about women.

I think I should have loved you presently

I think I should have loved you presently,
And given in earnest words I flung in jest;
And lifted honest eyes for you to see,
And caught your hand against my cheek and breast;
And all my pretty follies flung aside
That won you to me, and beneath your gaze,
Naked of reticence and shorn of pride,
Spread like a chart my little wicked ways.
I, that had been to you, had you remained,
But one more waking from a recurrent dream,
Cherish no less the certain stakes I gained,
And walk your memory's halls, austere, supreme,
A ghost in marble of a girl you knew
Who would have loved you in a day or two.

1920

Oh, think not I am faithful to a vow!

Oh, think not I am faithful to a vow!
Faithless am I save to love's self alone.
Were you not lovely I would leave you now:
After the feet of beauty fly my own.
Were you not still my hunger's rarest food,
And water ever to my wildest thirst,
I would desert you — think not but I would! —
And seek another as I sought you first.

But you are mobile as the veering air,
And all your charms more changeful than the tide,
Wherefore to be inconstant is no care:
I have but to continue on your side.
So wanton, light and false, my love, are you,
I am most faithless when I most am true.

1920

Millay may have written O, *think not* about her love relationship with the poet and activist Floyd Dell.

I shall forget you presently, my dear

I shall forget you presently, my dear,
So make the most of this, your little day,
Your little month, your little half a year,
Ere I forget, or die, or move away,
And we are done forever; by and by
I shall forget you, as I said, but now,
If you entreat me with your loveliest lie
I will protest you with my favourite vow.
I would indeed that love were longer-lived,
And oaths were not so brittle as they are,
But so it is, and nature has contrived
To struggle on without a break thus far, —
Whether or not we find what we are seeking
Is idle, biologically speaking.

1920

Only until this cigarette is ended

Only until this cigarette is ended,
A little moment at the end of all,
While on the floor the quiet ashes fall,
And in the firelight to a lance extended,
Bizarrely with the jazzing music blended,
The broken shadow dances on the wall,
I will permit my memory to recall
The vision of you, by all my dreams attended.

And then adieu,—farewell!—the dream is done.
Yours is a face of which I can forget
The colour and the features, every one,
The words not ever, and the smiles not yet;
But in your day this moment is the sun
Upon a hill, after the sun has set.

1920

Recuerdo

We were very tired, we were very merry—
We had gone back and forth all night on the ferry.
It was bare and bright, and smelled like a stable—
But we looked into a fire, we leaned across a table,
We lay on a hill-top underneath the moon;
And the whistles kept blowing, and the dawn came soon.

We were very tired, we were very merry—
We had gone back and forth all night on the ferry;
And you ate an apple, and I ate a pear,
From a dozen of each we had bought somewhere;
And the sky went wan, and the wind came cold,
And the sun rose dripping, a bucketful of gold.

We were very tired, we were very merry,
We had gone back and forth all night on the ferry.
We hailed, "Good morrow,[1] mother!" to a shawl-covered head,
And bought a morning paper, which neither of us read;
And she wept, "God bless you!" for the apples and pears,
And we gave her all our money but our subway fares.

1920

Millay based "Recuerdo" on her late-night perambulations through New York City with her fellow poet Salomón de la Selva (also included in this anthology). The Spanish word *recuerdo* means remembrance, recollection, or souvenir. Its use may reflect the native language of de la Selva, a citizen of Nicaragua. The poem makes a point of the liberated, cosmopolitan lifestyle of Jazz Age New York and the joys of heterosexual romance. But it also suggests, in the figure of the shawl-covered woman, the quiet suffering of those left behind by the economic boom.

1. Next day; morning.

Grown-up

Was it for this I uttered prayers,
And sobbed and cursed and kicked the stairs,
That now, domestic as a plate,
I should retire at half-past eight?

1920

Love is not blind. I see with single eye

Love is not blind. I see with single eye
Your ugliness and other women's grace.
I know the imperfection of your face, —
The eyes too wide apart, the brow too high
For beauty. Learned from earliest youth am I
In loveliness, and cannot so erase
Its letters from my mind, that I may trace
You faultless, I must love until I die.
More subtle is the sovereignty of love:
So am I caught that when I say, "Not fair,"
'Tis but as if I said, "Not here — not there —
Not risen — not writing letters." Well I know
What is this beauty men are babbling of;
I wonder only why they prize it so.

1923

I, being born a woman and distressed

I, being born a woman and distressed
By all the needs and notions of my kind,
Am urged by your propinquity to find
Your person fair, and feel a certain zest
To bear your body's weight upon my breast:
So subtly is the fume of life designed,
To clarify the pulse and cloud the mind,
And leave me once again undone, possessed.
Think not for this, however, the poor treason
Of my stout blood against my staggering brain,

I shall remember you with love, or season
My scorn with pity, — let me make it plain:
I find this frenzy insufficient reason
For conversation when we meet again.

1923

What lips my lips have kissed, and where, and why

What lips my lips have kissed, and where, and why,
I have forgotten, and what arms have lain
Under my head till morning; but the rain
Is full of ghosts tonight, that tap and sigh
Upon the glass and listen for reply,
And in my heart there stirs a quiet pain
For unremembered lads that not again
Will turn to me at midnight with a cry.
Thus in the winter stands the lonely tree,
Nor knows what birds have vanished one by one,
Yet knows its boughs more silent than before:
I only know that summer sang in me
A little while, that in me sings no more.

1923

To Inez Milholland

*Read in Washington, November eighteenth 1923, at the unveiling
Of a statue of three leaders in the cause of Equal Rights for Women*

Upon this marble bust that is not I
Lay the round, formal wreath that is not fame;
But in the forum of my silenced cry
Root ye the living tree whose sap is flame.
I, that was proud and valiant, am no more; —
Save as a dream that wanders wide and late,
Save as a wind that rattles the stout door,
Troubling the ashes in the sheltered grate.
The stone will perish; I shall be twice dust.
Only my standard on a taken hill
Can cheat the mildew and the red-brown rust

And make immortal my adventurous will.
Even now the silk is tugging at the staff:
Take up the song; forget the epitaph.

1923

Inez Milholland (1886–1916), like Millay, attended Vassar College, but she was suspended after organizing a women's suffrage meeting. In 1913 she led a women's rights demonstration in Washington, D.C., astride a white horse. A photograph of her became one of the movement's most memorable images. A socialist associated with *The Masses* journal, along with Helen Keller, Floyd Dell, Dorothy Day, Amy Lowell, and Carl Sandburg (the latter two included in this anthology), Milholland also opposed World War I on pacifist grounds. She collapsed while making a speech in Los Angeles and died a month later, the victim of untreated pernicious anemia. In 1923 Millay married Milholland's widower, a Dutch-American businessman named Eugen Boissevain.

Justice Denied in Massachusetts

Let us abandon then our gardens and go home
And sit in the sitting-room.
Shall the larkspur blossom or the corn grow under this cloud?
Sour to the fruitful seed
Is the cold earth under this cloud,
Fostering quack and weed, we have marched upon but cannot conquer;
We have bent the blades of our hoes against the stalks of them.

Let us go home, and sit in the sitting-room.
Not in our day
Shall the cloud go over and the sun rise as before,
Beneficent upon us
Out of the glittering bay,
And the warm winds be blown inward from the sea
Moving the blades of corn
With a peaceful sound.
Forlorn, forlorn,
Stands the blue hay-rack by the empty mow.
And the petals drop to the ground,
Leaving the tree unfruited.
The sun that warmed our stooping backs and withered the weed uprooted—
We shall not feel it again.
We shall die in darkness, and be buried in the rain.

What from the splendid dead
We have inherited—
Furrows sweet to the grain, and the weed subdued—
See now the slug and the mildew plunder.
Evil does overwhelm
The larkspur and the corn;
We have seen them go under.

Let us sit here, sit still,
Here in the sitting-room until we die;
At the step of Death on the walk, rise and go;
Leaving to our children's children this beautiful doorway,
And this elm,
And a blighted earth to till
With a broken hoe.

1928

"Justice Denied in Massachusetts" concerns the case of Nicola Sacco and Bartolomeo Vanzetti, anarchists who were executed for murder in Boston in 1927. They were convicted of robbery and murder but may well have been innocent. Many believed that the Italian immigrants were political and ethnic victims of the justice system. The governor refused to commute their sentence in spite of many appeals for clemency, including a personal plea by Millay. Female activists like Millay who were very involved in the case felt that Sacco and Vanzetti did not get a fair public hearing because they were poor immigrants and because their advocates were leftists and women.

To Elinor Wylie

(In answer to a question about her)

Oh, she was beautiful in every part!—
The auburn hair that bound the subtle brain;
The lovely mouth cut clear by wit and pain,
Uttering oaths and nonsense, uttering art
In casual speech and curving at the smart
On startled ears of excellence too plain
For early morning!—Obit. Death from strain;
The soaring mind outstripped the tethered heart.
Yet here was one who had no need to die
To be remembered. Every word she said,
The lively malice of the hazel eye

Scanning the thumb-nail close—oh, dazzling dead,
How like a comet through the darkening sky
You raced! . . . would your return were heralded.

1929

Millay wrote "To Elinor Wylie" for her friend and fellow poet (included in this anthology), who died on December 17, 1928, shortly before Millay was scheduled to give a public poetry reading at the Brooklyn Academy of Music. When Millay learned of Wylie's death, she paid tribute to her by telling the audience that a poet whom she regarded as greater than herself had died. She then proceeded to read Wylie's poems.

Love is not all: it is not meat nor drink

Love is not all: it is not meat nor drink
Nor slumber nor a roof against the rain;
Nor yet a floating spar to men that sink
And rise and sink and rise and sink again;
Love can not fill the thickened lung with breath,
Nor clean the blood, nor set the fractured bone;
Yet many a man is making friends with death
Even as I speak, for lack of love alone.
It well may be that in a difficult hour,
Pinned down by pain and moaning for release,
Or nagged by want past resolution's power,
I might be driven to sell your love for peace,
Or trade the memory of this night for food.
It well may be. I do not think I would.

1931

If in the years to come you should recall

If in the years to come you should recall,
When faint at heart or fallen on hungry days,
Or full of griefs and little if at all
From them distracted by delights or praise;
When failing powers or good opinion lost
Have bowed your neck, should you recall to mind
How of all men I honoured you the most,
Holding you noblest among mortal-kind:
Might not my love—although the curving blade
From whose wide mowing none may hope to hide,

Me long ago below the frosts had laid —
Restore you somewhat to your former pride?
Indeed I think this memory, even then,
Must raise you high among the run of men.

1931

Millay wrote *If in the years to come* to her husband.

And must I then, indeed, Pain, live with you

And must I then, indeed, Pain, live with you
All through my life? — sharing my fire, my bed,
Sharing — oh, worst of all things! — the same head? —
And, when I feed myself, feeding you, too?
So be it, then, if what seems true, is true:
Let us to dinner, comrade, and be fed: —
I cannot die till you yourself are dead,
And, with you living, I can live life through.
Yet have you done me harm, ungracious guest,
Spying upon my ardent offices
With frosty look; robbing my nights of rest;
And making harder things I did with ease.
You will die with me: but I shall, at best,
Forgive you with restraint, for deeds like these.

1942

And must I then, indeed, Pain, live with you exposes an interior fissure and an experience of psychic anguish that looks backward to the poetry of Emily Dickinson and forward to the work of Sylvia Plath and Anne Sexton.

DOROTHY PARKER
1893–1967

DOROTHY PARKER was known throughout America for her slashing wit as a poet, short story writer, and reviewer. She was also noted as a member of the celebrated Algonquin Round Table, a group of New York–based humorists and satirists. Such regulars as Robert Benchley, Alexander Woolcott, and Robert Sherwood and such frequent drop-ins as Edna Ferber, Tallulah Bankhead, and Harpo Marx gathered for lunch at a large round table in the dining room of Manhattan's Algonquin Hotel to take part in a daily ad lib interchange of wit.

Parker was born Dorothy Rothschild in West End, New Jersey—in her words, she was "a late unexpected arrival in a loveless family." Her mother died when she was four, and, after a childhood marked by bitterness and feelings of exclusion for her Jewish heritage, she left home at eighteen to seek her fortune in New York. In 1917, she was briefly married to the Hartford stockbroker Edwin Parker. The marriage did not last, but it left her, she later observed, with a "nice, clean name."

Working on the staff of such magazines as *Vanity Fair, Life,* and *The New Yorker,* Parker quickly achieved renown for a cynical brand of humor that was smartly in-the-know and seemed to embody the attitudes of the newly assertive and self-aware woman of the 1920s—though a note of insecurity always seemed to lurk in the background. Her first book of verse, *Enough Rope,* became an instant best-seller in 1926. It was followed by three successful sequels: *Sunset Gun* (1928), *Death and Taxes* (1931), and *Not So Deep as a Well* (1936). In the 1930s, Parker moved to Hollywood and with her second husband, Alan Campbell, wrote many screenplays, winning an Academy Award for her work with Campbell on the original *A Star Is Born* (1937). In the 1950s, Parker, a noted liberal, was brought before the House Un-American Activities Committee when she refused to implicate fellow writers. When she died in 1967, she left her entire estate to the NAACP. As a poet, Parker remains noted for light verse that incisively explored the foibles and ironies of love.

FURTHER READING

Marion Meade. *Dorothy Parker: What Fresh Hell Is This?* London: Heinemann, 1988.
Dorothy Parker. *The Portable Dorothy Parker.* New York: Viking, 1973.

General Review of the Sex Situation

Woman wants monogamy;
Man delights in novelty.
Love is a woman's moon and sun;
Man has other forms of fun.
Woman lives but in her lord;
Count to ten, and man is bored.
With this the gist and sum of it,
What earthly good can come of It.

1926

One Perfect Rose

A single flow'r he sent me, since we met.
  All tenderly his messenger he chose;
Deep-hearted, pure, with scented dew still wet—
  One perfect rose.

I knew the language of the floweret;
  "My fragile leaves," it said, "his heart enclose."
Love long has taken for his amulet
  One perfect rose.

Why is it no one ever sent me yet
  One perfect limousine, do you suppose?
Ah no, it's always just my luck to get
  One perfect rose.

1926

SALOMÓN DE LA SELVA
1893–1959

SALOMÓN DE LA SELVA was the first poet born in Latin America to publish a volume of English-language poetry in the United States. Born in Nicaragua to a physician's family, he came alone to the United States in 1904 or perhaps a few years later to live with a wealthy patron. After some college study, he taught Spanish and French at Williams College in Massachusetts. He became close friends with several U.S. and Latin American writers, including Edna St. Vincent Millay (who referred to him in her poem "Recuerdo," included in this anthology) and the great Nicaraguan poet Rubén Darío.

De la Selva published *Tropical Town and Other Poems* in 1918, when he was twenty-five. Such poems as "Tropical Town" and "Tropical Childhood" reflect his yearning for the beauty and culture of Nicaragua. "Deliverance," on the other hand, suggests his sense of being an outsider in the United States as well as his wish to fit in. Unhappy about the continued occupation of Nicaragua by the United States Marines, de la Selva moved to England soon after publication of his book, returning only briefly to New York and then spending the subsequent decades in Mexico, Nicaragua, Costa Rica, and Panama. During this period, he returned to his original Spanish for his poems and essays. A vocal opponent of both U.S. imperialism and Nicaraguan authoritarianism, he nonetheless accepted an ambassadorial position at the end of his life from the Nicaraguan dictator Anastasio Somoza. He died in Paris of a heart attack at the age of sixty-five. His poetry attests to the interconnectedness of the literature of the Americas.

FURTHER READING

Salomón de la Selva. *Antología mayor.* Ed. Julio Valle-Castillo. Managua: Editorial Nueva Nicaragua, 1993.
———. *Tropical Town and Other Poems.* Ed. Silvio Sirias. Houston: Arte Público Press, 1999.

Tropical Town

Blue, pink and yellow houses, and, afar,
The cemetery, where the green trees are.

Sometimes you see a hungry dog pass by,
And there are always buzzards in the sky.
Sometimes you hear the big cathedral bell,
A blindman rings it; and sometimes you hear
A rumbling ox-cart that brings wood to sell.
Else nothing ever breaks the ancient spell
That holds the town asleep, save, once a year,
The Easter festival . . .[1]

I come from there,
And when I tire of hoping, and despair
Is heavy over me, my thoughts go far,
Beyond that length of lazy street, to where
The lonely green trees and the white graves are.

1918

Like his friend Edna St. Vincent Millay, de la Selva resisted avant-garde modernist styles of innovation, fragmentation, and obscurity, preferring instead to breathe new life into traditional forms. This sonnet suggests both the poet's love of León, Nicaragua, his birthplace, and, in the image of the cemetery, his depression at being separated from it.

1. "The Easter festival, commonly known in Spanish as *Semana Santa,* solemnly commemorates the death and resurrection of Jesus with a week of ceremonies and processions" (Silvio Sirias).

Tropical Childhood

Toys I had, soldiers of lead and a sword of tin
And kites and tops; but I broke the silly sword
And melted the soldiers, and fast as a top may spin
And high as a kite may fly, I sent a word
Whirling and soaring: asking. I was so thin
And restless; scarcely spoke and hardly heard
What people gossiped, too busy with the din
Of that one answer that daily was deferred.

And so I grew, and one day saw the tears
That made my mother's cheek salty to kiss,
And looked behind me at the vanishing years,
And looked before me at the approaching tide,
And knew myself a turmoil of mysteries
And life a whirlwind rushing at my side.

1918

Deliverance

What am I doing, here, in New England?
All day long, till the end of the purple afternoon,
Watching to see, over the hills of New England,
The rising of the universal moon.

1918

E. E. CUMMINGS
1894–1962

E. E. CUMMINGS is most famous for his lively and playful experiments with poetic language. He made experimental modernism seem fun, accessible, and life-affirming. Cummings handled syntax and spelling with lighthearted adroitness, and he dropped initial capitals not only from the first lines of poems—as did Ezra Pound, William Carlos Williams, and Marianne Moore—but also from his name, sometimes signing his work "e. e. cummings." His work displays an irreverence for authority that is by turns playful and serious. He celebrates the joyful innocence of childhood; he consistently attacks the absurdity of war; and, in his erotic verse, he happily affirms the pleasures of love and sexuality.

Edward Estlin Cummings was born in Cambridge, Massachusetts. He attended Harvard, where his father taught sociology, receiving a B.A. in 1915 and an M.A. in 1916. During World War I, Cummings served as an ambulance driver in France, but French authorities placed him in a prison camp because he was friends with an American who had written a letter criticizing the war. He later recounted this experience in his memoir, *The Enormous Room* (1922). After the war, Cummings divided his time between Greenwich Village, where he became a friend of Williams and Moore, and Paris, where he met Pound and joined in the expatriate literary scene. His first book of poetry, *Tulips and Chimneys* (1923), a big success, was followed by *XLI Poems* and *&* (1925). In 1925 he won the Dial Award for service to American letters.

Cummings continued to publish steadily and successfully throughout his lifetime. He has sometimes been criticized for maintaining the popular style of eccentric experimentalism he initiated in his earliest books rather than expanding his stylistic and thematic horizons with the searching intensity of such contemporaries as Williams, Moore, and Pound. Yet Cummings's work remains widely read and admired today. Few poets have handled language with a similar talent for giving immediate joy. Moreover, Cummings remained a persistent champion of those endangered by superior force, as poems like "i sing of Olaf" reveal.

FURTHER READING

E. E. Cummings. *The Enormous Room.* 1922. Ed. Samuel Hynes. New York: Penguin, 1999.
———. *Selected Poems.* Ed. Richard Kennedy. New York: W. W. Norton, 1994.
Richard S. Kennedy. *Dreams in the Mirror: A Biography of E. E. Cummings.* 2nd ed. New York: W. W. Norton, 1994.
———. *E. E. Cummings Revisited.* New York: Twayne, 1994.
Rushworth M. Kidder. *E. E. Cummings: An Introduction to the Poetry.* New York: Columbia University Press, 1979.
Gary Lane. *I Am: A Study of E. E. Cummings' Poems.* Lawrence: University Press of Kansas, 1976.

All in green went my love riding

All in green went my love riding
on a great horse of gold
into the silver dawn.

four lean hounds crouched low and smiling
the merry deer ran before.

*   *   *

Fleeter be they than dappled dreams
the swift sweet deer
the red rare deer.

Four red roebuck at a white water
the cruel bugle sang before.

Horn at hip went my love riding
riding the echo down
into the silver dawn.

four lean hounds crouched low and smiling
the level meadows ran before.

Softer be they than slippered sleep
the lean lithe deer
the fleet flown deer.

Four fleet does at a gold valley
the famished arrows sang before.

Bow at belt went my love riding
riding the mountain down
into the silver dawn.

four lean hounds crouched low and smiling
the sheer peaks ran before.

Paler be they than daunting death
the sleek slim deer
the tall tense deer.

Four tall stags at a green mountain
the lucky hunter sang before.

All in green went my love riding
on a great horse of gold
into the silver dawn.

four lean hounds crouched low and smiling
my heart fell dead before.

1916

in Just-

in Just-
spring   when the world is mud-
luscious the little
lame balloonman

whistles   far   and wee

and eddieandbill come
running from marbles and
piracies and it's
spring

when the world is puddle-wonderful

the queer
old balloonman whistles
far   and   wee
and bettyandisbel come dancing

from hop-scotch and jump-rope and

it's
spring
and
    the

       goat-footed

balloonMan   whistles
far
and
wee

           1920

O sweet spontaneous

O sweet spontaneous
earth how often have
the
doting

*   *   *

                fingers of
purient philosophers pinched
and
poked

thee
,has the naughty thumb
of science prodded
thy

                beauty   .how
often have religions taken
thee upon their scraggy knees
squeezing and

buffeting thee that thou mightest conceive
gods
                (but
true

to the incomparable
couch of death thy
rhythmic
lover

                thou answerest

them only with

                    spring)

                                1920

Buffalo Bill 's

Buffalo Bill 's
defunct
            who used to
            ride a watersmooth-silver
                                    stallion
and break onetwothreefourfive pigeonsjustlikethat
                                        Jesus

*   *   *

he was a handsome man
                              and what i want to know is
how do you like your blueeyed boy
Mister Death

                                                            1920

the Cambridge ladies who live in furnished souls

the Cambridge ladies who live in furnished souls
are unbeautiful and have comfortable minds
(also,with the church's protestant blessings
daughters,unscented shapeless spirited)
they believe in Christ and Longfellow,[1]both dead,
are invariably interested in so many things—
at the present writing one still finds
delighted fingers knitting for the is it Poles?
perhaps.   While permanent faces coyly bandy
scandal of Mrs. N and Professor D
.... the Cambridge ladies do not care,above
Cambridge if sometimes in its box of
sky lavender and cornerless,the
moon rattles like a fragment of angry candy

                                                            1922

Cummings grew up in Cambridge, Massachusetts, where his father, a well-known Unitarian minister, taught at Harvard.

Poem,or Beauty Hurts Mr. Vinal

take it from me kiddo
believe me
my country,'tis of

you,land of the Cluett
Shirt Boston Garter and Spearmint

---

1. Henry Wadsworth Longfellow (1807–1882) was a popular nineteenth-century poet and a professor of modern languages at Harvard who was locally revered.

Girl With The Wrigley Eyes[1](of you
land of the Arrow Ide
and Earl &
Wilson
Collars)of you i
sing:land of Abraham Lincoln and Lydia E. Pinkham,[2]
land above all of Just Add Hot Water And Serve —
from every B.V.D.[3]

let freedom ring

amen.   i do however protest,anent[4] the un
-spontaneous and otherwise scented merde[5] which
greets one(Everywhere Why)as divine poesy per
that and this radically defunct periodical.[6]   i would

suggest that certain ideas gestures
rhymes,like Gillette Razor Blades
having been used and reused
to the mystical moment of dullness emphatically are
Not To Be Resharpened.[7] (Case in point

if we are to believe these gently O sweetly
melancholy trillers amid the thrillers
these crepuscular[8] violinists among my and your
skyscrapers — Helen & Cleopatra were Just Too Lovely,
The Snail's On The Thorn enter Morn and God's
In His andsoforth[9]

do you get me?)according
to such supposedly indigenous

1. Cluett Shirts, Boston Garters, and Wrigley's Spearmint Gum were popular trade names. Other trade names and advertising slogans appear throughout the poem, some of which are still current. Note that Cummings, who generally avoids the capitalization of initial letters, here uses initial capitals to denote these trade names and slogans.
2. Pinkham's was a patent medicine widely used for "female complaints." It had scant medicinal value but was 18 percent alcohol. Note the comic near-rhyme with Lincoln.
3. A still-active trade name for men's underwear. Note how "every B.V.D." rhymes comically with the actual words of "America": "from sea to shining sea."

4. Regarding, concerning.
5. Excrement (French).
6. Vinal edited the short-lived and artistically conservative poetry magazine *Voices*.
7. Old-fashioned straight razors were sharpened with a leather strop. Gillette's mass-produced safety razor blades were labeled "not to be resharpened."
8. Shadowy, dimly lit.
9. Parody of a song from Robert Browning's "Pippa Passes": "The lark's on the wing; / The snail's on the thorn; / God's in His heaven. / All's right with the world!"

throstles[10] Art is O World O Life
a formula:example,Turn Your Shirttails Into
Drawers and If It Isn't An Eastman It Isn't A
Kodak therefore my friends let
us now sing each and all fortissimo A-
mer

i

ca,I
love,
You. And there're a
hun-dred-mil-lion-oth-ers,like
all of you successfully if
delicately gelded(or spaded)[11]
gentlemen(and ladies)—pretty

littleliverpill-[12]
hearted-Nujolneeding-There's-A-Reason[13]
americans(who tensetendoned and with
upward vacant eyes,painfully
perpetually crouched,quivering,upon the
sternly allotted sandpile
—how silently
emit a tiny violetflavoured nuisance:Odor?

ono.[14]
comes out like a ribbon lies flat on the brush[15]

1922

In one of the earliest poems to make significant use of the language of popular culture, Cummings playfully yet persistently juxtaposes the trade names and slogans of American advertising with the patriotic language of the "Pledge of Allegiance" and Samuel F. Smith's song "America (My Country, 'Tis of Thee)." Mr. Harold Vinal was a traditional poet who served as the secretary of the Poetry Society of America—for Cummings, such archaic stylists wrote in a formulaic language much like the language of advertising. Such false poets, in his view, would find real beauty painful.

---

10. European thrush; hence, a nonnative singer.
11. Frequent mispronunciation of "spayed," the neutering of a female animal, as opposed to "gelding," the neutering of a male.
12. Carter's Little Liver Pills, a commercial laxative.
13. Nujol, another commercial laxative; There's

A-Reason: slogan for Post's Grape-Nuts cereal, which also promised to promote regularity.
14. Odor-ro-no was a toilet water sold as a deodorant.
15. Slogan for Colgate's Ribbon Dental Cream, one of the earliest tube toothpastes.

i sing of Olaf glad and big

i sing of Olaf glad and big
whose warmest heart recoiled at war:
a conscientious object-or[1]

his wellbelovéd colonel(trig[2]
westpointer most succinctly bred)
took erring Olaf soon in hand;
but—though an host of overjoyed
noncoms(first knocking on the head[3]
him)do through icy waters roll
that helplessness which others stroke
with brushes recently employed
anent[4] this muddy toiletbowl,
while kindred intellects evoke
allegiance per blunt instruments—
Olaf(being to all intents
a corpse and wanting any rag
upon what God unto him gave)
responds,without getting annoyed
"I will not kiss your fucking flag"

straightway the silver bird looked grave
(departing hurriedly to shave)

but—though all kinds of officers
(a yearning nation's blueeyed pride)
their passive prey did kick and curse
until for wear their clarion
voices and boots were much the worse,
and egged the firstclassprivates on
his rectum wickedly to tease
by means of skilfully applied
bayonets roasted hot with heat—
Olaf(upon what were once knees)
does almost ceaselessly repeat
"there is some shit I will not eat"

1. A person who refuses to serve in the military for religious or moral reasons.
2. Neat, trim, smart.
3. Noncoms: noncommissioned officers, such as sergeants.
4. Regarding, concerning (a legal term).

* * *

our president,being of which
assertions duly notified
threw the yellowsonofabitch
into a dungeon,where he died

Christ(of His mercy infinite)
i pray to see;and Olaf,too

preponderatingly because
unless statistics lie he was
more brave than me:more blond than you.

1931

CHARLES REZNIKOFF
1894–1976

CHARLES REZNIKOFF was an urban imagist, employing the economy and objectivity of experimental modernism while also providing the slice of life typical of realist and naturalist fiction. Working outside of the mainstream and away from the limelight, he produced some of the most humanly compelling poems of his time. Reznikoff's poetry celebrates in luminous detail the lives and feelings of the underprivileged, the immigrant, and the working poor. It unerringly locates the miraculous in the common, the paradisiacal in the ordinary, and the transforming moments of perception and grace embedded in even the most difficult lives. It testifies to the power of poetic language, stripped of affectation, to preserve the memory and confirm the value of such lives. Although Reznikoff's revelatory work has not yet received the wide audience it deserves, it has haunted the imagination of many devoted readers.

Reznikoff was born in Brooklyn, New York, the eldest child of Jewish immigrants who had escaped anti-Semitic pogroms in Russia. A brilliant student, he graduated high school several years early and entered the University of Missouri's school of journalism in 1910, at the age of sixteen, though he stayed for only a year. He received a law degree from New York University in 1915, at the age of twenty, and was admitted to the bar the following year. After practicing the law for only a few years, he quit in order "to use whatever mental energy I had for my writing." He took positions in sales and editing to support himself and to pay for the private printing of his first volumes of poetry. In 1930 he married Marie Syrkin (1899–1989), who was also to become a noted author. (Her historical study, *Blessed Is the Match*, tells of Jewish resistance during World War II.)

In 1931, Louis Zukofsky (also included in this anthology) published the "Objectivist" issue of *Poetry* magazine, which included Reznikoff's work and paid tribute to him as the progenitor of the objectivist movement, which prized the qualities of sincerity and objectivity. The newly formed Objectivist Press then published several of Reznikoff's books, none of which received extensive notice. In the Depression years, Reznikoff worked as an editor for the legal encyclopedia *Corpus Juris*, which provided him with material for a new style of documentary poetry, exemplified in "Testimony" and other works. He then spent several years as a script-reader and personal assistant in Hollywood, before returning to his beloved New York to work as a freelance writer and editor. In his later life, he continued to write poetry, while remaining in relative obscurity. One evening in 1976, at the age of eighty-one, he remarked to his wife, "You know I never made money but I have done everything that I most wanted to do." Then he had the heart attack that killed him.

In his long career, Reznikoff wrote many kinds of poems. His early, brief efforts, such as *The shopgirls leave their work*, employ imagistic language to evoke the sights and sounds of densely populated New York. These poems show the influence of Ezra Pound, William Carlos Williams, the Hebrew Bible, and Japanese haiku. Reznikoff said of them, "I believe in writing about the object itself, and I let the reader, or listener, draw his own conclusions." Related poems such as *She sat by the window opening into the airshaft* and *Four sailors on the bus, dressed in blue denim shirts* are permitted more space to round out their portraits. All of these New York poems, growing out of Reznikoff's daily walks through the city, present glimpses of working-class life observed in public spaces, factories, and tenement buildings. Focusing on moments of happiness and despair, they suggest the emotional and spiritual richness of lives often considered disparagingly, if they are considered at all. A powerful humanism illuminates these poems—and indeed all of Reznikoff's work.

In other poems, such as "Testimony" and *Holocaust*, Reznikoff innovated a new style of poetic composition, drawn from public records. These excruciatingly painful poems force the reader to acknowledge the injustices and to feel the agonies that form the woof and warp of human history. These documentary poems blur the distinctions between poetry and history, artistic making and material reality. They find a way to close the gap separating art from the lives people actually live.

In yet other poems, such as "Kaddish," Reznikoff explores his personal story and his family relations, diminishing the space between poetry and autobiography. These poems defy modernist dicta advocating impersonality, anonymity, and masks. In their introspection and domesticity, they look forward to the resurgence of personal poetry in a later generation of poets that included Robert Lowell and Sylvia Plath. Finally, poems such as "Te Deum" and *If the ship you are traveling on is wrecked* plumb Reznikoff's sense of spirituality, strongly informed by political egalitarianism and Jewish tradition. Reznikoff's spiritual work is suffused by tragic awareness. He knows that the "ship you are traveling on" is likely to be "wrecked." But his spirit is also marked by abiding hopefulness. He believes that "a plank may come floating your way," which "you may ride wave after wave." As he writes in "Epilogue," he feels "blessed / in the light of the sun and at the sight of the world / daily."

FURTHER READING

Charles Bernstein. "Reznikoff's Nearness." In *My Way: Speeches and Poems*, 197–228. Chicago: University of Chicago Press, 1999.

Michael Davidson. *Ghostlier Demarcations: Modern Poetry and the Material Word*. Berkeley: University of California Press, 1997.

Stephen Fredman. *A Menorah for Athena: Charles Reznikoff and the Jewish Dilemmas of Objectivist Poetry*. Chicago: University of Chicago Press, 2001.

Milton Hindus. *Charles Reznikoff: A Critical Essay*. Santa Barbara, Calif.: Black Sparrow Press, 1977.

Ranen Omer-Sherman. *Diaspora and Zionism in Jewish American Literature: Lazarus, Syrkin, Reznikoff, Roth*. Hanover, N.H.: University Press of New England, 2002.

Charles Reznikoff. *Holocaust*. Los Angeles: Black Sparrow Press, 1975.

——. *Poems, 1918–1975: The Complete Poems*. Ed. Seamus Cooney. Santa Rosa, Calif.: Black Sparrow Press, 1977.

——. *Selected Letters, 1917–1976*. Ed. Milton Hindus. Santa Barbara, Calif.: Black Sparrow Press, 1997.

On Brooklyn Bridge I saw a man drop dead

On Brooklyn Bridge I saw a man drop dead.
It meant no more than if he were a sparrow.
Above us rose Manhattan;
below, the river spread to meet sea and sky.

1918

On Brooklyn Bridge I saw a man drop dead and the succeeding six poems originally appeared in Reznikoff's first self-published volumes, *Rhythms* and *Rhythms II*. The poems apply imagistic techniques of conciseness, particularity, and objectivity to the cityscape rather than to a natural scene. Some of the poems, like this one and the one following, emphasize the bleakness of urban experience. Others, such as *My work done, I lean on the window-sill*, locate moments of beauty and resilience.

The shopgirls leave their work

The shopgirls leave their work
quietly.

Machines are still, tables and chairs
darken.

The silent rounds of mice and roaches begin.

1918

The shopgirls leave their work evokes the low-paying, labor-intensive world of garment and millinery piecework, staffed largely by immigrant women and their daughters. Compare this poem to *In the shop, she, her mother, and grandmother* and *The girls outshout the machines* (below).

Romance

The troopers are riding, are riding by,
the troopers are riding to kill and die
that a clean flag may cleanly fly.

They touch the dust in their homes no more,
they are clean of the dirt of shop and store,
and they ride out clean to war.

1918

My work done, I lean on the window-sill

My work done, I lean on the window-sill,
watching the dripping trees.
The rain is over, the wet pavement shines.
From the bare twigs
rows of drops like shining buds are hanging.

1918

I have not even been in the fields

I have not even been in the fields,
nor lain my fill in the soft loam,
and here you come blowing, cold wind.

1919

In the shop, she, her mother, and grandmother

In the shop, she, her mother, and grandmother,
thinking at times of women at windows in still streets,
of women reading, a glow on resting hands.

1919

The girls outshout the machines

The girls outshout the machines
and she strains for their words, blushing.

Soon she, too, will speak
their speech glibly.

1919

They have built red factories along Lake Michigan

They have built red factories along Lake Michigan,
and the purple refuse coils like congers[1] in the green depths.

1920

She sat by the window opening into the airshaft

She sat by the window opening into the airshaft,
and looked across the parapet[1]
at the new moon.

She would have taken the hairpins out of her carefully coiled hair,
and thrown herself on the bed in tears;
but he was coming and her mouth had to be pinned into a smile.
If he would have her, she would marry whatever he was.

A knock. She lit the gas and opened her door.
Her aunt and the man—skin loose under his eyes, the face slashed with wrinkles.
"Come in," she said as gently as she could and smiled.

1920

---

1. Large eels that can reach a length of ten feet.   1. Wall or barrier.

Still much to read, but too late

Still much to read, but too late.
I turn out the light.

The leaves of the tree are green beside the street-lamp;
the wind hardly blows and the tree makes no noise.

Tomorrow up early,
the crowded street-car, the factory.

1920

It had long been dark, though still an hour before supper-time

It had long been dark, though still an hour before supper-time.
The boy stood at the window behind the curtain.
The street under the black sky was bluish white with snow.
Across the street, where the lot sloped to the pavement,
boys and girls were going down on sleds.
The boys were after him because he was a Jew.

At last his father and mother slept. He got up and dressed.
In the hall he took his sled and went out on tiptoe.
No one was in the street. The slide was worn smooth and slippery — just right.
He laid himself on the sled and shot away. He went down only twice.
He stood knee-deep in snow:
no one was in the street, the windows were darkened;
those near the street-lamps were ashine, but the rooms inside were dark;
on the street were long shadows of clods of snow.
He took his sled and went back into the house.

1921

It had long been dark, though still an hour before supper-time concerns the experience of ethnic prejudice, specifically anti-Semitism. Stephen Fredman comments: "The poem manages to convey, through the skillful use of understatement and narrative jumping, a range of compelling emotions: loneliness, furtiveness, fear, desire, and exhilaration. In the social landscape portrayed by the poem, 'it had long been dark, though still an hour before supper-time,' for the wintry darkness of social exclusion has stained the entire day. At the end of the poem . . . the windows are dark. They reflect the light of the street lamps, but they reveal nothing of the beings who peer malevolently out of them during the day. For the Jewish boy, the mentality of anti-Semitism is opaque; he cannot penetrate the consciousness that sees him as Other." Fredman also sees the poem as an allegory of Reznikoff's position within the poetic community. Because "the boys were after him because he was a Jew," Reznikoff wrote poetry in the shadows, published mainly in Jewish magazines, and was forced to print his books at his own expense.

Permit me to warn you

Permit me to warn you
against this automobile rushing to embrace you
with outstretched fender.

1934

Testimony

1. The Sinking

The company had advertised for men to unload a steamer across the river. It was
    six o'clock in the morning, snowing and still dark.
There was a crowd looking for work on the dock;
and all the while men hurried to the dock.
The man at the wheel
kept the bow of the launch[1]
against the dock —
the engine running slowly;
and the men kept jumping from dock to deck,
jostling each other,
and crowding into the cabin.

Eighty or ninety men were in the cabin as the launch pulled away.
There were no lights in the cabin, and no room to turn — whoever was sitting
    down could not get up, and whoever had his hand up could not get it down,
as the launch ran in the darkness
through the ice,
ice cracking
against the launch
bumping and scraping
against the launch,
banging up against it,

---

1. A large utility boat.

until it struck a solid cake of ice,
rolled to one side, and slowly
came back to an even keel.

The men began to feel water running against their feet as if from a hose. "Cap,"[2]
    shouted one, "the boat is taking water! Put your rubbers on, boys!"
The man at the wheel turned.
"Shut up!" he said.
The men began to shout,
ankle-deep in water.
The man at the wheel turned
with his flashlight:
everybody was turning and pushing against each other;
those near the windows
were trying to break them,
in spite of the wire mesh
in the glass; those who had been near the door
were now in the river,
reaching for the cakes of ice,
their hands slipping off and
reaching for the cakes of ice.

2. *The Job*

Amelia was just fourteen and out of the orphan asylum; at her first job—in the
    bindery, and yes sir, yes ma'am, oh, so anxious to please.
She stood at the table, her blonde hair hanging about her shoulders, "knocking
    up" for Mary and Sadie, the stitchers
("knocking up" is counting books and stacking them in piles to be taken away).
There were twenty wire-stitching machines on the floor, worked by a shaft that
    ran under the table;
as each stitcher put her work through the machine,
she threw it on the table. The books were piling up fast
and some slid to the floor
(the forelady had said, Keep the work off the floor!);
and Amelia stooped to pick up the books—
three or four had fallen under the table
between the boards nailed against the legs.
She felt her hair caught gently;

2. Captain. Rubbers: overshoes.

put her hand up and felt the shaft going round and round
and her hair caught on it, wound and winding around it,
until the scalp was jerked from her head,
and the blood was coming down all over her face and waist.

3. *The Immigrants*

They had been married in Italy in May.
Her husband had been in America before,
but she had never been in this country;
neither had her husband's cousin.
The three of them had landed in New York City
that morning, and had taken a train north.
As they left the station, she carried a bundle, her husband a little trunk,
        and his cousin a satchel.
It was almost midnight and freezing cold.
Her husband had a paper on which an address was written.
He asked a man near the station the way,
but the man shook his head and walked on.

The saloon was still open, and her husband went inside.
The saloon-keeper knew the man they were looking for,
but he had moved.
Three men were sitting at a table, playing cards and drinking beer:
one was very short, the other dark
with curly hair and a cap on his head,
and the third was tall. That was Long John.

The saloon-keeper's wife poured her a little glass of anisette,
and the saloon-keeper put up two glasses of beer
for her husband and his cousin; and they warmed themselves at the stove.
The saloon-keeper said to the dark fellow with curly hair,
"Take them to my brother's—maybe he knows where the man lives." When
        they were gone,
Long John stood up and said,
"I think I'll get myself a little fresh air," and finished his beer.
Long John and the little fellow followed the others, overtook them,
and went along. Long John rang the door-bell, knocked and kicked at the door
until the saloon-keeper's brother—in his underwear—
opened the door, and all went in together.
The saloon-keeper's brother said to Madelina, "If you and your husband and
        the cousin
want to stay here tonight—

for going where the man you are looking for lives will take a little time—
you can stay in my place tonight. It's so late!
I'll put a mattress for the three of you in the kitchen."
Long John answered, "They will get there quickly—
we will go with them!" And the six went out,
Madelina, her husband and his cousin, Long John and the dark fellow with
     curly hair and the silent little fellow.
They had left the streets of the city
and were on the railroad tracks.
Long John went on ahead and the other two
who had been sitting with him in the saloon
walked behind. Madelina carried the bundle, her husband the little trunk,
     and his cousin the satchel.
She said at last, "When will we get there?"
Long John answered, "In four or five minutes.
You have walked so far, can't you walk a little longer?"
At last he stopped. "This is the place," he said.
Madelina looked about and saw only the railroad tracks
and the ground covered with snow.
"Is this the place? But I don't see any houses."
"They are only three or four steps further on."
Madelina turned to her husband. "Give them some money—
they have earned it." "No," said Long John,
"we don't want any money." And all at once
he had a pistol in his hand and was shooting.
Her husband started to run,
crying out, and holding his hands to the wound in his belly.
Madelina ran after him, until Long John caught her by the neck
and held her. Then the little fellow came up
and they took her back to where her husband's cousin was lying on the ground
dead, beside the satchel, the bundle, and the little trunk.

Long John said, "Don't cry! You've got to be my wife.
Don't think of your husband any more.
You should be glad to be my wife."
"Yes," said Madelina, "yes, yes."
He took the wedding ring from her finger,
but the rings on her other hand would not come off;
and they walked on in silence.
Long John told the other two to go ahead;
turning to Madelina,
he pushed her down on the snow.

*   *   *

Afterwards, they began to walk again,
and came up to the others; and all walked on until dawn.
In the morning, Long John saw the necklace.
"Give me your gold," he said. She took the necklace off and gave it to him.
They came, at last, to a car on a siding
in which was a store for the workers on the railroad,
and went up the little ladder.
The storekeeper knew Long John. He brought soap and water,
and Long John made Madelina wash her hands
and slipped the rings off.
The storekeeper called Long John aside and asked who she was.
"A whore," said Long John.
"You must go away," the storekeeper answered.
"If a foreman should come around, he'd kick if he saw you.
Warm yourselves a while—I'll make some coffee;
but then you must go away."
They were all silent until the coffee was ready.
Long John and his companions drank it,
but Madelina did not want any. She sat weeping.
Long John brought her a cup of coffee.
"Drink it," he said. "Never mind, never mind!"

4

Outside the night was cold, the snow was deep
on sill and sidewalk; but in our kitchen
it was bright and warm.
I smelt the damp clean clothes
as my mother lifted them from the basket,
the pungent smell of melting wax
as she rubbed it on the iron,
and the good lasting smell of meat and potatoes
in the black pot that simmered on the stove.
The stove was so hot it was turning red.
My mother lifted the lid of the pot
to stir the roast with a long wooden spoon:
Father would not be home for another hour.
I tugged at her skirts. Tell me a story!

Once upon a time (the best beginning!)
there was a rich woman, a baroness, and a poor woman, a beggar.

The poor woman came every day to beg and every day
the rich woman gave her a loaf of bread
until the rich woman was tired of it.
I will put poison in the next loaf, she thought,
to be rid of her.
The beggar woman thanked the baroness for that loaf
and went to her hut,
but, as she was going through the fields,
she met the rich woman's son coming out of the forest.
"Hello, hello, beggar woman!" said the young baron,
"I have been away for three days hunting
and am very hungry.
I know you are coming from my mother's
and that she has given you a loaf of bread;
let me have it—she will give you another."

"Gladly, gladly," said the beggar woman,
and, without knowing it was poisoned, gave him the loaf.
But, as he went on, he thought, I am nearly home—
I will wait.
You may be sure that his mother was glad to see him,
and she told the maids to bring a cup of wine
and make his supper—quickly, quickly!
"I met the beggar woman," he said,
"and was so hungry I asked for the loaf you gave her."
"Did you eat it, my son?" the baroness whispered.
"No, I knew you had something better for me
than this dry bread."
She threw it right into the fire,
and every day, after that, gave the beggar woman a loaf
and never again tried to poison her.
So, my son, if you try to harm others,
you may only harm yourself.

And, Mother, if you are a beggar, sooner or later,
there is poison in your bread.

1941

As a writer and editor at *Corpus Juris* (1930–34), Reznikoff worked every day with legal cases. He began to think that the cases amounted to a social history of the United States, "not from the standpoint of an individual, as in diaries, nor merely from the angle of the unusual, as in newspapers, but from every standpoint—as many standpoints as were provided by the witnesses themselves." Instead of the history celebrated in textbooks, the cases revealed narratives of suffering and injustice. Reznikoff used this material in multiple texts: first in a series of prose vignettes called *Testimony* (1934); then in this relatively short, four-part poem also called "Testimony"; and finally in two book-length poems called *Testimony: The United States, 1885–1890: Recitative* (1965) and *Testimony: The United States, 1891–1900: Recitative* (1968). Michael Davidson argues that in these texts, Reznikoff provides "a critical reappraisal of a unified national story," "a material record of diverse constituencies," and a poetic model that replaces "aesthetic language" with "social speech." It is noteworthy that in the fourth part of "Testimony," Reznikoff departs from his legal cases to recount a story told to him as a child by his mother, appending his own ironic moral to contest his mother's.

Kaddish

1

In her last sickness, my mother took my hand in hers
tightly: for the first time I knew
how calloused a hand it was, and how soft was mine.

2

Day after day you vomit the green sap of your life
and, wiping your lips with a paper napkin,
smile at me; and I smile back.
But, sometimes, as I talk calmly to others
I find that I have sighed — irrelevantly.

3

I pay my visit and, when the little we have to say is said,
go about my business and pleasures;
but you are lying these many weeks abed.
The sun comes out; the clouds are gone; the sky is blue;
the stars arise; the moon shines; and the sun shines anew
for me; but you are dying,
wiping the tears from your eyes —
secretly that I may go about my business and pleasures
while the sun shines and the stars rise.

4

The wind that had been blowing yesterday has fallen;
now it is cold. The sun is shining behind the grove of trees
bare of every leaf (the trees no longer brown

as in autumn, but grayish—dead wood until the spring);
and in the withered grass the brown oak leaves are lying, gray with frost.
"I was so sick but now—I think—am better."
Your voice, strangely deep, trembles;
your skin is ashen—
you seem a mother of us both, long dead.

5

The wind is crowding the waves down the river
to add their silver to the shimmering west.
The great work you did seems trifling now,
but you are tired. It is pleasant to close your eyes.
What is a street-light doing
so far from any street? That was the sun,
and now there is only darkness.

6

Head sunken, eyes closed,
face pallid,
the bruised lips parted;
breathing heavily,
as if you had been climbing flights of stairs,
another flight of stairs—
and the heavy breathing
stopped.
The nurse came into the room silently
at the silence,
and felt your pulse, and put your hand
beneath the covers,
and drew the covers to your chin,
and put a screen about your bed.
That was all:
you were dead.

7

Her heavy braids, the long hair of which she had been proud,
cut off, the undertaker's rouge
on her cheeks and lips,
and her cheerful greeting
silenced.

8

My mother leaned above me
as when I was a child.
What had she come to tell me
from the grave?
Helpless,
I looked at her anguish;
lifted my hand to stroke her cheek,
touched it and woke.

9

Stele[1]
Not, as you were lying, a basin beside your head
into which you kept vomiting; nor, as that afternoon,
when you followed the doctor slowly with hardly the strength to stand,
small and shrunken in your black coat;
but, as you half turned to me, before you went through the swinging door,
and lifted your hand, your face solemn and calm.

10

We looked at the light[2] burning slowly before your picture
and looked away;
we thought of you as we talked but could not bring ourselves to speak—
to strangers who do not care, yes,
but not among ourselves.

11

I know you do not mind
(if you mind at all)
that I do not pray for you
or burn a light
on the day of your death:
we do not need these trifles
between us—
prayers and words and lights.

1941

1. A carved stone slab or pillar, generally deco-   2. Of the mourner's (or yartzeit) candle.
rated with a relief sculpture on one face; used
as a monument by ancient Egyptians, Persians,
Greeks, and Mayans.

The Kaddish is the traditional Jewish mourner's prayer, recited by the bereaved in the synagogue and at home. It praises God's "great name" without mentioning death or offering explicit solace for loss. Reznikoff's "Kaddish," in contrast, dwells on the death of his beloved mother, Sarah Reznikoff, who is viewed as being above the ritual "prayers and words and lights." In a later generation, the identically titled "Kaddish" of Reznikoff's poetic inheritor, Allen Ginsberg, would also focus on the life and death of the poet's mother.

As I was wandering with my unhappy thoughts

As I was wandering with my unhappy thoughts,
I looked and saw
that I had come into a sunny place
familiar and yet strange.
"Where am I?" I asked a stranger. "Paradise."
"Can this be Paradise?" I asked surprised,
for there were motor-cars and factories.
"It is," he answered. "This is the sun that shone on Adam once;
the very wind that blew upon him, too."

1959

The speaker of *As I was wandering with my unhappy thoughts* discovers that even the most familiar spaces can become sacred. Ranen Omer-Sherman comments, "Reznikoff draws on the Hebrew Bible to imaginatively promote the attunement of the individual to his or her environment, suggesting that Paradise is wherever one lives fully in the present."

Te Deum

Not because of victories
I sing,
having none,
but for the common sunshine,
the breeze,
the largess[1] of the spring.

Not for victory
but for the day's work done

---

1. Generous bestowal of gifts.

as well as I was able;
not for a seat upon the dais[2]
but at the common table.

1959

The title, "Te Deum," means "thou God," the opening words of a Christian liturgical chant in praise of God, frequently used in celebratory musical settings. Milton Hindus remarks that "the contrast between the Latin (hymn) title and the meaning of the rest of the poem is striking," adding that what makes the poem memorable is "the 'message,' the solid democratic sense of it." Note also the poem's subtle rhymes (victories/breeze; sing/spring; none/done; able/table), alliterations (sing/sunshine/spring/seat), and wordplay (deum/day's/dais).

Epilogue

Blessed
in the light of the sun and at the sight of the world
daily,
and in all the delights of the senses and the mind;
in my eyesight blurred as it is
and my knowledge slight though it is
and my life brief though it was.

1959

Four sailors on the bus, dressed in blue denim shirts

Four sailors on the bus, dressed in blue denim shirts,
ill-fitting jackets,
shoddy trousers that do not match the jackets:
one a Negro, another has some Negro blood,
the other two white—Spanish or Portuguese.
The mulatto or octoroon is the eldest—
a handsome fellow in the thirties.
The others chatter away, laugh and talk,
but he says little
although they keep looking at him to say something.
He speaks once, briefly, dryly—
and the three burst out laughing with delight.

2. Raised platform for seats of honor.

*   *   *

One of the white men gives him a packet of photographs
to look at—snapshots;
and the other white man reaches for it.
The mulatto stops him with a gesture.
You would think the mulatto would slap his hand
or push him away
but he merely lifts his own hands
and keeps them lifted for a moment—
a moment in a dance.
Then when he has glanced through the pictures,
instead of giving them back or to his companion
who has snatched at them,
he offers them to a young woman seated nearby.

She is a stranger but her eyes
caught by the flicker of the photographs—
as anybody's would—
had strayed to them. And this time his gesture
has the grace of a man plucking a spray of flowers
from a bush he is passing
and giving them to the girl beside him.

1959

If the ship you are traveling on is wrecked

If the ship you are traveling on is wrecked,
a plank may come floating your way;
and on it you may ride wave after wave
until you walk again on dry land.

1969

If the ship you are traveling on is wrecked and the poem following are collages based on the
Talmud. The Talmud is an ancient book of Jewish laws, customs, and commentary that
holds a place in Jewish sacred tradition second only to the Hebrew Bible.

If you cannot look at the sun

If you cannot look at the sun—
only one of God's ministers—
how can you see God Himself?

1969

Free Verse

Not like flowers in the city
in neat rows or in circles
but like dandelions
scattered on a lawn.

1975

FROM *Holocaust*

Jewish women were lined up by German troops in charge of the territory,
told to undress,
and they stood in their undergarments.
An officer, looking at the row of women—stopped to look at a young woman—
tall, with long braided hair, and wonderful eyes.
He kept looking at her, then smiled and said,
"Take a step forward."
Dazed—as they all were—she did not move and he said again: "Take a step forward!
Don't you want to live?"
She took that step
and then he said: "What a pity to bury such beauty in the earth.
Go!
But don't look backwards.
There is the street to the boulevard.
Follow that."
She hesitated
and then began to walk as told.
The other women looked at her—
some no doubt with envy—
as she walked slowly, step by step.
And the officer took out his revolver
and shot her in the back.

✦   ✦   ✦

The soldier doing the shooting was sitting at the narrow end of the pit,
his feet dangling into it;
smoking a cigarette,
the machine-gun on his knees.

As each truck came, those who had been on it—
Jewish men, women, and children of all ages—
had to undress

and put their clothing at fixed places,
sorted in great piles—
shoes, outer clothing, and underwear.

The S.S. man at the pit
shouted to his comrade
and he counted off twenty, now completely naked,
and told them to go down the steps cut in the clay wall of the pit:
here they were to climb over the heads of the dead
to where the soldier pointed.
As they went towards the pit, a slender young woman with black hair,
passing a German civilian who was watching,
pointed to herself and said, "I am twenty-three."
An old woman with white hair
was holding a child about a year old
in her arms, singing to it and tickling it,
and the child was cooing with delight;
and a father was holding the hand of his little son—
—the child about to burst into tears—
speaking to the child softly, stroking his head
and pointing to the sky.

Bodies were soon heaped in the large pit,
lying on top of each other,
heads still to be seen and blood running over their shoulders;
but some were still moving,
lifting arms and turning heads.

1975

Written late in Reznikoff's life and published the year before his death, *Holocaust* documents the torture and murder of six million European Jews by the Nazis during World War II. Like "Testimony," this poem conflates poetry and moral witness. Reznikoff explained that he based the poem "on a United States government publication, *Trials of the Criminals before the Nuremberg Military Tribunal*, and the records of the [Adolph] Eichmann trial in Jerusalem." He added this explanation of Nazi methods of shooting people: "There were different techniques: some commanders lined up those to be shot and had them standing or kneeling on the edge of a pit, facing it; while others had those to be shot standing with their backs to the pit; and still others had them go into the pit while still alive and these were shot in the neck while standing or kneeling. This was the most efficient, for of those shot above the pit all did not fall into it and then the soldiers had the trouble of pushing them in; but if they were shot in the pit the next group to be shot could come at once and fall on the bleeding corpses. But whatever the method of execution, it was, to quote an official report, 'always honorable and done in a military manner.'"

GENEVIEVE TAGGARD
1894–1948

THE POLITICAL AND ECONOMIC turmoil of the 1930s may have produced as much activist poetry as the abolitionist movement of the mid-nineteenth century, and Genevieve Taggard stood at its center. Born in Waitsburg, Washington, she was raised primarily in Honolulu, Hawaii, by missionary parents. After graduating from the University of California, Berkeley, in 1919 and mingling in the socialist-literary circles of San Francisco, Taggard moved to New York City and helped found and edit the magazine *The Measure: A Journal of Verse*. She also published poetry in radical magazines such as the *Liberator* and *Masses* as well as little magazines and mass-circulation magazines, and she began collecting her work in volumes of poetry. Taggard committed herself to many social justice causes such as labor rights, civil rights, and women's issues, but by 1929 she had withdrawn from the public arena and begun teaching at women's colleges.

Her husband, the writer Robert L. Wolf, had a mental breakdown in 1931, and the couple divorced. Taggard then married Kenneth Durant, who worked for Tass, the news agency of the Soviet Union. Taggard rejoined leftist politics in the 1930s. Because Tass employed several Spanish Civil War veterans, she knew such poets as Edwin Rolfe well. She continued her political advocacy through her poetry until the end of her life in 1948, writing passionately about motherhood as well as labor strife and racial discrimination.

FURTHER READING

Julia Lisella, coordinator. Special feature on Genevieve Taggard. *How2* 2.1 (Spring 2003).
Genevieve Taggard. *Complete Poems, 1919–1938*. New York: Harper & Row, 1938.

Everyday Alchemy

Men go to women mutely for their peace;
And they, who lack it most, create it when
They make, because they must, loving their men,
A solace for sad bosom-bended heads. There
Is all the meager peace men get—no otherwhere;
No mountain space, no tree with placid leaves,
Or heavy gloom beneath a young girl's hair,
No sound of valley bell on autumn air

Or room made home with doves along the eaves,
Ever holds peace, like this, poured by poor women
Out of their heart's poverty, for worn men.

1919

With Child

Now I am slow and placid, fond of sun,
Like a sleek beast, or a worn one,
No slim and languid girl — not glad
With the windy trip I once had,
But velvet-footed, musing of my own,
Torpid, mellow, stupid as a stone.

You cleft me with your beauty's pulse, and now
Your pulse has taken body. Care not how
The old grace goes, how heavy I am grown,
Big with loneliness, how you alone
Ponder our love. Touch my feet and feel
How earth tingles, teeming at my heel!
Earth's urge, not mine, — my little death, not hers;
And the pure beauty yearns and stirs.

It does not heed our ecstasies, it turns
With secrets of its own, its own concerns,
Toward a windy world of its own, toward stark
And solitary places. In the dark
Defiant even now, it tugs and moans
To be untangled from these mother's bones.

1921

"With Child" was written the same year as Taggard's daughter, Marcia, was born.

To the Veterans of the Abraham Lincoln Brigade

Say of them
They knew no Spanish
At first, and nothing of the arts of war
At first,
          how to shoot, how to attack, how to retreat

How to kill, how to meet killing
At first.
Say they kept the air blue
Grousing and griping,
Arid words and harsh faces. Say
They were young;
The haggard in a trench, the dead on the olive slope
All young. And the thin, the ill and the shattered,
Sightless, in hospitals, all young.

Say of them they were young, there was much they did not know,
They were human. Say it all; it is true. Now say
When the eminent, the great, the easy, the old,
And the men on the make
Were busy bickering and selling,
Betraying, conniving, transacting, splitting hairs,
Writing bad articles, signing bad papers,
Passing bad bills,
Bribing, blackmailing,
Whimpering, meaching, garroting,—they
Knew and acted
                    understood and died.

Or if they did not die came home to peace
That is not peace.
                    Say of them
They are no longer young, they never learned
The arts, the stealth of peace, this peace, the tricks of fear;
And what they knew, they know.
And what they dared, they dare.

                                        1941

Taggard wrote this poem after veterans of the brigade, who had fought valiantly on the republican side as volunteers in the Spanish Civil War (1936–39), were questioned about their loyalty to the United States by the House Un-American Activities Committee.

JEAN TOOMER
1894–1967

JEAN TOOMER wrote one of the classic books of American literature when he penned *Cane* (1923). The volume alternates lyric poems with prose pieces. This remarkable, transgeneric collage combines features typical of both the Harlem Renaissance and the modernist movement, which were distinct but overlapping enterprises in the 1920s. Like other Harlem Renaissance texts by Claude McKay, Angelina Weld Grimké, and Countee Cullen, the poems of *Cane* employ traditional forms for new ends. They reveal black characters and culture in depth, while exposing a background of racial disparity. At the same time, *Cane* as a volume responds to many avant-garde imperatives. It is as experimental, fragmentary, imagistic, and boundary-crossing as William Carlos Williams's *Spring and All*. Finally, in its resonant humanism, *Cane* anticipates Toomer's eventual career as a religious searcher. Beyond exploring the landscape of African-American culture, the book meditates on some of the abiding dilemmas of the human spirit.

Toomer was born to racially mixed parents; his father left soon after Jean's birth, and his mother died when he was fifteen, after which he lived with grandparents. He grew up in Washington, D.C., and New Rochelle, New York, in a variety of black and white neighborhoods. Given his light-skinned appearance and his mixed African-American, European-American, and Native-American ancestry, he was able to live alternately as a black person and a white person. After graduation from high school, he attended five different colleges, including the University of Wisconsin and the City College of New York, but never received a degree. He began to write experimental poetry that was indebted to imagism, urbanism, and East Asian poetic forms. Critic Robert Jones calls this Toomer's "aesthetic period," an example of which is "Skyline," an impression of the New York skyline. During this period, Toomer also protested against fallacious racial stereotypes in a way that predicts his later career. Consider, for example, the following vignette:

> In Y. Don's laundry
> A Chinese baby fell
> And cried as any other.

In 1921 Toomer accepted a short-term appointment as superintendent of an African-American agricultural and industrial school in Sparta, Georgia. The experience inaugurated his brief but crucial black awareness period. Out of these four months came the first section of *Cane*: poetry and prose that portrayed the social, psychological, material, and spiritual lives of poor black farmworkers. In poems such as "Reapers," "Cotton Song," and "Song of the Son," the speaker bears witness to the difficult and often heroic struggles of an oppressed people whose culture and community sustain them amid adversity. In the second section of the volume, poems such as "Seventh Avenue" and "Her Lips Are Copper Wire" suggest the excitements and difficulties of life in African-American districts of Northern cities. Taken together, the texts provide a brilliant composite of African-American lifestyles and vocabularies—rural and urban, traditional and up to the moment.

Soon after *Cane* appeared in 1923, Toomer abandoned his racial subject matter and commenced a spiritual quest that would occupy him for the rest of his days. He had found that when living in the South and writing about black folk, "a deep part of my nature . . . sprang suddenly to life." Now, however, another aspect of his nature became primary: the wisdom seeker/speaker. He later commented, "Why people have expected me to write a second and a third and a fourth book like *Cane* is one of the queer misunderstandings of my life." Instead, he became, for a time, a follower of the European mystic George Gurdjieff, who advocated a personal transformation beyond ordinary life into a heightened state of awareness. Toomer proselytized for the movement in Harlem and Chicago, writing poems that reflected its philosophy. But in the mid-1930s, Toomer—now married, with a young daughter, and living in rural Pennsylvania—turned from Gurdjieff to the Quaker Society of Friends, a Christian denomination stressing pacificism, spiritual community, and direct communication with God. In 1940 he formally converted. For the next fifteen years Toomer wrote religious treatises, autobiographies, and such poems as "Our Growing Day," most of which remained unpublished until after his death.

Cane remains a masterpiece of both African-American culture and modernist structure. Toomer's subsequent attempt to move beyond racial categories seemed unrealistically idealistic to many of his contemporaries, though it may prove prophetic. His best writing illuminates social realities as it creates new forms and vocabularies for American poetry.

FURTHER READING

Robert B. Jones. *Jean Toomer and the Prison-House of Thought: A Phenomenology of the Spirit.* Amherst: University of Massachusetts Press, 1993.
Cynthia Earl Kerman and Richard Eldridge. *The Lives of Jean Toomer: A Hunger for Wholeness.* Baton Rouge: Louisiana State University Press, 1997.
Nellie McKay. *Jean Toomer, Artist.* Chapel Hill: University of North Carolina Press, 1984.
Jean Toomer. *Cane.* 1923; reprint, ed. Darwin T. Turner, New York: W. W. Norton, 1988.
———. *Collected Poems.* Ed. Robert B. Jones and Margery Toomer Latimer. Introduction by Robert B. Jones. Chapel Hill: University of North Carolina Press, 1988.
———. *The Wayward and the Seeking.* Ed. Darwin T. Turner. Washington, D.C.: Howard University Press, 1980.

Skyline

A cow-hoof imprint
pressed against the under-asphalt of
Fifth Avenue, sustains it

the osseous[1] teat of an inverted cow
spurts *s k y s c r a p e r s*
against a cloud
racing to
dusk,
and
it
sprays
    in
       num
         er
       ab
      le
blunt peaks against
the milky-way.

1921

"Skyline" uses imagism, visual pattern, and the witty metaphor of an upside-down cow being milked to evoke the New York skyline seen from Fifth Avenue at both dusk and night.

Reapers

Black reapers with the sound of steel on stones
Are sharpening scythes. I see them place the hones[1]
In their hip-pockets as a thing that's done,
And start their silent swinging, one by one.
Black horses drive a mower through the weeds,
And there, a field rat, startled, squealing bleeds.
His belly close to ground. I see the blade,
Blood-stained, continue cutting weeds and shade.

1923

"Reapers" is the first of eight poems (ending with "Her Lips Are Copper Wire") taken from Toomer's collage text, *Cane.* All the poems were written in 1921–22. Some were published

1. Composed of or resembling bone.   1. Whetstones used for sharpening blades.

in magazines slightly before their appearance in *Cane* in 1923. The first six poems, beginning with "Reapers," describe the world of African-American farmworkers in northern Georgia. The last two poems suggest the charged atmosphere of a black urban district in the Northeast. In "Reapers," an injured or killed rat suggests an analogy to the lives of the farmworkers themselves. The poem employs a very traditional form (iambic pentameter couplets) to describe a new subject matter.

November Cotton Flower

Boll-weevil's coming, and the winter's cold,
Made cotton-stalks look rusty, seasons old,
And cotton, scarce as any southern snow,
Was vanishing; the branch, so pinched and slow,
Failed in its function as the autumn rake;
Drouth fighting soil had caused the soil to take
All water from the streams; dead birds were found
In wells a hundred feet below the ground—
Such was the season when the flower bloomed.
Old folks were startled, and it soon assumed
Significance. Superstition saw
Something it had never seen before:
Brown eyes that loved without a trace of fear,
Beauty so sudden for that time of year.

1923

"November Cotton Flower," a sonnet, uses the unexpected appearance of natural beauty in a desolate scene as an extended metaphor for a psychologically and racially fearless woman.

Cotton Song

Come, brother, come. Lets lift it;
Come now, hewit! roll away!
Shackles fall upon the Judgment Day
But lets not wait for it.

God's body's got a soul,
Bodies like to roll the soul,
Cant blame God if we dont roll,
Come, brother, roll, roll!

*   *   *

Cotton bales are the fleecy way
Weary sinner's bare feet trod,
Softly, softly to the throne of God,
"We aint agwine t wait until th Judgment Day!

Nassur; nassur,
Hump.
Eoho, eoho, roll away!
We aint agwine t wait until th Judgment Day!"

God's body's got a soul,
Bodies like to roll the soul,
Cant blame God if we dont roll,
Come, brother, roll, roll!

1923

A work song, "Cotton Song" echoes the religious faith and rebellious undertone of such slave spirituals as "Roll, Jordan, Roll" and "Many Thousand Gone" (included in the first volume of this anthology). The workers perform backbreaking labor as they sing of freedom. The poem contains a passage of embedded quotation (lines 12–16) spoken in Southern black vernacular.

Song of the Son

Pour O pour that parting soul in song,
O pour it in the sawdust glow of night,
Into the velvet pine-smoke air to-night,
And let the valley carry it along.
And let the valley carry it along.

O land and soil, red soil and sweet-gum tree,
So scant of grass, so profligate of pines,
Now just before an epoch's sun declines
Thy son, in time, I have returned to thee,
Thy son, I have in time returned to thee.

In time, for though the sun is setting on
A song-lit race of slaves, it has not set;
Though late, O soil, it is not too late yet
To catch thy plaintive soul, leaving, soon gone,
Leaving, to catch thy plaintive soul soon gone.

* * *

O Negro slaves, dark purple ripened plums,
Squeezed, and bursting in the pine-wood air,
Passing, before they stripped the old tree bare
One plum was saved for me, one seed becomes

An everlasting song, a singing tree,
Caroling softly souls of slavery,
What they were, and what they are to me,
Caroling softly souls of slavery.

1922

The speaker, a visitor from the North but a spiritual "son" of the black South, observes people who are no longer literally "slaves" but whose lives are similar to those that slaves lived. He finds inspiration in songs and lives that he assumes are about to pass from the scene. Robert Jones comments that "Song of the Son" and the following poem, "Georgia Dusk," are "swan songs for the passing Afro-American folk spirit."

Georgia Dusk

The sky, lazily disdaining to pursue
    The setting sun, too indolent to hold
    A lengthened tournament for flashing gold,
Passively darkens for night's barbecue.

A feast of moon and men and barking hounds,
    An orgy for some genius of the South
    With blood-hot eyes and cane-lipped scented mouth,
Surprised in making folk-songs from soul sounds.

The sawmill blows its whistle, buzz-saws stop,
    And silence breaks the bud of knoll and hill,
    Soft settling pollen where plowed lands fulfill
Their early promise of a bumper crop.

Smoke from the pyramidal sawdust pile
    Curls up, blue ghosts of trees, tarrying low
    Where only chips and stumps are left to show
The solid proof of former domicile.

* * *

Meanwhile, the men, with vestiges of pomp,
    Race memories of king and caravan,
    High-priests, an ostrich,[1] and a juju-man,
Go singing through the footpaths of the swamp.

Their voices rise . . the pine trees are guitars,
    Strumming, pine-needles fall like sheets of rain . .
    Their voices rise . . the chorus of the cane
Is caroling a vesper to the stars . .

O singers, resinous and soft your songs
    Above the sacred whisper of the pines,
    Give virgin lips to cornfield concubines,
Bring dreams of Christ to dusky cane-lipped throngs.

                          1922

"Georgia Dusk" describes workers "making folk-songs from soul sounds." Their spiritual store includes "race memories" of African religion as well as "dreams of Christ." Robert Jones suggests that the smoke rising from the sawdust pile symbolizes the passing of an agricultural era, replaced by one of industry.

Portrait in Georgia

Hair — braided chestnut,
    Coiled like a lyncher's rope
Eyes — fagots,[1]
Lips — old scars, or the first red blisters,
Breath — the last sweet scent of cane,
And her slim body, white as the ash
    Of black flesh after flame.

                  1923

Seventh Street

Money burns the pocket, pocket hurts,
Bootleggers[1] in silken shirts,
Ballooned, zooming Cadillacs,
Whizzing, whizzing down the street-car tracks.

1. The flightless ostrich, the world's largest living bird, is native to Africa. Juju-man: juju is a West African charm or amulet thought to have magical powers. It is also the name of a West African musical form notable for percussive rhythms and natural sounds.

1. Bundle of sticks, i.e., of the sort used to burn a lynched person.

1. Those who deal illegally in alcohol. They thrived during Prohibition in the 1920s.

*   *   *

Seventh Street is a bastard of Prohibition and the War.[2] A crude-boned, soft-skinned wedge of nigger life breathing its loafer air, jazz songs and love, thrusting unconscious rhythms, black reddish blood into the white and whitewashed wood of Washington. Stale soggy wood of Washington. Wedges rust in soggy wood . . . Split it! In two! Again! Shred it! . . the sun. Wedges are brilliant in the sun; ribbons of wet wood dry and blow away. Black reddish blood. Pouring for crude-boned soft-skinned life, who set you flowing? Blood suckers of the War would spin in a frenzy of dizziness if they drank your blood. Prohibition would put a stop to it. Who set you flowing? White and whitewash disappear in blood. Who set you flowing? Flowing down the smooth asphalt of Seventh Street, in shanties, brick office buildings, theaters, drug stores, restaurants, and cabarets? Eddying on the corners? Swirling like a blood-red smoke up where the buzzards fly in heaven? God would not dare to suck black red blood. A Nigger God! He would duck his head in shame and call for the Judgment Day. Who set you flowing?

> Money burns the pocket, pocket hurts,
> Bootleggers in silken shirts,
> Ballooned, zooming Cadillacs,
> Whizzing, whizzing down the street-car tracks.

1922

"Seventh Street" frames an impressionistic prose poem within a traditionally rhyming refrain. Set in Washington, D.C., the poem contains startling images of speed, noise, criminality, money, and blood, all reflecting an edgy and heterogeneous urbanity.

Her Lips Are Copper Wire

> whisper of yellow globes
> gleaming on lamp-posts that sway
> like bootleg licker drinkers[1] in the fog
>
> and let your breath be moist against me
> like bright beads on yellow globes
>
> telephone the power-house
> that the main wires are insulate

---

2. World War I.
1. Those who get drunk on illegally distributed liquor during Prohibition.

*   *   *

(her words play softly up and down
dewy corridors of billboards)

then with your tongue remove the tape
and press your lips to mine
till they are incandescent

1923

The woman addressed in "Her Lips Are Copper Wires" has an electrical charge to her kiss. The poem's references to lamps and telephone wires play ironically off the natural imagery of English Renaissance love poems such as Thomas Campion's "There Is a Garden in Her Face." They also play more complexly off Shakespeare's sonnet "My mistress' eyes are nothing like the sun." Whereas Shakespeare compares his beloved's hair to "black wires" instead of the conventional "golden wires," Toomer compares his beloved's lips to "copper wire," which conducts electricity. The poem praises the woman's sexual energy rather than her passive beauty.

Our Growing Day

Awaken us to the long day of the spirit
To the sun more radiant than the eyes can see;
Bring us low, if we are falsely raised
   in conceit
Bathe us in bright humility
Sweeten us, if we are filled with bitterness
   and prejudice,
Plow us, if we are hard and encrusted,
Plow us deeply and make us ready to grow.

May the seeds of men, planted in the fertile
but dark earth, spring up and grow
   splendidly
Sending the issue of their growing upward
Towards the kingdom and outward
   to their brothers.

1988

This prayerful poem represents Toomer's final, Quaker period.

DADA

Dada was an international artistic and literary movement centered primarily in Zurich, Switzerland; Berlin, Hanover, and Cologne, Germany; Paris, France; Barcelona, Spain; and New York City. The word *dada* (French for "hobbyhorse") was chosen from a dictionary at random, suggesting the movement's interest in spontaneity and chance. Dada represents one extreme point of rebellion, innovation, and intensity within experimental modernism. In Dadaist texts, notions of tradition, linear rationality, and formal coherence are questioned and discarded. Instead, the texts are composed of a playful, improvised sequence of words. The poems blend iconoclasm with a venturesome exploration of the verbal resources of language itself. They emphasize outrageous juxtapositions, metaphors, puns, paradoxes, double meanings, wit, and nonsense. Appalled by the slaughter of World War I and opposed to bourgeois thinking, the Dadaists produced artworks that were freed from logical constraints and that challenged conventional notions of art and reality. Influenced by cubism in the visual arts, Dada had a wide range of associations and influences, including the work of Mina Loy, Gertrude Stein, and William Carlos Williams (all included in this anthology) as well as such later movements as surrealism, abstract expressionism, concrete poetry, conceptual art, and Beat poetry. It even appears in jazz and popular music—for example, in the song "Ja Da" (included in the "Jazz and Musical Theater Lyrics" entry in this anthology).

In New York, Dada flourished at the "291" gallery of the photographer Alfred Stieglitz and in the artistic circle of Walter Arensberg (1878–1954). Arensberg and his wife, Mary, were wealthy art collectors who purchased most of the works of the avant-garde French artist Marcel Duchamp (best known for his painting *Nude Descending a Staircase* and his ready-made *The Fountain*, which was simply a mass-produced porcelain urinal presented as an art object). In addition to supporting avant-garde art, Arensberg wrote Dadaist poems. He described such poems as being representative of "all that is young, alive, sporting." He thought that they should appeal to "all those who live without formula." One of his poems is included below.

Another leading Dadaist figure was the Baroness Else von Freytag-Loringhoven (1874–1927), referred to in Pound's *Cantos* as a woman living by "the principle of non-acquiescence." Mary Anne Caws describes her as an outlandish Dada character walking the New York streets, "the author of texts as bizarre as her outfits." She was once charged with assaulting her friend William Carlos Williams after having stalked him. Born on the Polish-German border under a different, less regal name, the abused child of a stonemason, she arrived in the United States in 1909, having already lived a life filled with name changes, job changes, husbands, and lovers. In 1913 she assumed her title of baroness through marriage to a man who soon left her. She remained in New York, working in menial jobs, modeling for artists, and committing petty crimes. She arrived at parties wearing a birdcage or a bustle with a taillight. She produced art objects out of garbage, and she improvised poems out of the words and images that chanced her way. In 1923 she returned to Europe, her ticket bought with money Williams gave her. In 1927 she died in Paris when someone, perhaps a former lover, snuck into her room and turned on the gas. Two of the baroness's poems appear below.

FURTHER READING

Mary Anne Caws. "Dada." In *Encyclopedia of American Poetry: The Twentieth Century*, ed. Eric L. Haralson, 169–70. Chicago: Fitzroy-Dearborn, 2001.

Irene Gammel. *Baroness Else*. Cambridge, Mass.: MIT Press, 2002.

Robert Motherwell, ed. *The Dada Painters and Poets: An Anthology*. Boston: G. K. Hall, 1981.

Francis Naumann. *New York Dada, 1915–23*. New York: Whitney/Abrams, 1994.

Ing

Walter Arensberg

Ing? Is it possible to mean *ing*?
Suppose
    for the termination in *g*
        a disoriented
        series
    of simple fractures
        in sleep
          Soporific
    has accordingly a value for soap
        so present to
        sew pieces.
        And *p* says: Peace is.
And suppose the *i*
    to be big in ing
    As Beginning.
        Then Ing is to ing
as aloud
    accompanied by times
and the meaning is a possibility
        of ralsis.

1917

"Ing" displays Arensberg's exuberant and iconoclastic wordplay, appearing in such forms as puns ("mean *ing*"), phonic repetitions ("Soporific," "soap," "so present"), homophones ("pieces," "peace is"), and invented words ("ralsis").

Appalling Heart

Else von Freytag-Loringhoven

City stir— —wind on eardrum— —
dancewind : herbstained — —
flowerstained— —silken— —rustling— —
tripping— —swishing— —frolicking— —
courtesing— —careening— —brushing— —
flowing— —lying down— —bending— —
teasing— —kissing : treearms— —grass— —
limbs— —lips.
City stir on eardrum— —.
In night lonely
peers— —:
moon— —riding !
pale— —with beauty aghast— —
too exalted to share !
in space blue— —rides she away from mine chest— —
illumined strangely— —
appalling sister !

Herbstained— —flowerstained— —
shellscented— —seafaring— —
foresthunting— —junglewise— —
desert gazing— —
rides heart from chest— —
lashing with beauty— —
afleet— —
across chimney— —
tinfoil river— —
to meet— —
another's dark heart— —

Bless mine feet !

1920

The kaleidoscopic text of "Appalling Heart" suggests a scene both urban and natural, and an interior life marked by psychic mobility and erotic desire.

Is It?

Else von Freytag-Loringhoven

It is— —is it— — ?
heart white sheet !
kiss it
flame beat !
in chest midst
print teeth
bite— —　　— —　　— —
this green
ponderous night.

1920

SONGS OF DISPLACEMENT, MIGRATION, AND WORK II

THE ORAL AND WRITTEN traditions of diverse communities offered fresh voices, images, and poetic forms from the nation's cultural margins on the subjects of displacement, migration, and work. Several communities found the United States inhospitable, especially the detainees at Angel Island in San Francisco, who left behind important poetry about their experiences. Such communities as the Chicanos filled their lyrics with stories about their struggles here. Poets from other groups—Asian Indians, Koreans, and Filipinos—often reflected upon their homelands. The poetry selections included here articulate not only the visions and lives of these specific communities but also the daily experiences of all immigrants arriving and settling in the nation at this time.

CORRIDOS

The corrido, a Chicano ballad or folk song, continued to be a crucial poetic form during the period of modernism. The corridos included here were written primarily between World War I and World War II and provide a unique insight into the experiences of Chicanos in the United States during this tumultuous time in American race relations and history. Race relations were incredibly conflicted, and this tension is mentioned in nearly all of the corridos. The corridos often functioned as a form of cultural self-defense against a blending of two antagonistic cultures. Many Latinos wanted to retain the humanistic values of their cultures in the face of an overpowering Americanization.

FURTHER READING

Maria Herrera-Sobek. *Northward Bound: The Mexican Immigrant Experience in Ballad and Song.* Bloomington: University of Indiana Press, 1993.

José E. Limón. *Mexican Ballads, Chicano Poems.* Berkeley: University of California Press, 1992.

Américo Paredes. *A Texas-Mexican Cancionero.* Urbana: University of Illinois Press, 1976.

Registro de 1918

Les cayeron sus tarjetas
al domicilio a cada uno,
se verificó el registro
del veintiuno al treinta y uno.

Adiós Laredo lucido
con sus torres y campanas,
pero nunca olvidaremos
a tus lindas mexicanas.

Ya nos llevan a pelear
a unas tierras muy lejanas,
y nos llevan a pelear
con las tropas alemanas.

Ya nos llevan a pelear
a distintas direcciones,
y nos llevan a pelear
con diferentes naciones.

¡Qué lejos es la travesía
sobre las olas del mar!
grande fuera mi alegría
si llegaré yo a triunfar.

Cuando andaba yo peleando
de toditos me acordaba
y más de mi pobre madre
que por mí tanto lloraba.

[TRANS.] Registration of 1918

The cards were sent
to each one's address,
the registration took place
from the twenty-first to the thirty-first.

Farewell sparkling Laredo[1]
with your towers and bells,
but we will never forget
your beautiful Mexican women.

Now they're taking us to fight
to faraway places
and they're taking us to fight
against the German forces.

Now they're taking us to fight
in different directions
and they're taking us to fight
against different nations.

How far is the journey
over the sea waves!
great would be my joy
if I could be victorious.

When I was in the battlefield
I would remember everyone,
especially my poor mother
who cried so much for me.

1. A town in Texas.

*   *   *

Adiós mis queridos padres
y la joven a quien yo amo,
ya cuando estemos en Francia
un suspiro les mandamos.

Adiós Laredo lucido
con sus torres y campanas,
pero nunca olvidaremos
a tus lindas mexicanas.

*   *   *

Farewell my beloved parents
and the young woman I love,
when we get to France
we'll send you a sigh.

Farewell sparkling Laredo
with your towers and bells,
but we will never forget
your beautiful Mexican women.

n.d.

"Registro de 1918" details the impact of World War I on a Chicano called to serve his country.

Nuevo Corrido de Laredo

I

Este es el mero corrido
de ese Laredo mentado,
cantando quiero decirles
por lo que aquí hemos pasado.

Este puerto de Laredo
es un puerto muy lucido,
donde se encuentra la mata
de esos hombres decididos.

Este pueblo de Laredo
es un pueblo muy mentado.
Los agentes de la ley
andan siempre con cuidado.

En este rancho de Brune
varias cosas han pasado,
contrabandistas y guardias
sus vidas las han jugado.

Los malos ésos de Laredo
nadie los puede negar,
se cambian bala por bala
y no los hacen rajar.

*   *   *

[TRANS.] New Corrido of Laredo

I

This is the corrido about the
celebrated town of Laredo,
I want to sing to you
about what goes on here.

This port of Laredo
is a very brilliant port
where you'll find the cradle
of those determined men.

This town of Laredo
is a very well-known town.
The officers of the law
always watch their step.

On the Brune ranch,
various incidents have occurred,
where smugglers and officers of the law
have gambled with their lives.

The bad men, those from Laredo,
no one can defy them,
they exchange bullet for bullet
and they don't give up.

*   *   *

Si va al juego yo le encargo,
con tu dinero se trata,
se tiene que poner chango
porque el que pierde arrebata.

Como dice cierto dicho:
"El périco siempre es verde,
gallo bucho nunca canta,
y la raza nunca pierde."
(se repite)

II

No solamente en hazañas
porque será criminal
decir que no se lucieron
en esta guerra mundial.

Aquí hay muchos mexicanos
que en esta guerra pelearon,
volvieron condecorados
por el valor que mostraron.

Unos también gasados,
otros les faltan las piernas,
pos que otras cosas sacaban
peleando causas ajenas.

No solamente en el frente
demostraron ser ufanos,
por eso en Laredo, Tejas,
aprecian los mexicanos.

El que conoce a Laredo
nunca lo puede negar
que en el puerto Río Bravo
hay mucho donde gozar.

El que le guste pasearse
goza de toda alegría,
que pase a Nuevo Laredo
y gozará noche y día.

* * *

If you go gambling, I warn you,
it is with your money that they deal,
one must be careful
because he who loses may get dangerous.

According to a certain saying:
"Parrots are always green,
the rooster never crows,
and the race never loses."
(repeat)

II

It would be criminal
were anyone to say
that your sons didn't shine
in the great world war.

There are many Mexicans here
who fought in the war,
they returned decorated
for the courage they demonstrated.

Some of them were gassed,
others are missing legs,
and many other things befell them
fighting foreign causes.

Not only at the front
did they demonstrate their valor,
for that reason in Laredo, Texas,
Mexicans are appreciated.

Anyone familiar with Laredo
could never deny
that in the port of Rio Bravo
there is much to enjoy.

One who appreciates going out
will find much joy,
so come to Nuevo Laredo
and you'll find pleasure, night and day.

* * *

Ya con ésta me despido,
meciéndome un anisado,
aquí terminé el corrido
de ese Laredo afamado.

Now with this I take my leave,
stirring a glass of anisette,
for here ends the corrido
of the celebrated town of Laredo.

n.d.

"Nuevo Corrido de Laredo" addresses the valor and heroism of Chicanos who fought for the United States in World War I. According to the ballad, Laredo has become a better place to live as a result of the veterans who reside there.

La Discriminación

Juan Gaytán

Con tristeza y sin remedio
voy a decir lo que siento
y sin referirme a nadie
para no hacer argumento,
solo culpo mi destino
con profundo sentimiento.

Nomás tan solo en pensar
en las discriminaciones
que sufrimos los Latinos
en ranchos y poblaciones,
nos distinguen como ovejas
algunos anglosajones.

Yo no me refiero a nadie
para no hacer argumento,
pertenezco a Estados Unidos
de seguro cien por ciento,
nadie me quita el derecho
pero guardo un sentimiento.

Yo nací en el estado de Tejas
y he crecido con afanes,
trabajando por la vida
y enriqueciendo rufianes
he sufrido los desprecios
de tejanos alemanes.

*   *   *

[TRANS.] Discrimination

It is with sadness and hopelessness
that I'm going to say what I feel,
I won't mention any names
so there won't be any arguments,
I can only blame my destiny
with a profound sense of grief.

Just to think about
the discrimination
that we Latins suffer
in the fields and towns,
we are looked upon as sheep
by some Anglo-Saxons.

I won't mention any names
so there won't be any arguments,
I belong to the United States
without a doubt, a hundred percent,
no one can take away that right
but nevertheless, I carry a grudge.

I was born in the state of Texas
and growing up has been a struggle,
while working to survive
I have enriched scoundrels,
I have suffered the disdain
of German Texans.

*   *   *

No me duele lo que soy
ni lamento mi desgracia
soy latino americano
y sin distinción de raza
yo peleé por igualdad
y la santa democracia.

¡O Diosito de mi vida!
de nosotros no te alejas,
y el señor Don Harry Truman
que oiga siempre nuestras quejas
como el caso de Longoria
en el estado de Tejas.

En mi despedida ruego
que me otorguen el perdón,
que en lo que digo no miento
y no distingo nación
que en todos los continentes
hay la discriminación.

I don't feel sorry about myself
nor do I pity my fate
I am Latin American
and regardless of race
I've fought for equality
and blessed democracy.

Oh, dear God of my life
you never abandon us
and Mr. Harry Truman
may he always hear our complaints
like the Longoria case[1]
in the state of Texas.

I hope in this my farewell
that you will excuse me
but what I say is true;
I won't single out any nation
since in all the continents
there is discrimination.

n.d.

The speaker of "La Discriminación" realizes that racism is a foe that every country must fight. The corrido suggests that the racism exhibited by Germany is prevalent in all countries, especially the United States.

Corrido de "Gregorio Cortez"

I

En el condado de El Carmen
miren lo que ha sucedido,
murió el *Sherife* Mayor
quedando Román herido.

Otro día por la mañana
cuando la gente llegó,
unos a los otros dicen
no saben quien lo mató.

[TRANS.] Corrido of "Gregorio Cortez"

I

In Carmen County
Look what happened
The sheriff died, leaving
Román wounded

The following morning
When people arrived
Some said to others
They don't know who killed him

1. Felix Longoria was killed in action during World War II. His wife encountered numerous instances of racism while she tried to organize his funeral. Then Senator Lyndon B. Johnson, who later became president of the United States, intervened with others to help her. Longoria was buried with full honors in Arlington National Cemetery.

*   *   *

Se anduvieron informando
como tres horas después,
supieron que el malhechor
era Gregorio Cortez.

Ya insortaron a Cortez
por toditito el estado
que vivo o muerto se aprehenda
porque a varios ha matado.

Decía Gregorio Cortez
con su pistola en la mano,
—No siento haberlo matado
al que siento es a mi hermano.—

Decía Gregorio Cortez
con su alma muy encendida,
—No siento haberlo matado
la defensa es permitida.—

Venían los americanos
que por el viento volaban,
porque se iban a ganar
tres mil pesos que les daban.

Siguió con rumbo a Gonzáles,
varios *sherifes* lo vieron,
no lo quisieron seguir
porque le tuvieron miedo.

Venían los perros *jaunes*
venían sobre la huella
Pero alcanzar a Cortez
era alcanzar a una estrella.

Decía Gregorio Cortez
—¿Pa' qué se valen de planes?
Si no pueden agarrar
ni con esos perros *jaunes*.—

*   *   *

They were investigating
And three hours later
They found out the wrongdoer
Was Gregorio Cortez.

Cortez was wanted
Throughout the state
Alive or dead apprehended
For he has killed several.

Said Gregorio Cortez
With his pistol in his hand,
"I do not regret killing him,
I regret my brother's death."

Said Gregorio Cortez
With his pistol in his hand,
"I'm not sorry I killed him
Self-defense is permitted."

Americans came
They flew like the wind
Because they were going to win
The three-thousand-peso reward.

They continued toward Gonzales
Several sheriffs saw him
They did not want to continue
Because they were afraid of him

Came the hound dogs
They came on his trail
But to reach Cortez
Was to reach a star.

Gregorio Cortez said,
"What's the use of plans
If you can't catch me
Even with those hound dogs."

II

Decían los americanos
—Si lo alcanzamos ¿qué le hacemos?
Si le entramos por derecho
muy poquitos volveremos.—

En el redondel del rancho
lo alcanzaron a rodear,
Poquitos más de trescientos
y allí les brincó el corral.

Allá por el Encinal
según lo a qui se dice
Se agarraron a balazos
y les mató otro *sherife*.

Decía Gregorio Cortez
con su pistola en la mano,
—No corran, rinches cobardes
con un solo mexicano.—

Giró con rumbo a Laredo
sin ninguna timidez,
—¡Síganme rinches cobardes,
yo soy Gregorio Cortez!—

Gregorio le dice a Juan
en el rancho del Ciprés,
—Platícame qué hay de nuevo,
yo soy Gregorio Cortez.—

Gregorio le dice a Juan,
—Muy pronto lo vas a ver,
anda háblale a los *sherifes*
que me vengan a aprehender.—

Cuando llegan los *sherifes*
Gregorio se presentó,
—Por la buena si me llevan
porque de otro modo no.—

    *   *   *

II

The Americans said,
"If we see him what shall we do to him,
If we face him head on
Very few will return."

In the ranch corral
They managed to surround him.
A little more than three hundred men
There he gave them the slip.

There around Encinal[1]
From all they say
They had a shoot-out
And he killed another sheriff.

Gregorio Cortez said,
With his pistol in his hand,
"Don't run, you cowardly Rangers,
I am Gregorio Cortez."

He turned toward Laredo
without any fear:
"Follow me, you cowardly Rangers,
I am Gregorio Cortez!"

Gregorio says to Juan
at the ranch of the Cypress:
"Tell me, what's new?
I am Gregorio Cortez."

Gregorio says to Juan,
"Very soon you will see,
Go and talk to the sheriffs
They should come and arrest me."

When the sheriffs came
Gregorio presented himself.
"You'll take me if I wish it,
Because there is no other way."

    *   *   *

---

1. A town in Texas.

Ya agarraron a Cortez
ya terminó la cuestión,
la pobre de su familia
la lleva en el corazón.

Ya con ésta me despido
con la sombra de un ciprés,
aquí se acaba cantando
la tragedia de Cortez.

Now they caught Cortez,
Now the case is closed,
His poor family
He carries in his heart.

With this I take my leave
In the shade of a cypress
Here we finish singing
The tragedy of Cortez.

n.d.

The "Corrido de 'Gregorio Cortez'" shows Cortez in a heroic light. It is generally assumed that Cortez killed the first sheriff accidentally. After that death, a witch hunt ensues in order to track Cortez and have him arrested or killed. Interestingly, the power struggle that is usually discussed in corridos is reversed here, with the Latino showing a strength that makes him stronger than the white characters.

Corrido de los Desarraigados

Señores, pongan cuidado
lo que es verdad yo les digo.
Como México no hay dos
por lindo, hermoso y florido.

Toditos los extranjeros
Lo tienen pa' su delirio.
Del cuarenta y tres atrás
no se hallaba complicado.

México, México era muy feliz
sincero, humilde y honrado.
Hasta que empezó a cruzar
la raza pa'l otro lado.

Contratistas y torqueros
pa' mi todos son iguales.
No más 'taban esperando
que pasaran nacionales.

Parecían lobos hambrientos
fuera de los matorrales.
Los creemos con honor
pero no los conocemos.

[TRANS.] Corrido of the Uprooted Ones

People, pay attention,
What I say is true.
There is no other country like Mexico,
Beautiful, lush, and green.

All the foreigners
Are amazed by Mexico.
Previous to 1943
There were no complications.

Mexico, Mexico was happy,
Sincere, humble, honest
Until our race started crossing
To the other side.

Contractors and truckers
To me they are all the same.
They were only waiting
For nationals to cross.

They resembled hungry wolves
Outside their thicket.
We believe they are honorable
But we don't know them.

*   *   *

Nos trabajan como esclavos	They work us like slaves
y nos tratan como perros.	And treat us like dogs.
No más falta que nos monten	All we need is for them to ride us
y que nos pongan el freno.	And to put the bridle on us.
Si alguno lo toma a mal	If someone doesn't like what I say
es que no lo ha conocido.	It's because he wasn't there.
Que se vaya a contratar	Let him go as a bracero[1]
a los Estados Unidos.	To the United States.
Y verá que va a trabajar	He will see that he will work
como un esclavo vendido.	Like a sold slave.
Antes éramos honrados	Before we were honorable men,
y de eso nada ha quedado.	Now we have lost it all.
Con eso del pasaporte	With our passports
nos creemos americanos	We think we are Americans
Pero tenemos el nombre	But we are called
de ser desarraigados.	The uprooted ones.
Allí les va la despedida	Here I bid farewell
a toditos mis paisanos	To all my countrymen.
Si quieren tener honor	If you want to have honor
no vayan al otro lado	Don't go to the other side
A mantener contratistas	To feed the contractors
y los troqueros hambrientos.	And hungry truckers.
	n.d.

The "Corrido de los Desarraigados" is extremely honest and confrontational. The speaker addresses his preference to be back in Mexico rather than experiencing Chicanos' poor quality of life in the United States.

Corrido de Tejas

Mi chinita me decía	My woman used to tell me,
Ya me voy para esa agencia—	"I am going to the agency—
a pasearme por el norte	I'll roam around the north
y para hacerle su asistencia.	And take care of you.

[TRANS.] Texas Corrido

*   *   *

---

1. A Mexican farmworker allowed to enter the United States to work for a short period of time.

De la parte donde estés
me escribes, no seas ingrato
y en contestación te mando
de recuerdos mi retrato.

Adiós estado de Tejas
con todo tu plantación,
me retiro de tus tierras
por no pizcar algodón.

Esos trenes del Tipi
que cruzan por la Lusiana
se llevan los mejicanos
para el estado de Indiana.

El día 22 de abril
a las dos de la mañana
salimos en un renganche
para el estado de Lusiana.

Adiós estado de Tejas
con toda tu plantación,
me despido de tus tierras
por no pizcar algodón.

Adiós Fort Worth y Dallas,
poblaciones sin un lago,
nos veremos cuando vuelva
de por Indiana y Chicago.

El enganchista nos dice
que no llevemos mujer,
para no pasar trabajos
y poder pronto volver.

"Wherever you may be,
Write to me, don't be forgetful;
And in reply I'll send you
My picture as a forget-me-not."

Good-bye, state of Texas,
With all your growing crops;
I am leaving your fields
So I won't have to pick cotton.

Those trains of the T & P[1]
That cross Louisiana
Carry the Mexicans
To the state of Indiana.

On the twenty-second of April
At two o'clock in the morning
We left on a labor contract
For the state of Louisiana.

Good-bye, state of Texas,
With all your growing crops;
I bid farewell to your fields
So I won't have to pick cotton.

Good-bye, Forth Worth and Dallas,
Cities without a lake;
We'll see each other when I return
From Indiana and Chicago.

The contractor tells us
Not to take a woman along,
So as to avoid difficulties
And so as to return soon.

n.d.

Deportados

Voy a contarles, señores,
voy a contarles, señores,
todo lo que yo sufrí,

[TRANS.] Deported

I am going to sing to you, gentlemen,
I am going to sing to you, gentlemen,
All about my sufferings

1. The Texas & Pacific Railroad.

cuando dejé yo a mi patria,
cuando dejé yo a mi patria,
por venirme a ese país.

Serían las diez de la noche,
serían las diez de la noche,
comenzó un tren a silbar;
oí que dijo mi madre
Ahí viene ese tren ingrate
Que a mi hijo se va a llevar.

Por fin sonó la campana,
por fin sonó la campana,
vámonos de la estación
no quiero ver a mi madre
llorar por su hijo querido,
por su hijo del corazón.

Cuando a Chihuahua llegamos
cuando a Chihuahua llegamos,
se notó gran confusión,
los empleados de la aduana,
los empleados de la aduana
que pasaban revisión.

Llegamos por fin a Juárez,
llegamos por fin a Juárez
ahí fue mi apuración
que dónde va, que dónde viene
cuánto dinero tiene
para entrar a esta nación.

Señores, traigo dinero,
señores, traigo dinero
para poder emigrar,
su dinero nada vale,
su dinero nada vale,
te tenemos que bañar.

Los güeros son muy maloras,
los gringos son muy maloras,
se valen de la ocasión,

When I left my native land,
When I left my native land,
In order to go to that country.

It must have been ten at night,
It must have been ten at night,
When a train began to whistle;
I heard my mother say,
"Here comes that hateful train
To take my son away."

Finally they rang the bell,
Finally they rang the bell.
"Let's go on out of the station;
I'd rather not see my mother
Weeping for her dear son,
The darling of her heart."

When we reached Chihuahua,
When we reached Chihuahua,
There was great confusion:
The customhouse employees,
The customhouse employees
Were having an inspection.

We finally arrived at Juárez,
We finally arrived at Juárez,
Where I had my inspection:
"Where are you going, where are you from,
How much money do you have
In order to enter this country?"

"Gentlemen, I have money,
Gentlemen, I have money
Enough to be able to emigrate."
"Your money is worthless,
Your money is worthless;
We'll have to give you a bath."

The blonds are very unkind;
The gringos are very unkind.
They take advantage of the chance

y a todos los mexicanos,
y a todos los mexicanos,
nos tratan sin compasión.

Hoy traen la gran polvadera,
hoy traen la gran polvadera
y sin consideración,
mujeres, niños y ancianos
los llevan a la frontera
los echan de esa nación.

Adiós, paisanos queridos,
adiós, paisanos queridos,
ya nos van a deportar
pero no somos bandidos
pero no somos bandidos
venimos a camellar.

Los espero allá en mi tierra,
los espero allá en mi tierra,
ya no hay más revolución;
vámonos, cuates queridos
seremos bien recibidos
en nuestra bella nación.

To treat all the Mexicans,
To treat all the Mexicans
Without compassion.

Today they are rounding them up,
Today they are rounding them up;
And without consideration
Women, children, and old folks
Are taken to the border
And expelled from that country.

So farewell, dear countrymen,
So farewell, dear countrymen,
They are going to deport us now,
But we are not bandits,
But we are not bandits,
We came to work.

I'll wait for you there in my country,
I'll wait for you there in my country
Now that there is no revolution;
Let us go, brothers dear,
We will be well received
In our own beautiful land.

n.d.

"Deportados" addresses the powerful political and cultural delineation between the United States and Mexico. In this corrido, U.S. citizens are viewed as cruel and selfish. Even the train that takes the speaker to the border is described by his mother as "hateful."

ANGEL ISLAND POETRY

While modernist poets were infatuated with orientalism, an estimated 250,000 Chinese and 150,000 Japanese immigrants were writing poetry to express their feelings about detainment, leaving behind an imaginative and historical record of their abuse at Angel Island, California. The age was openly prejudiced against Chinese and other Asian groups. *The Twentieth Century Annual Report of the Associated Charities of Boston* reported in 1899 that the Chinese in the city were regarded as "the most foreign of all foreigners." This racist sentiment was expressed in the federal Chinese Immigration Act, which for the first time banned a group solely on the basis of race and nationality, bringing the era of open immigration to a close. This same view led to the establishment of the Angel Island detention center in San Francisco Bay, through which one million immigrants passed from 1900 to 1940. They came not only from China and Japan but also from the Philippines, India, Korea, Russia, South and Central America, Mexico, Australia, New Zealand, and Canada. The longest periods of detention were reserved for Chinese immigrants in permissible categories (diplomats and family members).

Men, women, and children were held at the crowded, isolated, and barely habitable center for days, weeks, months, and sometimes even years. Among both the Chinese and Chinese Americans, Angel Island quickly became known as Devil's Island, as stories about abuses spread. The celebrated character of Mrs. Spring Fragrance, in Chinese-American writer Sui Sin Far's work of the period, tells her husband sarcastically that he should not worry about his "honored elder brother" being detained on Angel Island because "he is protected under the wing of the Eagle, the Emblem of Liberty." In spite of atrocious living conditions, poor food, lice, and mistreatment at the detention center as well as the general hostility of the public, the male detainees at the island refused to be silenced. Following the classical Chinese tradition of writing poems while in prison, they wrote or carved their grief, anger, courage, despair, and resignation in Chinese calligraphy on the painted walls. With only a few exceptions, this poetry was virtually unknown until the center was slated for demolition in 1970, and the writing was discovered just before the work was to begin. Approximately 135 poems have been recovered, and a new effort is under way to retrieve more poetry hidden under layers of paint.

The poetry is written in a classical Chinese style and includes couplets. The work was a communal effort; men borrowed lines, phrases, and images from one another to write and carve new poems. Some of the poets were well educated and used classical allusions. No poetry by female detainees survives. Men were placed in one barracks and the women and children in other quarters, which were destroyed by fire in 1940. That year Angel Island was turned into a center for Japanese prisoners of war.

While most of the poetry at Angel Island was written by Chinese detainees, the Japanese immigrants held there wrote poetry as well, which is not surprising, given the honored position of poetry in Japanese culture. American-born labor activist Karl G. Yoneda was detained at Angel Island because his family had moved back to Japan when his father became ill. While Yoneda was at the detention center, he wrote poems (using the pen name Kiyohi Hama) and later published them in the *San Francisco Nichibei* (issues of Februry 27, March 14, and March 24, 1927). Several of these English translations appear at the beginning of the selections included here. Yoneda not only experienced Angel Island detention but also was interned at Manzanar, the camp for Japanese Americans during World War II, until he volunteered for the U.S. Army.

FURTHER READING

Iris Chang. *The Chinese in America*. New York: Viking, 2003.

Mark Lai Him, Genny Lim, and Judy Yung. *Island: Poetry and History of Chinese Immigrants on Angel Island, 1910–1940*. Seattle: University of Washington Press, 1980.

Madeline Yuan-yin Hsu. *Dreaming of Gold, Dreaming of Home: Transnationalism and Migration between the United States and South China, 1882–1943*. Stanford, Calif.: Stanford University Press, 2000.

Erika Lee. *At American Gates: Chinese Immigration During the Exclusion Era, 1882–1934*. Chapel Hill: University of North Carolina Press, 2003.

Karen L. Polster. "Major Themes and Influences of the Poems at Angel Island." www.english.uiuc.edu/maps/poets/a_f/angel/polster.htm

Jingyu Wang. "Voices Caught between Worlds: Angel Island Poetry and Trans-Cultural Reading." Unpublished paper.

Japanese Angel Island Poetry

Angel Island—what a beautiful name

Kiyohi Hama

Angel Island—what a beautiful name
But there was no angel here
Only nameless prisoners of immigration.

n.d.

New Year's Day on Angel Island

Kiyohi Hama

New Year's Day on Angel Island
Is silent like a graveyard and nine Japanese deportees
Sitting together wrapped in blankets while I write poetry.

n.d.

New Year's Day came quietly and left silently

Kiyohi Hama

New Year's Day came quietly and left silently
I will soon be age twenty-one
No one can stop the sun.

n.d.

Chinese Angel Island Poetry

[TRANS.] Today is the last day of winter

今日爲冬末，
明朝是春分。
交替兩年景，
愁煞木樓人。

Today is the last day of winter,
Tomorrow morning is the vernal equinox.
One year's prospects have changed to another.
Sadness kills the person in the wooden building.

n.d.

[TRANS.] The insects chirp outside the four walls

四壁蟲喞喞，
居人多歎息。
思及家中事，
不覺淚沾滴。

The insects chirp outside the four walls.
The inmates often sigh.
Thinking of affairs back home,
Unconscious tears wet my lapel.

n.d.

[TRANS.] Leaving behind my writing brush and

留筆除劍到美洲，
誰知到此淚雙流？
倘若得志成功日，
定斬胡人草不留。

Leaving behind my writing brush and
　　removing my sword,[1] I came to America.
Who was to know two streams of tears would
　　flow upon arriving here?
If there comes a day when I will have
　　attained my ambition and become successful,
I will certainly behead the barbarians and
　　spare not a single blade of grass.

n.d.

---

1. Jingyu Wang points out that "brush" and "sword" are symbols of traditional Chinese intellectuals. When the poet says that he has left both his brush and his sword behind, he is indicating that he has left his life as a respected intellectual behind in China.

[TRANS.] If the land of the Flowery Flag
is occupied by us in turn

花旗旗其轉吾人佔據，
木樓樓留與天使還仇。

If the land of the Flowery Flag[1] is occupied by us in turn,
The wooden building will be left for the angel's revenge.

n.d.

[TRANS.] The low building with three beams
merely shelters the body

埃屋三椽聊保身，
嵛麓積愫不堪陳。
待得飛騰順遂日，
劃除關稅不論仁。

The low building with three beams[1] merely shelters the body.
It is unbearable to relate the stories[2] accumulated on the Island
slopes.
Wait till the day I become successful and fulfill my wish!
I will not speak of love[3] when I level the immigration station!

n.d.

[TRANS.] This is a message to those who live here
not to worry excessively

寄語同居勿過憂，
且把閒愁付水流。
小受折磨非是苦，
破嵛曾被島中囚。

This is a message to those who live here not to worry excessively.
Instead, you must cast your idle worries to the flowing stream.
Experiencing a little ordeal is not hardship.
Napoleon was once a prisoner on an island.

n.d.

This place is called an island of immortals

This place is called an island of immortals,[1]
When, in fact, this mountain wilderness is a prison.
Once you see the open net, why throw yourself in?
It is only because of empty pockets I can do nothing else.

n.d.

1. Colloquial Cantonese term for the United States.
1. Jingyu Wang suggests that the "beams" in the first line should be read as "rafters," the thin pieces of lumber that support the roof of the house. This interpretation allows one to read the reference as a comment ridiculing the weakness of the American-made roof. The first Chinese character in each of the poem's four lines can be read downward as "Angel Island awaiting its eradication."
2. "Stories" also can be translated as "feelings," according to Wang.
3. "Mercy" may be a more accurate translation, according to Wang.
1. Referring to Angel Island.

My grief, like dense clouds, cannot be dispersed

My grief, like dense clouds, cannot be dispersed.
Whether deliberating or being melancholy and bored,
I constantly pace to and fro.
Wang Can[1] ascended the tower but who pitied his sorrow?
Lord Yu[2] who left his country could only wail to himself.

n.d.

The young children do not yet know worry

The young children do not yet know worry.
Arriving at the Golden Mountain,[1] they were imprisoned in the wooden building.
Not understanding the sad and miserable situation before their eyes,
They must play all day like calves.

n.d.

[TRANS.] For one month I was imprisoned; my slippers never moved forward

乙月被囚履不前，

滿州輪來蒙古旋。

但得南洋登程日，

求活何須美利堅？

For one month I was imprisoned; my slippers never moved forward.
I came on the *Manchuria* and will return on the *Mongolia*.
But if I could make the trip to Nanyang,[1] I would.
Why should America be the only place to seek a living.

n.d.

[TRANS.] It was four days before the Chongyang Festival

重陽少四日：

香港付輪舟。

大家仍在此：

繫足將半秋。

It was four days before the Chongyang Festival[1]
When I transferred to a ship in Hong Kong.
Everybody is still here.
Our feet have been bound here for almost half an autumn.

n.d.

1. An official who became a refugee in Hubei Province and wrote poetry about his longing for home.
2. An official of the Liang dynasty in southern China who was detained in northern China when he was sent there as an envoy. He then served the succeeding Northern Zhou dynasty

and wrote about his longing for his home in the south.
1. Colloquial Chinese term for California.
1. Southeast Asia.
1. A festival that occurs on the ninth day of the ninth moon.

[TRANS.] My parents are old;
my family is poor

親老家貧：
寒來暑往。
無情白鬼：
悲憤填膺。

My parents are old; my family is poor.
Cold weather comes; hot weather goes.
Heartless white devils,
Sadness and anger fill my heart.

n.d.

[TRANS.] I went east to Asia;
I went west to Europe

東走亞兮西走歐：
南來北美苔禁愁。
任君入到囚困地：
若不流涕也低頭。

I went east to Asia; I went west to Europe.
I came to the South, to North America, where the
    harsh exclusion laws cause me worry.
Allowing you to enter the place of imprisonment,
Even if you don't shed tears, you will lower your head.

n.d.

[TRANS.] I raise my brush to write a poem
to tell my dear wife

舉筆寫詩我卿知：
昨夜三更嘆別離。
情濃囑語今猶在：
未知何日得旋歸。

I raise my brush to write a poem to tell my dear wife,
Last night at the third watch I sighed at being apart.
The message you gave with tender thoughts is still with me;
I do not know what day I can return home.

n.d.

[TRANS.] The silvery red shirt
is half covered with dust

銀紅衫子半蒙塵：
一盞殘燈伴此身。
却似梨花經已落：
可憐零落舊春時。

The silvery red shirt is half covered with dust.
A flickering lamp[1] keeps this body company.
I am like pear blossoms which have already fallen;
Pity the bare branches during the late spring.

n.d.

According to Jingyu Wang, red is a color for celebrations and happiness in Chinese culture, so this voyager wore a "red shirt" to mark his hope for safe passage and his joy on his journey

1. Wang suggests that the flickering lamp emphasizes the bleakness of the detainment.

to the United States. The "silvery" red shirt has lost its full color because of the grueling experience of the trip, symbolized by the dust. In a similar way, the poet himself is no longer happy. The fallen pear blossoms of line three are conventional symbols of feminine sorrow, asserts Wang. The last two lines of this poem are a variation on two well-known lines from "Song of Eternal Regret," a long narrative poem by the poet Bai Juyi of the T'ang dynasty: "Tears of loneliness glistened on her jade-skin cheeks / like pear blossoms tortured by spring's rain and breeze." Chinese male poets have frequently adopted feminine symbols and personae to express their feelings.

[TRANS.] Xishi always lives in golden houses

西施盡住黃金屋：

泥壁篷窗獨剩儂。

寄語樑間雙燕子：

天涯可有好房隆。

Xishi[1] always lives in golden houses;
Only the dirt walls and bamboo matted window are left for me.
I send a verbal message to the twin swallows between the
    rafters:
Is there a good room looming at the horizon?

               n.d.

[TRANS.] Having not yet crossed the Yellow River, my heart is not at peace

未過黃河心不息：

過了黃河雙淚流。

Having not yet crossed the Yellow River,[1] my heart is not at
    peace;
After crossing the Yellow River, a double stream of tears flow.

              1920s

ASIAN-INDIAN IMMIGRANT POETRY

In the early twentieth century, Asian Indians began migrating to the West Coast of the United States, where they worked in lumber and agriculture. The majority were Sikhs, and about one third were Muslims. From the beginning, the Indian immigrants challenged U.S. regulatory laws directed against Asians because they had migrated from a British colony. Indeed, a strong independence movement was under way to release India from British rule. In response to their growing numbers, U.S. local and federal governments enacted more regulations to control them. Unhappy with their lives here, about three thousand immigrants returned to India between 1920 and 1940. Those who remained organized themselves by re-

1. Chinese term that refers indirectly to "the American."

1. The Huang Ho, the second-longest river in China, starts in Tibet and flows to the Yellow Sea.

ligious affiliation into communities. Their poetry, which reflects their negative social experiences as well as their common bonds and interpersonal relations, has provided inspiration to later Indian-American poets.

FURTHER READING

Dhan Gopal Mukerji. *Caste and Outcast*. New York: E. P. Dutton, 1923.

Ved Prakash Vatuk and Sylvia Vatuk. "Protest Songs of East Indians on the West Coast, U.S.A." In *Thieves in My House: Four Studies in Indian Folklore of Protest and Change*, ed. Ved Prakash Vatuk. Varanasi, India: Vishwavidyalaya Prakashan, 1969.

Some push us around, some curse us

Some push us around, some curse us.
Where is your splendor and prestige today?
The whole world calls us black thieves,
The whole world calls us "coolie."[1]
Why doesn't our flag fly anywhere?
Why do we feel low and humiliated?
Why is there no respect for us in the whole world?

n.d.

Your hair is like a panther's shadow

Your hair is like a panther's shadow.
Your eyebrows are like the curve of a hawk's wings.

n.d.

KOREAN IMMIGRANT SONGS

Korean immigrants began to arrive on the U.S. West Coast in about 1900 and found themselves facing the same restrictions and discrimination as other Asian groups. Initially composed mostly of male laborers, this community was not large enough to form Koreatowns. After Japan annexed Korea in 1910, the first generation of Korean Americans faced Japanese colonialism if they returned to their homeland. Korean nationalist patriotism—and a desire to liberate their land from imperialism—soon became the bond that united this generation into an immigrant community. Their songs reflect their nostalgia for home and their enjoyment

---

1. A derogatory term for "Chinese."

of traditional love motifs. The songs have provided inspiration to later generations of Korean-American poets. During World War II, Korean-American men enlisted in large numbers because they saw the war as an opportunity to liberate Korea from Japanese colonialism.

FURTHER READING

Ronald Takaki. *Strangers from a Different Shore: A History of Asian Americans*. Boston: Back Bay Books, 1998.

Some loves are soft, others are rough

Some loves are soft, others are rough.
Some loves are deep like Kuwol Mountain.[1]
Other loves are so sad like the girl who sent her love to the army.
Some loves are secret.
What a delight! What a pleasure!
You can't help falling in love.

n.d.

Ari-rang, Ari-rang, A-ra-ri-yo

Ari-rang, Ari-rang, A-ra-ri-yo
He is going over the Ari-rang Hill[1]
Since he leaves me all alone
He'll have a pain in his foot without going very far.

n.d.

This song of loss and melancholy, sung by Korean immigrants, is a variant of a popular, late-nineteenth-century Korean folk song. In the song, a bereaved woman bids farewell to her lover who has either gone on a journey or died. She wishes that his feet will give him pain, as the sorrow of his leaving pains her.

FILIPINO POETRY AND SONGS

When the United States acquired the Philippines following the Spanish-American War, it declared Filipinos to be "American nationals" with permission to enter the country freely. Yet when they began to arrive, they were treated as if

---

1. A scenic mountain in what is now North Korea.
1. The name of numerous hills in Korea, including one on the outskirts of Seoul.

they were Asian immigrants. Coming with high hopes from the impoverished Spanish colony, Filipino men sought work all over the country but particularly on the West Coast, in California agriculture and Alaskan fishing and cannery industries. Their working conditions and wages were so poor that they realized they would probably never see their wives and families again. The poetry and songs included here reflect their homesickness and disillusionment, inspiring later Filipino poets such as Carlos Bulosan.

FURTHER READING

Ronald Takaki. *Strangers from a Different Shore: A History of Asian Americans*. Boston: Back Bay Books, 1998.

Song of the Alaskero

It's an unhappy fate
We face in Alaska.
Oh! what a hard fate!
Stale fat and ill-cooked fish,
Our one large daily dish
From the tight-fisted, mean Chink,
Give us stomachache.

We may curl and be brave
Beneath some blanket thick.
Yet oh! bitter cold!
And then at sunrise each day
Though dog tired we may be
Up we must go, quickly go
For another day.

n.d.

You were still waving, beloved

You were still waving, beloved
As I left you
To journey to another place
A white kerchief
You waved
Wet with tears
You couldn't help but cry
I promised it'll be a brief time perhaps
And I will return home

It's been only three months
Since then
To me, it's like
Three full years
And I count
Even hours now
Because my heart
Is filled with pain.

n.d.

Then why did I have to make

Then why did I have to make
A trip to this far land?
Oh! what a folly!
At home it's an easy life
For there's no work nor strife
Nor labor as hard to stand
As that in this land.

n.d.

The Filipino woman

The Filipino woman
Like the morning star
To see her brings joy
She offers radiance
And great beauty.

n.d.

PARLOR SONGS AND BALLADS

THROUGHOUT THE EARLY PART of the twentieth century, parlor songs continued to be one of the most popular genres in American music. Parlor songs were commonly used for courting and were played at parties. With the newly created phonograph (or gramophone, its trademarked name), more people could create their own musical entertainment, no longer needing to rely on someone to play the piano or another instrument to help lead them in their singing. Some of the parlor songs included racial stereotypes ("Bill Bailey, Won't You Please Come Home?") during a time when America's minstrel shows were still immensely popular. Parlor songs also dealt with lighter topics such as parted lovers ("Meet Me in St. Louis, Louis") and the national pastime of baseball ("Take Me Out to the Ball Game"). Songs with an Irish theme sold very well, especially to the Irish immigrants who were settling down in the United States and making economic strides. In the early decades, the songs appealed to their nostalgia for the homeland of Ireland, which was then still under British rule, and to the Irish independence movement that was gaining momentum.

The ballad, a narrative poem containing a refrain, was another popular song form of the era. This entry concludes with two African-American ballads that enjoyed great acclaim during the early twentieth century.

FURTHER READING

William Howland Kenney. *Recorded Music in American Life: The Phonograph and Popular Memory, 1890–1945*. Oxford: Oxford University Press, 1999.

Bird in a Gilded Cage

Arthur J. Lamb

The ballroom was filled with fashion's throng,
It shone with a thousand lights,
And there was a woman who passed along,
The fairest of all the sights,
A girl to her lover then softly sighed,
There's riches at her command;
But she married for wealth, not for love he cried,
Though she lives in a mansion grand.

CHORUS
She's only a bird in a gilded cage,
A beautiful sight to see,
You may think she's happy and free from care,
She's not, though she seems to be,
'Tis sad when you think of her wasted life,
For youth cannot mate with age,

And her beauty was sold,
For an old man's gold,
She's a bird in a gilded cage.

I stood in a churchyard just at eve',
When sunset adorned the west,
And looked at the people who'd come to grieve,
For loved ones now laid at rest,
A tall marble monument marked the grave,
Of one who'd been fashion's queen,
And I thought she is happier here at rest,
Than to have people say when seen.

1900

The lyrics of "Bird in a Gilded Cage," written by Arthur J. Lamb (1870–1928), illustrate the folly and public disdain associated with marrying for money.

Bill Bailey, Won't You Please Come Home?

Hughie Cannon

On one summer day . . .
Sun was shining fine . . .
The lady love of old Bill Bailey was
hanging clothes on de line
in her back yard . . .
and weeping hard . . .
She married a B. and G. brakeman
Dat took and throw'd her down.
Bellaring like a prune-fed calf,
wid a big gang hanging 'round;
And to dat crowd . . .
She yelled out loud: . . .

CHORUS

Won't you come home, Bill Bailey,
won't you come home?
She means de whole day long; . . .
I'll do de cooking, darling, I'll pay de rent:
I know I've done you wrong; . . .
'Member dat rainy eve dat I drove you out,

Wid nothing but a fine tooth comb?
I knows I'm to blame; well ain't dat a shame?
Bill Bailey, won't you please come home?

Bill drove by dat door . . .
in an automobile . . .
A great big diamond coach and fast-man,
hear dat big wench squeal "he's all alone." . . .
I heard her groan . . .
She holler'd thro' that door, "Bill Bailey, is you sore?
Stop a minute, won't you listen to me?
Won't I see you no more?" Bill winked his eye.
And he heard her cry: . . .

1902

Born in Detroit, Hughie Cannon (1877–1912), was a composer and vaudeville pianist. "Bill Bailey" was initially performed by minstrels and has subsequently been sung by many artists, including Louis Armstrong, Ella Fitzgerald, Bobby Darin, Pearl Bailey, and Patsy Cline.

In the Good Old Summer Time

Ren Shields

There's a time in each year
that we always hold dear,
Good old summer time;
With the birds and the treeses
and sweet scented breezes,
Good old summer time,
When your day's work is over
then you are in clover,
and life is one beautiful rhyme,
No trouble annoying,
each one is enjoying,
The good old summer time.

CHORUS

In the good old summer time,
In the good old summer time,
Strolling thro' the shady lanes,
With your baby mine;

You hold her hand and she hold yours
And that's a very good sign
That she's your tootsey wootsey in
The good old summer time.

To swim in the pool,
you'd play "hooky" from school,
Good old summer time;
You'd play "ring-a-rosie"
with Jim, Kate and Josie,
Good old summer time,
Those days full of pleasure,
we now fondly treasure,
when we never thought it a crime,
To go stealing cherries,
with face brown as berries,
Good old summer time.

1902

Ren Shields (1868–1913) was a vaudevillian from Chicago. When "In the Good Old Summer Time" was published, it immediately became a smash.

Meet Me in St. Louis, Louis

Andrew Sterling

When Louis came home to the flat,
He hung up his coat and his hat,
He gazed all around, but no wifey he found,
So he said, "Where can Flossie be at?"
A note on the table he spied,
He read it just once, then he cried.
It ran, "Louis dear, it's too slow for me here,
So I think I will go for a ride."

CHORUS

"Meet me in St. Louis, Louis,
Meet me at the fair,
Don't tell me the lights are shining
Any place but there;
We will dance the Hoochee Koochee,[1]

1. A belly dance.

I will be your tootsie wootsie,
If you will meet in St. Louis, Louis,
Meet me at the fair."

The dresses that hung in the hall
Were gone, she had taken them all;
She took all his rings and the rest of his things;
The picture he missed from the wall.
"What! Moving!" the janitor said,
"Your rent is paid three months ahead."
"What good is the flat?" said poor Louis. "Read that."
And the janitor smiled as he read.

1904

In this song "Louis" is pronounced "Louie." Andrew Sterling (1874–1955) wrote many memorable ragtime songs, and "Meet Me In St. Louis" became his greatest hit. The song even led to a 1944 motion picture by the same name, directed by Vincent Minnelli and starring Judy Garland.

Mary's a Grand Old Name

George M. Cohan

My mother's name was Mary, she was so good and true;
Because her name was Mary, she called me Mary too.
She wasn't gay or airy, but plain as she could be;
I hate to be contrary, and call myself Marie.

CHORUS (SUNG TWICE AFTER EACH VERSE)

For it is Mary, Mary, plain as any name can be;
But with propriety, society will say Marie;
But it was Mary, Mary, long before the fashions came,
And there is something there that sounds so square,
It's a grand old name.

Now, when her name is Mary, there is no falseness there;
When to Marie she'll vary, she'll surely bleach her hair.
Though Mary's ordinary, Marie is fair to see;
Don't ever fear sweet Mary, beware of sweet Marie.

1905

George M. Cohan (1878–1942) wrote this song for his play *Forty-five Minutes from Broadway*. The two hit songs from the play were "Mary's a Grand Old Name" and "So Long Mary."

Harrigan

George M. Cohan

Who is the man who will spend or will even lend?
Harrigan, That's Me!
Who is your friend when you find that you need a friend?
Harrigan, That's Me!
For I'm just as proud of my name, you see,
As an Emperor, Czar or a King could be.
Who is the man helps a man every time he can?
Harrigan, That's Me!

CHORUS

H - A - double R - I - G - A - N spells Harrigan
Proud of all the Irish blood that's in me; Divil a man can say a word agin me.
H - A - double R - I - G - A - N, you see,
Is a name that a shame never has been connected with, Harrigan, That's me!

Who is the man never stood for a gad about?
Harrigan, That's Me!
Who is the man that the town's simply mad about?
Harrigan, That's Me!
The ladies and babies are fond of me,
I'm fond of them, too, in return, you see.
Who is the gent that's deserving a monument?
Harrigan, That's Me!

1907

George M. Cohan composed "Harrigan" for his play *Fifty Miles from Boston*. He wrote the song about Edward Harrigan, who was part of the comedy team Harrigan and Hart. James Cagney memorably performed "Harrigan" in *Yankee Doodle Dandy* (1942), a film about Cohan's life.

Shine On, Harvest Moon

Jack Norworth

The night was mighty dark so you could hardly see,
For the moon refused to shine,
Couple sitting underneath a willow tree,
For love they pine,
Little maid was kinda 'fraid of darkness
So she said, "I guess I'll go,"

Boy began to sigh,
Looked up at the sky,
Told the moon his little tale of woe.

CHORUS

Oh, shine on, shine on, harvest moon up in the sky.
I ain't had no lovin'
Since January, February, June or July,
Snow time ain't no time to stay outdoors and spoon,
So, shine on, shine on, harvest moon,
For me and my gal.

I can't see why a boy should sigh, when by his side
Is the girl he love so true,
All he has to say is "Won't you be my bride,
For I love you,
Why should I be telling you this secret
When I know that you can guess,"
Harvest moon will smile,
Shine on all the while,
If the little girl should answer "Yes."

1908

Jack Norworth (1879–1959) was a songwriter, producer, and actor. He originally performed "Shine On, Harvest Moon" with his second wife, Nora Bayes (who wrote the music), in *The Follies of 1908*.

Take Me Out to the Ball Game

Jack Norworth

Katie Casey was baseball mad,
Had the fever and had it bad;
Just to root for the hometown crew,
Ev'ry sou Katie blew
On a Saturday, her young beau
Called to see if she if she'd like to go
To see a show but Miss Kate said,
"No, I'll tell you what you can do":

CHORUS

"Take me out to the ball game,
Take me out with the crowd.

Buy me some peanuts and crackerjack,
I don't care if I never get back,
Let me root, root, root for the home team,
If they don't win it's a shame.
For it's one, two, three strikes, you're out,
At the old ball game."

Katie Casey saw all the games,
Knew the players by their first names;
Told the umpire he was wrong,
All along good and strong
When the score was just two to two,
Katie Casey knew what to do,
Just to cheer up the boys she knew,
She made the gang sing this song:

1908

When Norworth wrote "Take Me Out to the Ball Game" at the age of twenty-nine, he had apparently never seen a baseball game.

By the Light of the Silvery Moon

Edward Madden

Place park, scene dark,
Silv'ry moon is shining thro' the trees;
Cast two, me, you,
Sound of kisses floating on the breeze.
Act one, begun,
Dialogue, "Where would you like to spoon?"
My cue, with you,
Underneath the silv'ry moon.

CHORUS

By the light of the silvery moon,
I want to spoon,
To my honey I'll croon love's tune,
Honey moon keep a-shining in June,
Your silv'ry beams will bring love dreams,
We'll be cuddling soon,
By the silvery moon.

✻   ✻   ✻

Act two, scene new,
Roses blooming all around the place;
Cast three, you, me,
Preacher with a solemn-looking face.
Choir sings, bell rings
Preacher: "You are wed forevermore."
Act two, all through,
Ev'ry night the same encore.

1909

Edward Madden (1978–1952) worked with many famous composers of the era, including Gus Edwards and Albert Von Tilzer.

Let Me Call You Sweetheart

Beth Slater Whitson

I am dreaming Dear of you
Day by day
Dreaming when the skies are blue
When they're gray;
When the silv'ry moonlight gleams
Still I wander on in dreams
In a land of love, it seems
Just with you.

CHORUS

Let me call you "Sweetheart" I'm in love with you.
Let me hear you whisper that you love me too.
Keep the lovelight glowing in your eyes so true.
Let me call you "Sweetheart" I'm in love with you.

Longing for you all the while
More and more
Longing for the sunny smile,
I adore;
Birds are singing far and near
Roses blooming ev'rywhere
You, alone, my heart can cheer
You just you.

1910

Beth Slater Whitson (1879–1930) was a poet and songwriter from Tennessee whose work has been acknowledged by the Songwriters Hall of Fame.

Peg O' My Heart

Alfred Bryan

Oh! my heart's in a whirl,
Over one little girl,
I love her, I love her, yes, I do,
Altho' her heart is far away,
I hope to make her mine some day,
Ev'ry beautiful rose, ev'ry violet knows,
I love her, I love her fond and true,
And her heart fondly sighs, as I sing to her eyes,
Her eyes of blue,
Sweet eyes of blue, my darling!

> CHORUS
> Peg O' My Heart,
> I love you,
> We'll never part,
> I love you, dear little girl,
> Sweet little girl,
> Sweeter than the rose of Erin,
> Are your winning smiles endearin',
> Peg O' My Heart,
> Your glances with Irish art entrance me,
> Come, be my own,
> Come, make your home in my heart.

When your heart's full of fears,
And your eyes full of tears,
I'll kiss them, I'll kiss them all away;
For, like the gold that's in your hair,
Is all the love for you I bear,
O, believe in me, do,
I'm as lonesome as you,
I miss you, I miss you all the day,
Let the light of love shine from your eyes into mine,
And shine for aye,
Sweetheart for aye, my darling!

1913

Alfred Bryan (1871–1958) was an early Tin Pan Alley lyricist who often collaborated with the composer Fred Fisher.

Frankie and Johnny

Frankie and Johnny were lovers,
   Lordy, how they could love,
Swore to be true to each other,
   True as the stars up above,
     He was her man, but he done her wrong.

Frankie went down to the corner,
   To buy her a bucket of beer,
Frankie says, "Mister Bartender,
   Has my lovin' Johnny been here?
     He is my man, but he's doing me wrong."

"I don't want to cause you no trouble
   Don't want to tell you no lie,
I saw your Johnny half-an-hour ago
   Making love to Nelly Bly.
     He is your man, but he's doing you wrong."

Frankie went down to the hotel
   Looked over the transom so high,
There she saw her lovin' Johnny
   Making love to Nelly Bly
     He was her man; he was doing her wrong.

Frankie threw back her kimono,
   Pulled out her big forty-four;
Rooty-toot-toot: three times she shot
   Right through that hotel door,
     She shot her man, who was doing her wrong.

"Roll me over gently,
   Roll me over slow,
Roll me over on my right side,
   'Cause these bullets hurt me so,
     I was your man, but I done you wrong."

Bring all your rubber-tired hearses,
   Bring all your rubber-tired hacks,
They're carrying poor Johnny to the burying ground
   And they ain't gonna bring him back,
     He was her man, but he done her wrong.

*   *   *

Frankie says to the sheriff,
   "What are they going to do?"
The sheriff he said to Frankie,
   "It's the 'lectric chair for you.
      He was your man, and he done you wrong."

"Put me in that dungeon,
   Put me in that cell,
Put me where the northeast wind
   Blows from the southeast corner of hell,
      I shot my man, 'cause he done me wrong."

n.d.

"Frankie and Johnny" may have been inspired by true events that occurred in Missouri on October 15, 1899, when a woman named Frankie Baker shot and killed Albert Britt. Bill Dooley, an African-American composer and pianist, may have written the song. The song was initially titled "Frankie and Albert" but later evolved into "Frankie and Johnny." The ballad and its oral history have many versions, however.

John Henry

When John Henry was a little fellow,
   You could hold him in the palm of your hand,
He said to his pa, "When I grow up
   I'm gonna be a steel-driving man,
      Gonna be a steel-driving man."

When John Henry was a little baby,
   Setting on his mammy's knee,
He said, "The Big Bend Tunnel on the C. & O. Road
   Is gonna be the death of me,
      Gonna be the death of me."

One day his captain told him
   How he had bet a man
That John Henry would beat his steam drill down,
   'Cause John Henry was the best in the land,
      John Henry was the best in the land.

John Henry kissed his hammer,
   White man turned on steam,

Shaker held John Henry's trusted steel,
 Was the biggest race the world had ever seen,
  Lord, biggest race the world ever seen.

John Henry on the right side
 The steam drill on the left,
"Before I'll let your steam drill beat me down,
 I'll hammer my fool self to death,
  Hammer my fool self to death."

John Henry walked in the tunnel,
 His captain by his side,
The mountain so tall, John Henry so small,
 He laid down his hammer and he cried,
  Laid down his hammer and he cried.

Captain heard a mighty rumbling,
 Said, "The mountain must be caving in,"
John Henry said to the captain,
 "It's my hammer swinging in de wind,
  My hammer swinging in de wind."

John Henry said to his shaker,[1]
 "Shaker, you'd better pray;
For if ever I miss this piece of steel,
 Tomorrow'll be your burial day,
  Tomorrow'll be your burial day."

John Henry said to his shaker,
 "Lordy, shake it while I sing,
I'm pulling my hammer from my shoulders down,
 Great Gawdamighty, how she ring,
  Great Gawdamighty, how she sing!"

John Henry said to his captain,
 "Before I ever leave town,
Gimme one mo' drink of dat tom-cat gin,
 And I'll hammer dat steam driver down,
  I'll hammer dat steam driver down."

John Henry said to his captain,
 "Before I ever leave town,

---

1. A shaker holds down the drill while the other person drills.

Gimme a twelve-pound hammer wid a whale-bone handle,
    And I'll hammer dat steam driver down,
        I'll hammer dat steam driver down."

John Henry said to his captain,
    "A man ain't nothing but a man,
But before I'll let dat steam drill beat me down,
    I'll die wid my hammer in my hand,
        Die wid my hammer in my hand."

The man that invented the steam drill
    He thought he was mighty fine,
John Henry drove down fourteen feet,
    While the steam drill only made nine,
        Steam drill only made nine.

"Oh, lookaway over yonder, captain,
    You can't see like me,"
He gave a long and loud and lonesome cry,
    "Lawd, a hammer be the death of me,
        A hammer be the death of me!"

John Henry had a little woman,
    Her name was Polly Ann,
John Henry took sick, she took his hammer,
    She hammered like a natural man,
        Lawd, she hammered like a natural man.

John Henry hammering on the mountain
    As the whistle blew for half-past two,
The last words his captain heard him say,
    "I've done hammered my insides in two,
        Lawd, I've hammered my insides in two."

The hammer that John Henry swung
    It weighed over twelve pound,
He broke, a rib in his left-hand side
    And his intrels fell on the ground,
        And his intrels fell on the ground.

John Henry, O, John Henry,
    His blood is running red,

Fell right down with his hammer to the ground,
Said, "I beat him to the bottom but I'm dead,
Lawd, beat him to the bottom but I'm dead."

When John Henry was laying there dying,
The people all by his side,
The very last words they heard him say,
"Give me a cool drink of water 'fore I die,
Cool drink of water 'fore I die."

John Henry had a little woman,
The dress she wore was red,
She went down the track, and she never looked back,
Going where her man fell dead,
Going where her man fell dead.

John Henry had a little woman,
The dress she wore was blue,
De very last words she said to him,
"John Henry, I'll be true to you,
John Henry, I'll be true to you."

"Who's gonna shoes yo' little feet,
Who's gonna glove yo' hand,
Who's gonna kiss yo' pretty, pretty cheek,
Now you done lost yo' man?
Now you done lost yo' man?"

"My mammy's gonna shoes my little feet,
Pappy gonna glove my hand,
My sister's gonna kiss my pretty, pretty cheek,
Now I done lost my man."

They carried him down by the river,
And buried him in the sand,
And everybody that passed that way
Said, "There lies a steel-driving man,
There lies a steel-driving man."

They took John Henry to the river,
And buried him in the sand,
And every locomotive come a-roaring by,
Says, "There lies a steel-drivin' man,
Lawd, there lies a *steel*-drivin' man."

    *   *   *

    Some say he came from Georgia,
        And some from Alabam,
    But it's wrote on the rock at the Big Bend Tunnel
        That he was an East Virginia man,
           Lord, Lord, an East Virginia man.

                              n.d.

The ballad of "John Henry" details the folk legend of John Henry, who worked on the Big Bend Tunnel in east Virginia in the 1870s. At the time of the tunnel's construction, it was the largest railroad tunnel in the United States. Many versions of the ballad exist.

WORLD WAR I–ERA SONGS

Many PATRIOTIC SONGS were written before, during, and immediately after World War I, as the United States watched war develop in Europe and then as the nation itself joined the Allies. Three selections here are by George M. Cohan, whose nationalistic fervor helped him write some of the most renowned songs of the era. In contrast, the lyrics of Cohan's contemporary, Irving Berlin, lack Cohan's fervor and idealism, perhaps because Berlin actually served in the military during the Great War. Lena Guilbert Ford's "Keep the Home Fires Burning" provides a woman's point of view from the homefront. The six songs included here illustrate Americans' innocence and optimism before becoming disillusioned by the reality of war.

FURTHER READING

Frederick G. Vogel, ed. *World War I Songs.* New York: McFarland, 1995.

Give My Regards to Broadway

George M. Cohan

Did you ever see two Yankees part up on a foreign shore,
When the good ship's just around about to start for Old New York once more?
With tear-dimmed eye they say goodbye, they're friends without a doubt;
When the man on the pier
Shouts "Let them clear," as the ship strikes out.

CHORUS

Give my regards to Broadway, remember me to Herald Square,[1]
Tell all the gang at Forty-second Street that I will soon be there;
Whisper of how I'm yearning
To mingle with the old time throng,
Give my regards to old Broadway and say that I'll be there e'er long.

Say hello to dear old Coney Isle,[2] if there you chance to be,
When you're at the Waldorf[3] have a smile and charge it up to me;
Mention my name ev'ry place you go, as 'round the town you roam;
Wish you'd call on my gal,
Now remember, old pal, when you get back home.

1904

"Give My Regards to Broadway" was written by George M. Cohan (1878–1942) for his play *Little Johnny Jones*. The play follows the romantic and legal troubles encountered by Johnny Jones, an American jockey who is accused of throwing the English Derby (a British horse race). This song is performed at the conclusion of the second act and highlights the jockey's longing to be back in America. The song took on a more somber tone and meaning for families and soldiers when the United States dropped its isolationist status in 1917 and sent troops to Europe to fight with the Allies.

You're a Grand Old Flag

George M. Cohan

There's a feeling comes a-stealing and it sets my brain a-reeling,
When I'm list'ning to the music of a military band.
Any tune like "Yankee Doodle" simply sets me off my noodle,
It's that patriotic something no one can understand.
"Way, down South in the land of cotton,"
Melody untiring,
Ain't that inspiring!
Hurrah! Hurrah!
We'll sing the jubilee,
And that's going some for the Yankees, by gum!

1. A building on 34th Street that housed the *New York Herald*.
2. Coney Island is a seaside resort in Brooklyn with an amusement park.

3. The Waldorf-Astoria was already a major New York hotel.

Red, White and Blue,
I am for you,
Honest, you're a grand old flag.

CHORUS

You're a grand old flag tho' you're torn to a rag,
And forever in peace may you wave.
You're the emblem of the land I love,
The home of the free and the brave,
Ev'ry heart beats true under Red, White and Blue,
Where there's never a boast or a brag;
"But should auld acquaintance be forgot,"
Keep your eye on the grand old flag.

I'm so cranky, hanky panky, I'm a dead square honest Yankee,
And I'm mighty proud of that old flag that flies for Uncle Sam.
Though I don't believe in raving ev'ry time I see it waving,
There's a chill runs up my back that makes me glad I'm what I am.
Here's a land with a million soldiers,
That's if we should need 'em,
We'll fight for freedom!
Hurrah! Hurrah!
For ev'ry Yankee Tar[1]
And old G.A.R.,[2] ev'ry stripe, ev'ry star,
Red, White and Blue,
Hats off to you,
Honest, you're a grand old flag.

                                                        1906

Originally appearing in the George M. Cohan play *George Washington, Jr.*, this patriotic song contains some of Cohan's best-known lyrics. During performances, the chorus is typically sung twice after every verse. Despite the apparent nationalistic fervor in Cohan's lyrics, he did employ hints of satire ("I don't believe in raving ev'ry time I see it waving").

---

1. "Yankee tar" refers to a sailor.
2. The Grand Army of the Republic, an organiza- tion dedicated to remembering the fallen Union soldiers of the Civil War.

Alexander's Ragtime Band

Irving Berlin

Oh, ma honey,
Oh, ma honey,
Better hurry and let's meander,
Ain't you goin',
Ain't you goin',
To the leader man, ragged meter man?
Oh, ma honey,
Oh, ma honey,
Let me take you to Alexander's grand stand, brass band,
Ain't you comin' along?

CHORUS

Come on and hear,
Come on and hear,
Alexander's ragtime band,
Come on and hear,
Come on and hear,
It's the best band in the land.
They can play a bugle call like you never heard before,
So natural that you want to go to war;
That's just the bestest band what am, honey lamb,
Come on along,
Come on along,
Let me take you by the hand,
Up to the man,
Up to the man who's the leader of the band,
And if you care to hear the Sewanee River[1] played in ragtime,
Come on and hear,
Come on and hear,
Alexander's ragtime band.

Oh, ma honey,
Oh, ma honey,
There's a fiddle with notes that screeches,
Like a chicken,
Like a chicken,
And the clarinet is a colored pet,

---

1. "Sewanee River" is a song by Stephen Foster.

Come and listen,
Come and listen,
To a classical band what's peaches, come now, somehow,
Better hurry along.

1911

During the 101 years of Irving Berlin's life (1888–1989), he wrote about fifteen hundred songs and became one of America's most popular and successful songwriters. After "Alexander's Ragtime Band" was published in 1911, it became Berlin's first international hit. Berlin's songwriting credits include "White Christmas," "There's No Business Like Show Business," and "God Bless America."

Keep the Home Fires Burning (Till the Boys Come Home)

Lena Guilbert Ford

They were summoned from the hillside,
They were called in from the glen,
And the Country found them ready
At the stirring call for men.
Let no tears add to their hardship,
As the Soldiers pass along
And although your heart is breaking,
Make it sing this cheery song.

REFRAIN

Keep the Home fires burning,
While your hearts are yearning,
Though your lads are far away
They dream of Home;
There's a silver lining
Through the dark cloud shining,
Turn the dark cloud inside out,
Till the boys come Home.

Over seas there came a pleading,
"Help a Nation in distress!"
And we gave our glorious laddies,
Honor made us do no less.
For no gallant Son of Freedom
To a tyrant's yoke should bend,
And a noble heart must answer
To the sacred call of "Friend!"

1914

The lyrics of "Keep the Home Fires Burning" by Lena Guilbert Ford (1870–1916) evoke the heartache felt by many families who yearned to see their sons return safely from the battlefields of the Great War. Ford was tragically killed in 1916 during a London air raid.

Over There

George M. Cohan

Johnnie get your gun,[1] get your gun, get your gun
Take it on the run, on the run, on the run
Hear them calling you and me
Ev'ry son of liberty
Hurry right away no delay go today
Make your daddy glad to have had such a lad
Tell your sweetheart not to pine
To be proud her boy's in line.

CHORUS

Over there — over there —
Send the word, send the word over there
That the Yanks are coming the Yanks are coming
The drums rum-tum-ming ev'rywhere —
So prepare
We'll be over we're coming over
And we won't come back till it's over over there.

Johnnie get your gun, get your gun, get your gun
Johnnie show the Hun[2] you're a son of a gun
Hoist the flag and let her fly
Yankee Doodle do or die
Pack your little kit show your grit do your bit
Yankees to the ranks from the towns and the tanks
Make your mother proud of you
And the old Red White and Blue.

1917

George M. Cohan was inspired to write "Over There" after the United States entered World War I on April 6, 1917. In 1936, "Over There" won Cohan a Congressional Medal of Honor.

---

1. "Johnny Get Your Gun" was the name of a popular song in the late 1800s. 2. A war propaganda term for a German soldier.

Oh! How I Hate to Get Up in the Morning

Irving Berlin

The other day I chanced to meet a soldier friend of mine,
He'd been in camp for sev'ral weeks and he was looking fine;
His muscles had developed and his cheeks were rosy red,
I asked him how he liked the life, and this is what he said:

CHORUS 1

"Oh! how I hate to get up in the morning,
Oh! how I'd love to remain in bed;
For the hardest blow of all, is to hear the bugler call;
You've got to get up, you've got to get up, you've got to get up this morning!
Some day I'm going to murder the bugler,
Some day they're going to find him dead;
I'll amputate his reveille, and step upon it heavily,
And spend the rest of my life in bed."

CHORUS 2

"Oh! how I hate to get up in the morning,
Oh! how I'd love to remain in bed;
For the hardest blow of all, is to hear the bugler call;
You've got to get up, you've got to get up, you've got to get up this morning!
Oh! boy the minute the battle is over,
Oh! boy the minute the foe is dead;
I'll put my uniform away, and move to Philadelphia,
And spend the rest of my life in bed."

A bugler in the army is the luckiest of men,
He wakes the boys at five and then goes back to bed again;
He doesn't have to blow again until the afternoon,
If ev'ry thing goes well with me I'll be a bugler soon.

1918

World War I had a profound impact on Irving Berlin's lyrics. He served in the military in 1917 and 1918.

PART TWO

✦

Second-Generation Modernisms

INTRODUCTION

A SECOND GENERATION of modernists, born between 1895 and 1906, began pro-
ducing poetry in the early 1920s. Whereas the first generation had innovated
forms and perspectives more or less on their own, as if stumbling in the dark toward
an elusive goal, the second generation had a different burden: to recognize and
remedy the first generation's limits and failures. Even more challenging, they
needed to recognize and build on the first generation's successes.

Social conditions were very different for the second generation. In contrast with
the pioneering generation that reached its maturity from the teens through the
1920s, marked by the trauma of World War I and the social changes associated with
the Jazz Age, the second generation reached its maturity from the 1920s through
the 1930s, as the Jazz Age gave way to the Great Depression and as the storm clouds
of a new world war darkened the horizon. The Depression, in particular, informed
the styles and values of the second generation of modernists. While many of the
pioneering modernists, coming from privileged backgrounds, had maintained
conservative or nostalgic notions about society and economics, many of the
second-generation modernists, writing from positions of poverty or marginality,
forged progressive or radical social agendas. Whereas many first-generation mod-
ernists had looked to myth for what Eliot called an "ordering device," or to form for
what Frost called "a momentary stay against confusion," the second-generation
modernists, as a group, felt accustomed to the confusions of modernity. They used
myth and form to express, explore, critique, or modify disorder rather than to con-
tain it or ward it off. If the initial buzz of first-generation innovations had died
down, the project of further transformations sustained the next generation.

Two large figures dominate current discourse about second-generation mod-
ernisms. The first, Langston Hughes, is generally regarded as the central poet of
the Harlem Renaissance. Whereas the pioneering generation of Harlem Renais-
sance poets such as McKay, Fauset, Johnson, and Grimké expressed new black
perspectives in traditional forms and standard English, Hughes produced a poetry
heavily influenced by the music, advertisements, casual conversation, and politi-
cal talk heard around him every day in Harlem. He introduced jazz and blues
motifs into his poetry as well as the vernacular language, boisterous dialogues,
and vigorous debates of the street, club, and café. Like the poetry of Whitman,

Williams, and Reznikoff, but even more so, Hughes's poetry incorporates social speech into the texture of American poetic discourse. Whereas the experimental modernists of the first generation tended to produce a visual poetry, epitomized by Pound's dictum of the "direct treatment of the thing," Hughes produced what Houston Baker calls a "sounding" discourse—a poetic style in lively conversation with the musical and vernacular culture of urban black life.

Inspired by Hughes's example, other second-generation Harlem Renaissance poets such as Sterling Brown, Countee Cullen, Arna Bontemps, and Gwendolyn Bennett (and the post-Renaissance poet Melvin B. Tolson) also explored the rich and paradoxical cultural life of African Americans. Like Hughes, they did so with an openness and confidence unavailable to first-generation Renaissance poets. All of them (except Cullen) were more willing to appropriate musical and vernacular motifs than were their precursors, and all of them were eager to subvert conventional proprieties. In the first generation only Grimké had dared to publish poems concerning the ambiguities of sexuality (Dunbar-Nelson kept such poems private); in the second generation, Hughes, Cullen, and Bennett all did so. Modernity, for Hughes and his cohort, centered on issues of sexuality as well as of race, class, and gender. Thus, second-generation Harlem Renaissance poets engaged in a dual process of social commentary and interior discovery.

Whereas Hughes was part of a vital poetic community, the other dominating figure of the second generation, Hart Crane, was something of a solitary figure. To be sure, he had friends, including Allen Tate, Jean Toomer, and Yvor Winters, and he read and was influenced by Eliot, Williams, and Stevens. But in many ways, Crane was on his own as he pursued modes of intense meditation that he found in the French symbolist poets, the nineteenth-century American symbolic writers, and the British Romantics and metaphysicals. Although Crane and Hughes did not know each other, and though their poetry is quite different in most ways, the two did share some traits. Both created a poetic language redolent of modernity. For example, both Crane and Hughes quoted from popular music and mentioned product brands. Both used the poetic medium to address personal and social issues: their own sexual ambiguities, their opposition to racial and class disparities. Crane, like Hughes, identified with the nation's poor and outcast, perhaps because of his own financial struggles and his position as a sexually active gay man. But Crane, perhaps more inward-looking than any other major poet of his time, sought to transform culture through a concept of poetic vision that moved from the inside out. Wearing the "splintered garland" of the "seer," he called forth an imagined "Belle Isle"; he sought to utter a capitalized "Word." He saw in his own verbal and imaginative skills something of the godlike power that Samuel Taylor Coleridge attributed to all great poets. While Hughes made poetry out of the verbal and sonic collisions he heard around him, Crane looked for inspiration within—to his own visionary and linguistic capacities. Whereas Hughes voyaged through social and political realities, Crane underwent an introspective voyage in which he risked everything.

Beyond these two poets, another significant new movement arose: objectivism. Emphasizing sincerity and objectivity, the movement grew out of, but superceded, the first-generation interest in imagism, particularly as theorized by Pound and practiced by H.D. and Williams. The objectivist group also took inspiration from the first-generation experimental modernist, Charles Reznikoff, whose early poetry included evocative images of working-class urban life. In fact, the objectivists considered Reznikoff an honorary member and Williams at least a tangential member. Louis Zukofsky organized the group, first in an issue of *Poetry* magazine and then in an anthology. Zukofsky's editions included his own poetry along with that of Williams, Reznikoff, Carl Rakosi, and George Oppen (the latter represented in the third volume of this anthology). Lorine Niedecker, who read the objectivist issue of *Poetry* with great excitement, soon became a member of the informal group as well, as did Kenneth Rexroth. Objectivists continued the imagists' interest in succinctness, "direct treatment of the thing," and metrical freedom, but they added new elements of their own: spontaneity, modesty, vernacular language, and a palpable sympathy for workers and the underprivileged. If imagist poems, especially as composed by Pound and H.D., read as though inscribed on stone shards or silk screens, the objectivist poems of Zukofsky, Rakosi, and Niedecker were more likely to resemble graffiti or to sound as if tossed off in conversation. Their discourse often seemed ripped apart and reassembled in a blender, with phrases missing and no matching edges. "The lines of this new song," Zukofsky once wrote, "are nothing / But a tune making the nothing full."

Such high-spirited but serious verbal experiments undermined the authority of conventional poetic forms and subject matters, as did the work of the Harlem Renaissance. Both movements opened the way for experimental movements later in the century: the Beats in the 1950s and 1960s, the Black Arts group in the 1960s and 1970s, and the Language poets in the 1980s to the present. Despite their differences, both the objectivists and the Harlem Renaissance poets proposed a poetry that would function critically and oppositionally to mainstream institutions. In this project they were joined by such social satirists as Kenneth Fearing and Melvin B. Tolson and by many of the popular poets and blues and jazz lyricists of the day. Rather than mourn the loss of an ordered and hierarchical past, as did the "high" modernists, these groups tended to look forward to a better and more democratic day.

A final group of lyric poets arose later in the 1930s: poets who, despite their admiration for the first-generation modernists, wished to modify or resist their experimental strategies. Allen Tate and Robert Penn Warren might be placed in a Southern wing of this grouping. Both poets belonged to the Southern "Fugitives" or "Agrarians" (along with first-generation poet John Crowe Ransom). Although they initially adopted a program of formal complexity and cultural conservatism indebted to Pound and Eliot, they later wrote more personal lyrics. Louise Bogan, Richard Eberhart, and Stanley Kunitz, who could belong in a Northeastern branch of this grouping, sought from the beginning to recover some of the lyric elements that the experimental poets had sacrificed: a consistent, personal voice and traditional meters and rhymes. Bogan, Eberhart, and Kunitz rejected experimental modernism's style of impersonality, fragmentation, obscurity, and juxtaposed images. They recovered a cohesive subject and perspective, preparing the way for the frankly personal and "confessional" lyrics of the mid-century and beyond.

Because the creation of blues, jazz, and musical theater songs closely paralleled the development of poetic modernisms, a rich interplay occurred between the genres, especially in the second modernist generation. Such lyricists as Bessie Smith, E. Y. "Yip" Harburg, Noble Sissle, and Cole Porter influenced the Harlem Renaissance poets, including Langston Hughes (who himself wrote lyrics for the musical stage), and a diversity of other poets ranging from Hart Crane and Melvin B. Tolson to the light versifiers Ogden Nash and Dorothy Parker. Moreover, poetic advances reciprocally influenced musical lyrics. For example, the verbal experiments of Dada were transformed into the jazz number "Ja Da," while protest poems by such writers as Kenneth Fearing and Langston Hughes were echoed in song lyrics by Harburg and Smith. In the second generation, the relations between written and musical discourse, between high art and popular art, became richer and more complicated than ever.

Both modernist generations produced poems and movements that were diverse, mutually entangled, and dynamic across time. Such second-generation modernists as Hughes, Crane, and the objectivists took the experimental project in vital new directions, combining the project's formal innovations with a newly critical social perspective. The second-generation lyric poets, on the other hand, sought to restore to modern expression some of the traditions that the experimentalists had shunted aside. The result is a second-generation discourse significantly different from that of the first but equally vigorous and contentious. These poems too fit Gertrude Stein's description of a modernist poetry that is at once "wonderfully beautiful" and "irritating annoying stimulating."

BLUES

THE BLUES is a signature form of U.S. and African-American culture. No other nation can claim the distinction of having developed a music exactly like it. Pain, frustration, displacement, mistreatment, and suffering are re-created and suspended within the space of blues performance. Blues lyrics enable people to endure and to resist with the help of humor—and a resolve that blurs into joy. While the blues today is generally recognized as a national cultural form, it originated in African-American society and cannot be separated from African-American identity and history. Its roots are essential to its being.

The patterns, themes, and emotions of the blues are unmistakable. Ethnomusicologist Jeff Todd Titon has stated that the blues are "best understood as a feeling." Words, phrases, or even whole stanzas are often altered from one performance to the next according to the musicians' inspiration. Such variety has led critic Houston Baker to suggest that blues singers may be considered as "translators" in the largest sense of the word because they take the text of another performer and transform it into something completely their own. The blues has become defined by its twelve-bar structure, its use of a 1-4-5 chord structure, and its invocation of a musical "turnaround" that returns the chord progression to its beginning. Although the earliest forms of the blues offered more freedom and variation in chord changes and lyrical progressions than does this definition, approximately ninety percent of all recorded blues songs fit this pattern.

Although no one person or place can be credited with being the inventor or the birthplace of the blues, such music was certainly being played and sung in the years just prior to the turn of the twentieth century. Texas, New Orleans, and particularly the Mississippi Delta region were all instrumental in shaping its sound. Despite efforts to link such regions with the origins of the blues, however, Ma Rainey reported that she first heard the blues being sung in Missouri in 1903. W. C. Handy considered himself the "Father of the Blues" for his role in performing and recording the blues. His "Yellow Dog Blues" resulted from two important encounters noted in his autobiography. While traveling the country as the orchestra leader of the Mahara Minstrels in 1903, he found himself waiting at a train station in Tutwiler, Mississippi. There he heard a young African-American man sliding a steel knife across guitar strings and singing about nothing more than getting ready to ride a train nicknamed the "Yellow Dog" by his fellow sharecroppers. Handy realized the potential for such music because, a year earlier in Cleveland, Mississippi, his traveling nine-piece orchestra had observed a local group receive more money and praise for performing a single tune with what he said was a "disturbing monotony" than the orchestra received for its entire evening performance. Handy copyrighted his blues tunes as early as 1912. Influenced by spirituals, field hollers, and work songs, the blues reached an enormous audience by the early 1920s undoubtedly because of Handy's efforts.

Nevertheless, African-American women such as Mamie Smith, Ma Rainey, Bessie Smith, Ida Cox, and Billie Holiday are the most responsible for the success of the blues. In 1920 Mamie Smith's recording of "Crazy Blues" sold an astonishing seventy-five thousand copies in one month. Bessie Smith's performances commanded as much as $2,000 a week in 1924, giving her the title "Empress of the Blues." But the blues was not isolated within the musical world. It often coexisted with other emerging genres, leading to new hybridized forms as blues musicians continued to experiment and to join with European-American musicians. Thomas A. Dorsey served as Ma Rainey's piano player in the 1920s but then turned his energies completely to gospel music. Jelly Roll Morton's "Mamie's Blues" invokes a blues tradition, yet his contributions also extend well into jazz and ragtime. One of his most important songs, "King Porter Stomp," was a swing music hit for Benny Goodman and his orchestra. Leadbelly's music blurs the line between blues and folk. He began performing with musicians such as Blind Lemon Jefferson and ended with Woody Guthrie in the early 1940s. Finally, Billie Holiday's performances point the way toward a rising jazz scene, and many of them from the 1940s to the 1960s brought new sophistication and unforgettable poignancy to the realm of popular music.

Although the blues eventually headed into the nation's mainstream musical culture, it continued to exert a powerful influence in African-American communities in the rural South and urban North through the Depression years, World War II, and well into the civil rights era. During the second half of the twentieth century, the blues remained a quintessential form of black culture, and it also became associated with white cultural production and mass consumption. Along with great African-American artists such as Willie Mae ("Big Mama") Thornton, Bo Diddley, and Jimi Hendrix, many successful European-American singers such as Elvis Presley, Bob Dylan, Janis Joplin, Kurt Cobain, and Bonnie Raitt integrated the blues into their distinct musical expressions.

FURTHER READING

Chris Albertson. *Bessie*. New Haven: Yale University Press, 2003.

Houston A. Baker, Jr. *Blues, Ideology, and Afro-American Literature*. Chicago: University of Chicago Press, 1984.

W. C. Handy. *Blues: An Anthology*. New York: Da Capo Press, 1990.

——. *Father of the Blues: An Autobiography*. Ed. Arna Bontemps. New York: Da Capo Press, 1991.

Sandra R. Lieb. *Mother of the Blues: A Study of Ma Rainey*. Amherst: University of Massachusetts Press, 1983.

Kip Lornell with Charles K. Wolfe. *The Legend and Life of Leadbelly*. New York: Da Capo Press, 1999.

Stuart Nicholson. *Billie Holiday.* Boston: Northeastern University Press, 1997.

Howard Reich with William Gaines. *Jelly's Blues: The Life, Music, and Redemption of Jelly Roll Morton.* New York: Da Capo Press, 2003.

Jeff Todd Titon. *Downhome Blues Lyrics.* Ed. Chris Frigon and Camille Roman. Boston: Twayne, 1981.

Yellow Dog Blues

W. C. Handy

Ever since Miss Susan Johnson lost her jockey, Lee,
There has been much excitement, more to be;
You can hear her moaning night and morn.
Wonder where my easy rider's gone?

Cablegrams come of sympathy,
Telegrams go of inquiry,
Letters come from down in "Bam"[1]
And ev'rywhere that Uncle Sam
Has even a rural delivery.
All day the phone rings but it's not for me.
At last good tidings fill our hearts with glee;
This message comes from Tennessee:

Dear Sue, your easy rider struck this burg today,
On a southbound rattler, sidedoor Pullman car.
See him here, and he was on the hog.[2]

Easy Rider's gotta stay away
He has to vamp it but the hike ain't far.
He's gone somewhere the Southern 'cross the Yellow Dog.[3]

1914

W. C. Handy (1873–1958) became regarded as the "Father of the Blues" as a result of his early publications of blues songs such as "Yellow Dog Blues." The son of a Baptist minister from Alabama, he taught music at A & M College in Huntsville, led his own orchestra on tours around the country, and played trumpet in a traveling minstrel group. Handy first began writing down the blues he heard in about 1903, and he published his first blues tune, "The Memphis Blues," in 1912.

1. "Bam" is an abbreviation for Alabama.
2. To be "on the hog" suggests that he was living a sexually licentious life.

3. "Yellow Dog" refers to the Yazoo Delta Railroad Line.

St. Louis Blues

W. C. Handy

I hate to see de evenin' sun go down
I hate to see de evenin' sun go down
Cause mah baby, he done lef' dis town

Feelin' tomorrow lak I feel today
Feelin' tomorrow lak I feel today
I'll pack mah trunk, an' make mah getaway

St. Louis woman wid her diamon' rings
Pulls dat man aroun' by her apron strings
'Twant for powder an' for store-bought hair
De man I love would not gone nowhere

Got de St. Louis blues, jes as blue as I can be
Dat man got a heart lak a rock cast in de sea
Or else he would not have gone so far from me

Been to de gypsy to get mah fortune tol'
To de gypsy, done got my fortune tol'
Cause I'm most wild 'bout mah jelly roll

Gypsy done tol' me, "Don't you wear no black"
Yes, she done tol' me, "Don't you wear no black
Go to St. Louis, you can win him back"

Help me to Cairo;[1] make St. Louis by mahself
Git to Cario, find my ol' frien', Jeff
Gwine to pin mahself close to his side
If I flag his train, I sho can ride

I loves dat man lak a schoolboy loves his pie
Lak a Kentucky Colonel loves his mint an' rye
I'll love mah baby till de day I die

You ought to see dat stovepipe brown o' mine
Lak he owns de Dimon' Joseph line
He'd make a cross-eyed 'oman go stone blind

Blacker than midnight, teeth lak flags of truce
Blackest man in de whole St. Louis

---

1. A Mississippi river town in southern Illinois.

Blacker de berry, sweeter is de juice. . . .
A black-headed gal make a freight train jump de track
Said, a black-headed gal make a freight train jump de track
But a long tall gal makes a preacher "Ball de Jack"[2]

Lawd, a blond-headed woman makes a good man leave the town
I said, a blond-headed woman makes a good man leave the town
But a red-headed woman makes a boy slap his papa down. . . .

1914

Although W. C. Handy first published this song, Bessie Smith's 1925 version with Louis Armstrong is the most well-known performance. The singer and the trumpeter use a call-and-response technique throughout the song. Smith's version includes only the first four stanzas of the above lyrics. The collaboration between Smith and Armstrong serves as a reminder of how closely linked jazz and blues were in the 1920s.

Beale Street Blues

W. C. Handy

I've seen the lights of gay Broadway,
Old Market Street, down by the Frisco Bay,
I've strolled the Prado,[1]
I've gambled on the Bourse,[2]
The seven wonders of the world I've seen,
And many are the places I have been.

Take my advice, folks,
And see Beale Street[3] first.
You'll see pretty browns in beautiful gowns,
You'll see tailor-mades and hand-me-downs,
You'll meet honest men and pick-pockets skilled,
You'll find that business never closes till somebody gets killed.

I'd rather be here than any place I know,
I'd rather be here than any place I know.
It's goin' to take the Sergeant
For to make me go.

2. A dance step of the 1920s.
1. Museum in Madrid, Spain.
2. The financial market in Paris.

3. The central gathering street for African Americans in Memphis, Tennessee.

*   *   *

Goin' to the river
Maybe, by and by,
Goin' to the river
And there's a reason why:
Because the river's wet,
And Beale Street's gone dry.

You'll see Hog Nose rest'rants and Chitlin' Cafes,
You'll see jugs and tell of by-gone days,
And places, once places, now just a sham,
You'll see Golden Balls[4] enough to pave the New Jerusalem.

Goin' to the river
Maybe, by and by,
Goin' to the river
And there's a reason why:
Because the river's wet,
And Beale Street's gone dry.

I'd rather be here than any place I know,
I'd rather be here than any place I know.
It's goin' to take the Sergeant
For to make me go.

Goin' to the river
Maybe, by and by,
Goin' to the river
And there's a reason why:
Because the river's wet,
And Beale Street's gone dry.

If Beale Street could talk, if Beale Street could talk[5]
Married men would have to take their beds and walk,
Except one or two who never drink booze,
And the blind man on the corner who sings the Beale Street Blues.

*   *   *

---

4. Golden Ball: the sign of a pawnshop. New Jeru-
salem: a reference to heaven made in Revelation
3:12.

5. James Baldwin's 1974 novel, *If Beale Street
Could Talk*, is based on this line.

I'd rather be here than any place I know,
I'd rather be here than any place I know.
It's goin' to take the Sergeant
For to make me go.

1917

W. C. Handy published this song. His favorite gathering place, the Monarch Club, was located on Beale Street, and a statue of him now stands in a nearby park named in his honor.

Crazy Blues

Perry Bradford

I can't sleep at night
I can't eat a bite—
'Cause the gal I love—
She don't treat me right.
She makes me feel so blue.
I don't know what to do.
Sometimes I sit and sigh
And then begin to cry
'Cause my best friend
Said her last good-bye.
There's a change in the ocean,
Change in the deep blue sea, my baby,
I'll tell you, folks, there ain't no change in me.
My love for that gal will always be.
Now I can read her letters.
I sure can't read her mind.
I thought she's lovin' me.
She's leavin' all the time.
Now I see my poor love was blind.
Now I got the crazy blues since my baby went away.
I ain't got no time to lose.
I must find her today.
Now the doctor's gonna do all that he can.
But what you're gonna need is an undertaker man.
I ain't had nothin' but bad news.
Now I got the crazy blues.

1920

Down-Hearted Blues

Lonie Austin and Alberta Hunter

Gee, but it's hard to love someone, when that someone don't love you,
I'm so disgusted, heartbroken too,
I've got those down-hearted blues.
Once I was crazy about a man, he mistreated me all the time,
The next man I see, he's got to promise to be mine, all mine.

Trouble, trouble, I've had it all my days,
Trouble, trouble, I've had it all my days,
It seems that trouble's going to follow me to my grave.

If I could only find the man, oh, how happy I would be,
To the Good Lord ev'ry night I pray, please send my man back to me
I've almost worried myself to death wond'ring why he went away,
But just wait and see, he's gonna want me back some sweet day.

World in a jug, the stopper's in my hand,
Got the world in a jug, the stopper's in my hand,
Going to hold it, baby, till you come under my command.

Say, I ain't never loved but three men in my life,
No, I ain't never loved but three men in my life,
'Twas my father, my brother, and the man who wrecked my life.

'Cause he mistreated me and he drove me from his door,
Yes, he mistreated me and he drove me from his door
But the Good Book says you'll reap just what you sow.

Oh, it may be a week and it may be a month or two,
Yes, it may be a week and it may be a month or two,
But the day you quit me, honey, it's coming home to you.

Oh, I walked the floor and I wrung my hands and cried,
Yes, I walked the floor and I wrung my hands and cried,
Had the down-hearted blues and couldn't be satisfied.

1922

Bessie Smith's 1923 version of this song sold 780,000 copies in the first six months of its release. Known as the "Empress of the Blues," Smith (1894–1937) became the highest-paid African-American entertainer in the country by 1924. She died in a car accident at the age of forty-three. Her grave remained unmarked until 1970 when Janis Joplin placed a headstone at the burial site.

See See Rider

Ma Rainey

See See Rider, see what you done done!
    Lord, Lord, Lord!
You made me love you, now your gal done come.
You made me love you, now your gal done come.

I'm goin' away, baby, I won't be back till fall.
    Lord, Lord, Lord!
Goin' away, baby, won't be back till fall.
If I find me a good man, I won't be back at all.
I'm gonna buy me a pistol just as long as I am tall.
    Lord, Lord, Lord!

Kill my man and catch the Cannonball.[1]
If he won't have me, he won't have no gal at all.

See See Rider, where did you stay last night?
    Lord, Lord, Lord!
Your shoes ain't buttoned, clothes don't fit you right.
You didn't come home till the sun was shinin' bright.

1924

Gertrude "Ma" Rainey (1886–1939) first recorded this song in 1924. Called the "Mother of the Blues," Rainey married the dancer, comedian, and singer William "Pa" Rainey at the age of eighteen and toured with him until the early 1930s.

Wild Women Don't Have the Blues

Ida Cox

I've got a disposition and a way of my own,
When my mind starts to kicking I let him find a new home,
I get full of good liquor, walk the street all night,
Go home and put my man out if he don't act right.
Wild women don't worry,
Wild women don't have the blues.

You never get nothing by being an angel child,
You'd better change your ways an' get real wild.

---

1. The train known as the Wabash Cannonball, traveling the line running from Cincinnati to New Orleans.

I wanta tell you something, I wouldn't tell you no lie,
Wild women are the only kind that ever get by.
Wild women don't worry,
Wild women don't have the blues.

1924

Ida Cox (1889–1967), who recorded this song, is sometimes considered the "uncrowned queen of the blues" because she is less known than Ma Rainey and Bessie Smith. She recorded more than one hundred songs between 1923 and 1940. She also wrote "Nobody Knows You When You're Down and Out," which was sung by many other singers, including Bessie Smith.

Friendless Blues

Mercedes Gilbert

Feel so low down an' sad Lawd,
Feel so low down an' sad Lawd,
Lost everything I had.

Ain't got no friend nowhere Lawd,
Ain't got no friend nowhere Lawd,
All by myself no one to care.

I met a man in my own home town,
In my own home town.
I met a man in my own home town,
Coaxed me away now he has thrown me down.
I want to see that Indian River shore,
Indian River shore.
I want to see that Indian River shore,
If I get back I'll never leave no more.

When I was home the door was never closed,
door was never closed.
When I was home the door was never closed.
Where my home is now the good Lawd only knows.
'Member the time when I was young and gay,
Had many friends hanging 'round me ev'ry day.

Money's all gone I'm so far from home,
I'm so far from home.

Money's all gone I'm so far from home,
far from home.
I just sit here all alone and cry an' moan,
cry an' moan.

Harlem men won't treat no gal right,
won't treat no gal right.
Harlem men won't treat no gal right,
no gal right.
They make you work all day and fight all night,
fight all night.

1926

Mercedes Gilbert (1889–1952) wrote the words for "Friendless Blues," and W. C. Handy (1873–1958) wrote the music. The song contemplates home from the vantage point of Harlem.

Mamie's Blues

Jelly Roll Morton

De Two-Nineteen done took mah baby away
Two-Nineteen took mah baby away
Two-Seventeen bring her back someday

Stood on the corner with her feets soakin' wet
Stood on the corner with her feets soakin' wet
Beggin' each an' every man that she met

If you can't give me a dollar, give me a lousy dime
Can't give me a dollar, give me a lousy dime
I wanna feed that hungry man of mine.

n.d.

Jelly Roll Morton (Ferdinand Joseph Lamothe; 1890–1941) based this song on one he remembered his New Orleans neighbor Mamie Desdoumes singing when he was very young. Probably the first African American to record with an all-white band, Morton sat in with the New Orleans Rhythm Kings in Chicago during a 1923 session. He was an unquestioned master on the piano who is most remembered as the first true theorist and composer of jazz. His "King Porter Stomp" was recorded by more than thirty different bands and supplied Benny Goodman with one of his biggest hits.

Young Woman's Blues

Bessie Smith

Woke up this mornin' when chickens was crowin' for days
And on the right side of my pilla my man had gone away
By the pilla he left a note reading I'm sorry Jane, you got my goat
No time to marry, no time to settle down
I'm a young woman and ain't done runnin' round
I'm a young woman and ain't done runnin' round

Some people call me a hobo, some call me a bum
Nobody knows my name, nobody knows what I've done
I'm as good as any woman in your town
I ain't high yeller, I'm a deep killa brown
I ain't gonna marry, ain't gonna settle down
I'm gonna drink good moonshine and run these browns down.

See that long lonesome road
Lord, you know it's gotta end
I'm a good woman and I can get plenty men.

1926

Bessie Smith began singing for money at age nine and toured the South with the Theater Owners' Booking Association as a teenager. In 1927 she gained notoriety when she successfully resisted a dozen members of the Ku Klux Klan who were poised to break up one of her performances in Concord, North Carolina.

Backwater Blues

Bessie Smith

When it rain five days an' de skies turned dark as night
When it rain five days an' de skies turned dark as night
Then trouble taken place in the lowland that night

I woke up this mornin', can't even get outa mah do'
I woke up this mornin', can't even get outa mah do'
That's enough trouble to make a po' girl wonder where she wanta go

Then they rowed a little boat about five miles 'cross the pond
They rowed a little boat about five miles 'cross the pond
I packed all mah clothes, th'owed 'em in, an' they rowed me along

*   *   *

When it thunder an' a-lightnin', an' the wind begin to blow
When it thunder an' a-lightnin', an' the wind begin to blow
An' thousan' people ain't got no place to go

Then I went an' stood up on some high ol' lonesome hill
I went an' stood up on some high ol' lonesome hill
An' looked down on the house where I used to live

Backwater blues done cause me to pack mah things an' go
Backwater blues done cause me to pack mah things an' go
Cause mah house fell down an' I cain' live there no mo'

O-o-o-oom, I cain' move no mo'
O-o-o-oom, I cain' move no mo'
There ain' no place fo' a po' ol' girl to go

1927

Bessie Smith knew a great deal about not having anyplace to go. Her father died when she was an infant, and her mother died when she was nine. She lived in a one-room shack in a district of Chattanooga, Tennessee, known as Blue Goose Hollow and in another section of town called Tannery Flats, where she was raised by her older sister Viola.

Prove It on Me Blues

Ma Rainey

Went out last night, had a great big fight,
Everything seemed to go on wrong;
I looked up, to my surprise,
The gal I was with was gone.

Where she went, I don't know,
I mean to follow everywhere she goes;
Folks said I'm crooked, I don't know where she took it,
I want the whole world to know:

They say I do it, ain't nobody caught me,
Sure got to prove it on me;
Went out last night with a crowd of my friends,
They must've been women, 'cause I don't like no men.

It's true I wear a collar and a tie,
Make the wind blow all the while;
They say I do it, ain't nobody caught me,
They sure got to prove it on me.

*   *   *

Say I do it, ain't nobody caught me,
Sure got to prove it on me;
I went out last night with a crowd of my friends,
They must've been women, 'cause I don't like no men.

Wear my clothes just like a fan,
Talk to the girls just like any old man;
'Cause they say I do it, ain't nobody caught me,
Sure got to prove it on me.

1928

Ma Rainey's lyrics suggest issues of lesbianism. A bisexual, Rainey married William "Pa" Rainey when she was eighteen years old. Her performance of this song sometimes included her strutting across the stage wearing men's clothing.

Goodnight Irene

I asked your mother for you
She told me that you was too young
I wish Good Lord I'd never seen your face
I'm sorry you was ever born

CHORUS

Irene goodnight, Irene goodnight
Goodnight Irene, goodnight Irene
I'll get[1] you in my dreams

Sometimes I live in the country
Sometimes I live in the town
Sometimes I have a great notion
To jump into the river and drown

Stop ramblin' and stop gamblin'
Quit stayin' out late at night
Go home unto your wife and your family
Sit down by the fireside bright

*   *   *

---

1. Alternative versions of this song sometime have either "see" or "kiss" in place of "get."

I love Irene, God knows I do
Love her until the sea runs dry
If Irene turns her back on me
I'm gonna take morphine and die.

1933

Huddie Ledbetter, or "Leadbelly" (1885–1949), first recorded this song for the Library of Congress in 1933. It may have been written by a songwriter in Cincinnati near the turn of the century. Accompanied by only his twelve-string guitar or accordion, Leadbelly became a touring companion of Blind Lemon Jefferson in the 1920s and a friend of Woody Guthrie in the early 1940s. The first and last verses of the song included here are often omitted. Recorded by various artists including the Grateful Dead, Van Morrison, Peter, Paul, and Mary, and the Indigo Girls, "Goodnight Irene" was a number-one hit for the Weavers in 1950, led by well-known folk musician Pete Seeger.

JAZZ AND MUSICAL THEATER LYRICS

ALTHOUGH THE NEW ORLEANS music scene of 1895 or the performance of Scott Joplin's "Maple Leaf Rag" in 1899 is sometimes cited as the beginning of jazz, little real agreement exists about the precise place and date that jazz originated. Most scholars agree, however, that in the early decades of the twentieth century a music now known as jazz evolved gradually from many kinds of music, including ragtime, African-American spirituals, marching band music, popular parlor songs, opera, European classical music, Native-American music, work songs, and the blues. The new form was characterized by free simultaneous improvisation by several instrumentalists and vocalists who used the opening notes of a piece as a starting point rather than following the song's notes exactly. As a result, jazz sounded like conversation because even the instrumental music attempted to reproduce the diverse sounds of the human voice.

Interestingly, about this same time a generation of future pioneering lyricists who would create American musical theater—a polyglot genre that both parallels and is intertwined inextricably with the development of jazz—was born in the Jewish neighborhoods on New York's Lower East Side. Such innovators as Ira Gershwin and E. Y. "Yip" Harburg grew up listening to the blues and jazz as well as minstrels, Yiddish theater, vaudeville, musical revues, operettas, Tin Pan Alley, parlor songs, and European music. Alongside such lyricists as Noble Sissle, Cecil Mack, Cole Porter, and P. G. Wodehouse (all of whom crossed racial and class barriers), they transformed the mass-produced lyrics of musical revues and vaudeville developed by giants like Irving Berlin and George M. Cohan into a sophisticated musical art form for film as well as stage that could respond to and improvise upon contemporary life.

Because the developments of jazz and theater songs closely paralleled the modernist era in poetry, they not only influenced Harlem Renaissance poets, including Langston Hughes (who also wrote for musicals). They also affected diverse poets writing during this time, ranging from Edna St. Vincent Millay, T. S. Eliot, William Carlos Williams, Vachel Lindsay, and Melvin B. Tolson to the light versifiers Ogden Nash and Dorothy Parker. Jazz and musical theater lyrics continue to shape poetry in the twenty-first century.

FURTHER READING

Ralph Ellison. *Shadow and Act.* 1964; reprint, New York: Vintage, 1995.

Sascha Feinstein. *Jazz Poetry: From the 1920s to the Present.* Westport, Conn.: Greenwood Press, 1997.

LeRoi Jones [Amiri Baraka]. *Blues People: Negro Music in White America.* New York: William Morrow, 1999.

Eric Porter. *What Is This Thing Called Jazz? African American Musicians as Artists, Critics, and Activists.* Berkeley: University of California Press, 2002.

Bernard Rosenberg and Ernest Harburg. *The Broadway Musical: Collaboration in Commerce and Art.* New York: New York University Press, 1993.

Deena Rosenberg. *Fascinating Rhythm: The Collaboration of George and Ira Gershwin.* New York: Dutton, 1991.

Gunther Schuller. *Early Jazz: Its Roots and Musical Development.* 1968; reprint, Oxford, Eng.: Oxford University Press, 1986.

———. *The Swing Era: The Development of Jazz, 1920–1945.* Oxford, Eng.: Oxford University Press, 1991.

Barry Ulanov. *A History of Jazz in America.* New York: Da Capo Press, 1972.

Martin Williams. *Jazz Tradition.* Oxford, Eng.: Oxford University Press, 1993.

Hello! My Baby

Joseph Howard

Hello! my baby,
hello! my honey,
hello! my ragtime gal;
Send me a kiss by wire,
baby, my heart's on fire!

✻   ✻   ✻

If you refuse me,
honey, you'll lose me,
then you'll be left alone.
Oh, baby, telephone
and tell me I'm your own.

1900

The lyricist Joseph Howard was touring in vaudeville in 1899 when he overheard a train porter talking to his girlfriend on the telephone. The conversation gave him the idea for this cake-walking ragtime song, which he wrote with his wife, Ida Emerson. When Howard sang it for the first time onstage, it became an instant success. Audiences related easily to the ragtime theme and the use of the telephone, both of which were considered new and exciting.

I've a Shooting Box in Scotland

Cole Porter

VERSE 1

Nowadays, it's rather nobby[1]
To regard one's private hobby
As the object of one's tenderest affections;
Some excel at Alpine climbing
Others have a turn for rhyming,
While a lot of people go in for collections.

Such as prints by Hiroshigi,[2]
Edelweiss[3] from off the Rigi,
Jacobean[4] soup tureens,
Early types of limousines,
Pipes constructed from a dry cob,
Baseball hits by Mister Ty Cobb,[5]
Locks of Mrs. Browning's hair,[6]
Photographs of Ina Claire,[7]

1. Nob: slang for a rich person, a fat cat.
2. Ando Hiroshige (1797–1858), Japanese woodblock-print artist, best known for his popular print "The Wave."
3. European mountain flower. Rigi: Swiss mountain.
4. From the time of King James I of England (reigned 1603–25).

5. Baseball's greatest star in 1916.
6. Elizabeth Barrett Browning (1806–1861), beloved British poet; married to poet Robert Browning.
7. American actress (1892–1985) on Broadway and in films.

First editions still uncut,
Daily pranks of Jeff and Mutt,[8]
Della Robbia[9] singing boys,
Signatures of Alfred Noyes,[10]
Fancy bantams,[11]
Grecian vases,
Tropic beetles,
Irish laces,
But my favorite pastime
Is collecting country places.

REFRAIN 1

I've a shooting box[12] in Scotland,
I've a chateau[13] in Touraine,
I've a silly little chalet
In the Interlaken Valley,[14]
I've a hacienda in Spain,
I've a private fjord in Norway,
I've a villa close to Rome,
And in traveling
It's really quite a comfort to know
That you're never far from home!

VERSE 2

Now it's really very funny
What an awful lot of money
On exorbitant hotels a chap can squander;
But I never have to do so,
Like resourceful Mister Crusoe,[15]
I can find a home however far I wander.

---

8. "Mutt and Jeff": a nationally popular comic strip originated by Bud Fisher.
9. Della Robbia Luca (ca. 1400–1482), Italian sculptor who worked in marble and glazed terra-cotta.
10. Popular British poet (1880–1958), a professor at Princeton from 1914.
11. Brightly colored miniature domestic fowl, originally imported from Bantam Java
12. A small country house used by hunters during the shooting season; a shooting lodge.

13. Castle or country house (French). Touraine: city in France's Loire Valley.
14. Valley in Switzerland surrounded by views of the Swiss mountains. A chalet is a summer cottage or country house in those mountains.
15. Robinson Crusoe, famous hero of the Daniel Defoe novel who was shipwrecked on a desert island and survived for many years.

REFRAIN 2

I've a bungalow at Simla,[16]
I've an island east of Maine,
If you care for hotter places,
I've an African oasis
On an uninhabited plain;
I've a houseboat on the Yangtze,[17]
I've an igloo up at Nome,[18]
Yes, in traveling
It's really quite a comfort to know
That you're never far from home!

1916

Cole Porter (1891–1964) was one of Broadway and Hollywood's leading lyricists and composers for more than four decades. His lyrics are noted for their adroit and surprising comic rhymes (he thought nothing of rhyming "soup tureens" with "limousines") and for their ironic sophistication and extraordinary range of topical reference. This early example of Porter's polished art was first performed at a campus musical (*Paranoia*, 1914) at Yale, where he was an undergraduate. It was showcased (slightly revised) in Porter's first Broadway musical, *See America First* (1916), and later received a memorable recording by Fred Astaire and Bing Crosby.

Till the Clouds Roll By

Jerome Kern and P. G. Wodehouse

VERSE 1

[She]   I'm so sad to think that I had to
Drive you from your home so coolly.

[He]   I'd be gaining nothing by remaining,
What would Missus Grundy say?
Her conventions, kindly recollect them!
We must please respect them duly.

[She]   My intrusion needs explaining;
I felt my courage waning.
Please, I beg don't mention it!
I should not mind a bit,
But it has started raining.

---

16. Resort city in India, in the foothills of the Himalayan Mountains.

17. The longest river in China.
18. Coastal city in northern Alaska.

REFRAIN

[Both]   Oh, the rain comes pitter, patter,
And I'd like to be safe in bed.
Skies are weeping, while the world is sleeping,
Trouble heaping on our head.
It is vain to remain and chatter,
And to wait for a clearer sky.
Helter skelter, I must fly for shelter
Till the clouds roll by.

VERSE 2

[She]   What bad luck, it's coming down in buckets;
Have you an umbrella handy?

[He]   I've a warm coat, waterproof, a storm coat,
I shall be alright, I know.
Later on, too, I will ward the grippe off,
With a little nip of brandy.

[She]   Or a glass of toddy draining,
You'd find that more sustaining.
Don't be worried, I entreat,
I've rubbers for my feet,
So I don't mind it raining.

[Both repeat refrain]

1917

Although Jerome Kern is known primarily as a composer, he collaborated with P. G. Wodehouse on the lyrics for this song and wrote the music as well. When the song was introduced in the musical show *Oh Boy!* in 1917, it became popular and has remained so. Kern's operatic-derived musical style combined with Wodehouse's wit and polish created a bridge between European operetta and a distinctively American theater song reflecting contemporary musical forms and life. In the 1940s, a film biography was made of Kern's life with the title *Till the Clouds Roll By*, which featured such box-office stars as Judy Garland, June Allyson, Lena Horne, Tony Martin, Van Johnson, and Van Heflin.

Ja Da

Bob Carleton

Ja Da, Ja Da,
Ja Da Ja Da jing jing jing.
Ja Da, Ja Da,

Ja Da Ja Da jing jing jing.
That's a funny little bit of melody
It's so soothing and appealing to me.
It goes Ja Da, Ja Da,
Ja Da Ja Da jing jing jing.

1918

"Ja Da" was written as a parody of the pseudo-Asian songs that were popular in the early twentieth century and followed the two major "Orientalist" successes, "Japanese Sandman" and "Hindustan." Some see in Bob Carleton's lyrics a relationship to modernist Dadaism, since they use syllables—or, more properly, sounds—for their own sake rather than for meaning. Dixieland bands took up the tune, and "Ja Da" became part of the Dixieland repertoire because it lent itself easily to collective improvisation. When the Latin cha-cha became popular during the 1950s, the lyrics were improvised upon and became "ja-da cha-cha-cha," giving the song yet another life within that Latino musical genre.

There's Magic in the Air

Ira Gershwin

Wise men all have come to this conclusion,
Magic is a fanciful delusion
But with them I can't agree,
For anyone can plainly see
You could put their notions in confusion.

REFRAIN

For there is magic in the air
When you're around.
In you a vision fair
I know I've found.
Your charm is so appealing,
It sets my mind a-reeling,
And makes my heart begin to jump and bound.
Of gloom I'm not aware
When you're around.
I lose my very care
Whene'er you're near, dear.
It's clear, dear,
There's magic in the air.

1918

In "There's Magic in the Air," Ira Gershwin reveals the lighthearted touch that he was developing sublimely for the most sentimental of topics on the Broadway stage. Regarded as arguably the lyricist who developed the art of the theater song to its highest level during the 1920s and excelled the most brilliantly in a witty versified speech, Gershwin and his frequent collaborator—his famous brother George—were the sons of middle-class Russian Jewish immigrants from St. Petersburg. They began collaborating in 1918 in such early musicals as *Half Past Eight*, which featured this song. E. Y. "Yip" Harburg, whose famous "Brother, Can You Spare a Dime?" and "Over the Rainbow" are also included in this entry, regarded Ira Gershwin as his lifelong close friend from their adolescence onward and his pivotal mentor in the art of writing song lyrics.

I'm Just Wild About Harry

Noble Sissle

I'm just wild about Harry
And Harry's wild about me.
The heavenly blisses of his kisses
Fill me with ecstasy.

He's sweet just like chocolate candy,
And just like honey from the bee.
Oh, I'm just wild about Harry
And he's just wild about,
Cannot do without,
He's just wild about me.

1921

With words by Noble Sissle and music by Eubie Blake, this ragtime strutting song was an instant success in the 1920s when it was introduced in the musical comedy *Shuffle Along*, the first all-African-American production to be a hit on Broadway.

Charleston

Cecil Mack

Charleston, Charleston,
Made in Carolina
Some dance, some prance
I'll say,
There's nothing finer than the

Charleston, Charleston,
Lord, how you can shuffle,

Ev'ry step you do
Leads to something new,
Man I'm telling you,
It's a lapazoo.

Buck dance, Wing dance,
Will be a back number,
But the Charleston, the new Charleston
That dance is surely a comer.

Some time,
You'll dance it one time,
The dance called the Charleston,
Made in South Caroline!

1923

This song accompanied the dance sensation known as the Charleston that replaced the shimmy and became the signature dance of the 1920s. Although the song was written and first performed in 1913, the dance that made it popular was introduced with it in the all-African-American revue *Runnin' Wild* in 1923. Cecil Mack wrote the words, and Jimmy Johnson composed the music.

Star Dust

Mitchell Parish

And now the purple dusk of twilight time
Steals across the meadows of my heart;
High up in the sky the little stars climb,
Always reminding me that we're apart.

You wandered down the lane and far away,
Leaving me a song that will not die;
Love is now the Star Dust of yesterday,
The music of the years gone by.

Sometimes I wonder why I spend the lonely night
Dreaming of a song?
The melody haunts my reverie,
And I am once again with you,
When our love was new
And each kiss an inspiration.

*   *   *

But that was long ago,
Now my consolation
Is in the Star Dust of a song.
Beside a garden wall,
When stars are bright,
You are in my arms,
The nightingale tells his fairy tale
Of paradise where roses grew.
Tho' I dream in vain,
In my heart it will remain:
My Star Dust melody,
The memory of love's refrain.

1929

Every dance band and orchestra had its signature pieces, and "Star Dust," with words by Mitchell Parish and music by Hoagy Carmichael, became associated with Artie Shaw and his orchestra in 1940 when they performed it for the first time. But the song was originally introduced in 1929. Carmichael had conceived of it as a ragtime piano piece because ragtime was very popular at the time. But Victor Young, an arranger for the Isham Jones Orchestra, decided to slow down the tempo and transform it into a ballad with words by Parish. Today there are more than one hundred different recorded versions of the song. While the Artie Shaw Orchestra was responsible for making "Star Dust" a household song, the tune received a great boost in popularity when the newspaper columnist Walter Winchell liked it so much that he mentioned it in nearly every column. Nat King Cole's version, often heard at the Copacabana Club in New York, is considered to be one of the most memorable.

It Don't Mean a Thing (If It Ain't Got That Swing)

Edward Kennedy "Duke" Ellington and Irving Mills

It don't mean a thing if it ain't got that swing.
Doo wah doo wah doo wah doo wah doo wah doo wah doo wah doo wah
It don't mean a thing all you got to do is sing.
Doo wah doo wah doo wah doo wah doo wah doo wah doo wah doo wah
It makes no diff'rence if it's sweet or hot,
Just give that rhythm ev'rything you've got.
Oh, it don't mean a thing if it ain't got that swing.
Doo wah doo wah doo wah doo wah doo wah doo wah doo wah doo wah
Oh, what good is melody, What good is music
If it ain't possessin' somethin' sweet.

It ain't the melody, It ain't the music.
There's somethin' else that makes the tune complete.
Oh! Don't mean a thing if ain't got that swing.
Doo wah doo wah doo wah doo wah doo wah doo wah doo wah doo wah

1932

This song, written by Edward Kennedy "Duke" Ellington and Irving Mills, encapsulates the immense popularity of swing music in the United States during the 1930s and 1940s as it replaced the hot jazz of the 1920s. The use of syllables to imitate the sound of instruments was widespread and gave singers the opportunity to improvise. Mills was also a major music manager and publisher who began life in the Jewish New York neighborhood on the East Side.

Brother, Can You Spare a Dime?

E. Y. "Yip" Harburg

They used to tell me
I was building a dream
And so I followed the mob
Where there was earth to plough
Or guns to bear
I was always there
Right on the job

They used to tell me
I was building a dream
With peace and glory ahead
Why should I be standing in line
Just waiting for bread?

CHORUS
Once I built a railroad,
Made it run
Made it race against time
Once I built a railroad
Now it's done
Brother, can you spare a dime?

Once I built a tower
To the sun
Brick and rivet and lime

Once I built a tower
Now it's done
Brother, can you spare a dime?

Once in khaki suits
Gee, we looked swell
Full of that Yankee Doodle-de-dum
Half a million boots went sloggin' thru hell
I was the kid with the drum

Say, don't you remember
They called me "Al"
It was "Al" all the time
Say, don't you remember
I'm your pal
Buddy, can you spare a dime?

1932

"Brother, Can You Spare a Dime?" with lyrics by E. Y. "Yip" Harburg and music by Jay Gorney, was written in the depths of the Great Depression and premiered in the musical *Americana* on Broadway in 1932. It reflects the pain of unemployment and the iniquities of working-class life. Harburg commented in Studs Terkel's *Hard Times* that the man in the song "is really saying: 'I made an investment in this country. Where the hell are my dividends?' . . . It doesn't reduce him to a beggar. It makes him a dignified human asking questions—and a bit outraged, too, as he should be." Some conservatives considered the song anti-capitalist propaganda and attempted to ban it from the radio, but it soon became popular as a sort of anthem of the Depression.

Over the Rainbow

E. Y. "Yip" Harburg

VERSE

When all the world is a hopeless jumble
And the raindrops tumble all around
Heaven opens a magic lane

When all the clouds darken up the skyway
There's a rainbow highway to be found
Leading from your windowpane
To a place behind the sun
Just a step beyond the rain

CHORUS

Somewhere over the rainbow
Way up high
There's a land that I heard of
Once in a lullaby

Somewhere over the rainbow
Skies are blue,
And the dreams that you dare to dream
Really do come true

Someday I'll wish upon a star
And wake up where the clouds are far behind me
Where troubles melt like lemon drops
Away above the chimney tops
That's where you'll find me

Somewhere over the rainbow
Bluebirds fly,
Birds fly over the rainbow
Why then oh why can't I?

If happy little bluebirds fly
Beyond the rainbow
Why oh why can't I?

1939

"Over the Rainbow," with words by E. Y. "Yip" Harburg and music by Harold Arlen, is quite possibly the best-known song in the entire American songbook. Sung with unforgettable poignancy by Judy Garland in the film *The Wizard of Oz* (1939), the lyric seems to speak of a girl's yearning for lost happiness and security. But the song has a communal message as well. Harburg was a well-known political liberal. The child of Jewish immigrants living on New York's Lower East Side, he grew up in poverty. As a young man, he developed an electrical appliance company, only to lose the business after the 1929 stock market crash. In desperation, he turned to writing song lyrics. "Over the Rainbow" reflects those dark times in the imagery of clouds and rain that dominates the initial verse (not sung in the film). The chorus evokes a compensatory vision of social utopia, a "land" where "troubles melt like lemon drops" and where "the dreams that you dare to dream really do come true." The movie was based on *The Wizard of Oz* by Frank Baum, but Harburg added the rainbow to the show. Among Harburg's great achievements in this musical film is the innovative use of song lyrics to develop both the characters and the plot so that everything in the production was integrated.

GOSPEL MUSIC stands somewhere between traditional African-American church hymns and popular songs such as the blues. This hybridized form came into its own during the 1930s. Instruments formerly consigned to the realms of "the devil" — tambourines, trombones, and trumpets — began to accompany the clapping, foot tapping, and swaying of church choirs and congregations. Church vocalists started to improvise their lyrics by relying on the verbal heights of shouts, moans, and half-cries as well as the solemn seriousness of spoken phrases. The call-and-response tradition of work songs also began to appear in gospel songs as lead vocalists called out to the accompanying choir, which assumed the duties of responding. Churches became sites of highly energetic worship, where half the service would sometimes be devoted to music. The common phrase "holy roller" became associated with such services because participants sometimes rolled on the floor in their excitement and praise.

Gospel music's increased popularity resulted in great part from the efforts of Thomas A. Dorsey. Dorsey was raised in the Baptist religious tradition and began his musical career as a piano player and writer, appearing with such artists as Ma Rainey, Tampa Red, and Lionel Hampton. In these early performances in blues and jazz settings, Dorsey sometimes appeared under the name of "Georgia Tom." Dorsey turned his attention exclusively to gospel music in 1929. His music was largely inspired by the example and innovations of C. Albert Tindley, whose hymns included "Stand by Me" (later appropriated in the 1960s) and "I'll Overcome" (which later became the classic "We Shall Overcome"). Because Dorsey served as the minister of music at the Pilgrim Baptist Church in Chicago, this city became synonymous with the early development of contemporary black gospel music. Dorsey made gospel music accessible by following the lead of blues legend W. C. Handy in offering his songs at affordable prices as individual sheets of music rather than in larger, more expensive collected volumes. While other gospel groups such as the Dinwiddie Colored Quartet (recorded in 1902) and men such as Homer Rodeheaver (who established Rainbow Records in 1916) clearly preceded Dorsey, the first great era of gospel was launched when Dorsey performed two of his songs in 1930 at the National Baptist Convention in Chicago. Dorsey was also responsible for training and accompanying several gospel stars, including Mahalia Jackson. His tours across the country from 1932 to 1944 under the title "Evenings with Dorsey" contributed immeasurably to the national awareness of this emerging musical genre.

As a result of a widespread desire to update and replace the inherited spirituals of previous generations, many gospel songs eventually achieved the status and popularity of major hits. "The Old Rugged Cross" is often found in the pages of current hymnals. "Take My Hand, Precious Lord" is still performed regularly. Across the country, young children attending churches recite variations on "This Little Light of Mine," while groups of Boy Scouts sing "Down by the Riverside" at their regular meetings.

FURTHER READING

Alan Lewens, dir. *Too Close to Heaven: The Story of Gospel Music.* Videocassette. Princeton, 1997.
Allan Moore, ed. *The Cambridge Companion to Blues and Gospel Music.* Cambridge, Eng.: Cambridge University Press, 2002.

The Old Rugged Cross

George Bennard

On a hill far away stood an old rugged cross,
The emblem of suffering and shame;
And I love that old cross, where the dearest and best
For a world of lost sinners was slain.

CHORUS

So I'll cherish the old rugged cross,
Till my trophies at last I lay down;
I will cling to the old rugged cross,
And exchange it someday for a crown.

Oh, that old rugged cross, so despised by the world,
Has a wondrous attraction for me;
For the dear Lamb of God left his glory above
To bear it to dark Calvary.

In the old rugged cross, stained with blood so divine,
A wondrous beauty I see;
For 'twas on that old cross Jesus suffered and died
To pardon and sanctify me.

To the old rugged cross I will ever be true,
Its shame and reproach gladly bear;
Then he'll call me some day to my home far away,
Where his glory forever I'll share.

1913

George Bennard (1873–1958) wrote the music and lyrics for this hymn, which is derived in part from Galatians 6:14. He served as an evangelist in Canada as well as throughout the United States, where he lived in Ohio, Michigan, and Wisconsin after having earlier worked for the Salvation Army in Illinois.

Take My Hand, Precious Lord

Thomas A. Dorsey

Precious Lord, take my hand,
Lead me on, let me stand,
I am tired, I am weak, I am worn.
Through the storm, through the night
Lead me on to the light,
Take my hand, precious Lord,
Lead me home.

When my way grows drear,
Precious Lord, linger near.
When my life is almost gone,
Hear my cry, hear my call,
Hold my hand lest I fall.
Take my hand, precious Lord,
Lead me home.

When the darkness appears
And the night draws near,
And the day is past and gone,
At the river I stand,
Guide my feet, hold my hand.
Take my hand, precious Lord,
Lead me home.

1932

Written by Thomas A. Dorsey (1899–1993) when his wife Nettie died while giving birth, "Take My Hand, Precious Lord" won great attention when it was performed by Mahalia Jackson. Dorsey worked closely with Jackson and adapted the music of George N. Allen's "Maitland" (1844) for this song. The son of a Baptist minister, he wrote more than two hundred songs during his lifetime for artists such as Tampa Red, Ma Rainey, and Bessie Smith.

This Little Light of Mine

Harry Dixon Loes and Avis B. Christiansen

Oh, this little light of mine,
I'm gonna let it shine.
This little light of mine,
I'm gonna let it shine.
This little light of mine,

I'm gonna let it shine.
Let it shine, shine, shine,
Let it shine.

All in my home,
I'm gonna let it shine.
All in my home,
I'm gonna let it shine.
All in my home,
I'm gonna let it shine.
Let it shine, shine, shine,
Let it shine.

God give it to me,
I'm gonna let it shine.
God give it to me,
I'm gonna let it shine.
God give it to me,
I'm gonna let it shine.
Let it shine, shine, shine,
Let it shine.

This little light of mine,
I'm gonna let it shine.
This little light of mine,
I'm gonna let it shine.
This little light of mine,
I'm gonna let it shine.
Let it shine, shine, shine,
Let it shine.

Everywhere I go,
I'm gonna let it shine.
Everywhere I go,
I'm gonna let it shine.
Everywhere I go,
I'm gonna let it shine.
Let it shine, shine, shine,
Let it shine.

n.d.

Harry Dixon Loes (1892–1965) wrote and composed this song with Avis B. Christiansen (b. 1895). The pair also wrote the hymns "Blessed Redeemer" and "Love Found a Way."

Down by the Riverside

I'm gonna lay down my sword and shield
Down by the riverside
Down by the riverside
Down by the riverside
I'm gonna lay down my sword and shield
Down by the riverside
Study war no more

CHORUS

I ain't gonna study war no more
Ain't gonna study war no more
I ain't gonna study war no more
I ain't gonna study war no more
Ain't gonna study war no more
Ain't gonna study war no more

I'm gonna put on my long white robes
Down by the riverside
Down by the riverside
Down by the riverside
I'm gonna put on my long white robes
Down by the riverside
Study war no more

I'm gonna meet all my friends who're gone
Down by the riverside
Down by the riverside
Down by the riverside
Gonna meet all my friends who're gone
Down by the riverside
Study war no more

I'm gonna put on my golden shoes
Down by the riverside
Down by the riverside
Down by the riverside
Gonna put on my golden shoes
Down by the riverside
Study war no more

*   *   *

I'm gonna meet my dear old mother
Down by the riverside
Down by the riverside
Down by the riverside
Gonna meet my dear old mother
Down by the riverside
Study war no more

n.d.

Recorded by such varied artists as Louis Armstrong, Patsy Cline, Elvis Presley, Sister Rosetta Tharpe, and Peter, Paul, and Mary, this song continues to be popular with many different peoples and groups.

EVARISTO RIBERA CHEVREMONT
1896–1974

EVARISTO RIBERA CHEVREMONT's poetry reflects the Puerto Rican cultural imperative of the early twentieth century to resist U.S. imperialism and influence. It does so by aligning itself with Spanish cultural models, including *modernismo* and other poetics sweeping across the Americas. Like other poets from the Creole bourgeoisie, Chevremont felt a deep nostalgia for Spain despite its often violent relationship with the island colony during the period of Spanish colonialism.

The selection included here reveals Chevremont's alliance with communism and socialism, which were burgeoning in Europe as well as in Latin American countries. A major revolution, for instance, began in Mexico in 1910. Chevremont advocates a masculinized proletariat, a "symphony of the hammers" to replace the sweet sounds of the piano, viola, and other instruments of the nobility and upper classes. Chevremont's interest in the sounds of industry aligns him with modern and avant-garde composers and poets in Europe who were including them in their work.

FURTHER READING

E. Mazan, ed. *Inventing a Word: An Anthology of Twentieth-Century Puerto Rican Poetry.* New York: Columbia University Press, 1980.
Alfredo Matula and Ivan Silen, eds. *The Puerto Rican Poets.* New York: Bantam, 1972.

La sinfonía de los martillos

En el silencio áspero retumban los martillos.
Es una nueva música de vigoroso ritmo.
Es música que expone, con masculino empuje,
La rígida grandeza del proletario espíritu.

En el silencio áspero retumban los martillos.

Oyendo las canciones eróticas y burdas,
de tono desmayado, se cansan los oídos.
El hombre de hoy reclama la brusca sinfonía
forjada por la mano brutal de nuestro siglo.

En el silencio áspero retumban los martillos.

Retumban en talleres de llama y humareda.
Retumban, anchurosos, potentes, los martillos.
Y, al retumbar, descubren el alma del acero.
El alma del acero se entrega en el sonido.

En el silencio áspero retumban los martillos.

Retumban los martillos, retumban los martillos.
Retumban, anchurosos, potentes, los martillos.
Y apagan las dulzuras del piano y de la viola,
sutiles instrumentos del enervador flúido.

En el silencio áspero retumban los martillos.

Gavotas, minuetos, romanzas y oberturas
denuncian una época de magistral estilo;
pero la sinfonía de los martillos dice
de la pujanza cruda de un tiempo vasto en ímpetus.

En el silencio áspero retumban los martillos.

No es hora del perfume, ni es hora de las citas.
No es hora del deleite, ni es hora de los vinos.
No es hora del poema de untuosos maquillajes.
Es hora del poema del músculo y del grito.

En el silencio áspero retumban los martillos.

*　　*　　*

Retumban los martillos, retumban los martillos.
Retumban, anchurosos, potentes, los martillos.
Retumban los martillos. Su ruda sinfonía
me enseña la energía compacta de lo físico.

En el silencio áspero retumban los martillos.

En el silencio áspero retumban los martillos.
Es una nueva música de vigoroso ritmo.
Es música que expone, con masculino empuje,
La rígida grandeza del proletario espíritu.

En el silencio áspero retumban los martillos.

[TRANS.] Symphony of the Hammers

In the turgid silence the hammers rumble.
A new music of powerful cadence.
Music that uncovers with masculine strength
the rigid grandeur of the proletarian spirit.

In the turgid silence the hammers rumble.

The ears tire of listening to the limp sounds
of the vulgar, erotic songs.
The man of today demands the brisk symphony
forged by the brutal hand of our century.

In the turgid silence the hammers rumble.

They rumble in factories of flame and smoke.
Vast and potent the hammers rumble.
And, rumbling, they discover the soul of steel.
The soul of steel melts into the sound.

In the turgid silence the hammers rumble.

The hammers rumble, the hammers rumble.
Vast and potent the hammers rumble.
And they muffle the sweetness of the piano and the viola,
subtle instruments of enervated flow.

In the turgid silence the hammers rumble.

*   *   *

Gavottes,[1] minuets, romances and overtures
denounce an epoch of masterful style;
but the symphony of the hammers tells
of the crude power of a vast expanse of time.

In the turgid silence the hammers rumble.

It is not the hour of perfume, nor the hour of dates.
It is not the hour of pleasure, nor the hour of wines.
It is not the hour of greasy makeup.
It is the hour of the poem of the muscle and the scream.

In the turgid silence the hammers rumble.

The hammers rumble, the hammers rumble.
Vast and potent the hammers rumble.
The hammers rumble. Their rude symphony
shows me the compact force of the physical.

In the turgid silence the hammers rumble.

In the turgid silence the hammers rumble.
A new music of powerful cadence.
Music that uncovers with masculine strength
the rigid grandeur of the proletarian spirit.

In the turgid silence the hammers rumble.

n.d.

Note how "Symphony of the Hammers" uses repetition to drown out the "limp" sounds of the musics that Chevremont believes are part of the past. The poem creates a new music appropriate to the new world dominated by the proletariat.

LOUISE BOGAN
1897–1970

Louise bogan was born in Livermore Falls, Maine, and her childhood was disturbed by the difficult relationship between her working-class parents. As Cheryl Walker notes, Bogan's mother, May, "was discontented with her husband and

---

1. Classical musical forms associated with such European composers as Wolfgang Amadeus Mozart, who wrote in the imperial court systems.

prone to clandestine extramarital affairs. Sometimes violent and hysterical, she was also unintentionally cruel to Louise, as when she abandoned her husband and children for extended periods of time." Bogan later complained of the "incredibly ugly mill towns of my childhood," and Walker suggests that "Bogan's visual memories of the New England towns she lived in are strangely infected by what must have been her emotional torment."

Bogan remained reticent about her troubled childhood, but the signs of emotional trauma — as registered in her austerely dark and haunted dream landscapes and her persistent attraction toward and recoiling from extreme emotion — keep reappearing in such poems as "Medusa" and "The Sleeping Fury." In these and other poems, female figures appear both as icons of power and as figures to appease or fear. Bogan observed that "once form has been smashed, it has been smashed for good, and once a forbidden subject has been released it has been released for good," and her poems display ambivalence about the maintenance or smashing of form and about the concealment or release of forbidden subjects. Yet many of Bogan's later poems work past her earlier resentment toward a sharply edged yet elegant tranquility.

Bogan attended Boston Girls' Latin School and spent a year at Boston University. She married, unhappily, at age nineteen in 1916, and soon separated. She was widowed in 1920 and remarried, again unhappily, in 1925 and divorced in 1937. Bogan reserved her best energies for her poetry and, increasingly in later years, for the literary criticism she wrote for the *New Yorker* and other journals. As her poem "The Alchemist" declares, "I burned my life, that I might find / A passion wholly of the mind." In praising the artistic result, her sometime companion, the poet Theodore Roethke, saw Bogan as a "true inheritor" of the great poetry of the past. He called her a poet who "writes out of the severest lyrical tradition in English," whose subjects are "love, passion, its complexities, its tensions, its betrayals," and whose obliquity—in never stating the experience directly in the poem—"brings Bogan close to Emily Dickinson and Marianne Moore." As W. H. Auden noted in a funeral eulogy, Bogan's life was a "struggle to wrest beauty and joy out of dark places."

FURTHER READING

Louise Bogan. *The Blue Estuaries: Poems, 1923–1968.* New York: Farrar, Straus & Giroux, 1968.

Elizabeth Frank. *Louise Bogan: A Portrait.* New York: Knopf, 1985.

Claire E. Knox. *Louise Bogan: A Reference Source.* Metuchen, N.J.: Scarecrow Press, 1990.

Theodore Roethke. *On the Poet and His Craft: Selected Prose.* Seattle: University of Washington Press, 1965.

Cheryl Walker. *Masks Outrageous and Austere: Culture, Psyche, and Persona in Modern Women Poets.* Bloomington: University of Indiana Press, 1991.

Medusa

I had come to the house, in a cave of trees,
Facing a sheer sky.
Everything moved,—a bell hung ready to strike,
Sun and reflection wheeled by.

When the bare eyes were before me
And the hissing hair,
Held up at a window, seen through a door.
The stiff bald eyes, the serpents on the forehead
Formed in the air.

This is a dead scene forever now.
Nothing will ever stir.
The end will never brighten it more than this,
Nor the rain blur.

The water will always fall, and will not fall,
And the tipped bell make no sound.
The grass will always be growing for hay
Deep on the ground.

And I shall stand here like a shadow
Under the great balanced day,
My eyes on the yellow dust, that was lifting in the wind,
And does not drift away.

1921

Medusa was, in Greek mythology, one of three hideous sisters, the Gorgons. She had snakes for hair, and her gaze could turn men into stone. When she was approached by Perseus, who slew her with the magical aid of the gods Athena and Hermes, she was surrounded by the bodies of petrified men. The poem re-creates the stony landscape that surrounded Medusa and her sisters.

Women

Women have no wilderness in them,
They are provident instead,
Content in the tight hot cell of their hearts
To eat dusty bread.

✳   ✳   ✳

They do not see cattle cropping red winter grass,
They do not hear
Snow water going down under culverts
Shallow and clear.

They wait, when they should turn to journeys,
They stiffen, when they should bend.
They use against themselves that benevolence
To which no man is friend.

They cannot think of so many crops to a field
Or of clean wood cleft by an axe.
Their love is an eager meaninglessness
Too tense, or too lax.

They hear in every whisper that speaks to them
A shout and a cry.
As like as not, when they take life over their door-sills
They should let it go by.

1922

The Alchemist

I burned my life, that I might find
A passion wholly of the mind,
Thought divorced from eye and bone,
Ecstasy come to breath alone.
I broke my life, to seek relief
From the flawed light of love and grief.

With mounting beat the utter fire
Charred existence and desire.
It died low, ceased its sudden thresh.
I had found unmysterious flesh —
Not the mind's avid substance — still
Passionate beyond the will.

1922

Bogan's alchemist may be a poet who magically yet painfully converts the lead of traumatic experience into the gold of art.

The Crows

The woman who has grown old
And knows desire must die,
Yet turns to love again,
Hears the crows' cry.

She is a stem long hardened,
A weed that no scythe mows.
The heart's laughter will be to her
The crying of the crows.

Who slide in the air with the same voice
Over what yields not, and what yields,
Alike in spring, and when there is only bitter
Winter-burning[1] in the fields.

1922

Henceforth, From the Mind

Henceforth, from the mind,
For your whole joy, must spring
Such joy as you may find
In any earthly thing,
And every time and place
Will take your thought for grace.

Henceforth, from the tongue,
From shallow speech alone,
Comes joy you thought, when young,
Would wring you to the bone,
Would pierce you to the heart
And spoil its stop and start.

Henceforth, from the shell,
Wherein you heard, and wondered
At oceans like a bell
So far from ocean sundered—
A smothered sound that sleeps
Long lost within lost deeps,

---

1. Farmers sometimes burn their fields in winter to remove excess vegetation and destroy harmful insects.

            *   *   *

Will chime you change and hours,
The shadow of increase,
Will sound you flowers
Born under troubled peace—
Henceforth, henceforth
Will echo sea and earth.

1931

Theodore Roethke considered "Henceforth, From the Mind" Bogan's masterpiece, "a poem that could be set beside the best work of the Elizabethans."

The Sleeping Fury

You are here now,
Who were so loud and feared, in a symbol before me,
Alone and asleep, and I at last look long upon you.

Your hair fallen on your cheek, no longer in the semblance of serpents,
Lifted in the gale; your mouth, that shrieked so, silent.
You, my scourge, my sister, lie asleep, like a child,
Who, after rage, for an hour quiet, sleeps out its tears.

The days close to winter
Rough with strong sound. We hear the sea and the forest,
And the flames of your torches fly, lit by others,
Ripped by the wind, in the night. The black sheep for sacrifice
Huddle together. The milk is cold in the jars.

All to no purpose, as before, the knife whetted and plunged,
The shout raised, to match the clamor you have given them.
You alone turn away, not appeased; unaltered, avenger.

Hands full of scourges,[1] wreathed with your flames and adders,
You alone turned away, but did not move from my side,
Under the broken light, when the soft nights took the torches.

At thin morning you showed, thick and wrong in that calm,
The ignoble dream and the mask, sly, with slits at the eyes,
Pretence and half-sorrow, beneath which a coward's hope trembled.

---

1. Whips.

*   *   *

You uncovered at night, in the locked stillness of houses,
False love due the child's heart, the kissed-out lie, the embraces,
Made by the two who for peace tenderly turned to each other.

You who know what we love, but drive us to know it;
You with your whips and shrieks, bearer of truth and of solitude;
You who give, unlike men, to expiation your mercy.

Dropping the scourge when at last the scourged advances to meet it,
You, when the hunted turns, no longer remain the hunter
But stand silent and wait, at last returning his gaze.

Beautiful now as a child whose hair, wet with rage and tears
Clings to its face. And now I may look upon you,
Having once met your eyes. You lie in sleep and forget me.
Alone and strong in my peace, I look upon you in yours.

                                                                    1936

In Greek myth, the Furies or Erinyes were avenging spirits in female form who bore whips and relentlessly (and unsleepingly) pursued those who had wronged the gods. Bogan's poem imagines someone addressing a "sleeping fury"—possibly in part a representation of her mother, seen now in the semblance of a child whose wrath is spent and who has returned to innocence.

Psychiatrist's Song

Those
Concerning whom they have never spoken and thought never to speak;
That place
Hidden, preserved,
That even the exquisite eye of the soul
Cannot completely see.[1]
But they are there:
Those people, and that house, and that evening, seen
Newly above the dividing window sash—
The young will broken
And all time to endure.

1. Freudian psychoanalysis rests on the theory that among neurotic patients repressed traumatic experience resides in the unconscious mind, hidden even from the sufferer, and that only uncovering and directly confronting this traumatic material—which even the "exquisite eye of the soul / cannot completely see"—will lead to cure.

* .* *

Those hours when murderous wounds are made,[2]
Often in joy.

I hear.
But far away are the mango trees (*the mangrove swamps, the mandrake root . . .*)
And the thickets of—are they palms?
I watch them as though at the edge of sleep.
I often journey toward them in a boat without oars,
Trusting to rudder and sail.
Coming to the shore, I step out of the boat; I leave it to its anchor;
And I walk fearlessly through the ripples of both water and sand.
Then the shells and the pebbles are beneath my feet.
Then these, too, recede,
And I am on firm dry land, with, closely waiting,
A hill all sifted over with shade
Wherein the silence waits.

Farewell, phantoms of flesh and of ocean!
Vision of earth
Heal and receive me.

                                                              1967

Bogan offers a mythic version of the psychoanalytic process of recovery through the confrontation with traumatic but repressed psychic material.

MELVIN B. TOLSON
1898–1966

BORN IN THE SMALL TOWN of Moberly, Missouri, Melvin Beaunorus Tolson graduated with honors from Lincoln University in Pennsylvania, then taught for forty years as a college instructor in Texas and as a professor of English at Langston University in Oklahoma. A four-term mayor of the town of Langston, he was deeply involved in the life of his university and community. Tolson's early poems,

---

2. Repressed traumatic experience, toward which the speaker journeys, psychically, in a "boat without oars."

such as "Dark Symphony," employ a straight-ahead style of public statement, mixing racial protest with inspirational moments. His later work, however, culminating in *Harlem Gallery*, explores black cultural life in a modernist style of complication, ellipsis, and condensation. *Harlem Gallery* challenges the traditions of both Afro-American poetics and Anglo-American modernism. This intellectually demanding but high-spirited text exemplifies a new kind of poetry that is still in the process of being absorbed and evaluated. It revises or "signifies on" African-American culture, world history, and modernist form in a way that strikes many readers as revolutionary.

Rita Dove specifies some of the characteristics of black speech embedded in *Harlem Gallery*: mimicry, humorously exaggerated language, spontaneity, the persona of the braggadocio, and the use of localized narratives to imply larger truths. She also suggests the complicated nature of Tolson's virtuoso style: "he mixes colloquial and literary references as well as dictions; irony and pathos, slapstick and pontification sit side by side. . . . Tolson is deliberately complicating our preconceived notions of cultural—and, by further comparison, existential—order." The poem explores two interrelated issues: the nature of African-American art and the conditions of African-American identity. Tolson had intended to compose four books of *Harlem Gallery*, which would have covered the whole range of African-American experience in the United States. When he died of cancer at the age of sixty-eight, he had completed only the first book.

FURTHER READING

Michael Bérubé. *Marginal Forces/Cultural Centers: Tolson, Pynchon, and the Politics of the Canon*. Ithaca, N.Y.: Cornell University Press, 1992.

Arthur P. Davis. *From the Dark Tower: Afro-American Writers, 1900–1960*. Washington, D.C.: Howard University Press, 1982.

Robert M. Farnsworth. *Melvin B. Tolson, 1898–1966: Plain Talk and Poetic Prophecy*. Columbia: University of Missouri Press, 1984.

Melvin B. Tolson. *"Harlem Gallery" and Other Poems*. Ed. Raymond Nelson. Introduction by Rita Dove. Charlottesville: University Press of Virginia, 1999.

FROM *Dark Symphony*

Andante Sostenuto

They tell us to forget
The Golgotha[1] we tread . . .
We who are scourged with hate,

---

1. The hill outside of Jerusalem where Jesus Christ was crucified; here used as a metaphor for African-American experience.

A price upon our head.
They who have shackled us
Require of us a song,
They who have wasted us
Bid us condone the wrong.

They tell us to forget
Democracy is spurned.
They tell us to forget
The Bill of Rights is burned.
Three hundred years we slaved,
We slave and suffer yet:
Though flesh and bone rebel,
They tell us to forget!

Oh, how can we forget
Our human rights denied?
Oh, how can we forget
Our manhood crucified?
When Justice is profaned
And plea with curse is met,
When Freedom's gates are barred,
Oh, how can we forget?

Tempo di Marcia

Out of abysses of Illiteracy,
Through labyrinths of Lies,
Across waste lands of Disease . . .
We advance!

Out of dead-ends of Poverty,
Through wildernesses of Superstition,
Across barricades of Jim Crowism . . .[2]
We advance!

With the Peoples of the World . . .
We advance!

1941

"Dark Symphony" is a sequence of six poems, of which "*Andante Sostenuto*" is the third and "*Tempo di Marcia*" the last. The sequence won the National Poetry Contest and was

2. Discrimination against people of color, especially blacks, by legal enforcement or traditional sanctions.

then published in the *Atlantic Monthly*. Each of the six poems has an Italian name indicating an appropriate musical tempo. *"Andante Sostenuto,"* which means a slow and sustained pace, employs stately repetitions and an ABAB rhyme scheme embedded in iambic trimeter lines. *"Tempo di Marcia,"* which means a march tempo, employs free verse bound together by a stirring refrain, "We advance!" Whereas *"Andante Sostenuto"* protests the failure of justice and democracy in America, *"Tempo di Marcia"* concludes the sequence on a militantly hopeful note. It foresees eventual victory for all people in their struggle against dehumanizing forces.

FROM *Harlem Gallery*

Lambda

From the mouth of the Harlem Gallery
came a voice like a
ferry horn in a river of fog:

"Hey, man, when you gonna close this dump?
Fetch highbrow stuff for the middlebrows who
don't give a damn and the lowbrows who ain't hip!
Think you're a little high-yellow[1] Jesus?"

No longer was I a boxer with a brain bruised
against its walls by Tyche's[2] fists,
as I welcomed Hideho Heights,[3]
the vagabond bard of Lenox Avenue,[4]
whose satyric[5] legends adhered like beggar's-lice.

"Sorry, Curator,[6] I got here late:
my black ma birthed me in the Whites' bottom drawer,
and the Reds[7] forgot to fish me out!"

His belly laughed and quaked
the Blakean[8] tigers and lambs on the walls.

---

1. Black or mixed-race person with a light brown complexion.
2. The goddess of chance in Greek myth.
3. A fictional black poet. His name comes from the musical signature of jazz entertainer Cab Calloway (1907–1994): "Hidee hidee hidee hi— hidee hidee hidee ho."
4. One of Harlem's main streets.
5. A satyr is a woodland creature in Greek myth, part human and part animal, associated with revelry, lust, and the imparting of wisdom.
6. The owner of the art gallery and cultural center called the Harlem Gallery; the narrator of the poem.
7. Communists or socialists.
8. Reference to English printmaker and poet William Blake (1757–1827), whose illustrated poems include "The Tyger" and "The Lamb."

Haw-Haw's[9] whale of a forefinger mocked
Max Donachie's[10] revolutionary hero, Crispus Attucks,
in the Harlem Gallery and on Boston Commons.
"In the beginning was the Word,"[11]
he challenged, "not the Brush!"
The scorn in the eyes that raked the gallery
was the scorn of an Ozymandias.[12]

The metal smelted from the ore of ideas,
his[13] grin revealed all the gold he had stored away.
"Just came from a jam session
at the Daddy-O Club," he said.
"I'm just one step from heaven
with the blues a-percolating in my head.
You should've heard old Satchmo[14] blow his horn!
The Lord God A'mighty made no mistake
the day that cat was born!"

Like a bridegroom unloosing a virgin knot,
from an inner pocket he coaxed a manuscript.
"Just given Satchmo a one-way ticket
to Immortality," he said. "Pure inspiration!"
His lips folded about the neck of a whiskey bottle
whose label belied its white-heat hooch.
I heard a gurgle, a gurgle—a death rattle.
His eyes as bright as a parachute light,[15]
he began to rhetorize in the grand style
of a Doctor Faustus[16] in the dilapidated Harlem Opera House:

King Oliver[17] *of New Orleans*
has kicked the bucket, but he left behind
old Satchmo with his red-hot horn

9. Perhaps a nickname for the ironic Hideho Heights.

10. One of the painters whose work is displayed in the gallery. Crispus Attucks (1723–1770): black hero of the Boston Massacre and the first American killed in the Revolution, whose portrait has been painted by Max Donachie.

11. Heights alludes here to the New Testament (John 1:1).

12. Egyptian king Ramses II (1279–1213 B.C.E.), a symbol of excessive pride, referred to as "Ozymandias" in a poem of that name by English poet Percy Bysshe Shelley.

13. Hideho Heights's.

14. Louis (Satchmo) Armstrong (1901–1971), one of the great trumpeters and coronetists in jazz history.

15. Military spotlight.

16. Lead character in *The Tragical History of Dr. Faustus* by English playwright Christopher Marlowe (1564–1593).

17. Joseph "King" Oliver (1885–1938), bandleader and coronetist who gave Louis "Satchmo" Armstrong his break. The italicized lines are Hideho Heights's speech or improvised poem.

to syncopate the heart and mind.
The honky-tonks in Storyville[18]
have turned to ashes, have turned to dust,
but old Satchmo is still around
like Uncle Sam's IN GOD WE TRUST.[19]

Where, oh, where is Bessie Smith[20]
with her heart as big as the blues of truth?
Where, oh, where is Mister Jelly Roll[21]
with his Cadillac and diamond tooth?
Where, oh, where is Papa Handy[22]
with his blue notes a-dragging from bar to bar?
Where, oh, where is bulletproof Leadbelly[23]
with his tall tales and 12-string guitar?

Old Hip Cats,
when you sang and played the blues
the night Satchmo was born,
did you know hypodermic needles in Rome
couldn't hoodoo him away from his horn?[24]
Wyatt Earp's[25] *legend, John Henry's, too,*
is a dare and a bet to old Satchmo
when his groovy blues put headlines in the news
from the Gold Coast to cold Moscow.

Old Satchmo's
gravelly voice and tapping foot and crazy notes
set my soul on fire.
If I climbed
the seventy-seven steps of the Seventh
Heaven,[26] *Satchmo's high C would carry me higher!*
Are you hip to this, Harlem? Are you hip?

---

18. A section of New Orleans where jazz was born in the first decade of the twentieth century.
19. Motto inscribed on U.S. currency.
20. Bessie Smith (1898–1937), great American blues singer.
21. Ferdinand La Menthe "Jelly Roll" Morton (1890–1941), innovative jazz composer, pianist, and bandleader.
22. W. C. Handy (1888–1949), composer and bandleader who changed American music by integrating blues into ragtime.
23. Huddie Ledbetter (1885–1949), traditional blues singer, guitarist, and composer.

24. "On June 23, 1959, while touring Italy, Armstrong suffered a severe heart attack and received considerable attention from the international press while he recovered at St. Peter's Hospital in Rome. He surprised everyone by appearing unannounced at a concert on July 4" (Raymond Nelson).
25. Wyatt Earp (1848–1929) was a legendary white lawman/outlaw in the American West. John Henry: legendary black hero, subject of a well-known folk ballad.
26. The ultimate of the seven heavens in Islamic tradition.

On Judgment Day, Gabriel[27] *will say*
after he blows his horn:
"I'd be the greatest trumpeter in the Universe,
if old Satchmo had never been born!"

FROM *Chi*

Despite his caricatures
of poets and poetasters,
Hideho's joy was Hasidic[28]
among the lives and works of the Masters—
old and new.
He himself was a sort of aged Istanbul
with a young Beyoglu.[29]

He didn't know
I knew
about the split identity
of the People's Poet—
the bifacial nature of his poetry:
the racial ballad in the public domain
and the private poem in the modern vein.

I had overheard the poet say:
"Reverend Eli, in a foxhole
with the banzai[30] in my ears,
one day
I collapsed from battle fatigue.
You know why?
Since I was unable to dig
the immortality of John Doe,[31]
fears
(not Hamlet's[32] . . . not Simon Legree's),

---

27. One of the archangels in Jewish, Christian, and Islamic tradition.

28. Hasidism (from the Hebrew word for "pious one") is a contemporary Jewish movement marked by mysticism, religious fervor, and direct communication with God. It was founded in twelfth-century Germany and revived by Baal Shem-Tov in eighteenth-century Poland.

29. The modern district of Istanbul, chief city of Turkey.

30. A Japanese salute, cheer, or shout. This passage alludes, either literally or metaphorically, to Heights's combat in the Pacific theater during World War II.

31. Arbitrary name for the anonymous man.

32. Hamlet is the tragic hero of *Hamlet, Prince of Denmark* by English playwright William Shakespeare (1564–1616). Simon Legree: the superstitious white villain of the novel *Uncle Tom's Cabin* by white abolitionist Harriet Beecher Stowe (1811–1896).

my fears
of oblivion made me realistic:
with no poems of Hideho's in World Lit—
he'd be a statistic!"

Poor Boy Blue,
the Great White World
and the Black Bourgeoisie
have shoved the Negro artist into
the white and not-white dichotomy,
the Afroamerican dilemma in the Arts—
the dialectic of
to be or not to be[33]
a Negro.

1965

Tolson wrote that his roots "are in Africa, Europe, and America," an assertion substantiated by the wide-ranging cultural allusions in *Harlem Gallery*. Although Tolson lived most of his adult life in Texas and Oklahoma, he visited New York frequently, and it is out of his experience of Harlem that his final long poem emerged. Tolson divided his poem into twenty-four parts, corresponding to the letters of the Greek alphabet. This anthology reprints all of "Lambda" and the first part of "Chi." Both of these sections are narrated by the curator of an art gallery in Harlem, a former art professor who is of "afroirishjewish origins." The narrator describes his encounters with another character named Hideho Heights, the "poet laureate of Harlem." Heights is a popular but authentic poet, a boisterous emotional and intellectual presence. According to Tolson's editor, Raymond Nelson, Heights may be based on Langston Hughes or Sterling Brown (both included in this anthology). He is the diametrical opposite of the learned and sequestered Tolson himself, yet Tolson portrays him with obvious affection and some degree of identification. In "Lambda," Heights poetically celebrates the jazz great Louis (Satchmo) Armstrong—and through him the depth and breadth of African-American artistry. In "Chi," the curator analyzes Height's own dualities: his "bifacial" poetry and his conflict between being a popular poet and a master of intricate, personal lyrics. Heights, in his contradictions and exuberance, exposes what Rita Dove calls "the predicament of being black and an artist in America."

33. Echo of a famous line in one of Hamlet's soliloquies: "To be or not to be: that is the question" (3.1.56). Hamlet is debating with himself the question of suicide and reflecting on the difficulties of moral choice. Heights is questioning to what extent his racial identity should determine the character of his poetry.

HART CRANE
1899–1932

INTENSE AND EXCITING, Hart Crane's poetry resists casual reading. It must be pored over, pondered, wrestled with, enjoyed and savored. Each phrase and image invites rereading and reconsideration. This innovative poetry is more than usually charged with meaning. It does not quite come into focus but remains a gorgeous and mysterious cascade of imaged words. Crane's influences were many: British writers (William Shakespeare, John Donne, William Blake); classic American writers (Edgar Allan Poe, Herman Melville, Walt Whitman, Emily Dickinson); French symbolist poets (Charles Baudelaire, Charles Rimbaud, Jules Laforgue); and the poet's modernist peers (James Joyce, Wallace Stevens, T. S. Eliot, Jean Toomer). Yet Crane did things with language and vision that were never done by anyone before him, and they have never been done again.

On one hand, Crane's poetry composes a self-enclosed verbal world of often astonishing beauty. In his essay "General Aims and Theories," Crane writes that his poems arise "on the organic principle of a 'logic of metaphor,' which antedates our so-called pure logic." By turns anguished and ecstatic, this figurative logic defeats ordinary reasoning to become something akin to a musical or visual structure, self-reflexively calling attention to its own forms and linguistic materials.

On the other hand, Crane's poetry comprises a social and spiritual quest. Aware of social contradiction, it seeks moments of prophecy that will somehow reconcile the poet and reader with the world, transcend the world through immersion in it, or change the world by changing our consciousness. The poems attempt to inscribe the conditions of modernity, but they also wish to reform and escape those conditions. An outsider, Crane speaks as a gay man in a homophobic culture, emphasizing social margins and shadows, celebrating underdogs and clowns. But he also speaks as a representative human being who would be a prophet, assimilating a range of experiences and striving for transformative vision. His language at times comes amazingly close to achieving this goal — and at other times reflects mournfully on its failure to do so.

Harold Hart Crane was born in Garrettsville, Ohio, the only child of a candy manufacturer who invented the Life Saver and disapproved of his son's "poetry nonsense" and a mother who alternately indulged and reproved him. A misfit in high school, Crane moved to New York City at the age of seventeen, ostensibly to prepare for college but actually to become a bohemian and poet. Irregularly employed as a mechanic, a soda jerk, and an advertising writer, he became actively and openly gay, with a stream of casual lovers and one enduring love relationship, with a sailor named Emil Opffer. Although penniless himself, Crane wrote occasional articles and advertising copy for *Fortune* magazine. He became friends with innovative cultural figures of the time: poets such as Allen Tate, Yvor Winters, and Jean Toomer (all included in this anthology) and critics such as Waldo Frank and Malcolm Cowley. Most importantly, he began to publish poems in some of the leading literary magazines of his day—*The Dial*, *The Little Review*, *Seven Arts*, and *Poetry*. He wrote with remarkable intensity. Once, when the words would not come, he hurled his typewriter out of a second-story window.

In 1926 Crane published his first volume of poetry, *White Buildings*. Apart from the rather straightforward and gentle "My Grandmother's Love Letters," the poems are packed with resonant, enigmatic images and with words that have multiple meanings. John Keats once advised poets to load every rift with ore, but no poet has ever done so to quite this degree. Crane's poems overflow with verbal and emotional energy. "Praise for an Urn," for example, mourns an artist-friend whose untimely death reveals both a common fate of artists and Crane's own frequent experience of loss and isolation. "Chaplinesque" pays tribute to an icon of American culture: Charlie Chaplin, an innovative film comic who, like Crane, identified himself with the marginalized and downtrodden. The major long text in *White Buildings*, "Voyages," is a sequence of poems comprising a quest that is at once linguistic, sexual, and spiritual. Reflecting both Crane's tumultuous love relationship with Emil Opffer and his excited reading of such quest texts as Melville's *Moby Dick* and Baudelaire's "Le Voyage," "Voyages" presents a poet-seer who can attain only a "splintered" garland of insight and recognition. Although he cannot locate "paradise" in either his troubled love affair or his flawed poetry, he finds sustenance in the ideal of poetic creation itself— "the unbetrayable reply / Whose accent no farewell can know."

Crane's next project, an epic sequence of poems called *The Bridge*, consumed the rest of his life. He undertook this poem as an answer to Eliot's *The Waste Land*, a poem he admired, especially for its mythic qualities, but which he considered "spiritually dead." Using the Brooklyn Bridge as its prime symbol, *The Bridge* seeks to restore meaning and unity to a fragmented and dissonant modern world. It attempts to subsume a heartless age of machinery and commercialism into a grand new visionary synthesis, one capable of changing everything. It wants to "lend a myth to God." Extending Whitman's idealistic, hopeful dream of America and modernity, the poem links past and present to future. It transforms the contemporary individual, whom society has rendered an isolated "bedlamite," into a whole and reconnected person, and it turns the inimical steel and concrete of the American infrastructure into a lovely "harp and altar" beyond time.

Crane did not live to write much poetry beyond *The Bridge*. Buffeted by poverty, failed relationships, and despair, he received a Guggenheim Fellowship to write his next proposed poem, an epic about Montezuma. He moved to Mexico, as much to escape his life problems in the United States as to research his new poem. In Mexico he began a tumultuous affair, the first heterosexual relationship of his life, with his friend Peggy Cowley, who was in Mexico to obtain a divorce from her husband Malcolm Cowley. The epic on Montezuma went unwritten, though Crane did pen one of his most beautiful and touching short poems, "The Broken Tower," in Mexico. Returning together to the United States on the steamship *Orizaba*, the couple quarreled one last time. Crane announced to Cowley, "I am utterly disgraced" — perhaps suggesting his sense of spiritual failure, or perhaps suggesting a kind of disconnection from love (his ambivalently loved mother was named, as it happens, "Grace"). He then jumped overboard, into the shark-infested waters of the Caribbean. As he sank into the sea, he lifted his arm, which observers interpreted as either an effort to seek rescue or a wave good-bye.

Hart Crane lived a tempestuous life of despair and ecstasy, of dysphoric rumination and creative triumph. He produced a poetry of exquisite richness and emotional fervor. It seems to elude its readers as it mysteriously draws them in, challenging and tempting them, evoking and yet exceeding their desire.

FURTHER READING

Warner Berthoff. *Hart Crane: A Re-Introduction*. Minneapolis: University of Minnesota Press, 1989.

Edward Brunner. *Splendid Failure: Hart Crane and the Making of "The Bridge."* Urbana: University of Illinois Press, 1985.

Hart Crane. *Complete Poems*, 2nd ed. Ed. Marc Simon. New York: Liveright, 2000.

———. *O My Land, My Friends: The Selected Letters of Hart Crane*. Ed. Langdon Hammer and Brom Weber. New York: Four Walls Eight Windows, 1997.

Clive Fisher. *Hart Crane: A Biography*. New Haven, Conn.: Yale University Press, 2002.

Langdon Hammer. *Hart Crane and Allen Tate: Janus-Faced Modernism*. Princeton: Princeton University Press, 1993.

Samuel Hazo. *Smithereened Apart: A Critique of Hart Crane*. Athens: Ohio University Press, 1963.

Herbert A. Leibowitz. *Hart Crane: An Introduction to the Poetry*. New York: Columbia University Press, 1968.

Paul Mariani. *The Broken Tower: A Life of Hart Crane*. New York: W. W. Norton, 1999.

Vincent Quinn. *Hart Crane*. Boston: Twayne, 1963.

Ernest Smith. *"The Imaged Word": The Infrastructure of Hart Crane's "White Buildings."* New York: Peter Lang, 1990.

Thomas Yingling. *Hart Crane and the Homosexual Text: New Thresholds, New Anatomies*. Chicago: University of Chicago Press, 1990.

In Shadow

Out in the late amber afternoon,
Confused among chrysanthemums,
Her parasol,[1] a pale balloon,
Like a waiting moon, in shadow swims.

1. Small sun umbrella.

* * *

Her furtive lace and misty hair
Over the garden dial distill
The sunlight—then withdrawing, wear
Again the shadows at her will.

Gently yet suddenly, the sheen
Of stars inwraps her parasol.
She hears my step behind the green
Twilight, stiller than shadows, fall.

"Come, it is too late—too late
To risk alone the light's decline:
Nor has the evening long to wait"—
But her own words are night's and mine.

1917

Crane wrote the enigmatic "In Shadow" when he was only seventeen years old. The poem begins, as Herbert Leibowitz has said, in the manner of a lovely Impressionist painting by Claude Monet. By the end, however, the poem's situation and meaning are, as Ernest Smith suggests, "unclear" and even "ominous." Does the woman speak the sentences quoted in the final stanza, or are they uttered by the poem's speaker? If they are the speaker's words, her reply is not quoted, though it is alluded to in the final line. Perhaps she affirms the necessity of risking night "alone"—that is, of furtively encountering the darkness of nature, the soul, or desire. Interestingly, her words are said to be not only "her own" but the night's and the speaker's hidden sentiments as well.

My Grandmother's Love Letters

There are no stars tonight
But those of memory.
Yet how much room for memory there is
In the loose girdle of soft rain.

There is even room enough
For the letters of my mother's mother,
Elizabeth,
That have been pressed so long
Into a corner of the roof
That they are brown and soft,
And liable to melt as snow.

* * *

Over the greatness of such space
Steps must be gentle.
It is all hung by an invisible white hair.
It trembles as birch limbs webbing the air.

And I ask myself:

"Are your fingers long enough to play
Old keys that are but echoes:
Is the silence strong enough
To carry back the music to its source
And back to you again
As though to her?"

Yet I would lead my grandmother by the hand
Through much of what she would not understand;
And so I stumble. And the rain continues on the roof
With such a sound of gently pitying laughter.

1920

While composing "My Grandmother's Love Letters," Crane wrote to a friend, "Grandma and her love letters are too steep climbing for hurried moments, so I don't know when I shall work on that again. As it is, I have a good beginning and I don't want any anti-climax effect. If I cannot carry it out any further, I may simply add a few finishing lines and leave it simply as a mood touched on." This poem, which Langdon Hammer considers Crane's first mature poem, concerns a grandson's ambiguous efforts to empathize with his grandmother's youthful self and, more generally, the difficulties of the historical imagination and the problematics of gender.

Chaplinesque

We make our meek adjustments,
Contented with such random consolations
As the wind deposits
In slithered and too ample pockets.

For we can still love the world, who find
A famished kitten[1] on the step, and know
Recesses for it from the fury of the street,
Or warm torn elbow coverts.[2]

---

1. Here perhaps a symbol of poetry or social vulnerability. Crane told his friend Gorham Munson that the kitten was inspired by T. S. Eliot's reference in "Preludes" to an "infinitely gentle, infinitely suffering thing."
2. Hiding places, shelters, or disguises.

*   *   *

We will sidestep, and to the final smirk
Dally[3] the doom of that inevitable thumb
That slowly chafes its puckered index toward us,
Facing the dull squint with what innocence
And what surprise!

And yet these fine collapses are not lies
More than the pirouettes of any pliant cane;
Our obsequies[4] are, in a way, no enterprise.
We can evade you, and all else but the heart:
What blame to us if the heart[5] live on.

The game enforces smirks; but we have seen
The moon in lonely alleys make
A grail of laughter of an empty ash can,[6]
And through all sound of gaiety and quest
Have heard a kitten in the wilderness.

1921

Charlie Chaplin (1889–1977) was a great film comedian and director. After seeing Chaplin's first feature film, *The Kid*, in 1921, Crane felt inspired to write a poetic tribute. Chaplin's screen alter ego, the "little tramp," typically wore a tight-fitting coat, pants that were too large and that had "too ample pockets," a battered derby, a small mustache, and a "cane." Always innocent, resilient, and good humored in defeat, he suggested to Crane the outcast status of the poet in modern society. Crane explained to a friend, "I am moved to put Chaplin with the poets (of today); hence the 'we.' In other words, he, especially in *The Kid*, made me feel myself, as a poet, as being 'in the same boat with' him. Poetry, the human feelings, 'the kitten,' is so crowded out of the humdrum, rushing, mechanical scramble of today that the man who would preserve them must duck and camouflage for dear life to keep them or keep himself from annihilation."

3. Postpone. Thumb: perhaps that of a policeman or other authority figure, or Death.
4. Funeral rites or acts of submission
5. Feelings of tenderness but also a pun on the poet's first name.

6. The rattle of an ash can sounds like laughter, which functions as a Holy Grail, a cup that in medieval legend had regenerative powers.

Praise for an Urn

In Memoriam: Ernest Nelson

It was a kind and northern face
That mingled in such exile guise
The everlasting eyes of Pierrot[1]
And, of Gargantua,[2] the laughter.

His thoughts, delivered to me
From the white coverlet and pillow,
I see now, were inheritances—
Delicate riders of the storm.

The slant moon on the slanting hill
Once moved us toward presentiments[3]
Of what the dead keep, living still,
And such assessments of the soul

As, perched in the crematory lobby,
The insistent clock commented on,
Touching as well upon our praise
Of glories proper to the time.

Still, having in mind gold hair,[4]
I cannot see that broken brow
And miss the dry sound of bees
Stretching across a lucid space.

Scatter these well-meant idioms
Into the smoky spring that fills
The suburbs, where they will be lost.[5]
They are no trophies of the sun.

1922

"Praise for an Urn" is an elegy for Crane's friend Ernest Nelson, a Norwegian-American painter who for economic reasons was forced to work in the lesser art of lithography. He died and was cremated in 1922. According to Samuel Hazo, "Crane saw in Nelson a symbol of his own condition as an artist."

1. The sad clown in French pantomime, frequently figured as well in French poetry, fiction, and visual and plastic arts. See "Complainte de Lord Pierrot" ("Complaint of Lord Pierrot") by Jules Laforgue (1860–1887).
2. The hero of *Gargantua and Pantagruel* by François Rabelais (ca. 1494–1553), this exuberant giant has a huge appetite for life.
3. Premonitions.
4. Nelson's.
5. The poem's memorializing words, like the ashes from the crematorium, will disappear.

Voyages

1

Above the fresh ruffles of the surf
Bright striped urchins[1] flay each other with sand.
They have contrived a conquest for shell shucks,[2]
And their fingers crumble fragments of baked weed
Gaily digging and scattering.

And in answer to their treble interjections
The sun beats lightning on the waves,
The waves fold thunder on the sand;
And could they hear me I would tell them:

O brilliant kids, frisk with your dog,
Fondle your shells and sticks, bleached
By time and the elements; but there is a line
You must not cross nor ever trust beyond it
Spry cordage[3] of your bodies to caresses
Too lichen-faithful[4] from too wide a breast.
The bottom of the sea is cruel.

2

—And yet this great wink of eternity,[5]
Of rimless floods, unfettered leewardings,[6]
Samite[7] sheeted and processioned where
Her undinal[8] vast belly moonward bends,
Laughing the wrapt[9] inflections of our love;

Take this Sea, whose diapason[10] knells
On scrolls of silver snowy sentences,[11]

---

1. Children.
2. Oyster shells.
3. Sticks on the beach or ropes on a ship; here, a metaphor for the children's limbs, flesh, nerves, and muscle.
4. A lichen is a compound composed of a fungus in symbiotic union with an alga; metaphorically, a close relationship.
5. The sea as a paradoxical symbol of momentary eternity. The imperative "Take" that begins the next stanza applies retroactively to this "wink of eternity."
6. Leeward is the point toward which the wind blows.

7. Heavy silk fabric threaded with gold that was produced in Greece in the Middle Ages.
8. An undine is a mythic female water spirit who acquires a soul if she marries a human being.
9. Enveloped or sheeted; also, rapt or awed. Our love: the speaker and his lover's.
10. A rich, full outpouring of melodious sound; the range of a musical instrument or voice; and either of two principal timbres of a pipe organ. Knell: slow ringing sound of a funeral bell.
11. The "silver snowy sentences," which carry both linguistic and judicial connotations, may allude to the white beaches of a seashore.

The sceptred terror of whose sessions rends
As her demeanors motion well or ill,
All but the pieties of lovers' hands.

And onward, as bells off San Salvador[12]
Salute the crocus lustres of the stars,[13]
In these poinsettia meadows of her tides,—
Adagios[14] of islands, O my Prodigal,
Complete the dark confessions her[15] veins spell.

Mark how her turning shoulders[16] wind the hours,
And hasten while her penniless rich palms
Pass superscription[17] of bent foam and wave,—
Hasten, while they are true,—sleep, death, desire,
Close round one instant in one floating flower.

Bind us in time, O Seasons clear, and awe.
O minstrel galleons of Carib fire,
Bequeath us to no earthly shore until
Is answered in the vortex of our grave
The seal's wide spindrift[18] gaze toward paradise.

3

Infinite consanguinity[19] it bears—
This tendered theme of you that light
Retrieves from sea plains where the sky
Resigns a breast that every wave enthrones;
While ribboned water lanes I wind
Are laved and scattered with no stroke
Wide from your side, whereto this hour
The sea lifts, also, reliquary[20] hands.

And so, admitted through black swollen gates
That must arrest all distance otherwise,—

---

12. The bells of a legendary cathedral sunken off the shore of San Salvador, El Salvador, in Central America.
13. The stars, perhaps as reflected in the sea, are metaphorically compared to crocus flowers.
14. Slow songs or dances. Crane explains the image in "General Aims and Theories" (below) as a reference to "the motion of a boat through islands clustered thickly, the rhythm of the motion, etc." Prodigal: generous or wandering; a reference to the speaker's lover.

15. The sea's.
16. Perhaps a metaphor for the sea's waves.
17. Something written above or on something.
18. Spray blown from a rough surf. Crane had originally written "findrinny" in place of "wide spindrift," but he could not find the word in any dictionary and replaced it at his editor's insistence. "Findrinny" appears once in Melville's *Moby Dick*, where Crane must have seen it.
19. Kinship, blood relationship.
20. Container holding relics.

Past whirling pillars and lithe pediments,[21]
Light wrestling there incessantly with light,
Star kissing star through wave on wave unto
Your body rocking!
                              and where death, if shed,
Presumes no carnage, but this single change,—
Upon the steep floor flung from dawn to dawn
The silken skilled transmemberment[22] of song;

Permit me voyage, love, into your hands . . .

4

Whose counted smile of hours and days, suppose
I know as spectrum of the sea and pledge
Vastly now parting gulf on gulf of wings
Whose circles bridge, I know, (from palms to the severe
Chilled albatross's[23] white immutability)
No stream of greater love advancing now
Than, singing, this mortality alone
Through clay aflow immortally to you.[24]

All fragrance irrefragibly,[25] and claim
Madly meeting logically in this hour
And region that is ours to wreathe again,
Portending eyes and lips and making told
The chancel[26] port and portion of our June—

Shall they[27] not stem and close in our own steps
Bright staves of flowers and quills today as I
Must first be lost in fatal tides to tell?

In signature of the incarnate word
The harbor shoulders to resign in mingling
Mutual blood, transpiring as foreknown
And widening noon within your breast for gathering

21. Ornamental low gables, typically triangular in shape.
22. A term Crane coined, suggesting both transformation and dismemberment.
23. A large seabird associated with cold climates and capable of staying aloft for long periods. An albatross plays a central role in "Rime of the Ancient Mariner" by Samuel Taylor Coleridge (1772–1834).
24. Poetry carries the speaker's love to his parted lover.
25. Undeniably.
26. Space near the altar of a church.
27. The waves.

All bright insinuations that my years have caught
For islands where must lead inviolably
Blue latitudes and levels of your eyes, —

In this expectant, still exclaim receive
The secret oar and petals of all love.[28]

5

Meticulous, past midnight in clear rime,[29]
Infrangible[30] and lonely, smooth as though cast
Together in one merciless white blade —
The bay estuaries[31] fleck the hard sky limits.

—As if too brittle or too clear to touch!
The cables of our sleep so swiftly filed,
Already hang, shred ends from remembered stars.
One frozen trackless smile . . .[32] What words
Can strangle this deaf moonlight? For we

Are overtaken. Now no cry, no sword
Can fasten or deflect this tidal wedge,
Slow tyranny of moonlight, moonlight loved
And changed . . . "There's

Nothing like this in the world," you say,
Knowing I cannot touch your hand and look
Too, into that godless cleft of sky
Where nothing turns but dead sands flashing.

"—And never to quite understand!" No,
In all the argosy[33] of your bright hair I dreamed
Nothing so flagless as this piracy.

*   *   *

28. Perhaps the speaker imagines a mysterious, sexual reunion with his lover; or perhaps he hopes that this poem will carry his love to his still-parted lover.

29. Frost.

30. Unbreakable.

31. Where the rivers meet the sea.

32. The frozen sea suggests the emotional separation of the speaker and his lover.

33. Fleet of ships or opulent supply. The word recalls the Greek myth of Jason and the Argonauts, a band of men who sailed in the ship *Argo* in search of the Golden Fleece —a goal both dangerous and rewarding.

But now
Draw in your head, alone and too tall here.
Your eyes already in the slant of drifting foam;
Your breath sealed by the ghosts I do not know:
Draw in your head and sleep the long way home.

6

Where icy and bright dungeons lift
Of swimmers their lost morning eyes,
And ocean rivers, churning, shift
Green borders under stranger skies,

Steadily as a shell secretes
Its beating leagues of monotone,
Or as many waters trough the sun's
Red kelson[34] past the cape's wet stone;

O rivers mingling toward the sky[35]
And harbor of the phoenix'[36] breast—
My eyes pressed black against the prow,
—Thy derelict and blinded guest

Waiting, afire, what name, unspoke,
I cannot claim: let thy waves rear
More savage than the death of kings,
Some splintered garland for the seer.[37]

Beyond siroccos[38] harvesting
The solstice thunders, crept away,
Like a cliff swinging or a sail
Flung into April's inmost day—

Creation's blithe and petalled word
To the lounged goddess[39] when she rose
Conceding dialogue with eyes
That smile unsearchable repose—

34. Joined timbers of a ship's keel. The word appears once in Whitman's "Song of Myself" (section 5).
35. The rivers may suggest time, sexuality, and death, whereas the sky may suggest eternity, heaven, and the absolute.
36. In Egyptian myth, a bird that lives for centuries, sets itself on fire, and then arises reborn from the ashes.
37. The poet, or "seer," wishes only a splintered garland or wreath—a broken and partial sign of his prophetic status.
38. Hot, dry winds of the Mediterranean.
39. Perhaps Aphrodite, Greek goddess of love.

* * *

Still fervid[40] covenant, Belle Isle,
—Unfolded floating dais[41] before
Which rainbows twine continual hair—
Belle Isle, white echo of the oar![42]

The imaged Word, it is, that holds
Hushed willows anchored in its glow.
It is the unbetrayable reply
Whose accent no farewell can know.

1926

Crane composed "Voyages" in the wake of such symbolist voyage poems as "Le Voyage" ("The Voyage") by Charles Baudelaire (1821–1867) and "Le Bateau ivre" ("The Drunken Boat") by Arthur Rimbaud (1854–1891). In such poems, the poetic speaker undergoes a voyage of discovery that may yield a wide variety of outcomes: disrupted senses, intellectual novelty, sexual passion, spiritual transcendence, poetic vision, a changed self, or death. All of these possibilities are present in Crane's "Voyages." The final five sections in the sequence were also precipitated by Crane's passionate and tumultuous love affair with Emil Opffer, a merchant seaman. Langdon Hammer suggests that "Voyages" attempts to undo the implied drowning of homosexual desire in Eliot's *The Waste Land* and to recover the sexual and spiritual "hope" buried by that poem.

To Brooklyn Bridge

How many dawns, chill from his rippling rest
The seagull's wings shall dip and pivot him,
Shedding white rings of tumult, building high
Over the chained bay waters Liberty[1]—

Then, with inviolate curve, forsake our eyes
As apparitional[2] as sails that cross
Some page of figures to be filed away;
—Till elevators drop us from our day . . .

* * *

40. Fervent. Covenant: agreement, perhaps a pledge of love. Belle Isle: an island off Labrador and a resort town in Louisiana; here, perhaps an image of paradise.
41. Platform for a throne or podium.
42. Image of the sea voyage, movement through the world, and perhaps male sexuality.

1. Flying over New York Harbor and the Statue of Liberty, the gull exemplifies a freedom denied the bay's shackled waters.
2. Ghostlike. Sails: perhaps sailboats glimpsed from an office window by a file clerk.

I think of cinemas, panoramic sleights[3]
With multitudes bent toward some flashing scene
Never disclosed, but hastened to again,
Foretold to other eyes on the same screen;

And Thee,[4] across the harbor, silver-paced
As though the sun took step of thee, yet left
Some motion ever unspent in thy stride,—
Implicitly thy freedom staying thee!

Out of some subway scuttle,[5] cell or loft
A bedlamite[6] speeds to thy parapets,
Tilting there momently,[7] shrill shirt ballooning,
A jest[8] falls from the speechless caravan.

Down Wall,[9] from girder into street noon leaks,
A rip-tooth of the sky's acetylene;[10]
All afternoon the cloud-flown derricks turn . . .
Thy cables breathe the North Atlantic still.

And obscure as that heaven of the Jews,
Thy guerdon . . .[11] Accolade thou dost bestow
Of anonymity time cannot raise:[12]
Vibrant reprieve and pardon thou dost show.

O harp and altar, of the fury fused,
(How could mere toil align thy choiring strings!)
Terrific threshold of the prophet's pledge,[13]
Prayer of pariah, and the lover's cry,—

Again the traffic lights[14] that skim thy swift
Unfractioned idiom, immaculate sigh of stars,
Beading thy path—condense eternity:
And we have seen night lifted in thine arms.

3. Skillful movements for purposes of deception or entertainment.
4. The Brooklyn Bridge, capitalized and addressed in the informal second person, implying sacredness and intimacy.
5. Deep bucket or quick pace; here, the subway exit.
6. Lunatic; literally, an inhabitant of Bedlam, a London insane asylum. Parapets: low protective walls at the base of the bridge.
7. Both momentarily and momentously.
8. Joke. That is, the crowd jokes as the man falls to his death, or the man *is* the joke.

9. Wall Street, New York's financial center.
10. Colorless gas used in metal cutting and welding and as an illuminant; here, a metaphor for the sun.
11. Reward.
12. Lift, gather, awaken, restore to life, and perhaps raze.
13. The prophet, and the pariah and the lover in the next line, are alternative embodiments of the poet.
14. Headlights of the cars crossing the bridge.

* * *

Under thy shadow by the piers I waited;
Only in darkness is thy shadow clear.
The City's fiery parcels[15] all undone,
Already snow submerges an iron year . . .

O Sleepless as the river under thee,
Vaulting the sea, the prairies' dreaming sod,[16]
Unto us lowliest sometime sweep, descend
And of the curveship[17] lend a myth to God.

1927

"To Brooklyn Bridge" was first published separately in 1927 and then gathered into Crane's epic sequence, *The Bridge*, in 1930. It serves as the epic's introductory poem, or "proem," introducing themes of modern desperation and urban despair as well as a concurrent quest for social harmony, aesthetic pleasure, and spiritual peace. Herbert Leibowitz comments, "Although the bridge is man-made, it has become something more than man; it is not exactly otherworldly, but it is not temporal either. It represents an indefinite eternal principle which is without the metaphysical furniture of traditional religions, which indefiniteness is its strength. . . . If the bridge 'condenses eternity,' it also attests to the unyielding grip in which time holds man; and if the bridge is a shimmering light of salvation, it paradoxically can be glimpsed only in darkness, and then only its shadow." Designed by John A. Roebling (1806–1869) and built from 1869 to 1883, the Brooklyn Bridge spans the East River between Brooklyn and Manhattan.

Van Winkle

Macadam,[1] gun-grey as the tunny's belt,
Leaps from Far Rockaway[2] to Golden Gate: *Streets spread*
Listen! the miles a hurdy-gurdy grinds—   *past store and*
Down gold arpeggios[3] mile on mile unwinds.   *factory—sped*
                                         by sunlight

Times earlier, when you hurried off to school,   *and her*
  —It is the same hour though a later day—   *smile . . .*[4]

15. The lit skyscrapers. Undone: the lights have been turned off in the wee hours of morning.
16. The bridge figuratively connects the ocean with the country's heartland.
17. Crane's coined word for the graceful arches of the bridge's suspension cables.
1. Road paved with crushed stones. Tunny: tuna.
2. An Atlantic beach community in New York. Golden Gate: The Golden Gate Bridge at the mouth of the San Francisco Bay in California.

3. Notes in succession.
4. The marginalia in this poem—and in several other poems in *The Bridge*—comment on the main action while composing a parallel text. Her smile: that of the female presence of the land, one of whose figurative incarnations is Pocahontas.

You walked with Pizarro[5] in a copybook,
And Cortes[6] rode up, reining tautly in —
Firmly as coffee grips the taste, — and away!

There was Priscilla's[7] cheek close in the wind,
And Captain Smith,[8] all beard and certainty,
And Rip Van Winkle bowing by the way, —
"Is this Sleepy Hollow,[9] friend — ?" And he —

Like Memory,
she is time's

And Rip forgot the office hours,
and he forgot the pay;
Van Winkle sweeps a tenement
way down on Avenue A, —

truant, shall
take you by
the hand . . .

The grind-organ says . . . Remember, remember[10]
The cinder pile at the end of the backyard
Where we stoned the family of young
Garter snakes under . . . And the monoplanes
We launched — with paper wings and twisted
Rubber bands . . . Recall — recall

the rapid tongues
That flittered from under the ash heap day
After day whenever your stick discovered
Some sunning inch of unsuspecting fibre[11] —
It flashed back at your thrust, as clean as fire.

And Rip was slowly made aware
that he, Van Winkle, was not here
nor there. He woke and swore he'd seen Broadway
a Catskill daisy chain[12] in May —

＊   ＊   ＊

5. Spanish conqueror (ca. 1475–1541) of the Incas of Peru.

6. Spanish conqueror (1485–1547) of the Aztecs of Mexico.

7. Priscilla Alden, colonial heroine of Henry Wadsworth Longfellow's "The Courtship of Miles Standish" (1858).

8. John Smith (ca. 1580–1631), founder of Jamestown, Virginia, whose life was purportedly saved by the Native-American woman Pocahontas.

9. The setting of Washington Irving's "The Legend of Sleepy Hollow" (1820).

10. Initiates passages based on Crane's memories of his Ohio childhood.

11. A snake.

12. Broadway appears to him as a chain of daisies from the Catskill Mountains of upstate New York.

So memory, that strikes a rhyme out of a box,
Or splits a random smell of flowers through glass[13] —
Is it the whip stripped from the lilac tree
One day in spring my father took to me,
Or is it the Sabbatical, unconscious smile
My mother almost brought me once from church
And once only, as I recall —?

It flickered through the snow screen, blindly
It forsook her at the doorway, it was gone
Before I had left the window. It
Did not return with the kiss in the hall.

Macadam, gun-grey as the tunny's belt,
Leaps from Far Rockaway to Golden Gate. . . .
Keep hold of that nickel for car-change,[14] Rip, —
Have you got your *"Times"* —?
And hurry along, Van Winkle — it's getting late![15]

1927

Rip Van Winkle, a character in a story by Washington Irving (1783–1859), sleeps for twenty years and wakes to find vast changes in his native land. In "Van Winkle," the poem's speaker initiates his quest for American roots and harmonies, which will be the focus of the rest of *The Bridge*. Writing to his patron, Otto Kahn, Crane explained, "The protagonist has left the room with his harbor sounds and is walking to the subway. The rhythm is quickened; it is a transition between sleep and the immanent tasks of the day. Space is filled with the music of a hand organ and fresh sunlight, and one has the impression of the whole continent — from Atlantic to Pacific — freshly arisen and moving. The walk to the subway arouses reminiscences of childhood, also the 'childhood' of the continental conquest, viz., the conquistadores, Priscilla, Capt. John Smith, etc. These parallelisms unite in the figure of Rip Van Winkle, who finally becomes identified with the protagonist, as you will notice, and who really boards the subway with the reader. He becomes the 'guardian angel' of the journey into the past." In subsequent poems of *The Bridge*, the protagonist ventures ever more deeply into the heart and soul of the nation, finally ending up back in the hellish "tunnel" of the subway system, to emerge with a renewed vision of the bridge, now fully realized as a "white, pervasive Paradigm" of "Love," an "Everpresence, beyond time."

---

13. Memory—including or especially the unhappy examples that follow — triggers poetry and the imagination.

14. Trolley fare.

15. Perhaps an echo of "Hurry up please, it's time" in T. S. Eliot's *The Waste Land* (1922).

Eternity

September—remember!
October—all over.
BARBADIAN ADAGE

After it was over, though still gusting balefully,
The old woman[1] and I foraged some drier clothes
And left the house, or what was left of it;
Parts of the roof reached Yucatan,[2] I suppose.
She almost—even then—got blown across lots
At the base of the mountain. But the town, the town!

Wires in the streets and Chinamen up and down
With arms in slings, plaster strewn dense with tiles,
And Cuban doctors, troopers, trucks, loose hens . . .
The only building not sagging on its knees,
Fernandez' Hotel, was requisitioned into pens
For cotted negroes, bandaged to be taken
To Havana[3] on the first boat through. They groaned.

But was there a boat? By the wharf's old site you saw
Two decks unsandwiched, split sixty feet apart
And a funnel high and dry up near the park
Where a frantic peacock rummaged amid heaped cans.
No one seemed to be able to get a spark
From the world outside, but some rumor blew
That Havana, not to mention poor Batabanó,[4]
Was halfway under water with fires
For some hours since—all wireless[5] down
Of course, there too.

　　　　　　　　　Back at the erstwhile house
We shoveled and sweated; watched the ogre sun
Blister the mountain, stripped now, bare of palm,
Everything—and lick the grass, as black as patent
Leather, which the rimed white wind had glazed.
Everything gone—or strewn in riddled grace—
Long tropic roots high in the air, like lace.

---

1. The caretaker of the house, Mrs. Sarah (Sally) Simpson,
2. Across the Caribbean's Yucatan Channel in Mexico, about 120 miles to the west.
3. Cuba's capital city.
4. Coastal region of southwestern Cuba, north of the Isla de Pinos.
5. Radio.

And somebody's mule steamed, swaying right by the pump,
Good God! as though his sinking carcass there
Were death predestined! You held your nose already
Along the roads, begging for buzzards, vultures . . .
The mule stumbled, staggered. I somehow couldn't budge
To lift a stick for pity of his stupor.

For I

Remember still that strange gratuity[6] of horses
—One ours, and one, a stranger, creeping up with dawn
Out of the bamboo brake[7] through howling, sheeted light
When the storm was dying. And Sarah saw them, too—
Sobbed, Yes, now—it's almost over. For they know;
The weather's in their noses. There's Don[8]—but that one, white
—I can't account for him! And true, he stood
Like a vast phantom maned by all that memoried night
Of screaming rain—Eternity!

Yet water, water!

I beat the dazed mule toward the road. He got that far
And fell dead or dying, but it didn't so much matter.

The morrow's dawn was dense with carrion[9] hazes
Sliding everywhere. Bodies were rushed into graves
Without ceremony, while hammers pattered in town.
The roads were being cleared, injured brought in
And treated, it seemed. In due time
The President sent down a battleship[10] that baked
Something like two thousand loaves on the way.
Doctors shot ahead from the deck in planes.
The fever was checked. I stood a long time in Mack's talking
New York with the gobs,[11] Guantanamo, Norfolk,—
Drinking Bacardi[12] and talking U.S.A.

1927

"Eternity," one of the least compacted poems Crane ever composed, takes its inspiration from his experience of riding out a hurricane on the Isla de Pinos (Isle of Pines), off Cuba's

6. Bonus or gift; something received without demand.
7. Thicket.
8. Their horse.
9. Dead and putrefying flesh.

10. U.S.S. *Milwaukee*, participating in Operation Rescue.
11. Sailors. Guantanamo: U.S. naval base in Cuba. Norfolk: U.S. naval base in Virginia.
12. A brand of rum.

southwestern coast in the Caribbean, in October 1926. The concluding lines suggest the return of a normal, human world after the terrifying yet somehow exhilarating destruction of the storm.

The Broken Tower

The bell-rope that gathers God at dawn[1]
Dispatches me as though I dropped down the knell
Of a spent day—to wander the cathedral lawn
From pit to crucifix, feet chill on steps from hell.

Have you not heard, have you not seen that corps
Of shadows in the tower, whose shoulders sway
Antiphonal carillons[2] launched before
The stars are caught and hived in the sun's ray?

The bells, I say, the bells break down their tower;
And swing I know not where. Their tongues engrave
Membrane through marrow, my long-scattered score
Of broken intervals . . .[3] and I, their sexton slave!

Oval encyclicals[4] in canyons heaping
The impasse high with choir. Banked voices slain!
Pagodas, campaniles[5] with reveilles outleaping—
O terraced echoes prostrate on the plain! . . .

And so it was I entered the broken world
To trace the visionary company of love, its voice
An instant in the wind (I know not whither hurled)
But not for long to hold each desperate choice.

My word I poured. But was it cognate, scored
Of that tribunal monarch of the air[6]
Whose thigh embronzes earth, strikes crystal Word
In wounds pledged once to hope—cleft[7] to despair?

1. The tolling of the morning Angelus bell in the Roman Catholic church, indicating that a devotion to the Annunciation is to be recited.
2. Bells producing alternating and harmonizing melodies.
3. Difference in musical pitch between two tones; here, perhaps an image of the speaker's fragmented creativity. Sexton: church caretaker and bell ringer.
4. Papal messages.
5. Bell towers. Reveilles: bugle or drum sounds to alert troops in the morning.
6. Perhaps the imagination conceived as a deity.
7. Stuck, adhering closely; or, conversely, split, divided.

* * *

The steep encroachments[8] of my blood left me
No answer (could blood hold such a lofty tower
As flings the question true?)—or is it she[9]
Whose sweet mortality stirs latent power?—

And through whose pulse I hear, counting the strokes
My veins recall and add, revived and sure
The angelus[10] of wars my chest evokes;
What I hold healed, original now, and pure . . .

And builds, within, a tower that is not stone
(Not stone can jacket heaven)—but slip
Of pebbles,—visible wings of silence sown
In azure circles, widening as they dip

The matrix of the heart, lift down the eye
That shrines the quiet lake and swells a tower . . .
The commodious, tall decorum of that sky
Unseals her earth, and lifts love in its shower.

1932

Crane wrote "The Broken Tower" in Mexico during the last year of his life, in the midst of his love affair with Peggy Baird Cowley. Cowley wrote to a friend that living with Crane "was like living with an erupting volcano." "The Broken Tower" was his last completed poem. Langdon Hammer comments, "For Crane, the entrance into poetry is imagined as a breaking or scattering of the whole of his desire, ambition, identity; it is a passage into structure that is, paradoxically, destructuring."

PROSE

FROM *General Aims and Theories*

. . . It is a terrific problem that faces the poet today—a world that is so in transition from a decayed culture toward a reorganization of human evaluations that there are few common terms, general denominators of speech that are solid enough or that ring with any vibration or spiritual conviction. The great

---

8. Trespasses, advancements beyond proper limits.
9. The object of the speaker's love, whether real or ideal.

10. Roman Catholic prayer that commemorates Christ's Incarnation; or the bell ringing that announces the prayer.

mythologies of the past (including the Church) are deprived of enough façade to even launch good raillery[1] against. Yet much of their traditions are operative still — in millions of chance combinations of related and unrelated detail, psychological reference, figures of speech, precepts, etc. These are all a part of our common experience and the terms, at least partially, of that very experience when it defines or extends itself.

The deliberate program, then, of a "break" with the past or tradition seems to me to be a sentimental fallacy. . . . The poet has a right to draw on whatever practical resources he finds in books or otherwise about him. He must tax his sensibility and his touchstone of experience for the proper selections of these themes and details, however — and that is where he either stands, or falls into useless archeology.

I put no particular value on the simple objective of "modernity." The element of the temporal location of an artist's creation is of very secondary importance; it can be left to the impressionist or historian just as well. It seems to me that a poet will accidentally define his time well enough simply by reacting honestly and to the full extent of his sensibilities to the states of passion, experience and rumination that fate forces on him, first hand. He must, of course, have a sufficiently universal basis of experience to make his imagination selective and valuable. His picture of the "period," then, will simply be a by-product of his curiosity and the relation of his experience to a postulated "eternity."

I am concerned with the future of America, but not because I think that America has any so-called par value as a state or as a group of people. . . . It is only because I feel persuaded that here are destined to be discovered certain as yet undefined spiritual quantities, perhaps a new hierarchy of faith not to be developed so completely elsewhere. And in this process I like to feel myself as a potential factor; certainly I must speak in its terms and what discoveries I may make are situated in its experience.

But to fool one's self that definitions are being reached by merely referring frequently to skyscrapers, radio antennae, steam whistles, or other surface phenomena of our time is merely to paint a photograph. I think that what is interesting and significant will emerge only under the conditions of our submission to and examination and assimilation of the organic effects on us of these and other fundamental factors of our experience. It can certainly not be an organic expression otherwise. And the expression of such values may often be as well accomplished with the vocabulary and blank verse of the Elizabethans as with the calligraphic tricks and slang used so brilliantly at times by an impressionist like Cummings.[2]

It may not be possible to say that there is, strictly speaking, any "absolute"

---

1. Banter, good-humored ridicule.
2. E. E. Cummings, a contemporary poet (included in this anthology).

experience. But it seems evident that certain aesthetic experience (and this may for a time engross the total faculties of the spectator) can be called absolute, inasmuch as it approximates a formally convincing statement of a conception or apprehension of life that gains our unquestioning assent, and under the conditions of which our imagination is unable to suggest a further detail consistent with the design of the aesthetic whole.

I have been called an "absolutist" in poetry, and if I am to welcome such a label it should be under the terms of the above definition. It is really only a *modus operandi*,[3] however, and as such has been used organically before by at least a dozen poets such as Donne,[4] Blake, Baudelaire, Rimbaud, etc. I may succeed in defining it better by contrasting it with the impressionistic method. The impressionist is interesting as far as he goes—but his goal has been reached when he has succeeded in projecting certain selected factual details into his reader's consciousness. He is really not interested in the *causes* (metaphysical) of his materials, their emotional derivations or their utmost spiritual consequences. A kind of retinal registration is enough, along with a certain psychological stimulation. And this is also true of your realist (of the Zola[5] type), and to a certain extent of the classicist, like Horace,[6] Ovid, Pope, etc.

Blake meant these differences when he wrote:

> We are led to believe in a lie
> When we see *with* not *through* the eye.[7]

The impressionist creates only with the eye and for the readiest surface of the consciousness, at least relatively so. If the effect has been harmonious or even stimulating, he can stop there, relinquishing entirely to his audience the problematic synthesis of the details into terms of their own personal consciousness.

It is my hope to go *through* the combined materials of the poem, using our "real" world somewhat as a spring-board, and to give the poem *as a whole* an orbit or predetermined direction of its own. I would like to establish it as free from my own personality as from any chance evaluation on the reader's part. (This is, of course, an impossibility, but it is a characteristic worth mentioning.) Such a poem is at least a stab at a truth, and to such an extent may be differentiated from other kinds of poetry and called "absolute." Its evocation will not be toward decoration or amusement, but rather toward a state of consciousness, an "innocence" (Blake) or absolute beauty. In this condition there may be discoverable under new forms certain spiritual illuminations, shining with a morality essentialized

3. Mode of operating.
4. John Donne (1572–1631), English metaphysical poet. William Blake (1757–1827): English Romantic poet. Charles Baudelaire (1821–1867): French symbolist poet. Arthur Rimbaud (1854–1891): French symbolist poet.
5. Émile Zola (1840–1902), French novelist.

6. Horace (65–8 B.C.E.), Roman lyric poet and satirist. Ovid (43 B.C.E.–ca. 17 C.E.): Roman poet. Alexander Pope (1688–1744): English poet and satirist.
7. Misquoted from William Blake's "Auguries of Innocence" (1803): "We are led to Believe a Lie / When we see not Thro' the Eye."

from experience directly, and not from previous precepts or preconceptions. It is as though a poem gave the reader as he left it a single, new *word*, never before spoken and impossible to actually enunciate, but self-evident as an active principle in the reader's consciousness henceforward.

As to technical considerations: the motivation of the poem must be derived from the implicit emotional dynamics of the materials used, and the terms of expression employed are often selected less for their logical (literal) significance than for their associational meanings. Via this and their metaphorical interrelationships, the entire construction of the poem is raised on the organic principle of a "logic of metaphor," which antedates our so-called pure logic, and which is the genetic basis of all speech, hence consciousness and thought-extension.

These dynamics often result, I'm told, in certain initial difficulties in understanding my poems. But on the other hand I find them at times the only means possible for expressing certain concepts in any forceful or direct way whatever. . . . When, in "Voyages" 2, I speak of "adagios of islands," the reference is to the motion of a boat through islands clustered thickly, the rhythm of the motion, etc. And it seems a much more direct and creative statement than any more logical employment of words such as "coasting slowly through the islands," beside ushering in a whole world of music. . . .

In manipulating the more imponderable phenomena of psychic motives, pure emotional crystallizations, etc., I have had to rely even more on these dynamics of inferential mention, and I am doubtless still very unconscious of having committed myself to what seems nothing but obscurities to some minds. . . .

I know that I run the risk of much criticism by defending such theories as I have, but as it is part of a poet's business to risk not only criticism — but folly — in the conquest of consciousness I can only say that I attach no intrinsic value to what means I use beyond their practical service in giving form to the living stuff of the imagination.

New conditions of life germinate new forms of spiritual articulation. And while I feel that my work includes a more consistent extension of traditional literary elements than many contemporary poets are capable of appraising, I realize that I am utilizing the gifts of the past as instruments principally; and that the voice of the present, if it is to be known, must be caught at the risk of speaking in idioms and circumlocutions sometimes shocking to the scholar and historians of logic. Language has built towers and bridges, but itself is inevitably as fluid as always.

1937

This essay, written in 1925, was published posthumously.

WEN I-TO [WEN JIAHUA]
1899–1946

W EN JIAHUA, writing under the pen name Wen I-To, is considered not only a significant Chinese-American modernist poet but also a pioneer in modern Chinese poetry. He was born in China and attended Qinghua University before deciding to study fine arts and literature in New York City in 1922. While he was in the United States writing and reading poetry in English, his first poetry collection, *Red Candle*, was published. Jiahua returned to China in 1925 to take a university teaching position. He continued to publish poetry, influenced by his time in the United States, and to pursue his studies of poetic form and classical Chinese poetry. He introduced free verse in his homeland, thereby modernizing Chinese poetry. Today he is studied as a major poetic figure in China.

Beginning in 1944, Jiahua pursued an increasingly political life. In 1946, he was assassinated, rumored to be one of the victims of Chiang Kai-shek's secret service because of allegations about his Communist leanings. As the poem included here illustrates, he was scornful of the mistreatment of the Chinese in the United States, and he was critical of the passivity of Chinese male immigrants.

FURTHER READING

Juliana Chang, ed. *Quiet Fire: A Historical Anthology of Asian American Poetry, 1892–1970.* New Brunswick, N.J.: Rutgers University Press, 1996.

The Laundry Song

(One piece, two pieces, three pieces,)
Washing must be clean.
(Four pieces, five pieces, six pieces,)
Ironing must be smooth.

I can wash handkerchiefs wet with sad tears;
I can wash shirts soiled in sinful crimes.
The grease of greed, the dirt of desire . . .
And all the filthy things at your house,
Give them to me to wash, give them to me.

Brass stinks so; blood smells evil.
Dirty things you have to wash.

Once washed, they will again be soiled.
How can you, men of patience, ignore them!
Wash them (for the Americans), wash them!

You say the laundry business is too base.
Only Chinamen are willing to stoop so low?
It was your preacher who once told me:
Christ's father used to be a carpenter.
Do you believe it? Don't you believe it?

There isn't much you can do with soap and water.
Washing clothes truly can't compare with building warships.
I, too, say what great prospect lies in this—
Washing the other's sweat with your own blood and sweat?
(But) do you want to do it? Do you want it?

Year in year out a drop of homesick tears;
Midnight, in the depth of night, a laundry lamp . . .
Menial or not, you need not bother,
Just see what is not clean, what is not smooth,
And ask the Chinaman, ask the Chinaman.

I can wash handkerchiefs wet with sad tears;
I can wash shirts soiled in sinful crimes.
The grease of greed, the dirt of desire . . .
And all the filthy things at your house,
Give them to me—I'll wash them, give them to me.

n.d.

Chinese immigrants were pushed into laundry work, one of the few occupations open to them. By 1900, one out of four employed Chinese-American men worked in a laundry. In the early decades of the new century, in such cities as San Francisco and New York, Chinese-American men often owned and operated the laundries, and their entire families worked in them to ensure their success.

ALLEN TATE
1899–1979

DISTINGUISHED BOTH as a poet and as a founder of the New Criticism, Allen Tate sought to breathe new life into traditional poetic forms. The more intricate the structure, the more it challenged and inspired him. In one of his essays, he argued that poetry "is the art of apprehending and concentrating our experience in the mysterious limitations of form." His poems convert raw experience into "knowledge / Carried to the heart" (as "Ode to the Confederate Dead" puts it), and they do so in a rhetoric remarkable for its condensation, ambiguity, and allusiveness. These poems are complex on every level—sonic, metrical, intellectual, and affective. If Tate wrote as "a man suffering from disbelief," he compensated for his terrifying sense of abandonment with some of the most ordered poetry of his century. He tied this difficult and intense poetic project to a conservative cultural critique. Raised in rural Kentucky, he looked askance on Northern urbanization, industrialization, and commercialization. He distrusted big business and big government. He yearned for an agrarian society, hierarchical and rooted in the soil, which he associated with the antebellum South and Jeffersonian democracy. Like many modernists influenced by Ezra Pound and T. S. Eliot, Tate tied a program of poetic innovation to cultural elitism.

John Orley Allen Tate was born in Winchester, Kentucky. He attended Vanderbilt University in Nashville, where he and his roommate Robert Penn Warren studied with John Crowe Ransom (both included in this volume). Tate joined Ransom's Fugitive group, which argued for conservative social and artistic ideals, based on notions of Southern regionalism and agrarianism. Tate later became a leading New Critic, theorizing and practicing a style of subtle close reading that proved especially illuminating on the densely written work of poets such as Eliot, Hart Crane, and Tate himself. Tate's poems written in the 1920s and 1930s depict both history and the human self as violent, fallen, divided, and tragic. "The Wolves" explores the brutish aspects of the human psyche. "The Mediterranean" meditates the downward spiral of Western civilization, whereas "Ode to the Confederate Dead" mourns the ravages of Southern history. In the 1950s, Tate composed "The Swimmers," a memory poem that takes a more critical view of Southern history than had previously been his custom.

Tate's poetry has suffered in reputation since his death, perhaps because its formal elements have seemed to some readers excessively complicated, perhaps because its cultural program has seemed provincial, and perhaps because Tate, especially in his early years, wrote prose that now seems racist and heterosexist. Yet Tate's best poems contain an excitement, a passion that lasts. Tate wrote poems as if his life depended on them—and as if the reader's does as well. At their strongest moments, the poems enter into some of the darkest spaces in human history and the human soul. When they enter that zone, they still have the power to shake us.

FURTHER READING

Langdon Hammer. *Hart Crane and Allen Tate: Janus-Faced Modernism*. Princeton: Princeton University Press, 1993.

Alexander Karanikas. *Tillers of a Myth: Southern Agrarians as Social and Literary Critics*. Madison: University of Wisconsin Press, 1969.

Louis D. Rubin, Jr. *The Wary Fugitives: Four Poets and the South*. Baton Rouge: Louisiana State University Press, 1978.

Radcliffe Squires. *Allen Tate: A Literary Biography*. New York: Pegasus, 1971.

Allen Tate. *Collected Poems: 1919–1976*. New York: Farrar, Straus & Giroux, 1977.

———. *Essays of Four Decades*. New York: William Morrow, 1959.

———. *The Fathers and Other Fiction*. Baton Rouge: Louisiana State University Press, 1977.

Thomas A. Underwood. *Allen Tate: Orpheus of the South*. Princeton: Princeton University Press, 2000.

The Wolves

There are wolves in the next room waiting
With heads bent low, thrust out, breathing
At nothing in the dark; between them and me
A white door patched with light from the hall
Where it seems never (so still is the house)
A man has walked from the front door to the stair.
It has all been forever. Beasts claw the floor.
I have brooded on angels and archfiends
But no man has ever sat where the next room's
Crowded with wolves, and for the honor of man
I affirm that never have I before. Now while
I have looked for the evening star at a cold window
And whistled when Arcturus[1] spilt his light,
I've heard the wolves scuffle, and said: So this
Is man; so—what better conclusion is there—
The day will not follow night, and the heart
Of man has a little dignity, but less patience
Than a wolf's, and a duller sense that cannot
Smell its own mortality. (This and other

---

1. One of the brightest stars in the night sky. Its name means "bear keeper" in Greek, a reflection of its visual position near the tail of the constellation Ursa Major (or Great Bear).

Meditations will be suited to other times
After dog silence howls his epitaph.)
Now remember courage, go to the door,
Open it and see whether coiled on the bed
Or cringing by the wall, a savage beast
Maybe with golden hair, with deep eyes
Like a bearded spider on a sunlit floor
Will snarl—and man can never be alone.

                    1931

"The Wolves" evokes a sense of nightmarish, existential terror as well as a notion of the wolfish quality of one's inner being. The speaker occupies a deserted house, perhaps the Gothic mansion of the self. He is not alone there only because—as a split, Freudian psyche—for company he has the beasts of his unconscious, which he finally feels he must confront.

The Mediterranean

Quem das finem, rex magne, dolorum?[1]

Where we went in the boat was a long bay
A slingshot wide, walled in by towering stone—
Peaked margin of antiquity's delay,
And we went there out of time's monotone:

Where we went in the black hull no light moved
But a gull white-winged along the feckless[2] wave,
The breeze, unseen but fierce as a body loved,
That boat drove onward like a willing slave:

Where we went in the small ship the seaweed
Parted and gave to us the murmuring shore,
And we made feast and in our secret need
Devoured the very plates Aeneas bore:[3]

Where derelict you see through the low twilight
The green coast that you, thunder-tossed, would win,
Drop sail, and hastening to drink all night
Eat dish and bowl to take that sweet land in!

---

1. "What end will you give, great king, to their troubles?" The goddess Venus says this to the supreme god, Jupiter, about her mortal son, Aeneas, and his followers (Virgil, *The Aeneid* 1.242).
2. Feeble.

3. When Aeneas and his band eat their food on slabs of bread, he recalls a prophecy that when they have so little food that they eat their tables, they will have found their new homeland (*The Aeneid* 7.115–27).

*   *   *

Where we feasted and caroused on the sandless
Pebbles, affecting our day of piracy,
What prophecy of eaten plates could landless
Wanderers fulfil by the ancient sea?

We for that time might taste the famous age
Eternal here yet hidden from our eyes
When lust of power undid its stuffless rage;
They, in a wineskin, bore earth's paradise.

Let us lie down once more by the breathing side
Of Ocean, where our live forefathers sleep
As if the Known Sea still were a month wide—
Atlantis howls but is no longer steep!

What country shall we conquer, what fair land
Unman our conquest and locate our blood?
We've cracked the hemispheres with careless hand!
Now, from the Gates of Hercules[4] we flood

Westward, westward till the barbarous brine
Whelms[5] us to the tired land where tasseling corn,
Fat beans, grapes sweeter than muscadine
Rot on the vine: in that land were we born.[6]

1933

In 1932 Tate and his first wife, the novelist Caroline Gordon, spent a year in France. That summer, according to Radcliffe Squires, they attended a beach party at Cassis, in a small cove of the Mediterranean Sea. As they ate and drank, their friend, the novelist Ford Madox Ford, commented that it must have been in such coves that Aeneas and his men had stopped to eat. Tate bought a copy of Virgil's *Aeneid* the next day, reread it for several weeks, and then began to compose "The Mediterranean." Tate's poem juxtaposes modern-day picnickers with Aeneas and his companions. After the Trojan War, Aeneas, a Trojan, embarked on an epic journey along the coasts of the Mediterranean to Italy, where he founded the city of Lavinium, becoming the ancestral father of the Romans.

4. The Strait of Gibraltar, leading from the Mediterranean Sea to the Atlantic Ocean.
5. Engulfs or submerges; here, also, propels.

6. The United States seen, perhaps ironically, as an extension of Aeneas' heroic journey and, implicitly, of the European heritage.

Ode to the Confederate Dead

Row after row with strict impunity
The headstones yield their names to the element,[1]
The wind whirrs without recollection;
In the riven troughs the splayed leaves[2]
Pile up, of nature the casual sacrament
To the seasonal eternity of death;
Then driven by the fierce scrutiny
Of heaven to their election in the vast breath,
They sough the rumour of mortality.[3]

Autumn is desolation in the plot
Of a thousand acres where these memories grow
From the inexhaustible bodies that are not
Dead, but feed the grass row after rich row.
Think of the autumns that have come and gone!—
Ambitious November with the humors of the year,
With a particular zeal for every slab,
Staining the uncomfortable angels[4] that rot
On the slabs, a wing chipped here, an arm there:
The brute curiosity of an angel's stare
Turns you, like them, to stone,
Transforms the heaving air
Till plunged to a heavier world below
You shift your sea-space blindly
Heaving, turning like the blind crab.[5]

Dazed by the wind, only the wind
The leaves flying, plunge

You[6] know who have waited by the wall
The twilight certainty of an animal,
Those midnight restitutions of the blood

1. The rows of gravestones yield their names to the weather. Like the dead and defeated soldiers whose bodies they mark, they are immune from further punishment.
2. The tangles of autumn leaves pile up in the troughs between the graves.
3. The rustling leaves murmur of mortality. Their sigh contrasts with metaphors of "sacrament" and "election," which suggest a doctrine of immortal life that the scene itself belies.
4. Stone statuary.
5. The oppressive, suffocating air seems to the speaker to have turned to water.
6. Possibly the fallen Confederate soldiers, or possibly other observers.

You know—the immitigable[7] pines, the smoky frieze
Of the sky, the sudden call: you know the rage,
The cold pool left by the mounting flood,
Of muted Zeno[8] and Parmenides.
You who have waited for the angry resolution
Of those desires that should be yours tomorrow,
You know the unimportant shrift[9] of death
And praise the vision
And praise the arrogant circumstance
Of those who fall
Rank upon rank, hurried beyond decision—
Here by the sagging gate, stopped by the wall.

        Seeing, seeing only the leaves
        Flying, plunge and expire

Turn your eyes to the immoderate past,
Turn to the inscrutable infantry rising
Demons out of the earth—they will not last.
Stonewall,[10] Stonewall, and the sunken fields of hemp,
Shiloh,[11] Antietam, Malvern Hill, Bull Run.
Lost in that orient of the thick-and-fast
You will curse the setting sun.

        Cursing only the leaves crying
        Like an old man in a storm

You hear the shout,[12] the crazy hemlocks point
With troubled fingers to the silence which
Smothers you, a mummy, in time.[13]

            *   *   *

---

7. Unchangeable or unimprovable. Frieze: decorative band or strip.
8. Greek philosopher (ca. 495–430 B.C.E.) who lived in Elea, Italy. Parmenides: another Greek philosopher (born ca. 515 B.C.E.) from Elea. Both philosophers maintained a distinction between the mutable world of appearance and ultimate reality. Paul Valéry's "Cimitière Marin," one of this poem's precursors, refers to Zeno as "cruel" rather than "muted."

9. Confession or absolution.
10. Thomas J. "Stonewall" Jackson (1824–1863), a Confederate general.
11. The place-name of a bloody Civil War battle of 1862, as are the other names in this line.
12. Perhaps an imagined shout in battle.
13. In "Narcissus as Narcissus" Tate explains that "the failure of the vision throws the man back upon himself, but . . . the human image is only that of preserved death (the mummy)."

                    The hound bitch
Toothless and dying, in a musty cellar
Hears the wind only.[14]

                    Now that the salt of their blood
Stiffens the saltier oblivion of the sea,
Seals the malignant purity of the flood,
What shall we who count our days and bow
Our heads with a commemorial woe
In the ribboned coats of grim felicity,
What shall we say of the bones, unclean,
Whose verdurous[15] anonymity will grow?
The ragged arms, the ragged heads and eyes
Lost in these acres of the insane green?
The gray lean spiders come, they come and go;
In a tangle of willows without light
The singular screech-owl's tight
Invisible lyric seeds the mind
With the furious murmur of their chivalry.

            We shall say only the leaves
            Flying, plunge and expire

We shall say only the leaves whispering
In the improbable mist of nightfall
That flies on multiple wing;
Night is the beginning and the end
And in between the ends of distraction
Waits mute speculation, the patient curse
That stones the eyes, or like the jaguar leaps
For his own image in a jungle pool, his victim.[16]
What shall we say who have knowledge
Carried to the heart? Shall we take the act
To the grave? Shall we, more hopeful, set up the grave
In the house? The ravenous grave?

            *   *   *

14. Possibly an echo of the "windy spaces" pervading Eliot's "Gerontion."
15. Green, verdant.
16. Tate comments, "This figure of the jaguar is the only explicit rendering of the Narcissus motif in the poem, but instead of a youth gazing into a pool, a predatory beast stares at a jungle stream and leaps to devour himself."

Leave now
The shut gate and the decomposing wall:
The gentle serpent,[17] green in the mulberry bush,
Riots with his tongue through the hush—
Sentinel of the grave who counts us all!

1937

Tate wrote "Ode to the Confederate Dead" in 1925–26, publishing an early version in 1927 and the final version in 1937. His best-known work, it is both an elegy for Southern Civil War soldiers and a revelation of the speaker's feelings of loss, estrangement, and failure. Standing just outside the locked gate of a military graveyard, he oscillates between observation and "mute speculation." Louis D. Rubin, Jr. comments, "The poem . . . is not about the dead Confederate soldiers at all; it is about the modern man's sense of being distanced from them." Tate himself, in an essay on the poem called "Narcissus as Narcissus," proposes that the poem "is 'about' solipsism, a philosophical doctrine which says that we create the world in the act of perceiving it; or about Narcissism."

The Swimmers

SCENE: *Montgomery County,
Kentucky, July 1911*

Kentucky water, clear springs: a boy fleeing
To water under the dry Kentucky sun,
His four little friends in tandem with him, seeing

Long shadows of grapevine wriggle and run
Over the green swirl; mullein[1] under the ear
Soft as Nausicaä's[2] palm; sullen fun

Savage as childhood's thin harmonious tear:
O fountain, bosom source undying-dead
Replenish me the spring of love and fear

And give me back the eye that looked and fled
When a thrush idling in the tulip tree
Unwound the cold dream of the copperhead.[3]

---

17. In "Narcissus as Narcissus" Tate identifies the serpent as "the ancient symbol of time," adding that "time is also death." Several critics, however, noting that the "serpent" is but a gentle, green silkworm, have seen more hopeful implications in the poem's conclusion

1. A wild plant with woolly leaves and spikes of yellow flowers.

2. The princess in Homer's *Odyssey* (book 6) who discovers the shipwrecked Odysseus and directs him to her father's palace.

3. Poisonous snake, which Northerners often associated with the Southern cause during the Civil War.

*   *   *

—Along the creek the road was winding; we
    Felt the quicksilver sky. I see again
    The shrill companions of that odyssey:

Bill Eaton, Charlie Watson, "Nigger"[4] Layne
    The doctor's son, Harry Duèsler who played
    The flute; and Tate, with water on the brain.

Dog-days: the dusty leaves where rain delayed
    Hung low on poison-oak and scuppernong,[5]
    And we were following the active shade

Of water, that bells and bickers all night long.
    "No more'n a mile," Layne said. All five stood still.
    Listening, I heard what seemed at first a song;

Peering, I heard the hooves come down the hill.
    The posse passed, twelve horse; the leader's face
    Was worn as limestone on an ancient sill.

Then, as sleepwalkers shift from a hard place
    In bed, and rising to keep a formal pledge
    Descend a ladder into empty space,

We scuttled down the bank below a ledge
    And marched stiff-legged in our common fright
    Along a hog-track by the riffle's[6] edge:

Into a world where sound shaded the sight
    Dropped the dull hooves again; the horsemen came
    Again, all but the leader: it was night

Momently and I feared: eleven same
    Jesus-Christers[7] unmembered and unmade,
    Whose Corpse had died again in dirty shame.

The bank then levelling in a speckled glade,
    We stopped to breathe above the swimming-hole;
    I gazed at its reticulated[8] shade

*   *   *

4. A nickname. The five boys named in this stanza are white.
5. Southern grapevine.
6. A rapid in a stream.
7. A lynch party composed of white evangelical Christians who have murdered an African American.
8. Netlike.

Recoiling in blue fear, and felt it roll
  Over my ears and eyes and lift my hair
  Like seaweed tossing on a sunk atoll.

I rose again. Borne on the copper air
  A distant voice green as a funeral wreath
  Against a grave: "That dead nigger there."

The melancholy sheriff slouched beneath
  A giant sycamore; shaking his head
  He plucked a sassafras twig and picked his teeth:

"We come too late." He spoke to the tired dead
  Whose ragged shirt soaked up the viscous flow
  Of blood in which It[9] lay discomfited.

A butting horse-fly gave one ear a blow
  And glanced off, as the sheriff kicked the rope
  Loose from the neck and hooked it with his toe

Away from the blood. —I looked back down the slope:
  The friends were gone that I had hoped to greet.[10] —
  A single horseman came at a slow lope

And pulled up at the hanged man's horny feet;
  The sheriff noosed the feet, the other end
  The stranger tied to his pommel[11] in a neat

Slip-knot. I saw the Negro's body bend
  And straighten, as a fish-line cast transverse
  Yields to the current that it must subtend.

The sheriff's Goddamn was a murmured curse
  Not for the dead but for the blinding dust
  That boxed the cortège[12] in a cloudy hearse

And dragged it towards our town. I knew I must
  Not stay till twilight in that silent road;
  Sliding my bare feet into the warm crust,

I hopped the stonecrop[13] like a panting toad
  Mouth open, following the heaving cloud
  That floated to the court-house square its load

9. The capitalization of the corpse, here and ear- 11. A knob at the front and top of a saddle.
lier, may suggest an identification of the mur- 12. A ceremonial procession, as at a funeral.
dered man with Jesus Christ. 13. Sedum, a succulent plant.
10. The boy's friends have run off.

* * *

Of limber corpse that took the sun for shroud.
　　There were three figures in the dying sun
　　Whose light were company where three was crowd.

My breath crackled the dead air like a shotgun
　　As, sheriff and the stranger disappearing,
　　The faceless head lay still. I could not run

Or walk, but stood. Alone in the public clearing
　　This private thing was owned by all the town,
　　Though never claimed by us within my hearing.[14]

1953

When Tate was eleven years old he experienced the events on which this poem is based. Here Tate moves away from the more impersonal poetics that established his reputation to recall a traumatic event from his childhood, going so far as to name himself, though wryly: "Tate, with water on the brain." The poem is written in terza rima, the stanza form of Dante's *Divine Comedy*. Each tercet begins and ends with lines that rhyme with the center line of the preceding tercet. Difficult and rarely used in English, this stanza form also appears in Percy Bysshe Shelley's "Ode to the West Wind."

YVOR WINTERS
1900–1968

YVOR WINTERS, one of the most influential critics of his time, began his career by displaying a vital interest in modernist experimentation. He praised the work of Wallace Stevens, William Carlos Williams, and Hart Crane. His own early poems have Native-American, Asian, and European echoes. As he matured, however, Winters moved to an anti-modernist position. He execrated formal experiment and excessive feeling, instead prizing logic, reason, morality, and restraint. Yet he did not advocate rationality from the perspective of one who was a stranger to emotion. On the contrary, he experienced intense sensual passion, as his poem "The Marriage" suggests, and he lived his life in the shadow of depression and madness, as his short story "The Brink of Darkness" and such poems as "By the Road to the Air-Base" and "A Dream Vision" imply. Rejecting modernist fragmentation

---

14. The white townspeople remain silent about the crime.

and obscurantism, which he termed "the fallacy of imitative form," he came to prefer the formal poets of the past. He particularly admired intellectually rigorous poets such as Fulke Greville and George Herbert (in the Renaissance) and Robert Bridges, Emily Dickinson, and Edwin Arlington Robinson (in the nineteenth century). Yet the cognitive sophistication of such poets subsists with intense and often dark emotions, just as in Winters's own work.

Arthur Yvor Winters grew up in Eagle Rock, California, then a suburb and now a neighborhood of Los Angeles. A brilliant student, he excelled in his classes, but his studies were interrupted by a bout of tuberculosis. Recovering in a New Mexican sanitorium, he began writing poetry, and he never stopped. After earning a B.A. and M.A. from the University of Colorado, Boulder, and a Ph.D. from Stanford, he accepted a job teaching English at Stanford, where he stayed until retirement. Married to the poet Janet Lewis, he had many disciples and just as many enemies. His poetry and criticism continue to influence a small cohort of devoted followers today. His writing is fascinating for the tensions it displays between innovation and tradition, and between feeling and the fear of feeling. In his late poem "A Dream Vision," he summed up his poetic achievement: "What I did was small but good."

FURTHER READING

Terry Comito. *In Defense of Winters: The Poetry and Prose of Yvor Winters*. Madison: University of Wisconsin Press, 1986.

Elizabeth Isaacs. *An Introduction to the Poetry of Yvor Winters*. Athens: Ohio University Press, 1981.

Yvor Winters. *In Defense of Reason*. Denver: Alan Swallow, 1947.

——. *Selected Poems*. Ed. Thom Gunn. New York: Library of America, 2003.

Two Songs of Advent

1

On the desert, between pale mountains, our cries—
Far whispers creeping through an ancient shell.

2

Coyote, on delicate mocking feet,
Hovers down the canyon, among the mountains,
His voice running wild in the wind's valleys.

Listen! listen! for I[1] enter now your thought.

1921

---

1. The coyote, a magical figure in Native-American tradition.

"Two Songs of Advent" come from Winters's early, experimentalist phase. Centering on the relationship between the earth and human consciousness, they reveal the strong influence of Native-American poetry. The coyote, for example, is a common figure in Indian myth and poetry of California and the Southwest. This figure was regarded as a creator, a culture hero, a magician, and a trickster. He could enter and transform beings and things. The first "Song of Advent" seems to suggest an East Asian influence as well.

The Hunter

Run! in the magpie's shadow.

1922

"The Hunter" and the four poems that follow derive from a sequence called *The Magpie's Shadow*. These poems combine a Native-American sense of the Western landscape with echoes of East Asian and French symbolist poetry. The magpie of western North America is a black-billed bird with an iridescent blue-green tail. Associated with freedom and speed, the magpie, like the coyote, appears frequently in Native-American art, masks, tales, and poems. Winters's use of the North American magpie contrasts with Gertrude Stein's reference to the Eurasian "magpie in the sky" in *Four Saints in Three Acts*.

The Shadow's Song

I am beside you, now.

1922

Cool Nights

At night bare feet on flowers!

1922

Sleep

Like winds my eyelids close.

1922

God of Roads

I, peregrine[1] of noon.

1922

---

1. Foreign, from abroad; a peregrine or cosmopolitan falcon.

The Marriage

Incarnate[1] for our marriage you appeared,
Flesh living in the spirit[2] and endeared
By minor graces and slow sensual change.
Through every nerve we made our spirits range.
We fed our minds on every mortal thing:
The lacy fronds of carrots in the spring,
Their flesh sweet on the tongue, the salty wine
From bitter grapes, which gathered through the vine
The mineral drouth[3] of autumn concentrate,
Wild spring in dream escaping, the debate
Of flesh and spirit on those vernal[4] nights,
Its resolution in naïve delights,
The young kids bleating softly in the rain —
All this to pass, not to return again.
And when I found your flesh did not resist,
It was the living spirit that I kissed,
It was the spirit's change in which I lay:
Thus, mind in mind we waited for the day.
When flesh shall fall away, and, falling, stand
Wrinkling with shadow over face and hand,
Still I shall meet you on the verge of dust
And know you as a faithful vestige[5] must.
And, in commemoration[6] of our lust,
May our heirs seal us in a single urn,
A single spirit never to return.

1931

"The Marriage" evokes the marital love of the speaker and his wife. The love at first takes the form of sexual desire and sensual pleasure, but with time, it becomes spiritual instead. The speaker prays that after death the couple's ashes may be sealed in the same funeral urn, "a single spirit never to return." Written in iambic pentameter couplets (and one triplet), the poem pays tribute to the form, vocabulary, and intricacy of Renaissance poetry.

1. Invested with bodily form.
2. The paradox of flesh and spirit is elaborated throughout the poem.
3. Drought, dryness.
4. Occurring in spring; youthful.
5. Visible mark of something no longer in existence.
6. Honor, celebration.

By the Road to the Air-Base

The calloused grass lies hard
Against the cracking plain:
Life is a grayish stain:
The salt-marsh hems my yard.

Dry dikes rise hill on hill:
In sloughs[1] of tidal slime
Shell-fish deposit lime,
Wild sea-fowl creep at will.

The highway, like a beach,
Turns whiter, shadowy dry:
Loud, pale against the sky,
The bombing planes hold speech.

Yet fruit grows on the trees;
Here scholars pause to speak;
Through gardens bare and Greek,
I hear my neighbor's bees.

1931

"By the Road to the Air-Base" contrasts the decay and violence of the surrounding natural and human scene with the fecundity and harmony of the scholar's garden. The title and first stanzas of the poem bear some resemblance to William Carlos Williams's earlier "Spring and All" (included in this volume).

A Dream Vision

What was all the talk about?
This was something to decide.
It was not that I had died.
Though my plans were new, no doubt,
There was nothing to deride.

I had grown away from youth,
Shedding error where I could;
I was now essential wood,
Concentrating into truth;
What I did was small but good.

1. Swamps; marshy backwaters.

*   *   *

Orchard tree beside the road,
Bare to core, but living still!
Moving little was my skill.
I could hear the farting toad
Shifting to observe the kill,

Spotted sparrow, spawn of dung,
Mumbling on a horse's turd,
Bullfinch, wren, or mockingbird
Screaming with a pointed tongue
Objurgation[1] without word.

1950

STERLING BROWN
1901–1989

STERLING BROWN combined a strong traditional education in literature with a sharply satirical eye and a keenly developed ear for African-American folklore and idiom to develop a compelling, energetically individual poetic voice. His poetic style melded elements from blues, jazz, spirituals, and work songs with a realist's urge to capture social life and circumstance, creating a style that was at once vividly dramatic, readily accessible, socially significant, and, at times, extremely funny. Brown was also an influential teacher, critic, and anthologist who, on each of these fronts, vigorously fought the stereotyping of African Americans then pervasive in American culture.

Sterling A. Brown was born in Washington, D.C., in 1901. His father, the Rev. Sterling N. Brown, taught at the School of Religious Studies at Howard University, where Brown would also later teach for many years. Brown's father was an associate of such leading figures in black history as Frederick Douglass, Booker T. Washington, and W. E. B. Du Bois. Brown was educated in Washington's segregated Dunbar High School at a time when it had an outstanding faculty, including the poets Angelina Weld Grimké and Jessie Redmon Fauset (also included in this anthology). Brown emerged from his early environment with a strong belief in the value

---

1. Reproach, denunciation.

of a distinctively African-American culture and a keen urge to communicate that value to others. Supported by a scholarship as Dunbar's top student, Brown attended Williams College, where he studied literature and graduated Phi Beta Kappa. He then went on to Harvard, receiving a master's degree in literature in 1923. Brown developed a keen interest in the new developments in modern American poetry. He was drawn particularly to the vivid expression of regional idiom and personal drama he found in the poetry of Robert Frost and Edwin Arlington Robinson, the rugged colloquial energy of Carl Sandburg and Vachel Lindsay, and the lively free-verse rhythms of imagists like Amy Lowell and H.D. (all but Robinson —who appears in the first volume—included in this anthology).

In 1926, Brown began teaching at Virginia Seminary and College in Lynchburg, Virginia, where his eager listening to local blues singers like Big Boy Davis— whose memory is celebrated in the early "When de Saints Go Ma'ching Home" —helped to shape a style rooted in African-American folk traditions. Brown came to believe, as Joanne V. Gabbin observes, that folk literature not only provided "a chronicle of the socio-historical experience of the group and a record of its spiritual struggle" but also served "as the surest aesthetic foundation for a Black literary tradition." Brown asserted that dialect, "or the speech of the people, is capable of expressing whatever the people are." By rooting one's work in black folklore, Brown maintained, the writer could present the specific forms of the culture and announce "the Negro's willingness to trust his own experience, his own sensibilities as to the definition of reality, rather than allow his masters to define these crucial matters for him."

Brown began teaching at Howard University in 1929, where he would influence several generations of students, including Gwendolyn Brooks and Amiri Baraka. Baraka called him a "repository of information and inspiration." Brown's first book of poetry, *Southern Road*, appeared in 1932. Brown published a series of important critical studies in the years that followed, including *Negro Poetry and Drama* (1937), *The Negro in American Fiction* (1937), and the anthology *The Negro Caravan* in 1941. A second volume of poetry, *No Hiding Place*, though finished in 1937, was persistently rejected by publishers; publication of his second book of poems, the ballad collection *The Last Ride of Wild Bill*, did not occur until 1975. Readers would have to wait until 1980 for the appearance of Brown's *Collected Poems*, edited by Michael Harper, to gain a comprehensive view of Brown's achievement as a poet.

FURTHER READING

Sterling A. Brown. *The Collected Poems*. Ed. Michael S. Harper. New York: Harper & Row, 1980.

———. *The Negro in American Fiction*. Washington, D.C.: Associates of Negro Folk Education, 1937; reprint ed., New York: Atheneum, 1969.

——. *Negro Poetry and Drama*. Washington, D.C.: Associates of Negro Folk Education, 1937;
   reprint ed., New York: Atheneum, 1969.
Joanne V. Gabbin. *Sterling A. Brown: Building the Black Aesthetic Tradition*. Charlottesville:
   University Press of Virginia, 1985.

When de Saints Go Ma'ching Home

*(To Big Boy Davis,[1] Friend.
In Memories of Days Before He Was
Chased Out of Town for Vagrancy.)*

I

He'd play, after the bawdy songs and blues,
After the weary plaints
Of "Trouble, Trouble deep down in muh soul,"
Always one song in which he'd lose the rôle
Of entertainer to the boys. He'd say,
"My mother's favorite." And we knew
That what was coming was his chant of saints,
"When de saints go ma'chin' home. . . ."
And that would end his concert for the day.

Carefully as an old maid over needlework,
Oh, as some black deacon, over his Bible, lovingly,
He'd tune up specially for this. There'd be
No chatter now, no patting of the feet.
After a few slow chords, knelling and sweet—
Oh when de saints go ma'chin' home,
Oh when de sayaints goa ma'chin' home. . . .
He would forget
The quieted bunch, his dimming cigarette
Stuck into a splintered edge of the guitar;
Sorrow deep hidden in his voice, a far
And soft light in his strange brown eyes;
Alone with his masterchords, his memories. . . .
      Lawd I wanna be one in nummer
      When de saints go ma'chin' home.
Deep the bass would rumble while the treble scattered high,
For all the world like heavy feet a-trompin' toward the sky,
With shrill-voiced women getting 'happy'

---

1. Davis was a wandering blues guitar player who made frequent appearances at Virginia Seminary and
College in Lynchburg and whose performances Brown both enjoyed and studied.

All to celestial tunes.
The chap's few speeches helped me understand
The reason why he gazed so fixedly
Upon the burnished strings.
For he would see
A gorgeous procession to 'de Beulah Land,'—
Of saints—his friends—*"a-climbi' fo' deir wings."*
Oh when de saints go ma'chin' home. . . .
Lawd I wanna be one o' dat nummer
When de saints goa ma'chin' home. . . .

II

There'd be—so ran his dream:
  "Ole Deacon Zachary
  With de asthmy in his chest,
  A-puffin' an' a-wheezin'
  Up de golden stair;
  Wid de badges of his lodges
  Strung acrost his heavin' breast
  An' de hoggrease jes' shinin'
  In his coal black hair. . . .

  "An' ole Sis Joe
  In huh big straw hat,
  An' huh wrapper flappin'
  Flappin' in de heavenly win',
  An' huh thin-soled easy walkers
  Goin' pitty pitty pat,—
  Lawd she'd have to ease her corns
  When she got in!"

Oh when de saints go ma'chin' home.
  "Ole Elder Peter Johnson
  Wid his corncob jes' a-puffin',
  An' de smoke a-rollin'
  Lak stormclouds out behin';
  Crossin' de cloud mountains
  Widout slowin' up fo' nuffin,
  Steamin' up de grade
  Lak Wes' bound no. 9.

    *   *   *

"An' de little brown-skinned chillen
Wid deir skinny legs a-dancin',
Jes' a-kickin' up ridic'lous
To de heavenly band;
Lookin' at de Great Drum Major
On a white hoss jes' a-prancin',
Wid a gold and silver drumstick
A-waggin' in his han'."
Oh when de sun refuse to shine
Oh when de mo-on goes down
          In Blood
"Ole Maumee Annie
Wid huh washin' done,
An' huh las' piece o' laundry
In de renchin' tub,
A wavin' sof' pink han's
To de much obligin' sun,
An' her feet a-moverin' now
To a swif' rud-a-dub;

"An' old Grampa Eli
Wid his wrinkle old haid,
A-puzzlin' over summut
He ain' understood,
Intendin' to ask Peter
Pervidin' he ain't skyaid,
'Jes' what mought be de meanin'
Of de moon in blood?' . . ."
When de saints go ma'chin' home. . . .

          III

"*Whuffolks*,"[2] he dreams, "*will have to stay outside*
Being so onery." But what is he to do
With that red brakeman who once let him ride
An empty going home? Or with that kind-faced man
Who paid his songs with board and drink and bed?
Or with the Yankee Cap'n who left a leg
At Vicksburg? *Mought be a place, he said,*

---

2. White folks.

Mought be another mansion fo' white saints,
A smaller one than his'n . . . not so gran'.
As fo' the rest . . . oh let 'em howl and beg.
Hell would be good enough—if big enough—
Widout no shade trees, lawd, widout no rain.
Whuffolks sho' to bring nigger out behin',
Excep'—"when de saints go ma'chin' home."

IV

Sportin' Legs would not be there—nor lucky Sam,
Nor Smitty, nor Hambone, nor Hardrock Gene,
An' not too many guzzlin', cuttin' shines,
Nor bootleggers to keep his pockets clean.
An' Sophie wid de sof' smile on her face,
Her foolin' voice, her strappin' body, brown
Lak coffee doused wid milk—she had been good
To him, wid lovin', money and wid food.—
But saints and heaven didn't seem to fit
Jes' right wid Sophy's Beauty—nary bit—
She mought stir trouble, somehow, in dat peaceful place
Mought be some dressed-up dudes in dat fair town.

V

Ise got a dear ole mudder,
She is in hebben I know—
He sees:
        Mammy,
        Li'l mammy—wrinkled face,
        Li'l brown eye, quick to tears—to joy—
        With such happy pride in her
        Guitar-plunkin' boy.
        Oh kain't I be one in nummer?

Mammy
With deep religion defeating the grief
Life piled so closely about her,
Ise so glad trouble doan last alway,
And her dogged belief
That some fine day
She'd go ma'chin'
When de saints go ma'chin' home.

*   *   *

He sees her ma'chin' home, ma'chin' along,
Her perky joy shining in her furrowed face,
Her weak and quavering voice singing her song—
The best chair set apart for her worn out body
In that restful place. . . .
    I pray to de Lawd I'll meet her
    When de saints go ma'chin' home.

VI

He'd shuffle off from us, always, at that,—
His face a brown study beneath his torn brimmed hat,
His broad shoulders slouching, his old box strung
Around his neck;—he'd go where we
Never could follow him—to Sophie probably,
Or to his dances in old Tinbridge flat.

                                        1927

Strong Men

The young men keep coming on
The strong men keep coming on.
SANDBURG

They dragged you from homeland,
They chained you in coffles,[1]
They huddled you in spoon-fashion in filthy hatches,
They sold you to give a few gentlemen ease.

They broke you in like oxen,
They scourged you,
They branded you,
They made your women breeders,
They swelled your numbers with bastards. . . .
They taught you the religion they disgraced.

You sang:
    Keep a-inchin' along
    Lak a po' inch worm. . . .

        *   *   *

---

1. A file of animals, prisoners, or slaves chained together.

You sang:
> *Bye and bye*
> *I'm gonna lay down dis heaby load. . . .*

You sang:
> *Walk togedder, chillen,*
> *Dontcha git weary. . . .*
>> The strong men keep a-comin' on
>> The strong men git stronger.

They point with pride to the roads you built for them,
They ride in comfort over the rails you laid for them.
They put hammers in your hands
And said — Drive so much before sundown.

You sang:
> *Ain't no hammah*
> *In dis lan',*
> *Strikes lak mine, bebby,*
> *Strikes lak mine.*

They cooped you in their kitchens,
They penned you in their factories,
They gave you the jobs that they were too good for,
They tried to guarantee happiness to themselves
By shunting dirt and misery to you.

You sang:
> *Me an' muh baby gonna shine, shine*
> *Me an' muh baby gonna shine.*
>> The strong men keep a-comin' on
>> The strong men git stronger. . . .

They bought off some of your leaders
You stumbled, as blind men will . . .
They coaxed you, unwontedly soft-voiced. . . .
You followed a way.
Then laughed as usual.

They heard the laugh and wondered;
Uncomfortable,
Unadmitting a deeper terror. . . .
>> The strong men keep a-comin' on
>> Gittin' stronger. . . .

*   *   *

What, from the slums
Where they have hemmed you,
What, from the tiny huts
They could not keep from you—
What reaches them
Making them ill at ease, fearful?
Today they shout prohibition at you
"Thou shalt not this"
"Thou shalt not that"
"Reserved for whites only"
You laugh.

One thing they cannot prohibit—
 The strong men . . . coming on
 The strong men gittin' stronger.
 Strong men. . . .
 Stronger. . . .

    1931

Slim Greer

 Listen to the tale
 Of Ole Slim Greer,
 Waitines' devil
 Waitin' here;

  Talkinges' guy
  An' biggest liar,
  With always a new lie
  On the fire.

 Tells a tale
 Of Arkansaw
 That keeps the kitchen
 In a roar;

  Tells in a long-drawled
  Careless tone,
  As solemn as a Baptist
  Parson's moan.

  *   *   *

How he in Arkansaw
Passed for white,
An' he no lighter
Than a dark midnight.

> Found a nice white woman
> At a dance,
> Thought he was from Spain
> Or else from France;

Nobody suspicioned
Ole Slim Greer's race
But a Hill Billy, always
Roun' the place,

> Who called one day
> On the trustful dame
> An' found Slim comfy
> When he came.

The whites lef' the parlor
All to Slim
Which didn't cut
No ice with him,

> An' he started a-tinklin'
> Some mo'nful blues,
> An' a-pattin' the time
> With No. Fourteen shoes.

The cracker listened
An' he spat
An' he said, "No white man
Could play like that. . . ."

> The white jane ordered
> The tattler out;
> Then, female-like,
> Began to doubt,

Crept into the parlor
Soft as you please,
Where Slim was agitatin'
The ivories.

*   *   *

Heard Slim's music —
An' then, hot damn!
Shouted sharp — "Nigger!"
An' Slim said, "Ma'am?"

She screamed and the crackers
Swarmed up soon,
But found only echoes
Of his tune;

'Cause Slim had sold out
With lightnin' speed;
"Hope I may die, sir —
Yes, indeed. . . ."

1931

Slim Lands a Job?

Poppa Greer happened
Down Arkansaw
An' ast for a job
At Big Pete's Cafe,

Big Pete was a six foot
Hard-boiled man
Wid a forty-four dungeon
In his han'.

"Nigger, kin you wait?"
Is what Pete ast;
Slim says, "Cap'n
I'm jes' too fast."

Pete says, "Dat's what
I wants to hire;
I got a slow nigger
I'm gonna fire —

Don't 'low no slow nigger
Stay roun' hyeah,
I plugs 'em wid my dungeon!"
An' Slim says, "Yeah?"

*   *   *

A noise rung out
  In rush a man
Wid a tray on his head
  An' one on each han'

Wid de silver in his mouf
  An' de soup plates in his vest
Pullin' a red wagon
  Wid all the rest. . . .

De man's said, "Dere's
  Dat slow coon now
Dat wuthless lazy waiter!"
  An' Slim says, "How?"

An' Slim threw his gears in
  Put it in high,
An' kissed his hand to Arkansaw,
  Sweetheart . . . good-bye!

                                1931

Ma Rainey

I

When Ma Rainey
Comes to town,
Folks from anyplace
Miles aroun',
From Cape Girardeau,
Poplar Bluff,
Flocks in to hear
Ma do her stuff;
Comes flivverin'[1] in,
Or ridin' mules,
Or packed in trains,
Picknickin' fools. . . .
That's what it's like,

---

1. Fliver: slang word for the popular Model-T Ford, derived from the vibrating sound it made when started.

Fo' miles on down,
To New Orleans delta
An' Mobile town,
When Ma hits
Anywheres aroun'.

II

Dey comes to hear Ma Rainey from de little river settlements,
From blackbottom cornrows and from lumber camps;
Dey stumble in de hall, jes a-laughin' an' a-cacklin',
Cheerin' lak roarin' water, lak wind in river swamps.

An' some jokers keeps deir laughs a-goin' in de crowded aisles,
An' some folks sits dere waitin' wid deir aches an' miseries,
Till Ma comes out before dem, a-smilin' gold-toofed smiles
An' Long Boy ripples minors on de black an' yellow keys.

III

O Ma Rainey,
Sing yo' song;
Now you's back
Whah you belong,
Git way inside us,
Keep us strong. . . .
O Ma Rainey,
Li'l an' low;
Sing us 'bout de hard luck
Roun' our do';
Sing us 'bout de lonesome road
We mus' go. . . .

IV

I talked to a fellow, an' the fellow say,
"She jes' catch hold of us, somekindaway.
She sang Backwater Blues one day:
　　　　'It rained fo' days an' de skies was dark as night,
　　　　Trouble taken place in de lowlands at night.

　　　　'Thundered an' lightened an' the storm begin to roll
　　　　Thousan's of people ain't got no place to go.

＊　＊　＊

'Den I went an' stood upon some high ol' lonesome hill,
An' looked down on the place where I used to live.'

An' den de folks, dey natchally bowed dey heads an' cried,
Bowed dey heavy heads, shet dey moufs up tight an' cried,
An' Ma lef' de stage, an' followed some de folks outside."

Dere wasn't much more de fellow say:
She jes' gits hold of us dataway.

1974

Gertrude "Ma" Rainey (1886–1939) was a popular singer who was sometimes termed the "Mother of the Blues." Noted for her powerful voice and compelling stage presence, she is generally credited with the rise in popularity of blues music in America. She performed and recorded with such noted jazz musicians as Louis Armstrong, Fletcher Henderson, and Coleman Hawkins.

LAURA RIDING
1901–1991

LAURA RIDING, who is also known by her married name, Laura (Riding) Jackson, was born Laura Reichenthal in New York City, the daughter of working-class Jews. Her immigrant father was a tailor, and her mother had gone nearly blind from working in sweatshops. Educated at Cornell, Riding became an avant-garde poet and prose writer whose work was influential and highly praised in the 1920s and 1930s. She wrote poetry noted for its intellectual intensity and difficulty. She thought that "a poem is an uncovering of truth." Condensed, knotty, and paradoxical, her poems aim to discover fundamental principles, but they also pinpoint the fissures in human knowledge, the way that truth remains hidden. "Helen's Burning," for example, exposes the failure of the observer's gaze to fathom the reality of a woman's existence. "The World and I" suggests the limits of language as it attempts to reflect the actual world. "The Wind Suffers" explores the painful and contradictory quality of human existence.

Riding was a friend of Hart Crane, Gertrude Stein, and the Fugitive group of poets including John Crowe Ransom and Allen Tate (all included in this

anthology). She was also the lover and writing partner of the British poet Robert
Graves, with whom she lived in England and Mallorca. Breaking with Graves, she
returned to the United States in 1939, where she married her second husband,
Schuyler Jackson, in 1941. The couple moved to Florida, where they became citrus
farmers and coauthors of linguistic studies. From then on, Riding wrote no more
poems. She came to think that poetry was too sensuous, patterned, and metaphori-
cal to succeed at conveying truth. She now argued that "poetry obstructs general
attainment to something better in our linguistic way-of-life than we have." Riding
devoted her last five decades to seeking lexical and linguistic methods of achieving
greater precision in writing and speech. She viewed poetry as "failing my kind of
seriousness," yet her poems remain important to readers who care about the pur-
suit of truth in poetic language.

FURTHER READING

Jeanne Heuving. "Laura (Riding) Jackson's 'Really New' Poem." In *Gendered Modernisms:
American Women Poets and Their Readers*, ed. Margaret Dickie and Thomas Travisano, 191–
213. Philadelphia: University of Pennsylvania Press, 1996.
Laura (Riding) Jackson. *Poems: A Newly Revised Edition of the 1938/1980 Collection*. Preface by
Mark Jacobs. New York: Persea Books, 2001.
Joyce Piell Wexler. *Laura Riding's Pursuit of Truth*. Athens: Ohio University Press, 1973.

Helen's Burning

Her beauty, which we talk of,
Is but half her fate.
All does not come to light
Until the two halves meet
And we are silent
And she speaks,
Her whole fate saying,
She is, she is not, in one breath.

But we tell only half, fear to know all
Lest all should be to tell
And our mouths choke with flame
Of her consuming
And lose the gift of prophecy.[1]

1938

In Greek myth, Helen of Troy was the beautiful daughter of the god Zeus and the mortal
woman Leda. Married to King Menelaus of Greece, Helen fled with the Trojan prince

---

1. Paradoxically suggests that knowing and telling everything would result in the loss of the power to
know and tell.

Paris. This flight caused the Trojan War, famously narrated in Homer's epic, the *Iliad*. "Helen's Burning" suggests the irreducible contradictions in Helen's nature and fate. It employs a discursive mode of tact, empathy, and identification rather than masculinist detachment and domination. The poem is comparable to H.D.'s "Helen" (also in this anthology).

The World and I

This is not exactly what I mean
Any more than the sun is the sun.
But how to mean more closely
If the sun shines but approximately?
What a world of awkwardness!
Perhaps this is as close a meaning
As perhaps becomes[1] such knowing.
Else I think the world and I
Must live together as strangers and die—
A sour love, each doubtful whether
Was ever a thing to love the other.
No, better for both to be nearly sure
Each of each—exactly where
Exactly I and exactly the world
Fail to meet by a moment, and a word.

1938

"The World and I" suggests Riding's lifelong quest to discover ways to "mean more closely"—that is, more accurately. If the self and the world must "live together as strangers," the speaker still wishes to understand exactly where the two "fail to meet." Yet reflecting the universal lack of correlation, the poem cannot even represent its central dilemma accurately, confessing at the outset, "This is not exactly what I mean."

The Wind Suffers

The wind suffers of blowing,
The sea suffers of water,
And fire suffers of burning,
And I of a living name.

As stone suffers of stoniness,
As light of its shiningness,
As birds of their wingedness,
So I of my whoness.

1. In a double sense: befits; changes into.

*   *   *

And what the cure of all this?
What the not and not suffering?
What the better and later of this?
What the more me of me?

How for the pain-world to be
More world and no pain?
How for the old rain to fall
More wet and more dry?

How for the willful blood to run
More salt-red and sweet-white?
And how for me in my actualness
To more shriek and more smile?

By no other miracles,
By the same knowing poison,
By an improved anguish,
By my further dying.

1938

"The Wind Suffers" meditates the contradictions, uncertainties, and sufferings of the human self. It makes abstract thought vivid through its verbal vitality, including such strategies as metaphor ("the wind"), condensation ("How for the pain-world to be . . . ?"), repetition ("As stone," "As light"), neologism ("whoness," "actualness"), open-ended interrogative ("What the better and later of this?"), and paradox ("more wet and more dry," "improved anguish").

GWENDOLYN BENNETT
1902–1981

GWENDOLYN BENNETT, an important poet of the Harlem Renaissance, wrote poems notable for their elegant lyric qualities. Whether they focus on racial issues, as does "Heritage," or the beauty and mystery of a black woman, as does "Street Lamps in Early Spring," the poems display a stylistic mastery of sound and image. Bennett was born in Texas but grew up in several different states. She studied fine arts at the Pratt Institute in New York, taught art at Howard University, and spent a year in Paris. Living in Harlem and Washington, D.C., during the height of the Harlem Renaissance, she was a close friend of Countee Cullen, Jessie Redmon Fauset, and Langston Hughes (all included in this anthology). Throughout these years she produced literary and graphic work for the movement's key magazines such as *Opportunity*, *Crisis*, and *Fire*!!. The death of her first husband in 1936 cut short her artistic career. Giving up poetry and art, she worked for many years for Consumers Union. She spent her final years running an antique shop with her second husband in rural Pennsylvania, where she died.

FURTHER READING

Walter C. Daniel and Sandra Y. Govan. "Gwendolyn Bennett." In *Afro-American Writers from the Harlem Renaissance to 1940*, ed. Trudier Harris and Thadious Davis, 3–7. Detroit: Gale, 1987.

Venetria K. Patton and Maureen Honey, eds. "Gwendolyn B. Bennett." In *Double-Take: A Revisionist Harlem Renaissance Anthology*, 506–19. New Brunswick, N.J.: Rutgers University Press, 2001.

Heritage

I want to see the slim palm-trees,
Pulling at the clouds
With little pointed fingers. . . .

I want to see lithe Negro girls
Etched dark against the sky
While sunset lingers.

I want to hear the silent sands,
Singing to the moon
Before the Sphinx[1]-still face. . . .

I want to hear the chanting
Around a heathen fire
Of a strange black race.

I want to breathe the Lotus flow'r[2]
Sighing to the stars
With tendrils drinking at the Nile. . . .

*   *   *

1. Creature with lion's body and human head, common to Egyptian and Greek myth.

2. A water lily in Egyptian culture and art; symbol of beauty, fertility, and pleasure.

I want to feel the surging
Of my sad people's soul,
Hidden by a minstrel-smile.

1923

"Heritage" associates African Americans with central Africa through the image of palm trees and with ancient Egypt through images of the Sphinx, the lotus, and the Nile. In the last line, the poem suggests that this proud African heritage is temporarily occluded by the minstrel-show demeanor that the United States has forced African Americans to adopt. Minstrel shows were an indigenous American theatrical entertainment that caricatured African-American culture. Initially performed by whites in blackface, the shows were increasingly performed by blacks after the Civil War. Minstrelsy alternated jokes, music, and dance, ultimately leading the way to vaudeville.

Street Lamps in Early Spring

Night wears a garment
All velvet soft, all violet blue . . .
And over her face she draws a veil
As shimmering fine as floating dew . . .
And here and there
In the black of her hair
The subtle hands of Night
Move slowly with their gem-starred light.

1926

ARNA BONTEMPS

1902–1973

Arna bontemps was a key figure in the Harlem Renaissance. A multifaceted writer, teacher, and thinker, he made important contributions as a novelist, poet, anthologist, historian, biographer, and literary scholar. As his friend Langston Hughes wrote in 1961, Bontemps was an authority on Negro life, literature, and folklore. Along with Hughes, Bontemps coedited *The Book of Negro Folklore* and *The Poetry of the Negro*. Although Bontemps is less known today for his poetry than for his other contributions, his best poems are remembered for their vivid evocations of African-American experience and aspirations.

Born in Alexandria, Louisiana, in 1902, Bontemps moved to the Watts section of Los Angeles at the age of three. He graduated from Pacific Union College in 1923. A short time after his graduation, Bontemps began publishing award-winning poems such as "A Black Man Talks of Reaping" in *The Crisis*, the magazine of the NAACP, which served as a launching pad for many of the young poets of the Harlem Renaissance. He moved to New York in 1926, where he taught for five years at the Harlem Academy and developed friendships with many of the leading figures of the Harlem Renaissance. His lifelong correspondence with Hughes, published in the selected *Letters, 1925–1967*, is of great importance. Moving to Huntsville, Alabama, in 1931, Bontemps taught at Oakville Junior College. He was dismissed by Oakville in 1934 because his radical writings and politics clashed with the school's conservative and religious views. He secured a graduate degree in library science in 1943, thereafter serving as head librarian at historically black Fisk University in Nashville. According to Hughes, Bontemps "built the Fisk University Library into one of the best libraries in the South." While he was teaching, pursuing graduate degrees, and heading a university library, Bontemps was also producing a steady stream of children's books, historical studies, biographies, and anthologies focused on black history and culture, including the still widely read *Black Thunder: Gabriel's Revolt: Virginia 1800* (1936), the story of an aborted slave rebellion led by Gabriel Prosser.

Most of Bontemps's poems were produced early in his long career and are notable for exploring problems of racial justice with an austere, meditative gravity. As Hughes noted in his 1961 tribute, "In the Days of Negro Renaissance in Harlem, his poetry attracted wide attention. His moving 'Nocturne at Bethesda' and 'A Black Man Talks of Reaping' have been used in innumerable commencement speeches and included in various anthologies." It is chiefly for these two poems that Bontemps remains known as a poet.

FURTHER READING

Arna Bontemps. *Personals*. New York: Dodd, Mead, 1980.

Arna Bontemps and Langston Hughes. *Letters, 1925–1967*. Ed. Charles H. Nichols. New York: Paragon House, 1980.

Kirkland C. Jones. *Renaissance Man from Louisiana: A Biography of Arna Wendell Bontemps*. Westport, Conn.: Greenwood Press, 1992.

A Black Man Talks of Reaping

I have sown beside all waters in my day.
I planted deep, within my heart the fear
That wind or fowl would take the grain away.
I planted safe against this stark, lean year.

*   *   *

I scattered seed enough to plant the land
In rows from Canada to Mexico
But for my reaping only what the hand
Can hold at once is all that I can show.

Yet what I sowed and what the orchard yields
My brother's sons are gathering stalk and root;
Small wonder then my children glean in fields
They have not sown, and feed on bitter fruit.

1926

Nocturne at Bethesda

I thought I saw an angel flying low,
I thought I saw the flicker of a wing
Above the mulberry trees; but not again.
Bethesda sleeps. This ancient pool that healed
A host of bearded Jews does not awake.

This pool that once the angels troubled does not move.
No angel stirs it now, no Saviour comes
With healing in His hands to raise the sick
And bid the lame man leap upon the ground.

The golden days are gone. Why do we wait
So long upon the marble steps, blood
Falling from our open wounds? and why
Do our black faces search the empty sky?
Is there something we have forgotten? some precious thing
We have lost, wandering in strange lands?

There was a day, I remember now,
I beat my breast and cried, "Wash me, God,
Wash me with a wave of wind upon
The barley; O quiet One, draw near, draw near!
Walk upon the hills with lovely feet
And in the waterfall stand and speak.

"Dip white hands in the lily pool and mourn
Upon the harps still hanging in the trees
Near Babylon along the river's edge,
But oh, remember me, I pray, before
The summer goes and rose leaves lose their red."

* * *

The old terror takes my heart, the fear
Of quiet waters and of faint twilights.
There will be better days when I am gone
And healing pools where I cannot be healed.
Fragrant stars will gleam forever and ever
Above the place where I lie desolate.

Yet I hope, still I long to live.
And if there can be returning after death
I shall come back. But it will not be here;
If you want me you must search for me
Beneath the palms of Africa. Or if
I am not there then you may call to me
Across the shining dunes, perhaps I shall
Be following a desert caravan.

I may pass through centuries of death
With quiet eyes, but I'll remember still
A jungle tree with burning scarlet birds.
There is something I have forgotten, some precious thing.
I shall be seeking ornaments of ivory,
I shall be dying for a jungle fruit.

      You do not hear, Bethesda.
O still green water in a stagnant pool!
Love abandoned you and me alike.
There was a day you held a rich full moon
Upon your heart and listened to the words
Of men now dead and saw the angels fly.
There is a simple story on your face;
Years have wrinkled you. I know, Bethesda!
You are sad. It is the same with me.

                              1926

The marble pool of waters at Bethesda in Jerusalem was considered to have healing powers
for the first person who stepped into it after an angel had stirred or "troubled" the waters.
According to the New Testament, Jesus found a man who had been sick for thirty-eight
years and who was too weak to step into the waters, so Jesus cured him, saying, "Rise, take
up thy bed, and walk" (John 5:2–9). Bontemps laments that no angel or savior seems ready
to cure long-suffering African Americans in like fashion.

KENNETH FEARING
1902–1961

Kᴇɴɴᴇᴛʜ ꜰᴇᴀʀɪɴɢ wrote poems notable for their cynical, amusing modernity and their ironic depictions of social iniquity. He included the sights and sounds of contemporary urban culture in his work, along with a jazzy tempo and a satirical tone. Mixing Marxism with journalistic panache, Fearing depicts a contemporary America stripped of its traditional myths, consumed by media images, and anxious and confused as it lurches toward the uncertain future. Like E. E. Cummings, Fearing brought a coruscating wit and an outsider's stance to the poetry of his time.

Born to a Protestant father and Jewish mother, Fearing grew up in Oak Park, Illinois. After his parents divorced, he was raised by an eccentric aunt. He studied at the University of Wisconsin, where he befriended Carl Rakosi (also included in this anthology). He then moved to New York City, taking odd jobs and working as a freelance writer. He drank heavily and lived hard and had numerous love affairs, two marriages, and one son. During these years, Fearing wrote popular fiction and published poems in the leftist *New Masses* as well as in mainstream magazines. His most successful novel was *The Big Clock* (1946), made into a film in 1948 and remade as *No Way Out* in 1987. In 1950, Fearing was subpoenaed by the U.S. attorney in Washington for questioning about his political activities. When asked if he belonged to the Communist Party, Fearing defiantly (and now famously) replied, "Not yet." Fearing's last years were spent in poverty, bitterness, and neglect. A lifelong smoker, he died of lung cancer at the age of sixty-one.

FURTHER READING

Rita Barnard. *The Great Depression and the Culture of Abundance*. Cambridge, Eng.: Cambridge University Press, 1995.

Kenneth Fearing. *Complete Poems*. Ed. Robert M. Ryley. Orono, Maine: National Poetry Foundation, 1994.

Dirge

1-2-3 was the number he played but today the number came 3-2-1;[1]
Bought his Carbide[2] at 30 and it went to 29; had the favorite at Bowie but the
track was slow —

1. In an illegal lottery.
2. Stock in Union Carbide Corporation, purchased at $30 a share. Bowie: a Maryland racetrack.

*   *   *

O executive type, would you like to drive a floating power, knee-action,
    silk-upholstered six?[3] Wed a Hollywood star? Shoot the course in 58?
    Draw to the ace, king, jack?
O fellow with a will who won't take no, watch out for three cigarettes on the same,
    single match; O democratic voter born in August under Mars, beware of
    liquidated rails—

Denouement[4] to denouement, he took a personal pride in the certain, certain way
    he lived his own, private life,
But nevertheless, they shut off his gas; nevertheless, the bank foreclosed;
    nevertheless, the landlord called; nevertheless, the radio broke,

And twelve o'clock arrived just once too often,
Just the same he wore one gray tweed suit, bought one straw hat, drank one straight
    Scotch, walked one short step, took one long look, drew one deep breath,
Just one too many,

And wow[5] he died as wow he lived,
Going whop to the office and blooie home to sleep and biff got married and bam
    had children and oof got fired,
Zowie did he live and zowie did he die,
With who the hell are you at the corner of his casket, and where the hell we going
    on the right-hand silver knob, and who the hell cares walking second from the
    end with an American Beauty[6] wreath from why the hell not,

Very much missed by the circulation staff of the New York Evening Post; deeply,
    deeply mourned by the B.M.T.[7]

Wham, Mr. Roosevelt; pow, Sears Roebuck; awk, big dipper; bop, summer rain;
Bong, Mr., bong, Mr., bong, Mr., bong.[8]

1934

A dirge is a funeral song, in this case ironically lamenting a businessman who may have committed suicide, having been ruined by the Great Depression of 1929. Fearing has been considered the poet laureate of the Depression. Robert Ryley adds that in poems like "Dirge," "iniquitous capitalism is made to seem almost incidental, the medium in which Americans of the Great Depression lived, and moved, and had their being."

---

3. An expensive automobile as described in advertising lingo. Course: golf course.
4. Resolution of a plot; outcome.
5. Slang expression popular in comic books, as are terms in succeeding lines such as "biff" and "bam."

6. Variety of rose.
7. New York subway line.
8. The tolling of the funeral bell.

Ad

WANTED: Men;
Millions of men are WANTED AT ONCE in a big new field;
NEW, TREMENDOUS, THRILLING, GREAT.

If you've ever been a figure in the chamber of horrors,
If you've ever escaped from a psychiatric ward,
If you thrill at the thought of throwing poison into wells, have heavenly
    visions of people, by the thousands, dying in flames —

YOU ARE THE VERY MAN WE WANT.
We mean business and our business is YOU.
WANTED: A race of brand-new men.

Apply: Middle Europe;
No skill needed;
No ambition required; no brains wanted and no character allowed.

TAKE A PERMANENT JOB IN THE COMING PROFESSION.
Wages: DEATH.

                                                            1938

"Ad" satirically depicts pre-war Nazi Germany.

Beware

Someone, somewhere, is always starting trouble,
Either a relative, or a drunken friend, or a foreign state.
Trouble it is, trouble it was, trouble it will always be.
Nobody ever leaves well enough alone.

It begins, as a rule, with an innocent face and a trivial remark:
"There are two sides to every question," or "Sign right here, on the dotted line,"
But it always ends with a crash of glass and a terrible shout —
No one, no one lets sleeping dragons sleep.

And it never happens, when the doorbell rings, that you find a troupe of houris[1]
    standing on your stoop.
Just the reverse.

---

1. Beautiful virgins awaiting Muslims in Paradise, according to traditional belief. Stoop: small porch.

So beware of doorbells. (And beware, beware of houris, too.)
And you never receive a letter that says: "We enclose, herewith, our check for a million."
You know what the letter always says, instead.
So beware of letters. (And anyway, they say, beware of great wealth.)

Be careful of doorbells, be cautious of telephones, watch out for genial strangers, and
    for ancient friends;
Beware of dotted lines, and mellow cocktails; don't touch letters sent specifically to you;
Beware, especially, of innocent remarks;
Beware of everything,
Damn near anything leads to trouble,
Someone is always, always stepping out of line.

1942

Art Review

Recently displayed at the Times Square Station, a new Vandyke[1] on the face-cream girl.
(Artist unknown. Has promise, but lacks the brilliance shown by the great masters of
    the Elevated age.)
The latest wood carving in a Whelan telephone booth, titled "O Mortal Fools WA
    9-5090," shows two winged hearts above an ace of spades.
(His meaning is not entirely clear, but this man will go far.)
A charcoal nude in the rear of Flatbush[2] Ahearn's Bar & Grill, "Forward to the
    Brotherhood of Man," has been boldly conceived in the great tradition.
(We need more, much more of this.)
Then there is the chalk portrait, on the walls of a waterfront warehouse, of a gentleman
    wearing a derby hat: "Bleecker Street Mike is a doublecrossing rat."
(Morbid, but powerful. Don't miss.)

Know then by these presents, know all men by these signs and omens, by these simple
    thumbprints on the throat of time,
Know that Pete, the people's artist, is ever watchful,
That Tuxedo Jim has passed among us, and was much displeased, as always,
That George the Ghost (no man has ever seen him) and Billy the Bicep boy will
    neither bend nor break,

---

1. A short, pointed beard, as seen in portraits by
Flemish painter Anthony Van Dyck (1599–1641).
Someone has drawn the beard on the face of a
young woman in a subway station ad.

2. A section of Brooklyn.

That Mr. Harkness of Sunnyside still hopes for the best, and has not lost his
 human touch,
That Phantom Phil, the master of them all, has come and gone, but will return,
 and all is well.

1943

This poem uses the language of art reviews to pay ironic tribute to the graffiti artists of
New York.

LANGSTON HUGHES
1902–1967

WHILE LANGSTON HUGHES has for many years been considered a major Ameri-
can poet, the leading name in Harlem Renaissance poetry, and a premier poet of
the political left, even those accolades have tended to obscure his broader legacy
as an international poet. Early in his career, Hughes decided that an African-
American poet should serve as moral witness to exploitation and as historian of the
African diaspora. As his life progressed, his agenda became ever more inclusive —
reaching across boundaries of race, class, gender, sexual orientation, and national
identity. Today, writers and readers view him as a model of social and cultural pro-
test against such practices as colonialism, imperialism, environmental neglect and
assault, sexism, and unfair labor relations. This list is likely to grow as a projected
seventeen-volume complete edition of his writings is published. Such "closeted"
aspects of his life as his long-term intimate same-sex relationships are now being
revealed and interpreted. The incredible vitality of his writing across many genres
is beginning to be recognized.

 Hughes was born in Joplin, Missouri, in 1902 in a racially segregated society
where lynching was a growing problem. Indeed, a lynching occurred in Joplin
only months after his birth. This white supremacist environment had a profound
impact on Hughes early in his life, and it influenced his poetry. He wrote more
than twenty poems on lynching alone. Hughes was descended from a distin-
guished African-American family. The first husband of his maternal grandmother
died at Harpers Ferry fighting with abolitionist John Brown. His bullet-riddled
shawl was brought home to Hughes's grandmother, and she used it to cover her
grandson when he slept. Her second husband (Hughes's maternal grandfather)
was prominent in Kansas politics during Reconstruction until he was driven out by

racism. His maternal great-uncle John Mercer Langston was a congressman from Virginia, the founding dean of the Howard University Law School, and one of the most famous African Americans of the nineteenth century. One of Hughes's great-grandfathers was a European-American planter in Virginia.

Hughes grew up in poverty, living mostly with his maternal grandmother after his parents divorced. To escape racism, his father immigrated to Mexico, where he became a wealthy businessman. His mother moved from city to city in search of work as a journalist and stenographer. By the time Hughes graduated from high school, he had lived in four Midwestern cities: Joplin, Missouri; Lawrence, Kansas; Lincoln, Illinois; and Cleveland, Ohio. In his late teens, he also spent time with his father in Mexico, which gave him an international perspective on racist restrictions in the lives of African Americans. In Mexico, he was often treated as though he were a Mexican and given equal accommodations with whites (for instance, on trains). He also studied Spanish and used it to learn about Mexican life in both Mexico and the United States.

An eclectic reader, Hughes was strongly influenced by a diverse range of poets. He admired the free verse of Edgar Lee Masters, Vachel Lindsay, Amy Lowell, and especially Carl Sandburg. But his favorite American poet was Walt Whitman. Among African-American poets and intellectuals, he was impressed by Claude McKay, Alain Locke, W. E. B. Du Bois, and James Weldon Johnson. Both Du Bois and Johnson mentored him. African-American singers, however, captivated him more than any writer, especially in the way they depicted working-class African-American life after the Reconstruction. But Hughes used any form, regardless of origin, that he felt would fit his artistic needs. Already a published poet in his late teens, Hughes attended Columbia University for one year in 1921 with the financial support of his father, but he spent most of his time exploring the world of Harlem. Uncomfortable at the university, he decided to take a series of working-class jobs such as delivery boy and mess boy on a ship. He then joined the crew of a merchant ship and traveled to the Caribbean, Africa, and Europe. He stayed for a while in Paris, working at odd jobs. By 1926, he had published *The Weary Blues*, his first collection of poetry, with Alfred A. Knopf, a mainline New York publisher. In 1929 he graduated from Lincoln University in Pennsylvania, an African-American institution.

Following graduation, Hughes embarked on a stellar literary career that lasted until his death in 1967. Unlike most poets, he was able to support himself through his writing. Beginning with the Scottsboro case of 1931, in which nine male African-American teenagers were falsely accused of raping two white women, and were nearly lynched as a result, Hughes devoted many poems and a great deal of his time to campaigning against lynching. Although he was responsible for helping to eradicate the practice, he died before lynching had completely stopped. He also wrote about many other issues of exploitation, such as the plight of sharecroppers and the rape of African-American women by European-American men. Early in his career he drew attention to labor exploitation in Africa as well, and he continued to focus on this international problem. In the 1930s, he traveled to the Soviet Union, to produce a film that never reached completion, and to China and Japan as well. During the Spanish Civil War of 1936–39, he traveled as a journalist to Spain, reporting on the military atrocities and racism he observed there. At the end of his life in the 1960s, he wrote about the violence directed at civil rights workers. In short, his poetry—as well as other writing—offers a rich documentation of chapters of history that were often ignored or marginalized in mainstream history during his lifetime.

Hughes was notably inventive in his use of cultural styles and materials in his poetry. He eagerly adapted blues and jazz forms as well as other African-American oral traditions that included stories that mainstream history generally overlooked. Breaking from European-American traditions that other Harlem Renaissance poets worked assiduously to master, Hughes parodied advertising, urban argot, journalese, and other forms of popular culture. His poetry was accompanied by more illustrations than was the work of any other poet in the period, as he enthusiastically combined these two cultural genres in an effort to tell his stories vividly. In addition to his use of oral and visual cultural forms, Hughes also relied on the performing arts, especially drama, to create a multi-voiced poetry. His poems absorb the energy of the world around him—the discourses of popular culture, the conversations heard on the street and in homes and public places, the variant languages coursing through African-American life and the American experience.

By the end of Hughes's life, he had authored or edited more than eighty books and plays. This oeuvre included twelve volumes of poetry as well as the play *The Mulatto*, which was the longest-running African-American production on Broadway until Lorraine Hansberry's *A Raisin in the Sun* in the 1950s. Hughes founded three theaters and created many more plays as well as novels, autobiographies, libretti for opera and gospel music shows, scripts for film and television, children's books, translations, histories, and anthologies. He invented a character named Jesse B. Semple, shortened to Simple, an African-American laborer with funny and sometimes wise things to say about black life in urban America. Hughes wrote these hugely successful "Simple stories" in a weekly column for the *Chicago Defender* and other newspapers between 1942 and 1962. He collected them in a series of books, including *The Best of Simple* (1961).

Although Hughes was greatly loved by many readers and writers in his lifetime, he was reviled by politically conservative opponents. As he escalated his campaign against lynching, for example, he drew more and more attention from right-wing groups as well as from the Federal Bureau of Investigation (FBI). At the outset of the Cold War, he was under investigation for his earlier leftist affiliations. Like William Carlos Williams, he was not permitted to assume the position of Poetry

Consultant to the Library of Congress, a position now known as Poet Laureate. In 1953, Senator Joseph McCarthy forced Hughes to testify about his politics, and he was attacked by the House Un-American Activities Committee (HUAC), though he was never prosecuted. Shaken by such pressures, he issued a volume of his selected poetry in 1959 in which he toned down his politics, and he wrote more patriotic poetry. He was not allowed to travel outside of the country until 1960, when he rejoined the international poetry circuit. His work at the end of his life represents a return to his earlier, pre-HUAC thinking. Langston Hughes has left a legacy of rich involvement in the working-class cultures swirling around and through African Americans and indeed all of the United States and the world. He has also become the image of a poet who combines artistic innovation and vitality with joyful humor and humanity and the effective expression of social conscience.

FURTHER READING

Houston A. Baker, Jr. *Modernism and the Harlem Renaissance*. Chicago: University of Chicago Press, 1989.

Faith Berry. *Langston Hughes: Before and Beyond Harlem*. Westport, Conn.: Hill, 1983.

Michael G. Cooke. *Afro-American Literature in the Twentieth Century: The Achievement of Intimacy*. New Haven, Conn.: Yale University Press, 1984.

Nathan Huggins. *Harlem Renaissance*. Oxford: Oxford University Press, 1973.

Langston Hughes. *Collected Poems*. Ed. Arnold Rampersad. New York: Vintage, 1995.

George Hutchinson. *The Harlem Renaissance in Black and White*. Cambridge, Mass.: Harvard University Press, 1997.

David Levering Lewis. *When Harlem Was in Vogue*. New York: Alfred Knopf, 1981.

R. Baxter Miller. *The Art and Imagination of Langston Hughes*. Lexington: University Press of Kentucky, 1989.

Venetria Patton and Maureen Honey, eds. "Langston Hughes." In *Double-Take: A Revisionist Harlem Renaissance Anthology*, 458–505. New Brunswick, N.J.: Rutgers University Press, 2001.

Arnold Rampersad. *The Life of Langston Hughes*. 2 vols. New York: Oxford University Press, 1988, 2002.

Robert Shulman. *The Power of Political Art: The 1930s Literary Left Reconsidered*. Chapel Hill, N.C.: University of North Carolina Press, 2000.

Steven Tracy. *Langston Hughes and the Blues*. Urbana: University of Illinois Press, 1988.

Steven Watson. *The Harlem Renaissance: Hub of African-American Culture, 1920–1931*. New York: Pantheon, 1995.

The Negro Speaks of Rivers

I've known rivers:
I've known rivers ancient as the world and older than the flow of human blood
in human veins.

My soul has grown deep like the rivers.

*   *   *

I bathed in the Euphrates[1] when dawns were young.
I built my hut near the Congo[2] and it lulled me to sleep.
I looked upon the Nile[3] and raised the pyramids above it.
I heard the singing of the Mississippi when Abe Lincoln[4] went down to New
    Orleans, and I've seen its muddy bosom turn all golden in the sunset.

I've known rivers:
Ancient, dusky rivers.

My soul has grown deep like the rivers.

1921

"The Negro Speaks of Rivers" is one of Hughes's most famous poems and, with its strong sense of pride, a signature poem of the Harlem Renaissance. It can be read as his first anti-lynching poem because he wrote it as he headed toward Texas on a train during a period of many lynchings following World War I. When the poem appeared in *The Crisis* in 1921, Hughes dedicated it to black liberationist intellectual W. E. B. Du Bois. Du Bois was not only the general editor of *The Crisis* but also the founder of the NAACP in Harlem. Jessie Redmon Fauset (also included in this anthology), the literary editor of *The Crisis*, greatly encouraged Hughes.

Negro

I am a Negro:
    Black as the night is black,
    Black like the depths of my Africa.

I've been a slave:
    Caesar[1] told me to keep his door-steps clean.
    I brushed the boots of Washington.[2]

I've been a worker:
    Under my hand the pyramids[3] arose.
    I made mortar for the Woolworth Building.[4]

---

1. River considered the cradle of ancient Babylonian civilization, flowing from present-day Turkey through Syria and Iraq into the Persian Gulf.
2. River flowing from the present-day Democratic Republic of the Congo in central Africa into the Atlantic Ocean.
3. River associated with classic Egyptian civilization, flowing from the Sudan through Egypt into the Mediterranean Sea.
4. Abraham Lincoln is said to have decided to abolish slavery after a trip to New Orleans. Many slaves were sold up and down the Mississippi River.

1. Emperor Augustus Caesar of the Roman Empire subjugated ancient Egypt, turning its inhabitants into slaves.
2. George Washington, the first U.S. president, owned slaves.
3. Laborers, not the pharaohs, built the pyramids for which Egypt is famous.
4. New York skyscraper built in 1910 and for a while the tallest building in the world. It was nicknamed the "Cathedral of Commerce,"

    *   *   *

I've been a singer:
  All the way from Africa to Georgia
  I carried my sorrow songs.
  I made ragtime.

I've been a victim:
  The Belgians cut off my hands in the Congo.[5]
  They lynch me still in Mississippi.[6]

I am a Negro:
  Black as the night is black,
  Black like the depths of my Africa.

                 1922

During his travels to Africa, Hughes linked African-American history and experience to the African experience with European imperialism and slavery, the economic exploitation of workers, and the violent subjugation of colonized peoples. In "Negro," his repetition of the first stanza in the poem's conclusion may reflect an African experience that both surprised and upset him. Because he was a mulatto, many Africans did not believe that he was like them. Yet he wanted very much to feel a deep connection to them—hence, his emphasis on the fact that he, too, is "black as the night is black."

Danse Africaine

The low beating of the tom-toms,[1]
The slow beating of the tom-toms,
    Low . . . slow
    Slow . . . low—
    Stirs your blood.
    Dance!
A night-veiled girl[2]
    Whirls softly into a

5. Hughes undoubtedly learned about the mutilation of hands when he visited the Congo, then a Belgian colony. When the Congolese resisted their colonizers' recruitment as forced mining labor, their hands were cut off, or other mutilations occurred. Arthur Conan Doyle, the creator of Sherlock Holmes, wrote *The Crime of the Congo* in 1909, which included photographs of people with cut-off hands, in an effort to stop the Belgian practice.

6. Lynching of African Americans occurred in the United States, especially in the South, Midwest, and West, throughout the early part of the twentieth century. Mississippi saw five hundred recorded lynchings between the 1800s and 1955. During the 1920s, the number of lynchings escalated.

1. Two-sided, two-toned drums used in many cultures, including African, Chinese, and Native American.

2. The veil suggests that the woman is doing a slow, hypnotic belly dance.

Circle of light.
Whirls softly . . . slowly,
Like a wisp of smoke around the fire —
And the tom-toms beat,
And the tom-toms beat,
And the low beating of the tom-toms
Stirs your blood.

1922

"Danse Africaine" evokes a sensual scene of Moorish dancing that Hughes observed in his travels to northern Africa.

Jazzonia

Oh, silver tree!
Oh, shining rivers of the soul!

In a Harlem cabaret
Six long-headed jazzers play.
A dancing girl whose eyes are bold
Lifts high a dress of silken gold.

Oh, singing tree!
Oh, shining rivers of the soul!

Were Eve's[1] eyes
In the first garden
Just a bit too bold?
Was Cleopatra[2] gorgeous
In a gown of gold?

Oh, shining tree!
Oh, silver rivers of the soul!

In a whirling cabaret
Six long-headed jazzers play.

1923

Hughes enjoyed listening to jazz and the blues in Harlem clubs, finding the music a great source of pleasure, cultural dissent, wisdom, uncensored history, and hope. He often wrote

1. Refers to Eve's seductiveness with Adam in the Garden of Eden in Genesis. Some scholars locate the historical Eden in the Tigris and Euphrates River Valley in present-day Iraq.
2. The Egyptian queen Cleopatra was considered a seductive beauty. She died from the sting of an asp, a poisonous snake, rather than become subjugated to Caesar, and she instructed her servants to lay her body out in her queenly attire.

while he listened. In "Jazzonia," his attempt to adapt jazz to poetry, he appears to link the African-American female jazz dancer with the North African female dancer in "Danse Africaine."

Justice

That Justice is a blind goddess
Is a thing to which we black are wise.
Her bondage hides two festering sores
That once perhaps were eyes.

1923

Hughes makes it clear in "Justice" that he will devote his poetry to writing/righting the flawed justice arranged by those in power. Robert Shulman has tied this poem to Hughes's campaign on behalf of nine teenaged boys in Scottsboro, Alabama, who were convicted of raping two white women on the basis of false testimony. "Justice" appears as the opening to four of Hughes's Scottsboro poems and a verse play published in his booklet *Scottsboro Limited* to raise money for the Scottsboro Defense Fund. Shulman's copy of the booklet is inscribed by Hughes to Tom Mooney, a white labor organizer who was unjustly jailed in 1916 for a bombing incident and was the subject of repeated "Free Tom Mooney" campaigns. The images of the "blind goddess" and "festering sores" are central to Hughes's Scottsboro essay, "Southern Gentlemen, White Prostitutes, Mill Owners, and Negroes." Shulman points out that Hughes changed "black" to "poor" to shift the emphasis to class when he published the poem in 1938 in a Communist publication for workers.

The Weary Blues

Droning a drowsy syncopated tune,
Rocking back and forth to a mellow croon,
    I heard a Negro play.
Down on Lenox Avenue[1] the other night
By the pale dull pallor of an old gas light
    He did a lazy sway . . .
    He did a lazy sway . . .
To the tune o' those Weary Blues.
With his ebony hands on each ivory key
He made that poor piano moan with melody.
    O Blues!
Swaying to and fro on his rickety stool

---

1. A major thoroughfare in Harlem, now called Adam Clayton Powell Boulevard.

He played that sad raggy tune like a musical fool.
    Sweet Blues!
Coming from a black man's soul.
    O Blues!

In a deep song voice with a melancholy tone
I heard that Negro sing, that old piano moan —
    "Ain't got nobody in all this world,
    Ain't got nobody but ma self.
    I's gwine to quit ma frownin'
    And put ma troubles on the shelf."
Thump, thump, thump, went his foot on the floor.
He played a few chords then he sang some more —
    "I got the Weary Blues
    And I can't be satisfied.
    Got the Weary Blues
    And can't be satisfied —
    I ain't happy no mo'
    And I wish that I had died."
And far into the night he crooned that tune.
The stars went out and so did the moon.
The singer stopped playing and went to bed
While the Weary Blues echoed through his head.
He slept like a rock or a man that's dead.

                                                    1925

"The Weary Blues," one of Hughes's most famous poems, reflects on the power of the blues to transform isolated pain into solace, art, and a sense of human connection. The poem reveals the musician's cultural despair and his creative gift, and it demonstrates the poet-speaker's parallel artistic ability to observe, empathize, and transform. The "weary blues" that the musician performs becomes a vital presence in his listeners and in the poem itself. This blues number seems influenced by the blues sung by Ethel Waters, King Oliver, and one of Hughes's favorites, Bessie Smith. (See the "Blues" entry in this anthology.) Note how Hughes goes beyond representing the musician in performance, suggesting that he has a weary life outside of the performance. By 1925, European Americans were flooding to Harlem clubs and to all-African-American musical productions on Broadway, but they often knew nothing about the performers except what they saw in the performances because they immediately returned home to their racially segregated lives. This poem employs a mixture of dictions — sophisticated ("syncopated") and vernacular ("fool") — to explore what Michael Cooke calls "the paradoxes of self-veiling."

Song to a Negro Wash-Woman

Oh, wash-woman
Arms elbow-deep in white suds,
Soul washed clean,
Clothes washed clean,
I have many songs to sing you
Could I but find the words.

Was it four o'clock or six o'clock on a winter afternoon, I saw you wringing out
    the last shirt in Miss White Lady's kitchen? Was it four o'clock or six o'clock?
    I don't remember.

But I know, at seven one spring morning you were on Vermont Street with a
    bundle in your arms going to wash clothes.
And I know I've seen you in the New York subway in the late afternoon coming
    home from washing clothes.

Yes, I know you, wash-woman.

I know how you send your children to school, and high-school, and even college.
I know how you work to help your man when times are hard.
I know how you build your house up from the washtub and call it home.
And how you raise your churches from white suds for the service of the
    Holy God.

I've seen you singing, wash-woman. Out in the backyard garden under the apple
    trees, singing, hanging white clothes on long lines in the sunshine.
And I've seen you in church on Sunday morning singing, praising your Jesus
    because some day you're going to sit on the right hand side of the Son of
    God and forget you ever were a wash-woman. And the aching back and the
    bundles of clothes will be unremembered then.

Yes, I've seen you singing.

So for you,
O singing wash-woman,
For you, singing little brown woman,
Singing strong black woman,
Singing tall yellow woman,
Arms deep in white suds,
Soul washed clean,
Clothes washed clean,

For you I have
Many songs to sing
Could I but find the words.

1925

Many African-American women worked as washerwomen during the day in the homes of European Americans to support their families. Compare this poem with the poetry about laundries written by Chinese Americans—for example, Wen I-To's "The Laundry Song."

Desire

Desire to us
Was like a double death,
Swift dying
Of our mingled breath,
Evaporation
Of an unknown strange perfume
Between us quickly
In a naked
Room.

1925

Venetria Patton and Maureen Honey suggest that "Desire" has a same-sex subtext.

Poem [2]

(To F. S.)

I loved my friend.
He went away from me.
There's nothing more to say.
The poem ends,
Soft as it began,—
I loved my friend.

1925

Venetria Patton and Maureen Honey believe "Poem [2]" suggests a same-sex love affair.

To Midnight Nan at Leroy's

Strut and wiggle,
    Shameless gal.
Wouldn't no good fellow
    Be your pal?

Hear dat music . . .
    Jungle night.
Hear dat music . . .
    And the moon was white.

Sing your Blues song,
    Pretty Baby.
You want lovin', . . .
    And you don't mean maybe.

Jungle lover . . .
    Night black boy . . .
Two against the moon
    And the moon was joy.

Strut and wiggle,
    Shameless Nan.
Wouldn't no good fellow
    Be your man?

                1926

Bound No'th Blues

Goin' down de road, Lord,
Goin' down de road.
Down de road, Lord,
Way, way down de road.
Got to find somebody
To help me carry this load.
Road's in front o' me
Nothin' to do but walk.
Road's in front o' me
Walk . . . and walk . . . and walk.
I'd like to meet a good friend
To come along an' talk.
Road, road, road, O!

Road, road, . . . road, . . . road, road!
Road, road, road, O!
On de No'thern road.
These Mississippi towns ain't
Fit fer a hoppin' toad.

1926

This poem first appeared in *Opportunity*. Six additional lines were added later between "To come along an' talk" and "Road, road, road, O!"

Song for a Dark Girl

Way Down South in Dixie[1]
   (Break the heart of me)
They hung my dark young lover[2]
   To a cross roads tree.

Way Down South in Dixie
   (Bruised body high in air)
I asked the white Lord Jesus
   What was the use of prayer.

Way Down South in Dixie
   (Break the heart of me)
Love is a naked shadow
   On a gnarled and naked tree.

1927

The number of lynchings increased during the 1920s, one of the worst periods in race relations since the Civil War. By 1925, the resurrected Ku Klux Klan had five million members.

Christ in Alabama

Christ is a nigger,
Beaten and black:
O, bare your back.

*   *   *

1. This is the last line of the popular minstrel song "Dixie," which became a patriotic song of the Southern Confederacy during and after the Civil War. Here it is used ironically.

2. This line was later changed to "They hung my black young lover."

Mary is His Mother:
Mammy of the South,[1]
Silence your mouth.

God's His Father:
White Master above,
Grant us your love.

Most holy bastard
Of the bleeding mouth:
    Nigger Christ
    On the cross
    Of the South.

1931

"Christ in Alabama" was illustrated by Hughes's male companion Zoe Ingram, who depicted a black Christ to accompany the text when it first appeared in *Contempo*. Hughes used the poem in his pamphlet *Scottsboro Limited* on behalf of the Scottsboro defendants. The reliance on the language of Christianity is aimed at its hypocritical use by the culture of racism. By the time the poem appeared in December 1931, the accused Scottsboro teenagers were in jail, and many sharecroppers who had demanded their release were injured or dead, as a result of a police raid on a meeting of the Alabama Share Croppers Union. Several protesting sharecroppers were lynched afterwards. Communist organizers and the International Labor Defense, an arm of the party, had helped the sharecroppers organize in order to escape their lives of forced farm labor. Under pressure from HUAC, Hughes toned down the poem for *Selected Poems* in 1959. Compare this original version to similar poems such as "Justice" and "Goodbye Christ."

Come to the Waldorf-Astoria

FINE LIVING . . . a la carte??

LISTEN, HUNGRY ONES!

Look! See what *Vanity Fair*[1] says about the new Waldorf-Astoria: "All the luxuries
    of private home . . ."
Now, won't that be charming when the last flop-house[2] has turned you down this
    winter? Furthermore:

1. Perhaps Hughes draws a parallel between Mary and the mammy because both had husbands who were not the fathers of their child. Christ's father is God, whereas the father of the mammy's child is the white plantation master. Slave Bibles, which the slaves were forced to learn, emphasized that the plantation master was also deific.

1. *Vanity Fair* continues to publish for elite audiences today.
2. The flop-houses in Manhattan were in the area known as the Bowery. During this time, more than twenty-five thousand men sought beds every night in about one hundred lodging houses, paying for them with their daily earnings.

"It is far beyond anything hitherto attempted in the hotel world . . ." It cost twenty-
eight million dollars. The famous Oscar Tschirky is in charge of banqueting.
Alexandre Gastaud is chef. It will be a distinguished background for society.
So when you've got no place else to go, homeless and hungry ones, choose the
Waldorf as a background for your rags—
(Or do you still consider the subway after midnight good enough?)

ROOMERS

Take a room at the new Waldorf, you down-and-outers—sleepers in charity flop-houses
where God pulls a long face, and you have to pray to get a bed.
They serve swell board[3] at the Waldorf-Astoria.
Look at this menu, will you:

GUMBO CREOLE

CRABMEAT IN CASSOLETTE

BROILED BRISKET OF BEEF

SMALL ONIONS IN CREAM

WATERCRESS SALAD

PEACH MELBA

Have luncheon there this afternoon, all you jobless.
Why not?
Dine with some of the men and women who got rich off of your labor, who clip
coupons with clean white fingers because your hands dug coal, drilled stone,
sewed garments, poured steel—to let other people draw dividends and live easy.
(Or haven't you had enough yet of the soup-lines and the bitter bread of charity?)
Walk through Peacock Alley[4] tonight before dinner, and get warm, anyway. You've got
nothing else to do.

EVICTED FAMILIES

All you families put out in the street: Apartments in the Towers are only $10,000 a year.
(Three rooms and two baths.) Move in there until times get good, and you can do
better. $10,000 and $1.00 are about the same to you, aren't they?
Who cares about money with a wife and kids homeless, and nobody in the family
working? Wouldn't a duplex high above the street be grand, with a view of the
richest city in the world at your nose?
"A lease, if you prefer; or an arrangement terminable at will."

    ♣   ♣   ♣

---

3. Meals.   4. A cocktail lounge in the hotel.

NEGROES

O, Lawd, I done forgot Harlem!

Say, you colored folks, hungry a long time in 135th Street—they got swell music at
the Waldorf-Astoria. It sure is a mighty nice place to shake hips in, too. There's
dancing after supper in a big warm room. It's cold as hell on Lenox Avenue. All
you've had all day is a cup of coffee. Your pawnshop overcoat's a ragged banner on
your hungry frame. . . . You know, down-town folks are just crazy about Paul
Robeson.[5] Maybe they'd like you, too, black mob from Harlem. Drop in at the
Waldorf this afternoon for tea. Stay to dinner. Give Park Avenue a lot of darkie[6]
color—free—for nothing! Ask the Junior Leaguers to sing a spiritual for you. They
probably know 'em better than you do—and their lips won't be so chapped with
cold after they step out of their closed cars in the undercover driveways.

Hallelujah! under-cover driveways!

Ma soul's a witness for de Waldorf-Astoria!

(A thousand nigger section-hands keep the road-beds[7] smooth, so investments in
railroads pay ladies with diamond necklaces staring at Sert[8] murals.)

Thank God A-Mighty!

(And a million niggers bend their backs on rubber plantations,[9] for rich behinds to ride
on thick tires to the Theatre Guild tonight.)

Ma soul's a witness!

(And here we stand, shivering in the cold, in Harlem.)

Glory be to God—

De Waldorf-Astoria's open!

EVERYBODY

So get proud and rare back, everybody! The new Waldorf-Astoria's open!

(Special siding for private cars from the railroad yards.)

You ain't been there yet?

(A thousand miles of carpet and a million bath rooms.)

What's the matter? You haven't seen the ads in the papers? Didn't you get a card? Don't
you know they specialize in American cooking?

Ankle on down to 49th Street at Park Avenue. Get up off that subway bench tonight
with the evening POST for cover! Come on out o' that flop-house! Stop shivering
your guts out all day on street corners under the El.

Jesus, ain't you tired yet?

---

5. An African-American singer, actor, and spokes-man for the left.
6. An offensive term for an African American.
7. Roads covered with train tracks.
8. José María Sert y Badia (1874–1945) was a Span-ish painter commissioned to do the murals for the Rockefeller Center in New York after Diego Ri-

vera was dismissed for creating Marxist-inspired murals.
9. Rubber plantation workers are highly exploited even today, working twelve-hour days. Their wages are kept very low so that they are dependent on the plantation owners for housing and their basic needs.

*   *   *

CHRISTMAS CARD

Hail Mary, Mother of God!
The new Christ child of the Revolution's about to be born.
(Kick hard, red baby, in the bitter womb of the mob.)
Somebody, put an ad in Vanity Fair quick!
Call Oscar of the Waldorf—for Christ's sake!
It's almost Christmas, and that little girl—turned whore because her belly was too
    hungry to stand it any more—wants a nice clean bed for the Immaculate
    Conception.
Listen, Mary, Mother of God, wrap your new born babe in the red flag of Revolution:
The Waldorf-Astoria's the best manger we've got.
For reservations: Telephone
                    Eldorado 5-3000.

                                  1931

"Come to the Waldorf-Astoria" originally appeared in the leftist journal *New Masses* in December 1931 as a parody of an advertisement in the elite magazine *Vanity Fair*. In its first publication, the poem was accompanied by satiric sketches of limousines, upper-class women and gentlemen, and partygoers above a crowd of grim-faced workers. Hughes states that he frequently walked by the Waldorf-Astoria, which had opened that year as "the world's grandest and largest hotel" on Park Avenue, and thought about the fact that no African Americans were hired there and none admitted as guests. He felt that this segregated world acted as though there were no economic depression, while millions of poorly treated workers were underpaid, jobless, and/or homeless. This poem appeared the same year that the Scottsboro Trial took place and shows Hughes's move leftward as he sought solutions to African-American problems. In the poem Hughes draws attention to the disparity between the elite class's fascination with African-American culture and its willful ignorance of the exploitation of workers, including African-American workers, to finance its lifestyle.

Goodbye Christ

    Listen, Christ,
    You did alright in your day, I reckon—
    But that day's gone now.
    They ghosted you up a swell story, too,
    Called it Bible—
    But it's dead now,
    The popes and the preachers've
    Made too much money from it.
    They've sold you to too many

*　*　*

Kings, generals, robbers, killers—
Even to the Tzar and the Cossacks,
Even to Rockefeller's Church,
Even to THE SATURDAY EVENING POST.
You ain't no good no more.
They've pawned you
Till you've done wore out.

Goodbye,
Chris Jesus Lord God Jehova,
Beat it on away from here now.
Make way for a new guy with no religion at all—
A real guy named
Marx Communist Lenin Peasant Stalin Worker ME—

I said, ME!

Go ahead on now,
You're getting in the way of things, Lord.
And please take Saint Gandhi[1] with you when you go,
And Saint Pope Pius,[2]
And Saint Aimee McPherson,[3]
And big black Saint Becton[4]
Of the Consecrated Dime.
And step on the gas, Christ!
Move!

Don't be so slow about movin'!
The world is mine from now on—
And nobody's gonna sell ME
To a king, or a general,
Or a millionaire.

1932

Hughes wrote "Goodbye Christ" during his trip to the Soviet Union. In it he contemplates the difference between his treatment in a "Godless" country and his treatment back home.

1. Mohandas Gandhi (1869–1948) led the Indian movement for independence from British rule and advocated nonviolence.
2. Piux XI (1857–1939) headed the Roman Catholic Church and opposed the left.
3. Aimee McPherson (1890–1944) was an American evangelist accused of monetary and sexual improprieties. Her followers picketed Hughes at a book luncheon in Pasadena, California. While a sound truck played "God Bless America," they passed out this poem and then marched into the luncheon, disrupting it. Hughes left to avoid further problems.
4. George Becton led a religious sect in Harlem that was funded through so-called consecrated dimes until he was murdered in 1933.

He refers specifically to the Christian language used by American racist and lynching culture to justify itself. The poem first appeared in *The Negro Worker* in 1932, probably without Hughes's knowledge. It was then republished without his permission in *The Saturday Evening Post* in 1940 as part of a long crusade against him by the political right and the FBI. Under pressure from HUAC and other members of Congress in the 1950s, Hughes wrote a disclaimer about his politics and this poem.

Letter from Spain
ADDRESSED TO ALABAMA

> Lincoln Battalion
> International Brigades,
> November Something, 1937.

Dear Brother at home:

We captured a wounded Moor[1] today.
He was just as dark as me.
I said, Boy, what you been doin' here
Fightin' against the free?

He answered something in a language
I couldn't understand.
But somebody told me he was sayin'
They nabbed him in his land

And made him join the fascist army
And come across to Spain.
And he said he had a feelin'
He'd never get back home again.

He said he had a feelin'
This whole thing wasn't right.
He said he didn't know
The folks he had to fight.

> And as he lay there dying
> In a village we had taken,
> I looked across to Africa
> And seed foundations shakin'.

*   *   *

1. A North African Muslim.

'Cause if a free Spain wins this war,
The colonies, too, are free —
Then something wonderful'll happen
To them Moors as dark as me.

I said, I guess that's why old England
And I reckon Italy, too,
Is afraid to let a workers' Spain
Be too good to me and you —

'Cause they got slaves in Africa —
And they don't want them to be free.
Listen, Moorish prisoner, hell!
Here, shake hands with me!

I knelt down there beside him,
And I took his hand —
But the wounded Moor was dyin'
And he didn't understand.

Salud,
Johnny

1937

Hughes spent about six months visiting loyalist troops in Spain during the Spanish Civil War. He gave "Letter from Spain" to Edwin Rolfe to publish in *Volunteers for Liberty*, the magazine of the International Brigades. In the poem he connects the fascist dictators Franco and Mussolini to imperialism, working-class exploitation, and racism. While members of the black Lincoln Battalion objected to Hughes's use of a sharecropping dialect because they were all educated, the dialect suited his goal of linking U.S. sharecroppers with other exploited workers. When the poem was republished in *The Daily Worker* in 1938, its accompanying illustration made the Spanish peasant plowing the fields and the U.S. sharecropper look nearly indistinguishable. All of the troops from the United States were volunteers because the U.S. government did not militarily support the struggle against Franco.

PROSE

First published in *The Nation*, "The Negro Artist and the Racial Mountain" became the manifesto of the Harlem Renaissance. It addresses the role that racism plays in determining what is desirable in both art and life in the United States. As Hughes argues, African Americans are taught not to see themselves, or to see themselves as being as white as possible. Consider the historical context in which

Hughes was writing. During the 1920s, a virulent white supremacy group called the Ku Klux Klan was reinvigorated, growing to several million members and including women as well as men. Klan chapters were even part of college and university campus life. The Klan marched publicly in many parts of the country, including Washington, D.C. Not surprisingly, lynching and other acts of racist violence became more widespread. Rather than back away from their African and African-American heritage, however, Hughes urges artists to embrace it.

The Negro Artist and the Racial Mountain

One of the most promising of the young Negro poets said to me once, "I want to be a poet—not a Negro poet," meaning, I believe, "I want to write like a white poet"; meaning subconsciously, "I would like to be a white poet"; meaning behind that, "I would like to be white." And I was sorry the young man said that, for no great poet has ever been afraid of being himself. And I doubted then that, with his desire to run away spiritually from his race, this boy would ever be a great poet. But this is the mountain standing in the way of any true Negro art in America—this urge within the race toward whiteness, the desire to pour racial individuality into the mold of American standardization, and to be as little Negro and as much American as possible.

But let us look at the immediate background of this young poet. His family is of what I suppose one would call the Negro middle class: people who are by no means rich yet never uncomfortable nor hungry—smug, contented, respectable folk, members of the Baptist church. The father goes to work every morning. He is a chief steward at a large white club. The mother sometimes does fancy sewing or supervises parties for the rich families of the town. The children go to a mixed school. In the home they read white papers and magazines. And the mother often says "Don't be like niggers" when the children are bad. A frequent phrase from the father is, "Look how well a white man does things." And so the word white comes to be unconsciously a symbol of all the virtues. It holds for the children beauty, morality, and money. The whisper of "I want to be white" runs silently through their minds. This young poet's home is, I believe, a fairly typical home of the colored middle class. One sees immediately how difficult it would be for an artist born in such a home to interest himself in interpreting the beauty of his own people. He is never taught to see that beauty. He is taught rather not to see it, or if he does, to be ashamed of it when it is not according to Caucasian patterns.

For racial culture the home of a self-styled "high-class" Negro has nothing better to offer. Instead there will perhaps be more aping of things white than in a less cultured or less wealthy home. The father is perhaps a doctor, lawyer, landowner, or politician. The mother may be a social worker, or a teacher, or she may do nothing and have a maid. Father is often dark but he has usually married the lightest woman he could find. The family attend a fashionable church where few really colored faces are to be found. And they themselves draw a color line. In the North they go to white theaters and white movies. And in the South they have at least two cars and a house "like white folks." Nordic manners, Nordic faces, Nordic hair, Nordic art (if any), and an Episcopal heaven. A very high mountain indeed for the would-be racial artist to climb in order to discover himself and his people.

But then there are the low-down folks, the so-called common element, and they are the majority — may the Lord be praised! The people who have their nip of gin on Saturday nights and are not too important to themselves or the community, or too well fed, or too learned to watch the lazy world go round. They live on Seventh Street in Washington or State Street in Chicago and they do not particularly care whether they are like white folks or anybody else. Their joy runs, bang! into ecstasy. Their religion soars to a shout. Work maybe a little today, rest a little tomorrow. Play awhile. Sing awhile. O, let's dance! These common people are not afraid of spirituals, as for a long time their more intellectual brethren were, and jazz is their child. They furnish a wealth of colorful, distinctive material for any artist because they still hold their own individuality in the face of American standardizations. And perhaps these common people will give to the world its truly great Negro artist, the one who is not afraid to be himself. Whereas the better-class Negro would tell the artist what to do, the people at least let him alone when he does appear. And they are not ashamed of him — if they know he exists at all. And they accept what beauty is their own without question.

Certainly there is, for the American Negro artist who can escape the restrictions the more advanced among his own group would put upon him, a great field of unused material ready for his art. Without going outside his race, and even among the better classes with their "white" culture and conscious American manners, but still Negro enough to be different, there is sufficient matter to furnish a black artist with a lifetime of creative work. And when he chooses to touch on the relations between Negroes and whites in this country with their innumerable overtones and undertones, surely, and especially for literature and the drama, there is an inexhaustible supply of themes at hand. To these the Negro artist can give his racial individuality, his heritage of rhythm and warmth, and his incongruous humor that so often, as in the Blues, becomes ironic laughter mixed with tears. But let us look again at the mountain.

A prominent Negro clubwoman in Philadelphia paid eleven dollars to hear Raquel Meller[1] sing Andalusian popular songs. But she told me a few weeks

---

1. Raquel Meller (1888–1962) was a Spanish singer who sang Andalusian, or southern Spanish, songs.

before she would not think of going to hear "that woman," Clara Smith,[2] a great black artist, sing Negro folksongs. And many an upper-class Negro church, even now, would not dream of employing a spiritual in its services. The drab melodies in white folks' hymnbooks are much to be preferred. "We want to worship the Lord correctly and quietly. We don't believe in 'shouting.' Let's be dull like the Nordics," they say, in effect.

The road for the serious black artist, then, who would produce a racial art is most certainly rocky and the mountain is high. Until recently he received almost no encouragement for his work from either white or colored people. The fine novels of Chesnutt[3] go out of print with neither race noticing their passing. The quaint charm and humor of Dunbar's[4] dialect verse brought to him, in his day, largely the same kind of encouragement one would give a sideshow freak (A colored man writing poetry! How odd!) or a clown (How amusing!).

The present vogue in things Negro, although it may do as much harm as good for the budding colored artist, has at least done this: it has brought him forcibly to the attention of his own people among whom for so long, unless the other race had noticed him beforehand, he was a prophet with little honor. I understand that Charles Gilpin[5] acted for years in Negro theaters without any special acclaim from his own, but when Broadway gave him eight curtain calls, Negroes, too, began to beat a tin pan in his honor. I know a young colored writer, a manual worker by day, who had been writing well for the colored magazines for some years, but it was not until he recently broke into the white publications and his first book was accepted by a prominent New York publisher that the "best" Negroes in his city took the trouble to discover that he lived there. Then almost immediately they decided to give a grand dinner for him. But the society ladies were careful to whisper to his mother that perhaps she'd better not come. They were not sure she would have an evening gown.

The Negro artist works against an undertow of sharp criticism and misunderstanding from his own group and unintentional bribes from the whites. "O, be respectable, write about nice people, show how good we are," say the Negroes. "Be stereotyped, don't go too far, don't shatter our illusions about you, don't amuse us too seriously. We will pay you," say the whites. Both would have told Jean Toomer[6] not to write *Cane*. The colored people did not praise it. The white people did not buy it. Most of the colored people who did read *Cane* hate it. They are afraid of it. Although the critics gave it good reviews the public

2. Clara Smith (1897–1935) was an American blues singer.

3. Charles Chesnutt (1858–1932) was an African-American novelist and short-story writer.

4. Paul Laurence Dunbar (1872–1906), included in the first volume of this anthology, was an African-American poet and short-story writer.

5. Charles Gilpin (1878–1930) was an African-American actor and singer.

6. Jean Toomer (1894–1967), included in this anthology, wrote *Cane*, a modernist volume that mixed poetry and fiction.

remained indifferent. Yet (excepting the work of Du Bois[7]) *Cane* contains the finest prose written by a Negro in America. And like the singing of Robeson,[8] it is truly racial.

But in spite of the Nordicized Negro intelligentsia and the desires of some white editors we have an honest American Negro literature already with us. Now I await the rise of the Negro theater. Our folk music, having achieved world-wide fame, offers itself to the genius of the great individual American Negro composer who is to come. And within the next decade I expect to see the work of a growing school of colored artists who paint and model the beauty of dark faces and create with new technique the expressions of their own soul-world. And the Negro dancers who will dance like flame and the singers who will continue to carry our songs to all who listen — they will be with us in even greater numbers tomorrow.

Most of my own poems are racial in theme and treatment, derived from the life I know. In many of them I try to grasp and hold some of the meanings and rhythms of jazz. I am sincere as I know how to be in these poems and yet after every reading I answer questions like these from my own people: Do you think Negroes should always write about Negroes? I wish you wouldn't read some of your poems to white folks. How do you find anything interesting in a place like a cabaret? Why do you write about black people? You aren't black. What makes you do so many jazz poems?

But jazz to me is one of the inherent expressions of Negro life in America: the eternal tom-tom beating in the Negro soul — the tom-tom of revolt against weariness in a white world, a world of subway trains, and work, work, work; the tom-tom of joy and laughter, and pain swallowed in a smile. Yet the Philadelphia clubwoman is ashamed to say that her race created it and she does not like me to write about it. The old subconscious "white is best" runs through her mind. Years of study under white teachers, a lifetime of white books, pictures, and papers, and white manners, morals, and Puritan standards made her dislike the spirituals. And now she turns up her nose at jazz and all its manifestations — likewise almost everything else distinctly racial. She doesn't care for the Winold Reiss[9] portraits of Negroes because they are "too Negro." She does not want a true picture of herself from anybody. She wants the artist to flatter her, to make the white world believe that all Negroes are as smug and as near white in soul as she wants to be. But, to my mind, it is the duty of the younger Negro artist, if he accepts any duties at all from outsiders, to change through the force of his art that old

7. W. E. B. Du Bois (1868–1963) was a leading African-American author, intellectual, and protest movement founder. His work appears in the first volume of this anthology.
8. Paul Robeson (1898–1976) was an African-American singer, actor, and activist.

9. Winold Reiss (1886–1953) was a German-born American painter known for his portraits of African Americans and Native Americans.

whispering "I want to be white," hidden in the aspirations of his people, to "Why should I want to be white? I am a Negro—and beautiful!"

So I am ashamed for the black poet who says, "I want to be a poet, not a Negro poet," as though his own racial world were not as interesting as any other world. I am ashamed, too, for the colored artist who runs from the painting of Negro faces to the painting of sunsets after the manner of the academicians because he fears the strange un-whiteness of his own features. An artist must be free to choose what he does, certainly, but he must also never be afraid to do what he might choose.

Let the blare of Negro jazz bands and the bellowing voice of Bessie Smith[10] singing Blues penetrate the closed ears of the colored near-intellectuals until they listen and perhaps understand. Let Paul Robeson singing "Water Boy," and Rudolph Fisher[11] writing about the streets of Harlem, and Jean Toomer holding the heart of Georgia in his hands, and Aaron Douglas[12] drawing strange black fantasies cause the smug Negro middle class to turn from their white, respectable, ordinary books and papers to catch a glimmer of their own beauty. We younger Negro artists who create now intend to express our individual dark-skinned selves without fear or shame. If white people are pleased we are glad. If they are not, it doesn't matter. We know we are beautiful. And ugly too. The tom-tom cries and the tom-tom laughs. If colored people are pleased we are glad. If they are not, their displeasure doesn't matter either. We build our temples for tomorrow, strong as we know how, and we stand on top of the mountain, free within ourselves.

1926

OGDEN NASH

1902–1971

OGDEN NASH was the most popular author of humorous verse of the mid-twentieth century. Known for an incisively whimsical, breezily sardonic view of the world and for the outrageous rightness of his rhymes, Nash created a style that was uniquely his own. Born in Rye, New York, in 1902, he was working at Double-

10. Bessie Smith (1894–1937) was one of Hughes's favorite blues singers.
11. Rudolph Fisher (1897–1934) was an African-American novelist and short-story writer.

12. Aaron Douglas (1899–1979) was an African-American artist.

day Page publishers in 1930 when he dashed off a nonsense poem juxtaposing the tedium of responsible work against the irresponsible joy of ludicrous rhyme. He threw his "doggerel" in the trash, then thought again. Retrieving the poem, he sent it to *The New Yorker*, which promptly published it. He was instantly popular, and his first book of verse, *Hard Lines*, followed quickly in 1931 and went through many printings. In 1932, he joined the editorial staff of *The New Yorker*, which continued to publish his work with regularity for the next four decades. Nash went on to write many volumes and collections. He also authored a humorous narrative text for Saint-Saens's musical suite *The Carnival of the Animals*, which has been recorded many times and continues to be widely performed.

FURTHER READING

Ogden Nash. *I Wouldn't Have Missed It: Selected Poems*. New York: Little Brown, 1975.
David Stuart. *The Life and Rhymes of Ogden Nash*. Lanham, Md.: Madison Books, 2000.

Reflections on Ice-Breaking

Candy
Is dandy
But liquor
Is quicker.

1931

The Turtle

The turtle lives twixt plated decks
Which practically conceal its sex.
I think it clever of the turtle
In such a fix to be so fertile.

1931

Columbus

Once upon a time there was an Italian,
And some people thought he was a rapscallion,
But he wasn't offended,
Because other people thought he was splendid,
And he said the world was round,
And everybody made an uncomplimentary sound,

But his only reply was Pooh,
He replied, Isn't this fourteen ninety-two?
It's time for me to discover America if I know my chronology,
And if I discover America you owe me an apology,
So he went and tried to borrow some money from Ferdinand
But Ferdinand said America was a bird in the bush and he'd rather have a berdinand,
But Columbus' brain was fertile, it wasn't arid,
And he remembered that Ferdinand was unhappily married,
And he thought, there is no wife like a misunderstood one,
Because if her husband thinks something is a terrible idea she is bound to think it a
    good one,
So he perfumed his handkerchief with bay rum and citronella,
And he went to see Isabella,
And he looked wonderful but he had never felt sillier,
And she said, I can't place the face but the aroma is familiar,
And Columbus didn't say a word,
All he said was, I am Columbus, the fifteenth-century Admiral Byrd,
And, just as he thought, her disposition was very malleable,
And she said, Here are my jewels, and she wasn't penurious like Cornelia the mother
    of the Gracchi, she wasn't referring to her children, no, she was referring to her
    jewels, which were very very valuable,
So Columbus said, Somebody show me the sunset and somebody did and he set sail
    for it,
And he discovered America and they put him in jail for it,
And the fetters gave him welts,
And they named America after somebody else,
So the sad fate of Columbus ought to be pointed out to every child and every voter,
Because it has a very important moral, which is, Don't be a discoverer, be a promoter.

                                                                            1934

COUNTEE CULLEN
1903–1946

COUNTEE CULLEN made a huge cultural impact early in his life, winning poetry prizes in his late teens and publishing his first, very successful book of poetry, *Color*, at the age of twenty-two. An early star of the Harlem Renaissance, he wrote poems that expressed with more immediacy than anyone else's the social dilemmas and interior conflicts experienced by African Americans. "Incident," for example, suggests the lingering wound caused by white supremacy, whereas "Heritage" explores an African American's ambivalences toward both Africa and his homeland. "Yet Do I Marvel" crystallizes the challenges faced by the African-American poet: "Yet do I marvel at this curious thing: / To make a poet black, and bid him sing!"

Cullen believed that he had more to gain from "the rich background of English and American poetry" than from his African inheritance, yet he also found that in his joys and sorrows, "I feel as a Negro." His poems rigorously adhere to European-American traditions of structure and style, exemplifying what Houston Baker has called "mastery of form." Nevertheless, the poems' subtle allusions to black consciousness and racial inequity reveal a complementary strategy that Baker terms the "deformation of mastery." Cullen described himself poetically as "a rank conservative, loving the measured line and the skillful rhyme." He reserved his rebellious impulses for matters exterior to poetic form: primarily race awareness but also hints of homosociality and enduring melancholia.

Born Countee Porter, the poet was raised in Baltimore by his paternal grandmother. When he was fifteen, his grandmother died and he was adopted by a Harlem clergyman and his wife, Frederick and Carolyn Cullen. Grateful for their kindness, Countee Cullen nevertheless chafed against their austere ways, viewing them as Christians and himself as a "pagan." He graduated with honors from the predominantly white De Witt Clinton High School, graduated Phi Beta Kappa from New York University, and received his M. A. from Harvard, where he studied British poetry with the noted critic and poet Robert Hillyer, an archconservative in matters of form. He spent the 1920s publishing his poetry, and he also edited a landmark anthology of African-American poetry and worked as assistant editor of the major black journal *Opportunity*. During this decade, he married his first wife, Nina Du Bois, the daughter of W. E. B. Du Bois. But only two months after the wedding, Cullen left for France with his lifelong companion, Harold Jackman, and without his wife. He and his wife divorced two years later.

The 1930s witnessed a decline in Cullen's career. He published poetry and a novel but received lukewarm reviews. His creative urge waned. To support himself, he took a job teaching French and creative writing at Frederick Douglass Junior High School in New York. One of his students was James Baldwin, who grew up to be a famous writer himself. Cullen married a second time and continued to produce new writing: several children's books and a coauthored play. He died of uremia at the age of forty-two. Like John Keats, one of the English poets he most admired, Cullen had produced his great work at a very young age.

FURTHER READING

Houston A. Baker, Jr. *Afro-American Poetics: Revisions of Harlem and the Black Aesthetic*. Madison: University of Wisconsin Press, 1988.

———. *Modernism and the Harlem Renaissance*. Chicago: University of Chicago Press, 1987.

Countee Cullen. *My Soul's High Song: The Collected Writings*. Garden City, N.Y.: Doubleday-Anchor, 1990.

———, ed. *Caroling Dusk: An Anthology of Verse by Black Poets*. New York: Harper & Row, 1927.

Arthur P. Davis. *From the Dark Tower: Afro-American Writers, 1900–1960*. Washington, D.C.: Howard University Press, 1974.

Alan Shucard. *Countee Cullen*. Boston: Twayne, 1984.

Tableau

Locked arm in arm they cross the way,
    The black boy and the white,
The golden splendor of the day,
    The sable pride of night.

From lowered blinds the dark folk stare,
    And here the fair folk talk,
Indignant that these two should dare
    In unison to walk.

Oblivious to look and word
    They pass, and see no wonder
That lightning brilliant as a sword
    Should blaze the path of thunder.

1924

"Tableau" uses the ballad stanza traditional to English-language poetry. The poem is written in iambics, with lines that alternate between four feet and three feet, and with an ABAB rhyme scheme. The vocabulary and imagery are traditional as well, though the racial subject and perspective are not. Houston Baker observes that the poem uses nature imagery to underline the social contrast of black and white. He ascribes the relationship of the two boys to "the camaraderie of youth." The friendship could also be seen in the light of Cullen's lifelong relationship with Harold Jackman.

Yet Do I Marvel

I doubt not God is good, well-meaning, kind,
And did He stoop to quibble could tell why
The little buried mole continues blind,
Why flesh that mirrors Him must some day die,
Make plain the reason tortured Tantalus[1]

---

1. In Greek myth, a king forced to stand in neck-high water that flowed away when he tried to drink; over his head hung fruits that wafted away when he tried to grasp them.

Is baited by the fickle fruit, declare
If merely brute caprice dooms Sisyphus[2]
To struggle up a never-ending stair.
Inscrutable His ways are, and immune
To catechism[3] by a mind too strewn
With petty cares to slightly understand
What awful brain compels His awful hand.
Yet do I marvel at this curious thing:
To make a poet black, and bid him sing!

1925

This Shakespearean sonnet integrates Cullen's cosmic irony and pessimism with a specific sense of the black poet's situation. The final couplet suggests that he must endure the tortures of a Tantalus or a Sisyphus.

Incident

Once riding in old Baltimore,
   Heart-filled, head-filled with glee,
I saw a Baltimorean
   Keep looking straight at me.

Now I was eight and very small,
   And he was no whit bigger,
And so I smiled, but he poked out
   His tongue, and called me, "Nigger."

I saw the whole of Baltimore
   From May until December;
Of all the things that happened there
   That's all that I remember.

1925

"Incident" recalls the speaker's initiation from innocence into the experience of racial prejudice.

2. In Greek myth, a king who was eternally punished by having to push a boulder up a hill only to have it roll down again just as he reached the summit.

3. Reasoning.

Heritage

(For Harold Jackman)

What is Africa to me:
Copper sun or scarlet sea,
Jungle star or jungle track,
Strong bronzed men, or regal black
Women from whose loins I sprang
When the birds of Eden[1] sang?
One three centuries removed
From the scenes his fathers loved,
Spicy grove, cinnamon tree,
What is Africa to me?

So I lie,[2] who all day long
Want no sound except the song
Sung by wild barbaric birds
Goading massive jungle herds,
Juggernauts[3] of flesh that pass
Trampling tall defiant grass
Where young forest lovers lie,
Plighting troth beneath the sky.
So I lie, who always hear,
Though I cram against my ear
Both my thumbs, and keep them there,
Great drums throbbing through the air.
So I lie, whose fount of pride,
Dear distress, and joy allied,
Is my somber flesh and skin,
With the dark blood dammed within
Like great pulsing tides of wine
That, I fear, must burst the fine
Channels of the chafing net
Where they surge and foam and fret.

Africa? A book one thumbs
Listlessly, till slumber comes.
Unremembered are her bats

---

1. Paradisiacal garden of Genesis 2–3
2. Recline, rest; but perhaps also speak deceptively, make a false statement.

3. In Hindu belief, the Juggernaut is a sacred idol carried on a large cart before which believers would throw themselves.

Circling through the night, her cats
Crouching in the river reeds,
Stalking gentle flesh that feeds
By the river brink; no more
Does the bugle-throated roar
Cry that monarch claws have leapt
From the scabbards[4] where they slept.
Silver snakes that once a year
Doff the lovely coats you wear,
Seek no covert[5] in your fear
Lest a mortal eye should see;
What's your nakedness to me?
Here no leprous[6] flowers rear
Fierce corollas[7] in the air;
Here no bodies sleek and wet,
Dripping mingled rain and sweat,
Tread the savage measures of
Jungle boys and girls in love.
What is last year's snow to me,
Last year's anything? The tree
Budding yearly must forget
How its past arose or set—
Bough and blossom, flower, fruit,
Even what shy bird with mute
Wonder at her travail there,
Meekly labored in its hair.
One three centuries removed
From the scenes his fathers loved,
Spice grove, cinnamon tree,
What is Africa to me?

So I lie, who find no peace
Night or day, no slight release
From the unremittent beat
Made by cruel padded feet
Walking through my body's street.
Up and down they go, and back,
Treading out a jungle track.

---

4. Sheaths for swords; here, lions' or tigers' dens.   6. Scaly. Rear: raise.
5. Hiding place.   7. Inner whorls of flowers.

So I lie, who never quite
Safely sleep from rain at night—
I can never rest at all
When the rain begins to fall;
Like a soul gone mad with pain
I must match its weird refrain;
Ever must I twist and squirm,
Writhing like a baited worm,
While its primal measures drip
Through my body, crying, "Strip!
Doff this new exuberance.
Come and dance the Lover's Dance!"
In an old remembered way
Rain works on me night and day.

Quaint, outlandish heathen gods
Black men fashion out of rods,
Clay, and brittle bits of stone,
In a likeness like their own,
My conversion came high-priced;
I belong to Jesus Christ,
Preacher of humility;
Heathen gods are naught to me.

Father, Son, and Holy Ghost,
So I make an idle boast;
Jesus of the twice-turned cheek,[8]
Lamb of God, although I speak
With my mouth thus, in my heart
Do I play a double part.
Ever at Thy glowing altar
Must my heart grow sick and falter,
Wishing He I served were black,
Thinking then it would not lack
Precedent of pain to guide it,
Let who would or might deride it;
Surely then this flesh would know
Yours had borne a kindred woe.

8. In the Sermon on the Mount, Jesus Christ says, "Whosoever shall smite thee on thy right cheek, turn to him the other also" (Matthew 5:39).

Lord, I fashion dark gods, too,
Daring even to give You
Dark despairing features where,
Crowned with dark rebellious hair,
Patience wavers just so much as
Mortal grief compels, while touches
Quick and hot, of anger, rise
To smitten cheek and weary eyes.
Lord, forgive me if my need
Sometimes shapes a human creed.

All day long and all night through,
One thing only must I do:
Quench my pride and cool my blood,
Lest I perish in the flood.
Lest a hidden ember set
Timber that I thought was wet
Burning like the dryest flax,
Melting like the merest wax,
Lest the grave restore its dead.
Not yet has my heart or head
In the least way realized
They and I are civilized.

1925

"Heritage," Cullen's masterpiece, explores racial and emotional ambivalence. Its key line, "What is Africa to me?," is far from a rhetorical question. Although the speaker describes reading a book about Africa "listlessly," the detail and fervor of his African evocations testify to his passionate interest in the continent. Moreover, he insistently links his African cultural heritage to his hidden and frustrated emotional needs: primarily sexual desire but also feelings of anger and rebellion. He contrasts his ascetic Christian morality with an imagined sexual freedom associated with the African past. He wishes to "dance the Lover's Dance" in an "old remembered way." Significantly, Cullen dedicated this poem to his longtime companion, Harold Jackman (1901–1961). Born in London, Jackman was educated in New York public schools, where he first met Cullen. The two attended New York University together and ultimately became fellow teachers in the New York school system. After Cullen's death, Jackman established an archive in the poet's honor at Atlanta University. After Jackman's death, the archive was renamed the Countee Cullen/Harold Jackman Memorial Collection.

Sacrament

She gave her body for my meat,
    Her soul to be my wine,
And prayed that I be made complete
    In sunlight and starshine.

With such abandoned grace she gave
    Of all that passion taught her,
She never knew her tidal wave
    Cast bread on stagnant water.

                    1925

For a Lady I Know

She even thinks that up in heaven
    Her class lies late and snores,
While poor black cherubs rise at seven
    To do celestial chores.

                    1925

"For a Lady I Know" and the poem that follows it, "For One Who Gayly Sowed His Oats,"
are two of Cullen's condensed and ironic "Epitaphs."

For One Who Gayly Sowed His Oats

My days were a thing for me to live,
    For others to deplore;
I took of life all it could give:
    Rind, inner fruit, and core.

                    1925

From the Dark Tower

(To Charles S. Johnson)

We shall not always plant while others reap
The golden increment of bursting fruit,
Not always countenance, abject and mute,
That lesser men should hold their brothers cheap;
Not everlastingly while others sleep

Shall we beguile their limbs with mellow flute,
Not always bend to some more subtle brute;
We were not made eternally to weep.

The night whose sable breast relieves the stark,
White stars is no less lovely being dark,
And there are buds that cannot bloom at all
In light, but crumple, piteous, and fall;
So in the dark we hide the heart that bleeds,
And wait, and tend our agonizing seeds.

1926

According to Arthur Davis, "From the Dark Tower" moves from an anguished sense of being exiled to "a mystic faith in a new world and a better day for the oppressed." Charles Spurgeon Johnson (1893–1956), to whom the sonnet is dedicated, was an eminent sociologist and editor of *Opportunity*, the journal for which Cullen served as assistant editor and columnist. Zora Neale Hurston called Johnson "the Father of the New Negro Renaissance."

Nothing Endures

Nothing endures,
Not even love,
Though the warm heart purrs
Of the length thereof.

Though beauty wax,
Yet shall it wane;
Time lays a tax
On the subtlest brain.

Let the blood riot,
Give it its will;
It shall grow quiet,
It shall grow still.

Nirvana gapes
For all things given;
Nothing escapes,
Love not even.

1929

LORINE NIEDECKER

1903–1970

LORINE NIEDECKER thought of her poetry as a "condensery." Her poems condensed the sounds and sights of rural Wisconsin, where she was born and spent most of her life. Her poems also condensed her roving consciousness, which focused alternately on the natural world around her and on the domestic world of family and neighbors in which she was engaged. Finally, her poems condensed language itself, in the minimalist manner of East Asian and Native-American poems as well as of Emily Dickinson, Adelaide Crapsey, and William Carlos Williams. Niedecker eschewed personal disclosure, preferring instead to experiment with both the objective and the nonreferential capacities of poetic language. Yet despite herself, she was also drawn to the subjective "I," an aspect of her creative urge that she criticized but could not forego. Vivid, unpretentious, and unusual, Niedecker's poems juxtapose their carefully chosen yet spontaneous-seeming words against the white space of the page. They provide an image of human utterance lonely in the surrounding silences: poetry arising within the vast spaces of the American heartland and, indeed, the infinitude of the cosmos.

Niedecker lived an isolated life. An only child, she grew up on marshy Black Hawk Island on Lake Koshkonong, near the small town of Fort Atkinson, Wisconsin. Winters were harsh. Niedecker's father supported the family by fishing, tending bar, and renting cabins. Her mother had lost her hearing in childbirth and suffered from depression and blindness as well. Niedecker attended Beloit College for several years but was called back to the family to care for her mother. A marriage in her twenties ended when both Niedecker and her husband lost their jobs in the Depression. Niedecker moved back in with her parents, working odd jobs that ranged from library assistant, stenographer, and writer in the Federal Writers' Project to cleaning woman. She lived with her parents until their death in the early 1950s, and after that she lived alone, in a small cabin without plumbing. In 1963, at the age of fifty-nine, she married Albert Millen, moving into his home in Milwaukee the following year. She died of a stroke in 1970, just as her poetry was receiving its first significant signs of recognition.

In the 1920s, Niedecker had become interested in poets associated with the imagist project, such as Ezra Pound, H.D., Amy Lowell, and Wallace Stevens (all included in this anthology). Then in 1931 she excitedly read the "Objectivist" issue of *Poetry* magazine, which contained work by poets—such as Louis Zukofsky, Charles Reznikoff, and Carl Rakosi (also included in this anthology)—who thought of themselves as the imagists' successors. Niedecker wrote to Zukofsky, the issue's editor, and thereby initiated a lifelong friendship. Niedecker's poetry shares some qualities with that of the objectivists: verbal play, spare and bare language, an avoidance of ego, and a focus on concrete particulars. But her poetry goes its own way, too—in its frequent flights toward surrealism or personal expression, and in its idiosyncrasies. Niedecker's poems are written in a personal style and never according to a program. They reveal what avant-garde poetry looks and sounds like when crafted by a gifted woman living among the marshes, trees, flowers, and people of a remote corner of the Upper Midwest.

FURTHER READING

Joseph M. Conte. "Sounding and Resounding Anew: Louis Zukofsky and Lorine Niedecker." In *Unending Design*, 141–63. Ithaca, N.Y.: Cornell University Press, 1991.

George Hart. "My Life by Water." In *Encyclopedia of American Poetry: The Twentieth Century*, ed. Eric L. Haralson, 513–14. Chicago: Fitzroy Dearborn, 2001.

Michael Heller. *Conviction's Net of Branches: Essays on the Objectivist Poets and Poetry*. Carbondale: Southern Illinois University Press, 1985.

Lorine Niedecker. *Collected Works*. Ed. Jenny Penberthy. Berkeley: University of California Press, 2002.

Jenny Penberthy, ed. *Lorine Niedecker: Woman and Poet*. Orono, Maine: National Poetry Foundation, 1996.

Marjorie Perloff. "Canon and Loaded Gun: Feminist Poetics and the Avant-Garde." In *Poetic License*, 31–52. Evanston, Ill.: Northwestern University Press, 1990.

Young girl to marry

Young girl to marry,
winds the washing harry.[1]

1936

Young girl to marry, like many of Niedecker's poems, employs a concentrated style to evoke the everyday existence of people around her.

Remember my little granite pail?

Remember my little granite pail?
The handle of it was blue.
Think what's got away in my life—
Was enough to carry me thru.

1946

Along with the following four poems, *Remember my little granite pail?* was written in the 1930s but not published until the 1940s, when Niedecker's work began to be noticed. The

---

1. Plague or trouble.

poem demonstrates Niedecker's concern for what she called "the hard, clear image, the thing you could put your hand on." Joseph Conte comments, "I have seen the 'granite' of the pail glossed as 'enamel,' but certainly that stone and the blue of the Rock River and Lake Koshkonong, which flowed past and frequently flooded the Niedecker cabin on Black Hawk Island, are the most prominent topological features of her region."

I said to my head, Write something.

I said to my head, Write something.
It looked me dead in the face.
Look around, dear head, you've never read
of the ground that takes you away.
Speed up, speed up, the frosted windshield's a fern spray.

1946

The speech rhythms and vocabulary of *I said to my head, Write something* are complemented by the playful use of rhyme, consonance, and image.

The museum man!

The museum man!
I wish he'd taken Pa's spitbox!
I'm going to take that spitbox out
and bury it in the ground
and put a stone on top.
Because without that stone on top
it would come back.

1946

In letters to Louis Zukofsky and others, Niedecker indicated that she based this poem on the "direct, simple speech" of her mother, Daisy.

A monster owl

A monster owl
out on the fence
flew away. What
is it the sign
of? The sign of
an owl.

1946

Well, spring overflows the land

Well, spring overflows the land,
floods floor, pump, wash machine
of the woman moored to this low shore by deafness.

    Good-bye to lilacs by the door
    and all I planted for the eye.
    If I could hear—too much talk in the world,
    too much wind washing, washing
    good black dirt away.

Her hair is high.
Big blind ears.

    I've wasted my whole life in water.
    My man's got nothing but leaky boats.
    My daughter, writer, sits and floats.

                  1946

Niedecker's mother suffered from deafness and other ailments. Her father, Henry, rented fishing boats, among other occupations.

My friend tree

My friend tree
I sawed you down
but I must attend
an older friend
the sun

    1961

Niedecker wrote to Louis Zukofsky's son, Paul, "Here is one of the tree workers way up near the top of my big ash tree. . . . They did it with ropes and a gasoline-run saw. $90 well spent. I hail the sun and the moon. . . . I still have 14 trees on my lawn. But you do have a feeling about destroying a tree."

Poet's work

Grandfather
    advised me:
        Learn a trade

*   *   *

I learned
      to sit at desk
           and condense

No layoff
      from this
           condensery
              1963

"Poet's work," like "My Life by Water," below, adopts William Carlos Williams's triadic line, evidenced in his "The Descent" (included in this anthology). Marjorie Perloff points out that Niedecker based her final, invented word, "condensery," on nouns such as "dairy," "nursery," and "pantry"—settings for domestic labor.

I married

I married

in the world's black night
for warmth
        if not repose.
        At the close—
someone.

I hid with him
from the long range guns.
        We lay leg
        in the cupboard, head
in closet.

A slit of light
at no bird dawn—
        Untaught
        I thought
he drank

too much.
I say
        I married
        and lived unburied.
I thought—
           1968

In *I married*, Niedecker explains why, at age fifty-nine, she married Albert Millen, a house-painter with no literary interests, who spent considerable time in taverns. The poem may be read as a paean to domestic companionship as a method of living "unburied." Or, especially considering the poem's last line, it may be read as a critique of such a solution.

Popcorn-can cover

Popcorn-can cover
screwed to the wall
over a hole
    so the cold
can't mouse in
    1969

He lived—childhood summers

He lived—childhood summers
    thru bare feet
then years of money's lack
    and heat

beside the river—out of flood
    came his wood, dog,
woman, lost her,[1] daughter—
    prologue

to planting trees. He buried carp[2]
    beneath the rose
where grass-still
    the marsh rail goes.

To bankers on high land
    he opened his wine tank.
He wished his only daughter
    to work in the bank

      *   *   *

1. Perhaps a reference to the death of Niedecker's mother, though the slant rhyme with "daughter" suggests a distance between father and daughter as well.

2. Niedecker's father was a carp fisherman, among his other occupations.

but he'd given her a source
to sustain her—
a weedy speech,[3]
a marshy retainer.[4]

1969

Niedecker composed *He lived—childhood summers* in the early 1950s, toward the end of her father's life. The poem suggests the muted, even bleak, drama of his life story in relation to that of "his only daughter."

What horror to awake at night

What horror to awake at night
and in the dimness see the light.
    Time is white
    mosquitoes bite
I've spent my life on nothing.

The thought that stings. How are you, Nothing,
sitting around with Something's wife.
    Buzz and burn
    is all I learn
I've spent my life on nothing.

I'm pillowed and padded, pale and puffing
lifting household stuffing—
    carpets, dishes
    benches, fishes
I've spent my life in nothing.

1969

What horror to awake at night may be compared to other modernist confrontations with mortality and nothingness, such as Robert Frost's "Desert Places," Adelaide Crapsey's "November Night," and Wallace Stevens's "The Snow Man" (all included in this anthology). Louis Zukofsky particularly praised the poem's uses of sound. Note also the enigmatic prepositional shift in the final line.

---

3. Reference to the daughter's poetic vocation.
4. Several different meanings apply: something that keeps her; a fee; a servant or dependent; a dental device that makes speech "weedy."

My Life by Water

My life
      by water—
            Hear

spring's
      first frog
            or board

out on the cold
      ground
            giving

Muskrats
      gnawing
            doors

to wild green
      arts and letters
            Rabbits

raided
      my lettuce
            One boat

two—
      pointed toward
            my shore

thru birdstart[1]
      wingdrip
            weed-drift

of the soft
      and serious—
            Water
            1969

Niedecker wrote to a friend about "My Life by Water": "I used to feel that I was goofing off unless I held only to the hard, clear image, the thing you could put your hand on, but now I dare do this reflection." George Hart observes that in this poem, "rhyme is eschewed; the

1. The first of three successive compound nouns, invented for the occasion, enigmatic but resonant with the delicacy and loneliness of life lived along the water.

poet sings through alliteration, consonance, and assonance. The syntax is also radically condensed. . . . The number of stanzas that begin with prepositions reveals how Niedecker's compression actually gets more music into—and out of—fewer words, while also producing multiple or indeterminate meanings. . . . The details are precise and vivid—the sound of frog or board, the gnawing muskrats, the boats pointed toward shore—but they also contribute to 'a state of consciousness,' one that all readers may share."

Frog noise

Frog noise
suddenly stops

Listen!
They turned off
their lights

1976

Frog noise adapts the five-part form and compressed, imagistic style of Japanese haiku. Compare, for example, this famous haiku by Matsuo Bashō (1644–1694): "Old pond: / frog jump in / water sound."

CARL RAKOSI
1903–2004

UNPRETENTIOUS AND DOWN TO EARTH, Carl Rakosi's poetry aims for clarity and spontaneity. It explores everyday life and feeling while reveling in the capacity of language to be both playful and succinct. Rakosi was part of the objectivist group of the 1930s, which included Louis Zukofsky, Lorine Niedecker, and Charles Reznikoff (also in this anthology). He brought closely observed details and vernacular melodies to the center of his project. Like the other objectivists, Rakosi respected Ezra Pound's theoretical insistence on the "direct treatment of the thing," but he came to feel that Pound's *Cantos* were "disastrous," exemplifying grandiosity and pretense. Instead, he looked to Wallace Stevens, E. E. Cummings, and William Carlos Williams for inspiration. He also shared the impetus of many second-generation modernists toward neorealism and social justice. His poetry celebrates the uncommon person leading a common life. It focuses on the peripheral vision, the intellectual curiosity, the moments of humor and pleasure, and the delight in language that can make such a life a meaningful adventure.

Rakosi was born in Berlin, Germany, the son of Hungarian Jews. His parents divorced, and at the age of seven, Rakosi migrated to the American Midwest to live with his father and stepmother. Arising from such a disrupted childhood, Rakosi distinguished himself in school, earning a B.A. and M.A. in English from the University of Wisconsin and a master's of social work from the University of Pennsylvania. He supported himself, his wife, Leah, and their children by working as a social worker and psychotherapist. He concluded a distinguished career in social work by serving as executive director of the Jewish Family and Children's Service in Minneapolis.

From his time in college, Rakosi considered writing his true calling. He was prominently featured in Zukofsky's 1931 "Objectivist" issue of *Poetry* magazine. But in 1941, Rakosi stopped reading and writing poetry, finding that in a busy life, he simply did not have the time and energy to continue. As someone drawn to Marxist ideas about literature, he also experienced a crisis about the value of lyric poetry in a time of war and social deprivation. When he first quit writing poetry, he "had all sorts of physical symptoms and a dreadful depression," but he ultimately found that "life goes on and fills up with other things." Several years before his retirement in 1968, however, Rakosi came to think that poetry exists in the private life of the individual rather than in the world of social values. Inspired by a letter from a young poet named Andrew Crozier, he began to write poetry again. He became increasingly prolific as the decades went on, publishing a dozen books of poetry after 1968, including four while in his nineties, and achieving a level of acclaim denied him in his earlier years. He spent the last part of his life in the Sunset District of San Francisco, living with companion Marilyn Kane. His career demonstrates how much a gifted poet can achieve in later years.

FURTHER READING

Michael Heller, ed. *Carl Rakosi: Man and Poet*. Orono, Maine: National Poetry Foundation, 1993.

Ming-Qian Ma. "Be Aware of 'The Medusa's Glance': The Objectivist Lens and Carl Rakosi's Poetics of Strabismal Seeing." In *The Objectivist Nexus*, ed. Rachel Blau DuPlessis and Peter Quartermain. Tuscaloosa: University of Alabama Press, 1999.

Carl Rakosi. *Collected Poems*. Orono, Maine: National Poetry Foundation, 1986.

ZZZZZ

nasturtium[1] petals alight:

20 watts of tangerine

shaded by green

leaf

a meticulous parasol

by Hokusai[2]

the orangey alpha[3]

and the green omega

of the bee's world.

1941

"ZZZZZ" focuses on the particularity of nature in a typically objectivist manner. It adopts the bee's perspective without explicit interference from the "I" of the poet. Nevertheless, one feels the subtle influence of the speaker's consciousness in the allusions to electric wattage, a parasol by Hokusai, and the alpha and omega of the Greek alphabet.

L'Chayim

I felt
the foetus stir
a foot
below my wife's
breast

and woke
the neighbours
with my shouting
(a day
for silly asses)

and greeted
my first-born:
"Listen, I am

---

1. South American plant, now commonly grown in the United States, prized for its brightly hued (including tangerine) flowers and its parasol-shaped leaves.

2. Katsushika Hokusai (1760–1849), the greatest Japanese artist and printmaker of the *ukiyo-e* ("pictures of the floating world") school.

3. Alpha and omega are the first and last letters of the Greek alphabet; hence, a figure of speech indicating the beginning and the end.

your provider.
Let us get to know
each other."

1941

"L'Chayim" means "to life" in both Hebrew and Yiddish. The phrase is generally used as a toast. This poem suggests the Jewish ambience of Rakosi's life as well as his interest in specific perceptions and emotions, his humor, and his joie de vivre.

Lying in Bed on a Summer Morning

How pleasant are the green
and brown tiles
of my neighbour's roof.
The branches of his elm tree
stretch across
and make a delightful
composition,
        the angle
of the roof
    the exact plane
which the branch needs
to be interesting.
Le mot juste? la branche juste![1]

And you, my dark spruce,
dominate the left side
of this composition.
You are clannish but authentic
and stand, uncompromising,
for the family of trees.

And all at once the early birds
all break out chirping
as when the bidding opens
on the stock exchange.
          Then one,
the long sweet warble
of a finch.

---

1. The precise word? the precise branch! (French).

Oh stay! . . . .

And then a chant from down the street,
two boys triumphant,
very small in thick glasses:
"We got a bird nest! We got a bird nest!"
But a younger brother,
left behind and clobbered
when the mother was not looking,
saw his chance to singsong back
(ah, sweet revenge):

"But

a woodpecker didn't make that nest!"

A contrary air.
It is gone.
And the blue sky,

clear as in Genesis,[2]

holds.

What is there between us?[3]
an abstract air. . . .
a state sans question

or inquietude. . . .

something light

as a country air

yet serious as gold
or man sui generis.[4]

1967

"Lying in Bed on a Summer Morning" is the first poem Rakosi composed when he returned to writing in 1965. He had received an inquiry from an admirer named Andrew Crozier and thought, "Was it *possible* I could write again? This time it was possible. I would be free [retired] in two years, and with great joy I started." The poem celebrates everyday human realities.

2. The first book of the Hebrew Bible.   4. Of his own kind; unique (Latin).
3. Perhaps between the speaker and the world.

Objectivist Lamp

goddess,

           ivory carved

Japanese

      lady,

hands crossed

         over breast,

holding

        on her head

electric bulbs

      and batik[1]

lamp shade.

1981

Concerning "Objectivist Lamp," Ming-Qian Ma comments: "Here the lamp is an object perceived but not, as Rakosi would say, aggrandized. The poem outlines a process in which language's transitive, nominating impulse is nullified at its inception, and the mirage of seeing is shattered at the moment of its suggestiveness and taken over by the detail of seeing. . . . What can be identified, then, is only the material out of which this 'goddess' is made: 'ivory carved.' Although 'goddess' is further specified by its apposition of 'Japanese / lady,' it is nothing more than the same physical substance that relates them, thus frustrating any attempt to see beyond the appearance. In a like manner, the ghost of a symbolic gesture suggestively promised in 'hands crossed / over breast, / holding / on her head' is driven away by the rather banal 'electric bulbs / and batik / lamp shade.'"

Old Lovers

Bubeleh,[1]

        if you will be

good-natured,

          I can be

wise.

1986

1. Hand-dyed in Javanese style.
1. Yiddish term of endearment, literally "little grandmother."

RICHARD EBERHART
1904–Present

THOUGHTFUL AND CONTEMPLATIVE, Richard Eberhart's poems focus on issues of life and death, decay and regeneration, body and soul. "The Groundhog," for example, uses the chance discovery of a dead animal as an opportunity to ponder the consciousness of mortality. Poems about World War II deepen and intensify Eberhart's exploration of the meanings of death and continuance. "Dam Neck, Virginia," confronts the stunning contradictions between spiritual and aesthetic perception on the one hand and organized violence on the other. "The Fury of Aerial Bombardment" is at once a prayer, a protest, and a lament for the dead. Eberhart's work sustains a concerted effort to find redemption in a landscape of loss.

Eberhart wrote poems notable for their interplay of intricate forms with deliberately rough-hewn rhythms and diction. "The Fury of Aerial Bombardment," for instance, begins with a traditional rhyme scheme (ABBA) that becomes increasingly frayed as it progresses. Moreover, the poem goes out of its way to substitute speech rhythms for iambic pentameter, while the vocabulary ranges from the traditional ("God") to the contemporary ("aerial bombardment") to the weird ("shock-pried"). Mixing observation with meditation, Eberhart's poetry seems indebted to English Romantic poets, such as William Wordsworth. But in its accessibility, subjective cohesion, and resemblance to good prose, it also seems to look ahead to poets of the generation after his own, such as Robert Lowell and Randall Jarrell. Whatever its glances backward and forward, Eberhart's poetry breaks from modernist styles of experiment and impersonality by grounding itself in the present knowable moment.

Eberhart was born in Austin, Minnesota, the son of a businessman and a housewife. He received his B.A. from Dartmouth College in New Hampshire and a B.A. and M.A. from Cambridge University in England. By his mid-twenties he was already publishing poetry and establishing his career. In the 1930s he taught at St. Mark's School in Southborough, Massachusetts, where one of his teenaged students (a notably unruly one) was Robert Lowell. In 1941 Eberhart married Elizabeth Butcher, with whom he had two children. During World War II he served as a lieutenant commander in the U.S. Naval Reserve. He taught aerial gunnery at several different bases, an experience vividly reflected in his war poems. After the war he worked for a time as an executive in the Butcher Polish Company in Boston, founded the Poets' Theatre in Cambridge, Massachusetts, and ultimately served as professor of English and poet-in-residence at Dartmouth College. Among his many honors in a notably long career are the Shelley Memorial Prize, the Bollingen Prize, the Frost Medal, and the Pulitzer Prize.

FURTHER READING

Richard Eberhart. *Collected Poems, 1930–1986.* New York: Oxford University Press, 1988.
Bernard F. Engel. *Richard Eberhart.* New York: Twayne, 1971.
Joel Roache. *Richard Eberhart: The Progress of an American Poet.* New York: Oxford University Press, 1971.

The Groundhog

In June, amid the golden fields,
I saw a groundhog lying dead.
Dead lay he; my senses shook,
And mind outshot our naked frailty.
There lowly in the vigorous summer
His form began its senseless change,
And made my senses waver dim
Seeing nature ferocious in him.
Inspecting close his maggots' might
And seething cauldron of his being,
Half with loathing, half with a strange love,
I poked him with an angry stick.
The fever[1] arose, became a flame
And Vigour circumscribed[2] the skies,
Immense energy in the sun,
And through my frame a sunless trembling.
My stick had done nor[3] good nor harm.
Then stood I silent in the day
Watching the object, as before;
And kept my reverence for knowledge
Trying for control, to be still,
To quell the passion of the blood;
Until I had bent down on my knees
Praying for joy in the sight of decay.
And so I left; and I returned
In Autumn strict of eye, to see
The sap gone out of the groundhog,
But the bony sodden hulk remained.
But the year had lost its meaning,
And in intellectual chains

1. May refer to the activity of the maggots, stirred up by the stick.
2. Drew a circle around, surrounded.
3. Neither.

I lost both love and loathing,
Mured[4] up in the wall of wisdom.
Another summer took the fields again
Massive and burning, full of life,
But when I chanced upon the spot
There was only a little hair left,
And bones bleaching in the sunlight
Beautiful as architecture;
I watched them like a geometer,[5]
And cut a walking stick from a birch.
It has been three years, now.
There is no sign of the groundhog.
I stood there in the whirling summer,
My hand capped a withered heart,
And thought of China and of Greece,
Of Alexander[6] in his tent;
Of Montaigne[7] in his tower,
Of Saint Theresa[8] in her wild lament.

                    1936

Bernard Engel calls "The Groundhog" Eberhart's "most deeply moving recognition of the universality of death."

Dam Neck, Virginia

Anti-aircraft[1] seen from a certain distance
On a steely blue night say a mile away
Flowers on the air absolutely dream-like,
The vision has no relation to the reality.

The floating balls of light are tossed easily
And float out into space without a care,
They the sailors of the gentlest parabolas[2]
In a companionship and with a kind of stare.

4. Walled (a neologism based on the French *murer*, to wall up).
5. Geometrician, a person skilled in geometry.
6. Alexander the Great (356–323 B.C.E.), the Greek warrior and emperor.
7. Michel de Montaigne (1533–1592), a French essayist.

8. St. Theresa of Avila (1515–1582), a Spanish nun and mystic who wrote spiritual classics.
1. That is, ammunition fired by machine guns.
2. Bowl-shaped curves.

          *   *   *

They are a controlled kind of falling stars,
But not falling, rising and floating and going out,
Teaming together in efflorescent[3] spectacle
Seemingly better than nature's: man is on the lookout.

The men are firing tracers,[4] practising at night.
Each specialist himself precision's instrument,
These expert prestidigitators[5] press the luminence
In knowledge of and ignorance of their doing.

They do not know the dream-like vision ascending
In me, one mile away: they had not thought of that.
Huddled in darkness behind their bright projectors
They are the scientists of the skill to kill.

As this sight and show is gentle and false,
The truth of guns is fierce that aims at death.
Of war in the animal sinews[6] let us speak not,
But of the beautiful disrelation of the spiritual.

1947

Eberhart served as a gunnery instructor at Dam Neck, Virginia, during World War II. Note the way that the slant-rhyme scheme of the initial four stanzas mysteriously fades away in the final two.

The Fury of Aerial Bombardment

You would think the fury of aerial bombardment
Would rouse God to relent; the infinite spaces
Are still silent. He looks on shock-pried faces.[1]
History, even, does not know what is meant.

You would feel that after so many centuries
God would give man to repent; yet he can kill
As Cain[2] could, but with multitudinous will,
No farther advanced than in his ancient furies.

---

3. Flowerlike.
4. Projectiles containing a chemical substance that causes them to trail fire, making their path visible.
5. Magicians. Luminence: radiating light.
6. Tendons, sources of physical strength.

1. Perhaps faces that were peered into or detached by wartime trauma.
2. According to the Jewish and Christian Bibles, Cain killed his brother Abel, thereby becoming the first murderer (Genesis 4:1–16).

*   *   *

Was man made stupid to see his own stupidity?
Is God by definition indifferent, beyond us all?
Is the eternal truth man's fighting soul
Wherein the Beast ravens in its own avidity?

Of Van Wettering I speak, and Averill,[3]
Names on a list, whose faces I do not recall
But they are gone to early death, who late[4] in school
Distinguished the belt feed lever from the belt holding pawl.[5]

1947

According to Bernard Engel, Eberhart believed that World War II was a "just war," but he still could not "square . . . with Christianity" the fact that he taught "thousands of young men to kill" by firing machine guns. Upon learning that several of his students had died in battle, he wrote the first three stanzas of "The Fury of Aerial Bombardment" as a kind of prayer and the final stanza two weeks later.

LOUIS (LITTLE COON) OLIVER
1904–1991

LOUIS OLIVER is a member of an early-twentieth-century generation of poets who have provided crucial models to contemporary Native-American poets such as Joy Harjo. His poetry expresses reverence for the natural world, the family, and the community. A Creek born in Oklahoma, Oliver traces his ancestry to the Golden Raccoon Clan, who lived originally near the Chattahoochee River in Alabama before the tribes were subjugated and removed to reservations. His lyrical poetry is both pastoral and idyllic, but also pragmatic.

FURTHER READING

Duane Niatum, ed. *Harper's Anthology of 20th Century Native American Poetry*. San Francisco: HarperSanFrancisco, 1988.

3. Soldiers the speaker has trained who thereafter died in the war.

4. Recently.

5. Parts of a gun.

Empty Kettle

I do not waste what is wild
I only take what my cup
   can hold.
When the black kettle gapes
   empty
and children eat roasted acorns
   only,
it is time to rise-up early
   take no drink—eat no food
   sing the song of the hunter.
I see the Buck—I chant
   "He-hebah-Ah-kay-kee-no!"
My arrow, no woman has ever touched,
   finds its mark.
I open the way for the blood to pour
   back to Mother Earth
    the debt I owe.
My soul rises—rapturous
   and I sing a different song,
    I sing,
    I sing.

               n.d.

The Horned Snake

The snake snatched
   its single horn clipped
    for strong medicine,
to be used on a warrior
   or a chief who,
facing a volley of death
   from bullets
would be brave, unflinching
   —untouched.

When moon looked the other way,
   eclipsed,
and stillness—stark-naked
   stillness

made ears ring,
the snake bobbed up from
the wildest of wild springs
—gave its horn
to the medicine
man.

n.d.

LOUIS ZUKOFSKY
1904–1978

BRILLIANT AND DARING, Louis Zukofsky extended the spirit of innovation among the second generation of modernist poets. He was an important intellectual leader, editing an "Objectivist" volume of *Poetry* magazine in 1931 that created a movement, or at least an affinity group, that also included Carl Rakosi, Charles Reznikoff, Lorine Niedecker, and tangentially William Carlos Williams (all included in this anthology). The objectivist enterprise invoked the particularity of objects, freed from the interference of the poet's ego. Objectivist poems offered, as Zukofsky put it, "the detail, not mirage, of seeing, of thinking with things as they exist." The poems employed the vocabulary of common speech but not its syntax, aiming to produce a musical and visual structure rather than to communicate information. Zukofsky was as forceful an artist as he was a theorist. He breathed new life into ancient forms, as in "'Mantis,'" and he invented collages like nothing heard or seen before, as in "I's (pronounced *eyes*)." His poetry carries the modernist spirit of experimentation to new places. His poems could be more allusive than Pound's, more extemporaneous than Williams's, more precise than Moore's, more abstract than Stevens's, and more difficult than Stein's. Hugh Kenner once observed that we will probably still be sorting out Zukofsky's poems in the twenty-second century.

Growing up in a Jewish working-class family in New York's Lower East Side, the son of Russian immigrants, Zukofsky spoke primarily Yiddish at home. An outstanding student, he received his B.A. and M.A. from Columbia University, where he wrote his master's thesis on the late-nineteenth-century essayist and autobiographer Henry Adams. In the 1930s, Zukofsky lived a bohemian life in New York, publishing poems and manifestos in literary magazines, involving himself in progressive political activities, and becoming a close friend of and advisor to William Carlos Williams. He married his wife, Celia, a composer and translator, in 1939.

The couple had a son in 1943: Paul, a violin prodigy, grew up to be a noted violinist and conductor. During this period Zukofsky achieved prominence among the cognoscenti as an avant-garde poet and theorist, largely as a result of his having edited the "Objectivist" issue of *Poetry* magazine and then, a year later, *An "Objectivist" Anthology* (1932). Yet, because his poetry was so difficult, he was not able to publish his first volume of poetry until 1941.

After a stint (1935–42) in the Depression-era Federal Writers' Project, Zukofsky became an instructor at the Polytechnic Institute of Brooklyn, where he continued to work for nineteen years (1947–66). During and after this period, he published numerous volumes of short poems and his great long poem called "A." "A" includes twenty-four sections or movements, one of which is reprinted in this anthology. Written over the course of many decades, "A" embeds fifty years' public and personal experience into a vast mosaic or symphony of words. In the 1960s and 1970s, Zukofsky finally received a few well-earned honors, but he was never widely read or sufficiently celebrated. Nevertheless, poets ranging from Pound and Williams (in the generation before his) to Robert Duncan, Robert Creeley, and the Language poets (in the generations after his) have treasured his work. He has been called not simply a poet's poet but a "poet's poet's poet." In 1972, the Zukofskys moved from New York City to Long Island, to be close to their son. Louis Zukofsky was still writing innovative poetry when he died in Port Jefferson, New York, in 1978.

FURTHER READING

Barry Ahearn. *Zukofsky's "A": An Introduction.* Berkeley: University of California Press, 1983.
Rachel Blau DuPlessis and Peter Quartermain, eds. *The Objectivist Nexus: Essays in Cultural Poetics.* Tuscaloosa: University of Alabama Press, 1999.
Mark Scroggins. *Louis Zukofsky and the Poetry of Knowledge.* Tuscaloosa: University of Alabama Press, 1998.
Sandra Kumamoto Stanley. *Louis Zukofsky and the Transformation of a Modern American Poetics.* Berkeley: University of California Press, 1994.
Louis Zukofsky. "A." Berkeley: University of California Press, 1978.
———. *Complete Short Poetry.* Foreword by Robert Creeley. Baltimore: Johns Hopkins University Press, 1991.
———. *Prepositions: The Collected Critical Essays.* Expanded edition. Foreword by Hugh Kenner. Berkeley: University of California Press, 1981.

"Mantis"

Mantis! praying mantis! since your wings' leaves
And your terrified eyes, pins, bright, black and poor
Beg—"Look, take it up" (thoughts' torsion)! "save it!"
I who can't bear to look, cannot touch,—You—
You can—but no one sees you steadying lost
In the cars' drafts on the lit subway stone.

*   *   *

Praying mantis, what wind-up brought you, stone
On which you sometimes prop, prey among leaves
(Is it love's food your raised stomach prays?), lost
Here, stone holds only seats on which the poor
Ride, who rising from the news may trample you—
The shops' crowds a jam with no flies in it.

Even the newsboy who now sees knows it
No use, papers make money, makes stone, stone,
Banks, "it is harmless," he says moving on—You?
Where will he put *you*? There are no safe leaves
To put you back in here, here's news! too poor
Like all the separate poor to save the lost.

Don't light on my chest, mantis! do—you're lost,
Let the poor laugh at my fright, then see it:
My shame and theirs, you whom old Europe's poor
Call spectre, strawberry, by turns; a stone—
You point—they say—you lead lost children—leaves
Close in the paths men leave, saved, safe with you.

Killed by thorns (once men), who now will save you
Mantis? what male love bring a fly, be lost
Within your mouth, prophetess, harmless to leaves
And hands, faked flower,—the myth is: dead, bones, it
Was assembled, apes wing in wind: On stone,
Mantis, you will die, touch, beg, of the poor.

Android,[1] loving beggar, dive to the poor
As your love would even without head to you,
Graze like machined wheels, green, from off this stone
And preying on each terrified chest, lost
Say, I am old as the globe, the moon, it
Is my old shoe, yours, be free as the leaves.

Fly, mantis, on the poor, arise like leaves
The armies of the poor, strength: stone on stone
And build the new world in your eyes, Save it!

                                                    1934

"'Mantis'" begins with the speaker's observation of a praying mantis, an insect with upraised
forelegs that give it the appearance of being in prayer. The mantis appears in the unlikely set-

---

1. A mobile robot in a human form.

ting of a New York subway, triggering the speaker's meditation on perception, ecology, and the oppression and liberation of the poor. The poem is a sestina, an intricate form invented by the Provençal poet Arnaut Daniel (fl. 1180–1200). According to Mark Scroggins, "The requirements of the form are clearly specified and rigorously bind the poet. There is no conventional rhyme, but the line-end words of the first six-line stanza are reshuffled in each succeeding stanza until the sixth, when they reach the limit of their combinatory possibilities. . . . The sixth stanza is followed by a three-line coda, . . . in which all six of the key words reappear, half in line-end positions and half somewhere within the lines."

Anew 10

What are these songs
straining at sense —
you the consequence?

1946

Part of a forty-three-poem sequence called *Anew*, this poem questions the relationship among poetry, music, meaning, and reader.

Anew 20

The lines of this new song are nothing
But a tune making the nothing full
Stonelike become more hard than silent
The tune's image holding in the line.

1946

This self-reflexive poem is concerned with its own language, filling the perceptual void with its graven melody. An example of syllabic verse, the poem contains nine syllables per line. Zukofsky admired Marianne Moore, who made syllabic verse famous in the 1920s.

Anew 21

Can a mote[1] of sunlight defeat its purpose
When thought shows it to be deep or dark?

See sun, and think shadow.

1946

Anew 21 poses scientific explanation (light as particle or wave) or perhaps simply errant thought (light as dark) against physical perception (light as sun).

1. Particle or speck (usually of dust).

H. T.

Being driven after the hearse thru suburbs —
   the dead man who had been good
   and by a coincidence my father-in-law,
I sped by shop signs:
   Handel, Butcher, Shelley, Plumber
a beautiful day, blue wintry sky
such is this world.

1956

"A"-11

for Celia and Paul

River[1] that must turn full after I stop dying
Song, my song, raise grief to music
Light as my loves' thought, the few sick
So sick of wrangling: thus weeping,
Sounds of light, stay in her keeping
And my son's face — this much for honor.[2]

Freed by their praises who make honor dearer
Whose losses show them rich and you no poorer[3]
Take care, song, that what stars' imprint you mirror
Grazes their tears; tears draw speech from their nature or
Love in you — faced to your outer stars — purer
Gold[4] than tongues make without feeling
Art new, hurt old: revealing
The slackened bow as the stinging
Animal dies, thread gold stringing
The fingerboard pressed in my honor.

---

1. Perhaps tears flowing from the eyes of Celia and Paul after Zukofsky's death. Perhaps also a reference to the Bronx River, beside which the Zukofskys lived for years. The Bronx River appears in Joseph Rodman Drake's nineteenth-century elegy, "Bronx," which along with Cavalcanti's ballad underlies this movement.
2. This word concludes each verse-paragraph, as it concludes the opening stanzas of Guido Cavalcanti's "Perch'io non spero."
3. Barry Ahearn compares this line to a consoling sentence about grief in Henry James's story "The Altar of the Dead": "People were not poor, after all, whom so many losses could overtake; they were positively rich when they had so much to give up."
4. Spiritual rather than material gold, as in the alchemical writings of Paracelsus (1493–1541). Tongues: perhaps tongues of refining flame.

* * *

Honor, song, sang the blest is delight knowing
We overcome ills by love.[5] Hurt, song, nourish
Eyes, think most of whom you hurt. For the flowing
River   's poison[6] where what rod blossoms. Flourish
By love's sweet lights and sing *in them I flourish.*
No, song, not any one power
May recall or forget, our
Love to see your love flows into
Us. If Venus lights, your words spin, to
Live our desires lead us to honor.[7]

Graced, your heart in nothing less than in death,[8] go—
I, dust—raise the great hem of the extended
World that nothing can leave; having had breath go
Face my son, say: 'if your father offended
You with mute wisdom,[9] my words have not ended
His second paradise[10] where
His love was in her eyes where
They turn, quick for you two—sick
Or gone cannot make music
You set less than all. Honor

His[11] voice in me, the river's turn that finds the
Grace in you, four notes[12] first too full for talk, leaf
Lighting stem, stems bound to the branch that binds the
Tree,[13] and then as from the same root we talk, leaf
After leaf of your mind's music, page, walk leaf
Over leaf of his thought, sounding
His happiness: song sounding

5. Compare Baruch Spinoza's "Hatred should be overcome by love" (*Ethics* 4:73n).
6. Perhaps the mourners' river of tears. Rod: compare Aaron's flowering rod, symbolizing spiritual fertility, in Numbers 17:8 of the Hebrew Bible.
7. Compare Spinoza's "We are led in life principally by the desire of honor" (*Ethics* 4:52n).
8. Compare Spinoza's "A free man thinks of nothing less than of death" (*Ethics* 4:67).
9. Barry Ahearn comments: "To Paul 'mute' would signify the clip attached to the [violin] that deadens its resonance. 'Mute wisdom' would be

Louis's occasionally heavy-handed direction of Paul's upbringing."
10. Perhaps the paradise of art. Compare Paracelsus' "The striving for wisdom is the second paradise of the world."
11. Perhaps Cavalcanti's.
12. Reference to the movement's four guiding spirits: Guido Cavalcanti, Baruch Spinoza, Paracelsus, and either Henry James or Joseph Rodman Drake.
13. Compare "a well-remembered face in each old tree" in Joseph Rodman Drake's "Bronx."

The grace that comes from knowing
Things, her love our own showing
Her love in all her honor.'

1959

"A" was Zukofsky's masterwork, a poem of over eight hundred pages, begun in 1928 and completed in 1974. Musical in structure and reference, the poem is notable for the depth of its personal and social vision, the range of its forms and styles, and the diversity of its possible meanings. Zukofsky wrote "A-11," the eleventh of twenty-four sections or movements, in 1950–51. In this movement, he leaves behind the social concerns that had dominated the previous movements, turning instead to a lyric celebration of family life. He bids an imagined farewell to his wife and son after his own death. In conceiving this movement, Zukofsky found his principal inspiration in an Italian love ballad, "Perch'io non spero," by Guido Cavalcanti (ca. 1255–1300). Overall, "A"-11 communicates an uplifting sense that we "overcome ills by love" and "flourish / By love's sweet lights."

I's (*pronounced* eyes)

Hi Kuh,[1]

those
gold'n bees
are I's,

eyes,

skyscrapers.

*

Red azaleas
        make this
        synagogue
Not the
        other way
        round.

*

---

1. Pun on "haiku," a succinct Japanese poetic form. *Kuh* is also both German for "cow" and a last name. Zukofsky suggested that this line refers to a cow glimpsed on a billboard or in a vision, though it could also be a sight of New York skyscrapers.

Fiddler Age Nine[2]
(with brief- and violin-case)

Sir Attaché[3] Détaché

*

HARBOR

The winds
agitating
the
waters.

*

FOR

Four tubas
or
two-by-four's.[4]

*

Angelo

the Superintendent's
Porto Rican Helper—

See
I work
alread' start roof pla'form
ñ scratching floor
on
Eight

if
I
can do
you
good.

---

2. Refers to a photograph of Zukofsky's son, Paul, the violinist.
3. Attached; a diplomatic official; or a briefcase (French). Détaché: detached, removed, indiffer-ent; on temporary assignment; or a kind of violin bowing (French).
4. Sonically inverts "four tubas."

＊

SEVEN DAYS A WEEK

A
good man
when everybody
is draping
the flag on a holiday
he's behind a box

or stamp or information
window in the
Post Office.

＊

TREE—SEE?

—I see
by
your tree

—What
do you
see[5]

＊

A SEA

the
foam
claws

cloys
close

＊

---

5. A question in a letter Lorine Niedecker wrote to Zukofsky.

ABC

He has wit[6] —
but who has more —

who looks
some way more

withal[7]

than
one eye

weeps, his voice

*

AZURE

Azure[8]
as ever
adz aver[9]
1963

The eleven parts of this sequence were originally composed as separate short poems and later combined. Sandra Kumamoto Stanley comments that the title of "I's (pronounced *eyes*)" suggests that "the act of being is not only the act of seeing but also the act of linguistic free play." The poem is replete with both acts of perception and plays on words: for example, *bees / I's / eyes / skyscrapers, see / sea / ABC*, and *azure / as ever / adz aver*.

CARMEN CELIA BELTRÁN

1905–2002

CARMEN CELIA BELTRÁN was born in Durango, Mexico, but fled with her family to the United States when the Mexican Revolution began in 1910. By the time the revolution ended nearly fourteen years later, Beltrán had settled in Arizona, which became her permanent home. She published not only poetry but also radio plays.

6. Humor, canniness, clear perception.
7. Besides, nevertheless (archaic).
8. Perhaps the blue sky.

9. Advertisements aver or affirm; an adz is also a curved tool for chiseling and a hieroglyph.

An actress as well as a writer, she enjoyed a career in both radio and the theater. Beltrán's poetry reflects her preoccupation with her homeland of Mexico, often focusing on national themes or patriotic "moments," such as September 15, the Mexican Day of Independence. She uses poetry as cultural self-defense against forgetting her Chicana heritage. In "Flores Secas/Dried Flowers," she honors a world of memory and dreaming that might remind some readers of the contemporary Latina writer Isabel Allende.

FURTHER READING

Tey Diana Reybodollo and Eleana S. Rivero, eds. *Infinite Divisions: An Anthology of Chicana Literature*. Tucson: University of Arizona Press, 1993.

Flores Secas

Mis ensueños fueron siempre
    deslumbrantes mariposas
que jamás quedaron presas
    en el cáliz de una flor,
porque al roce de sus alas
    los claveles y las rosas
marchitándose perdieron
    su fragancia y su color.

En mi huerto sólo quedan
    unas blancas tuberosas
que mis sueños incitaron
    con sus galas y su olor,
las conservo, y así secas
    esas flores luminosas
con sus pétalos perfuman
    los recuerdos de un amor!

Fué un amor maravilloso!
    Embriagándome de anhelo
escalé los arreboles
    en la bóveda del cielo . . .
y después que el espejismo
    de mi senda se alejó,
el recuerdo lo revive
    descorriendo un tenue velo.

[TRANS.] Dried Flowers

My fantasies were always
    dazzling butterflies
that were never imprisoned
    in the calyx of a flower,
because with the friction of their wings
    the carnations and the roses
withered, losing
    their fragrance and their color.

In my orchard there remained only
    some white tuberoses
which incited my dreams
    with their elegance and their smell;
I save them, and thus dried
    these luminous flowers
with their petals perfume
    the memories of a love!

It was a marvelous love!
    Drunk with eagerness
I scaled the red clouds
    in the arch of the sky . . .
and after the mirage
    distanced itself from my path,
the memory revives it
    drawing along a tenuous veil.

* * *

Fue como ave peregrina
    que bajó en un raudo vuelo
a la fuente que a su paso
    un remanso le brindó . . .

* * *

It was like a wandering bird
    that flew down in a rapid flight
to the spring which instantly
    tranquil water bestowed . . .

                    n.d.

STANLEY KUNITZ
1905–Present

STANLEY KUNITZ helped redirect American poetry from the intellectualism, opacity, and verbal density that typifies much experimental modernist writing toward a more transparent, personal, and visionary use of language. Although he has been called a "post-confessional" poet—since he began writing most of his autobiographical poetry a decade after poets such as Robert Lowell and Anne Sexton initiated the movement in about 1960—he might also be considered a "pre-confessional poet" because his early poetry forecast the entire enterprise. Most of Kunitz's best poems forego the impersonal masks made famous by Ezra Pound and T. S. Eliot in order to mine personal relations and childhood memory. Unlike nineteenth-century poems that idealize the family, Kunitz's poems freely expose anger, grief, and pain as well as a search for meaning and forgiveness. Breaking from both nineteenth-century and high modernist inheritances, these poems helped establish a kind of personal lyric that is still with us today.

Kunitz was born to a Jewish family in Worcester, Massachusetts. Before his birth, his father committed suicide, an event that would haunt the poet's life and writing. Kunitz grew up in middle-class surroundings with his mother, who owned a sewing shop, and his two sisters, Sarah and Sophia. He then attended Harvard University, where he earned his B.A. and M.A. Unable to attain an academic position because of the anti-Semitism of his day, he worked in editing and began publishing his poems. As a result of the recognition he received as a poet, he eventually obtained a variety of academic appointments, most enduringly at Columbia University, where he taught for more than twenty years (1963–85). Living with his wife and daughter in New York City and Cape Cod, he founded both the New York Poets House and the Provincetown Fine Arts Work Center, where he helped numerous young artists and writers get their start. Over the years, his poetry earned many awards, including the Pulitzer Prize (1959) and the National Medal of the Arts (1993). In 2000, at the age of ninety-five, he served as the poet laureate of the United States.

FURTHER READING

Marie Henault. *Stanley Kunitz*. Boston: Twayne, 1980.

Stanley Kunitz. *Collected Poems*. New York: W. W. Norton, 2000.

Gregory Orr. *Stanley Kunitz: An Introduction to the Poetry*. New York: Columbia University Press, 1985.

The Portrait

My mother never forgave my father
for killing himself,
especially at such an awkward time
and in a public park,
that spring
when I was waiting to be born.
She locked his name
in her deepest cabinet
and would not let him out,
though I could hear him thumping.
When I came down from the attic
with the pastel portrait in my hand
of a long-lipped stranger
with a brave moustache
and deep brown level eyes,
she ripped it into shreds
without a single word
and slapped me hard.
In my sixty-fourth year
I can feel my cheek
still burning.

1971

"The Portrait" reveals a moment of violence between mother and son resulting from their conflicting reactions to the father's absence. In an interview, Kunitz explained that the poem reveals "the nature of the sorrows of childhood, the sorrows of my childhood. There was a cloud that hung over our house in Worcester, and it took me almost fifty years before I could face it in a poem."

KENNETH REXROTH
1905–1982

Robert hass has said that Kenneth Rexroth seems to have "invented the culture of the West Coast." Although the culture of the American West Coast actually goes back to pre-Columbian times, Rexroth did reinvigorate it with his ecological, erotic, and social meditations as well as his passionate engagement with East Asian poetry and religion. He began as a member of the experimental objectivist movement, founded in 1930 by Louis Zukofsky and inspired by the examples of William Carlos Williams, Ezra Pound, and Charles Reznikoff (all included in this anthology). "Lyell's Hypothesis Again," though written in a subsequent style, shows the residual influence of that movement in its attention to unadorned natural details. In the 1950s and 1960s, Rexroth was a leading member of what Michael Davidson has called "the San Francisco Renaissance," a collage of literary and political countercultural communities. During this period, Rexroth translated Asian poetry and championed such alternative poets as Mina Loy, Robert Creeley, Denise Levertov, Allen Ginsberg, and Gary Snyder. "The Love Poems of Marichiko," written after two extended trips to Japan, demonstrates Rexroth's abiding interest in Asian culture as well as his continued reliance on natural phenomena as conveyors of emotional meaning.

Kenneth Rexroth grew up in South Bend, Indiana, and Chicago, Illinois, where he was orphaned in his early teens. Largely self-educated, he left for California at the age of twenty-one. In the 1920s, he worked as a forest ranger, farmworker, factory hand, brothel owner, and union organizer. In the 1930s and 1940s, he was active in progressive and radical political circles and worked as a hospital orderly. He also produced a multitude of poems, paintings, and essays, publishing the first of many books in 1940. Married four times and father of two daughters, he became a well-known public figure in the 1950s and 1960s, speaking on the radio and writing columns for the *Nation*, the *San Francisco Examiner*, and the *Bay Guardian*. From 1968 on, he taught at the University of California, Santa Barbara, living in nearby Montecito, on California's south-central coast. Catholic eulogies, Buddhist chants, and countercultural poems were performed at his funeral. He left a poetic legacy notable for its ecological and transcultural awareness.

FURTHER READING

Lee Bartlett. *Kenneth Rexroth*. Boise, Idaho: Boise State University Press, 1988.
Michael Davidson. *The San Francisco Renaissance*. Cambridge, Eng.: Cambridge University Press, 1989.
Robert Hass. *Twentieth-Century Pleasures: Prose on Poetry*. New York: Ecco Press, 1984.
Kenneth Rexroth. *Collected Poems*. Port Townsend, Wash.: Copper Canyon Press, 2002.
Eliot Weinberger. "At the Death of Kenneth Rexroth." *Sagetrieb* 2.3 (1983): 45–52.

Lyell's Hypothesis Again

*An Attempt to Explain the Former Changes of
the Earth's Surface by Causes Now in Operation*
SUBTITLE OF LYELL, *PRINCIPLES OF GEOLOGY*

1

The mountain road ends here,
Broken away in the chasm where
The bridge washed out years ago.
The first scarlet larkspur[1] glitters
In the first patch of April
Morning sunlight. The engorged creek
Roars and rustles like a military
Ball. Here by the waterfall,
Insuperable[2] life, flushed
With the equinox, sentient[3]
And sentimental, falls away
To the sea and death. The tissue
Of sympathy and agony
That binds the flesh in its Nessus' shirt;[4]
The clotted cobweb of unself
And self; sheds itself and flecks
The sun's bed with darts of blossom
Like flagellant[5] blood above
The water bursting in the vibrant
Air. This ego by personal
Tragedy and the vast
Impersonal vindictiveness
Of the ruined and ruining world,
Pauses in this immortality,
As passionate, as apathetic,
As the lava flow that burned here once;
And stopped here; and said, "This far
And no further." And spoke thereafter
In the simple diction of stone.

1. Common name for delphinium, a plant with blue flowers, the calyx and petals of which resemble a spur.
2. Incapable of being overcome.
3. Having the power of sensuous perception.

4. In Greek myth, a shirt dipped in the poisoned blood of the centaur Nessus; when the hero Heracles put it on, it killed him.
5. Beaten or beating.

2

Naked in the warm April air,
We lie under the redwoods,
In the sunny lee[6] of a cliff.
As you kneel above me I see
Tiny red marks on your flanks
Like bites, where the redwood cones
Have pressed into your flesh.
You can find just the same marks
In the lignite[7] in the cliff
Over our heads. *Sequoia*
Langsdorfii[8] before the ice,
And *sempervirens*[9] afterwards
There is little difference,
Except for all those years.
Here in the sweet, moribund
Fetor[10] of spring flowers, washed,
Flotsam and jetsam together,
Cool and naked together,
Under this tree for a moment,
We have escaped the bitterness
Of love, and love lost, and love
Betrayed. And what might have been,
And what might be, fall equally
Away with what is, and leave
Only these ideograms[11]
Printed on the immortal
Hydrocarbons of flesh and stone.

1944

"Lyell's Hypothesis Again" takes its inspiration from Rexroth's camping expeditions in the California wilderness with his second wife, Marie Kass. The poem combines descriptions of nature, natural history, ecology, mysticism, and eroticism. Sir Charles Lyell (1797–1875), author of *Principles of Geology* (1830), was a Scottish geologist who discovered that all

6. Shelter.
7. Brown coal intermediate between peat and bituminous coal.
8. Fossilized form of an ancient sequoia tree, a tall Western conifer.
9. Present-day form of the coastal sequoia or coast redwood, the tallest tree in the world, an evergreen conifer found in the coastal ranges of central and northern California and southern Oregon.
10. Stench.
11. Written symbols of East Asian languages, representing ideas or objects directly.

features of the earth's surface result from physical, chemical, and biological processes occurring over time. His book laid the foundation for evolutionary biology as well as modern geology.

FROM *The Love Poems of Marichiko*

1

I sit at my desk.
What can I write to you?
Sick with love,
I long to see you in the flesh.
I can write only,
"I love you. I love you. I love you."
Love cuts through my heart
And tears my vitals.
Spasms of longing suffocate me
And will not stop.

3

Oh the anguish of these secret meetings
In the depth of night,
I wait with the shoji[1] open.
You come late, and I see your shadow
Move through the foliage
At the bottom of the garden.
We embrace—hidden from my family.
I weep into my hands.
My sleeves are already damp.
We make love, and suddenly
The fire watch[2] loom up
With clappers and lantern.
How cruel they are
To appear at such a moment.
Upset by their apparition,[3]
I babble nonsense
And can't stop talking
Words with no connection.

---

1. Sliding door with paper panes.   3. Ghostly appearance.
2. Fire patrol.

16

Scorched with love, the cicada[4]
Cries out. Silent as the firefly,
My flesh is consumed with love.[5]

18

Fires
Burn in my heart.
No smoke rises.
No one knows.

24

I scream as you bite
My nipples, and orgasm
Drains my body, as if I
Had been cut in two.

25

Your tongue thrums[6] and moves
Into me, and I become
Hollow and blaze with
Whirling light, like the inside
Of a vast expanding pearl.

31

Some day in six inches of
Ashes will be all
That's left of our passionate minds,
Of all the world created
By our love, its origin
And passing away.[7]

32

I hold your head tight between
My thighs, and press against your

4. Flying insect that produces a shrill sound.
5. "Based on a geisha song in many forms" (Rexroth).
6. To play on a stringed instrument; alternatively, to thread.

7. "Echoes the Buddhist sutra, Samyutta Nikaya, II, 3, 8" (Rexroth).

Mouth, and float away
Forever, in an orchid
Boat[8] on the River of Heaven.

33

I cannot forget
The perfumed dusk inside the
Tent of my black hair,
As we awoke to make love
After a long night of love.[9]

34

Every morning, I
Wake alone, dreaming my
Arm is your sweet flesh
Pressing my lips.

38

I waited all night.
By midnight I was on fire.
In the dawn, hoping
To find a dream of you,
I laid my weary head
On my folded arms,
But the songs of the waking
Birds tormented me.[10]

41

On the mountain,
Tiring to the feet,
Lost in the fog, the pheasant
Cries out, seeking her mate.[11]

---

8. "'Orchid boat' is a metaphor for the female sexual organ" (Rexroth).
9. "Echoes Yosano Akiko" (Rexroth).
10. "Ono no Komachi (834–888) is certainly Japan's greatest woman poet. Marichiko echoes her most famous poem" (Rexroth).
11. "Echoes an anonymous poem usually attributed to Hitomaro" (Rexroth).

49

Once again I hear
The first frogs sing in the pond.
I am overwhelmed by the past.

59

I hate this shadow of a ghost
Under the full moon.
I run my fingers through my greying hair,
And wonder, have I grown so thin?

60

Chilled through, I wake up
With the first light. Outside my window
A red maple leaf floats silently down.
What am I to believe?
Indifference?
Malice?
I hate the sight of coming day
Since that morning when
Your insensitive gaze turned me to ice
Like the pale moon in the dawn.

1974

"The Love Songs of Marichiko" is an original sequence composed by Rexroth. Marichiko is an invented character, but for years Rexroth pretended that she was an actual poet living in Japan. He wrote that "Marichiko is the pen name of a contemporary young woman who lives near the temple of Marishi-ben in Kyoto." He explained that Marishi-ben is a Buddhist goddess of the dawn and sexual bliss, a patron of "geisha, prostitutes, women in childbirth, and lovers, and, in another aspect, once of samurai." Rexroth commented that many of Marichiko's poems "turn religious verse into erotic, and she also turns traditional geisha songs into visionary poems," adding that the sequence forms "a sort of little novel." One might argue that in adopting the voice of a young Japanese woman, this white, middle-aged male poet was performing an act of empathy and cultural exchange. But one might also worry whether, in so doing, he was stereotyping, patronizing, and appropriating another national culture. Eliot Weinberger comments, "Most of the imagery is pastoral and the undressed clothes are traditional. The narrator is defined only in relation to her lover, and of her lover we learn absolutely nothing, including gender. . . . It is America's first Tantric poetry: through passion, the dissolution of the world . . . and the final dissolution of passion itself."

ROBERT PENN WARREN
1905–1989

ROBERT PENN WARREN was born in Guthrie, Kentucky, in 1905 to a well-educated and supportive family. At the age of sixteen, he entered Vanderbilt University, where he became the youngest member of the group of Southern poets called the Fugitives, which included John Crowe Ransom and Allen Tate (both included in this anthology). Warren's first poems appeared in *The Fugitive*, a magazine that the group published from 1922 to 1925. The Fugitives advocated the rural Southern agrarian tradition and based their poetry and critical perspective on a balance between classical aesthetic ideals and the possibilities recently opened up by experimental modernism. From 1925 to 1927, Warren taught at the University of California, Berkeley, where he earned a master's degree. After studying at Oxford as a Rhodes scholar, he returned to the United States in 1930. He then taught at Vanderbilt, Louisiana State, the University of Minnesota, and Yale University. With Cleanth Brooks, he wrote *Understanding Poetry* (1938), a textbook that championed New Critical approaches—particularly the close reading of the individual poem and the importance of irony, ambiguity, and the poem's dramatic occasion or situation. This text widely influenced the study of poetry in America for the next several decades.

Though regarded as one of the best poets of his generation, Warren was for many years better known as a novelist. He received great acclaim for *All the King's Men*, a fictional reexamination of the career of Governor Huey Long, the Louisiana demagogue, which won the Pulitzer Prize for fiction in 1947. As his Southern background was exchanged for a later life spent in New England, with homes in Connecticut and Vermont, Warren's youthful advocacy for the ways of the traditional South gradually gave way to more liberal views. At the same time, his poetry became less formal and more expansive, garnering even higher critical acclaim: his *Promises: Poems, 1954–1956* won many awards, including the National Book Award and the Pulitzer Prize. A prolific fiction writer, critic, anthologist, and biographer, Warren began to devote ever more of his creative energy to verse. The vast majority of his extensive poetic oeuvre was published after 1960.

Warren's verse continuously explores the problem of the individual seeking knowledge in a world that is at once dark, ambiguous, and beautiful. He has a particular talent for the long, meditative lyric sequence. And the protagonists of Warren's long meditative sequences, including "Tale of Time," *Audubon: A Vision*, and "A Way to Love God," are searchers who find uncertainty, pain, and loveliness in the world and an echoing doubt, grief, and yearning for beauty and knowledge in their own natures. At their most powerful, Warren's poems affirm the self in all of its uncertainty.

Warren earned a third Pulitzer Prize in 1979, this time for *Now and Then: Poems, 1976–1978*. In 1985 Warren became the first U.S. poet laureate, a position formerly known as the Poetry Consultant to the Library of Congress. His contributions to American letters as poet, novelist, critic, and educator would be difficult to overestimate.

FURTHER READING

Joseph Blotner. *Robert Penn Warren: A Biography*. New York: Random House, 1997.

James H. Justus. *The Achievement of Robert Penn Warren*. Baton Rouge: Louisiana State University Press, 1981.

David Madden, ed. *The Legacy of Robert Penn Warren*. Baton Rouge: Louisiana State University Press, 2000.

Randolph Runyon. *The Braided Dream: Robert Penn Warren's Late Poetry*. Lexington: University Press of Kentucky, 1990.

Robert Penn Warren. *The Collected Poems of Robert Penn Warren*. Ed. John Burt. Baton Rouge: Louisiana State University, 1998.

Tale of Time

I. What Happened

It was October. It was the Depression. Money
Was tight. Hoover[1] was not a bad
Man, and my mother
Died,[2] and God
Kept on, and keeps on,
Trying to tie things together, but

It doesn't always work, and we put the body
Into the ground, dark
Fell soon, but not yet, and oh,
Have you seen the last oak leaf of autumn, high,
Not yet fallen, stung
By last sun to a gold
Painful beyond the pain one can ordinarily
Get? What

1. Herbert Hoover was the U.S. president from 1929 to 1932. He presided over the earliest and darkest years of the Great Depression.

2. Warren's mother, Ruth Penn Warren, a schoolteacher who encouraged Warren's love of reading, died in Hopkinsville, Kentucky, in October 1931. Warren, then twenty-six, and already launched on a career as a teacher and writer, was at her bedside throughout her final illness. His poem, published in 1966, contemplates this event and its lingering implications from a distance of thirty-five years. As he wrote the poem, Warren was older than his mother was when she died.

       *　　*　　*

Was there in the interim
To do, the time being the time
Between the clod's *chunk* and
The full realization, which commonly come only after
Midnight? That

Is when you will go to the bathroom for a drink of water.
You wash your face in cold water.
You stare at your face in the mirror, wondering
Why now no tears come, for
You had been proud of your tears, and so
You think of copulation, of
Fluid ejected, of
Water deeper than daylight, of
The sun-dappled dark of deep woods and
Blood on green fern frond, of
The shedding of blood, and you will doubt
The significance of your own experience. Oh,
Desolation—oh, if
You were rich!
You try to think of a new position. Is this

Grief? You pray
To God that this be grief, for
You want to grieve.

This, you reflect, is no doubt the typical syndrome.

But all this will come later.
There will also be the dream of the eating of human flesh.

II. The Mad Druggist

I come back to try to remember the faces she saw every day.
She saw them on the street, at school, in the stores, at church.
They are not here now, they have been withdrawn, are put away,
They are all gone now, and have left me in the lurch.

I am in the lurch because they were part of her.
Not clearly remembering them, I have therefore lost that much
Of her, and if I do remember,
I remember the lineaments only beyond the ice-blur and soot-smutch

*   *   *

Of boyhood contempt, for I had not thought they were real.
The real began where the last concrete walk gave out
And the smart-weed crawled in the cracks, where the last privy canted to spill
Over flat in the rank-nourished burdock,[3] and would soon, no doubt,

If nobody came to prop it, which nobody would do.
The real began there: field and woods, stone and stream began
Their utterance, and the fox, in his earth, knew
Joy; and the hawk, like philosophy, hung without motion, high, where the sun-blaze
    of wind ran.

Now, far from Kentucky, planes pass in the night, I hear them and all, all is real.
Some men are mad, but I know that delusion may be one name for truth.
The faces I cannot remember lean at my bed-foot, and grin fit to kill,
For we now share a knowledge I did not have in my youth.

There's one I remember, the old druggist they carried away.
They put him in Hoptown, where he kept on making his list—
The same list he had on the street when he stopped my mother to say:
"Here they are, Miss Ruth, the folks that wouldn't be missed,

"Or this God-durn town would be lucky to miss,
If when I fixed a prescription I just happened to pour
Something in by way of improvement." Then leaned in that gray way of his:
"But you—you always say something nice when you come in my store."

In Hoptown he worked on his list, which now could have nothing to do
With the schedule of deaths continuing relentlessly,
To include, in the end, my mother, as well as that list-maker who
Had the wit to see that she was too precious to die:

A fact some in the street had not grasped—nor the attending physician, nor God, nor I.

III. Answer Yes or No

Death is only a technical correction of the market.[4]
Death is only the transfer of energy to a new form.
Death is only the fulfillment of a wish.

Whose wish?

3. A tall and prickly wild plant that grows throughout the United States.
4. The sort of dismissive statement economists might make to minimize the effect of the stock market crash of 1929, which provoked the Great Depression.

IV. *The Interim*

1

Between the clod and the midnight
The time was.
There had been the public ritual and there would be
The private realization,
And now time was, and

In that time the heart cries out for coherence.
Between the beginning and the end, we must learn
The nature of being, in order
In the end to be, so

Our feet, in first dusk, took
Us over the railroad tracks, where
Sole-leather ground drily against cinders, as when
Tears will not come. She

Whom we now sought was old. Was
Sick. Was dying.[5] Was
Black. Was.
Was: and was that enough? Is
Existence the adequate and only target
For the total reverence of the heart?

We would see her who,
Also, had held me in her arms.
She had held me in her arms,
And I had cried out in the wide
Day-blaze of the world. But

Now was a time of endings.

What is love?

2

Tell me what love is, for
The harvest moon, gold, heaved
Over the far woods which were,
On the black land black, and it swagged over

---

5. Warren and his father, brother, and sister have crossed to the other side of the tracks to visit an African-American woman, perhaps a former servant, who, like his mother, is dying.

The hill-line. That light
Lay gold on the roofs of Squigg-town, and the niggers
Were under the roofs, and
The room smelled of urine.
A fire burned on the hearth;
Too hot, and there was no ventilation, and

You have not answered my question.

3

Propped in a chair, lying down she
Could not have breathed, dying
Erect, breath
Slow from the hole of the mouth, that black
Aperture in the blackness which
Was her face, but
How few of them are really
Black, but she
Is black, and life
Spinning out, spilling out, from
The holes of the eyes: and the eyes are
Burning mud beneath a sky of nothing.
The eyes bubble like hot mud with the expulsion of vision.

I lean, I am the
Nothingness which she
Sees.

Her hand rises in the air.
It rises like revelation.
It moves but has no motion, and
Around it the world flows like a dream of drowning.
The hand touches my cheek.
The voice says: *you.*

I am myself.

The hand has brought me the gift of myself.

4

I am myself, and
Her face is black like cave-blackness, and over
That blackness now hangs death, gray

Like cobweb over the blackness of a cave, but
That blackness which she is, is
Not deficiency like cave-blackness, but is
Substance.
The cobweb shakes with the motion of her breath.

My hand reaches out to part that grayness of cobweb.

My lips touch the cheek, which is black.
I do not know whether the cheek is cold or hot, but I
Know that
The temperature is shocking.
I press my lips firmly against that death,
I try to pray.

The flesh is dry, and tastes of salt.

My father has laid a twenty-dollar bill on the table.
Secretly.
He, too, will kiss that cheek.

   5
We stand in the street of Squigg-town.
The moon is high now and the tin roofs gleam.
My brother says: *The whole place smelled of urine.*
My father says: *Twenty dollars—oh, God, what*
Is twenty dollars when
The world is the world it is!

The night freight is passing.
The couplings clank in the moonlight, the locomotive
Labors on the grade.
The freight disappears beyond the coal chute westward, and
The red caboose light disappears into the distance of the continent.
It will move all night into distance.

My sister is weeping under the sky.
The sky is enormous in the absoluteness of moonlight.

These are factors to be considered in making any final estimate.

   6
There is only one solution. If
You would know how to live, here

Is the solution, and under
My window, when ice breaks, the boulder now
Groans in the gorge, the foam swirls, and in
The intensity of the innermost darkness of steel
The crystal blooms like a star, and at
Dawn I have seen the delicate print of the coon-hand in silt by the riffle.

Hawk-shadow sweetly sweeps the grain.
I would compare it with that fugitive thought which I can find no word for.

   7

Planes pass in the night. I turn
To the right side if the beating
Of my own heart disturbs me.
The sound of water flowing is
An image of Time, and therefore
Truth is all and
Must be respected, and
On the other side of the mirror into which,
At morning, you will stare, History

Gathers, condenses, crouches, breathes, waits. History
Stares forth at you through the eyes which
You think are the reflection of
Your own eyes in the mirror.
Ah, Monsieur du Miroir!

Your whole position must be reconsidered.

   8

But the solution: You
Must eat the dead.
You must eat them completely, bone, blood, flesh, gristle, even
Such hair as can be forced. You
Must undertake this in the dark of the moon, but
At your plenilune[6] of anguish.

Immortality is not impossible,
Even joy.

6. Full moon.

V. What Were You Thinking, Dear Mother?

What were you thinking, a child,[7] when you lay,
At the whippoorwill hour, lost in the long grass,
As the sun, beyond the dark cedars, sank?
You went to the house. The lamps were now lit.

What did you think when the evening dove mourned,
Far off in those sober recesses of cedar?
What relevance did your heart find in that sound?
In lamplight, your father's head bent at his book.

What did you think when the last saffron
Of sunset faded beyond the dark cedars,
And on noble blue now the evening star hung?
You found it necessary to go to the house,

And found it necessary to live on,
In your bravery and in your joyous secret,
Into our present maniacal century,
In which you gave me birth, and in

Which I, in the public and private mania,
Have lived, but remember that once I,
A child, in the grass of that same spot, lay,
And the whippoorwill called, beyond the dark cedars.

VI. Insomnia

1

If to that place. Place of grass.
If to hour of whippoorwill, I.
If I now, not a child. To.
If now I, not a child, should come to
That place, lie in
That place, in that hour hear
That call, would
I rise,
Go?

Yes, enter the darkness. Of.
Darkness of cedars, thinking

---

7. In this section, Warren imagines his mother as a young child.

You there, you having entered, sly,
My back being turned, face
Averted, or
Eyes shut, for
A man cannot keep his eyes steadily open
Sixty years.

I did not see you when you went away.

Darkness of cedars, yes, entering, but what
Face, what
Bubble on dark stream of Time, white
Glimmer un-mooned? Oh,
What age has the soul, what
Face does it wear, or would
I meet that face that last I saw on the pillow, pale?
I recall each item with remarkable precision.

Would the sweat now be dried on the temples?

2

What would we talk about? The dead,
Do they know all, or nothing, and
If nothing, does
Curiosity survive the long unravelment? Tell me

What they think about love, for I
Know now at long last that the living remember the dead only
Because we cannot bear the thought that they
Might forget us. Or is
That true? Look, look at these—
But no, no light here penetrates by which
You might see these photographs I keep in my wallet. Anyway,
I shall try to tell you all that has happened to me.

Though how can I tell when I do not even know?

And as for you, and all the interesting things
That must have happened to you and that
I am just dying to hear about—

But would you confide in a balding stranger
The intimate secret of death?

3

Or does the soul have many faces, and would I,
Pacing the cold hypothesis of Time, enter
Those recesses to see, white,
Whiter than moth-wing, the child's face
Glimmer in cedar gloom, and so
Reach out that I might offer
What protection I could, saying,
"I am older than you will ever be"—for it
Is the child who once
Lay lost in the long grass, sun setting.

Reach out, saying: "Your hand—
Give it here, for it's dark and, my dear,
You should never have come in the woods when it's dark,
But I'll take you back home, they're waiting."
And to woods-edge we come, there stand.

I watch you move across the open space.
You move under the paleness of new stars.
You move toward the house, and one instant,

A door opening, I see
Your small form black against the light, and the door
Is closed, and I

Hear night crash down a million stairs.
In the ensuing silence
My breath is difficult.

Heat lightning ranges beyond the horizon.

That, also, is worth mentioning.

4

Come,
Crack crust, striker
From darkness, and let seize—let what
Hand seize, oh!—my heart, and compress
The heart till, after pain, joy from it
Spurts like a grape, and I will grind
Teeth on flint tongue till
The flint screams. Truth
Is all. But

*   *   *

I must learn to speak it
Slowly, in a whisper.

Truth, in the end, can never be spoken aloud,
For the future is always unpredictable.
But so is the past, therefore

At wood's edge I stand, and,
Over the black horizon, heat lightning
Ripples the black sky. After
The lightning, as the eye
Adjusts to the new dark,
The stars are, again, born.

They are born one by one.

1966

A contemplation by Warren of the death of his mother thirty-five years earlier, this poetic
sequence is also a lyric contemplation of effects and implications of time and change.

FROM *Audubon: A Vision*

II. *The Dream He Never Knew the End Of*

[A]

Shank-end of day, spit of snow, the call,
A crow, sweet in distance, then sudden
The clearing: among stumps, ruined cornstalks yet standing, the spot
Like a wound rubbed raw in the vast pelt of the forest. There
Is the cabin, a huddle of logs with no calculation or craft:
The human filth, the human hope.[1]

Smoke,
From the mud-and-stick chimney, in that air, greasily
Brims, cannot lift, bellies the ridgepole, ravels
White, thin, down the shakes, like sputum.

*   *   *

1. Based on an incident in the upper Midwestern plains from the spring of 1812 and described in Audu-
bon's *Ornithological Journals*.

                                    He stands,
Leans on his gun, stares at the smoke, thinks: "Punk-wood."[2]
Thinks: "Dead-fall half-rotten." Too sloven,
That is, to even set axe to clean wood.

                                    His foot,
On the trod mire by the door, crackles
The night-ice already there forming. His hand
Lifts, hangs. In imagination, his nostrils already
Know the stench of that lair beyond
The door-puncheons.[3] The dog
Presses its head against his knee. The hand
Strikes wood. No answer. He halloos. Then the voice.

    [B]

What should he recognize? The nameless face
In the dream of some pre-dawn cock-crow—about to say what,
Do what? The dregs
Of all nightmare are the same, and we call it
Life. He knows that much, being a man,
And knows that the dregs of all life are nightmare.

Unless.

Unless what?

    [C]

The face, in the air, hangs. Large,
Raw-hewn, strong-beaked, the haired mole
Near the nose, to the left, and the left side by firelight
Glazed red, the right in shadow, and under the tumble and tangle
Of dark hair on that head, and under the coarse eyebrows,
The eyes, dark, glint as from the unspecifiable
Darkness of a cave. It is a woman.

She is tall, taller than he.
Against the gray skirt, her hands hang.

            *   *   *

---

2. A small piece of kindling, often made of rotting
wood and sometimes used to start a fire when
striking flint against steel.

3. Pieces of broad, heavy, roughly dressed timber
with one face finished flat; here, used to frame a
door.

"Ye wants to spend the night? Kin ye pay?
Well, mought as well stay then, done got one a-ready,
And leastwise, you don't stink like no Injun."

[D]

The Indian,
Hunched by the hearth, lifts his head, looks up, but
From one eye only, the other
An aperture below which blood and mucus hang, thickening slow.

"Yeah, a arrow jounced back off his bowstring.
Durn fool—and him a Injun." She laughs.

                              The Indian's head sinks.
So he turns, drops his pack in a corner on bearskin, props
The gun there. Comes back to the fire. Takes his watch out.
Draws it bright, on the thong-loop, from under his hunter's-frock.
It is gold, it lives in his hand in the firelight, and the woman's
Hand reaches out. She wants it. She hangs it about her neck.

And near it the great hands hover delicately
As though it might fall, they quiver like moth-wings, her eyes
Are fixed downward, as though in shyness, on that gleam, and her face
Is sweet in an outrage of sweetness, so that
His gut twists cold. He cannot bear what he sees.

Her body sways like a willow in spring wind. Like a girl.

The time comes to take back the watch. He takes it.
And as she, sullen and sunken, fixes the food, he becomes aware
That the live eye of the Indian is secretly on him, and soundlessly
The lips move, and when her back is turned, the Indian
Draws a finger, in delicious retardation, across his own throat.

After food, and scraps for his dog, he lies down:
In the corner, on bearskins, which are not well cured,
And stink, the gun by his side, primed and cocked.

Under his hand he feels the breathing of the dog.

The woman hulks by the fire. He hears the jug slosh.

[E]

The sons come in from the night, two, and are
The sons she would have. Through slit lids
He watches. Thinks: "Now."

　　　　　　　The sons
Hunker down by the fire, block the firelight, cram food
Into their large mouths, where teeth
Grind in hot darkness, their breathing
Is heavy like sleep, he wants to sleep, but
The head of the woman leans at them. The heads
Are together in firelight.

He hears the jug slosh.

　　　　　　Then hears,
Like the whisper and *whish* of silk, that other
Sound, like a sound of sleep, but he does not
Know what it is. Then he knows, for,
Against the firelight, he sees the face of the woman
Lean over, and the lips purse sweet as to bestow a kiss, but
This is not true, and the great glob of spit
Hangs there, glittering, before she lets it fall.

The spit is what softens like silk the passage of steel
On the fine-grained stone. It whispers.

When she rises, she will hold it in her hand.[4]

[F]

With no sound, she rises. She holds it in her hand.
Behind her the sons rise like shadow. The Indian
Snores. Or pretends to.

　　　　　　He thinks: "Now."

　　　　　　　　　And knows

He has entered the tale, knows
He has entered the dark hovel
In the forest where trees have eyes, knows it is the tale

---

4. The woman, witchlike, has stolen his gold watch and apparently plans, with her sons, to murder Audubon and the injured Indian.

They told him when he was a child, knows it
Is the dream he had in childhood but never
Knew the end of, only
The scream.

[G]

But no scream now, and under his hand
The dogs lies taut, waiting. And he, too, knows
What he must do, do soon, and therefore
Does not understand why now a lassitude
Sweetens his limbs, or why, even in this moment
Of fear — or is it fear? — the saliva
In his mouth tastes sweet.

"Now, now!" the voice in his head cries out, but
Everything seems far away, and small.

He cannot think what guilt unmans him, or
Why he should find the punishment so precious.

It is too late. Oh, oh, the world!

Tell me the name of the world.

[H]

The door bursts open, and the travelers enter:
Three men, alert, strong, armed. And the Indian
Is on his feet, pointing.

He thinks
That now he will never know the dream's ending.

[I]

Trussed up with thongs, all night they lie on the floor there.
The woman is gagged, for she had reviled them.
All night he hears the woman's difficult breath.

Dawn comes. It is gray. When he eats,
The cold corn pone[5] grinds in his throat, like sand. It sticks there.

Even whiskey fails to remove it. It sticks there.

---

5. Small oval cake of corn bread, either baked or fried, that can be dry when cold.

* * *

The leg-thongs are cut off the tied-ones. They are made to stand up.
The woman refuses the whiskey. Says: "What fer?"
The first son drinks. The other
Takes it into his mouth, but it will not go down.

The liquid drains, slow, from the slack of the mouth.

[J]

They stand there under the long, low bough of the great oak.
Eastward, low over the forest, the sun is nothing
But a circular blur of no irradiation, somewhat paler
Than the general grayness. Their legs
Are again bound with thongs.

They are asked if they want to pray now. But the woman:
"If'n it's God made folks, then who's to pray to?"
And then: "Or fer?" And bursts into laughing.

For a time it seems that she can never stop laughing.

But as for the sons, one prays, or tries to. And one
Merely blubbers. If the woman
Gives either a look, it is not
Pity, nor even contempt, only distance. She waits,

And is what she is,

And in the gray light of morning, he sees her face. Under
The tumbled darkness of hair, the face
Is white. Out of that whiteness
The dark eyes stare at nothing, or at
The nothingness that the gray sky, like Time, is, for
There is no Time, and the face
Is, he suddenly sees, beautiful as stone, and

So becomes aware that he is in the manly state.

[K]

The affair was not tidy: bough low, no drop, with the clients[6]
Simply hung up, feet not much clear of the ground, but not

---

6. The woman and her sons (the clients) are being lynched by Audubon's rescuers, apparently as rough
frontier justice for this crime or for crimes previously committed.

Quite close enough to permit any dancing.
The affair was not quick: both sons long jerking and farting, but she,
From the first, without motion, frozen
In a rage of will, an ecstasy of iron, as though
This was the dream that, lifelong, she had dreamed toward.

                                  The face,

Eyes a-glare, jaws clenched, now glowing black with congestion
Like a plum, had achieved,
It seemed to him, a new dimension of beauty.

  [L]

There are tears in his eyes.
He tries to remember his childhood.
He tries to remember his wife.
He can remember nothing.

His throat is parched. His right hand,
Under the deerskin frock, has been clutching the gold watch.

The magic of that object had been,
In the secret order of the world, denied her who now hangs there.

He thinks: "What has been denied me?"
Thinks: "There is never an answer."

Thinks: "The question is the only answer."

He yearns to be able to frame a definition of joy.

  [M]

And so stood alone, for the travelers
Had disappeared into the forest and into
Whatever selves they were, and the Indian,
Now bearing the gift of a gun that had belonged to the hanged-ones,
Was long since gone, like smoke fading into the forest,
And below the blank and unforgiving eye-hole
The blood and mucus had long since dried.

He thought: "I must go."

                        But could not, staring
At the face, and stood for a time even after
The first snowflakes, in idiotic benignity,

Had fallen. Far off, in the forest and falling snow,
A crow was calling.

         So stirs, knowing now
He will not be here when snow
Drifts into the open door of the cabin, or,
Descending the chimney, mantles thinly
Dead ashes on the hearth, nor when snow thatches
These heads with white, like wisdom, nor ever will he
Hear the infinitesimal stridor[7] of the frozen rope
As wind shifts its burden, or when

The weight of the crow first comes to rest on a rigid shoulder.

IV. *The Sign Whereby He Knew*

[A]

His life, at the end, seemed — even the anguish — simple.[8]
Simple, at least, in that it had to be,
Simply, what it was, as he was,
In the end, himself and not what
He had known he ought to be. The blessedness! —

To wake in some dawn and see,
As though down a rifle barrel, lined up[9]
Like sights, the self that was, the self that is, and there
Far off but in range, completing that alignment, your fate.

Hold your breath, let the trigger-squeeze be slow and steady.

The quarry lifts, in the halo of gold leaves, its noble head.

This is not a dimension of Time.

[B]

In this season the waters shrink.

       ✻   ✻   ✻

---

7. Whistling sound when breathing.
8. Audubon contemplates his life from the perspective of old age.
9. During his ornithological explorations, Audubon traveled with little more than his sketchbooks and gun. He shot the birds he was contemplating so that he could draw and study them in close detail, although his paintings always show them dramatically alive. Now Audubon imagines himself as standing in the rifle sights, stalked, inevitably, by age and time.

The spring is circular and surrounded by gold leaves
Which are fallen from the beech tree.

Not even a skitter-bug disturbs the gloss
Of the surface tension. The sky

Is reflected below in absolute clarity.
If you stare into the water you may know

That nothing disturbs the infinite blue of the sky.

[C]

Keep store, dandle babies, and at night nuzzle
The hazelnut-shaped sweet tits of Lucy,[10] and
With the piratical mark-up of the frontier, get rich.[11]

But you did not, being of weak character.

You saw, from the forest pond, already dark, the great trumpeter swan
Rise, in clangor, and fight up the steep air where,
At the height of last light, it glimmered, like white flame.

The definition of love being, as we know, complex,
We may say that he, after all, loved his wife.

The letter, from campfire, keelboat,[12] or slum room in New Orleans,
Always ended, "God bless you, dear Lucy." After sunset,

Alone, he played his flute in the forest.

[D]

Listen! Stand very still and,
Far off, where shadow
Is undappled, you may hear

The tushed boar grumble in his ivy-slick.

Afterward, there is silence until
The jay, sudden as conscience, calls.

10. Audubon married Lucy Bakewell in 1808. She later composed a biography of her famous husband.
11. The once-impoverished Audubon became wealthy from the international success of *Birds of America* and later books.

12. A flat-bottomed wooden boat of shallow draft; in Audubon's time, a workhorse on America's rivers and canals.

*   *   *

The call, in the infinite sunlight, is like
The thrill of the taste of—on the tongue—brass.

[E]

The world declares itself. That voice
Is vaulted in—oh, arch on arch—redundancy of joy, its end
Is its beginning, necessity
Blooms like a rose. Why,

Therefore, is truth the only thing that cannot
Be spoken?

It can only be enacted, and that in dream,
Or in the dream become, as though unconsciously, action, and he stood,

At dusk, in the street of the raw settlement, and saw
The first lamp lit behind a window, and did not know
What he was. Thought: "I do not know my own name."

He walked in the world. He was sometimes seen to stand
In perfect stillness, when no leaf stirred.

Tell us, dear God—tell us the sign
Whereby we may know the time has come.

VI. Love and Knowledge

Their footless dance
Is of the beautiful liability of their nature.
Their eyes are round, boldly convex, bright as a jewel,
And merciless. They do not know
Compassion, and if they did,
We should not be worthy of it. They fly
In air that glitters like fluent crystal
And is hard as perfectly transparent iron, they cleave it
With no effort. They cry
In a tongue multitudinous, often like music.

He slew them, at surprising distances, with his gun.[13]
Over a body held in his hand, his head was bowed low,
But not in grief.

---

13. Audubon first shot the birds that he later drew and painted.

* * *

He put them where they are, and there we see them:
In our imagination.

What is love?

One name for it is knowledge.

VII. *Tell Me a Story*

[A]

Long ago, in Kentucky, I, a boy,[14] stood
By a dirt road, in first dark, and heard
The great geese hoot northward.

I could not see them, there being no moon
And the stars sparse. I heard them.

I did not know what was happening in my heart.

It was the season before the elderberry blooms,
Therefore they were going north.

The sound was passing northward.

[B]

Tell me a story.

In this century, and moment, of mania,
Tell me a story.

Make it a story of great distances, and starlight.

The name of the story will be Time,
But you must not pronounce its name.

Tell me a story of deep delight.

1968

John James Audubon (1785–1851) was one of the most important American naturalists of the nineteenth century. Of Haitian-French extraction, Audubon moved to Pennsylvania in 1803 and later to Kentucky, where he failed in several businesses, pleading bankruptcy in 1819. Profoundly interested in studying and painting birds, Audubon traveled with his family in 1820 to Louisiana, where his wife served as a governess to make ends meet while

14. Warren speaks now in his own voice, recalling his youth.

Audubon began the extensive field studies and exact yet dramatic drawings that would lead to the triumphant publication, from 1826 to 1838, of his *Birds of America*, which remains a standard work. Warren's *Audubon*, visionary in character, unfolds not as a conventional narrative but rather as a series of visualized moments from Audubon's life in which he—representing both the artist and the pioneer—contemplates problems of knowledge, identity, and emotional ambivalence in the face of the wayward power and uncertainty of nature, other people, and his own impulses.

A Way to Love God

Here is the shadow of truth, for only the shadow is true.
And the line where the incoming swell from the sunset Pacific
First leans and staggers to break will tell all you need to know
About submarine geography, and your father's death rattle
Provides all biographical data required for the *Who's Who* of the dead.

I cannot recall what I started to tell you, but at least
I can say how night-long I have lain under stars and
Heard mountains moan in their sleep. By daylight,
They remember nothing, and go about their lawful occasions
Of not going anywhere except in slow disintegration. At night
They remember, however, that there is something they cannot remember,
So moan. Theirs is the perfected pain of conscience, that
Of forgetting the crime, and I hope you have not suffered it. I have.

I do not recall what had burdened my tongue, but urge you
To think on the slug's white belly, how sick-slick and soft,
On the hairiness of stars, silver, silver, while the silence
Blows like wind by, and on the sea's virgin bosom unveiled
To give suck to the wavering serpent of the moon; and,
In the distance, in *plaza, piazza, place, platz*, and square,
Boot heels, like history being born, on cobbles bang.

Everything seems an echo of something else.

And when, by the hair, the headsman held up the head
Of Mary of Scots,[1] the lips kept on moving,
But without sound. The lips,
They were trying to say something very important.

1. Mary Stuart, Queen of Scotland (1542–1587), fled her country to England after being forced to abdicate in 1567. Held almost as a prisoner by her cousin Queen Elizabeth I, she was implicated in a plot to overthrow the English crown and was beheaded in 1587. Her son became King James I of England on Elizabeth's death in 1603.

*   *   *

But I had forgotten to mention an upland
Of wind-tortured stone white in darkness, and tall, but when
No wind, mist gathers, and once on the Sarré at midnight,
I watched the sheep huddling. Their eyes
Stared into nothingness. In that mist-diffused light their eyes
Were stupid and round like the eyes of fat fish in muddy water,
Or of a scholar who has lost faith in his calling.

Their jaws did not move. Shreds
Of dry grass, gray in gray mist-light, hung
From the side of a jaw, unmoving.

You would think that nothing would ever again happen.

That may be a way to love God.

1975

WORLD WAR II
INTERNMENT CAMP POETRY

IMMEDIATELY AFTER the bombing of Pearl Harbor, American citizens with Japanese backgrounds—as well as many with German, Italian, Bulgarian, Czech, Hungarian, Romanian, and other ancestry—found themselves targeted by the U.S. government as "enemy aliens" if they lived on the West Coast or were seen as a threat to national security. The 120,000 Japanese Americans, after suffering a range of abuses and indignities, were forcibly removed from their homes with only what they could carry. They were then taken in trains to detention centers that often were little more than racetracks, where families were housed in horse stalls that had not even been cleaned before their arrival. After this temporary stop, they were again put on trains and shipped to concentration camps scattered in remote areas of several states for the duration of the war. The camp internees, forced to live surrounded by barbed wire and armed guards, lost millions of dollars in property as well as their jobs.

A federal government report declared in 1983 that the internment of the Japanese Americans was not justified by military necessity, and a civil liberties act provided each survivor with $20,000 tax-free restitution and a government apology.

The report stated that the broad historical causes were racial prejudice, war hysteria, and a failure of political leadership. In 2004, historian Brian Masaru Hayashi argued in his study, *Democratizing the Enemy: The Japanese American Internment,* that even more important than these causes may have been U.S. plans for the postwar occupation of Japan as well as the issue of land development in the American West.

The federal intervention in the lives of Japanese communities known as "Japantowns" in many West Coast cities also disrupted the rich and varied literary cultures of these communities — especially the poetry clubs that produced haiku, senryu (which is structurally like haiku but focuses more on the human condition and politics), and tanka. Both traditional haiku and the newer kaiko haiku, which allowed poets to more freely express their feelings, were popular. Kaiko haiku moved away from the restrictive expressions of scenery and objective subtleness demanded and valued by classical haiku. Before the war, poetry clubs had met weekly or monthly as men, women, and children carried on the Japanese custom of daily writing poems, often in both Japanese and English.

Poets tried to continue writing in the internment camps in spite of oppressive conditions. Some of them published their work in camp-sponsored newspapers and journals; others waited until after the war to share their work publicly. Some wrote under their actual names; others adopted pen names. They wrote in many different poetic modes, from traditional Japanese forms to American free verse. They reflected on the difficulties of their daily lives in the camps as well as on their feelings and concerns. The selections here are meant to suggest the poetry's wide range of ideas, feelings, forms, styles, and subjects. By continuing to write, to meet in groups, and to publish, these poets offered important role models to the generation of children in the camps who later became poets — for example, Janice Mirikitani, who lived at Heart Mountain Concentration Camp in Wyoming, and Lawson Inada, who lived at Topaz Concentration Camp in Utah.

Although manuscripts of poetry from the Japanese-American internment have been collected for some time now and are still being located, research work has just begun with respect to Italian Americans, German Americans, and others who were similarly treated and imprisoned during the war and to those from Latin America who were arrested, shipped to the United States, and held in camps. These internment histories have been denied, repressed, and guarded in shame until recently, as lawmakers and historians have started to seek redress and to publish accounts of these experiences. More than 10,000 Italian immigrants who were not yet citizens were forcibly evacuated from their homes on the West Coast and relocated. Others were forced to observe a curfew and could not enter communities if their presence posed a national security risk. This restriction meant that many could not travel more than five miles from their residences during the war without police permission. Such interventions separated families and cost citizens their jobs and sometimes their lives. Italian fishermen, especially in California, were required to surrender their boats to the U.S. Coast Guard. More than 2,000 fishermen on the West Coast were interrogated, and about 300 were sent to Fort Missoula, Montana, which held more than 10,000 Germans and German Americans during the war. About twenty camps around the country held these individuals, and a number of detention centers, including Ellis Island, also existed.

Twelve Latin American nations responded to the U.S. directive that they arrest Axis residents. More than 4,000 German Latin Americans were arrested at one point. Figures vary on the number of arrests and internments, but about 3,000 Japanese, Germans, and Italians from Latin America apparently spent some time in U.S. internment camps. Peru, for instance, provided a large number of internees, mostly Japanese.

While many U.S. citizens of Japanese, German, and Italian backgrounds suffered in camps during World War II, males as well as females from these communities also enlisted in the U.S. armed services in large numbers. Italian Americans made up the largest ethnic group to serve in the war. The war contributions of all these groups have been widely acknowledged, for they were invaluable to the success of the Allies. Yet military records did not make resettlement easy once the camps closed. The vigilante violence that had greeted these groups at the beginning of the war at times threatened them again as they attempted to reestablish their free civilian lives.

The poetry selections included here offer glimpses of the Japanese-American internment experience. Perhaps they can also serve to suggest what other groups of internees endured, at least until their own poetry can be located and published alongside this work.

FURTHER READING

Violet Kazue (Matsuda) de Christoforo, ed. and trans. *May Sky: There Is Always Tomorrow: An Anthology of Japanese American Concentration Camp Kaiko Haiku*. Los Angeles: Sun & Moon Press, 1997.

Roger Daniels. *Asian America: Chinese and Japanese in the United States Since 1850*. Seattle: University of Washington Press, 1988.

———. *Japanese Americans: From Relocation to Redress*. Salt Lake City: University of Utah Press, 1986.

———. *Prisoners without Trial: Japanese American Internment*. New York: Hill and Wang, 1993.

Lawrence DiStasi, ed. *Una Storia Segreta: The Secret History of Italian American Evacuation and Internment during World War II*. With a preface by Sandra Gilbert. New York: Heyday Books, 2001.

Stephen Fox. *America's Invisible Gulag: A Biography of German-American Internment and Exclusion: Memory and History*. New York: Peter Lang, 2000.

———. "Un-Civil Liberties: Italian Americans Under Siege during World War II." Upublish .com, 2000. Reprinted from *The Unknown Internment*. New York: Twayne, 1990.

C. Harvey Gardiner. *Pawns in a Triangle of Hate: The Peruvian-Japanese and the United States*. Seattle: University of Washington Press, 1981.

Brian Masaru Hayashi. *Democratizing the Enemy: The Japanese American Internment*. Princeton: Princeton University Press, 2004.

Jerre Mangione. *An Ethnic at Large: A Memoir of America in the Thirties and Forties*. New York: Putnam, 1970.

Janice Mirikitani, ed. *Ayumi: A Japanese-American Anthology*. San Francisco: Japanese-American Anthology Committee, 1980.

Jiro Nakano and Kay (Nakano) Yokoyama, ed. and trans. *Poets Behind Barbed Wire*. Honolulu: Bamboo Ridge Press, 1983.

Gary Okihiro. *Whispered Silences: Japanese-Americans and World War II*. Photos by Joan Myers. Seattle: University of Washington Press, 1996.

U.S. Commission on Wartime Relocation and Internment of Civilians. *Personal Justice Denied*. Washington, D.C.: Government Publications Office, 1983.

Distorted Sun

Akira Togawa

Over a purple covered mountain
the distorted sun is rising.
Green trees cover the foot of the mountain.
The whole sky is blue.
My daughter, 5 years old,
painted the picture with colored pencils.

Each morning she wakes
in early darkness.
Still cold her small hands
grip a cup of hot cocoa for breakfast.
Later, joining a circle
around a fire
in a vacant lot far away
from the block
she watches the sunrise
above mountains to the East.

The natural presence of the desert
seeped into her mind
is born in her children's painting.

Ah, my helpless daughter,
your father is almost crying.
During the long, long trip over the desert
crowded in a train, destination unknown,

you held a Shirley Temple doll.
Your parents were embarrassed to hear you wish
   "I want to go to Los Angeles."
   "I want to go home!"

You survived that burning jigoku.[1]
Though fragile,
every day you attended kindergarten
and began to enjoy life in the desert.
Can you imagine your father's gladness?

Ah, my daughter,
my dearest innocent child,
remember this unusual life.
You may live long,
but this life may never come again.

Pray with your mother and father
that the day will come soon
when the distorted sun you painted
becomes big and round
and the peaceful sunlight penetrates
everyone's heart all over the world.

                                 n.d.

In "Distorted Sun," Akira Togawa (born 1903) describes the long train trip to the intern-
ment camp in the desert at Poston, Arizona. At the camp, his daughter attended kindergar-
ten with the other schoolchildren there. Shirley Temple dolls, created and named after the
famous golden-curled child-actress, were very popular.

In Topaz

Toyo Suyemoto [Kawakami]

Can this hard earth break wide
  The stiff stillness of snow
And yield me promise that
  This is not always so?

       *   *   *

1. Hell.

Surely, the warmth of sun
 Can pierce the earth ice-bound,
Until grass comes to life
 Outwitting barren ground!

1943

Toyo Suyemoto [Kawakami] (1916–2003) was taken first to Tanforan Racetrack in northern California in April 1942. From there she was transported by train to Topaz Concentration Camp in central Utah. This poem originally appeared in *Trek Literary Magazine* in the camp.

Hokku

Toyo Suyemoto [Kawakami]

The geese flew over
At dusk—I shivered, not with
Cold, but sense of loss.

Where do the geese go?
Can they escape from autumn
And return to spring?

Let me follow them:
The birds know better than I
Which way leads to spring.

n.d.

[Untitled]

Sojin Takei

MP o matasete
nare ga totonoeshi
namoida komorishi
kaban no omoki

[TRANS.] Untitled

While the MP's wait
You fill my suitcase
And spill your tears.
How heavy its weight.

1946

[Untitled]

Sojin Takei

takazora wa
saku naki mama ni
yugarasu
izuchi hatenami
tobitsu kieyuku

[TRANS.] Untitled

There is no fence
High up in the sky.
The evening crows
Fly up and disappear
Into the endless horizon.

1946

Prisoner

Muin Pzaki

prisoner
dressed as I am
a snowy wind

n.d.

Prisoner and the poems that follow are senryu and tanka describing the camp experience.

Stepping through snow

Oshio

stepping through snow
in predawn haste
a kitchen worker

n.d.

Since the day of internment

Sasabune

since the day of internment
sitting on his ass
the go[1] player

n.d.

---

1. A board game.

Dimples

Sasabune

dimples
so clearly seen
dream of my grandchild

n.d.

Shouldering

Taro Katay

shouldering
a house without a husband
letter from my wife

n.d.

Taro Katay was sent first to Tanforan and then interned at Topaz in Utah. He later volunteered for the U.S. Army.

Hay spread for

Hokko

hay spread for
movie viewing
beneath spring stars

n.d.

Sprinkling

Hokko

sprinkling
sprinkling
but the dust does not stay down

n.d.

Is this to be?

Rokaku

Is this to be?
My child, toward Japan
points a gun

n.d.

The days when I laughed

Hakkaku

the days when I laughed
are forgotten, three times
spring has passed

n.d.

Birds

Gensui

birds
living in the cage
human spirit

n.d.

Thorns of the iron fence

Kyokusui

thorns of the iron fence
pointed inward
toward camp

n.d.

Passed guard tower

Kyotaro Komuro

passed guard tower
without glancing up
before summer daybreak

n.d.

Passed guard tower and the poems that follow are kaiko haiku, a contemporary variant of traditional haiku.

Want to be with children

Kyotaro Komuro

want to be with children
playing in water
of irrigation ditch

n.d.

Withered grass on ground

Shonan Suzuki

withered grass on ground
army tank creaking
in the wind

n.d.

Moon shadows on internment camp

Shonan Suzuki

moon shadows on internment camp
I hear the cries of geese
again this year

n.d.

Young grass red and shriveled

Hakuro Wada

young grass red and shriveled
wide sandy flat
and gritty wind

n.d.

Released seagull

Hakuro Wada

released seagull
after writing NIPPON in red on its belly
summer morning in highlands

n.d.

Even the croaking of frogs

Hakuro Wada

even the croaking of frogs
comes from outside the barbed wire fence
this is our life

n.d.

[Untitled]

Keiho Soga

ikameshiki
nijyu no saku no
kanata niwa
murasaki niou
yama manekiori

[TRANS.] Untitled

Beyond the forbidding fence
Of doubled barbed wire,
The mountain,
Aglow with purple,
Sends us its greetings

1957

[Untitled]

Keiho Soga

junjitso no
uchi ni ryoyu
mitari yukinu
kono tatkai no
hate o mizushite

[TRANS.] Untitled

Within just ten days
Three fellow internees
Depart from this world
Never to see
The end of this war.

1957

ABOUT THE EDITORS

Steven Gould Axelrod is Professor of English at the University of California, Riverside. He has won his university's Distinguished Teaching Award and has held the NEH Chair in Teaching Excellence. He has also served as the English department chair. He specializes in American poetry, having written about such poets as Emily Dickinson, Wallace Stevens, William Carlos Williams, Elizabeth Bishop, Robert Lowell, Gwendolyn Brooks, and Sylvia Plath. Among his books are *Robert Lowell: Life and Art* (Princeton University Press, 1978), which was nominated for a Pulitzer Prize, and *Sylvia Plath: The Wound and the Cure of Words* (John Hopkins University Press, 1990). Books he has edited include (with Helen Deese) *Robert Lowell: New Essays on the Poetry* (Cambridge University Press, 1986), *Critical Essays on Wallace Stevens* (G. K. Hall, 1988), *Critical Essays on William Carlos Williams* (G. K. Hall/Macmillan, 1995), and *The Critical Response to Robert Lowell* (Greenwood Press, 1999). He has also published more than fifty articles. He is president of the Robert Lowell Society.

Camille Roman is Professor of English Emeritus at Washington State University in Pullman and holds affiliate faculty positions in American Studies, Women's Studies, and the Honors College. She also has been a visiting scholar at Brown University and Potchefstromse Universiteit, South Africa. She has published a dozen books offering interdisciplinary and transcultural studies of American poetry, twentieth-century music, and the gender and language debate. Her work includes *Elizabeth Bishop's World War II–Cold War View* (Palgrave/Macmillan, 2001, 2004) and *The Women and Language Debate: A Sourcebook* (Rutgers University Press, 1993), coedited with Suzanne Juhasz and Cristanne Miller. She is founding coeditor with Chris D. Frigon of Twayne's Music Series and coedited volumes on down-home blues lyrics (1981), Carlos Chávez (1983), Sonny Rollins (1983), Claude Debussy (1983), black women composers (1983), the Beatles (1983), Olivier Messiaën (1984), and Lester Young (1985). She is a member of the editorial board of *Twentieth-Century Literature* and president-elect of The Robert Frost Society. She also has published essays on Amy Lowell, Robert Frost, Edna St. Vincent Millay, Louise Bogan, Frank O'Hara, Sylvia Plath, Elizabeth Bishop, and D. H. Lawrence as well as the vocal artist Billie Holiday.

Thomas Travisano is Professor of English at Hartwick College, Oneonta, New York. His most recent publication is an edition of the correspondence of Elizabeth Bishop and Robert Lowell entitled *Words in Air* (Farrar, Straus and Giroux, 2008). He has written *Elizabeth Bishop: Her Artistic Development* (University of Virginia Press, 1988) and *Midcentury Quartet: Bishop, Lowell, Jarrell, Berryman, and the Making of a Postmodern Aesthetic* (University of Virginia Press, 1999) and is co-editor of *Gendered Modernisms: American Women Poets and Their Readers* (University of Pennsylvania Press, 1996). He is cofounder and first president of the Elizabeth Bishop Society and from 1995 to 1997 was director of The American Century Project, an NEH-funded humanities project.

COPYRIGHTS AND PERMISSIONS

INDEX